The Routledge Handbook of Second Language Acquisition and Language Testing

This *Handbook*, with 45 chapters written by the world's leading scholars in second language acquisition (SLA) and language testing, dives into the important interface between SLA and language testing: shared ground where researchers seek to measure second language performance to better understand how people learn their second languages. The *Handbook* also reviews how to best measure and evaluate the second language (L2) learners' personal characteristics, backgrounds, and learning contexts to better understand their L2 learning trajectories. Taking a transdisciplinary approach to research, the book builds upon recent theorizing and measurement principles from the fields of applied linguistics, cognitive science, psychology, psycholinguistics, psychometrics, educational measurement, and social psychology. The *Handbook* is divided into six key sections: (1) Assessment concepts for SLA researchers, (2) Building instruments for SLA research, (3) Measuring individual differences, (4) Measuring language development, (5) Testing specific populations, and (6) Measurement principles for SLA researchers.

Paula Winke is a Professor of Second Language Studies and TESOL at Michigan State University, USA, where she specializes in the assessment of language proficiency for practical uses and the measurement of individual differences for SLA research.

Tineke Brunfaut is a Professor of Linguistics and English Language at Lancaster University, UK, where she specializes in language testing and second language reading and listening.

ROUTLEDGE HANDBOOKS IN SECOND LANGUAGE ACQUISITION

Susan M. Gass and Alison Mackey, Series Editors
Kimberly L. Geeslin, Associate Editor

The Routledge Handbooks in Second Language Acquisition are a comprehensive, must-have survey of this core sub-discipline of applied linguistics. With a truly global reach and featuring diverse contributing voices, each handbook provides an overview of both the fundamentals and new directions for each topic.

The Routledge Handbook of Second Language Acquisition and Pragmatics
Edited by Naoko Taguchi

The Routledge Handbook of Second Language Acquisition and Corpora
Edited by Nicole Tracy-Ventura and Magali Paquot

The Routledge Handbook of Second Language Acquisition and Language Testing
Edited by Paula Winke and Tineke Brunfaut

For more information about this series, please visit:https://www.routledge.com/Second-Language-Acquisition-Research-Series/book-series/RHSLA

The Routledge Handbook of Second Language Acquisition and Language Testing

Edited by Paula Winke and Tineke Brunfaut

Routledge
Taylor & Francis Group
NEW YORK AND LONDON

First published 2021
by Routledge
52 Vanderbilt Avenue, New York, NY 10017

and by Routledge
2 Park Square, Milton Park, Abingdon, Oxon, OX14 4RN

Routledge is an imprint of the Taylor & Francis Group, an informa business

Library of Congress Cataloging-in-Publication Data
Names: Winke, Paula Marie, editor. | Brunfaut, Tineke, editor.
Title: The Routledge handbook of second language acquisition and language testing/edited by Paula Winke and Tineke Brunfaut.
Description: New York: Routledge, 2020. |
Series: The Routledge handbooks
in second language acquisition | Includes bibliographical references and index. |
Identifiers: LCCN 2020028661 (print) | LCCN 2020028662 (ebook)
Subjects: LCSH: Second language acquisition. | Language and languages–Study and teaching–Foreign speakers. | Language and languages–Ability testing.
Classification: LCC P118.2 .R684 2020 (print) | LCC P118.2 (ebook) | DDC 418.0071–dc23
LC record available at https://lccn.loc.gov/2020028661
LC ebook record available at https://lccn.loc.gov/2020028662

ISBN: 978-1-138-49068-0 (hbk)
ISBN: 978-1-351-03478-4 (ebk)

Typeset in Times New Roman
by Deanta Global Publishing Services, Chennai, India

Contents

Figures

Tables

Acknowledgements

There are numerous individuals to whom we are grateful. First we thank the chapter authors of this *Handbook*, presented alphabetically in the Author Biographies list, many of whom also served as peer reviewers of the other chapters. We appreciate the authors' enthusiasm for this volume and the chapters, their special attention to details, and for working with us throughout the entire publication-writing process. Second, we would like to thank our graduate students at Michigan State University (MSU) and Lancaster University who helped us in the preparation and organization of the manuscripts and their many associated files. In particular, we would like to thank Dylan Burton, who served as the longest-running project manager on this edited volume, and who saw the project through to the final finish. Thank you to Ryo Maie, who served as the project manager during the first phase of the project. We also thank Daniel R. Isbell and Dustin Crowther who additionally provided early input on the project, as did many of our SLA and language testing colleagues at MSU and Lancaster University. Third, we are grateful to individuals from the fields of SLA and language testing who served as additional reviewers of the chapters: Robert M. DeKeyser, Valentina Denzel, Jonathan Henner, Ute Knoch, Geoffrey T. LaFlair, Robert J. Mislevy, Carsten Roever, Charles W. Stansfield, Nicole Tracy-Ventura, and Sara Cushing Weigle. Where authors were more specialized in language testing than SLA, we sent their chapters to SLA researchers for review, and vice versa. The peers' tips and suggestions to authors, and to us, bettered the reach and cross-pollinating depth of the chapters. Fourth, we would like to thank Susan Gass and Alison Mackey, who trusted us with this project and provided oversight, important feedback, and encouragement as series editors. And we would like to thank Ze'ev Sudry and Helena Parkinson at Routledge for their support, assistance, and understanding at each stage of the book development process. Producing a book with 45 chapters was absolutely a full-time job at various stages, and thus we also thank our home teams: Paul, Erika, and Sonja Stokstad for Paula; and Hannes, Casper and Simon Pretorius for Tineke. We do this work with you in mind.

Contributors

Riikka Alanen is Professor of Foreign Language Education in the Department of Teacher Education of the University of Jyväskylä in Finland. Her research interests include L2 learning and teaching as mediated activity. Together with her colleagues at the University of Jyväskylä, she has investigated the development and assessment of L2 writing proficiency in multilingual contexts, specializing in the development of EFL writing proficiency.

Samantha Ayers-Glassey, BSc, is currently employed as a research assistant with Dr Peter MacIntyre at Cape Breton University, Canada, where she recently completed her undergraduate honour's degree in psychology. Her general research interests include cognitive neuroscience, attention, and emotion regulation, topics which she will be pursuing as a MA candidate at the University of Waterloo in the fall.

Kathleen M. Bailey is a Professor of Applied Linguistics at the Middlebury Institute of International Studies at Monterey (MIIS), USA. She has served as the president of TESOL and the American Association for Applied Linguistics. Since 2009 she has been the President and the Chairman of the Board of Trustees of The International Research Foundation (TIRF) for English language education.

Jayanti Banerjee is a language assessment professional and researcher. In her current role, she guides the development of language tests, monitors test quality assurance, and suggests and advises on strategies for product improvement. Her main research interests are related to the assessment of speaking and listening in a second language. In addition, she is interested in the interpretation and use of test scores for decision making and in how test takers interact with test tasks.

Aaron Olaf Batty is an Associate Professor at Keio University in Fujisawa, Japan. He received his PhD in linguistics from Lancaster University. He has published on vocabulary, speaking, and listening assessment, and is currently interested in the impact of nonverbal communicative cues on video listening test performance. He employs item response theory, especially many-facet Rasch models, in most of his work, and sits on the board of the Pacific Rim Objective Measurement Society.

Tej K. Bhatia is Professor of Linguistics and Director of South Asian languages at Syracuse University, Syracuse, New York, USA. He has been Director of the Linguistic Studies Program and Acting Director of Cognitive Sciences at his university. Currently, he is also a Faculty Fellow, Forensic Sciences and National Security Institute. He is a recipient of the Chancellor's Citation Award for excellence in research. He has delivered key-note and featured-speaker addresses nationally and internationally. He has published 16 books and over 300 book chapters and articles.

Eveline Boers-Visker is a sign language teacher within a bachelor program for sign language teachers and interpreters in the Netherlands. She researches L2 sign language acquisition, with a focus on the modality specific features that come with learning a language in a new modality.

Amanda Brown is an Associate Professor of Linguistics at Syracuse University, USA. She investigates the psycholinguistic effects of multilingualism in speech and gesture and associated implications for language pedagogy and assessment, and teacher preparation. She teaches courses in L2 teaching/learning and holds administrative positions in graduate programs in linguistics and language teaching.

Tineke Brunfaut is a Professor in Linguistics and English Language at Lancaster University (UK), where she specializes in language testing and second language reading and listening. Her main research interests are: cognitive and affective factors and processes in language testing, methodology in language testing research, and language test development. She is a recipient of the ILTA Best Article Award, the e-Assessment Award for Best Research, and the TOEFL Outstanding Young Scholar Award.

J. Dylan Burton is a PhD student in the Second Language Studies program at Michigan State University, USA, and editorial assistant for the journal Language Testing with co-editors Paula Winke and Luke Harding. He holds an MA in Language Testing from Lancaster University. Dylan's research interests include the development and validation of speaking tests, rater cognition, and nonverbal behavior. His research has been published in Language Assessment Quarterly and System.

Carol A. Chapelle is Distinguished Professor of Liberal Arts and Sciences at Iowa State University, USA. She is editor of the Encyclopedia of Applied Linguistics (Wiley, 2013) and of the Cambridge Applied Linguistics Series. She is past president of the American Association for Applied Linguistics and former editor of TESOL Quarterly and Language Testing. Her research investigates the use of technology in language learning and assessment, the topic of many of her books and research articles.

Mark Chapman is Director of Test Development at WIDA, University of Wisconsin-Madison, USA, where he leads language test development projects in the US K-12 context. His research interests include second language writing assessment and validation research for assessments of young learners' language development. He has a PhD in second language writing assessment from the Centre for Research in English Language Learning and Assessment at The University of Bedfordshire, UK.

Liying Cheng, PhD, is Professor and Director of the Assessment and Evaluation Group (AEG) at the Faculty of Education, Queen's University, Canada. Her primary research interests are the impact of large-scale testing on instruction, the relationships between assessment and instruction, and the academic and professional acculturation of international and new immigrant students, workers, and professionals to Canada.

Troy L. Cox, PhD, is a faculty member in the Linguistics Department at Brigham Young University, USA, and serves as the Associate Director of the Center for Language Studies. He is also a certified ACTFL oral proficiency trainer and has used his testing expertise as a forensic linguist and in test development projects in a number of different languages. His research interests include proficiency testing, the integration of technology with assessment, objective measurement, and self-assessment.

Dustin Crowther is an Assistant Professor in the Department of Second Language Studies at the University of Hawai'i at Mānoa, USA. His research interests include second language pronunciation, mutual intelligibility in multilingual and multicultural contact, World Englishes, and research methodologies. His research has been published in a wide range of journals, including Studies in Second Language Acquisition, The Modern Language Journal, TESOL Quarterly, and the Journal of Second Language Pronunciation. He recently co-edited a volume on methodologies in World Englishes inquiry with Drs. Peter De Costa and Jeffrey Maloney (Routledge).

Dan P. Dewey, Professor of Linguistics at Brigham Young University, USA, received a PhD in Second Language Acquisition from Carnegie Mellon University, USA. His research focuses largely on language acquisition in settings other than the classroom (study abroad, internships, foreign language housing, autonomous online learning, and so forth). His recent research addresses social interaction, anxiety, motivation, self-regulation and individual differences in SLA.

Karen J. Dunn is a Senior Researcher in Measurement and Evaluation at the British Council. Dr Dunn works on analysing operational data for the British Council's suite of English language tests (Aptis), as well as in-depth research into scoring and validity issues. She is also involved in projects addressing a range of language assessment issues, specialising in statistical analysis using latent variable models.

Kathrin Eberharter attained her teaching degree in English as a Foreign Language and German, after that, she worked for the national Austrian exam-reform project. She has an MA in Language Testing and currently holds a research position at the University of Innsbruck, Austria. Kathrin is enrolled in Lancaster University's Applied Linguistics PhD programme and her current interests are in the areas of assessing productive skills, language assessment literacy, and integrating literary studies and foreign language assessment.

Glenn Fulcher is Professor of Applied Linguistics and Language Assessment at the University of Leicester, UK. He has published widely, and his books include "Testing Second Language Speaking" (2003), "Language Testing and Assessment" (Routledge, 2007), "Practical Language Testing" (Hodder, 2010), "The Routledge Handbook of Language Testing" (Routledge, 2012), and "Language Testing Re-examined" (Routledge, 2015). In 2014 he was awarded a National Teaching Fellowship for his contribution to language assessment literacy for his website, http://languagetesting.info.

Dana Gablasova is Senior Lecturer at the Department of Linguistics and English Language, Lancaster University, UK. Her research interests include corpus-based approaches to the study of language learning, teaching, and assessment with special interest in formulaic language and spoken production. She is the lead developer of the Trinity Lancaster Corpus of L2 spoken English. Her research appeared in journals such as Applied Linguistics, The Modern Language Journal, Language Learning, and English for Specific Purposes.

Evelina D. Galaczi is Head of Research Strategy at Cambridge Assessment English, UK. She has worked in English language education for over 25 years and her key areas of expertise are the assessment of speaking skills, the role of technology in learning and assessment, and ways of empowering teachers to be successful practitioners in the digital age. She has a strong track record of academic publications and presentations at international conferences. Evelina received her Master's and Doctorate degrees from Columbia University, USA.

Anthony Green is Professor in Language Assessment and Director of the Centre for English Language Learning and Assessment at the University of Bedfordshire, UK. His publications include "Exploring Language Assessment and Testing" (Routledge), an introductory guide to this field for teachers and students. He also has extensive practical experience as a test developer, examiner and consultant to testing agencies.

Rita Green has been involved in the field of language testing since the mid-1980s acting as a trainer, consultant and/or researcher on projects for a wide range of organisations including the British Council, DfID, the Thai Ministry of Foreign Affairs, EUROCONTROL and Lancaster University. She is particularly interested in training language test developers; the role statistical analyses play in task development and the assessment of listening. She has run Language Testing at Lancaster (LTL) since 2001.

Stefan Th. Gries is Professor of Linguistics, an affiliate in the Department of Spanish and Portuguese, and member of the Center for Responsible Machine Learning (CRML) at the University of California, Santa Barbara, USA. He is an Honorary Liebig-Professor (since 2011) at the Justus Liebig University Giessen, where he maintains a 25% position as Professor of Corpus Linguistics. For five years (1999–2004), he was at the University of Southern Denmark. Dr Gries researches learner corpora and how they can be best used in L2 psycholinguistics research.

Luke Harding is a Professor in the Department of Linguistics and English Language at Lancaster University UK. His research interests are in language assessment and applied linguistics more broadly, particularly listening assessment, pronunciation and intelligibility, language assessment literacy, and the challenges of World Englishes and English as a Lingua Franca for language assessment. He is currently co-editor of the journal Language Testing.

Claudia Harsch is a Professor at the University of Bremen, Germany, specialising in language learning, teaching and assessment. She has worked in Germany and in the UK, and is active in teacher training worldwide. Her research interests focus on areas such as language assessment, educational evaluation and measurement, intercultural communication, and the implementation of the CEFR. Claudia was president of the European Association of Language Testing and Assessment between 2016–2019.

Tobias Haug studied sign linguistics at Hamburg University, Germany, and Deaf Education at Boston University, USA, where he received his masters (Deaf Education) in 1998. In 2009 he earned his PhD (sign linguistics) at Hamburg University, Germany. In 2017, he completed a distance master in language testing from Lancaster University, UK. From 1998 to 2004 he worked as a sign language interpreter and researcher. Since 2004 he has been the Program Director of the sign language interpreter program in Zurich, Switzerland. One of his research interests is sign language assessment and sign language interpreting.

Ching-Ni Hsieh is Research Scientist at the Assessment and Learning Technology Research and Development Division at Educational Testing Service, USA. She received her PhD in Second Language Studies from Michigan State University, USA, and Master's in English Language Teaching from the University of Nottingham, UK. Her research and development interests include assessing young language learners, speaking assessment, automated speech scoring and feedback, and technology-enhanced language learning, with a specific focus on adaptive language learning using AI-powered capabilities.

Ari Huhta is a Professor of Language Assessment in the Centre for Applied Language Studies at the University of Jyväskylä, Finland. His research interests include assessments that support learning (e.g., diagnostic and formative assessment), computer-based assessment, development of reading and writing, as well as combining second language acquisition research and language testing perspectives in research.

Yo In'nami is a Professor of English at Chuo University, Japan. He is interested in meta-analytic inquiry into the variability of effects and the longitudinal measurement of change in language proficiency. His publication has appeared in English Teaching & Learning, International Journal of Testing, Language Assessment Quarterly, Language Learning, Language Testing, Language Testing in Asia, System, and TESOL Quarterly.

Chihiro Inoue is a Senior Lecturer at the Centre for Research in English Language Learning and Assessment, University of Bedfordshire, UK. Her research interests lie in the task design, rating scale development and the criterial features of learner language. She has been involved in numerous test development and validation projects around the world and has published a book, book chapters and journal articles in Language Assessment Quarterly, Assessing Writing, and the Language Learning Journal.

Daniel R. Isbell is an Assistant Professor in the Department of Second Language Studies at the University of Hawai'i at Mānoa, USA. Dan's primary area of interest is language assessment, with specific research foci in proficiency testing, diagnostic assessment, and the rating of performance assessments. His other interests include second language pronunciation, the measurement of implicit and explicit L2 knowledge, technology in language teaching and learning, and methodology in second language research.

Janina Iwaniec is a Senior Lecturer in TESOL at the University of Bath, UK. Her research interests include language learning motivation in foreign and second language contexts, gender roles in language learning, and the role of contextual factors in language learning. She has published in System, Journal of Multilingual and Multicultural Development, European Journal of Applied Linguistics and the Language Learning Journal.

Eun Hee Jeon is an Associate Professor of English at the University of North Carolina at Pembroke (UNCP), USA. She teaches various courses in TESOL, applied linguistics, and linguistics at the undergraduate and graduate level at UNCP. Her research interests include second language (L2) reading comprehension, L2 proficiency, and research methods.

Glyn Jones is a freelance consultant in language learning and assessment. An EFL teacher by background, he worked extensively in the fields of Self Access Learning and Computer Assisted Language Learning before specialising in assessment. He has worked as a test development manager for two major awarding bodies, and as a senior researcher in language assessment. At the time of writing he is completing a PhD in Linguistics at Lancaster University, UK.

Alan Juffs is Professor of Linguistics and Director of the English Language Institute at the University of Pittsburgh, USA. His research interests include the lexicon, language processing, morpho-syntax, working memory, ESL materials development, and the use of online tools for language education. He has taught ESL in France, China, Japan, Canada, and the USA. His most recent research focus is using learner corpora to track language development in an intensive English program.

Nahal Khabbazbashi is a Senior Lecturer in Language Assessment at the Centre for Research in English Language Learning and Assessment (CRELLA), University of Bedfordshire, UK. She holds a DPhil in Education and an MSc in Applied Linguistics and Second Language Acquisition from the University of Oxford. Her work appears in Language Testing (2020; 2017), Language and Education (2019), and the Studies in Language Testing series (Moeller, Creswell, and Saville, eds. 2016).

Rie Koizumi is an Associate Professor of English at Juntendo University, Japan, and a Vice Secretary General of the Japan Language Testing Association (JLTA). Her research interests include assessing and modeling second language ability, performance, and development. She has published her work in Language Testing, Language Assessment Quarterly, System, Assessment in Education: Principles, Policy & Practice, and other journals.

Judit Kormos is a Professor in Second Language Acquisition at Lancaster University, UK. She was a key partner in the award-winning DysTEFL project sponsored by the European Commission and is a lead educator in the Dyslexia and Foreign Language Teaching massive open online learning course offered by FutureLearn. She is the co-author of the book "Teaching languages to students with specific learning differences" (Multilingual Matters) with Anne Margaret Smith. She has published widely on the effect of dyslexia on learning additional languages including a new book entitled "The second language learning processes of students with specific learning difficulties" (Routledge).

Benjamin Kremmel researches and teaches language learning, teaching, and assessment at the University of Innsbruck, Austria, where he is the head of the Language Testing Research Group Innsbruck (LTRGI). His research interests are in assessment of L2 lexical knowledge and L2 reading skills, as well as in language assessment literacy. His research has been published in Language Testing, Language Assessment Quarterly, Applied Linguistics, PlosOne and TESOL Quarterly.

Folkert Kuiken is Professor Emeritus of Dutch as a Second Language and Multilingualism at the University of Amsterdam, the Netherlands, and Academic Director of the Institute for Dutch Language Education at that same university. His research interests include the effect of task complexity and interaction on SLA, Focus on Form, and the relationship between linguistic complexity and functional adequacy. He (co)authored and (co)edited various books, including "Dimensions of L2 performance and proficiency" (Housen, Kuiken & Vedder, 2012).

Santi B. Lestari is a doctoral student in Language Testing at Lancaster University, UK. Her doctoral study is funded by the Indonesia Endowment Fund for Education. She has an MA in ELT with a specialisation in testing and assessment from the University of Warwick, and her study was funded by the A. S. Hornby Educational Trust scholarships. Her research interests include L2 writing assessment, integrated tasks, and raters' cognitive processes.

Peter D. MacIntyre is a Professor of Psychology at Cape Breton University, Canada. His research areas include the psychology of language and communication. He has published numerous articles and chapters on language anxiety, willingness to communicate, motivation and other topics. He has co-authored or co-edited books including "Optimizing Language Learners' Nonverbal Behavior: From Tenet to Technique," "Positive Psychology in SLA," "Motivational Dynamics in Language Learning," and "Capitalizing on Language Learner Individuality."

Margaret E. Malone is Director of Assessment, Research and Development at ACTFL and Director of the Assessment and Evaluation Language Resource Center and Research Professor at Georgetown University, USA. Her research focuses on understanding language assessment uses and applications, oral proficiency and study abroad.

Todd H. McKay is an instructor in the Specialized English Language Programs unit of St. George's University, Grenada, West Indies. Todd's areas of expertise are in language testing, program evaluation, task-based language teaching, and applied measurement.

Akira Murakami is a Birmingham Fellow at the Department of English Language and Linguistics, University of Birmingham, UK. His main research interests include second language acquisition, corpus linguistics and quantitative data analysis for applied linguistics research. Prior to joining Birmingham in 2018, he worked as a post-doctoral researcher at the Universities of Birmingham, Cambridge and Tübingen.

Fumiyo Nakatsuhara is a Reader in Language Assessment at CRELLA, the University of Bedfordshire, UK. Her research interests include the nature of co-constructed interaction in speaking tests, task design and rating scale development. Fumiyo has recently published the book, "The Discourse of the IELTS Speaking Test" (with P. Seedhouse, 2018, CUP) and an article in Language Assessment Quarterly (2017). She has carried out a number of international testing projects, working with ministries, universities and examination boards.

Gabriele Pallotti is Professor of Language teaching methodology at the University of Modena and Reggio Emilia, Italy. He is member of the Executive Committee of the European Second Language Association (Eurosla) and the editor of the Eurosla Studies series. His research focusses on L2 interaction and socialization, interlanguage analysis, linguistic complexity, methodology and epistemology in applied linguistics.

Magali Paquot is a permanent FNRS research associate at the Centre for English Corpus Linguistics, Language and Communication Institute, UCLouvain, Belgium. She is co-editor in chief of the International Journal of Learner Corpus Research and a founding member of the Learner Corpus Research Association. Her research interests include learner corpus research, linguistic complexity, phraseology, crosslinguistic influence, English for Academic Purposes, and pedagogical lexicography.

Amos Paran is Professor of TESOL, University College London Institute of Education, UK. He started his career teaching EFL in secondary schools in Israel and writing EFL coursebooks. His main interests are using literature in EFL and reading in EFL. His publications include "Testing the Untestable in Language Education" (Multilingual Matters, 2010) and "Literature" (OUP, 2016). He is a tutor on the free MOOC, Teaching EFL/ESL Reading: A Task-Based Approach and co-convenor of the AILA research network, Literature in Language Learning and Teaching (https://lilltresearch.net).

Ana Pellicer-Sánchez is an Associate Professor of Applied Linguistics and TESOL at the UCL Institute of Education (UK). Her research interests centre around the teaching and learning of vocabulary in a second and foreign language, with a particular focus on the use of psycholinguistic techniques to investigate the process of vocabulary acquisition. Her most recent research examines the incidental acquisition of single words and multi-word expressions from reading using the eye-tracking technique.

Aek Phakiti is an Associate Professor in TESOL in the Sydney School of Education and Social Work at the University of Sydney, Australia. His research interests focus on current issues in language testing and assessment, second language acquisition, and research methods. His research has been published in journals, such as Language Learning, Language Testing and Language Assessment Quarterly.

John Pill is a Lecturer in the Department of Linguistics and English Language at Lancaster University, UK. He teaches on the MA in Language Testing programme and is involved in Lancaster's research partnership with Trinity College London. He completed his doctoral studies at the University of Melbourne. His research interests include specific-purpose language testing, particularly in healthcare and academic contexts, speaking assessment, and language assessment literacy.

Luke Plonsky is Associate Professor of Applied Linguistics at Northern Arizona University, USA, where he teaches courses in second language acquisition and research methods. His work in these and other areas has resulted in over 80 articles, book chapters, and books. Luke is Senior Associate Editor of Studies in Second Language Acquisition, Managing Editor of Foreign Language Annals, Co-Editor of de Gruyter Mouton's Series on Language Acquisition, and Co-Director of the IRIS Database (iris-database.org).

Ulla Ratheiser teaches English Literature and Cultural Studies at Innsbruck University, Austria. Her research interests are Postcolonial Studies, contemporary migrant literature and, more recently, the use of literature in second language acquisition.

Hayo Reinders (www.innovationinteaching.org) is Professor of TESOL and Chair of Research at Anaheim University in the USA and Professor of Applied Linguistics at KMUTT in Thailand. His interests are in the areas of autonomy, technology, teacher education and out-of-class learning. He edits a book series for Palgrave Macmillan and is editor of the journal Innovation in Language Learning and Teaching.

Andrea Révész is a Professor of Second Language Acquisition at the UCL Institute of Education, University College London, UK. Her research interests lie at the interface of second language (L2) acquisition, instruction and assessment. Her current research investigates the roles of tasks and individual differences in L2 development and assessment, and the cognitive processes underlying L2 writing, reading, and listening performance.

Karen Roehr-Brackin is a Reader in the Department of Language and Linguistics at the University of Essex in the UK. She works in the area of second language acquisition. Her research interests include explicit and implicit knowledge and learning as well as the role of individual learner differences such as language learning aptitude, working memory and cognitive/learning style in adult and child second language learning.

John Rogers is an Assistant Professor in the Department of English Language Education at the Education University of Hong Kong. His research interests include the development and measurement of implicit and explicit knowledge, quantitative research methods, as well as issues related to task-based language teaching and instructed second language acquisition.

Olena Rossi is a doctoral student and associate lecturer at Lancaster University, UK, specialising in language testing. She has an MA in Language Testing, and her main research interests are item-writing, item-writer training, and assessment literacy for test stakeholders. Her PhD research study investigates item-writer training in order to gain insights into the nature of item-writing skills and their development.

Gila A. Schauer is Professor of English and Applied Linguistics at the University of Erfurt, Germany. She received her PhD from the University of Nottingham, England. She is the author of "Interlanguage pragmatic development: The study abroad context" (Continuum/Bloomsbury, 2009) and "Teaching and Learning English in the Primary School: Interlanguage Pragmatics in the EFL context" (Springer, 2019), as well as of several articles and book chapters.

Rob Schoonen (PhD) is Chair Professor of Applied Linguistics in the Department of Linguistics of the Radboud University Nijmegen, the Netherlands. His research concerns (psycholinguistic) aspects of language proficiency, both language comprehension and language production, and also the assessment of language proficiency. He holds a PhD in Psychology from the University of Amsterdam, the Netherlands.

Cameron Smart is an English Language Assessment Development Manager at the Hong Kong Examinations and Assessment Authority. He has been working in the field of EFL teaching and testing for the last 30 years. He has a PhD in Applied English Linguistics from the University of Birmingham. His interests lie in the application of linear unit grammar and linear unit discourse analysis and the use of learner corpora in test development and analysis of test takers' performance.

Young-A Son is a Data Analytics and Assessment Specialist in the Center for Educational Effectiveness at the University of California, Davis, USA. Her research interests include the assessment of heritage and foreign language learners with emphasis on less commonly taught languages, such as Korean. More specifically, her research focuses on examining the validity of the use of language tests and other indicators of language proficiency for research as well as instructional purposes.

Patti Spinner is an Associate Professor at Michigan State University, USA. Her work centers on the second language acquisition of grammar, in particular morphological marking such as gender and number agreement. Her work has appeared in journals such as Language Learning, Second Language Research, and Studies in Second Language Acquisition.

Carol Spöttl has taught English language, literature and assessment to undergraduates in the School of Education at the University of Innsbruck, Austria, and been extensively involved in in-service teacher training in these areas in several European countries. She led the project to reform the school leaving exam in foreign languages in Austria and set up the Language Testing Research Group at the University of Innsbruck where she is currently based.

Yuichi Suzuki is Associate Professor in the Department of Cross-Cultural Studies at Kanagawa University, Japan. His research interests include validity of measurements for explicit and implicit knowledge, the interface issue, automatization, optimal schedules for vocabulary and grammar learning, and aptitude-treatment interaction. His research has been published in international journals such as Studies in Second Language Acquisition, Language Learning, Bilingualisms: Language and Cognition, Language Teaching Research, and Applied Psycholinguistics.

Lynda B. Taylor is Visiting Professor at the Centre for Research in English Language Learning and Assessment (CRELLA), University of Bedfordshire, UK. With over 35 years' experience of theoretical and practical issues in language learning, teaching and assessment, she has provided expert assistance for major test development projects worldwide. She presents on language testing and assessment issues at international workshops and conferences and has published widely in academic journals and volumes in the field.

Veronika Timpe-Laughlin is a Research Scientist in the *Center for Language Education and Assessment Research* at Educational Testing Service, USA. Her research interests include L2 pragmatics and task-based language teaching, as well as teaching and assessing young language learners. Veronika has recently published in Language Assessment Quarterly, Language Teaching, and Intercultural Pragmatics and is the co-author of the 2017 book "Second Language Educational Experiences for Adult Learners" (Routledge). Prior to joining ETS, Veronika taught in the English Department at TU Dortmund University, Germany.

Beppie van den Bogaerde, originally a Teacher of English and a translator/interpreter in English and Dutch, later studied general linguistics and did a PhD on Interaction and Input in Deaf Families, with a focus on L1 acquisition of Dutch and Sign Language of the Netherlands (NGT) by deaf and hearing children. Subsequently she worked on L2 acquisition of NGT by adult learners, and looked into interpreter practices, as well as bimodal bilingual education and the sociology of the Deaf Community in the Netherlands.

Kris Van den Branden is a Professor of linguistics and teacher educator at the University of Leuven, Belgium. He is the co-editor (together with Koen Van Gorp) of the journal TASK and the academic promotor of the Centre for Language and Education. He was the first President of the International Association for Task-based Language Teaching.

Ineke Vedder is senior researcher at the University of Amsterdam (Amsterdam Center for Language and Communication), the Netherlands. She is co-editor of the *Eurosla Studies* book series of the European Second Language Association. Her research interests include instructed SLA (particularly L2 Italian), L2 and L1 writing, and the relationship between complexity, accuracy, and fluency and functional adequacy. She (co) authored and (co) edited various books (e.g. Kuiken, Housen & Vedder, 2012).

Zhisheng (Edward) Wen, PhD, is an Associate Professor at Macao Polytechnic Institute, Macau SAR, China. He has teaching and research interests in second language acquisition, psycholinguistics and cognitive sciences. His latest books include "Working memory in second language acquisition and processing" (2015, Multilingual Matters), "Working memory and second language learning" (2016, Multilingual Matters), "Language aptitude" (Routledge, 2019) and "Researching L2 task performance and pedagogy" (2019, John Benjamins). His forthcoming book is "The Cambridge handbook of working memory and language."

Paula Winke is a Professor in the Second Language Studies Program (SLS) at Michigan State University, USA. She researches and teaches language testing and individual differences. She is co-editor of the journal Language Testing and co-director of the SLS Eye-tracking Labs. She has received the CALICO article of the year award (2009), the TESOL International Distinguished Researcher award (2012), and the American Association of Applied Linguistics article of the year award (2020).

Junko Yamashita is a Professor at Graduate School of Humanities, Nagoya University, Japan. She has a Ph.D. from Lancaster University, UK. Her primary research fields are L2 reading and lexical processing including factors that affect L2 reading comprehension, teaching and assessment of L2 reading skills and its components, and the cross-linguistic influence on the acquisition of L2 reading and lexical processing. Her publications appear in many journals and several book chapters.

Monique Yoder is a PhD student in the Second Language Studies Program (SLS) at Michigan State University, USA. She is an affiliate faculty member in the MA TESOL program with LCC International University in Lithuania. Her research interests include classroom-based language assessment, language assessment literacy, second language writing assessment, test-taker responses, and the intersection of language assessment and language education policy.

Hyung-Jo Yoon is an Assistant Professor in the Department of Linguistics/TESL at California State University, Northridge, USA. His research interests include second language writing, corpus linguistics, and language assessment. His work has been published in Assessing Writing,

Journal of Second Language Writing, System, TESOL Quarterly, etc. He developed the automated processing tool, Authorial Voice Analyzer, that analyzes the quantity and quality of interactional metadiscourse.

Soo Jung Youn is an Assistant Professor in the English Education Department at Daegu National University of Education, Korea. Her research interests include language testing and assessment, L2 pragmatics, interactional competence, task-based language teaching, and mixed methods research. Her research has been recently published in Language Testing, System, Applied Linguistics Review, and Journal of English for Academic Purposes.

Ying Zheng is an Associate Professor in Modern Languages and Linguistics at the University of Southampton, UK. Before joining the University of Southampton in 2013, Ying worked as a Psychometrician and Director of Research (2009–2013) in the Language Testing Division of Pearson, London. She obtained her MEd (2005) and PhD (2009) in Cognitive Studies from Queen's University, Canada, specializing in Second Language Testing and Assessment.

1

Perspectives on "Knowing" a Second Language

What Are We Seeking to Measure?

Paula Winke & Tineke Brunfaut

Background

Learning a second, additional, or foreign language—the process of which we henceforth call *second language acquisition* (SLA) or L2 learning—is a human endeavor that has been, and always will be, taking place because humans are social beings who interact, forge relationships, and want to understand one another in the present, past, and future. As described by Gass and Mackey (2012, p. 3), individuals vary in how they learn second languages, have various capabilities to learn, and have various levels and types of ultimate (end-state) learning outcomes. A difficulty, Gass and Mackey stressed, is in trying to account for individual and contextually bound differences in L2 learning and L2 learning outcomes. That is where SLA researchers step in; they endeavor to measure SLA in order to document, describe, explain and predict L2 learning and its outcomes. SLA researchers work to "consider as many relevant factors as possible" to understand "what it means to know a second language" (Gass & Mackey, 2012, p. 3). Doing so can shed light on large, philosophical issues, such as "*the nature of the human mind and intelligence*" (Doughty & Long, 2003, p. 5, emphasis original). Or, field-specifically, SLA research can help develop, optimize, and substantiate L2 learning theories. On a practical level, SLA research can reveal important information that can be applied by pedagogues who develop classroom methods, materials, and tests.

Critical to understanding SLA research is knowing that *language* itself is a latent trait that must be somehow measured to investigate specific SLA theory. Language is holistically unobservable except through manifest observations: that is, through instances of people's language performances, captured through various observational techniques. To study or research L2 learning achievement (through empirical, cross-sectional, or experimental research designs) or trajectories (through longitudinal designs) has, therefore, at its heart the measurement of second languages at their various stages and within their developmental contexts; contexts that comprise methodological, social, cultural, and physical elements, that likewise interface with human cognition and emotions, and that are time bound.

Without a doubt, SLA researchers can (and do) study important SLA factors without directly measuring the L2: Extremely significant qualitative, descriptive, and empirical studies have investigated the circumstances, socio-cultural affordances, and practices that strongly influence, shape, or hinder SLA. Such research is particularly virtuous in uncovering important information about nascent SLA concepts. For example, Norton and De Costa (2018) stressed the urgent need for SLA researchers to conduct ethnographic studies to understand how race is implicated in teachers' experiences of language-teacher legitimacy (p. 95), and how educational policy impacts language teachers' practices and their identity constructions (p. 100). Such field-expanding research may not necessarily involve direct measurement of language, but rather may involve nuanced qualitative investigations into complex social and transnational constructs, such as *agency* and *legitimacy*, that shape SLA. Language testing researchers, such as Shohamy (2013), have entered into such inquiry by positioning language tests as policy elements that delegitimize and marginalize L2 learners, turning tests from information providers about L2 constructs to covariates that can strongly affect the SLA process. Such qualitative research has extreme value and requires transparency, but perhaps not strict empirical replicability (see Markee, 2017; Polio, 2012), as its findings can contribute uniquely to the field of SLA and keep SLA (and, we think, language testing) from being myopic (see Firth & Wagner, 2007, p. 801). As explained by Norris and Ortega (2008), different theories within SLA conceptualize L2 learning from different perspectives, and concomitantly, "measurement practices differ systematically according to the varying theoretical premises" (p. 718). Thus, we stress that SLA and language testing overlap, but not entirely; however, as Shohamy (2013) has shown, even when one is in a research area where SLA and language testing seem to *not* overlap, indeed, they can.

Within the incredibly broad and interdisciplinary field of SLA, one *specific* line of research is to employ experimental methodologies and statistical techniques to uncover and understand empirically replicable L2 outcomes, patterns, and their influencers. This line of research has a durable quantitative side, and most often necessitates robust and valid *measurements* of the L2, typically using tests, as well as necessitating robust and valid measurements of the constructs hypothesized to influence the L2's development. As explained by Saito (2004), understanding "variability in second/foreign language (L2) performance has long been a central issue in SLA" (p. 30). And this is where SLA *and* language testing strongly converge. Language testing expertise is useful in these SLA pursuits because defining and measuring the constructs of language ability are at the core of language testing.

Foundations that Bridge SLA and L2 Testing

Links between SLA research and L2 testing research have existed since the beginning of the field of SLA. The two areas have developed in tandem, and have emerged over the years as two parallel-running, reciprocal disciplines (Shohamy, 2000). We do not venture to write that SLA and language testing are distinct and separate disciplines (see Davies, 2012; Douglas, 2001, who seemed to suggest so), but rather we opine and observe, alongside many others who have done so in the past (i.e., Bachman, 1988; Bachman & Cohen, 1998; Gu, 2014; Huhta et al., 2014), that SLA and language testing are strongly *interfaced*, that is, synthetically connected by shared goals and methods. As noted by the Douglas Fir Group, or DFG (2016), and commentary on the DFG work, transdisciplinary work, such as that done by SLA and language testing researchers, can "achieve a wider and more holistic understanding than is possible from one vantage point alone" (Hult, 2019, p. 136). "True collaboration between language testers or measurement specialists and measurement-informed SLA researchers" (Norris & Ortega, 2008, p. 749) is a golden ticket to expand the broader fields of SLA and applied linguistics, as described by Kunnan and Lakshmanan (2006, pp. 91–92), because language testing researchers have built skills to accurately and validly measure L2 development and its mediating constructs, while SLA researchers have researched new constructs and contexts, and developed new hypotheses, to probe deeper and further into the mechanisms of SLA (Shohamy, 2000). As noted by Alderson et al. (2017, p. 380), SLA researchers and language assessment practitioners/researchers have long benefited from their collaborations, and together they better explore constructs that constitute or contribute to L2 development.

For example, *interactional competence* (see Galaczi & Taylor, Chapter 32, this volume) and *willingness-to-communicate* (MacIntyre & Ayers-Glassey, Chapter 18, this volume) are constructs within SLA and within language testing that seemingly influence each other. These constructs are latent traits that can be measured through tests, which record instances of them. Repeated testing of the constructs, respectively, from the same individuals, strung together, side-by-side and over time, can measure the constructs' parallel or non-parallel change or development within the measurement time frame and test-administration context(s). The longitudinal data can inform SLA growth theories, such as whether, how much, when, and why (and specifically for whom) willingness-to-communicate affects the development of interactional competence, and vice versa. A statistical model, such as a cross-lagged panel model or a longitudinal structural equation model, could be used to test such theories, if the model's mathematical assumptions concerning the data are met. Foundationally, the measurements of the constructs must be robust and sensitive enough to document differences in the constructs' developments both within and between cases over time (Spolsky, 2000, p. 547), a measurement consideration that researchers with their psychometric hats on can investigate. In sum, it is these shared constructs, and the desire to measure them well, that bind SLA and language testing.

An important point to keep in mind, as science has shown, is that no single measure of a latent trait is ever a perfectly accurate and reliable measure of that trait. The general call is to test more than once (as more estimates will better represent the underlying construct), and as many times as would be practical and beneficial. However, the number of times to test should be driven by information that is educationally, cognitively, socially, and ethically construed. Different kinds of tests can be viewed as tapping into latent traits from different angles, thus providing different information about the traits. Some tests or assessments may measure various aspects of a latent trait better than others. Theorists can debate whether various measurements of a trait *should* produce converging information, or if measures that provide diverging information may be revealing novel areas of the trait, such as a new sub-construct that will need further definition and exploration. SLA and assessment specialists must speculate together how much measurement unreliability is acceptable in measuring their shared constructs (see Swain, 1993), because it could be the case that when a measurement is not perfect, it can still produce scores that are useful or valuable for specific types of theorizing, or for particular real-world, decision-making purposes. At the interface of SLA and language testing, a well-informed balance between construct measurement and theory can be found.

Different from the 20th century, a modern balance also necessitates social responsibility in research and measurement (McNamara, 2001; McNamara & Roever, 2006), methodological transparency and open-science data reporting practices (Marsden et al., 2018), and evidence that tests are appropriate for the test takers who take them, lest the test takers' scores will not be valid for any uses (Chapelle, 2020; Weir, 2005). Test scores should *not* be used for purposes for which the tests were not intended (Joint Committee on Testing Practices, 2013), and language testers and SLA researchers should be vocal and guard against inappropriate test administrations that provide false or meaningless (random; unreliable) information about language learners (see, for example, Macqueen et al., 2019; Winke & Zhang, 2019). Testing and SLA research, therefore, must have higher standards, better objectivity, and be socially responsible and accountable in ways that they did not need to be two decades ago. These efforts have called for tighter bonds between SLA and language testing.

Key Concepts

Constructs: In science, psychology, and the social sciences, including SLA and language testing, *constructs* are theoretical terms for things humans know (or believe) are real, but that are unobservable, like intelligence, memory, attention, language knowledge, L2 literacy skills, or implicit grammatical knowledge. All scientific theory refers to *constructs*, and not the assessments used to measure them. (See the key concepts in Chapter 2, this volume, for more definitions on assessment constructs.)

Latent traits: *Latent traits* are a special type of construct. A latent trait is a relatively *stable instance* of a construct that changes (emerges and/or dissipates) over time (with time being variously defined; for example, over the period of three hours, six months, or across the span of one's life), such as a person's L2 knowledge, L2 literacy skills, or motivation for L2 learning.

Measures: *Measures*, or tests, can be used to tap into a latent trait. A measure or test collects or records a *manifest observation* (or observable performance) of the latent trait.

Measurement assumptions: In testing, the relationship between the observable, stable performance that was measured and the unobservable latent trait is described by a mathematical function. As such, latent trait estimation or modeling is mathematical (see Hambleton & Cook, 1977). Statistical analyses or latent trait modeling in SLA are based on *mathematical assumptions* about the measurement data, such as the data being normally distributed, and not skewed. Researchers must consider whether the test data satisfy (or will satisfy) the assumptions of the mathematical tests or models to which they wish to apply the data, which can drive sampling or measurement decisions, and demarcate the questions that one may be able to answer with the data.

Key Issues

The primary scope of this *Handbook* is on the modern interface between SLA and language testing: the shared ground where researchers seek to measure L2 constructs to better understand SLA. We asked authors who are SLA researchers, language testing researchers, or both to come together and write about key issues that lie at the current cross-roads of the two specializations. While the topics in this *Handbook* have always benefited from cross-pollination, we believed it was time for explicit sharing. We divided the book into six key parts: (I) Assessment concepts for SLA researchers, (II) Building instruments for SLA research, (III) Measuring individual differences, (IV) Measuring language development, (V) Testing specific populations, and (VI) Measurement principles for SLA researchers.

In the first part, the authors discuss important assessment concepts that may not be reviewed enough within SLA. This includes language assessment validity (Chapelle, Chapter 2), and how researchers can, and should, validate the interpretations of their language assessments (Révész & Brunfaut, Chapter 3). SLA researchers often use common yardsticks for describing L2 proficiency and language growth, such as the A1 through C2 proficiency levels from the Common European Framework of Reference for Languages (CEFR); thus, Part I describes and contextualizes the creation and uses of various national and international scales and their frameworks (Harsch & Malone, Chapter 4). Due to corpora's exponentially rising influence on language testing and SLA, this part also includes a chapter on how corpora can be used for and are benefitting language assessments (Gablasova, Chapter 5). The part ends with a chapter on SLA researcher assessment literacy, which shines light on the ubiquity of measurement within SLA studies, and how and why SLA researchers need to know as much about measurement as they can; so that they can be better designers, implementers, and consumers of language tests and SLA research (Harding & Kremmel, Chapter 6).

In the second part, authors discuss how to build instruments for SLA research, along with suggestions and tips on the administrative and scoring procedures related to tests and surveys. An overview is provided of vital steps in test design (Green & Fulcher, Chapter 7) and of prevailing task types (Banerjee, Lestari & Rossi, Chapter 8). Particular attention is given to the importance of item and Likert-scale construction (Jones, Chapter 9; Phakiti, Chapter 10), and test trialing and piloting (Green, Chapter 11). The last two chapters in this section (Kuiken & Vedder, Chapter 12; Pill & Smart, Chapter 13) overview and describe instruments and methods for guiding raters' scoring of speaking and writing performances to ensure that the scores provided by raters are as consistent, meaningful, and objective as possible.

Part III dives into the measurement of individual differences that are well known to affect SLA, factors such as L2 aptitude (Roehr-Brackin, Chapter 14), motivation (Iwaniec & Dunn, Chapter 15), working memory (Wen, Juffs & Winke, Chapter 16), anxiety (Cheng & Zheng, Chapter 17), and willingness to communicate (MacIntyre & Ayers-Glassey, Chapter 18). The authors discuss old and trusted, as well as new and cutting-edge, methods for measuring these factors in a variety of learner types (e.g., children versus adults; low versus high L2 proficiency). Each of these chapters draws heavily on the fields of psychology, cognitive psychology, cognitive science, and psycholinguistics, and they are meant to serve as guides in the measurement of other individual differences that were not covered, due to space constraints, in this volume.

Part IV overviews, intensely, constructs that are commonly assessed through language testing: complexity, accuracy, and fluency (CAF; Pallotti, Chapter 19); vocabulary (Kremmel & Pellicer-Sánchez, Chapter 20); grammar (Spinner, Chapter 22); and L2 listening, speaking, reading, and writing (Batty, Chapter 26; Nakatsuhara, Inoue & Khabbazbashi, Chapter 27; Jeon & Yamashita, Chapter 25; Yoon & Burton, Chapter 28, respectively). But within this part, the authors also delve into constructs that are more often embraced by and assessed by SLA researchers than language testers, constructs that language testers should investigate with more rigor: such as pragmatics (Timpe-Laughlin & Youn, Chapter 24), phonology (Crowther, Chapter 23), lexicogrammar (Paquot, Gries & Yoder, Chapter 21), interactional competence (Galaczi & Taylor, Chapter 32), implicit and explicit L2 knowledge (Isbell & Rogers, Chapter 29), L2 literary competency (Paran, Spöttl, Ratheiser & Eberharter, Chapter 31), and intercultural competence (Schauer, Chapter 34). It furthermore includes a chapter on task-based language assessment (Van den Branden, Chapter 30). Finally, this part has strong insights on how (and why it is important) to document and evaluate L2 learning that occurs *outside* of the language classroom or language lab (Reinders & Bailey, Chapter 35), and how to use robust and informative self-assessments for L2 research (Cox & Dewey, Chapter 36).

Part V concerns the people who are assessed. Language testing and SLA research provide information about humans and social conditions (see Brown & Harris, 2016), thus it is important to always robustly define who is tested in SLA and language testing research, and to consider the implications for how to best assess their language ability. This part provides particular attention and coverage of bilingual and multilingual learners (Brown & Bhatia, Chapter 37), young (child) language learners (Hsieh & Chapman, Chapter 38), L2 learners with specific learning difficulties (Kormos & Taylor, Chapter 39), heritage language learners (Son, Chapter 40), and sign language learners (Haug, Boers-Visker & van den Bogaerde, Chapter 41).

And finally, in Part VI, authors expertly review measurement principles for SLA research. The topics include statistical modeling of SLA theories, and how, mathematically, the models connect test performances to the underlying constructs (In'nami & Murakami, Chapter 42). The authors divulge how researchers can create equivalent and parallel forms for pre-test, post-test, and delayed post-test (and longitudinal) research designs (Suzuki & Koizumi, Chapter 43). The part rounds off with a discussion of reliability and validity reporting practices, and generalizability issues, in SLA and language testing research that are important to consider (McKay & Plonsky, Chapter 44; Schoonen, Chapter 45).

In sum, this volume points toward the important overlapping and mutually beneficial work being done in the fields of SLA and language testing. The volume shows how these are not distinct, separate fields, but rather areas of expertise that are often shared in working toward a common goal: To map and understand the ever-expanding and undulating landscapes of L2 learning, and the people who occupy and are affected by the landscapes within which they live and learn.

Recommendations for Practice

Each of the chapters in this volume have recommendations for practice. Our main recommendation is for SLA researchers and language testing researchers to share ideas. It is quite obvious to us that many researchers in the fields of SLA and applied linguistics are dual language testers and SLA/applied linguistics researchers. Individuals such as ourselves, and many of the authors of chapters in this edited volume, wear both SLA and language testing hats (albeit often with varying balances). At times, we (Paula and Tineke) research SLA processes, and at other times, we investigate how to make better L2 tests, or we do both at the same time. Each area of research stems from overlapping (but not 100% so) histories, sets of literature, and methodological tools. On the other hand, each area has *pipelines in* that flow particularly strongly: SLA is fed strongly, one could say, by education, psychology, and cognitive science, while language testing is fed strongly, one could say, by educational measurement. To keep your feet in both fluid fields of SLA and language testing, we recommend the following:

- Occasionally attend a conference, workshop, or webinar, or presentation that is not squarely in the "camp" with which you most associate yourself (SLA or language testing). Doing so will help you spread your horizons, and help you see how others are, on a macro level, investigating the same topics you are interested in, but perhaps just from a different angle, or within a different research tradition.
- Instead of learning everything across the two overlapping disciplines, engage in co- and multi-author projects that combine researchers with various strengths and skills in SLA and language testing.
- Avoid thinking that paradigms cannot or should not overlap (see Polio, 2012). There is room for everyone at the L2 research table, and all work on describing and understanding L2 learning contexts and constructs benefits the overall modern movement of SLA theory.

Recommended Readings

We obviously highly recommend the chapters in this volume, which each have further recommended readings at the end of them. Below, we list four books we think that SLA researchers and language testing researchers should have on hand. These are recent or highly influential works that make the interface between SLA and language testing more transparent.

American Educational Research Association, American Psychological Association, & National Council on Measurement in Education. (2014). *Standards for educational and psychological testing*. American Educational Research Association.

To promote excellent test development, useful and meaningful test scores, and the rights of test takers, the AERA, APA, and NCME have continually published updated versions of this book since 1985. This newest 2014 version guides test developers and researchers through test accountability issues, how and why tests must be equally accessible to all examinees, and why researchers should empirically analyze test takers' response processes (through, for example, verbal reports or eye-movement recordings) to validate test constructs and test-score uses.

Aryadoust, V., & Raquel, M. (Eds.), *Quantitative data analysis for language assessment*, Volume 1 (*Fundamental techniques*; 2019) and Volume 2 (*Advanced methods*; 2020). Routledge.

This two-volume set overviews fundamental and advanced techniques, respectively, for analyzing results from language assessments. Topics covered include item analysis, item response theory, differential item functioning, *t* tests, ANOVA, MANCOVA, linear regression, factor analysis, hierarchical and structural equation modeling, and longitudinal multilevel modeling.

Dimova, S., Yan, X., & Ginther, A. (2020). *Local language testing: Design, implementation, and development*. Routledge.

This book is a basic primer in language test creation and validation research that every language tester and SLA researcher should have. The book will help graduate students and novice researchers create, select, or adapt measures for their specific research purposes, formulate procedures for efficient and effective test administration, adopt and apply rating scales, and train and employ raters. Most timely is a section devoted to data collection, data management, and meaningful and ethical score reporting.

Stanley, K. (2017). *Validating psychological constructs: Historical, philosophical, and practical dimensions*. Palgrave Macmillan.

Kathleen Stanley does an excellent job describing concisely and in a reader-friendly manner the historical developments and contemporary theorizing on construct validation theory within psychological and educational testing. She explains how construct validation theory is not just for testing, but also for understanding all aspects of research on psychological phenomena.

References

Alderson, J. C., Brunfaut, T., & Harding, L. (2017). Bridging assessment and learning: A view from second and foreign language assessment. *Assessment in Education: Principles, Policy and Practice*, *24*(3), 379–387. https://doi.org/10.1080/0969594X.2017.1331201

Bachman, L. F. (1988). Language testing-SLA research interfaces. *Annual Review of Applied Linguistics*, *9*, 193–209. https://doi.org/10.1017/s0267190500000891

Bachman, L. F., & Cohen, A. D. (1998). *Interfaces between second language acquisition and language testing research*. Cambridge University Press.

Brown, G. T. L., & Harris, L. R. (Eds.). (2016). *Handbook of human and social conditions in assessment*. Routledge.

Chapelle, C. (2020). *Argument-based validation in testing and assessment*. SAGE Publications.

Davies, A. (2012). Review of the book Linguistic relativity in SLA: Thinking for speaking, by Z. H. Han & T. Cadierno, Eds. *Language Testing*, *29*(1), 156–160. https://doi.org/10.1177/0265532211417208

Doughty, C. J., & Long, M. H. (2003). The scope of inquiry and goals of SLA. In C. J. Doughty & M. H. Long (Eds.), *The handbook of second language acquisition* (pp. 3–16). Blackwell. https://doi.org/10.1002/9780470756492.ch1

Douglas, D. (2001). Performance consistency in second language acquisition and language testing research: A conceptual gap. *Second Language Research*, *17*(4), 442–456. https://doi.org/10.1177/026765830101700408

Firth, A., & Wagner, J. (2007). Second/foreign language learning as a social accomplishment: Elaborations on a reconceptualized SLA. *The Modern Language Journal*, *91*(S1), 800–819. https://doi.org/10.1111/j.1540-4781.2007.00670.x

Gass, S. M., & Mackey, A. (2012). Introduction. In S. M. Gass & A. Mackey (Eds.), *The Routledge handbook of second language acquisition* (pp. 1–4). Routledge.

Gu, L. (2014). At the interface between language testing and second language acquisition: Language ability and context of learning. *Language Testing*, *31*(1), 111–133. https://doi.org/10.1177/0265532212469177

Hambleton, R. K., & Cook, L. L. (1977). Latent trait models and their use in the analysis of educational test data. *Journal of Educational Measurement*, *14*(2), 75–96. http://www.jstor.com/stable/1434009

Huhta, A., Alanen, R., Tarnanen, M., Martin, M., & Hirvelä, T. (2014). Assessing learners' writing skills in a SLA study: Validating the rating process across tasks, scales and languages. *Language Testing*, *31*(3), 307–328. https://doi.org/10.1177/0265532214526176

Hult, F. M. (2019). Toward a unified theory of language development: The transdisciplinary nexus of cognitive and sociocultural perspectives on social activity. *The Modern Language Journal*, *103*, 136–144. https://doi.org/10.1111/modl.12527

Joint Committee on Testing Practices. (2013). Code of fair testing practices in education. In R. M. Kaplan & D. P. Saccuzzo (Eds.), *Psychological testing: Principles, applications, and issues* (pp. 635–639). Wadsworth Cengage Learning.

Kunnan, A. J., & Lakshmanan, U. (2006). *Editorial. Language Assessment Quarterly*, *3*(2), 91–95. https://doi.org/10.1207/s15434311laq0302_1

Macqueen, S., Knoch, U., Wigglesworth, G., Nordlinger, R., Singer, R., & Brickle, R. (2019). The impact of national standardized literacy and numeracy testing on children and teaching staff in remote Australian Indigenous communities. *Language Testing*, *36*(2), 265–287. https://doi.org/10.1177/0265532218775758

Markee, N. (2017). Are replication studies possible in qualitative second/foreign language classroom research? A call for comparative re-production research. *Language Teaching*, *50*(3), 367–383. https://doi.org/10.1017/S0261444815000099

Marsden, E., Morgan-Short, K., Thompson, S., & Abugaber, D. (2018). Replication in second language research: Narrative and systematic reviews and recommendations for the field. *Language Learning*, *68*(2), 321–391. https://doi.org/10.1111/lang.12286

McNamara, T. (2001). Language assessment as social practice: Challenges for research. *Language Testing*, *18*(4), 333–349. https://doi.org/10.1177/026553220101800402

McNamara, T., & Roever, C. (2006). *Language testing: The social dimension*. Blackwell.

Norris, J., & Ortega, L. (2008). Defining and measuring SLA. In C. J. Doughty & M. H. Long (Eds.), *The handbook of second language acquisition* (pp. 716–761). Blackwell. https://doi.org/10.1002/9780470756492.ch21

Norton, B., & De Costa, P. I. (2018). Research tasks on identity in language learning and teaching. *Language Teaching*, *51*(1), 90–112. https://doi.org/10.1017/S0261444817000325

Polio, C. (2012). No paradigm wars please! *Journal of Second Language Writing*, *21*(3), 294–295. https://doi.org/10.1016/j.jslw.2012.05.008

Saito, H. (2004). Language testing and SLA research: Some issues concerning task difficulty. *The Japan Language Testing Association Journal*, *6*, 30–39. http://jlta2016.sakura.ne.jp/wp-content/uploads/2015/10/JLTA_Journal_Contents06.pdf

Shohamy, E. (2000). The relationship between language testing and second language acquisition, revisited. *System*, *28*(4), 541–553. https://doi.org/10.1016/S0346-251X(00)00037-3

Shohamy, E. (2013). The discourse of language testing as a tool for shaping national, global, and transnational identities. *Language and Intercultural Communication*, *13*(2), 225–236. https://doi.org/10.1080/14708477.2013.770868

Spolsky, B. (2000). Language testing in The Modern Language Journal. *The Modern Language Journal*, *84*(4), 536–552. https://www.jstor.org/stable/330305

Swain, M. (1993). Second language testing and second language acquisition: Is there a conflict with traditional psychometrics? *Language Testing*, *10*(2), 193–207. https://doi.org/10.1177/026553229301000205

The Douglas Fir Group. (2016). A transdisciplinary framework for SLA in a multilingual world. *The Modern Language Journal*, *100*, 19–47. https://doi.org/10.1111/modl.12301

Weir, C. J. (2005). *Language testing and validation: An evidence-based approach*. Palgrave Macmillan.

Winke, P., & Zhang, X. (2019). How a third-grade reading retention law will affect ELLs in Michigan, and a call for research on child ELL reading development. *TESOL Quarterly*, *53*(2), 529–542. https://doi.org/10.1002/tesq.481

Part I

Assessment Concepts for SLA Researchers

2

Validity in Language Assessment

Carol A. Chapelle

Background

The field of SLA is largely concerned with describing second language knowledge and explaining how it develops over time, but at least the latter goal requires empirical research. Writing about empirical research in SLA, Ellis's view in 2005 was that there had been "little real progress in achieving the second goal because of a general failure to address how learners' L2 knowledge can be measured" (Ellis, 2005, p. 142). Because assessment of learners' language knowledge, performance, or some aspect of ability is central to second language acquisition research, validation should be of central importance for the credibility of research results. The need for careful attention to assessment methods has heightened over the past decade with the open science initiatives that have made research instruments publically available and are encouraging the dissemination of research results among SLA researchers and beyond.

But how can a researcher validate assessment practices when the subject of validation in language assessment itself includes a complex set of practices, statistical methods, frameworks, and theoretical perspectives? A look for guidance from within the language assessment literature results in at least a dozen books with almost as many frameworks, perspectives, and even more pieces of advice for justifying the validity of test use. Moreover, their overarching concern is the use of language assessments for decision-making about individuals or programs in, for example, educational or professional contexts. Researchers in SLA can detect a dissonance between their interests and those of language testers, who tend to work with the broadly defined constructs, statistical techniques requiring large numbers of test takers, and considerations of the social consequences of decision making. Moreover, the field of language testing does not express a consensus validation method that can be readily applied by anyone willing to read a single book. These issues raise questions about the use of conceptions of validity and validation in language testing for investigating validity in SLA research. How can an SLA researcher begin to assess the relevance of validation practices used in language assessment?

In this chapter I offer a basis for addressing this question by outlining some areas of general agreement in language assessment about validation. Underlying this chapter is the perspective stated by Douglas (2001):

> In both language testing and SLA studies, practitioners make inferences about the state of a learner's interlanguage, i.e., the abilities underlying language performance, based on

> systematic observation of an elicited performance. It follows from this that both language tests and SLA elicitation devices should be held to similar standards of validity.
>
> (Douglas, 2001, p. 442)

The process of making inferences based on performance describes what users do with both *tests* and *assessments*, and therefore I use these terms interchangeably in this chapter. In the first part of this chapter I introduce the foundational concepts in educational and psychological measurement that underlie the various presentations of validity in language assessment. I then identify key issues for applying current validation practices in SLA research, and I offer advice for practice.

Foundations of Validity

Common ground about validation in language testing today stems from a paper by Messick (1989) that has been influential in educational and psychological measurement as well as in language testing. Despite the fact that pre-Messick concepts, expressions, and perspectives still appear in language testing, for the most part, Messick's presentation of validity is accepted in language testing today. Messick's paper, which covers a range of issues from philosophy of science to empirical research design and the values inherent in assessment, is useful for understanding validity in language testing.

Messick defined validity as a unitary concept defined as "an overall evaluative judgment of the degree to which empirical evidence and theoretical rationales support the adequacy and appropriateness of interpretations and actions based on test scores" (Messick, 1989, p. 13). Messick's unitary view of validity contrasts with the idea that there are three or more *types* of validity. Messick explained, "because content- and criterion-related evidence contribute to score meaning, they have come to be recognized as aspects of construct validity. In a sense, then, this leaves only one category, namely, construct-related evidence" (Messick, 1989, p. 20). Messick's distinction between "types of validity" and "types of evidence" is disregarded by some language testers (Weir, 2005). Nevertheless, the distinction is important because, as Messick explained, the types-of-validities approach leads the validation process astray by prompting researchers to see a test as having a certain type of validity rather than seeing a need to present theoretical rationales and evidence for interpretations and uses of a test, in accordance with his definition.

Construct validity is central to Messick's definition of validity, because validation seeks evidence for the construct meaning of the test score. From an assessment perspective, the technical sense of the word *construct* is a meaningful interpretation of performance consistency. "The key point is that in educational and psychological measurement inferences are drawn from scores, a term used here in the most general sense of any coding or summarization of observed consistencies on a test, questionnaire, observation procedure, or other assessment device" (Messick, 1989, p. 14). Scores are interpreted to have meanings such as implicit grammatical knowledge, vocabulary ability, or working memory, for example. Conducting validation research requires the construct the test is intended to assess to be defined in sufficient detail to be used to guide development of assessments and to formulate hypotheses about how those assessments will perform. Validation research serves as an empirical check as to how well the construct theory accounts for, or explains, results (Cronbach & Meehl, 1955; Cronbach, 1971).

Beyond construct validity, validation needs to take into account issues of relevance and utility, value implications, and the social consequences of testing. These three other facets of validity are not considered types of validity, but rather additional aspects of test interpretation and use that researchers or language test developers need to include in a validity investigation. Messick's four-faceted definition expanded validity inquiry beyond the technical concerns normally associated with quantitative research methodology (Campbell & Fiske, 1959) and moved validity into the domains of values and social practice.

By thinking outside the technical box, Messick engaged the *philosophy of science* in his discussion of validity, which in turn ignited debates over ontological, epistemological and axiological aspects of validation in educational and psychological assessment (e.g., Borsboom, 2006; Markus & Borsboom, 2013). Put simply, the ontological debate centers around whether the process of testing seeks the truth about the individuals tested, or evidence about useful constructs. The epistemological question raised is whether inferences from a given test can be proven to be valid by demonstrating statistically that the response data fit the measurement model of the construct, or whether inferences must be supported through a variety of evidence to be used in a judgment about validity. The axiological dimension centers on whether the process of validation should be considered as value-neutral (as the truth/proof side wishes) or as value-laden (as the utility/evidence side would do). Messick's use of the expression "evaluative judgment" signals his affiliation with the utility/evidence side of the debate, which is largely the position taken in the field of language testing.

Messick's definition of validity has played a significant role in educational and psychological testing as demonstrated by its overall acceptance by the Joint Committee of the American Education Research Association, American Psychological Association, and the National Council on Measurement in Education, which is responsible for producing and updating the *Standards for Educational and Psychological Testing* (AERA, APA, & NCME, 2014), referred to as the *Standards* hereafter. The *Standards* expresses a consensus view of these three professional organizations, which arguably affect practice throughout the world (Zumbo, 2014), including the international field of language testing.

Bachman's (1990) seminal work, *Fundamental Considerations in Language Testing*, drew heavily on these central threads of Messick's discussion of validity, and eventually, Messick's perspectives took root in language testing (e.g., McNamara & Roever, 2006). However, with only a few exceptions (e.g., Chapelle, 1994, 1998; Douglas, 2001), Messick's influence went unnoticed in SLA. Even in language testing, Messick's validity framework was recognized as too complex to guide validation practices. Instead, Bachman's work set into motion two decades of framework building in language testing with attempts to put into practice the broad concerns laid out by Messick (Bachman & Palmer, 1996, 2010; Norris, 2008; Weir, 2005). Perhaps the best known, Bachman and Palmer's (1996) test usefulness framework has been used to guide validation studies (Chapelle et al., 2003) and is still used to introduce concepts in language testing to teachers.

Like language testers, researchers in other areas of educational and psychological measurement are interested in applying Messick's ideas (Newton & Shaw, 2014). To address this need, argument-based validity has been developed primarily by Kane (1992, 2001, 2006, 2013) as a pragmatic approach for putting into practice Messick's perspective on validity. According to Kane, "to validate an interpretation or use of measurements is to evaluate the rationale, or argument, for the claims being made, and this in turn requires a clear statement of the proposed interpretations and uses and critical evaluation of these interpretations and uses" (Kane, 2006, p. 17). Kane outlined a process of validation that begins with a set of claims that the tester wants to make about test interpretation and use, rather than with a set of criteria or qualities that have been set by someone else. The process continues with research required to support the inferences that need to be made to draw the conclusions, which serve as claims in the validity argument. Finally, the results of research are interpreted in view of the degree of support they offer their respective inferences, and an overall judgment is made about the validity of the claimed interpretations and uses of the test. Argument-based validity, as presented by Kane across a number of papers from the early 1990s, has been influential in language testing (Bachman, 2005; Chapelle et al., 2008, 2010; Cheng & Sun, 2015; Llosa, 2008; Norris, 2008; Youn, 2015).

Key Concepts

Test content: The material appearing on the test used to elicit performance from the test taker. Content appears as listening or reading passages, texts to be completed, or individual multiple-choice items, for example.

Performance: The test takers' spoken or written language (or other responses) produced in response to test prompts.

Reliability: The consistency or stability of test scores. Reliability refers to test scores, not to tests. Reliability can be estimated in a number of different ways, each of which takes into account different types of error (inconsistency).

Construct: A meaningful interpretation, or explanation, of performance consistency. Constructs can be posited to be real entities or constructions created by testers, or a combination of the two.

Target context: The context of interest to test score users when they interpret test scores; the domain where test takers are expected to be able to perform if they achieve high test scores.

Test use: Actions and decisions taken on the basis of test results (e.g., placement into an instructional program, certification for a job, continuation of research, conclusion about a research question).

Consequences: Results emanating from test use, including increased knowledge in the field, students placed at an appropriate level, education of teachers about important aspects of language.

Values: Judgments about importance, worth, or usefulness of aspects of testing including an approach to construct definition, the selection of test content, the identification of research participants.

Inference: A deduction or logical step taken in moving from grounds consisting of an observation or accepted statement to a conclusion consisting of new knowledge.

Claim: A statement about the proposed interpretation for a particular purpose of testing that requires support from evidence.

Warrant: A statement whose credibility needs to be substantiated to support an inference.

Key Issues

Key issues in applying argument-based validity in both language assessment and SLA research stem from the understanding of validity articulated by Messick (1989). As the *Standards* put it, "statements about validity should refer to particular interpretations for specified uses" of tests (AERA, APA, & NCME, 2014, p. 1). Since it is the interpretations and uses of the test that are the objects of validation, "it is incorrect to use the unqualified phrase 'the validity of the test'" (AERA, APA, & NCME, 2014, p. 1). In other words, validity is not treated as a quality or entity that can be attributed to a test and carried with the test for all prospective uses and in all contexts. Instead, validity refers to an argument that includes particular claims about the interpretations and uses of the test. The key issues in validity are found in the concepts required to build such arguments, the most basic of which is inference.

Inferences Underlie Assessment Use

An inference is a logical step taken in moving from an observation or accepted statement to a new insight or understanding. The new understanding obtained from construct-related inferences in language testing includes conclusions that the test user draws about the learner's language knowledge, performance, or ability (Chalhoub-Deville et al., 2006). SLA researchers are typically interested in drawing inferences about precise aspects of learners' knowledge such as implicit

Table 2.1 Inferences and their meanings with the types of claims that each leads to in a validity argument

Inference	*Meaning in a Validity Argument*	*General Claim Serving as Conclusion**
Consequence Implication	• The test user believes that the stated positive consequences will result from intended test use.	• Test score use results in positive consequences.
Utilization	• The test user concludes that the test scores will serve well for their stated use.	• The test scores are useful for their intended purpose.
Extrapolation	• The test user accepts that the score meaning extends to the target context.	• The test scores represent the performance of interest in the target context.
Explanation	• The test user surmises that the score meaning is explained by the defined construct.	• The test scores reflect the intended construct.
Generalization	• The test user concludes that the test has produced reliable scores in relevant research contexts.	• Scores reflect performance consistency.
Evaluation	• The test user trusts that relevant test takers' performance has been summarized accurately in scores.	• The test scores accurately summarize relevant performance.
Domain Definition	• The test user accepts that the analysis of the domain of interest has been carried out adequately to create relevant assessment tasks with appropriate content.	• Appropriate observations of test takers' performance has been obtained.

* A validity argument for a particular test interpretation and use would contain a tailored version of these general claims to address the specific testing purpose.

knowledge of certain grammatical features; making precise inferences requires stating a precise construct definition (Ellis, 2005). A construct-related inference, called explanation, is only one of several inferences made when an assessment is interpreted and used (Chapelle et al., 2010).

Table 2.1 presents seven types of inferences that test users may make when they interpret test scores for particular uses. The meaning of each inference is given in Table 2.1 in addition to the wording of a general claim that each inference would lead to in a validity argument. For example, when a generalization inference is made, the test user concludes that the test has produced reliable scores, which allows for a claim that the scores reflect performance consistency. Since a construct is a meaningful interpretation of performance consistency observed on an assessment, this claim is needed to serve as the basis, or grounds, for the inference about the construct, which is called the explanation inference. In language testing, it is not unusual to see validity arguments with six or seven inferences, but the number and type of inferences depends on the assessment and its purpose. Kane did not specify a certain number of inferences that validity arguments must contain.

Validation Research Investigates Inferences

Identifying inferences that underlie interpretation and use of assessments is important because validation research investigates the validity of these inferences. The distinction between investigating the *validity of the test* and the *validity of inferences* is important because the former results in problematic conclusions. For example, Erlam's (2006) validation study of an elicited imitation task as a measure of L2 implicit knowledge concluded that "results suggest that as a measure of implicit language knowledge, [the test] has both validity and reliability" (p. 489). If the test itself has the attributes of validity and reliability, can anyone create the grammaticality judgment test in the model of Erlam's and use it for any purpose requiring a language test? Can it be used for making university admissions decisions, precluding, for example, the need for the IELTS, which was developed by the University of Cambridge Examination Syndicate in the UK?

Someone looking to SLA research for a convenient assessment for university admissions should, of course, be advised to more carefully consider the adequacy of what the test measures in view of the intended test use. The test itself does not have validity. If the prospective test user is serious about validating the intended interpretations and uses, the user would need to identify the claims and inferences underlying the new test use. The relevant claims would be something like claims one through seven below. The inference leading to each claim is given in parentheses.

1. The EI test yields positive consequences for test takers and test users (consequence implication).
2. The test scores are useful for distinguishing among students who are more and less ready linguistically for university study (utilization).
3. The test scores reflect the levels of language performance that students are likely to display in their academic work (extrapolation).
4. The scores reflect the varying levels of implicit language knowledge of the test takers (explanation).
5. The scores reflect performance consistency (generalization).
6. The scores accurately summarize performance relevant to implicit language knowledge (evaluation).
7. The domain of implicit language knowledge was adequately analyzed to create test tasks that elicit relevant performance (domain definition).

The validation research driven by such claims could include the following: 1) Interviews with students about their test preparation practices if the new test were instituted, 2) observations of the performance of students who would be admitted based on EI test scores, 3) correlations of EI test scores with scores on language performance in university classes, 4) retrospective interviews of test taking processes, 5) estimation of internal consistency reliability taking into account the number of test tasks, 6) item analysis to calculate difficulty, discrimination, and model fit, 7) focus group conducted with content experts to explore the range of content coverage desired for a test. These are examples of the variety of qualitative and quantitative methods that can be undertaken for validation. The choice of method and specific study design depends on the detail in the validity argument.

Research Results Show (Lack of) Support for Inferences

Validation results need to be interpreted in terms of what they mean for the inferences in a validity argument that specifies the claims, inferences, and warrants in need of support for the specified test use. Gutiérrez's (2013) investigation of a grammaticality judgment test (GJT) illustrated the need for the specifics of the validity argument to guide the interpretation of results. Gutiérrez introduced the GTJs as being used in past decades of research "in SLA as a measure of learners' linguistic ability in the L2" (p. 425). If a validation study is to be undertaken to assess the support for the claim that a GJT assesses linguistic ability in the L2, the meaning of "linguistic ability in the L2" needs to be defined more precisely, and the warrants underlying the inference to be made need to be specified. However, in the paper, the logic linking linguistic ability in the L2 with implicit and explicit grammatical knowledge is not presented. Nor is the precise validity claim that is investigated in the study. The final paragraph of the discussion of the construct allows readers to infer that the claim is about implicit knowledge because it indicates that previous researchers have "expressed their concerns regarding timed GJTs as a valid measure of implicit knowledge" (p. 429). Based on this introduction and the research that was carried out, the validity

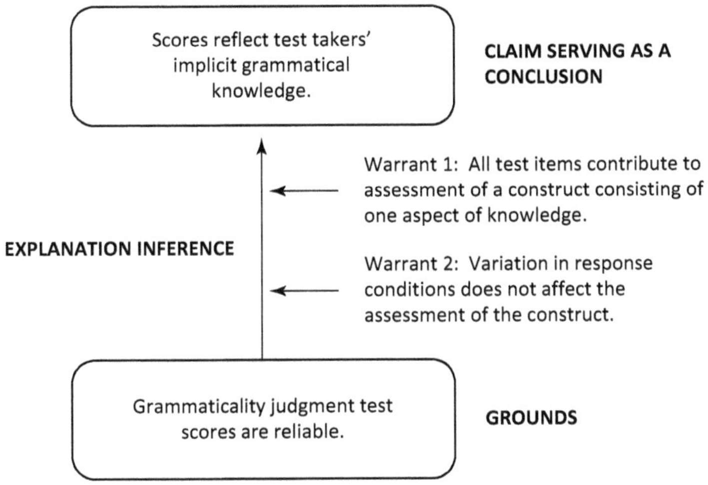

Figure 2.1 Outline of an argument supporting the claim that scores on a grammaticality test should be interpreted as an assessment of implicit grammatical knowledge.

claim with its inference, warrants and conclusion might be presented using the argument-based validity notation outlined in Figure 2.1.

Figure 2.1 illustrates the logic underlying the study which investigates whether or not support is found for an inference underlying the claim that the scores on the GJT reflect test takers' implicit grammatical knowledge. Specifically, the two warrants state the empirically testable statements that, if supported by the data, would warrant the explanation inference leading to the claim. The warrants are that all the test items contribute to assessment of a single construct and that variation in response conditions does not affect the assessment of the construct. Support for neither warrant was found. The lack of support for Warrant 1 was interpreted from the processing differences found for the two types of items and from data indicating that the items with grammatical and ungrammatical sentences loaded on different factors. The author concluded that "differences may be interpreted as [indicating] these two types of sentences [are] measures of implicit and explicit knowledge, respectively" (p. 444). The lack of support for Warrant 2 was interpreted from the finding that "the two dimensions of time pressure and task stimulus significantly affect the L2 learners' performance on those tests" (p. 444).

If the study had been framed as shown in Figure 2.1 (as an argument containing statements in need of support of a stated claim), interpretation of the results for the validity of the GJT as a measure of implicit grammatical knowledge in SLA research could have been stated in the conclusion of the article. A clear statement about validity would be useful in the conclusion of an article whose title is "The construct validity of grammaticality judgment tests as measures of implicit and explicit knowledge." Lacking such clarity, however, the author's conclusion about construct validity appears to be, "the results of the study also emphasize the need to verify whether or not the instruments used in a study actually measure what they are intended to measure" (Gutiérrez, 2013, p. 445).

Recommendations for Practice

The issues of identifying inferences, planning relevant research, and making clear interpretations are likely to increase in importance for SLA research going forward. These issues are not new in the field (e.g., Bachman & Cohen, 1998; Chalhoub-Deville et al., 2006), but technology has expanded both the types of assessments used and their accessibility to a broad array of prospective users in the field and beyond. In this environment, where clarity is needed about the justified interpretations and uses of assessments, individual researchers might be advised as follows:

- (Re)learn the basics. Fundamental characteristics of assessment and reporting of assessment results need to be learned before undertaking assessment in research. Purpura et al. (2015) provided a list of assessment-related errors commonly appearing in SLA research articles (e.g., reporting the wrong reliability estimates). It will be difficult to move the field forward without some common ground in assessment knowledge among researchers. In short, research cannot be interpreted unless assessment results can be interpreted.
- Understand your purpose, audience and context. To write the specific statements required for a validity argument, researchers need to be able to express the specific characteristics of the interpretations and uses of the assessment tasks they are working with. Context-specific statements are needed. Assessments do not attain validity by being used in previous studies.
- Explain the rationale for context-specific assessment decisions reported in research. Rationales are needed for choices made during assessment construction, adaption, or adoption; for sample selection; for the logic behind statistical calculations; and for the selection of precisely what results are reported. Rationales are key to dialogue about assessment practices and they serve as educational tools for graduate students and for other researchers. Writing rationales requires an understanding of the basics of assessment and the goals of research. Rationales for interpretations and uses need to stem from rationales underlying test development (Mislevy & Haertel, 2006; Nichols et al., 2015).
- Investigate statements rather than entities. Statements appear as claims and warrants in validity arguments. Entities are multifaceted concepts such as reliability and validity. When validity, or construct validity, as a noun phrase is investigated, the degree to which results offer support is not obvious. Statements are needed because they express a proposition, which the research results can be interpreted as supporting or not supporting.
- Interpret validation research results to elucidate the degree of support they provide for the claims in the validity argument. Such interpretations can be made only to the extent that the intended validity argument has been clearly stated.
- Examine the validity arguments in previous research. Progress is made in the study of complex constructs and their development over time by a community of researchers who are able to communicate about the detail of their research endeavor. Communication about assessment requires the concepts and language that are up to the task in addition to researchers who are able to use it.

In this era of open science, research results and instruments are made physically available to anyone who wants to use them. The impetus has never been greater for addressing the theoretical, methodological, and ethical dimensions of assessment use in SLA research. The international flow of information equally provides language testers and SLA researchers with access to and responsibility for availing themselves of established practices in educational and psychological testing. In the *Standards*, validity is defined as "the degree to which evidence and theory support the interpretations of test scores for proposed uses of test scores" (AERA, APA, & NCME, 2014, p. 1). If such widely-used statements of practice are not relevant to SLA research, alternative frames of reference need to be articulated.

In a review article on validation in language assessment in 1999, I predicted that in the future "language testing researchers [could] be expected to be more closely allied with these views [in the *Standards*] than ever before. As a consequence, [I suggested that] for applied linguists who think that 'the validity of a language test' is its correlation with another language test, now is a good time to reconsider" (Chapelle, 1999, p. 265). Twenty-plus years hence, evidence suggests that SLA researchers are engaging with issues of validation for some assessments, as detailed in Résvész and Brunfaut, Chapter 3, this volume. With this interest demonstrated by researchers and more clarity about the concepts and tools available in argument-based validation today, the time may be ideal to increase the clarity of validation practices in SLA research.

Recommended Readings

Chapelle, C. A. (forthcoming). *Argument-based validation in testing and assessment*. SAGE Publications.

Chapelle defines the concepts in assessment required to develop and use validity arguments by situating them historically. She illustrates how these basic concepts in assessment are made more precise and contextually relevant by developing them into claims, inferences and warrants in validity arguments.

Lissitz, R. W. (Ed.). (2009). *The concept of validity: Revisions, new directions and applications*. Information Age Publishing, Inc.

Lissitz gathers some of the key validity researchers in educational and psychological testing to present a variety of perspectives on validity. This may be a good starting point for researchers wishing to better understanding the academic context of validation research.

Ercikan, K., & Pellegrino, J. W. (Eds.). (2017). *Validation of score meaning in the next generation of assessments*. The National Council on Measurement in Education.

This volume explores the use of test takers' process data in validation research. Process data (e.g., gathered through think alouds, eye-tracking, and response latency data) are used in second language acquisition research for making inferences about learning, language knowledge and strategic processes. This volume introduces a different perspective on how such data can be used in validation research and in doing so may suggest an expanded use for data that SLA researchers currently work with.

References

American Education Research Association, American Psychological Association, & The National Council on Measurement in Education. (2014). *Standards for educational and psychological testing*. American Education Research Association.

Bachman, L. F. (1990). *Fundamental considerations in language testing*. Oxford University Press.

Bachman, L. F. (2005). Building and supporting a case for test use. *Language Assessment Quarterly*, *2*(1), 1–34. https://doi.org/10.1207/s15434311laq0201_1

Bachman, L. F., & Cohen, A. D. (Eds.). (1998). *Second language acquisition and language testing interfaces*. Cambridge University Press.

Bachman, L. F., & Palmer, A. S. (1996). *Language testing in practice*. Oxford University Press.

Bachman, L. F., & Palmer, A. S. (2010). *Language assessment in practice*. Oxford University Press.

Borsboom, D. (2006). The attack of the psychometricians. *Psychometrika*, *71*, 425–440. https://doi.org/10.1007/s11336-006-1447-6

Campbell, D. T., & Fiske, D. W. (1959). Convergent and discriminant validation by the multitrait-multimethod matrix. *Psychological Bulletin*, *56*(2), 81–105. https://doi.org/10.1037/h0046016

Chalhoub-Deville, M., Chapelle, C. A., & Duff, P. (2006). *Inference and generalizability in applied linguistics: Multiple perspectives*. John Benjamins Publishing.

Chapelle, C. (1994). Are C-tests valid measures for L2 vocabulary research? *Second Language Research*, *10*(2), 157–187. https://doi.org/10.1177/026765839401000203

Chapelle, C. (1998). Construct definition and validity inquiry in SLA research. In L. F. Bachman & A. D. Cohen (Eds.), *Second language acquisition and language testing interfaces* (pp. 32–70). Cambridge University Press.

Chapelle, C. A. (1999). Validity in language assessment. *Annual Review of Applied Linguistics*, *19*, 254–272. https://doi.org/10.1017/S0267190599190135

Chapelle, C. A., Chung, Y.-R., Hegelheimer, V., Pendar, N., & Xu, J. (2010). Designing a computer-delivered test of productive grammatical ability. *Language Testing*, *27*(4), 443–469. https://doi.org/10.1177/0265532210367633

Chapelle, C. A., Enright, M. E., & Jamieson, J. (2008). *Building a validity argument for the test of English as a foreign language*. Routledge.
Chapelle, C. A., Enright, M. E., & Jamieson, J. (2010). Does an argument-based approach to validity make a difference? *Educational Measurement: Issues and Practice*, *29*(1), 3–13. https://doi.org/10.1111/j.1745-3992.2009.00165.x
Chapelle, C. A., Jamieson, J., & Hegelheimer, V. (2003). Validation of a web-based ESL test. *Language Testing*, *20*(4), 409–439. https://doi.org/10.1191/0265532203lt266oa
Cheng, L., & Sun, Y. (2015). Interpreting the impact of the Ontario Secondary School Literacy Test on second language students within an argument-based validation framework. *Language Assessment Quarterly*, *12*(1), 50–66. https://doi.org/10.1080/15434303.2014.981334
Cronbach, L. (1971). Test validation. In R. L. Thorndike (Ed.), *Educational measurement* (2nd ed., pp. 443–507). American Council on Education.
Cronbach, L. J., & Meehl, P. E. (1955). Construct validity in psychological tests. *Psychological Bulletin*, *52*(4), 281–302. https://doi.org/10.1037/h0040957
Douglas, D. (2001). Performance consistency in second language acquisition and language testing: A conceptual gap. *Second Language Research*, *17*(4), 442–456. https://doi.org/10.1177/02676583010 1700408
Ellis, R. (2005). Measuring implicit and explicit knowledge of a second language a psychometric study. *Studies in Second Language Acquisition*, *27*(2), 141–172. https://doi.org/10.1017/S0272263105050096
Erlam, R. (2006). Elicited imitation as a measure of L2 implicit knowledge: An empirical validation study. *Applied Linguistics*, *27*(3), 464–491. https://doi.org/10.1093/applin/aml001
Gutiérrez, X. (2013). The construct validity of grammaticality judgment tests as measures of implicit and explicit knowledge. *Studies in Second Language Acquisition*, *35*(3), 423–449. https://doi.org/10.1017/S0272263113000041
Kane, M. T. (1992). An argument-based approach to validity. *Psychological Bulletin*, *112*(3), 527–535. https://doi.org/10.1037/0033-2909.112.3.527
Kane, M. T. (2001). Current concerns in validity theory. *Journal of Educational Measurement*, *38*(4), 319–342. https://doi.org/10.1111/j.1745-3984.2001.tb01130.x
Kane, M. T. (2006). Validation. In R. Brennen (Ed.), *Educational measurement* (4th ed., pp. 17–64). Praeger and Greenwood Publishing.
Kane, M. T. (2013). Validating the interpretations and uses of test scores. *Journal of Educational Measurement*, *50*(1), 1–73. https://doi.org/10.1111/jedm.12000
Llosa, L. (2008). Building and supporting a validity argument for a standards-based classroom assessment of English proficiency based on teacher judgments. *Educational Measurement: Issues and Practice*, *27*(3), 32–42. https://doi.org/10.1111/j.1745-3992.2008.00126.x
Markus, K. A., & Borsboom, D. (2013). *Frontiers of test validity theory: Measurement, causation, and meaning*. Routledge.
McNamara, T., & Roever, C. (2006). *Language testing: The social dimension*. Blackwell Publishing.
Messick, S. (1989). Validity. In R. L. Linn (Ed.), *Educational measurement* (3rd ed., pp. 13–103). Macmillan Publishing Company.
Mislevy, R. J., & Haertel, G. D. (2006). Implications of evidence-centered design for educational testing. *Educational Measurement: Issues and Practice*, *25*, 6–20. https://doi.org/10.1111/j.1745-3992.2006.00075.x
Newton, P. E., & Shaw, S. D. (2014). *Validity in educational & psychological assessment*. Sage Publications.
Nichols, P., Ferrara, S., & Lai, E. (2015). Principled design for efficacy: Design and development for the next generation tests. In H. Jiao & R. W. Lissitz (Eds.), *The next generation of testing: Common core standards, smarter-balanced, PARCC, and the nationwide testing movement* (pp. 49–81). Information Age Publishing.
Norris, J. (2008). *Validity evaluation in foreign language assessment*. Peter Lang.
Purpura, J., Brown, J., & Schoonen, R. (2015). Improving the validity of quantitative measures in second language research. In J. M. Norris, S. Ross, & R. Schoonen (Eds.), *Improving and extending quantitative reasoning in second language research: Currents in language learning* (Vol. 2). Wiley-Blackwell. https://doi.org/10.1111/lang.12112
Weir, C. (2005). *Language testing and validation: An evidence-based approach*. Palgrave Macmillan.
Youn, S. J. (2015). Validity argument for assessing L2 pragmatics in interaction using mixed methods. *Language Testing*, *32*(2), 199–225. https://doi.org/10.1177/0265532214557113
Zumbo, B. (2014). What role does, and should, the test *Standards* play outside of the United States of America? *Educational Measurement: Issues and Practice*, *33*(4), 4–12. https://doi.org/10.1111/emip.12052

3

Validating Assessments for Research Purposes

Andrea Révész & Tineke Brunfaut

Background

When SLA researchers design or adapt an assessment for research purposes, a key concern is to validate the interpretations of the assessment. As elaborated upon by Chapelle (Chapter 2, this volume), validation in this context refers to the process of obtaining evidence for the claims made about research instruments in view of their intended use and in view of their appropriateness for the research population. It involves collecting information which demonstrates that accurate interpretations are made on the basis of the scores achieved on the assessment. If research instruments are flawed due to issues with validity, any conclusions reached about SLA theory and L2 instruction will lack credibility.

There have been repeated calls for attributing greater importance to validation work in the field of SLA (e.g., Chapelle, 1994, 1999; Douglas, 2001; Norris & Ortega, 2003, 2012; Shohamy, 2000). As early as the 1990s, Chapelle (1994, 1999) emphasised the need to validate SLA instruments for their proposed research purposes, and illustrated and discussed how measurement theory could be applied to the validation of assessments within SLA. An important contribution in SLA-related validation work was the publication of Norris and Ortega's (2003) measurement framework, which aimed to provide a detailed guide to validity considerations and practices in order to address concerns in validity evaluation in SLA. Another valuable resource is Purpura, Brown, and Schoonen's (2015) article, which demonstrated how Kane's (2006, 2013) influential validity framework can be utilised to justify interpretation of scores obtained through the use of SLA elicitation devices.

Likely due to these publications, there is an increasing recognition of the importance of validating research instruments among SLA researchers. However, validation practices often still remain insufficiently aligned with published guidelines for good practice in developing, using and evaluating research instruments (Purpura et al., 2015; Schmitt, Nation, & Kremmel, 2019). With the ultimate aim of improving current validation practices in SLA, this chapter introduces some key frameworks that can be utilised in SLA research, provides illustrative examples of how an argument can be built for validating SLA assessments, and gives some recommendations to guide future research.

Key Concepts

Construct: Entity that is deduced from theory or observation but cannot be directly measured.

Construct underrepresentation: An assessment that fails to measure key aspects of the construct and is thus too narrow in what it assesses. The scores only partly represent the intended construct, and inferences about learners' ability based on these scores may be incorrect.

Construct-irrelevant variance: An assessment that is systematically influenced by factors unrelated to the construct. The scores include systematic measurement error due to factors other than the intended construct, and score interpretations may be incorrect.

Grounds or datum: Data that is available.

Claim: Statement about intended interpretation based on data.

Qualifier: Specification of the extent to which the claim applies.

Warrant: Justification for the claim, based on the grounds/datum.

Backing: Evidence that corroborates the warrant.

Rebuttal: Statement that describes a situation where the claim would not be sustained; counterclaim.

Interpretation/use argument: Network of inferences and assumptions leading from observed data to interpretations.

Validity argument: A structure that provides the evidence needed in support of and against a proposed interpretation.

Key Issues

Measurement and Validation Frameworks

In SLA validation research, a principal aim is to seek construct-related evidence for the research instruments. When SLA researchers design empirical research studies, they often develop assessments that intend to measure constructs such as knowledge, development, memory, or aptitude, which come from theory or are deduced from observations but cannot be measured directly. Thus, as part of validation, researchers need to gauge how appropriately and precisely the interpretations based on the assessment match a construct's theoretical definition, and to what extent that construct definition accounts for learners' results on the assessment. In particular, two main threats need to be considered: *construct underrepresentation* and *construct-irrelevant variance* (American Educational Research Association, American Psychological Association, & National Council on Measurement in Education, 2014). Construct underrepresentation refers to a situation where an assessment does not succeed in capturing key aspects of the construct because the assessment does not adequately sample all aspects of performance required to make inferences about the construct. For example, a grammaticality judgement test (GJT) would suffer from construct underrepresentation if it only included items targeting a small number of grammatical features but claimed to test L2 learners' grammatical competence as a whole. In this case, construct underrepresentation could be resolved by designing a more comprehensive GJT entailing a broader spectrum of target grammatical features, or by modifying the claim about what the test measures to include only those aspects of grammar actually tested. Construct-irrelevant variance occurs when assessments are systematically influenced by factors that are not relevant to the construct assessors intend to measure. In other words, the assessment entails extraneous variables. For example, if in a GJT some items were misspelled, this could cause construct-irrelevant variance since some learners might classify these as ungrammatical when, in fact, they showed orthographical and/or lexical issues (which are not the intended construct of the assessment).

To help SLA researchers avoid construct underrepresentation and construct-irrelevant variance in their assessments, Norris and Ortega (2003) provided a comprehensive guide for developing and using SLA research tools. Their six-stage measurement framework explains how to proceed through each stage to achieve warranted interpretations about the construct under investigation. The first three stages are concerned with the conceptualisation of the measurement process. In particular, the first step involves defining the construct, that is, what exactly researchers would like to investigate in light of the interpretations or conclusion they would like to reach. Such construct definitions should signal the theoretical assumptions on which they are based and need to be specific so that they can be linked to observable behaviours. For example, a researcher might decide to examine the role of phonological short-term memory (PSTM) in L2 listening, where the construct of PSTM could be derived from Baddeley's (1986) multidimensional model of working memory. The second step entails identifying the behaviours to be observed with a view to supplying sufficient evidence in support of the intended construct interpretations and to avoid construct underrepresentation. The process of associating behaviours with constructs is ideally informed by the collective theoretical knowledge and empirical work in the field. For example, in the case of PSTM, a well-established behaviour associated with this particular construct is the ability to repeat sound sequences immediately after they have been heard. Then, in the third step, the researcher specifies the tasks or situations that will be used to elicit or observe the target behaviours. Key to this stage is a careful consideration of whether the tasks/situations can indeed generate the envisioned type of evidence. For example, in the study of PSTM and listening, the researcher might decide to employ non-word or digit span tests, in which participants need to reproduce series of non-words or numbers increasing in length, to assess PSTM.

In the next three stages of Norris and Ortega's (2003) measurement framework, the outcomes of the conceptualisation process are proceduralised. The behaviours are elicited through careful operationalisation and administration of the research instruments, that is, the actual elicitation devices are developed and then employed to collect the data. To ensure construct representation in the research instruments, researchers need to make sure that the tasks fully capture the behaviours they plan to elicit. For example, if the aim is to measure whether learners' ability to use an L2 construction has improved as a result of an instructional treatment, it is advisable to obtain evidence through a range of tasks creating various contexts for the use of the target feature. There are also several potential sources of error at this stage (e.g., unclear instructions, noisy computer lab), which can be pre-empted through careful piloting of instruments and data collection procedures, to ensure consistent and comparable results (see, for example, Bachman & Palmer, 2010; Mackey & Gass, 2016 for overviews). Once behaviours have been elicited, the observations are coded and/or scored with regard to aspects that are relevant to the constructs examined. Important to achieving validity at this point is to develop a coding and/or scoring scheme that is well aligned with the construct definition. For example, if the goal of the study is to capture syntactic complexity, researchers will need to employ a variety of measures to capture the multidimensional nature of this construct rather than a single index (e.g., Bulté & Housen, 2012). Coding and scoring consistency is a further priority, which can be facilitated through careful coder and rater selection and training, and checking coder and scorer reliability (see Révész, 2012). It is also crucial at this stage to provide statistical evidence that the instruments function as intended, for instance, in the form of internal consistency reliability estimates (Bachman, 2004; Green, 2013). These reliability measures themselves also need to be chosen carefully, since unsuitable ones are sometimes used or their assumptions not checked (see Chapelle, Chapter 2, this volume). Finally, the scores obtained on the assessments need to be subjected to proper statistical analyses to interpret scores in relation to the research questions (Norris et al., 2015; Plonsky, 2013). If the statistical analyses are not appropriately selected and rigorously conducted, interpretations from the instruments may be skewed, misleading, or simply incorrect.

In sum, Norris and Ortega's (2003) framework provides guidance for designing and implementing research instruments that are appropriate to reach meaningful interpretations about theoretical constructs. After all, an important purpose of using the instruments is to empirically test SLA theories. A limitation of Norris and Ortega's (2003) framework, however, is its lack of emphasis on validating the *use* of the instruments. While this is a general weakness of the framework, it constitutes a drawback especially in the context of SLA studies that investigate the effectiveness of L2 instructional treatments. When applied to such situations, the framework does not direct researchers to substantiate whether the interpretations reached are warranted for the relevant learner populations and instructional contexts (Drackert, 2015a). Purpura et al. (2015) and Drackert (2015a) convincingly argue that Kane's (2006, 2013) argument-based validation framework can successfully address this limitation as it provides a framework for evaluating both intended interpretations and uses of assessments.

Kane's (2006, 2013) argument-based approach draws on Toulmin's (1958) six-component model of argument, explained in Table 3.1. Kane (2006, 2013) called for building an argument along the following two stages:

a. Drawing up an *interpretation/use argument* (IUA) about the proposed interpretations and uses of the assessment, i.e., the plan. This means specifying the series of claims made in the

Table 3.1 Toulmin's argument components

Component	*Definition*	*SLA example*
Data/ Grounds	Facts or evidence that can be utilised to verify or refute the argument made.	Second language data elicited through a research instrument.
Claim	Statement which entails conclusions and intended interpretations that are deduced based on the data.	If a group of L2 learners achieves higher scores on a test assessing their knowledge of a target L2 feature after being exposed to one type of instructional treatment than another group of learners receiving a different type of treatment, the claim could be that the former treatment was more effective.
Qualifier	Specification of the conditions under which the claim applies.	The advantage observed for one of two instructional treatments applies only if there were no initial differences in the two groups' knowledge of the target construction.
Warrant or inference	Linking of claims and data, including a set of assumptions.	Inference related to the reliability of coding procedures and the internal consistency of the research instruments: If the coding process and instruments prove reliable, we could conclude that the instrument produces consistent results, thus providing evidence for the claim.
Backing	Corroborations of the assumptions entailed in the warrants, involving the provision of theoretical and/ or empirical evidence in support of them.	Backing for scoring and instrument reliability could be provided by calculating coder and instrument reliability statistics.
Rebuttal	Counter-argument that describes situations where the argument would not be sustained.	The better performing group in an experimental study might receive additional instruction in their regular language class, which could account for their higher gains.

interpretation/use argument, including inferences about the domain description, evaluation or scoring, generalisation, explanation, extrapolation, and utilisation (see Chapelle, Chapter 2, this volume for a description of these stages). If the validation process yields evidence against any of the claims, the research instrument under scrutiny will be put to doubt.

b. Providing a *validity argument* which evaluates the appropriateness of the claims outlined in the interpretation/use argument (IUA) through accumulating theoretical and empirical evidence against or in support of the intended interpretations and uses, i.e., the actual argument.

Purpura et al. (2015) proposed that "the appropriateness and adequacy of evidence needed in a validity argument be determined by the purpose of the study, the research claims we would like to make, and the consequences of using the scores for the intended research purposes" (p. 49), arguing that it may not be practical or possible to gather and analyse data to test all claims. They emphasise, however, that it is important for researchers to be aware of the claims implicated in their research instruments and to take into account whether they have or have not provided evidence for the relevant claims when interpreting their research findings.

Issues in Validation in SLA

Against this background, we now turn to three issues in SLA validation work: how to proceed with validating theory-derived research instruments, how to validate research instruments for various uses, and how to plan validation as an integral phase of SLA research studies.

Validating Theory-Derived Research Instruments. Here, we describe how SLA researchers could approach the validation of research instruments that are constructed on the basis of SLA theory. We clarify this with examples from the context of research on implicit and explicit learning, since probably the most comprehensive and influential validation work in SLA has concerned the development of measures of implicit and explicit knowledge to inform the long-standing theoretical controversy regarding the relationship between these types of knowledge.

Ellis and colleagues (Ellis, 2005; Ellis et al., 2009) initiated work into the validation of interpretations based on measures of implicit and explicit knowledge. Although not explicitly following Norris and Ortega's (2003) measurement framework, the steps the researchers took exemplify the stages outlined in that model. Drawing on existing theoretical and empirical work, Ellis et al. derived a constellation of observable behaviours assumed to be associated with implicit and explicit knowledge. Through this process, implicit knowledge came to be defined as intuitive, procedural, systematic, automatic, non-verbalisable, and developmentally-constrained, and explicit knowledge as conscious, declarative, actively controlled, verbalisable, and learnable at any age. Next, they designed a battery of assessments to elicit the observable behaviours associated with the construct definitions of implicit and explicit knowledge. An elicited imitation task, an oral narrative task, and a timed GJT were constructed to tap implicit knowledge, and an untimed GJT and a metalinguistic knowledge test were developed to gauge explicit knowledge. Then, a series of studies was conducted to test whether the assessments were indeed successful in eliciting behaviours linked to the constructs of implicit and explicit knowledge (e.g., more versus less systematic behaviour), i.e., whether the assessments' interpretations would be valid. In addition, statistical analyses were carried out to test the hypothesised links between the participants' performance on the assessments and their relationships to other factors assumed to be related to the theoretical constructs (e.g., age of starting to learn the L2). Based on the results of the project, the researchers concluded that the instruments could be used as valid measures of implicit and explicit knowledge. As Norris and Ortega (2012) noted, Ellis and colleagues' project serves as a useful example for future validation work, in several respects. First, the researchers defined the constructs—in this case, implicit and explicit knowledge—synthesising previous theoretical and empirical work, thereby arriving at construct definitions that reflected researchers' shared knowledge in the domain. Also, they assessed hypothesised links between the tests that were aligned with theoretical assumptions and expectations shared within the research community.

The project, however, has also been subjected to criticisms, some of which are relevant from the perspective of validation. In particular, several concerns have been raised regarding the appropriateness of the factor analyses conducted. Isemonger (2007) argued that confirmatory rather than exploratory factor analysis should have been employed in Ellis (2005) given that *a priori* hypotheses were made regarding the nature of the constructs assessed by the instruments. Although Ellis and Loewen (2007) addressed this limitation in a follow-up study, further issues have been highlighted by Vafaee et al. (2017), who pointed out that rival models were not tested in the factor analysis. From the perspective of Kane's argument-based approach, it could be argued that Ellis and colleagues' work lacked consideration and evaluation of some key rebuttals. To address this shortcoming and to test new, theoretically derived, comprehension-based measures of implicit knowledge, Vafaee et al. (2017) performed a new study to validate the interpretations drawn from measures of implicit and explicit knowledge. The results challenged the findings of previous research, indicating that while self-paced reading and word-monitoring tasks appear to measure implicit knowledge, timed GJTs may not constitute tests of implicit knowledge. This line of research provides an excellent example of how ongoing validation work, building on previous attempts to operationalise key constructs in the field, can lead to the development of more and more refined instruments that allow for more appropriate interpretations about the constructs of interest.

Validating Research Instruments for Various Uses. In SLA research, instruments that have been used with a certain learner population for one purpose in one study are often utilised in new studies for a different purpose and with different groups of participants. This practice, in and of itself, is not questionable. However, the problem is that researchers often borrow instruments without validating them for the populations and uses in their own research; that is, they fail to make sure that the instruments enable reaching warranted interpretations about the learners and contexts they investigate.

Drawing on Drackert (2015a), we illustrate how researchers can validate SLA research instruments for different uses and how Kane's (2006, 2013) argument-based approach to validity can be utilised in validating SLA assessments. Drackert (2015a) set out to validate a Russian elicited imitation (EI) test as a proficiency assessment for two uses: (1) controlling for participants' initial oral proficiency at the beginning of a study and (2) screening participants into a study on the basis of their overall listening and speaking proficiency. In validating the EI test for the first use, Drackert took the following steps. The project started with specifying the intended test context and use, followed by the development of the test and the construction of the interpretation/use argument. As shown in Figure 3.1, the first inference in the interpretation/use argument concerned the elicitation of test performance, which for example comprised assumptions about test administration procedures, test delivery quality, and comprehensibility of instructions. This inference is not specified in Kane's (2006) original model, but was added by Drackert given that data elicitation is a crucial stage in SLA research. The second, *scoring/evaluation* inference entailed assumptions about the monitoring of the choice of test items, the development of the scoring rubric, and the consistency of scoring. In the third, *generalisation* inference, the assumptions were related to the reliability of the test, the appropriateness of the sample size, and the consistency of the test across educational settings and different first language backgrounds. The assumptions under the fourth inference, *extrapolation*, were derived from previous theoretical and empirical work, and outlined expected statistical relationships of the EI test to relevant background variables and self-assessments of L2 skills. The last inference, *utilisation*, specified the uses for which the test had been validated.

Once the interpretation/use argument had been developed, Drackert posed a number of evaluation questions, listed in Figure 3.2. Then, the process of building the validity argument began

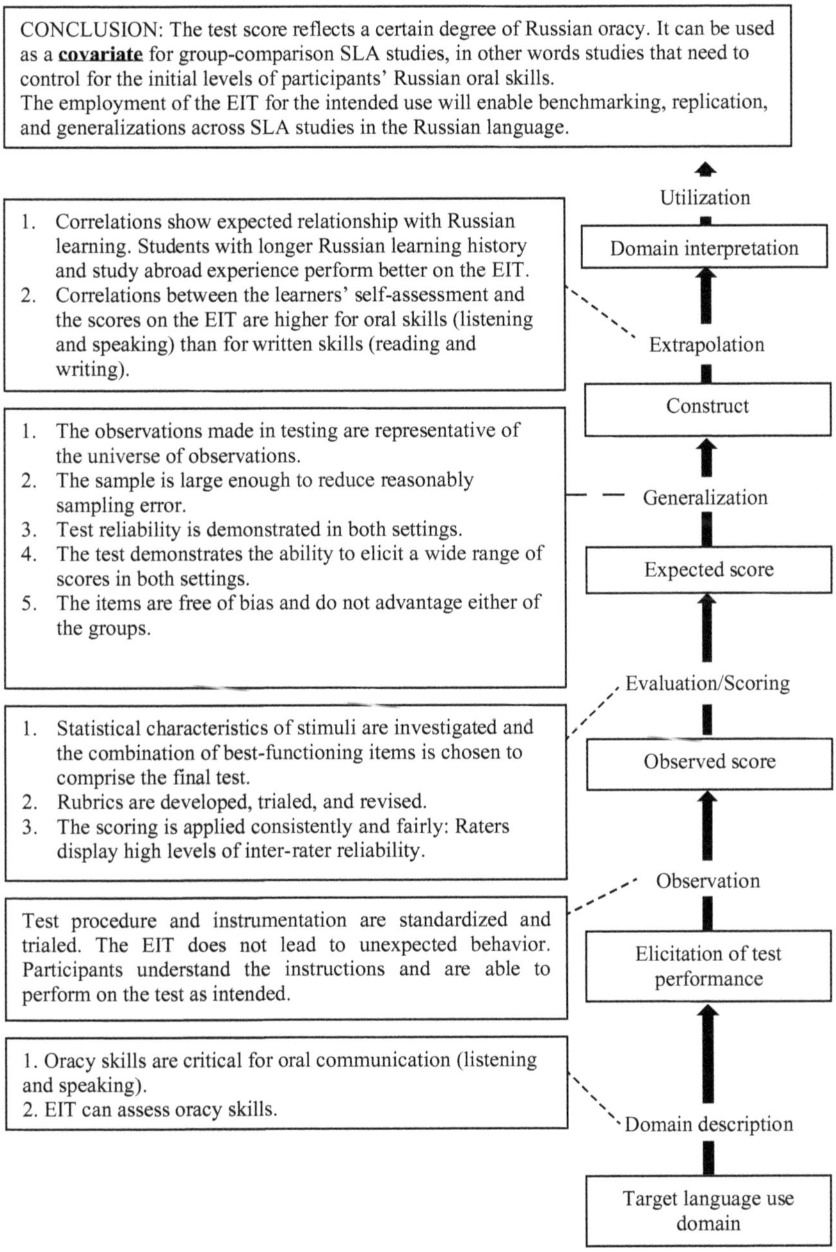

Figure 3.1 Interpretation/use argument 1: EIT scores as a covariate (Drackert, 2015a, p. 112).

through addressing the evaluation questions. Drackert administered the EI test and a background questionnaire to 97 Russian-FL learners in the USA and Germany. The results were subjected to a range of statistical analyses, including descriptive statistics and differential item functioning, item response theory, correlational and interrater reliability analyses, to answer the evaluation questions. The findings confirmed that the EI test can reliably be used for one purpose, to control for initial levels of Russian oral proficiency in SLA studies.

To investigate whether the test can also be used for selecting participants for SLA studies based on their listening and speaking proficiency, a second validation study ensued. This

1. Which combination of items differentiates most accurately and reliably between learners of different levels of oracy skills in Russian? [...]
2. Is the scoring rubric used appropriately, in particular: Are all points of the rubric utilized? Do raters display high inter-rater reliability? [...]
3. Does the test function independently of the educational setting?
   3.1. Does the test function reliably in two educational settings? [...]
   3.2. Does the test demonstrate the ability to elicit a wide range of scores in both settings? [...]
   3.3. Are the items free of bias for both learner groups? [...]
4. Are there any substantial correlations between the length of studying Russian, study/residence abroad, frequency of use of Russian, age of first exposure, and the scores on the EIT? [...]
5. Are the correlations between the learners' self-assessment and the scores on the EIT higher for oral skills (listening and speaking) than for written skills (reading and writing)? [...]

Figure 3.2 Questions posed to evaluate the interpretation/use argument (from Drackert, 2015a, p. 114).

study followed the same overall design, starting with the construction of the interpretation/use argument, followed by deducing and investigating evaluation questions based on the interpretation/use argument. Sixty-seven learners of Russian in the USA took the EI test, a Russian speaking test, a C-test, and a listening comprehension test. Results from an array of descriptive and inferential statistical analyses showed that the test can distinguish between four levels of Russian-FL speaking proficiency and predict a threshold for listening ability at the intermediate level.

To sum up, Drackert's work shows that Kane's argument-based approach to validity can act as a framework for validating SLA research instruments for different uses. For additional worked examples of the argument-based approach in L2 instrument development and validation, we refer the reader to Voss (2012) and Kremmel (2017).

Integrating Instrument Validation into Research Designs. Finally, we demonstrate how researchers can integrate validation of the instruments used in SLA research into the design of smaller-scale SLA studies through an example. For the past two decades a lot of instructed SLA research has explored the effects of task complexity (i.e., inherent cognitive demands of tasks) on L2 outcomes measures such as complexity, accuracy and fluency in order to test cognitive models of task-based language learning (Robinson, 2001; Skehan, 2009). Until recently, a methodological weakness in existing research was that no evidence was provided in support of task complexity manipulations. Researchers typically designed a complex and simple version of a task (e.g., one with more and one with less reasoning demands), but failed to test whether the task version designed to be more cognitively demanding was indeed more cognitively complex. In response to calls to address this shortcoming (Norris & Ortega, 2003; Révész, 2014), more and more studies now include independent measures of cognitive load or mental effort into their design (e.g., Baralt, 2013; Révész et al., 2014; Zalbidea, 2017), such as subjective self-ratings, subjective time estimations, dual-task methodology and expert judgments. Some researchers have also trialled various ways to assess task-generated cognitive load (e.g., Révész et al., 2016; Sasayama, 2016) to inform future task complexity validation practices. Figure 3.3 provides an illustration of a possible argument structure for studies with independent measures of task complexity, hypothesising that the task version created to be more complex is indeed more cognitively demanding.

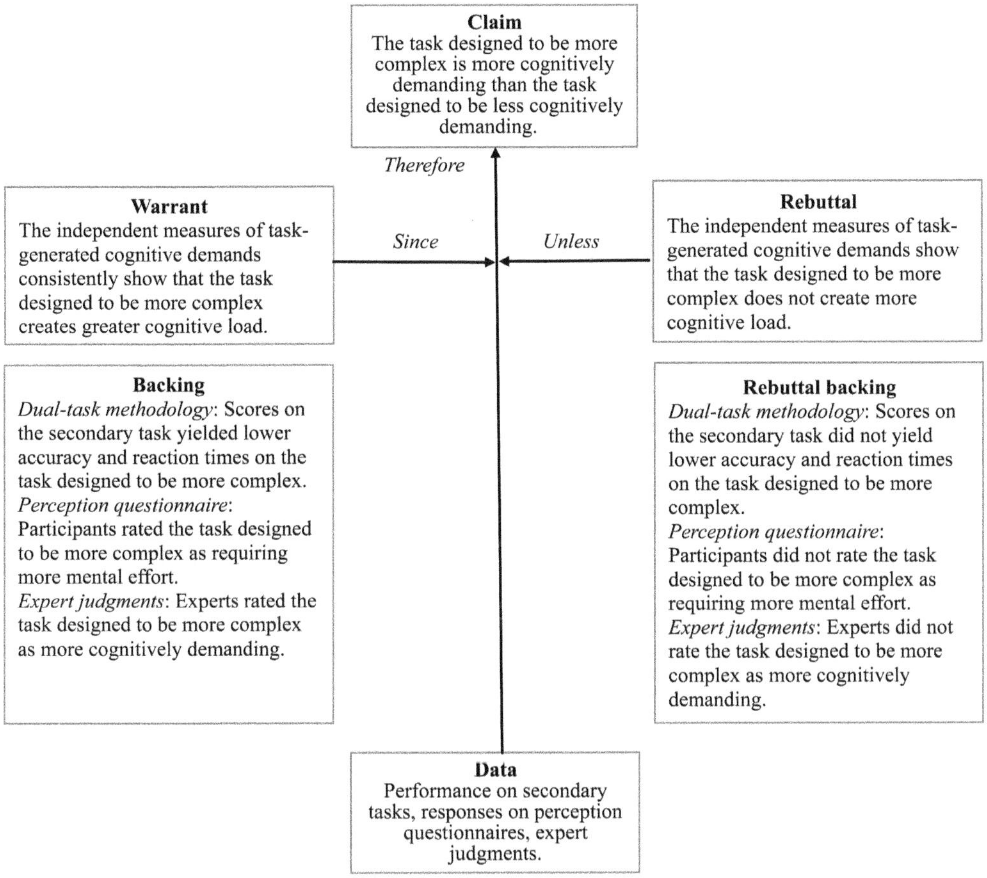

Figure 3.3 Argument structure (based on Purpura et al., 2015).

Recommendations for Practice

With the ultimate goal of improving validation practices within the field, we would like to end this paper with some practical recommendations that may guide SLA researchers when constructing and validating research instruments. Several of the suggestions made below mirror the comments put forward by Chapelle (Chapter 2, this volume) and other researchers in the context of broader methodological discussions in the field (Ercikan & Pellegrino, 2017; Marsden & Plonsky, 2018; Norris & Ortega, 2003, 2012; Norris et al., 2015; Plonsky & Gass, 2011; Purpura et al., 2015).

- When designing an empirical study, consider each step outlined in Norris and Ortega's (2003) measurement framework (construct definition, behaviour identification, task specification, behaviour elicitation, observation scoring, data analysis). Draw up an interpretation/use argument and formulate evaluation questions for each stage and a plan for the validation argument (Kane, 2006, 2013). Make sure to provide evidence in support of the claims in the interpretation/use argument while considering possible ways to provide rebuttals against the evidence provided. An example of how this can be done was provided in the previous section. In short, evidence for the validity of each stage of the measurement process should be given rather than assumed.

- In particular, keep the target construct in mind at all times and carefully evaluate whether your instrument operationalises it in a sufficiently comprehensive manner (to avoid construct underrepresentation) and does not require or involve the use of other knowledge, skills or abilities (to avoid construct-irrelevant variance).
- Construct underrepresentation, or even misrepresentation, is something to look out for when measuring constructs. Checking for representation problems could be done through, for example, validation work that investigates learners' cognitive-response processes (Nicols & Huff, 2017). That is, researchers can collect data on how learners mentally process and work through items during assessments through, for example, think-alouds, retrospective interviews, eye-tracking, or key-stroke-log methods, as explained by Nicols and Huff, and use that data to verify the mental processes assumed to underlie scores.
- When it is not possible to collect and analyse data to address claims put forward in the validity argument, highlight this and take it into account when interpreting research findings.
- Do not assume that tests which have been validated for one purpose with one population of learners in one context will also be valid for a different purpose, a different population of learners, and/or a different setting. Instruments need to be validated for their intended purposes, populations, and contexts.
- Follow the guidelines for reporting quantitative methods and results outlined in Norris et al. (2015). This will enable fellow researchers to replicate previous research as well as evaluate and critique the validity of it.
- Share your instruments and data in open-access repositories such as IRIS—a digital repository of instruments for research into second language learning and teaching (https://www.iris-database.org/iris/app/home/index), accompanied by the original publication/dissertation with information on the purpose, population and context in which the instruments were used and data generated. This will not only allow other researchers to better assess the validity of research instruments and designs used in previous research but also facilitate ongoing validation endeavours aimed at the refinement of SLA elicitation devices (see, for example, continuous validation work on the development of implicit and explicit knowledge measures).

Recommended Readings

Drackert, A. (2015b). *Validating language proficiency assessments in second language acquisition research: Applying an argument-based approach.* Peter Lang.

This monograph provides a step-by-step illustration of how Kane's argument-based approach to validation can be applied to developing and validating SLA assessments.

Norris, J., & Ortega, L. (2003). Defining and measuring SLA. In C. J. Doughty & M. H. Long (Eds.), *The handbook of second language acquisition* (pp. 717–761). Blackwell.

This chapter discusses key stages in the SLA measurement process with a view to achieving validity and reliability.

Purpura, J. E., Brown, J. D., & Schoonen, R. (2015). Improving the validity of quantitative measures in second language research. *Language Learning, 65*(S1), 37–75. https://doi.org/10.1111/lang.12112

This article shows how to construct a validity argument for an SLA research instrument, and also highlights typical pitfalls in SLA research with respect to validity.

References

American Educational Research Association, American Psychological Association, & The National Council on Measurement in Education. (2014). *Standards for educational and psychological testing*. American Psychological Association.

Bachman, L. F. (2004). *Statistical analyses for language assessment*. Cambridge University Press.

Bachman, L. F., & Palmer, A. S. (2010). *Language assessment in practice*. Oxford University Press.

Baddeley, A. D. (1986). *Working memory*. Oxford University Press.

Baralt, M. (2013). The impact of cognitive complexity on feedback efficacy during online versus face-to-face interactive tasks. *Studies in Second Language Acquisition*, *35*(4), 689–725. https://doi.org/10.1017/S0272263113000429

Bulté, B., & Housen, A. (2012). Defining and operationalising L2 complexity. In A. Housen, F. Kuiken, & I. Vedder (Eds.), *Dimensions of L2 performance and proficiency: Investigating complexity, accuracy and fluency in SLA* (pp. 21–46). John Benjamins.

Chapelle, C. A. (1994). Are C-tests valid measures for L2 vocabulary research? *Second Language Research*, *10*(2), 157–187. https://doi.org/10.1177/026765839401000203

Chapelle, C. A. (1999). Validity in language assessment. *Annual Review of Applied Linguistics*, *19*(1), 254–272. https://doi.org/10.1017/S0267190599190135

Douglas, D. (2001). Performance consistency in second language acquisition and language testing: A conceptual gap. *Second Language Research*, *17*(4), 442–456. https://doi.org/10.1177/026765830101700408

Drackert, A. (2015a). *Applying an argument-based approach for validating language proficiency assessments in second language acquisition research: the elicited imitation test for Russian*. (Unpublished doctoral dissertation). Georgetown University.

Ellis, R. (2005). Measuring implicit and explicit knowledge of a second language a psychometric study. *Studies in Second Language Acquisition*, *27*(2), 141–172. https://doi.org/10.1017/S0272263105050096

Ellis, R., & Loewen, S. (2007). Confirming the operational definitions of explicit and implicit knowledge in Ellis (2005): Responding to Isemonger. *Studies in Second Language Acquisition*, *29*(1), 119–126. https://doi.org/10.1017/S0272263107070052

Ellis, R., Loewen, S., Elder, C., Erlam, R., Philp, J., & Reinders, H. (2009). *Implicit and explicit knowledge in second language learning, testing and teaching*. Multilingual Matters.

Ercikan, K., & Pellegrino, J. W. (Eds.). (2017). *Validation of score meaning for the next generation of assessments: The use of response processes*. Routledge.

Green, R. (2013). *Statistical analyses for language testers*. Palgrave Macmillan.

Isemonger, I. M. (2007). Operational definitions of explicit and implicit knowledge: Response to R. Ellis (2005) and some recommendations for future research in this area. *Studies in Second Language Acquisition*, *29*(1), 101–118. https://doi.org/10.1017/S0272263107070040

Kane, M. T. (2006). Validation. In R. L. Brennan (Ed.), *Educational measurement* (4th ed., pp. 17–64). American Council of Education and Praeger Series on Higher Education.

Kane, M. T. (2013). Validating the interpretations and uses of test scores. *Journal of Educational Measurement*, *50*(1), 1–73. https://doi.org/10.1111/jedm.12000

Kremmel, B. (2017). *Development and initial validation of a diagnostic computer-adaptive profiler of vocabulary knowledge* (Unpublished doctoral dissertation). University of Nottingham.

Mackey, A., & Gass, S. M. (2016). *Second language research: Methodology and design*. Routledge.

Marsden, E., & Plonsky, L. (2018). Data, open science, and methodological reform in second language acquisition research. In A. Gudmestad & A. Edmonds (Eds.), *Critical reflections on data in second language acquisition* (pp. 219–228). John Benjamins.

Nicols, P., & Huff, K. (2017). Assessments of complex thinking. In K. Ercikan & J. W. Pellegrino (Eds.), *Validation of score meaning for the next generation of assessments: The use of response processes* (pp. 63–74). Routledge.

Norris, J., & Ortega, L. (2003). Defining and measuring SLA. In C. J. Doughty & M. H. Long (Eds.), *The handbook of second language acquisition* (pp. 717–761). Blackwell.

Norris, J. M., & Ortega, L. (2012). Assessing learner knowledge. In S. M. Gass & A. Mackey (Eds.), *The Routledge handbook of second language acquisition* (pp. 573–589). Routledge.

Norris, J. M., Plonsky, L., Ross, S. J., & Schoonen, R. (2015). Guidelines for reporting quantitative methods and results in primary research. *Language Learning*, *65*(2), 470–476. https://doi.org/10.1111/lang.12104

Plonsky, L. (2013). Study quality in SLA: An assessment of designs, analyses, and reporting practices in quantitative L2 research. *Studies in Second Language Acquisition*, *35*(4), 655–687. https://doi.org/10.1017/S0272263113000399

Plonsky, L., & Gass, S. (2011). Quantitative research methods, study quality, and outcomes: The case of interaction research. *Language Learning*, *61*(2), 325–366. https://doi.org/10.1111/j.1467-9922.2011.00640.x
Purpura, J. E., Brown, J. D., & Schoonen, R. (2015). Improving the validity of quantitative measures in second language research. In J. M. Norris, S. Ross, & R. Schoonen (Eds.), *Improving and extending quantitative reasoning in second language research: Currents in language learning* (Vol. 2). Wiley-Blackwell. https://doi.org/10.1111/lang.12112
Révész, A. (2012). Coding second language data validity and reliability. In A. Mackey & S. M. Gass (Eds.), *Research methods in second language acquisition* (pp. 203–221). Blackwell Publishing Ltd.
Révész, A. (2014). Towards a fuller assessment of cognitive models of task-based learning: Investigating task-generated cognitive demands and processes. *Applied Linguistics*, *35*(1), 87–92. https://doi.org/10.1093/applin/amt039
Révész, A., Michel, M., & Gilabert, R. (2016). Measuring cognitive task demands using dual-task methodology, subjective self-ratings, and expert judgments: A validation study. *Studies in Second Language Acquisition*, *38*(4), 703–737. https://doi.org/10.1017/S0272263115000339
Révész, A., Sachs, R., & Hama, M. (2014). The effects of task complexity and input frequency on the acquisition of the past counterfactual construction through recasts. *Language Learning*, *64*(3), 615–650. https://doi.org/10.1111/lang.12061
Robinson, P. (2001). Task complexity, cognitive resources, and syllabus design: A triadic framework for examining task influences on SLA. In P. Robinson (Ed.), *Cognition and second language instruction* (pp. 287–318). Cambridge University Press.
Sasayama, S. (2016). Is a 'complex' task really complex? Validating the assumption of cognitive task complexity. *The Modern Language Journal*, *100*(1), 231–254. https://doi.org/10.1111/modl.12313
Schmitt, N., Nation, P., & Kremmel, B. (2019). Moving the field of vocabulary assessment forward: The need for more rigorous test development and validation. *Language Teaching*, *53*(1), 109–120. https://doi.org/10.1017/S0261444819000326
Shohamy, E. (2000). The relationship between language testing and second language acquisition revisited. *System*, *28*, 541–553. https://doi.org/10.1016/S0346-251X(00)00037-3
Skehan, P. (2009). Modeling second language performance: Integrating complexity, accuracy, fluency, and lexis. *Applied Linguistics*, *30*(4), 510–532. https://doi.org/10.1093/applin/amp047
Toulmin, S. E. (1958). *The uses of argument*. Cambridge University Press.
Vafaee, P., Suzuki, Y., & Kachinske, I. (2017). Validating grammaticality judgment tests: Evidence from two new psycholinguistic measures. *Studies in Second Language Acquisition*, *39*(1), 59–95. https://doi.org/10.1017/S0272263115000455
Voss, E. (2012). *A validity argument for score meaning of a computer-based ESL academic collocational ability test based on a corpus-drive approach to test design* (Unpublished doctoral dissertation). Iowa State University.
Zalbidea, J. (2017). 'One task fits all'? The roles of task complexity, modality, and working memory capacity in L2 performance. *The Modern Language Journal*, *101*(2), 335–352. https://doi.org/10.1111/modl.12389

4

Language Proficiency Frameworks and Scales

Claudia Harsch & Margaret E. Malone

Background

Proficiency is a complex and useful construct to measure language outcomes, track student progress, and provide a common language for students, instructors, administrators and other stakeholders to talk about second/foreign language curricula, teaching, and assessment. In this chapter, we focus first on defining proficiency from a historical perspective. We then trace the permutations of proficiency during the past 60 years via the chronological development of three sets of what may be the oldest, modern-day proficiency frameworks and scales: the Interagency Language Roundtable (ILR) scale, the ACTFL Proficiency Guidelines (ACTFL) and the Common European Framework of Reference (CEFR). We address ways that these frameworks and scales have evolved to reflect different needs, contexts, and audiences. These reference points, used nationally and internationally in both different and overlapping settings, have had direct and indirect impacts on language teaching and learning, as well as testing. In addition, we address the value the different frameworks and scales bring to language testing situations from both a local and global perspective, and to SLA research and language learning. Finally, we provide recommendations on how scales and their accompanying tests, philosophies, and proficiency development frameworks provide washback to teaching and learning. We discuss how the frameworks can affect curricula, classroom assessments, and student self-assessments.

Key Concepts

Language proficiency: A measure of language ability described through performance observations. It is nested in language-use contexts, and is often used for decision-making purposes.

Proficiency scale: A one-dimensional, graduated series of language ability descriptors of language proficiency, arranged vertically according to a hypothetical scheme of acquisition rank or order.

Proficiency framework: A multi-dimensional range of language competences, contexts, and functions arranged horizontally with corresponding vertical ability scales for each horizontal element, some of which may overlap.

Language standards: The alignment of curricula, syllabi, tasks, texts, assessments, and other pedagogical resources onto proficiency scales and frameworks, which articulate and guide hypothesized language development.

Proficiency tests: Measurements of language ability relative to specific, real world uses, often aligned empirically to proficiency scales and frameworks through standard-setting procedures.

Key Issues

Defining Language Proficiency

Defining a model of language proficiency is an essential part of assessing language proficiency. When applied to language, proficiency addresses the extent to which an individual can use language in a real-life situation (see Davies, et al., 1999). Bachman (1990, p. 16) defined language proficiency as "knowledge, competence, or ability in the use of a language." The distinction between "knowledge" and "competence" is often used to contrast what the learner knows or understands in the language versus how well they can perform or demonstrate their competence. Also, while earlier definitions of proficiency often failed to explore the sociolinguistic and cultural implications of proficiency, an important contribution of Bachman's work has been the recognition of sociolinguistic, illocutionary, and pragmatic competence as core to language proficiency. Knowing and demonstrating competence in vocabulary, grammar, and phonology is necessary but not sufficient; learners must also be able to cope with various social situations when speaking and writing. Such situations require learners to not only communicate accurately, but also effectively, with different interlocutors in varied settings.

Frameworks or models of proficiency usually encompass two dimensions, a horizontal one where relevant skills and task-related aspects of proficiency are defined, and a vertical scale, along which these components are described in ascending degrees or levels, thus outlining an *increase* in proficiency: in other words, a hierarchical model of how language proficiency *grows*. Ideally, such a system of ascending levels would describe the development of proficiency by depicting stages in SLA which language learners will go through as they advance in proficiency. Identifying these stages then facilitates the instruction and teaching of second or foreign languages within the context for which the framework was created by providing the instructors with the articulated framework for curricula and progression. The benchmarks and thresholds within the framework and scale can also serve to measure progress and abilities.

Three Influential Proficiency Frameworks and Scales

Although there are many proficiency frameworks and scales used across the world for classroom uses and for international tests, there are three long-established ones that are used to describe language proficiency in multiple languages across the world. These three, in the order in which they were created, are the ILR scale, the ACTFL Proficiency Guidelines, and the illustrative scales of the CEFR (for a detailed review, see Cox et al., 2018). We describe these three in detail below. While not discussed here, others, such as the Canadian Language Benchmarks for Canada's adult learners of English and French, China's Standards of English Language Ability, and the WIDA Consortium's English Language Proficiency Standards for child English language learners, are also important and are rapidly developing into full-blown frameworks of proficiency with integrated standards, assessments, and curricular materials for instruction. For more information on the latter, we refer the reader to Jezak (2017), NEEA (n.d.) and WIDA (2014), respectively.

ILR Scale. First released in the late 1950s, the ILR scale was developed by the US Foreign Service Institute (FSI) as a set of criteria to measure the speaking, listening, and reading abilities of US foreign service officers before they were sent to the field (Herzog, 2003; Lowe, 1985; National Academies of Sciences, Engineering, and Medicine, 2020). With the advent of the Cold War, the US government needed personnel to communicate with host country staff, and no reliable tests existed that allowed such personnel to demonstrate their ability to communicate in languages other than English. FSI staff observed the language used and needed to conduct State Department business overseas and were charged with creating a scale that measured a range of proficiency from "none" to that of an educated native speaker (Liskin-Gasparro, 1982, 1984). The result was the ILR scale and the FSI's accompanying Oral Proficiency Interview (OPI), which currently is given in 60 to 80 languages (National Academies of Sciences, Engineering, and Medicine, 2020). The ILR scale includes six levels (0–5) with plus levels (+) at each level except 5 to demonstrate a performance far above the base level that is not yet sustained at the following level. The level 5 is based on an educated native speaker (and is rarely used today, as described in the National Academies report), and the level 0 means "no demonstrated proficiency." For many government positions, a minimum of a 3, indicating professional-level proficiency, on one or more domains is required. The development of the ILR scale was based in utility; to measure the extent to which diplomats and other government employees could use the language in the target culture to conduct their work in the target language and culture.

The ILR scale and accompanying OPI represented a novel approach to measuring language. At the time of their creation, grammar translation and audiolingualism were emphasized in language teaching; the OPI's face-to-face testing of speaking proficiency, with the core of the assessment including the performance of mock tasks that mirrored those the test taker may experience later on the job, stood in stark contrast to these methods. The OPI was conducted by a tester, who elicited the language from the candidate and was observed and double-rated by an examiner, a process still used in the US government today.

The ILR scale was adopted across a number of US government agencies and focused primarily on language proficiency within the professional context. Over time, language professionals in higher education tried to adopt the scale for their own purposes, but found that students were unlikely to reach professional levels of proficiency within the classroom and with only limited full-immersion opportunities. Moreover, the scale did not describe adequately the kind of progress students make in academic settings. As Carroll (1967) discovered, even language majors attained, at most, a 2+ level (later labeled as Advanced High on the ACTFL scale) in any domain. Thus, using the ILR scale in academic environments meant that more than half of the scale was unlikely to be used; a new system was needed.

ACTFL Proficiency Guidelines. The ACTFL Proficiency Guidelines were developed to meet the needs of an academic and less proficient audience than that of the ILR (Liskin-Gasparro, 1984). Released in 1982, the Guidelines' initial development was funded by a grant from the US Department of Education. Although based on the ILR scale, the ACTFL developers expanded definitions for lower levels of proficiency beyond those of the ILR, and the ACTFL Guidelines were used to adapt the existing Oral Proficiency Interview (OPI) for non-government settings; primarily students in post-secondary programs who were generally native speakers of English learning second languages.

The ACTFL Guidelines and accompanying ACTFL OPI tester training efforts in multiple languages across the US (Liskin-Gasparro, 1982, 1984) had a meaningful impact on language teaching and learning in the US. Instead of a numeric scale, the ACTFL Guidelines use terms; Novice, Intermediate, Advanced, and Superior, with three levels initially at Novice and Intermediate and later at Advanced. The Superior level includes the ILR levels 3–5. In addition, the ACTFL Guidelines across the domains of listening, speaking, reading, and writing were used as a platform to promote proficiency, in contrast to audiolingualism, which was still the norm at the time (Liskin-Gasparro, 1982, 1984). One main premise of the ACTFL Guidelines was and is a functional approach to what students can do with the language. Another underlying premise is that of the sympathetic interlocutor; in other words, how much effort must the listener make to understand the speaker? As proficiency increases, the Guidelines describe an increasingly unsympathetic listener. The unsympathetic listener, then, indicates that culture and pragmatics play a more important role in the communication at higher levels. Finally, in addition to these qualities, the Guidelines are known for the non-compensatory inverted pyramid, in which the highest level, Superior, is at the top, and the lowest, Novice, is at the bottom. The idea behind the inverted pyramid is that speakers generally possess all the abilities of the level or levels below, in addition to the level at which their performance is rated, although strong empirical evidence for this theory is needed, as anecdotal cases contrary to the theory have been pointed out (i.e., the US Foreign Service Officer who can discuss nuclear disarmament within intergovernmental groups, but who cannot discuss what he or she does for fun on the weekend, either due to a lack of contextual vocabulary or experience or both) (Figure 4.1).

The Guidelines were substantially overhauled and re-released in 1999 to emphasize three instead of two sublevels at the Advanced level and again in 2012 to emphasize the Distinguished level, a level above Superior. At present, the ACTFL Guidelines form the basis for most US State world language standards and are used to rate most tests of world language proficiency in the United States. However, only ACTFL and its testing arm, LTI, conduct certified ACTFL tests that can be used for licensure and official governmental purposes.

Common European Framework of Reference (CEFR). In Europe, endeavors to describe language proficiency within a large-scale framework started in the 1970s by the Council of Europe (CoE), a human rights organization, to enhance communication and mobility across Europe (Trim, 2001). Taking a functional-notional approach, van Ek published the *Threshold Level* in 1975, which described what language learners need to be able to do in order to function independently in a second or foreign language environment. This was followed by *Waystage* (van Ek & Alexander, 1977), which described an intermediate proficiency stage. Based on this early work focusing on English and French, the CoE commissioned the development of a framework of language proficiency with the intention to "provide a common basis … for the description of

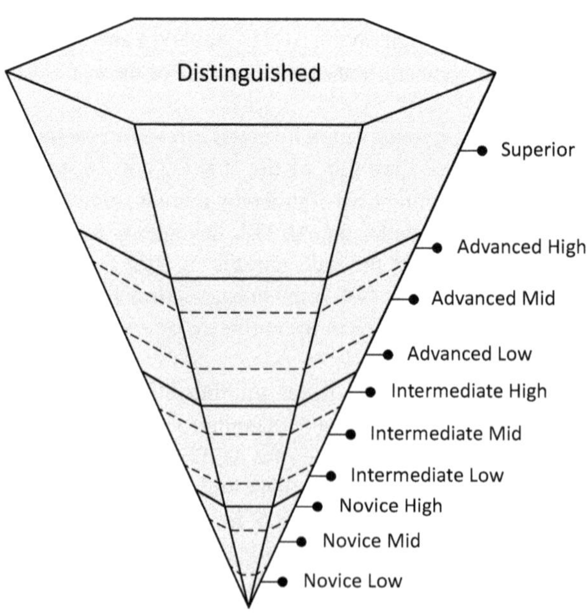

Figure 4.1 ACTFL proficiency scale.

objectives, content and methods … of courses, syllabuses and qualifications" (CoE, 2001, p. 1). The resulting CEFR (CoE, 2001) is a language- and context-independent framework describing relevant aspects of language learning and use, language teaching, communicative tasks, curricula, assessment and language policy. The CEFR is a language policy tool that aims to increase transparency, provide a metalanguage for stakeholder communication, and enable mutual recognitions of qualifications and exams across Europe. At its core, the CEFR provides a descriptive proficiency scale system, that depicts relevant horizontal aspects of proficiency (differentiated for receptive, productive and interactive skills as well as for several linguistic competences) on six ascending levels (A1 and A2 describe beginning proficiency, where A2 represents *Waystage*; B1 and B2 describe independent usage, with B1 corresponding to *Threshold*; C1 and C2 represent mastery). This proficiency framework and accompanying illustrative scales for language learning, teaching, and assessment was recently updated and widened by the *Companion Volume* (CoE, 2018a), which contains additional descriptors for existing scales, as well as a whole new set of scales for the concept of mediation, amongst other additions.

The CEFR scales are based on over 40 existing proficiency scales (North, 2002) and on expert-derived level descriptions (*Threshold*, *Waystage*); meanwhile, the more recent *Companion* descriptors are mainly based on expert descriptions. The descriptors of the CEFR and its *Companion* were empirically scaled: Teachers (and other language professionals in case of the *Companion*) were asked to estimate the descriptors' difficulty levels, and these estimations were subjugated to statistical analyses, resulting in the six ascending proficiency levels. Nevertheless, the theoretical foundation of the CEFR remains one of its weak points (e.g., Cumming, 2009; Hulstijn, 2007). While the CEFR proficiency concept is based on models of communicative competence (e.g., Bachman & Palmer, 1996; and Canale & Swain, 1981), the descriptors themselves are based "on professional consensus rather than empirical evidence" (Harsch, 2014, p. 156). North (2007), however, stressed the importance of involving practitioners in the development of such a framework, rather than basing it on SLA theories. Hence, while the levels were derived from expert estimation and quantitative analyses, the ascending order of the levels is not a validated, theoretical description of second language acquisition, nor does it describe proficiency development precisely.

Comparing ILR, ACTFL, and CEFR. When the CEFR was released in 2001, there were no official correspondences between the ILR, ACTFL, and CEFR scales (Tschirner, 2012). Meanwhile, research was conducted that aimed at aligning the three frameworks (ILR, ACTFL and CEFR). In 2010, ACTFL worked to establish relationships with European testing organizations to explore crosswalks among the three scales. Over several years and multiple meetings, including working groups comprised of users of both scales, cooperative studies were conducted to compare and align the scale systems, with differing outcomes. Tschirner (2012) reported a set of standard setting studies to align ACTFL and CEFR scales, and based on additional studies by the team headed by Tschirner, ACTFL published the following alignment table for the receptive and productive skills:

As Table 4.1 shows, the alignment is currently uni-directional; that is, a score on an ACTFL-certified test can be converted to a CEFR level but not the reverse. In addition, one issue with directly comparing different proficiency systems, of course, is that of the tests used within each system. In the US, regardless of language, the only official ILR tests come from the US government (or ACTFL) and the only certified ACTFL tests are administered via ACTFL's testing arm, Language Testing International (LTI). This situation contrasts with CEFR contexts; there is no official body in Europe or elsewhere that would endorse tests that are aligned to the CEFR. Rather, test providers and exam boards develop their own tests and conduct their own CEFR alignment studies. Hence the quality, nature, and difficulty of tests that claim alignment to the CEFR levels vary by language and even country. Although some work has been conducted to align these frameworks, more research and collaboration would benefit language learners who

Table 4.1 ACTFL and CEFR level alignment (ACTFL, n.d., p. 4)

ONE-DIRECTIONAL ALIGNMENT: Receptive Skills – Reading and Listening		*ONE-DIRECTIONAL ALIGNMENT: Productive Skills – Speaking and Writing*	
Rating on ACTFL Assessment (LPT, RPT or L&Rcat)	*Corresponding CEFR Rating*	*Rating on ACTFL Assessment (OPI, OPIc or WPT)*	*Corresponding CEFR Rating*
Distinguished	C2		
Superior	C1.2	Superior	C2
Advanced High	C1.1	Advanced High	C1
Advanced Mid	B2	Advanced Mid	B2.2
Advanced Low	B1.2	Advanced Low	B2.1
Intermediate High	B1.1	Intermediate High	B1.2
Intermediate Mid	A2	Intermediate Mid	B1.1
Intermediate Low	A1.2	Intermediate Low	A2
Novice High	A1.1	Novice High	A1
Novice Mid	0	Novice Mid	0
Novice Low	0	Novice Low	0

need to transfer a test result from one system to another in order to receive credit for studying abroad or to communicate the language gain made.

Implications for Second Language Acquisition and Language Testing

Proficiency scales and their frameworks provide a common reference point and metalanguage to facilitate communication about models of proficiency development amongst stakeholders; not the least, to compare curricula, standards, exams, and educational outcomes within and across educational contexts, and to enhance mutual recognition of learning benchmarks, exam-outcomes, and qualifications. Within an educational system, proficiency scales such as those of the CEFR can serve as a reference point for the constructive alignment of curricula, teaching objectives, learning outcomes, educational standards, and assessment (Little & Erickson, 2015). Thinking of an evaluative circle that starts with curricula and goals, continues to teaching and learning, moves on to summative assessment of outcomes, and finally comes back to evaluating curricula and goals based on course effectiveness, all three proficiency scales have been and continue to be used to help inform all stages of this circle. For example, curricula and goals can be derived from the CEFR: Teaching materials and activities can be designed to reflect the goals and be presented in a progression that mirrors the stages in the proficiency framework. Continuous formative assessment and feedback can be oriented towards the goals and how to reach them. Self- and peer-assessments can use the self-assessment grids from the CEFR. Summative assessment of learning outcomes can be aligned to the same proficiency framework, so that the evaluation of whether teaching and learning activities lead to the intended goals takes places within one framework. Thus, frameworks like the CEFR can inform teaching, learning, and assessment so that their constructive alignment within one proficiency framework can lead to positive washback. This same process is used in US Kindergarten through 12th grade (K-12) schools and institutions of higher education with the ACTFL Guidelines.

Focusing more specifically on assessment and evaluation, proficiency scales like ACTFL's can facilitate the comparison of different approaches to evaluate teaching effectiveness and learning outcomes. In the classroom, for example, internal teacher-, peer- and self-assessments can use the same criteria, albeit in different forms. In order to keep assessment tools manageable, teachers can use a selection of descriptors or levels of a scale system. For learners, relevant descriptors can be presented as checklists to facilitate peer- and self-assessment. Here, tools like the aforementioned CEFR self-assessment grid and the *European Language Portfolio* (CoE, n.d.), which also operates within the CEFR framework, can be employed. Thus, the different agents in the classroom can meaningfully compare and reflect their angles on learner performance, development and proficiency. Similar tools, such as the ACTFL/NCSSFL Can-Do Statements and LinguaFolio (https://ncssfl.org/linguafolio2020/) provide the basis for student self-assessment, goal setting, and accountability.

To relate internal assessment to external evaluation, proficiency frameworks and scales can serve as common reference points to compare internal assessment outcomes with external evaluation tools such as large-scale educational monitoring studies. In Germany for example, the educational standards that describe expected learning outcomes at the end of schooling were derived from the CEFR. Likewise in the United States, expected K-12 and university-level learning is often articulated on the ACTFL scale. Curricula in both contexts were and are revised to reflect certain CEFR or ACTFL proficiency levels and language use domains. School-leaving or exit/graduation exams operationalize specific aspects and levels of the scales. Hence internally, the scales serve as a common reference point to define and assess learning outcomes. In addition, Germany uses an external educational monitoring system where CEFR-aligned standardized tests are used to assess learner proficiency of school students at regular intervals. Moreover, teachers are provided annually with standardized diagnostic language tests aligned to the CEFR. Thus, informal internal assessment by teachers and learners can be related to and compared with standardized external assessment results, whereby learning outcomes can be evaluated from a variety of relevant angles, thus adding reliability and validity to the evaluation. This can serve as valuable feedback for teachers regarding teaching effectiveness, for learners regarding their development, and for educational stakeholders regarding quality monitoring and maintaining standards. The ACTFL Assessment for Performance toward Proficiency in Languages (AAPPL) has served a similar function in US K-12 schools. As teachers develop curricula and plan assessments, they align their proficiency goals to the ACTFL Guidelines. To measure student progress toward such goals, many schools, districts and states use the AAPPL as a standardized measure.

Normative Effects

While proficiency scales were intended to provide a descriptive scheme that has to be adapted for different languages, contexts and purposes, they are nevertheless being used for normative purposes. The CEFR has been criticized as being a normative tool and arbitrary standard to produce uniformity (e.g., Spolsky, 2008). Such criticism is partly based on the fact that all major exam bodies and test providers world-wide, as well as many course book providers, have aligned their tests and materials to international scales such as those of the CEFR or ACTFL, thus creating the impression of a "common standard." Some providers follow the procedures outlined in the *Manual for Relating Examinations to the CEFR* (CoE, 2009a) with academic rigor, others less so. This seemingly simple alignment of very different exams and materials to a common set of reference levels may create the impression that the proficiency scale levels are a valid set of standards that can be applied directly to all sorts of language requirements, contexts and purposes, such as university entrance requirements, language requirements for taking up a certain profession, or language requirements for immigration. For example, a recent survey has shown that in Europe, university admissions tend to set entry requirements at CEFR level B2 by following what their colleagues in other countries and universities do, rather than by conducting a needs analysis for their specific contexts and languages (Deygers et al., 2018). Or, while language requirements for immigration purposes are often expressed in terms of CEFR levels and the proficiency tests used for immigration might be aligned to the CEFR, they may not be validated for this purpose. Hence, proficiency scales have a huge potential for exerting normative effects on stakeholders.

This effect may partly be caused by the fact that proficiency scales provide a relatively simple and linear model of language proficiency that represents a hugely complex construct on a limited number of levels. Using these levels as a "given standard" involves much fewer resources than conducting a needs analysis for a given context. Often, the necessary expertise for such a needs analysis is not given, and more than often, decisions are influenced by policies and competitors, but not by sound science. To counteract this effect, stakeholders must be supported by professional associations to understand the implications and dangers of misusing a proficiency framework as a "given standard", and to understand why local analyses of contexts, participants and requirements need to be conducted and disseminated, as, for example, Harsch (2014) argued.

Standard Setting Implications

Proficiency frameworks and scales can serve as common reference points for local or international tests. Here, test items, tasks, performances, criteria or rubrics, and outcomes can be specified and described with reference to the proficiency scale categories and levels. In a next step, test scores can be formally aligned to an established proficiency scale via so-called standard setting methods. Thereby, the levels of the external proficiency scale are projected onto the internal test score scale via expert judgments and statistical methods. This adds qualitative meaning to the quantitative test scores and enhances score interpretation and transparency. Notwithstanding the advantages of such alignment, the procedures involved contain inherently subjective aspects. The main ones concern the interpretation of the meaning of a proficiency level; the understanding of what it means to be at a proficiency level; and the fact that different standard setting methods lead to differing outcomes. We discuss these three issues in turn.

The interpretation of the meaning of a given proficiency level takes place at every step of test development, scoring, and standard setting. Context-independent proficiency scales such as those of the CEFR have to be interpreted locally and adapted to the specific context in which a test operates. Different test providers will interpret the proficiency levels and descriptors differently, which leads to differing test specifications, formats, rubrics and scoring approaches. To counteract this unavoidably subjective interpretation, transparent documentation can facilitate communicating how a certain proficiency level was interpreted in a certain context for certain purposes.

The second issue concerns differences in the understanding of what it means to have reached a certain proficiency level (Harsch, 2019). The question here is how many test items of a certain difficulty or proficiency level a test taker must pass to be classified as proficient at the given level. The question can be phrased from a statistical perspective by asking the test taker's probability of completing, with mastery, the tasks at a given proficiency level. For classification, should the probability be 50 or 80%? A related question is whether the items used for judging mastery should be located at the beginning, middle or upper end of a given proficiency level. Unfortunately, there is no consensus amongst researchers or test providers on the answers to these questions, and different standard setting projects use different approaches. At the same time, professional associations such as the American Psychological Association or the European Association for Language Testing and Assessment (www.ealta.eu.org/guidelines.htm) have published recommendations that tests undergo such rigorous review and standard setting before release.

A third issue addresses the reality that different standard setting methods may yield differing results. Not only do different projects show differences in their understanding of what it means to attain a level, different statistical methods also lead to differing results, as do different expert panels. Hence, standard setting projects must justify their choices of approaches and methods, and they must transparently document their interpretations, specifications, procedures, and outcomes. This allows an evaluation of the meaningfulness and soundness of the alignment.

There is a vast body of literature on methodological aspects and research projects on standard setting (e.g., Cizek, 2012; or, see Harsch, 2014, for a brief overview of projects in the European context). In Europe, the CoE has addressed the need for guidance in this area by publishing the aforementioned *Manual* (CoE, 2009a) and its technical supplements (CoE, 2009b). Regarding ILR and ACTFL-certified tests, regular standard-setting studies are carried out following state-of-the-art procedures and involving professional psychometricians and subject matter experts.

Recommendations for Practice

Proficiency scales and their vertical levels depict an inherent implication of how language learners develop, progress, and manage to communicate in ever more complex and demanding situations. There is an inextricable link between such a progression and theories of SLA: They inform and validate each other. We acknowledge that the three scales reviewed here were not based on SLA theories, but rather on descriptions of language behavior, as Brindley (1998) pointed out when discussing the ACTFL and ILR scales, and we agree with him that this may lead to issues with the scales' construct validity. Nevertheless, even if a scale system is not based on SLA theories, or on longitudinal observation of learner development and language acquisition, the ascending levels and their underlying progression provide descriptions that can be meaningful for learning, teaching, and assessment, as we have discussed above.

The connection between proficiency assessment and SLA research has been recognized for a long time (e.g., Byrnes, 1987; Bachman & Cohen, 1998). Byrnes, for example, argued with regard to employing the ACTFL Guidelines that "the assessment procedure can become a source of data for future SLA research" (1987, p. 44). Not only can such assessment data be analyzed for SLA purposes, but if SLA research employs assessment tools that are aligned to a proficiency scale (see 2.3 above), the proficiency levels of SLA research-study participants can be compared across different settings. Nonetheless, the scale needs to validly reflect language development to be meaningful in SLA research.

Recently, investigations of the relationship between proficiency levels and SLA have gained momentum. In Europe, the Second Language Acquisition & Testing in Europe (SLATE) network brings together researchers interested "in the relationship between second/foreign language development, levels of second-language proficiency, and language testing research" (n.d.). Bartning et al. (2010) gave an overview of aspects that the networks investigates, such as cohesive devices and CEFR levels, appropriacy and accuracy in written learner texts at different CEFR levels, or task complexity in listening. Some projects aim to underpin the CEFR levels with empirical evidence on the development of particular linguistic features, such as the Cefling project in Finland using Finnish and English corpora. Another corpora-based approach is the English Profile program (https://www.englishprofile.org/), a series of projects that aim to describe "what aspects of English are typically learned at each CEFR level" and to bring corpus linguistics, pedagogy, and assessment together to inform "teachers, curriculum developers, course-book authors and test writers what is suitable for learning at each level" (Cambridge University Press, 2015). In the US, two National Foreign Language Resource Centers are exploring separate and combined efforts to establish such corpora in languages other than English.

Another angle in both testing and SLA research is the link between language behavior and the tasks that elicit such behavior. Studies on task demands in SLA (Robinson, 2001) have successfully informed test development and validation (e.g., Harsch & Rupp, 2011). Here, findings from SLA research and selected CEFR features contributed to developing test specifications and tasks operationalizing certain difficulty-determining characteristics. The task characteristics could then be used to confirm and explain empirically derived task difficulties, thus contributing to task validation. More research is needed, however, to systematize task demands across proficiency levels for the three frameworks and their scales reviewed here.

Currently, the CEFR and ACTFL scales are being applied to describe SLA outcomes and development with young learners. With reference to the CEFR, a bank of descriptors focusing on young learners has recently been added with descriptors "drawn from European Language Portfolios and other sources and mapped to the extended set of illustrative descriptors of the CEFR, organized by CEFR level" (CoE, 2018b, p. 3). The ACTFL Guidelines are currently used with the AAPPL to describe the language of upper elementary, middle and high school students. However, more research is needed on child SLA to fully understand how ACTFL and CEFR-related scales can be applied to the assessment of very young learners (or whether they should be), and whether more fine-grained levels are needed. Indeed, newer scales and frameworks are being developed specifically for children and their immediate learning contexts which are unique to the countries in which the learning is taking place. For example, China's Standards of English Language Ability for children through adults, and the United States' WIDA Consortium's English Language Proficiency Standards for child English language learners were developed out of a need to have proficiency scales and frameworks (with accompanying standards, materials, and tests) that fit the demographics, curricula, and learning goals and trajectories within those specific populations. Further areas of common interest in proficiency assessment and SLA are the role of cognitive processes in different stages of development, the influence of multilingualism on the development of a further language, the relation between intercultural competences and language proficiency, or differential effects of real-world vs. teaching vs. testing tasks at different proficiency stages. Here, SLA studies could yield important insights into characteristics that are direly needed to expand the existing proficiency scales and frameworks.

In sum, proficiency scales and frameworks have the potential to provide a common language that SLA researchers can use to describe language learners and contextual characteristics of language learning. Moreover, test instruments that operationalize a proficiency scale allow SLA researchers to transparently assess their study participants' proficiency levels, thereby facilitating comparisons of study results across different contexts. Such proficiency assessment data can also be used to confirm SLA hypothesis, and SLA findings can be employed to enhance existing proficiency scales and inform proficiency assessment.

Recommended Readings

Bartning, I., Martin, M., & Vedder, I. (Eds.). (2010). *Communicative proficiency and linguistic development: Intersections between SLA and language testing research*. EUROSLA Monograph Series (Vol. 1). http://www.eurosla.org/monographs/EM01/EM01home.php

This volume contains a series of empirical studies carried out to bridge the gap between notions of communicative proficiency as operationalized in the CEFR and notions of language development held by SLA researchers.

Cizek, G. J. (Ed.). (2012). *Setting performance standards: Foundations, methods, and innovations* (2nd ed.). Routledge. https://doi.org/10.4324/9780203848203

This volume is a must-read for those aligning pedagogical instruments to language proficiency frameworks and scales. It provides one of the most in-depth explanations of the theoretical issues surrounding standard setting and offers a set of tools for practitioners to align curricula, learning, and testing to proficiency frameworks and scales.

Tschirner, E. (Ed.). (2012). *Aligning frameworks of reference in language testing: The ACTFL proficiency guidelines and the common European framework of reference*. Stauffenburg Verlag.

This volume is dedicated to linking understanding and interpretation of performance standards between the two most influential international proficiency frameworks—the CEFR and the ACTFL Proficiency Guidelines.

References

American Council on the Teaching of Foreign Languages. (n.d.). *Assigning CEFR ratings to ACTFL assessments.* http://www.actfl.org/sites/default/files/reports/Assigning_CEFR_Ratings_To_ACTFL_Assessments.pdf

Bachman, L. (1990). *Fundamental considerations in language testing.* Oxford University Press.

Bachman, L. F., & Cohen, A. D. (Eds.). (1998). *Interfaces between second language acquisition and language testing research.* Cambridge University Press.

Bachman, L. F., & Palmer, A. S. (1996). *Language testing in practice: Designing and developing useful language tests.* Oxford University Press.

Bartning, I., Martin, M., & Vedder, I. (Eds.). (2010). *Communicative proficiency and linguistic development: Intersections between SLA and language testing research.* EUROSLA Monograph Series (Vol. 1). http://www.eurosla.org/monographs/EM01/EM01home.php

Brindley, G. (1998). Describing language development? Rating scales and SLA. In L. F. Bachman & A. D. Cohen (Eds.), *Interfaces between second language acquisition and language testing research* (pp. 112–140). Cambridge University Press.

Byrnes, H. (1987). Proficiency as a framework for research in second language acquisition. *The Modern Language Journal, 71*(1), 44–49. https://doi.org/10.1111/j.1540-4781.1987.tb01054.x

Cambridge University Press. (2015). *English profile—What the CEFR means for English.* http://www.englishprofile.org/

Canale, M., & Swain, M. (1981). A theoretical framework for communicative competence. In A. S. Palmer, P. Groot, & G. Trosper (Eds.), *The construct validation of tests of communicative competence* (pp. 31–36). TESOL.

Carroll, J. (1967). Foreign language proficiency levels attained by language majors near graduation from college. *Foreign Language Annals, 1*(2), 131–151. https://doi.org/10.1111/j.1944-9720.1967.tb00127.x

Cizek, G. J. (Ed.). (2012). *Setting performance standards: Foundations, methods, and innovations* (2nd ed.). Routledge. https://doi.org/10.4324/9780203848203

Council of Europe. (n.d.). *European language portfolio (ELP).* Council of Europe. https://www.coe.int/en/web/portfolio

Council of Europe. (2001). *A common European framework of reference for language learning and teaching.* Cambridge University Press.

Council of Europe. (2009a). *Relating language examinations to the 'Common European framework of reference for languages: Learning, teaching, assessment' (CEFR): A manual.* Council of Europe Language Policy Division. https://www.coe.int/en/web/common-european-framework-reference-languages/relating-examinations-to-the-cefr

Council of Europe. (2009b). *Reference supplement to the manual for relating language examinations to the CEFR.* Council of Europe Language Policy Division. https://www.coe.int/en/web/common-european-framework-reference-languages/additional-material

Council of Europe. (2018a). *European framework of reference for languages: Learning, teaching, assessment: Companion volume with new descriptors.* Council of Europe. https://rm.coe.int/cefr-companion-volume-with-new-descriptors-2018/1680787989

Council of Europe (2018b). *Collated representative samples of descriptors of language competences developed for young learners (volume 1: ages 7–10; volume 2: ages 11–15.* Council of Europe. https://www.coe.int/en/web/common-european-framework-reference-languages/bank-of-supplementary-descriptors

Cox, T., Malone, M. E., & Winke, P. M. (2018). Future directions in assessment: Influences of standards and implications for language learning. *Foreign Language Annals, 51*(1), 104–115. https://doi.org/10.1111/flan.12326

Cumming, A. (2009). Language assessment in education: Tests, curricula and teaching. *Annual Review of Applied Linguistics, 29,* 90–100. https://doi.org/10.1017/S0267190509090084

Davies, A., Brown, A., Elder, C., Hill, K., & Lumley, T. (1999). *Dictionary of language testing.* Cambridge University Press.

Deygers, B., Zeidler, B., Vilcu, D., & Hamnes Carlsen, C. (2018). One framework to unite them all? Use of the CEFR in European university entrance policies. *Language Assessment Quarterly, 15*(1), 3–15. https://doi.org/10.1080/15434303.2016.1261350

Harsch, C. (2014). General language proficiency revisited: Current and future issues. *Language Assessment Quarterly, 11*(2), 152–169. https://doi.org/10.1080/15434303.2014.902059

Harsch, C. (2019). What it means to be at a CEFR level: Or why my Mojito is not your Mojito—On the significance of sharing Mojito recipes. In A. Huhta, N. Figueras, & G. Erickson (Eds.), *Developments in language education: a memorial volume* (pp. 76–93). EALTA and University of Jyväskylä. http://www.ealta.eu.org/resources.htm

Harsch, C., & Rupp, A. (2011). Designing and scaling level-specific writing tasks in alignment with the CEFR: A test-centered approach. *Language Assessment Quarterly*, *8*(1), 1–34. https://doi.org/10.1080/15434303.2010.535575

Herzog, M. (2003). Impact of the proficiency scale and the Oral Proficiency Interview on the foreign language program at the Defense Language Institute Foreign Language Center. *Foreign Language Annals*, *36*, 566–571. https://doi.org/10.1111/j.1944-9720.2003.tb02146.x

Hulstijn, J. (2007). The shaky ground beneath the CEFR: Quantitative and qualitative dimensions of language proficiency. *The Modern Language Journal*, *91*(4), 663–667. https://doi.org/10.1111/j.1540-4781.2007.00627_5.x

Jezak, M. (2017). *Language is the key: The Canadian language benchmarks model*. University of Ottawa Press. https://library.oapen.org/bitstream/handle/20.500.12657/31313/631397.pdf

Liskin-Gasparro, J. E. (1982). *ETS oral proficiency testing manual*. Educational Testing Service.

Liskin-Gasparro, J. E. (1984). The ACTFL proficiency guidelines: Gateway to testing and curriculum. *Foreign Language Annals*, *17*(5), 475–489. https://doi.org/10.1111/j.1944-9720.1984.tb01736.x

Little, D., & Erickson, G. (2015). Learner identity, learner agency, and the assessment of language proficiency: Some reflections prompted by the Common European Framework of Reference for Languages. *Annual Review of Applied Linguistics*, *35*, 120–139. https://doi.org/10.1017/S0267190514000300

Lowe, P. (1985). The ILR proficiency scale as a synthesizing research principle: The view from the mountain. In C. J. James (Ed.), *Foreign language proficiency in the classroom and beyond* (pp. 9–49). National Textbook.

National Academies of Sciences, Engineering, and Medicine. (2020). *A principled approach to language assessment: Considerations for the U.S. Foreign Service Institute*. National Academies Press. https://doi.org/10.17226/25748

NEEA. (n.d). *China standards of English language ability*. National Educational Examination Authority, Ministry of Education, P.R. China. http://cse.neea.edu.cn/html1/folder/1505/244-1.htm

North, B. (2002). Developing descriptor scales of language proficiency for the CEF common reference levels. In J. C. Alderson (Ed.), *Common European framework of reference for languages: Learning, teaching, assessment. Case studies* (pp. 87–105). Council of Europe. https://rm.coe.int/168069f403

North, B. (2007). The CEFR illustrative descriptor scales. *The Modern Language Journal*, *91*(4), 656–659. https://doi.org/10.1111/j.1540-4781.2007.00627_3.x

Robinson, P. (Ed.). (2001). *Cognition and second language instruction*. Cambridge University Press.

Second Language Acquisition & Testing in Europe Network. (n.d.). *What is SLATE?*

Spolsky, B. (2008). Introduction: *Language Testing* at 25: Maturity and responsibility? *Language Testing*, *25*(3), 297–305. https://doi.org/10.1177/0265532208090153

Trim, J. (2001). *The work of the Council of Europe in the field of modern languages, 1957–2001*. http://www.ecml.at/Portals/1/resources/John%20Trim%20collection/Trim_TheWorkOfTheCouncilOfEurope_ModernLanguages_1957_2001.pdf

Tschirner, E. (Ed.). (2012). *Aligning frameworks of reference in language testing: The ACTFL proficiency guidelines and the common European framework of reference*. Stauffenburg Verlag.

van Ek, J. A. (1975). *The threshold level in a European unit/credit system for modern language learning by adults*. Council of Europe.

van Ek, J. A., & Alexander, L. G. (1977). *Waystage*. Council of Europe.

WIDA. (2014). *The WIDA standards framework and its theoretical foundations*. Board of Regents of the University of Wisconsin System. https://wida.wisc.edu/sites/default/files/resource/WIDA-Standards-Framework-and-its-Theoretical-Foundations.pdf

5

Corpora for Second Language Assessments

Dana Gablasova

Background

Language corpora are electronic datasets that contain samples of language use and provide evidence about how language is used in real, meaning-oriented communication, both spoken and written. Corpora can range in size from tens of thousands to billions of words, and can be used to describe different linguistic contexts (settings) and/or groups of language users. Language samples in corpora are coded (annotated) with information about the users and the setting and are searchable according to these variables (such as gender, age, proficiency level, genre, or exam mark awarded). Due to the size of the evidence, corpus-based research can use sophisticated statistical methods to test theories of language use and to produce models of language learning and production, thus complementing findings from classroom-based and experimental research on SLA.

The robust analysis of patterns in learner production makes corpora and corpus methods a valuable resource in language testing as well, contributing to its core objective of "the systematic gathering of language-related behavior in order to make inferences about language ability and capacity for language" (Chapelle & Plakans, 2013, p. 241). Corpora have been a steady presence in the fields of language acquisition and language testing for several decades (Barker, 2013). Since the 1990s, when Charles Alderson (1996) first identified a range of potential corpus applications in language testing, several major examination boards (e.g., the British Council, Cambridge Assessment English, ETS, Pearson and Trinity College London) commissioned the creation of corpora either based on their exams or based on language of a particular domain in order to develop and revise their tests. Moreover, the topic of corpus-based approaches to language assessment has appeared in major reference books in the fields of applied linguistics (e.g., Taylor & Barker, 2008; Barker, 2012; Barker et al., 2015; Nesi, 2016), and papers using corpus-based research with implications for language assessment have become increasingly common in specialised language testing journals such as *Language Testing* (e.g., Cushing, 2017) and *Language Assessment Quarterly* (e.g., Paquot, 2018; Pan & Qian, 2017; Park, 2014), as well as in major journals in applied linguistics (e.g., Staples et al., 2017, 2018; Wisniewski, 2017). Over this period of time, corpora have been used with an increasing range of applications in language assessment, contributing to each stage of the test development cycle (see Green & Fulcher, Chapter 7, this volume on the cycle) such as defining the construct, developing test items, validation of tests, and test revision.

Key Concepts

Corpus linguistics: A versatile method of language analysis based on robust empirical evidence provided by corpora, electronic datasets containing samples of real language use.

Corpus evidence: Different types of language production (e.g., spoken, written, online, and multimodal) which complement other major sources of data in learner language research such as introspection, metalinguistic judgements, and observed language use, both elicited and naturally-occurring.

L2 variation: Systematic patterns in L2 use revealing variation in the processes and outcomes of L2 acquisition, which may be linked with variables in L2 learner profiles (e.g., L1 background and learning history) to explain the individual and group-related differences in language learning.

Key Issues

This section first describes corpora and corpus methods of particular relevance to SLA and language testing. Then, it focuses on direct applications of these tools to language assessments. Throughout the section, examples from recent SLA and testing research and practice are provided to illustrate the application of these corpus tools.

Corpora

Corpora are computer-searchable collections of language samples, selected to represent specific populations of language users or specific contexts of use (McEnery et al., 2006). Corpora can represent different modes of communication—written, oral, online, multimodal, or sign communication. Here, I discuss three types of corpora most relevant for studies on SLA and language testing.

Corpora Representing Production of L1/Expert Users. These corpora are usually employed in SLA and language testing research to investigate the target use of language, often providing reference points for evaluating L2 production. The L1 corpora can be further subdivided into general and specialised corpora, each with a different purpose (McEnery et al., 2006). General L1 corpora are typically very large as they seek to represent language use in a very broadly defined domain (e.g., all of spoken British English) and contain samples from different genres and registers found in this domain (e.g., formal communication, informal conversations, institutional discourse). An example of this type of corpus is the spoken component of the British National Corpus 2014 (Love et al., 2017), which contains ten million words of informal conversations of British English from the 2010s. These general corpora are particularly useful when establishing overall distributions of linguistic features, providing information on frequency of occurrence and co-occurrence of these features in language use which can be used to guide instrument/test development as well as rating scale development—whether for SLA research or language testing purposes (Cushing, 2017; Barker, 2013).

Specialised corpora, which are of varying sizes due to their specialised nature (ranging from thousands to millions of words), seek to represent language use in a more narrowly defined domain, for example, in a particular genre such as written academic language (Nesi, 2016) or healthcare communication (e.g., Staples, 2015). Many of these corpora are based on L1 use in the target domain; however, recognising that not all L1 users have the same level of linguistic knowledge and experience across different domains (e.g., Hulstijn, 2015), some of the corpora only include language from the expert users of language in the domain. Specialised corpora are especially useful for exploring the target language domains, both in order to understand the typical language use in these domains and to draw on the corpus examples when writing or revising test items and selecting input materials (such as readings). This enables researchers and test developers "to base their testing tasks more closely on authentic rather than contrived language and texts" (Taylor & Barker, 2008, p. 246). For example, Pearson commissioned the creation of the Pearson International Corpus of Academic English (PICAE) (Ackermann et al., 2011) to be used in the development of the Pearson Test of English Academic (PTE Academic) while ETS commissioned the development of the TOEFL 2000 Spoken and Written Academic Language Corpus (T2K-SWAL) (Biber et al., 2006) to revise the Test of English as a Foreign Language (TOEFL).

Corpora Representing Production from L2 Users Of The Target Language. These corpora, which are sometimes referred to as "learner corpora", are a group of specialised corpora that represent different types of L2 production and usually contain information (metadata) about different speaker characteristics, such as L2 proficiency level, L1 background, and information about L2 learning history (McEnery et al., 2006). Users can search and analyse these corpora according to these variables, observing their effect on the patterns in L2 use. The language in these corpora can represent either specific, narrowly defined tasks or a more broadly defined genre (e.g., academic writing). Examples of two corpora that represent learners from a broad range of L1 backgrounds and proficiency levels but with a different target language are: i) the EF-Cambridge Open Language Database (EFCAMDAT) (https://corpus.mml.cam.ac.uk/efcamdat2/public_html/) containing 83 million words and consisting of assignments written online by learners of English, and ii) the Guangwai Lancaster Chinese Learner Corpus (https://www.sketchengine.eu/guangwai-lancaster-chinese-learner-corpus/) representing spoken and written production from learners of Chinese. The latter corpus is fully error-tagged, and can also act as a corpus representing language use in exams, as it contains a large component of language elicited and marked under exam conditions.

Corpora Representing Production From Test-Takers in an Exam Setting. A special subcategory of L2 specialised corpora,[1] which are of particular relevance to language testing, are corpora representing language use from an exam context. An example of such a corpus is the Trinity Lancaster Corpus of L2 English production based on the Graded Examinations in Spoken English (GESE) developed and administered by Trinity College London (Gablasova et al., 2019). The corpus contains over four million words from 2,000 transcriptions of speaking exam performances and is searchable according to a number of variables including speaker (e.g., age, educational level, L1 background, and L2 proficiency) and exam characteristics (e.g., marks for each speaking task). Other such exam corpora are, for example, the Cambridge Learner Corpus (e.g., Park, 2014) which contains 16 million words from exams administered by Cambridge Assessment English (2.9 million words of this corpus are freely accessible; https://www.sketchengine.eu/cambridge-learner-corpus/), and the TOEFL iBT corpus (e.g., Biber et al., 2016) created from the TOEFL iBT Public Use Dataset made available by ETS.

In addition to providing insights into L2 production, these corpora are particularly useful for investigating issues directly applicable to language testing such as interaction between test-takers and examiners and the effect of individual characteristics on the test-takers' ability to demonstrate their linguistic knowledge. Bachman and Palmer (1996, pp. 64–65) identified several variables that can affect exam performance, such as test-takers' personal characteristics (e.g., gender, age, and education) or the characteristics of the task (e.g., test-takers' familiarity with the topic). Exam corpora that contain the relevant set of variables allow examining the effect of these characteristics on test performance. For example, Gablasova et al. (2017) used the Trinity Lancaster Corpus to examine the effect of task variables on pragmatic choices of test-takers. The study compared test-takers' stance-taking strategies in two GESE tasks which differ in terms of topic familiarity and speaker role, finding the effect of task significant. As Taylor and Barker (2008) summarise, exam corpora can act as "archives", enabling language testers "to address key issues such as comparability across test forms, rater training and standardisation, standard setting and maintenance of standards over time, and investigation of test bias across different test-taker populations" (p. 247).

Corpus Methods and Corpus Information

A range of techniques is used to identify patterns in corpora that are relevant for SLA and language testing purposes (see Brezina & Gablasova, 2017 for an overview of key corpus methods). One of the key functions of corpora is to provide information about *frequency of (co)occurrence* of linguistic features; this information is particularly useful in research on second language use as it highlights typical (most frequent) linguistic features (e.g., the most frequent words, multi-word units, grammatical structures or most frequent errors) characteristic of a particular domain of language or a group of speakers. The results of this analysis are often reported in the form of frequency-ranked lists enabling instrument/test developers to consider the frequency of words or lexico-grammatical structures when developing research instruments, language tests, or rating scales (Römer, 2017), or in order to control level of difficulty in instrument/test instructions and in items (Taylor & Barker, 2008). For example, the PICAE corpus was analysed to produce the Collocations wordlist (Ackermann et al., 2011), which was then used to inform the development of the PTE Academic test. The target linguistic features can be further explored with the aid of *concordance analysis*, in which all instances of the target items found in the corpus are listed with their context, revealing larger lexico-grammatical patterns in which they tend to occur. Concordancing is especially useful when describing target-like use as well as when deciding on acceptability of use. A particular type of co-occurrence of linguistic items is *collocation*, a systematic occurrence of lexical and/or grammatical items in each other's neighbourhood (for a review of corpus-based collocation research in SLA see Gablasova et al., 2017b). *Collocation analysis* is very effective at identifying multi-word expressions, which have been used to distinguish native and non-native users of language, and can be used to create items for research instruments and language tests, as well as for rating L2 performance (Paquot, 2018; Taylor & Barker, 2008; Paquot, Gries, & Yoder, Chapter 21, this volume). Finally, *multidimensional analysis* (e.g., Biber et al., 2016) is used to identify meaningful lexico-grammatical clusters and, based on these, to create a linguistic profile of a certain domain. This approach has been very fruitful in both test development and validation.

Application of Corpus Methods in L2 Research and Testing

Corpora and corpus methods can be integrated into different stages of the instrument development or language testing cycle, contributing to instrument/test development as well as validation. This section discusses several areas in the assessment of language ability that can benefit (and have already benefitted) from corpus analysis.

Instrument/Test Development. When developing a language assessment instrument, it is crucial to gain an in-depth understanding of the linguistic requirements that language learners or test-takers should possess in order to perform successfully in the target environment. This understanding of the target language use (TLU) lies at the heart of effective test development and the ability to generalise from the test performance to real-life contexts (Bachman & Palmer, 1996). Test developers therefore use a variety of ways to collect primary data about how language is actually used in target domains such as interviews with experts (Douglas, 2014). Corpus findings can complement these strategies and considerably enhance our understanding of the TLU as they are based on principled collections of language samples from the target area, allowing test creators to move beyond their intuitions and personal experience with language (Taylor & Baker, 2008). In practical terms, corpora can contribute to three major areas of test development—whether for L2 research or testing purposes: defining the test construct, producing test materials, and developing the rating scales.

Describing the test construct is an essential step in producing L2 research instruments and tests that are useful and effective (Bachman & Palmer, 1996). Corpus evidence can provide a better understanding of the TLU, helping with a clear and accurate definition of the construct to be measured. For example, corpora are useful when describing new domains that have not yet been systematically described (e.g., blog posts as a new genre), as well as refining descriptions of more fully established domains. To illustrate the point both the PICAE and T2K-SWAL have been constructed to inform the development of specific tests of academic English (see above). Corpus-based analysis can also inform a re-evaluation of more general constructs such as that underlying spoken competence. Römer (2017), for example, investigated the role of formulaic language in spoken communication and its representation in rating scales of several major exams (e.g., the TOEFL iBT, the IELTS, and the Cambridge English: Advanced exam). The study demonstrated that while formulaic units played a major role in spoken language found in a large corpus of L1 speakers, formulaic knowledge was not treated systematically in the construct definitions of the reviewed exams and their rating scales.

Instrument and test development is another area that can benefit from corpus data. General as well as specialised L1/expert corpora help to identify the most typical (frequent and recurring) features of a TLU that can be included in the assessment of the language of this TLU. Also, these corpora contain a variety of authentic examples from the TLU which can be sampled for instrument/test input materials and items, thus enhancing correspondence between the language in the instrument/test and the target environment. In addition to directly using corpora to provide material for research instruments and tests, L1/expert corpora can assist with checking how similar the items are to authentic language use (e.g., Staples et al., 2018). Learner corpora represent a good source of information about the most typical errors found in L2 production which can serve as distractor options in research instruments and tests (Cushing, 2017).

Finally, learner corpora are of particular relevance for developing rating scales to analyse and score L2 language performances, as such corpora provide information about typical patterns of language use (e.g., lexical and grammatical complexity as well as errors) at different levels of language proficiency and can help validate "test writer intuitions about language features and frequencies associated with different proficiency levels" (Taylor & Barker, 2008, p. 246). These detailed, corpus-based accounts of L2 knowledge have the potential to inform the description of different levels of expected L2 (test) performance (e.g., Paquot, 2018).

Instrument/Test Validation. As stated above, language assessments should be based on a good understanding of language use in the target domain; likewise, it is crucial that L2 research instruments and tests succeed in eliciting language similar to that of the intended target construct or TLU. This is necessary for the construct validity of the instruments and tests and their ability to draw inferences about second language acquisition or to predict whether test-takers will be able to successfully communicate in the TLU. As Bachman and Palmer (1996, p. 9) put it, "in order for a particular language test to be useful for its intended purposes, test performance must correspond in demonstrable ways to language use in non-test situations." Construct validation is another key area where SLA and language testing can benefit considerably from corpus analysis employed to establish the correspondence between language elicited in instruments/tests and the target construct/ TLU. For example, a number of corpus-based studies have addressed this dimension of language testing, with several of these focusing on the comparison of language produced in the TOEFL iBT test and the target academic domains. For instance, Staples et al. (2013) used the TWL2-SWK corpus for this comparison, noting differences between the corpus data and test-taker performances in terms of formulaic language. Staples et al. (2018) compared L2 writing in the TOEFL iBT with a corpus of student academic writing, reporting differences between the two corpora with respect to a range of lexico-grammatical features related to, for example, stance and information density. Using several reference corpora, LaFlair and Staples (2017) and Staples, LaFlair and Egbert (2017) examined the validity of a high-stakes test of spoken English, the Michigan English Language Assessment Battery (MELAB), a type of oral proficiency interview, reporting a number of differences between the test and language typical of the domains to which it should be generalisable (e.g., spoken academic discourse or face-to-face conversations).

In addition to evaluating the construct validity of existing language assessments, corpora have been used to examine the validity of a widely used and influential scale of language proficiency, the Common European Framework of Reference (CEFR). For example, Wisniewski (2017) investigated how learner corpora can contribute both to a better understanding of language use at different CEFR levels as well as how they can be used to empirically validate the CEFR's illustrative scales. In another example, Thewissen (2013) examined the differences between CEFR levels by analysing errors typical for the B1 to C2 proficiency levels, relying on empirical evidence from a written learner corpus. Finally, Paquot (2018), using both L1 and learner corpora, investigated how incorporation of phraseological competence could enhance the validity and effectiveness of CEFR levels.

Examiner Impact and Examiner Training. While the quality of the test development process is crucial for the construct validity and usefulness of a test, examiners play a vital role in interactive spoken test delivery, influencing test-takers' language production and co-constructing the outcome of the test (Brown, 2013). Exam corpora are an invaluable resource for investigating the impact of examiner characteristics and behaviour on the candidate's exam performance, a topic that has been traditionally of interest to language testers (e.g., Brown, 2003, 2013). These corpora make it possible to examine the effect of linguistic as well as social variables (e.g., age, gender, and cultural background) on the interaction in spoken exams. Corpus-based studies of exam performances and scores awarded can also contribute to our understanding of how different aspects of the language produced in the exam (e.g., content and linguistic properties of test-takers' contributions) affect examiners' perceptions and ratings of candidates' linguistic abilities, and reveal what plays a role in examiner decision-making, complementing existing knowledge in this area (e.g., Sato, 2012; Taguchi, 2011).

These insights are useful in examiner training for specific tests as well as for improving examiner skills and sensitivity to linguistic and social issues in interaction in general. Transcripts selected from exam corpora provide a good opportunity to highlight both routine and atypical situations during the exams as well as offering examples of good practice. It should not be difficult to integrate them into examiner training, for example, as discussion points or model situations to resolve, in order to increase consistency in dealing with test-taker reactions.

While this last application area of corpora has so far mainly focused on examiners in operational language testing situations, it should be pointed out that it could equally provide relevant insights into the impact of L2 researcher behaviour in SLA or testing studies, e.g., when eliciting spoken samples from learners through learner-researcher interaction, or when interviewing participants.

Recommendations for Practice

Working with a suitable corpus lies at the heart of any meaningful and informative corpus-based analysis. When doing and interpreting corpus-based SLA or language testing research, it is essential to carefully and critically evaluate the representativeness of the corpus and to consider its suitability with respect to the research aims (Biber, 1993; Egbert, 2017). Corpus representativeness is one of the most crucial concepts in corpus linguistics and refers to the fact that language samples in a corpus are selected in a principled way to represent a certain type of language (e.g., a genre) and/or a group of language users (e.g., advanced L2 learners of Spanish). The corpus then acts as a sample of language use defined by these criteria (McEnery et al., 2006). In this section, three major issues affecting the quality of corpus-based L2 research are discussed, with corresponding recommendations provided.

First, when assessing the representativeness of a learner corpus and its suitability for SLA and language testing purposes, researchers should pay special attention to how the L2 proficiency of the learners, as recorded in the corpus metadata, was established. Despite its significance in language learning research, information available about L2 proficiency in the corpus metadata has been recently identified as one of the most problematic variables in learner corpus research because it is often not measured reliably and can be based on indirect, proxy variables such as years spent learning the L2 (Carlsen, 2012). This makes it difficult to accurately estimate what L2 level is represented in the corpus and to interpret findings from these corpora (Callies et al., 2014). For example, when comparing production of L2 speakers from different L1 backgrounds to find what typical errors are associated with their L1s, L2 proficiency established through indirect measures makes it difficult to determine whether any observed differences between the groups are indeed due to the linguistic background, or to different L2 mastery (or both).

Second, it is important to carefully reflect on the features of corpus design and representativeness in comparative corpus studies, which account for much of corpus-based L2 research (Granger, 2015). In order for the results to be meaningful, the corpora to be compared should be similar in all major aspects, and differ only with respect to the variable whose effect we wish to observe. This is often not the case in corpus-based learner research when, for example, general corpora of L1 use such as the BNC are compared to specialised, learner corpora, representing language from a specific task. Results of such comparisons should be treated with caution. Gablasova et al. (2017a) demonstrated that even if corpora of L1 speakers, representing similar linguistic contexts (informal speech), are compared, there tend to be statistically significant differences between the language use in these corpora. The differences found when comparing corpora should therefore be examined critically, with special attention paid to the degree of comparability of the corpora used.

Finally, language samples in L1 corpora used as a reference point (baseline) in comparative studies with L2 learners, or used as a source of information about L1 use, should be examined carefully. As demonstrated by psycholinguistic research (e.g., Andringa & Dąbrowska, 2019), language knowledge can vary considerably across L1 speakers, often in relation to education and literacy levels, and not all L1 speakers use the language to the same (high) standard (Hulstijn, 2015). L1 corpora should therefore not be used for benchmarking purposes by default, and their selection should be clearly justified; alternatively, a corpus representing expert use of language could be employed. Overall, as Egbert (2017) emphasises, the researchers who wish to use corpora "should be careful to learn about the sampling design and practices of existing corpora before using them for research and follow sound principles of corpus design and sampling when constructing a new corpus" (p. 560).

Note

1 It should be noted that these corpora are not necessarily limited to L2 users, as various professionals also take exams of domain-specific language competence in their first language (e.g., healthcare professionals).

Recommended Reading

Brezina, V. (2018). *Statistics in corpus linguistics: A practical guide*. Cambridge University Press.

This book offers a practical guide for doing corpus analysis for research purposes, and is organised according to major linguistic topics. The companion website (http://corpora.lancs.ac.uk/stats/) provides a user-friendly interface for performing all language analyses described in the book.

Staples, S., LaFlair, G. T., & Egbert, J. (2017). Comparing language use in oral proficiency interviews to target domains: Conversational, academic, and professional discourse. *The Modern Language Journal*, *101*(1), 194–213. https://doi.org/10.1111/modl.12385

This paper illustrates the use of corpora in the analysis of the TLU and the application of the findings in test validation.

Tracy-Ventura, N., & Paquot, M. (2021). *The Routledge handbook of SLA and corpus linguistics*. Routledge.

Published in the same series as the present handbook, this volume provides a comprehensive introduction to corpus linguistics topics directly relevant to L2 research.

References

Ackermann, K., De Jong, J. H. A. L., Kilgarriff, A., & Tugwell, D. (2011). The Pearson International Corpus of Academic English (PICAE). In *Proceedings of corpus linguistics conference*. University of Birmingham, 20–22 July 2011.

Alderson, J. C. (1996). Do corpora have a role in language assessment? In J. A. Thomas & M. H. Short (Eds.), *Using corpora for language research: Studies in honour of Geoffrey Leech* (pp. 248–59). Longman.

Andringa, S. J., & Dąbrowska, E. (2019). Individual differences in first and second language ultimate attainment and their causes. *Language Learning*, *69*(s1), 5–12. https://doi.org/10.1111/lang.12328

Bachman, L. F., & Palmer, A. (1996). *Language testing in practice: Designing and developing useful language tests*. Oxford University Press.

Barker, F. (2012). Corpus-based testing. In C. A. Chapelle (Ed.), *The encyclopedia of applied linguistics* (pp. 1360–1366). Wiley-Blackwell. https://doi.org/10.1002/9781405198431.wbeal0263

Barker, F. (2013). Using corpora to design assessment. In A. J. Kunnan (Ed.), *The companion to language assessment* (pp. 1013–1028). Wiley-Blackwell. https://doi.org/10.1002/9781118411360.wbcla102

Barker, F., Salamoura, A., & Saville, N. (2015). Learner corpora and language testing. In S. Granger, G. Gilquin, & F. Meunier (Eds.), *The Cambridge handbook of learner corpus research* (pp. 511–533). Cambridge University Press. https://doi.org/10.1017/CBO9781139649414.023c

Biber, D. (1993). Representativeness in corpus design. *Literary and Linguistic Computing*, *8*(4), 243–257.

Biber, D., Conrad, S., Reppen, R., Byrd, P., & Helt, M. (2006). The Spoken and Written Academic Language (SWAL) corpus. In D. Biber (Ed.), *University language: A corpus-based study of spoken and written registers* (pp. 23–31). John Benjamins. https://doi.org/10.1075/scl.23

Biber, D., Gray, B., & Staples, S. (2016). Predicting patterns of grammatical complexity across language exam task types and proficiency levels. *Applied Linguistics*, *37*(5), 639–668. https://doi.org/10.1093/applin/amu059

Brezina, V., & Gablasova, D. (2017). The corpus method. In. J. Culpeper, P. Kerswill, R. Wodak, T. McEnery, & F. Katamba (Eds.), *English language: Description, variation and context* (2nd ed.). Palgrave Macmillan.

Brown, A. (2003). Interviewer variation and the co-construction of speaking proficiency. *Language Testing*, *20*(1), 1–25. https://doi.org/10.1191/0265532203lt242oa

Brown, A. (2013). Interlocutor and rater training. In G. Fulcher & F. Davidson (Eds.), *The Routledge handbook of language testing* (pp. 427–439). Routledge.

Callies, M., Díez-Bedmar, M. B., & Zaytseva, E. (2014). Using learner corpora for testing and assessing L2 proficiency. In P. Leclercq, H. Hilton, & A. Edmonds (Eds.), *Measuring L2 proficiency: Perspectives from SLA* (pp. 71–90). Multilingual Matters. https://doi.org/10.21832/9781783092291-007

Carlsen, C. (2012). Proficiency level: A fuzzy variable in computer learner corpora. *Applied Linguistics*, *33*(2), 161–183. https://doi.org/10.1093/applin/amr047

Chapelle, C. A., & Plakans, L. (2013). Assessment and testing: Overview. In C. A. Chapelle (Ed.), *The encyclopaedia of applied linguistics* (pp. 240–244). Wiley-Blackwell. https://doi.org/10.1002/9781405198431.wbeal0603

Cushing, S. T. (2017). Corpus linguistics in language testing research. *Language Testing*, *34*(4), 441–449. https://doi.org/10.1177/0265532217713044

Douglas, D. (2014). *Understanding language testing*. Routledge.

Egbert, J. (2017). Corpus linguistics and language testing: Navigating uncharted waters. *Language Testing*, *34*(4), 555–564. https://doi.org/10.1177/0265532217713045

Gablasova, D., Brezina, V., & McEnery, T. (2017a). Exploring learner language through corpora: Comparing and interpreting corpus frequency information. *Language Learning, 67*(1), 130–154. https://doi.org/10.1111/lang.12226
Gablasova, D., Brezina, V., & McEnery, T. (2017b). Collocations in corpus-based language learning research: Identifying, comparing, and interpreting the evidence. *Language Learning, 67*(1), 155–179. https://doi.org/10.1111/lang.12225
Gablasova, D., Brezina, V., & McEnery, T. (2019). The Trinity Lancaster Corpus: Development, description and application. *International Journal of Learner Corpus Research, 92*, 8–28. https://doi.org/10.1075/scl.92.02gab
Gablasova, D., Brezina, V., McEnery, T., & Boyd, E. (2017). Epistemic stance in spoken L2 English: The effect of task type and speaker style. *Applied Linguistics, 38*(5), 613–637. https://doi.org/10.1093/applin/amv055
Granger, S. (2015). Contrastive interlanguage analysis: A reappraisal. *International Journal of Learner Corpus Research, 1*(1), 7–24. https://doi.org/10.1075/ijlcr.1.1.01gra
Hulstijn, J. H. (2015). *Language proficiency in native and non-native speakers: Theory and research*. John Benjamins. https://doi.org/10.1075/lllt.41
LaFlair, G. T., & Staples, S. (2017). Using corpus linguistics to examine the extrapolation inference in the validity argument for a high-stakes speaking assessment. *Language Testing, 34*(4), 451–475. https://doi.org/10.1177/0265532217713951
Love, R., Dembry, C., Hardie, A., Brezina, V., & McEnery, T. (2017). The spoken BNC2014. *International Journal of Corpus Linguistics, 22*(3), 319–344. https://doi.org/10.1075/ijcl.22.3.02lov
McEnery, T., Xiao, R., & Tono, Y. (2006). *Corpus-based language studies: An advanced resource book*. Routledge.
Nesi, H. (2016). Corpus studies in EAP. In K. Hyland & P. Shaw (Eds.), *The Routledge handbook of English for academic purposes* (pp. 230–241). Routledge.
Pan, M., & Qian, D. D. (2017). Embedding corpora into the content validation of the grammar test of the National Matriculation English Test (NMET) in China. *Language Assessment Quarterly, 14*(2), 120–139. https://doi.org/10.1080/15434303.2017.1303703
Paquot, M. (2018). Phraseological competence: A missing component in university entrance language tests? Insights from a study of EFL learners' use of statistical collocations. *Language Assessment Quarterly, 15*(1), 29–43. https://doi.org/10.1080/15434303.2017.1405421
Park, K. (2014). Corpora and language assessment: The state of the art. *Language Assessment Quarterly, 11*(1), 27–44. https://doi.org/10.1080/15434303.2013.872647
Römer, U. (2017). Language assessment and the inseparability of lexis and grammar: Focus on the construct of speaking. *Language Testing, 34*(4), 477–492. https://doi.org/10.1177/0265532217711431
Sato, T. (2012). The contribution of test-takers' speech content to scores on an English oral proficiency test. *Language Testing, 29*(2), 223–241. https://doi.org/10.1177/0265532211421162
Staples, S. (2015). Examining the linguistic needs of internationally educated nurses: A corpus-based study of lexico-grammatical features in nurse–patient interactions. *English for Specific Purposes, 37*, 122–136. https://doi.org/10.1016/j.esp.2014.09.002
Staples, S., Biber, D., & Reppen, R. (2018). Using corpus-based register analysis to explore the authenticity of high-stakes language exams: A register comparison of TOEFL iBT and disciplinary writing tasks. *The Modern Language Journal, 102*(2), 310–332. https://doi.org/10.1111/modl.12465
Staples, S., Egbert, J., Biber, D., & McClair, A. (2013). Formulaic sequences and EAP writing development: Lexical bundles in the TOEFL iBT writing section. *Journal of English for Academic Purposes, 12*(3), 214–225. https://doi.org/10.1016/j.jeap.2013.05.002
Staples, S., LaFlair, G. T., & Egbert, J. (2017). Comparing language use in oral proficiency interviews to target domains: Conversational, academic, and professional discourse. *The Modern Language Journal, 101*(1), 194–213. https://doi.org/10.1111/modl.12385
Taguchi, N. (2011). Rater variation in the assessment of speech acts. *Pragmatics, 21*(3), 453–471. https://doi.org/10.1075/prag.21.3.08tag
Taylor, L., & Barker, F. (2008). Using corpora for language assessment. In E. Shohamy & N. H. Hornberger (Eds.), *Encyclopaedia of language and education: Language testing and assessment* (pp. 241–254). Springer. https://doi.org/10.1007/978-0-387-30424-3_179
Thewissen, J. (2013). Capturing L2 accuracy development patterns: Insights from an error-tagged EFL learner corpus. *The Modern Language Journal, 97*(S1), 77–101. https://doi.org/10.1111/j.1540-4781.2012.01422.x
Wisniewski, K. (2017). Empirical learner language and the levels of the Common European Framework of Reference. *Language Learning, 67*(S1), 232–253. https://doi.org/10.1111/lang.12223

6

SLA Researcher Assessment Literacy

Luke Harding & Benjamin Kremmel

Background

The basic premise of this chapter is that second language acquisition (SLA) researchers require a level of language assessment literacy to perform their role. "Language assessment literacy" (LAL) here refers to a set of knowledge and skills required to carry out assessment-related tasks and activities (see "Key concepts" below). LAL is clearly of central importance to the type of research which draws on formal test instruments to measure language proficiency and development, such as studies which employ pre-/post-test designs, longitudinal studies, or factorial designs where language proficiency is a dependent or an independent variable. In this sense, the measurement concerns of SLA research and the measurement-related components of LAL align.

Our premise, however, is contentious for two reasons. First, SLA researchers are not a homogeneous group; SLA research covers a wide range of epistemologies and ontologies, from positivist, laboratory-based experimental research to interpretative, classroom-based ethnographic studies. It follows that some varieties of SLA research may have more direct interface with assessment matters than others. Second, assessment literacy is itself a multidimensional construct which includes not only technical skills related to measurement quality but also knowledge of the principles of assessment, beliefs about assessment practices and, importantly, awareness of the consequences of assessment. A comprehensive LAL is therefore also important for understanding the role of assessment within broader ecologies of language learning. For example, a deep understanding of test washback may be vital to interpreting environmental influences on language learning in a particular classroom setting. Similarly, understanding learners' beliefs about assessment may be key to understanding their motivation to learn. For all SLA researchers, the ability to understand and critique claims based on assessment data will be an important element of a broader set of research skills.

The purpose of this chapter is therefore to explore the concept of language assessment literacy as it applies to SLA researchers. In the next section, "Key issues," we first provide an overview of current approaches to LAL in the field of language assessment. We then survey papers which have connected with issues of LAL in the SLA literature and present the results of a pilot study into the general LAL needs of SLA researchers. Next, we turn to "Recommendations for practice," where we discuss the ways in which language assessment literacy could form a more substantial part of SLA researcher training. Finally, we call for closer collaboration between SLA researchers and those who identify as language testing researchers and practitioners, arguing that there are problems with language testing practice which would benefit from a perspective more informed by SLA. We also argue that assessment practices within SLA will be aided by a shift within language testing towards the principles of Open Science.

Key Concepts

Assessment: In this chapter we define assessment broadly as a type of evaluation or judgement which leads to decision-making. Language assessment can span more structured types (such as a vocabulary size test), through evaluations of language performance (e.g., role-play tasks), to incidental and informal types of judgement (providing corrective feedback or recasts). Tests form one subset of assessment types.

Language assessment literacy: Commonly known in the language testing literature as "LAL," language assessment literacy refers to the repertoire of knowledge and skills that individuals require in order to carry out relevant assessment-related tasks. For test developers, this repertoire is likely to be multifaceted and comprehensive. For other stakeholders such as teachers, this repertoire may be more specific.

SLA researcher: We define "SLA researcher" here broadly as any individual involved in conducting research with a view to understanding how second languages are learned, how second languages develop, what factors influence second language learning, and how second languages can best be taught.

Key Issues

Current Perspectives on Language Assessment Literacy

Language assessment literacy is still a relatively new area of interest in the field of language assessment. Having emerged in general education (e.g., through foundational articles by Stiggins, 1991, and Popham, 2009), the notion of assessment literacy was taken up in the field of language testing by Brindley (2001), Davies (2008), Inbar-Lourie (2008), and Taylor (2009) among others. These early papers typically placed the focus of LAL on a key stakeholder group—language teachers—and sought to theorise what LAL should entail, where it was lacking, and how it might best be enhanced among professional educators. Language teachers have remained a focus of much of the subsequent research on LAL (e.g., Baker & Riches, 2018; Fulcher, 2012; Lam, 2015; Malone, 2013; Vogt & Tsagari, 2014; Yan et al., 2018). The scope of LAL enquiry, however, has also broadened to include a range of other stakeholders involved in assessment including language teacher educators (Villa Larenas, 2019), students of language assessment (Jeong, 2013), language testing and assessment researchers and developers (Kremmel & Harding, 2020), admissions officers (Baker, 2016; O'Loughlin, 2013), and policy makers (Deygers & Malone, 2019; Pill & Harding, 2013).

The diversification of research across contexts and stakeholder groups has also led to a deeper theoretical understanding of the nature of LAL. Based on this growing canon of LAL scholarship, current understandings of language assessment literacy hold that (a) LAL is multi-componential, (b) LAL comprises a developmental continuum, and (c) different stakeholders may require different levels of expertise upon this developmental continuum in order to carry out their assessment-related tasks effectively. The notion that LAL is multi-componential emerged in early work such as Brindley (2001), in which five components of LAL were identified, and in Davies (2008), where LAL was broken down into knowledge, principles, and practice. Various components and associated labels have been discussed in the literature since, including Inbar-Lourie's (2008) framing of LAL around three key questions (the "what," the "how," and the "why" of assessment), Fulcher's (2012) three components of practical knowledge, procedural/theoretical knowledge, and socio-historical understanding of language assessment, and the multidimensional models discussed in Taylor (2013) and Kremmel and Harding (2020, see below).

Alongside the componential view of LAL, Pill and Harding (2013) introduced a developmental perspective to LAL models and suggested (based on an existing model for mathematical literacy) that LAL might develop on a continuum from illiteracy to nominal, functional, procedural, and ultimately multidimensional literacy. While their initial model was intended as a complementary view of LAL to modular approaches, recent research has tried to integrate the two perspectives to describe how different components of LAL might develop, or rather how the needs of different stakeholder groups might differ as to the developmental level or depth of knowledge required in each of the components. This latter idea emerged early in a paper by Taylor (2009), and was given more weight in a follow-up (2013) in which Taylor speculated on different profiles for stakeholders, including test writers, test users, and assessment researchers. Taylor proposed eight components, synthesised from the literature, and speculated varying profiles of knowledge which would enable the different stakeholder groups to carry out their relevant assessment-related duties. These eight components included: 1) knowledge of theory, 2) technical skills, 3) principles and concepts, 4) language pedagogy, 5) sociocultural values, 6) local practices, 7) personal beliefs/attitudes, and 8) scores and decision making. As an illustration, Taylor hypothesised that language-testing researchers would need the highest level of knowledge across all eight dimensions, whereas test users would need a high level of knowledge about scores and decision-making, but lower levels of technical skills in designing tests and analysing test score data.

In attempting to empirically validate these stipulated hypothetical dimensions, Kremmel and Harding (2020) followed an approach that combined the multi-componential and developmental views of LAL in a large-scale survey of the self-identified LAL needs of different stakeholder groups. Their resulting factor analytic model yielded nine empirically derived components of LAL, described in Table 6.1 below. These nine components confirmed, and in some cases challenged, the speculative dimensions proposed by Taylor (2013).

LAL Needs in SLA Research

It will be clear from the review of literature described above that there has not yet been a specific focus within LAL research on SLA researchers as a key stakeholder group. This does not mean, however, that other relevant research has not touched upon this particular population. There is now an established tradition of research and commentary on the measurement knowledge required of SLA researchers, which has a clear connection to the notion of LAL, even if it is not framed in those precise terms. In an important contribution to the literature in this area, Chapelle (1998) described the connection between language testing and SLA thus: "In second language acquisition (SLA) research, some form of measurement is frequently used to produce empirical evidence for hypotheses about the nature and development of communicative competence" (p. 32). Chapelle went on to delineate two aspects of measurement of key relevance to SLA researchers: (1) defining the construct of measurement, and (2) validating the measure (i.e., determining whether the measure is a "valid indicator of the construct" (p. 32). Chapelle charted a range of frameworks and methods which can be used to either conceptualise constructs or conduct validity research. A useful, clear example of the application of validity concerns in second language research can be seen in Chapelle's earlier (1994) paper querying the use and interpretation of C-test scores as vocabulary measures. A similar type of argument has been advanced by Read (2007), who noted that SLA researchers could "learn from language testing the importance of evaluating the reliability of their elicitation instruments, and the need to consider carefully how adequately they have operationalised their theoretical constructs" (p. 22). Once again, readers see

Table 6.1 Factor labels and descriptions drawn from LAL survey (Kremmel & Harding, 2020)

Factor	*Description*
(1) Developing and administering language assessments	Covers knowledge and skills in designing and administering appropriate tasks, developing scoring keys and rating scales (rubrics), and training others within the assessment cycle (e.g., rater training).
(2) Assessment in language pedagogy	Understanding of the relationship between language teaching, learning and assessment, as well as the selection and use of appropriate assessments, including also peer- and self-assessments.
(3) Assessment policy and local practices	Knowledge about the alignment of language assessments with local educational or accreditation systems and related legal regulations within local/national educational contexts.
(4) Personal beliefs and attitudes	Involves the ability to reflect upon how one's attitudes and beliefs might influence, or conflict with, assessment practices.
(5) Statistical and research methods	Knowledge of, and skills in using, statistical and other research procedures to evaluate the quality of items and tasks, and to analyse the quality of tests (pre- and post-administration).
(6) Assessment principles and interpretation	Refers to the understanding of key theoretical concepts like validity or reliability and how they relate to, and inform, score interpretation and use.
(7) Language structure, use and development	Targets how knowledgeable one is about theories (constructs) of language and communication, including theories of language learning and the nature of language proficiency.
(8) Washback and preparation	The awareness or knowledge of the influence of assessments on teaching and learning materials or on learning itself in classroom contexts.
(9) Scoring and rating	Knowledge or skill in scoring open-ended and closed-response questions, and in applying a rating scale appropriately.

here the twin notions of construct definition and evaluation of the technical quality of research instruments as fundamental aspects of SLA practice.

More recently, these issues have been comprehensively discussed in an article by Purpura et al. (2015), who identified a number of common problematic measurement issues across SLA research studies. Purpura et al. identified four main categories of "mistake" with respect to measurement, including construct definition and reliability (as discussed above), as well as test development/scoring, and use of appropriate methods of statistical analysis. A summary of the issues they highlighted is shown in Table 6.2.

It is worth noting the prominence of concerns about reliability in Table 6.2. Although listed as a separate category, reliability is also woven into concerns about test development (insufficient items for a robust measure; inter-coder agreement). In fact, the need for better reliability in research practices generally (and better knowledge about reliability among researchers) has been commented on by numerous researchers discussing study quality in SLA. For example, Chaudron (2001) found low reliability in classroom SLA research; Russell and Spada (2006) noted the importance of instrument and inter-rater reliability; and Plonsky and Gass (2011) critiqued reporting practices around reliability (though noted good practices in SLA interaction research) (see also Norris & Ortega, 2000; Plonsky, 2013).

We cannot easily generalise from the observation that reliability reporting practices require improvement to a claim that SLA researchers do not have sufficient knowledge about how to calculate reliability; reporting practices may be more associated with following disciplinary conventions of the time. But LAL may play a role in broadening the methodological options for examining reliability within SLA research. As a case in point, it has long been recognised in the

Table 6.2 Practical measurement issues for applied linguistics researchers (drawn from Purpura et al., 2015, pp. 73–75)

Categories	*Mistakes*
Test development	Creating a measure that has too few items
	Failure to adequately describe coding and scoring procedures
Describing and analysing measurement data	Failing to calculate or report descriptive statistics
	Forgetting to check and meet assumptions of normality, equal variances, etc.
	Using a criterion referenced test with parametric statistics
Reliability	Failing to calculate or report reliability statistics
	Unintentionally creating unreliable scores
	Reporting the wrong reliability estimates
Validity	Inaccurately targeting the intended construct
	Failing to test precisely what is needed to maximise the power of the study

field of language assessment that Rasch measurement theory, and particularly applications for rating designs such as many-facet Rasch measurement, provide advanced and powerful tools for managing the natural variability of human raters in awarding scores or judging performance. Adjusted measures, known as "fair scores," may be usefully employed as the dependent variable in situations where multiple ratings have been provided, as they take into account the variations in individual raters' levels of severity. However, there have only been a few studies in the SLA literature which have drawn on these methods. For example, a keyword search for "Rasch" in one flagship journal for the field—*Studies in Second Language Acquisition*—returned only two articles which had employed this methodology (Révész, 2009; Révész & Brunfaut, 2013). The advantages of Rasch measurement are one example of where greater familiarity with techniques common in language assessment may prove beneficial to SLA researchers.

Returning to the question of LAL, it is possible to connect some of the recommendations regarding measurement quality in SLA to different components of LAL. If one extrapolates from Purpura et al.'s (2015) list of issues to the dimensions identified in Kremmel and Harding's (2020) study (see Figure 6.1), one would envisage strong representation here in the areas of *Developing and administering language assessments*, *Statistical and research methods*, *Assessment principles and interpretation*, and *Scoring and rating*. Given the existing interface between SLA and pedagogical and linguistic concerns, one would also anticipate a strong set of requirements in the areas of *Assessment in language pedagogy*, and *Language structure, use and development*. We predict that areas which may have less direct applicability for general SLA research, but which may be of relevance to certain research topics, would be *Washback and test preparation*, *Assessment policy and local practices*, and *Personal beliefs and attitudes related to assessment*. These latter three areas may be of crucial importance in understanding language learning development within the complex ecology of educational systems which maintain a heavy testing focus and thus guide curriculum decisions, teaching focus and method, and student motivation and self-regulation.

As with Taylor's (2013) hypotheses, our own suggestions above remain speculative, and require a deeper exploration of the specific LAL needs of SLA practitioners. This area of research is abbreviated as LAL for SLA, or, more colloquially, as LAL4SLA.

LAL4SLA: A Work-in-Progress

In addressing the research gaps above, we are currently conducting a research project which seeks to gather the peer- and self-assessments of SLA researchers using the LAL survey described in Kremmel and Harding (2020). In this ongoing study we have kept the original 71 items from

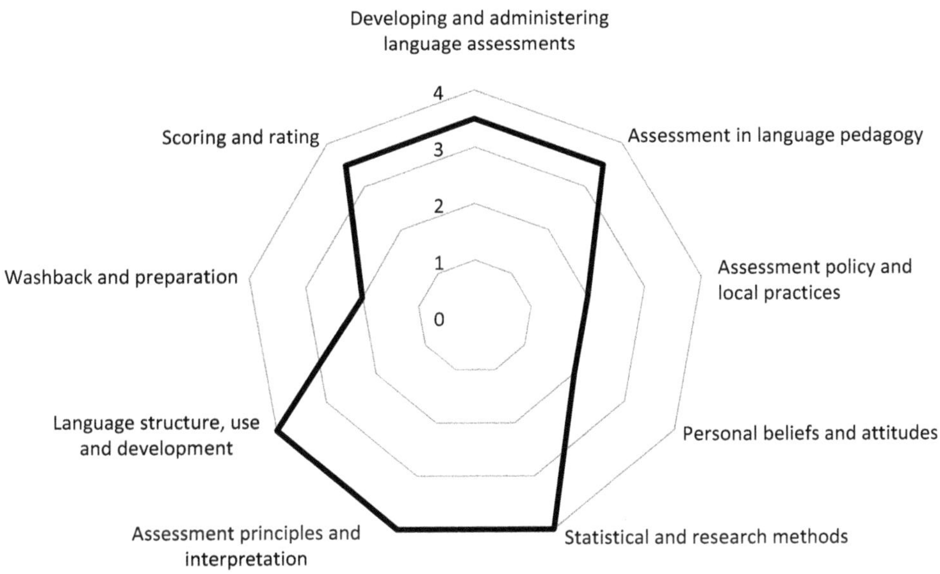

Figure 6.1 Hypothetical LAL profile for SLA researchers based on components defined in Kremmel and Harding (2020).

our initial survey (http://wp.lancs.ac.uk/ltrg/projects/language-assessment-literacy-survey); however, we have changed some preceding information in order to collect data on the career stage of our respondents (i.e., whether they were a "first stage researcher" [up to PhD level]; a "recognised researcher;" an "established researcher;" or a "leading researcher;" following: https://euraxess.ec.europa.eu/europe/career-development/training-researchers/research-profiles-descriptors). As with our initial survey, we also invited the respondents to complete a self-assessment once they had completed the peer needs-analysis. Participants responded to all of the 71 items on a five-point scale on which 0 = not knowledgable/skilled at all, 1 = slightly knowledgeable/skilled, 2 = moderately knowledgable/skilled, 3 = very knowledgeable/skilled, 4 = extremely knowledgable/skilled.

Although this project is still in its nascent stage, a consideration of the results of the pilot study revealed some interesting patterns. The pilot data presented here is drawn from 25 participants who completed the survey in full, representing eleven countries and several areas of specialisation within SLA (vocabulary acquisition, CALL, ISLA, CLIL, psycholinguistics, TBLT, attrition). The pilot respondents also represented different career stages: first-stage researcher (n=17), recognised researcher (n=2), established researcher (n=6). We recognise that much of the prescriptive advice above (e.g., demonstrating reliability of the instrument for the population under study) cannot be fulfilled. Therefore, we do not seek to extrapolate our findings here to the pre-established factors described in Table 6.1, or to draw interpretations based on scale sub-scores. Rather, we present these initial findings at the item-level in order to describe interesting patterns that may later be confirmed through a research study which is broader in scope.

Table 6.3 shows that in the pilot data, strongly endorsed survey items (where the median response was 4) demonstrated a clear orientation towards measurement concerns (measurement error and validity), interpretation of results, and construct knowledge.

Weakly endorsed items where the median response was 2 (Table 6.4) also followed an expected direction in focusing on the types of assessment knowledge that would be more relevant for classroom teachers using assessment to promote learning, more localised concerns for

Table 6.3 Strongly-endorsed items from pilot study (N = 25)

Item	Mdn
How to interpret measurement error	4
How to interpret what a particular score says about an individual's language ability	4
How language skills develop (e.g., reading, listening, writing, speaking)	4
How foreign/second languages are learned	4
The concept of validity (how well an assessment measures what it claims to measure)	4
Making decisions about what aspects of language to assess	4

Table 6.4 Weakly-endorsed items from pilot study (N = 25)

Item	Mdn
How to use assessments to motivate student learning	2
How to use peer-assessment	2
How to determine if a language assessment aligns with a local system of accreditation	2
The history of language assessment	2
The assessment traditions in your local context	2
The relevant legal regulations for assessment in your local area	2

those who seek to implement assessments within specific educational systems, and the history of language assessment.

While these results are limited in their generalisability, they provide some initial evidence that SLA researchers do distinguish between different elements of LAL which may be more or less relevant to their practice in hypothesised directions, and this is promising for further research in this vein.

Recommendations for Practice

In the first section of this chapter, we proposed that language assessment literacy is an important part of the repertoire of research skills for second language acquisition researchers, but we also problematised this notion in light of the different needs that SLA researchers may have depending on their epistemological approach to conducting research. In the second part of the chapter, we surveyed the current field of language assessment literacy research, charting developments in the conceptualisation and scope of LAL. While SLA researchers have not featured as a stakeholder group of interest within research to date, we noted that a parallel commentary on study quality in SLA has clear overlaps with the concerns of LAL, particularly with respect to measurement. An initial pilot study to some extent reflected the view that LAL components related to measurement and construct definition are of central concern to SLA researchers.

Drawing these various threads together, it is possible to identify some obvious, core LAL priorities for SLA practitioners. One challenge in making recommendations for practice, however, is in determining where such topics might be introduced within the professional trajectory of SLA researchers. Given that many active researchers will require doctoral-level education, and that more advanced methods-based instruction will occur during PhD candidature, we imagine that the following recommendations would be most applicable to doctoral-level research training programs. We therefore propose the following recommendations for those involved in training or mentoring future SLA practitioners (supervisors, programme chairs, textbook authors, etc.). For clarity, we divide the recommendations into "conceptual knowledge" (the theoretical knowledge that must be mastered) and "technical skills" (the techniques that will require more hands-on training):

Core Conceptual Knowledge

Construct Definition

Theoretical and abstract conceptualisation or definition of what is intended or claimed to be measured. A clear understanding of Messick's (1989) concepts *construct under-representation* and *construct-irrelevant variance*.

Reliability

Understanding consistency of measurement/scoring and its importance in various dimensions (e.g., internal consistency, inter- and intra-rater reliability), and being able to discern between different types of reliability evidence most appropriate for a given context. More advanced techniques such as Rasch measurement would be useful additions to SLA doctoral training.

Measurement Error

Awareness that true scores might differ from observed scores and what might cause this divergence, an understanding of the statistical procedures used for evaluating error, and awareness of how to interpret and report measurement error.

Validity and Validation

An understanding of current validity theories (e.g., argument-based approaches or socio-cognitive validity theory) and their relevance for the development and evaluation of measures within SLA research conditions, as well as a firm understanding of the types of evidence required to be able to demonstrate the quality of measures empirically, either through quantitative or qualitative methods.

Other key conceptual knowledge areas regarding language development and theories of learning are likely to be developed independently of any assessment training, and are in fact already likely to be much more comprehensive for SLA researchers than the type of training language testers may receive in similar areas (see discussion below).

Core Technical Skills

Novice SLA researchers would benefit from training in the following key techniques related to assessment:

- Development of test specifications: translating theoretical constructs into operational test instruments (see Davidson & Lynch, 2002; Green & Fulcher, Chapter 7, this volume).
- Item writing: awareness of best-practice in developing tasks and items (e.g., multiple-choice questions; speaking test prompts), and developing an ability to critically evaluate item quality (see Banerjee, Lestari, & Rossi, Chapter 8; Jones, Chapter 9, this volume).
- Item analysis: calculating basic (also called classical, as in Classical Test Theory) statistics such as facility value and discrimination index manually or through relevant software (see Carr, 2011; Green, 2013).
- Test development: following best-practice processes of item moderation/revision, test-trialling (see Green, Chapter 11, this volume), and analysis (see Chapters 42–45, this volume).
- Calculating internal reliability (see McKay & Plonsky, Chapter 44, this volume).
- Calculating inter-rater agreement/reliability.

There are numerous books which now exist and would function well as foundational texts for this element of core assessment training for SLA researchers (e.g., Bachman & Palmer, 2010; Fulcher, 2012).

Critical Knowledge: Beyond the Core

Although assessment may often be viewed as more aligned with a positivist approach to SLA research, there are domains in which more critical approaches to language assessment might overlap with critical SLA research. For example, proficiency frameworks, tests and testing regimes often exert an influence on language learning and teaching in real-world settings. Understanding the socio-political character of tests and their role within educational policy is therefore fundamental. Thus, in addition to the core knowledge identified above, there is a range of ancillary assessment topics that have direct relevance to a range of SLA researchers, and where knowledge should ideally be developed in addition to the more measurement-focused elements described above:

- standards and frameworks (their uses and limitations)
- the impact of tests on key variables of interest in SLA (e.g., motivation, self-efficacy)
- the role of tests within the ecology of the L2 classroom
- the relationship between tests and systems of power within wider educational systems and their influence on language learning at the micro-level

At the same time, we argue that a fundamental LAL is required for all SLA researchers in order to be critical readers of research papers which draw on more positivist paradigms. For example, a classroom-based ethnographic researcher investigating pronunciation instruction and learner identity may still include in their literature review a discussion of studies on pronunciation conducted in lab-based environments. It is important to have the requisite skills to appraise the quality of instruments used in those studies, and—in the case of pronunciation—to be able to critically examine the connection between instrumentation and a hypothesised construct (e.g., whether it is native-like development, or a more nuanced intelligibility construct).

Future Directions

Our remit in this chapter was to discuss SLA researcher assessment literacy, and not necessarily to focus on language testing researchers' SLA literacy. It should be clear, however, that the flow of knowledge should be bidirectional across these two sub-disciplines, and that there is much for language testing researchers to learn from the field of SLA regarding language constructs and the development of L2 proficiency. A clear example is provided in the various critiques made of the CEFR (e.g., Fulcher, 2004), a tool which has had significant impact on the practices of language testers in Europe and beyond, but has been critiqued for being atheoretical with respect to current theories of language development within SLA. We have argued elsewhere that one of the most fundamental components of LAL for language test developers, researchers, teachers and others is knowledge of language: how it is learned and how it is used. SLA researchers are acutely aware that languages are learned differently according to the various individual factors, one being age of the learner. However, in language testing contexts, the CEFR scale is sometimes applied to learners of any age in describing language development, an approach that may be viewed with scepticism from those with research agendas that investigate SLA processes across age groups. The constructs of language testing need to be constantly challenged, and for this to happen there needs to be more cross-fertilisation between the fields of SLA and language assessment. Finally, newer forms of learning-oriented assessment (such as diagnostic assessment) may provide a key site for cross-pollination of ideas of this kind. Diagnostic assessment requires a deep understanding of second language acquisition processes (trajectories of development, feedback effectiveness, treatment evaluation) and age constraints, as well as a thorough understanding of language test construction and evaluation. Enhancing LAL on both sides will lead to much richer and more useful diagnostic instruments in the future.

A final point—also related to cross-fertilisation—is that one substantial barrier to developing better assessment practices in SLA research is the paucity of freely-available assessment tools for researchers to use, particularly those which measure general language proficiency. In the absence of such instruments, SLA researchers may resort to designing their own tests of complex constructs, or they may use inappropriate existing tests for research purposes (as a case in point, at Lancaster University we receive intermittent requests, always refused, from researchers to use Dialang—a diagnostic language assessment instrument—for the purposes of measuring proficiency for research purposes). SLA research has seen a recent shift towards the principles of Open Science, with language testing also starting to follow this lead. The IRIS Repository, set up to share resources among SLA researchers, is an innovative resource in service to the Open Science model. However IRIS, or similar repositories recommended and vetted by international Open Science consortia, such as Open Science (https://cos.io/), could also in the future function as crucial sites for enhancing LAL by providing spaces for the sharing of test materials which are no longer live, but which have sufficient validity evidence to warrant ongoing use for research purposes, or for sharing specifications for instruments which researchers can then follow to create tests for their research. Researchers and test developers are recommended to deposit their instruments, anonymised data, and directions for use within a repository or as a supplemental file that can be accessed for downloading. Each file should ideally be immutable, time stamped, sufficiently explained as to its intended purposes (within metadata to the files), and accessible via a digital object identifier (https://www.doi.org/), or DOI.

Recommended Readings

Chapelle, C. (1998). Construct definition and validity inquiry in SLA research. In L. F. Bachman & A. D. Cohen (Eds.), *Interfaces between second language acquisition and language testing* (pp. 32–70). Cambridge University Press.

This chapter presents a comprehensive discussion of the application of language testing measurement theory to SLA practice. Although the chapter is now over twenty years old the points raised are still of fundamental importance to considerations of LAL in SLA research.

Inbar, O. (Ed.). (2013). Language assessment literacy (special issue). *Language Testing*, *30*(3), 301–415. https://doi.org/10.1177/0265532213480126

This special issue remains the most comprehensive collection of articles to date covering the range and depth of language assessment literacy across different stakeholders. Although second language acquisition researchers are not studied explicitly, the discussions across the articles within form a basis for understanding the nature and scope of language assessment literacy.

Purpura, J. E., Brown, J. D., & Schoonen, R. (2015). Improving the validity of quantitative measures in applied linguistics research. *Language Learning*, *65*(S1), 37–75. https://doi.org/10.1111/lang.12112

This article provides a highly-useful and well-argued overview of measurement concerns in SLA and the particular areas where future research training should focus. A good deal of the recommendations presented in this chapter were informed by this article, which provides perhaps the best existing treatment of assessment issues in SLA scholarship.

References

Bachman, L. F., & Palmer, A. S. (2010). *Language assessment in practice: Developing language assessments and justifying their use in the real world.* Oxford University Press.

Baker, B. (2016). Language assessment literacy as professional competence: The case of Canadian admissions decision makers. *Canadian Journal of Applied Linguistics*, *19*(1), 63–83. https://journals.lib.unb.ca/index.php/CJAL/article/view/23033
Baker, B. A., & Riches, C. (2018). The development of EFL examinations in Haiti: Collaboration and language assessment literacy development. *Language Testing*, *35*(4), 557–581. https://doi.org/10.1177/0265532217716732
Brindley, G. (2001). Language assessment and professional development. In C. Elder, A. Brown, E. Grove, K. Hall, N. Iwashita, T. Lumley, T. F. Mcnamara, & K. O'Loughlin (Eds.), *Experimenting with uncertainty: Essays in honour of Alan Davies* (pp. 126–136). Cambridge University Press.
Carr, N. A. (2011). *Designing and analysing language tests*. Oxford University Press.
Chapelle, C. (1994). Are C-tests valid measures for L2 vocabulary research? *Second Language Research*, *10*(2), 157–187. https://doi.org/10.1177/026765839401000203
Chaudron, C. (2001). Progress in language classroom research: Evidence from The Modern Language Journal, 1916–2000. *The Modern Language Journal*, *85*(1), 57–76. https://doi.org/10.1111/0026-7902.00097
Davidson, F., & Lynch, B. (2002). *Testcraft: A teacher's guide to writing and using language test specifications*. Yale University Press.
Davies, A. (2008). Textbook trends in teaching language testing. *Language Testing*, *25*(3), 327–347. https://doi.org/10.1177/0265532208090156
Deygers, B., & Malone, M. E. (2019). Language assessment literacy in university admission policies, or the dialogue that isn't. *Language Testing*. https://doi.org/10.1177/0265532219826390
Fulcher, G. (2004). Deluded by artifices? The common European framework and harmonization. *Language Assessment Quarterly: An International Journal*, *1*(4), 253–266. https://doi.org/10.1207/s15434311laq0104_4
Fulcher, G. (2012). Assessment literacy for the language classroom. *Language Assessment Quarterly*, *9*(2), 113–132. https://doi.org/10.1080/15434303.2011.642041
Green, R. (2013). *Statistical analysis for language testers*. Palgrave Macmillan.
Inbar-Lourie, O. (2008). Constructing a language assessment knowledge base: A focus on language assessment courses. *Language Testing*, *25*(3), 385–402. https://doi.org/10.1177/0265532208090158
Jeong, H. (2013). Defining assessment literacy: Is it different for language testers and non-language testers? *Language Testing*, *30*(3), 345–362. https://doi.org/10.1177/0265532213480334
Kremmel, B., & Harding, L. (2020). Towards a comprehensive, empirical model of language assessment literacy across stakeholder groups: Developing the language assessment literacy survey. *Language Assessment Quarterly*, *17*(1), 100–120. https://doi.org/10.1080/15434303.2019.1674855
Lam, R. (2015). Language assessment training in Hong Kong: Implications for language assessment literacy. *Language Testing*, *32*(2), 169–197. https://doi.org/10.1177/0265532214554321
Malone, M. E. (2013). The essentials of assessment literacy: Contrasts between testers and users. *Language Testing*, *30*(3), 329–344. https://doi.org/10.1177/0265532213480129
Messick, S. (1989). Validity. In R. L. Linn (Ed.), *Educational measurement* (3rd ed., pp. 13–104). Macmillan.
Norris, J. M., & Ortega, L. (2000). Effectiveness of L2 instruction: A research synthesis and quantitative meta-analysis. *Language Learning*, *50*(3), 417–528. https://doi.org/10.1111/0023-8333.00136
O'Loughlin, K. (2013). Developing the assessment literacy of university proficiency test users. *Language Testing*, *30*(3), 363–380. https://doi.org/10.1177/0265532213480336
Pill, J., & Harding, L. (2013). Defining the language assessment literacy gap: Evidence from a parliamentary inquiry. *Language Testing*, *30*(3), 381–402. https://doi.org/10.1177/0265532213480337
Plonsky, L. (2013). Study quality in SLA: An assessment of designs, analyses, and reporting practices in quantitative L2 research. *Studies in Second Language Acquisition*, *35*(4), 655–687. https://doi.org/10.1017/S0272263113000399
Plonsky, L., & Gass, S. (2011). Quantitative research methods, study quality, and outcomes: The case of interaction research. *Language Learning*, *61*(2), 325–366. https://doi.org/10.1111/j.1467-9922.2011.00640.x
Popham, W. J. (2009). Assessment literacy for teachers: Faddish or fundamental? *Theory into Practice*, *48*(1), 4–11. https://doi.org/10.1080/00405840802577536
Read, J. (2007). Towards a new collaboration: Research in SLA and language testing. *New Zealand Studies in Applied Linguistics*, *13*(1), 22–35.
Révész, A. (2009). Task complexity, focus on form, and second language development. *Studies in Second Language Acquisition*, *31*(3), 437–470. https://doi.org/10.1017/S0272263109090366
Révész, A., & Brunfaut, T. (2013). Text characteristics of task input and difficulty in second language listening comprehension. *Studies in Second Language Acquisition*, *35*(1), 31–65. https://doi.org/10.1017/S0272263112000678

Russell, J., & Spada, N. (2006). The effectiveness of corrective feedback for second language acquisition: A meta-analysis of the research. In J. Norris & L. Ortega (Eds.), *Synthesizing research on language learning and teaching* (pp. 131–164). Benjamins.
Stiggins, R. J. (1991). Assessment literacy. *Phi Delta Kappan, 72*(7), 534–539.
Taylor, L. (2009). Developing assessment literacy. *Annual Review of Applied Linguistics, 29*, 21–36. https://doi.org/10.1017/S0267190509090035
Taylor, L. (2013). Communicating the theory, practice and principles of language testing to test stakeholders: Some reflections. *Language Testing, 30*(3), 403–412. https://doi.org/10.1177/0265532213480338
Villa Larenas, S. (2019, March 4–8). *Understanding teacher educators' language assessment literacy: Practices while training pre-service English teachers in Chile* [Paper presentation]. Language Testing Research Colloquium (LTRC) 41st Annual Conference, Atlanta, GA, United States.
Vogt, K., & Tsagari, D. (2014). Assessment literacy of foreign language teachers: Findings of a European study. *Language Assessment Quarterly, 11*(4), 374–402. https://doi.org/10.1080/15434303.2014.960046
Yan, X., Zhang, C., & Fan, J. J. (2018). "Assessment knowledge is important, but…": How contextual and experiential factors mediate assessment practice and training needs of language teachers. *System, 74*, 158–168. https://doi.org/10.1016/j.system.2018.03.003

Part II

Building Instruments for SLA Research

7
Test Design Cycle

Anthony Green & Glenn Fulcher

Background

To produce meaningful results, SLA research requires carefully designed instruments and procedures that can be shown to measure features of interest to the researcher. This priority is shared with language testing, which must demonstrate that the information provided by an assessment meets the needs of the people who will base important decisions on the results (see Chapelle, Chapter 2, this volume). Targets for SLA research often include language learning aptitude (see Roehr-Brackin, Chapter 14, this volume), proficiency, achievement, or progress (traditionally measured through language tests), but may also involve a wide variety of attitudes, behaviours and attributes believed to affect language acquisition ranging from working memory span (see Wen, Juffs, & Winke, Chapter 16, this volume) to personality and motivation (see Iwaniec & Dunn, Chapter 15, this volume).

Drawing on techniques developed for psychological and educational measurement originating in the mental tests devised over 100 years ago by such early psychologists as Wundt, Galton and Cattell (Rust & Golombok, 2014), this chapter introduces SLA researchers and language testers to the language test design cycle, a set of systematically interrelated activities intended to ensure that assessment instruments and procedures (including research instruments, such as questionnaires as well as tests) consistently fulfil their intended purposes.

Based on a clear description of the rationale for using the assessment, the test design cycle involves:

- defining what is to be assessed or measured
- techniques for collecting relevant information within practical constraints
- deciding how the assessment should be administered
- collecting evidence to establish whether the assessment is working as intended

The quality of assessment is enhanced when there is a clear plan for design, development and administration. If properly conceived, executed and documented, the process is also opened to scrutiny, a prerequisite for confidence in the results.

SLA researchers often design and develop their own instruments. Alternatively, they may adopt or adapt instruments developed by others, drawing on collections such as the IRIS Repository (Marsden et al., 2016). When researchers develop their own instruments, the test design cycle can help to guide them through the process. When they are considering adopting instruments developed by others, the cycle can inform conclusions about the applicability and technical qualities of the available options.

Key Concepts

Reliability: The consistency of test scores across time, context, forms and makers.

Validity: The extent to which we may trust the inferences we draw about test taker ability, depending upon the theory upon which the test is based, and the quality of the evidence that supports the claims we make for the meaning of test scores.

Constructs: The knowledge, skills, or abilities that we claim the test measures.

Criterion: The real-world languages behaviours, performances, or practices to which we wish to make a prediction based upon test scores.

Key Issues

The assessment design cycle consists of a number of steps, starting from a careful consideration of the purpose of the assessment and culminating in a decision about the test taker, learner, or research participant. These are summarised in Figure 7.1. Although this is presented as a sequence, each step may have implications for the steps before as well as for those that follow. For example, changes to the design or scoring procedure of a questionnaire item made at the evaluating and prototyping stage may prompt changes to the specification and construct definition. Green (2014) shows how each step in the cycle should be clearly documented—both to inform the next step and to provide evidence in support of the validity of the instrument.

Assessment Purpose

A clear and explicit statement of the purpose of an assessment is a prerequisite for the investigation of validity. Not only is it important to know the use for which an assessment was designed, it is also essential to know what it should not be used for. The idea of a purely generic test makes its validation impossible. Assessment purpose is therefore the first thing that needs to be established in the test design cycle. Like research questions in a study, all else follows from this clear and explicit articulation of intended use. Cureton (1951, p. 621) provides the classic definition of purpose:

> Validity is always validity for a particular purpose. It indicates how well the test serves the purpose for which it is used. Purpose, in turn, has at least two aspects. One of these concerns the function to be appraised; the other, the nature of the group in which the appraisal is to be made.

This encapsulates what we intend to assess (constructs and/or behaviours), and who we are going to test (the population for whom the test is relevant). What it does not include, but is of critical importance, are the predictions we wish to make on the basis of the test score. For as Carroll (1961/1965, p. 314) correctly argues: "The purpose of language testing is always to render information to aid in making intelligent decisions about possible courses of action."

Traditionally, the purpose of a test is broken down into five types. Diagnostic tests are used to identify learning problems; aptitude tests are intended to discover if a test taker has the potential to learn a language; proficiency tests are summative assessments of language competence;

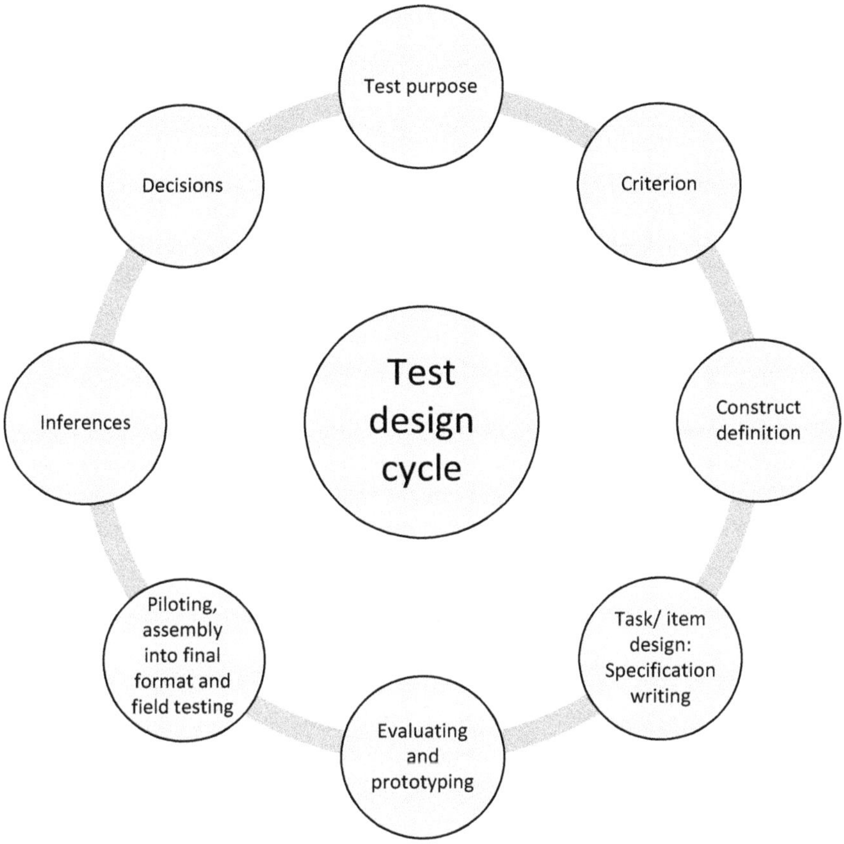

Figure 7.1 The test design cycle. Adapted from Fulcher (2010, p. 94).

placement tests are used to place new students into suitable classes; achievement tests assess whether learners have mastered what has been taught in a particular programme of study, and so are based on the curriculum used within a school. However, it is now much more common to think of the purpose of a test being more specific to language use within a particular domain. For example, the purpose of the Occupational English Test (OET) is to assess whether test takers have acquired the necessary language to communicate successfully as a health professional within a hospital setting (see https://www.occupationalenglishtest.org/).

Test Criterion

One element of test purpose is a statement of the predictions that we wish to make on the basis of test scores. The process involves the use of test tasks that generate evidence which can be given a score, and from the score test users make inferences about the likelihood of successful language use in some concurrent or future non-test context. The situation to which we make an inference, or prediction, is the test criterion.

All inferencing relies upon the test criterion, for without a criterion it is not possible to form a hypothesis of the type "Evidence X from test Y is predictive of behaviour/ability Z" (Fulcher, 2015, p. 21). Current approaches to validation that rely upon the Toulmin/Kane argument approach implicitly or explicitly assume the need for an explicit test criterion (Bachman,

2005). This approach requires the construction of an argument that links evidence from research to claims that support the main interpretation of test scores, which is often omitted when tests are used in SLA research. As Chapelle (1998) argues, SLA research needs to include evidence regarding content relevance, item behaviour, task analysis, the relationship between scores and other measures of similar and different constructs, and data regarding the generalisability of outcomes across people, contexts, and interventions.

A criterion may be one of the following: ability to read first year undergraduate business English texts; make patient notes in daily nursing activities; politely greet and deal with customer requests at a supermarket service desk; manage air traffic in a busy control tower. These are specific criteria which guide test design and lay the ground for specific hypotheses that can be tested in validation studies. The more opaque the criterion, the more "validity chaos" is introduced to the test design cycle. As Chalhoub-Deville and Fulcher (2003) state:

> "If limitless applications are intended, it becomes challenging—if not impossible—to delineate and accommodate all the knowledge, skills, and processes salient in different contexts. Moreover, an assessment that suits all purposes creates validation chaos. In such a situation it is not clear what research evidence should be targeted or given priority."
>
> (p. 502)

Construct Definition

The definition of the construct is another critical element of the statement of test purpose that drives assessment design and development (Green, 2014). The notion of a "construct" is endemic to human activity of all kinds. We use abstract nouns to describe things that we cannot observe, but which are important to us. These include "love" and "kindness", "evil" and "despair". We know what these words mean intuitively as *concepts*. We use them in daily life on the assumption that others will understand us.

But if we were to start listing the observable manifestations of any of these concepts we would start to find variations across individuals and cultures. The same is true of concepts in language education and assessment such as "fluency", "intelligibility", or "accuracy". These terms cease to be *concepts* and become *constructs* when we define them in such a way that they can be *measured* (Fulcher, 2010). Sometimes this is called an *operational definition*, because it tells an assessor what to look for in order to assign a number on a scale to behaviours that are indicative of the degree of presence or absence of the construct. One example of a behavioural indicator of fluency that is frequently used in research is the pause, which is the place and length of silence during a speaking turn. Some positions and durations are "unnatural" and therefore indicators of language processing problems that are typical of less proficient learners.

Task/Item Design: Specification Writing

Thinking through the purpose of an assessment, considering what might constitute an appropriate criterion and developing a construct definition can be time-consuming, but these steps are essential to the interpretation of results. One needs only compare a language test from sixty years ago (such as the English Proficiency Test Battery: EPTB) with one from thirty years ago (the English Language Testing System: ELTS) and one designed more recently (such as the current version of the International English Language Testing System: IELTS) (all reviewed in Davies, 2008) to recognise that the history of language assessment has involved constant re-evaluation of the nature of language and that test instruments are regularly revised and updated to reflect developments (see Winke & Brunfaut, Chapter 1, this volume). Equally, comparing two contemporary tests such as the British Council *Aptis* test (www.britishcouncil.org/exam/aptis) and the *Pearson*

Test of English: General (https://qualifications.pearson.com/en/qualifications/pearson-test-of-english/pearson-test-of-english-general.html) would reveal differences in how test designers think about and represent language abilities.

Even if a researcher intends to adopt instruments developed by others, they will need to build up a clear understanding of how the construct has been conceptualised in those instruments. They will need to understand how that interpretation of the construct relates to the way the construct is conceived and operationalised by other researchers, who may have developed alternative means of measuring it. They will also need to reflect on the extent to which that interpretation of the construct reflects or conflicts with their own understanding.

One example of how challenging it can be to create assessment tasks that reflect the ways in which people use language in their daily lives is the discourse completion task. Because it is much more convenient to work with written tasks than to observe learners interacting spontaneously under natural conditions, researchers interested in pragmatics have sometimes employed written discourse completion tasks that ask learners to indicate how they would respond in a range of scenarios, each presented in the form of a short, scripted dialogue with a slot at the end for the learner to write their answer. It was assumed that responses to these tasks would give the researcher an unambiguous picture of how people would respond to similar scenarios in real life. Unfortunately, experience has shown that what people write in written discourse completion tasks is often very different from what they say under more natural conversational conditions. In other words, as Kasper (2000) observed, written discourse completion tasks seem to indicate "what L2 learners know rather than what they can do under the much more demanding conditions of conversational encounters" (p. 330). A researcher interested in measuring *knowledge* of pragmatic principles might find that written discourse completion tasks serve their purpose reasonably well, but one interested in real-world pragmatic *behaviours* might reject them (see Timpe-Laughlin & Youn, Chapter 24, this volume).

If researchers intend to adapt an existing instrument, or to develop a research instrument for themselves, they will need to design tasks capable of eliciting convincing evidence of the abilities, behaviours or attributes that they wish to learn about. This will involve decisions about:

- The extent to which conditions should be controlled: available options range from observing behaviour in naturally occurring situations to highly constrained experimental tasks such as tests of word recognition speed or working memory span.
- The variety, number or extent of observations to be made. Because the use of different methods can have a substantial impact on the nature of the response, it is often helpful to use a range of methods to address a research question. Collecting multiple observations, or including large numbers of items on a test or questionnaire is likely to improve reliability, but may overburden participants.
- The nature of any materials or resources that learners will be expected to engage with.
- How learners are expected to respond, and which aspects of their behaviour should be categorised and recorded.
- Whether and how responses or behaviours should be counted, scored and aggregated.

Whatever choices are made, it is important to demonstrate that there is a principled relationship between the assessment construct and the design of the tasks and procedures: Why are these tasks, administered under these conditions and scored, analysed or evaluated in this way? Why is this the most appropriate means of obtaining relevant evidence?

Specifications are documents that describe and explain the purpose of the assessment and the constructs it is intended to address (see Green, 2014, Chapter 3; Fulcher, 2010, Chapter 5). They provide details of the number and types of item used, how these are constructed and presented, how participants or test takers are expected to respond, the conditions under which the assessment is administered, and procedures used for analysis or scoring. One of their main functions is to enable replication. In large-scale assessment, they facilitate the production of multiple forms of a test that will each cover similar content, employing similar tasks that are likely to be similarly challenging for test takers. For research instruments and procedures, they help other researchers considering adoption of an instrument to judge its suitability for their research focus, or to create new material that follows the same principles.

A good specification is the explicit statement of the rationale for an inference to be made from successful performance on the item or task to the construct, and from the construct to the criterion (Fulcher, 2010, pp. 134–135).

Evaluating and Prototyping

Once the preliminary decisions have been taken about the format of the assessment, the kinds of task to be used and how test writers should go about sourcing appropriate materials (such as texts or recordings), the draft specifications should be evaluated by people who have not been directly involved in their development. It is helpful to have the perspectives of a range of those with an interest in the assessment, from experts or fellow researchers, to members of the population who will take the assessment and who will be the focus of the research who can provide insights into how the proposed assessment reflects the construct. Do they find the instructions clear and unambiguous? Do they find the length and timing of the tasks to be reasonable? Are scoring keys clear and accurate? Are any rating scales easy to use and do they capture the key qualities of performance?

After passing through this initial scrutiny, tasks and items can be taken forward for prototyping. Where evaluation involves looking at and critiquing material, prototyping involves using it in practice. A draft version of the assessment is compiled and reviewed, based on the specifications. Small groups of perhaps three to ten research participants take the assessment or respond to the questions. It is also helpful to involve those who will be involved in the administration and scoring of the assessment, or the coding of responses. The key issue at this stage is whether the responses given by learners or research participants are in line with what the designers intended. Feedback is obtained from participants on how they arrived at their responses or on aspects of the experience that they found engaging or confusing. This is then used to refine the material. Naturally, issues identified at this stage will have implications for the specifications and these will also need to be revised to reflect the lessons learned.

Piloting, Assembly into Final Format, and Field Testing

When sufficient items have successfully passed through the prototyping and evaluation processes, they can be collated into complete test or questionnaire forms and given to a much larger number of learners or participants so that statistical information can be collected. This group should not include those who will eventually take the assessment but should otherwise be as similar as possible to them (i.e., have a similar age and gender profile, educational background etc.). The administration and scoring procedures should also follow the intended guidelines as closely as possible. This try-out of the assessment is referred to as piloting (see Green, Chapter 11, this volume). It not only provides another opportunity to establish whether the individual items are working as intended, but also to establish that the instrument as a whole gives the expected results and to check that administration and scoring procedures are effective.

It is generally recommended that around 20% to 30% more material should be piloted than will be used operationally. It is important to ensure that sufficient material has been prepared, has passed through the earlier stages of the cycle and is piloted to allow for a proportion of the material to be rejected. If more than 20% of the material proves to be problematic at this stage, it is likely that aspects of the assessment will need to be reconsidered. Techniques for evaluating pilot assessment performance are described in Green (2014) and Fulcher (2010).

Following successful piloting, the best of the material can be compiled into a final, operational form. It is important that the assembly of the operational form should also be carefully evaluated to ensure that the content fully reflects the specifications; that the items represent an appropriate balance of topics or content areas; that common issues are avoided (such as the content of one question giving away, influencing or cueing the answer to another); and that instructions and the presentation of the material will be clear to all test takers or research participants. Ideally, a further round of piloting, or "field testing", should be carried out at this point with the assessment in its operational form to confirm that it is now ready to be used for its intended purpose.

Once an assessment or research instrument becomes operational, any new material should go through evaluation, prototyping and piloting and any new form of the test or instrument should be reviewed and field tested. It cannot be assumed that a new form, written from the same specifications, will produce equivalent results to the original: this also needs to be investigated (see Suzuki & Koizumi, Chapter 43, this volume). The creation of instruments that can be shown to give equivalent results is especially important in SLA and language testing research studies with pre- and post-test designs.

Inferences and Decisions

Inferences, decisions, and the consequences that flow from them are of central importance to SLA researchers, just as they are for test developers and together define the purpose of an assessment or research instrument. Researchers need to be as confident as possible that their instruments have worked well enough to justify their interpretation of the results. If others are to be persuaded to share the researcher's confidence, a compelling argument must be presented, justifying use of the instrument or procedure (see Chapelle, Chapter 2; Révész & Brunfaut, Chapter 3, this volume).

It is also important to be able to demonstrate that use of a research instrument has not had damaging consequences. Issues of privacy and confidentiality may be involved and, equally, it may be important to acknowledge the contribution made by colleagues or by participants to a research study. Research results may be misinterpreted or misrepresented by the media or may be used to justify inequitable policies. Researchers need to consider whose interests their findings may serve and to anticipate and work to prevent or mitigate negative effects. Ethical guidelines are available that may serve to guide the work of SLA researchers such as the British Association for Applied Linguistics (BAAL) Recommendations on Good Practice in Applied Linguistics (BAAL, 2016) or, specifically for testing, the International Language Testing Association (ILTA) Code of Ethics (ILTA, 2000).

Recommendations for Practice

Insights into SLA derived from research often have important implications for language teaching and assessment, encouraging new thinking about objectives and methods. Equally, tests, as instruments for collecting evidence of learner language, sometimes on a massive scale, may serve as useful sources of SLA data. However, the value of the evidence that each provides is constrained by the quality of the instruments and techniques employed and of the thought that informs them. Our key recommendation is that SLA researchers, language testers and those seeking to benefit from potential insights will gain from the use of systematic procedures designed to warrant, document, and demonstrate careful and systematic development of the assessment instruments and attention to the likely consequences of their use. This requires following the steps of the test design cycle outlined in the Key Issues section above, including the advice and considerations formulated there for each step. When information is lacking on matters such as how a construct is conceptualised, how instruments operationalise that construct and the extent to which they measure it consistently, the value of the results must be questioned.

Testing Tips

- Keep good records at every stage. A key purpose of a well-conceived testing cycle is to drive quality and improvement. Effective documentation is essential as it provides the basis for reflection and planning further developments. It is important not only to have detailed and very clearly written documents setting out the procedures to be followed, but also to keep records of how well each step in the cycle has functioned on each occasion.
- Work with colleagues when designing new items or tasks for a test, as individuals often do not see problems with their own items. Groups bring critical insights to the process of test creation that result in better outcomes.
- Write specifications for each item/task type. Whenever you alter the item/task because of feedback from others or statistical information from piloting, update the specifications and record the reasons for the change. These contribute to the evidence for a validation argument.
- Try out items/tasks with small numbers of learners before you start using a test for real data collection or decision making. Often called "prototyping", the aim is to uncover problems that test takers may have with the item so that we can remove them before we proceed to use them in a live test situation.

Recommended Readings

Lane, S., Raymond, M. R., Haladyna, T. M., & Downing, S. M. (2015). Test development process. In Lane, S., Raymond, M. R., & Haladyna, T. M. (Eds.), *Handbook of test development* (pp. 3–18). Routledge.

This chapter from a standard general-purpose guide to the practice of educational assessment is based on the widely used *Standards for Educational and Psychological Testing* (American Educational Research Association (AERA), American Psychological Association & National Council on Measurement in Education, 2014). It is not specifically concerned with languages, but sets out 12 essential components of any test development.

Fulcher, G. (2010). *Practical language testing*. Hodder Education.

For those wishing to pursue the topic of this chapter and to develop their own language tests, Chapters 4 to 6 in particular offer a much fuller and more detailed discussion of the value of test design cycles in language assessment.

Green, A. (2014). *Exploring language assessment and testing*. Routledge.

This book provides a practical and straightforward introduction to language assessment issues with guidance on designing, developing, and using assessments. It offers flexible, step by step processes for improving the quality of tests and assessment systems to make them fairer and more accurate.

References

BAAL: British Association for Applied Linguistics. (2016). *Recommendations on good practice in applied linguistics*. https://baalweb.files.wordpress.com/2016/10/goodpractice_full_2016.pdf

Bachman, L. F. (2005). Building and supporting a case for test use. *Language Assessment Quarterly*, *2*(1), 1–34. https://doi.org/10.1207/s15434311laq0201_1

Carroll, J. B. (1965). Fundamental considerations in testing English language proficiency of foreign students. In R. N. Allen & H. B. Campbell (Eds.), *Teaching English as a second language: A book of readings* (pp. 313–330). McGraw Hill. (Original work published 1961)

Chalhoub-Deville, M., & Fulcher, G. (2003). The oral proficiency interview and the ACTFL guidelines: A research agenda. *Foreign Language Annals*, *36*(4), 498–506. https://doi.org/j.1944-9720.2003.tb02139.x

Chapelle, C. (1998). Construct definition and validity enquiry in SLA research. In L. F. Bachman & A. D. Cohen (Eds.), *Interfaces between second language acquisition and language testing research*. Cambridge University Press.

Cureton, E. E. (1951). Validity. In E. F. Lindquist (Ed.), *Educational measurement*. American Council on Education.

Davies, A. (2008). *Assessing academic English: Testing English proficiency, 1950–1989: The IELTS solution*. Cambridge University Press.

Fulcher, G. (2010). *Practical language testing*. Hodder Education.

Fulcher, G. (2015). *Re-examining language testing: A philosophical and social inquiry*. Routledge.

Fulcher, G., & Davidson, F. (2009). Test architecture, test retrofit. *Language Testing*, *26*(1), 123–144. https://doi.org/10.1177/0265532208097339

Green, A. (2014). *Exploring language assessment and testing*. Routledge.

ILTA: International Language Testing Association. (2000). *Code of ethics for ILTA*. https://www.iltaonline.com/page/CodeofEthics

Kasper, G. (2000). Data collection in pragmatics research. In H. Spencer-Oatey (Ed.), *Culturally speaking*. Continuum.

Marsden, E., Mackey, A., & Plonsky, L. (2016). The IRIS repository: Advancing research practice and methodology. In A. Mackey & E. Marsden (Eds.), *Advancing methodology and practice: The IRIS repository of instruments for research into second languages* (pp. 1–21). Routledge.

Rust, J., & Golombok, S. (2014). *Modern psychometrics: The science of psychological assessment*. Routledge.

8

Choosing Test Formats and Task Types

Jayanti Banerjee, Santi B. Lestari & Olena Rossi

Background

A central challenge in SLA and language testing research concerns the alignment of theoretical constructs and techniques used for their measurement so that a particular data elicitation instrument measures the intended construct in a comprehensive (construct representation), relevant (construct relevance), and reliable manner. Discussing SLA research, Norris and Ortega (2003) argued that any study should start from defining the construct in specific and measurable terms of observable behavior (see also Révész & Brunfaut, Chapter 3, this volume). As pointed out by Shohamy (1999), for decades the focus of language testing research, in fact, has been on defining the construct of language ability, and nowadays there is a clear understanding that any test development should start with defining the construct to be measured. The next step, as outlined by Norris and Ortega (2003), involves the specification of data collection techniques, such as test tasks, that can be used to elicit the targeted behaviour. This implies "the careful analysis of tasks/situations in order to determine whether they can provide the behavioural evidence required of them" (Norris & Ortega, 2003, p. 721). Given that tasks are at the heart of language testing activity, a large amount of expertise has been built up, both in operational language testing and research, on the targeted selection of test formats and task types.

In this chapter, we offer guidance on how to design, select, and evaluate test formats and task types that are best suited to measure particular constructs. The breadth of foci in SLA and language testing research precludes an exhaustive catalogue of task types or test formats; instead, we describe some of the main formats and task types available. Although our discussion primarily relates to measuring learner language, the advice also applies to tools for measuring other constructs SLA and language testing researchers might be interested in, such as learner aptitude or motivation.

Key Concepts

Test format: The general design of a research instrument or a test.

Task type: The activities or tasks that learners have to do in a test. A test or a research instrument might consist of several task types which are often classified according to the response required from learners.

Selected-response tasks: Task types where learners are presented with answer options and required to select one or more correct ones. An example is multiple-choice tasks.

Constructed-response tasks: Task types that require learners to produce a response, which allows for assessment of learners' ability to produce language. The required responses range from a word or a short phrase to essays used to assess learners' writing ability, or oral interviews to assess their speaking ability.

Direct testing: Testing learners' skills or abilities by requiring them to directly perform the skills intended to be measured. Direct testing is usually associated with performance assessment of productive language skills (i.e., speaking and writing).

Indirect testing: Testing learners' skills by measuring their performance on abilities believed to underlie the targeted skills. An inference about learners' skills is then made on the basis of their performance on the underlying abilities. For example, an indirect test of writing ability might include a multiple-choice or a true/false task requiring learners to choose correct grammar, spelling or punctuation forms, or to identify errors.

Key Issues

Whether selecting ready-made instruments or designing new ones, several key issues should be considered. These include selecting test formats and/or task types appropriate to the SLA study or language test's aims, and considering the effect the choice has on the construct of the test and learner performance.

Test Format Choice

A test format has three main facets: mode of delivery, components assessed, and proficiency levels assessed. Firstly, for instance, a test can be delivered in a paper-based or a computer-based mode. Secondly, tests also differ in the aspects of language they assess. For instance, they may offer four separate sections/components, each focusing on a different language skill (speaking, listening, reading, and writing) and providing separate scores for each section. Alternatively, tests might integrate different skills, requiring learners to first listen to a talk or discussion and then write or speak about it, or perhaps write about a passage that they have read. Integrated tests might have a single score outcome to represent the main underlying construct (such as one score for integrated writing, whereby the definition of writing includes the reading of materials that inform the writing), or multiple scores to represent the various underlying skills involved. An example of an integrated test is the Canadian Academic English Language (CAEL) test (https://www.cael.ca/). Some tests may also separately assess grammatical and vocabulary knowledge, in addition to one or more language skills. For instance, the Michigan English Placement Test comprises four sections: grammar, vocabulary, listening comprehension, and reading comprehension (https://michiganassessment.org/institutions/products-services/michigan-ept/). A third test format facet is how the test distinguishes between learners of different proficiency levels. Some tests are multi-level; all learners sit for the same test and are awarded different scores or bands according to their performance (e.g., the IELTS test, https://www.ielts.org). Other tests are graded; learners select the most appropriate test level for their present ability and receive a pass or a fail at that level. An example of graded tests is the Cambridge English Qualifications suite which offers tests at the CEFR A2, B1, B2, C1, and C2 levels (https://www.cambridgeenglish.org/exams-and-tests/qualifications/general/).

Task Type Choice

In this section, we provide a brief overview of the main task types available. The strengths and the challenges associated with each are extensively described in the literature—see Alderson et al. (1995), Haladyna and Rodriguez (2013), and Hughes and Hughes (2020) for examples. Below, we discuss key issues related to each task type. Table 8.1 lists frequently-used selected-response task types.

The **multiple-choice** task type is so ubiquitous that it receives specific attention in Jones (Chapter 9, this volume), with a detailed discussion of its uses, design problems, and recommendations for item-writing.

Yes/No or **True/False** tasks allow for fast and straightforward marking using a scoring key. At the same time, because there are only two options, learners have a 50% chance to answer correctly by guessing, so the learners' true ability is not revealed in the test scores. To reduce guessing, a third option—"Not Given"—is often introduced. However, the difference between "False" and "Not Given" might not be obvious, particularly for listening tasks where learners cannot revisit the recording to confirm their choices (Green, 2014). The difference between "True" and "Not Given" can be disputable due to inferring from a text, thus risking a double key. In addition, tasks with a "Not Given" option are more difficult to write.

Matching tasks (Figure 8.1) are particularly useful for assessing reading and listening comprehension, especially to assess global processing (understanding the gist or main idea). At lower proficiency levels or with younger learners, picture-matching can be useful. At higher levels, header-paragraph matching is a useful format. The key thing to keep in mind is that, if the number of answers available is the same as the number of items (e.g., four words to match to four images), once three of the items have been matched correctly to their answer, the fourth item is

Table 8.1 Selected-response task types: An overview

Multiple-choice	Normally consists of a stem/question and several response options, and is the most common selected-response task type (see also Chapter 9, this volume).
Yes/No—True/False	Learners choose between the two responses so, in effect, it is a multiple-choice task with two options. Sometimes a third option, Not Given (i.e., the information is not in the text), is included.
Matching	Can be based on pictures, diagrams, words, phrases or whole paragraphs (*Figure 8.1*). Learners match pictures, words, or propositions from one list to words or propositions in another list. Learners may also be asked to match paragraph headers to the correct paragraph or to label a diagram from a list of words or phrases (e.g., https://ielts-up.com/reading/diagram-completion-1.html).
Ordering/sequencing	Can be used to order words in a sentence, sentences in a text, or paragraphs in a text (e.g., Aptis Reading test task 2, https://www.britishcouncil.org/exam/aptis/practice-material/reading-test).
Banked cloze	A selected-response version of the fill-in-the-blank task type (see below for gapped cloze). The learner is given a paragraph in which words have been deleted. The deletions can be principled, with the aim of assessing specific language features (banked gap-fill) or can be based on the systematic deletion of every n^{th} word. The learner's task is to restore the words in the blanks by selecting from a bank of words (e.g., https://pearsonpte.com/wp-content/uploads/2014/10/Tutorial.pdf, p. 20).
Acceptability judgment	One variant of an acceptability judgment task is a **grammaticality judgment test (GJT)**. Learners are presented with a sentence and asked to judge whether and/or to what extent it is grammatical. Another variant is a **Yes/No vocabulary** task in which learners are presented with a list of words, some of which are genuine words and others are pseudo-words. The learners identify those that they consider to be genuine words (e.g., the Vocabulary Size Placement Test used in Dialang, https://dialangweb.lancaster.ac.uk/).

Match each picture to the name of the animal. There is one extra name which you do not need to use.

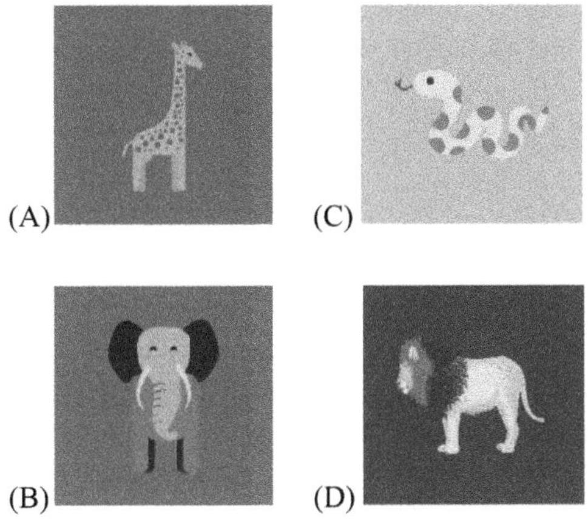

(1) Giraffe

(2) Zebra

(3) Elephant

(4) Lion

(5) Snake

Figure 8.1 Example of a matching task.

correct by default. Therefore, it is important to offer more possible answers than the number of items, and to ensure that the extra answers are not correct for any of the items.

Ordering tasks (also sometimes called **sequencing**) are widely used to assess textual coherence and cohesive devices. It is most appropriate in computer-based testing where learners can drag-and-drop text elements and check-read the text afterwards. The main challenge in producing ordering tasks is to ensure that only one sequence of words/sentences is correct. Decisions also need to be made on how to score the responses, since one incorrectly placed element will lead to all subsequent elements also being placed incorrectly. Therefore, partial credit might be given for correctly ordering some elements of a sequence, and a full score for ordering the whole sequence correctly.

Cloze tests, including **banked cloze** or **banked gap-fill**, allow for testing a variety of constructs, although careful consideration of the target construct is needed when designing banked cloze items, as both the positioning of the gap and the options offered in the bank will determine what the item is testing, for example, whether it is testing reading comprehension or vocabulary/grammar more narrowly. In addition, McCray and Brunfaut (2018) detected differences in how lower- and higher-scoring learners completed banked gap-fills, with the former relying more on local reading and lower-level cognitive processing. It is also important to ensure that each word in a bank fits only one gap. Similar to matching tasks, there should be more words in the bank than gaps in the text, which lexically and grammatically distract, to eliminate guessing.

Acceptability judgment tasks, often with Likert scales, are used extensively in SLA research. In particular, GJTs are often used to measure implicit vs explicit learning (see Isbell & Rogers, Chapter 29, this volume), with several previous studies suggesting that untimed GJTs measure explicit knowledge (EK) while timed GJTs measure implicit knowledge (IK) (see e.g., Bowles, 2011; Ellis & Loewen, 2007). These findings have been criticized in a recent factor analysis study which concluded that "GJTs are too coarse to be measures of IK, and that the different types of GJTs measure different levels of EK" (Vafaee et al., 2017, p. 60). As for Yes/No vocabulary tasks, they are useful in gaining quick insights into learners' vocabulary size—a large number of items can be administered in a time- and resource-efficient manner. However, the results are usually too imprecise to inform research or high-stakes assessment. Indeed, in the Dialang test, the Vocabulary Size Placement Test uses this task type as a "filter" to then present learners with a lower- vs mid- vs high-proficiency test. Scoring these tasks can be complicated because of the four types of responses they produce (yes/no to real words, yes/no to non-words). Several scoring methodologies based on reaction time and responses to non-words have been proposed with no single methodology found to suit all learners and all testing situations (Pellicer-Sánchez & Schmitt, 2012).

A range of constructed-response task types is also available, with frequently-used ones listed in Table 8.2.

Table 8.2 Constructed-response task types: An overview

Gapped cloze	A constructed-response version of banked-cloze tasks (see above). The task requires a one-word response by filling blanks in a text (e.g., Cambridge English B2 First for Schools, Reading and Use of English paper: https://www.cambridgeenglish.org/exams-and-tests/first-for-schools/exam-format/).
C-test	Another version of the fill-in-the-blank task type (*Figure 8.2*). Instead of deleting whole words, only part of the word is deleted (see Grotjahn, 1987, for instructions on how to develop C-tests).
Short-answer questions	Require learners to produce a word, phrase, or short sentence in response to an open-ended question (*Figure 8.3*).
Direct writing	Typically presents the learner with a prompt (*Figure 8.4*) or can include a table or graph to interpret (e.g., IELTS Academic Writing Task 1, graph description: https://www.ielts.org/about-the-test/test-format). The learner is expected to compose a written response. Alternatively, a continuation task, whereby the learner reads an incomplete story and then writes what follows in the story.
Sentence building	A speaking task type whereby the learner hears different phrases presented in random order and must mentally rearrange them to utter a complete sentence (cf. van Moere, 2012).
Elicited imitation	Learners hear a sentence and must repeat it as accurately as possible. Sentences typically increase in complexity, length, or speed of delivery.
Reading aloud	Learners read a short passage aloud (e.g., the Versant English Speaking Test: https://www.pearson.com/english/versant/tests/english-speaking-test.html).
Picture description	This speaking task type can involve a single image, several images for comparison, or a story board. The task can be completed by one learner, in pairs, or groups where each learner takes responsibility for describing a part of a picture or one picture in a series.
Information gap	This speaking task type is typically used when learners are paired or put in small groups. They each have some information which they must share with their partner(s). These tasks can also have a decision-making element. The speaking test of the Examination for the Certificate of Proficiency in English (ECPE: https://michiganassessment.org/institutions/products-services/ecpe/) requires learners to exchange information about four different options and then negotiate which option they prefer.
Oral proficiency interview (OPI)	The learner takes part in a one-to-one interview with an interlocutor who also usually acts as an examiner. OPIs can be delivered face-to-face or online where questions are pre-recorded and delivered via computer, for example the ACTFL Oral Proficiency Interview (https://www.actfl.org/professional-development/assessments-the-actfl-testing-office/oral-proficiency-assessments-including-opi-opic).
Summary task	Summary tasks are one form of integrated tasks. Learners are required to produce an oral or written summary of a passage they have read/listened to.

While **gapped cloze** tests are a popular task type, it is still unclear whether they measure reading comprehension at the sentence or text level or both, or are indicators of overall language proficiency (see Trace, 2020 for an up-to-date overview). Gapped cloze tasks are also challenging to design. Firstly, it is not easy to ensure that each gap has only one answer. Additionally, selecting words from the text to create the gaps should be done carefully since some gaps are difficult to fill if one does not know the original text.

C-tests (Figure 8.2) were originally developed to test global language proficiency and have been shown to be a good way to differentiate learners; that is why they are often used for placement testing. However, there is some controversy about what exactly C-tests measure (see Drackert & Timukova, 2019 for an up-to-date discussion). Newer work on C-testing (see https://aelrc.georgetown.edu/research/current-projects/c-tests/) calls for computer-adaptive C-tests to help ensure learners receive texts at the appropriate level of difficulty. On a practical level, correct responses can sometimes be found in the surrounding text.

Short-answer questions (Figure 8.3) are particularly common and versatile for assessing reading and listening comprehension; they can test literal meaning, inferencing, local/global meaning, careful/expeditious/search processing, etc. Guessing is less likely than with multiple-choice items. However, short-answer questions can be very time-consuming to mark, and spelling errors might obfuscate correctness of the meaning of answers. It is also challenging to arrive at a consistent marking scheme, as there might be acceptable answers unforeseen by the item writer.

Direct writing tasks (Figure 8.4) elicit an extended writing sample to assess learners' overall writing ability. This can tap into a variety of genres (e.g., narrative, argumentative, formal report, transactional correspondence). A risk is that learners with less background knowledge on the topic produce responses that are less well developed. Also, learners cannot usually produce more than one or two pieces of writing in one sitting, which narrows the range of language that might be elicited. In the case of the continuation task, Shi et al. (2020) found that different prompt types affected learners' performance in terms of scores and linguistic features of the response, and their writing strategies. Yoon and Burton (Chapter 28, this volume) detail key issues regarding the design of direct writing tasks.

Bats

Bats have an interesting way of looking at their world. They are noctur___, which me___ they a__ most act__ at ni__. They do__ use the__ eyes t_ find th__ way aro___ at ni___. Instead th__ use a spe___ skill call___ echolocation wh___ allows th__ to h____ for fo__. It al__ helps th__ to av___ obstacles in th___ path a_ they f__ in t__ dark.

Figure 8.2 Example of a C-test task.

Where did the speaker first meet the girl? ______________________________

Figure 8.3 Example of a short-answer question.

The local supermarket has decided to stop providing bags for customers' groceries. From now on, people must bring their own bags when they go shopping. What do you think of this new policy? Explain your opinion, giving specific reasons to support your view.

Figure 8.4 Example of a direct writing prompt.

Task types that require speaking range from fairly controlled to offering learners more scope to speak creatively. Among more controlled task types are sentence building, elicited imitation, and reading aloud. The **sentence building** task type offers insights into learners' morphosyntactic knowledge. Arguably, this task type tests short-term memory more than it does speaking proficiency. Additionally, because the sentences are presented aurally, a learner's performance on the task might be affected by their listening proficiency.

While **elicited imitation** tasks are used extensively in SLA research, there is no strong consensus on what they actually measure. It is typically considered a good measure of verbal working memory but can also offer insights into a learner's chunking ability (cf. Buck, 2001). Van Moere (2012) reported how this task type is used to measure phonological accuracy, fluency, and grammatical accuracy. Like the sentence building task, it possibly tests short-term memory more so than speaking proficiency. The interference of a learner's listening proficiency on their task performance may be of concern as well. Additionally, reliable scoring of learners' performances on this task can be problematic.

Reading aloud tasks are an economical tool for assessing learners' pronunciation, intonation, and aspects of connected speech on the same text. This task type lends itself to the use of automated speech scoring due to highly predictable responses (Zechner & Evanini, 2019). A possible source of concern is that learners' reading ability can interfere with their reading aloud. Even native speakers vary considerably in their ability to read aloud.

Picture description and information gap tasks offer learners the opportunity to create unique utterances. Single images in **picture description** tasks are useful for eliciting descriptions, while story boards can be used to elicit narratives. Like other constructed-response task types, these can be time-consuming to mark, and it is difficult to arrive at a consistent mark scheme.

As **information gap** tasks involve paired or group speaking, they can capture interactional facets of speaking proficiency such as turn taking, collaboration, or meaning negotiation. These tasks do not always elicit a wide range of language, however. Alderson et al. (1995) stated that, in many instances, "the questioner might be able to get away with using the perfectly acceptable, 'How about …?'" (p. 62). Therefore, their ability to measure real conversation ability needs further examination.

Oral proficiency interviews are often claimed to measure learners' communicative competence in the target language. However, Brown (2003) noted that the interlocutor's elicitation procedures and feedback may affect the learner's performance. Whether or not this is irrelevant to the construct depends on how communicative competence is defined. If the construct definition includes navigating different questioning techniques as in real-life communication, then the varying interlocutor behaviours can arguably be considered construct-relevant. The concern would then be to standardise the marking of learners' performances.

As a form of integrated tasks, **summary tasks** closely resemble real-life language activities where two or more language skills are used together. This improved task authenticity, however, may pose a challenge in construct definition and, in turn, marking. If a learner produces a poor summary, it will not be easy to identify whether this is due to misunderstanding the input material or poor writing/speaking skills. Some tests use summary tasks as a measure of productive skills, while others as a measure of receptive skills, or a combination.

Task Effects

The choice of task format and/or task type potentially has consequences for the measurement of the intended constructs. A long-standing issue in task selection is that "the method used for testing a language ability may itself affect the student's score" (Alderson et al., 1995, p. 44). For instance, although multiple-choice and constructed-response task types were found to measure a very similar construct, provided that they use equivalent stems (Rodriguez, 2003), the use of either of the two may contribute to different relative difficulty of the test. In'nami and Koizumi's (2009) meta-analysis on the effects of multiple-choice and short-answer questions on L1 reading,

L2 reading and L2 listening test performance indicated that MC was easier than short-answer questions in L1 reading and L2 listening. One possible implication suggested by the researchers is to use MC if an easier test is desirable.

The construction of test items or tasks may also have an effect on the elicitation of the targeted construct. Brunfaut and McCray (2015) found that the way items within the same task type are developed may fundamentally shift the construct. One of the task types (banked gap-fills) from the test under scrutiny in their study intended to measure short-text reading comprehension skills. However, learners solved some items by primarily using collocation and syntactic knowledge. This was probably enabled by the distractors in the bank that gave away some lexico-grammatical clues. Therefore, the researchers emphasized the importance of clear and specific guidance for item writers to mitigate against this potential threat to test validity.

Test or task delivery conditions may contribute to variance in a learner's performance. The effect of test delivery mode on writing performance has been widely investigated (see Yoon & Burton, Chapter 28, this volume). While learners have typically indicated they prefer the computer-based mode, findings in terms of effects on the performances themselves vary. It is therefore important to evaluate one's research context and population in terms of computer literacy and broader educational characteristics. For example, when it concerns young children and/or learners taking the tests in languages they normally handwrite and therefore do not have keyboarding skills in (e.g., Yigitoglu, 2016), test delivery conditions seem to matter. Kim et al. (2019), for instance, found that the paper test mode was the optimum delivery condition for first and second graders. Therefore, requiring these learners to take computer-based writing tests might introduce construct-irrelevant variance (a variable extraneous to the targeted construct which affects measurement outcome). In speaking tests, on the other hand, only small performance differences have been found in relation to delivery modes such as face-to-face versus semi-direct online (Kiddle & Kormos, 2011) or face-to-face versus video-conferencing mediated (Nakatsuhara et al., 2017b).

Rating conditions, in relation to delivery modes, may also introduce construct-irrelevant variance. Findings are mixed regarding effects on scores resulting from computer- vs paper-based writing. For speaking tests, Nakatsuhara et al. (2017a) found that audio-only ratings of speaking performances were remarkably lower than ratings on the basis of video recordings. The verbal data suggested that raters found visual information in the videos helpful in comprehending the candidates' speech and in providing non-verbal contexts. Therefore, it is important to consider not only delivery mode effects on learners and their performance, but also on raters and ratings.

Another task delivery condition which might present variance in a learner's performance concerns planning time (see Ellis, 2005). Research into the effects of planning on speaking performance has variable findings, with some suggesting that the amount of planning time had only negligible effects (e.g., Wigglesworth & Elder, 2010), and others revealing that planning effects are dependent on other factors including task demand and learners' proficiency level (e.g., Wigglesworth, 1997; O'Grady, 2019), as well as when planning time is allowed (i.e., pre-task planning versus on-line planning) (Yuan & Ellis, 2003). A central consideration to whether and when to allow planning time is the target construct. Nitta and Nakatsuhara (2014), for example, found that pre-task planning appeared to lower learners' interactional patterns in paired speaking tasks. As interactional competence was the intended construct of the test, allowing pre-task planning inadvertently deprived learners of performing to the best of their ability.

Recommendations for Practice

Here, we offer practical suggestions for ensuring that tests and tasks used as data collection instruments are of such quality that they guarantee "that the data collected can unambiguously address the question that is being asked" (Hudson & Llosa, 2015, p. 76).

In many circumstances, developing research instruments from scratch is deemed impractical due to constraints such as time and budget. It then becomes important to study the various existing options available. Some test materials are available to researchers upon request (e.g., the Mandarin C-test developed by the Assessment and Evaluation Language Resource Center (AELRC) at Georgetown University https://aelrc.georgetown.edu/research/current-projects/c-tests/). IRIS, a digital repository of instruments and materials for research into second languages (Marsden et al., 2016) is available at www.iris-database.org and hosts a large number of research instruments including language tests. When making a selection, it is vital to evaluate whether the instrument is fit for purpose in terms of target construct representation and intended use (as well as for the population and proficiency level), and to consider the strengths and weaknesses of the task format and type.

It is also necessary to review studies validating the use of the instruments, and studies that have used them. For example, the vocabulary size tests developed by Nation and colleagues (https://www.wgtn.ac.nz/lals/about/staff/paul-nation#vocab-tests) have been widely validated and used with different learner populations. While using a well-known, validated instrument will give confidence in its quality, a validity argument for an existing instrument is not automatically transferable when the instrument is used in a new context. It should be kept in mind that validity is not a property of the instrument per se, but what matters is the validity of the inferences made on the basis of learners' performances on the said instrument (see also Chapelle, Chapter 2; Révész & Brunfaut, Chapter 3, this volume).

Frequently though, an existing instrument cannot be used unaltered due to the different conditions for which it was originally developed, such as learner population, measurement purpose, or research design. Decisions then need to be made on potential modifications, whether content-related (using only part of the instrument that fits the defined purpose, modifying or even substituting some items from the instrument, or modeling after a certain test format or design to write new items), or non-content related (e.g., test delivery and test layout adaptations). Extra care should be taken to ensure that any adaptation will preserve the ecological validity of the data collection methods (i.e., the correspondence between the research conditions and the real-life settings) and that it will not lead to construct-irrelevant variance. Therefore, following the modification of an instrument, it is necessary to pilot the adapted version, analyse the pilot data, make any necessary changes, and re-pilot the revised version. This is important because any validation studies conducted on the original instrument cannot be assumed to apply to the modified version.

In some cases, a new instrument will need to be developed for one's research purposes. In operational testing, the first step in developing any new test task is producing task specifications. This might also be relevant in research contexts if more than one test version is required, or if more than one task of the same type is used in the test. This is because developing tasks from specifications, rather than modeling them on each other, will ensure that the test/task versions produce comparable results. Advice on this can be found in Green and Fulcher (Chapter 7, this volume). Furthermore, as explained more elaborately in Green (Chapter 11, this volume), the test then needs to be piloted. Prior to this, each task could be pre-piloted with one or more colleagues or students by asking them to do the task as learners; as pilots can be time-consuming and costly, pre-piloting will already help eliminate some flaws (Rossi & Brunfaut, 2019).

Developing a test task often requires specialist knowledge as each task type carries with it pitfalls which an experienced item writer knows how to avoid. For instance, as mentioned earlier, matching tasks should offer more possible answers than the number of items to avoid matching by default. Similar recommendations can be made for each task type discussed in this chapter. Therefore, before embarking on test development, it is advisable to consult a reliable item writing guide which provides item writing advice for relevant task types. Jones (Chapter 9, this volume) constitutes a good guide for developing multiple-choice items, while Haladyna and Rodriguez

(2013) provide guidance on developing and validating a broad range of selected-response and constructed-response task types.

Several item-writing principles, however, hold for every task type, most importantly construct validity, as a task can only contribute to valid assessment if it correctly reflects what the researcher wants to measure, and if the resulting score reflects only the construct of assessment, and nothing else. When designing a test task, two problems have to be watched out for. First, to avoid construct-irrelevant variance, the task designer has to ensure that no variable extraneous to the construct of assessment will affect the assessment outcomes. For example, including complex vocabulary in a grammar task might skew the results for those learners whose vocabulary knowledge is insufficient, although the task itself is only aimed at testing grammar. Second, construct underrepresentation occurs when an important aspect of the construct is not included in the task design. As a simple example, a task aimed at testing the knowledge of question construction in English will have to include several aspects of the construct including the word order and the use of auxiliary verbs, while a task that only focuses on the use of question words will underrepresent the construct.

In this chapter, we discussed considerations that SLA researchers and language testers should bear in mind while adopting, adapting, or developing new testing/research instruments. We hope that the chapter has brought to light the importance of using a suitable test format and task type to produce valid learner assessment and research results, as the choice of the testing/research instrument can have a substantial effect on the findings.

Testing Tips

- Consider the construct to be tested. Choose a task type/test format that will enable testing the construct in a comprehensive and targeted manner.
- Use a variety of task types in one testing/research instrument to balance out the strengths and challenges of each.
- Consider the potential effects of different task types and task delivery conditions on learners' performances.
- Consider your resources when deciding whether to develop a test task from scratch, adapt, or adopt an existing task.
- If you decide to develop your own task, start with producing task specifications.
- Consult item writing recommendations for each specific task type you want to produce.
- Pre-pilot (sometimes called alpha testing), pilot (beta test) and, if necessary, develop an iterative plan to re-pilot (delta test) each newly developed or adapted task. Conduct analysis of the pilots and make any necessary revisions to the task at each stage. This will increase measurement success at launch and over the lifespan of the assessment.

Recommended Readings

Green, A. (2014). *Exploring language assessment and testing: Language in action*. Routledge.

Chapters 5 and 6 of this book offer guidance on assessing language skills and knowledge, and the chapter companion (http://cw.routledge.com/textbooks/rial/data/task_and_response_types.pdf) provides commentaries and examples of different task types.

Haladyna, T., & Rodriguez, M. C. (2013). *Developing and validating test items*. Routledge.

This handbook provides comprehensive guidance on producing a range of selected-response and constructed-response task types. Detailed tips for each task type are provided, with multiple illustrative examples.

Hughes, A., & Hughes, J. (2020). *Testing for language teachers* (3rd ed.). Cambridge University Press.

This book overall provides practical guidance on developing language tests, and Chapter 8 in particular discusses the most-commonly used task types.

References

Alderson, J. C., Clapham, C., & Wall, D. (1995). *Language test construction and evaluation*. Cambridge University Press.

Bowles, M. A. (2011). Measuring implicit and explicit linguistic knowledge. *Studies in Studies in Second Language Acquisition*, 33, 247–271. https://doi.org/10.1017/ S0272263110000756

Brown, A. (2003). Interviewer variation and the co-construction of speaking proficiency. *Language Testing, 20*(1), 1–25. https://doi.org/10.1191/0265532203lt242oa

Brunfaut, T., & McCray, G. (2015). *Looking into test-takers' cognitive processes whilst completing reading tasks: A mixed-method eye-tracking and stimulated recall study*. British Council ARAGs Research Reports Online. https://www.britishcouncil.org/sites/default/files/brunfaut_and_mccray_report_final_0.pdf

Buck, G. (2001). *Assessing listening*. Cambridge University Press.

Drackert, A., & Timukova, A. (2019). What does the analysis of C-test gaps tell us about the construct of a C-test? A comparison of foreign and heritage language learners' performance. *Language Testing, 37*(1), 107–132. https://doi.org/10.1177/0265532219861042

Ellis, R. (Ed.). (2005). *Planning and task performance in a second language*. John Benjamins Publishing.

Ellis, R., & Loewen. S. (2007). Confirming the operational definitions of explicit and implicit knowledge in Ellis (2005). *Studies in Second Language Acquisition*, 29, 119–126. https://doi.org/10.1017/S0272263107070052

Grotjahn, R. (1987). How to construct and evaluate a C-test: A discussion of some problems and some statistical analyses. In R. Grotjahn, C. Klein-Braley, & D. K. Stevenson (Eds.), *Taking their measure: The validity and validation of language tests* (pp. 219–253). Brockmeyer.

Haladyna, T., & Rodriguez, M. C. (2013). *Developing and validating test items*. Routledge.

Hudson, T., & Llosa, L. (2015). Design issues and inference in experimental L2 research. *Language Learning, 65*(S1), 76–96. https://doi.org/10.1111/lang.12113

Hughes, A. & Hughes, J. (2020). *Testing for language teachers* (3rd ed.). Cambridge University Press.

In'nami, Y., & Koizumi, R. (2009). A meta-analysis of test format effects on reading and listening test performance: Focus on multiple-choice and open-ended formats. *Language Testing, 26*(2), 219–244. https://doi.org/10.1177/0265532208101006

Kiddle, T., & Kormos, J. (2011). The effect of mode of response on a semidirect test of oral proficiency. *Language Assessment Quarterly, 8*(4), 342–360. https://doi.org/10.1080/15434303.2011.613503

Kim, A. A., Lee, S., Chapman, M., & Wilmes, C. (2019). The effects of administration and response modes on grade 1–2 students' writing performance. *TESOL Quarterly, 53*(2), 482–513. https://doi.org/10.1002/tesq.495

Marsden, E., Mackey, A., & Plonsky, L. (2016). The IRIS repository: Advancing research practice and methodology. In A. Mackey & E. Marsden (Eds.), *Advancing methodology and practice: The IRIS repository of instruments for research into second languages* (pp. 1–21). Routledge.

McCray, G., & Brunfaut, T. (2018). Investigating the construct measured by banked gap-fill items: Evidence from eye-tracking. *Language Testing, 35*(1), 51–73. https://doi.org/10.1177/0265532216677105

Nakatsuhara, F., Inoue, C., Berry, V., & Galaczi, E. (2017a). Exploring the use of video-conferencing technology in the assessment of spoken language: A mixed-methods study. *Language Assessment Quarterly, 14*(1), 1–18. https://doi.org/10.1080/15434303.2016.1263637

Nakatsuhara, F., Inoue, C., & Taylor, L. (2017b). *An investigation into double-marking methods: Comparing live, audio and video rating of performance on the IELTS speaking test*. The IELTS Partners: British Council, IDP: IELTS Australia and Cambridge English Language Assessment. https://www.ielts.org/-/media/research-reports/ielts_online_rr_2017-1.ashx

Nitta, R., & Nakatsuhara, F. (2014). A multifaceted approach to investigating pre-task planning effects on paired oral test performance. *Language Testing, 31*(2), 147–175. https://doi.org/10.1177/0265532213514401

Norris, J., & Ortega, L. (2003). Introduction: A framework for understanding measurement in SLA research. In C. J. Doughty & M. H. Long (Eds.), *The handbook of second language acquisition* (pp. 717–761). https://doi.org/10.1002/9780470756492.ch21

O'Grady, S. (2019). The impact of pre-task planning on speaking test performance for English-medium university admission. *Language Testing*, *36*(4), 505–526. https://doi.org/10.1177/0265532219826604

Pellicer-Sánchez, A., & Schmitt, N. (2012). Scoring yes-no vocabulary tests: Reaction time vs. nonword approaches. *Language Testing*, *29*(4), 489–509. https://doi.org/10.1177/0265532212438053

Rodriguez, M. C. (2003). Construct equivalence of multiple-choice and constructed-response items: A random effects synthesis of correlations. *Journal of Educational Measurement*, *40*(2), 163–184. https://doi.org/10.1111/j.1745-3984.2003.tb01102.x

Rossi, O., & Brunfaut, T. (2019). Test item writers. In J. I. Liontas (Ed.), *The TESOL encyclopaedia of English language teaching* (pp. 1–7). John Wiley & Sons. https://doi.org/10.1002/9781118784235.eelt0981

Shi, B., Huang, L., & Lu, X. (2020). Effect of prompt type on test-takers' writing performance and writing strategy use in the continuation task. *Language Testing*, *37*(3). https://doi.org/10.1177/0265532220911626

Shohamy, E. (1999). How can language testing and SLA benefit from each other? The case of discourse. In L. Bachman & A. Cohen (Eds.), *Interfaces between second language acquisition and language testing research* (pp. 156–176). Cambridge University Press. https://doi.org/10.1017/CBO9781139524711.009

Trace, J. (2020). Clozing the gap: How far do cloze items measure? *Language Testing*, *37*(2), 235–253. https://doi.org/10.1177/0265532219888617

Vafaee, P., Suzuki, Y., & Kachisnke, I. (2017). Validating grammaticality judgement tests. *Studies in Second Language Acquisition*, *39*(1), 59–95. https://doi.org/10.1017/S0272263115000455

Van Moere, A. (2012). A psycholinguistic approach to oral language assessment. *Language Testing*, *29*(3), 325–344. https://doi.org/10.1177/0265532211424478

Wigglesworth, G. (1997). An investigation of planning time and proficiency level on oral test discourse. *Language Testing*, *14*(1), 85–106. https://doi.org/10.1177/026553229701400105

Wigglesworth, G., & Elder, C. (2010). An investigation of the effectiveness and validity of planning time in speaking test tasks. *Language Assessment Quarterly*, *7*(1), 1–24. https://doi.org/10.1080/15434300903031779

Yigitoglu, N. (2016). The role of writing in learning less-commonly-taught languages in Turkey. *The Journal of the National Council of Less Commonly Taught Languages*, *19*, 1–30. http://www.newsite.ncolctl.org/images/writing-in-learning-less-commonly-taught-languages-in-Turkey.pdf

Yuan, F., & Ellis, R. (2003). The effects of pre-task planning and on-line planning on fluency, complexity and accuracy in L2 monologic oral production. *Applied Linguistics*, *24*(1), 1–27. https://doi.org/10.1093/applin/24.1.1

Zechner, K., & Evanini, K. (2019). *Automated speaking assessment: Using language technologies to score spontaneous speech*. Routledge. https://doi.org/10.4324/9781315165103

9
Designing Multiple-Choice Test Items

Glyn Jones

Background

Multiple-choice (MC) items have been a staple of large-scale testing since the 1920s (Fulcher, 2014). Their continuing popularity is largely due to the ease with which they can be administered and marked. Answering a MC item is a very simple mechanical operation—ticking a box or circling a number on paper; on a computer they can be answered with a mouse or touch screen. Marking MC items is also a simple operation. On paper it can be done very quickly by untrained staff. On a computer or with an optical character reader it happens instantaneously. *Good* MC items, however, are difficult to write. The benefits of ease of administration and marking therefore tend to be offset by the time and effort required to produce the items in the first place.

Key Concepts

Multiple-choice item: A question with a restricted choice of possible answers.
Stem: The main text of MC items directing test takers to the options, generally in the form of a grammatical question or an incomplete statement.
Options: Alternative possible answers listed in random order below the stem.
Key: The option which provides the correct answer to the question or the missing piece that correctly completes the stem.
Distractors: Options that represent incorrect responses.

Key Issues

In this section, I outline some of the issues which one should consider when contemplating using MC items in language testing or research. These concern:

- inherent properties of MC items, such as their vulnerability to guessing and test-wise strategies
- their scope and validity: What aspects of language ability can they assess? How well do they assess them?

- washback
- the ideal number of options

Guessing

A key disadvantage of MC items is that it is possible for test takers to answer correctly by blind guessing, and the probability of a lucky guess is higher the fewer options there are. This is clearly a threat to validity. Since it is difficult to know whether test takers' correct answers are the result of guessing, this is an unavoidable source of error. However, it is widely thought that test takers don't blindly guess except if they are running out of time at the end of a test (Rodriguez, 2005) or as a last resort after exhausting all other available strategies (Rupp et al., 2006). This is partly borne out by empirical studies such as Farr et al. (1990), who found that test takers seldom resorted to random guessing, or to test-wise strategies, when answering reading comprehension items. Further, Currie and Chiramanee (2010) found that blind guessing accounted for only 6.7% of answer choices in a MC grammar test.

Test-wise Strategies

Another potential threat to validity is posed by test takers' use of test-wise strategies. Coaching institutions and self-help books (e.g., Merritt, 2006; Poundstone, 2015) offer tips for test takers on how to exploit common features of MC items to choose the right option without actually knowing the answer. Part of the art of item writing lies in knowing and blocking these strategies.

Scope and Validity

Hughes (2003) lists as one of the limitations of MC items that "the technique tests only recognition knowledge," and cautions:

> A multiple choice grammar test score, for example, may be a poor indicator of someone's ability to use grammatical structures. The person who can identify the correct response in [an item] may not be able to produce the correct form when speaking or writing. This is in part a question of construct validity; whether or not grammatical knowledge of the kind that can be demonstrated in a multiple choice test underlies the productive use of grammar.
>
> (p. 60)

The notion "recognition knowledge" deserves some scrutiny. MC items cannot elicit a truly original response, since the correct answer is inevitably there on the page or screen. An important consequence for language testing and research is therefore that MC items cannot be used for the direct assessment of productive skills: speaking and writing.

However, identifying the key in a MC item is not necessarily the result of straightforward recognition. Rather, most MC items can be seen as problems that offer a number of alternative solutions. The cognitive processes required to solve the problem, and so choose the correct solution from among the options, may be quite complex. Thus, although MC items cannot test productive *skills*, they are by no means limited to testing *passive* knowledge.

From this standpoint, MC items—as used in second language research and testing—can be divided into two categories:

- Stand-alone items, where the problem is encapsulated in the item itself, and where the cognitive process may indeed consist in instantaneous recognition but more often involves forming a judgment based on the application of some rule or principle.

- Comprehension items, where the problem relates to a text (such as a reading passage or video), external to the item itself, and where the cognitive process involves understanding the text at some level.

Stand-alone items are generally used to assess aspects of ability that are hypothesized to underlie language competence, for example:

- grammatical knowledge
- vocabulary
- pragmatics (what to say in specific situations or to achieve specific goals)
- discourse (how to link ideas in a conversation or written text)
- phonological recognition (e.g., being able to distinguish between *ship* and *sheep* in English)

Whether test developers can draw inferences regarding language *use* from such evidence is a matter of construct validity (Hughes, 2003). Purpura (2004), writing about grammar items, claims:

> There is … nothing innately 'bad' about this or any test task, as long as it successfully elicits instances of performance from which valid inferences about grammatical ability can be made for the testing purpose.
>
> (p. 129)

Making a correct judgment about the grammaticality of a particular combination of stem and option is indeed an instance of a certain kind of performance, from which test developers may be able to infer that the test taker is able to apply a certain grammatical rule in written receptive mode. The important thing is thus to be clear and explicit about the construct being tested by a particular set of MC items, and its limitations.

The above considerations also apply to other discrete-item methods of testing these abilities, but this does not mean that different methods are interchangeable. Whatever exercise of judgment the item demands, the fact of choosing among options, rather than producing the answer from one's own resources, has an effect on outcomes. Studies comparing different item types have generally found that MC items are easier than equivalent constructed-response items (e.g., short-answer questions, in which test takers write the answer rather than simply identifying it on the page or screen), but that scores are highly intercorrelated (Cheng, 2004; Currie & Chiramanee, 2010; In'nami & Koizumi, 2009; Rodriguez, 2003). From this, the researchers concluded that the various items tap into the same constructs. However, Currie and Chiramanee (2010), who investigated test takers' cognitive processes by means of verbal reports, found that in over 25% of cases test takers had answered MC items correctly on the basis of partial knowledge (the chosen option seemed most likely to be correct), and in a similar number of cases by eliminating the distractors. As these strategies are not available when attempting constructed-response items, Currie and Chiramanee concluded that, although there was a high correlation between scores on the two item formats, they actually assessed different constructs.

Comprehension items are used to test language use, albeit receptive rather than productive use. Here, too, there is a question of construct validity: To what extent does the language use demonstrated in solving the item resemble the kind of language use required in reading or listening in real life? The answer depends on what aspects of real-life comprehension test developers wish to assess. It is possible to design MC items that target higher-level reading skills such as understanding of global meaning (e.g., see Pearson, 2012, pp. 96–97 for a list of skills that may be targeted by MC items in PTE Academic), but research suggests that they generally tend to induce test takers to approach text in a way that is focused on low-level comprehension. For example, Farr et al. (1990) used verbal reports to study the strategies deployed by American college students when taking an MC reading comprehension test. They found that the dominant strategies involved using the questions to home in on specific regions of the text. They concluded that "multiple-choice tests are valid as at least one type of reading" (Farr et al., 1990, p. 223), namely reading to find specific information. At the same time, they caution that there may be no single test method that can assess all the kinds of reading that people engage in in real life. In a similar study, Rupp et al. (2006) found that test takers' reading strategies were strongly influenced by properties of the item, especially the degree of similarity or plausibility of options, and did not necessarily correspond to the type of reading purpose that the item writer had in mind.

Washback

The pressure to prepare learners for a MC test might induce teachers to devote large amounts of class time to practicing MC items. Given the limitations of scope and validity of MC items discussed above, this would constitute a harmful washback effect, assuming that the goal of instruction is developing an all-round profile of communicative language skills. At worst, teachers may resort to coaching test-wise strategies at the expense of effective teaching. However, research into the impact of MC tests on teaching and learning seems inconclusive. Alderson and Hamp-Lyons (1996), investigating the possible washback effect of the TOEFL exam, found that while the form of the test can have an effect on teaching methods, the effect is not inevitable, and varies from teacher to teacher and according to institutional circumstances.

Number of Options

Haladyna (2004) advises us to "use as many choices as possible but three seems to be a natural limit" (p. 112). Rodriguez (2005), who reviewed the results of 27 studies conducted over a period of 80 years, found that most studies concluded that three was the optimum number of options. The rationale for this varied from study to study, but common factors were that:

- Item discrimination (the extent to which items are answered correctly by more able test takers and incorrectly by less able test takers) and reliability (the extent to which the test yields consistent scores on repeated administrations) generally improve as the number of options increase, however whereas the step from two to three options produces a considerable improvement in these properties, the step from three to four produces a much smaller difference (and the difference is smaller still when the number of options is increased to five). Thus it is argued that it is not worth the additional work of devising a third distractor.
- In many cases it is simply not possible to devise more than two *plausible* distractors.
- Items with three options take less time to answer than those with four, so more three-option items can be administered in a given time, which makes for higher reliability.

Rodriguez's (2005) own conclusion is that one should write "as many plausible distractors as feasible" but that "in most cases only three are feasible" (p. 10).

More recently, Lee and Winke (2012) compared the results from administering three-, four- and five-option variants of the same tests in a second language learning context. They found that three-option tests were significantly easier than the equivalent four-option tests, but not consistently less discriminating or reliable. Seinhorst (2008) found no significant differences in difficulty, reliability or discrimination between three- and four-option variants of the same test. He further found that average completion time for the three-option variant was 9% less than for the four-option variant, leading him to suggest that three options make for more efficient information gathering.

The above studies contrasted test versions with different option numbers. However, according to Frary (1995) one may even vary the number of options within the same test: "There is no psychometric advantage to having a uniform number, especially if doing so results in options that are so implausible that no one or almost no one marks them" (p. 1).

Regarding the *plausibility* of distractors, it is worth noting that this can be gauged empirically once items have been pre-tested with a group of trial test takers. A plausible distractor will be chosen by some of the less able test takers. If nobody chooses a distractor then clearly nobody found it plausible. It should be dropped or replaced.

Recommendations for Practice

There are several excellent how-to guides to writing MC items in general (e.g., Frary, 1995; Fulcher, 2014; Haladyna, 2004; Haladyna & Downing, 1989; Spaan, 2007), as well as books that include advice on the use of MC items in language testing (e.g., Alderson, 2000; Alderson et al., 1995; Buck, 2001; Fulcher, 2010; Hughes, 2003; Purpura, 2004; Read, 2000). Here, I outline some of the most important recommendations as they apply to language testing and research. First, I make some recommendations that can be applied to most types of MC items, whether stand-alone or for comprehension. I then offer some that apply specifically to reading and listening comprehension items.

The Stem

The stem should be either a question requiring an answer (see Example 4) or an incomplete statement (see Examples 1 and 2). Haladyna (2004) prefers the question format, claiming that this is clearer than the incomplete statement format. He also cautions "never to leave a blank in the middle or at the beginning of the stem. These *blankety-blank* formats are difficult for students to read" (Haladyna, 2004, pp. 69–70). Both of these injunctions may be valid when assessing knowledge of a content subject domain, but when testing language, where linguistic form *is* the subject domain, they do not necessarily hold. Often, the construct that educators or researchers want to assess is the ability to select the correct form to fit a particular context, and filling a gap in that context is the clearest and most economical way of signaling this.

The Key

There must be one and only one correct answer. This may sound obvious, but it is easy to miss an instance of an answer that may be acceptable in a different context from the one that you, the item writer, had in mind. This is a reason to trial the items with colleagues before administering them to test takers (Alderson et al., 1995).

The key should not stand out as being different in any obvious way from the distractors (Fulcher, 2014). In particular, it should not be noticeably longer. This is not always easy to achieve. Particularly with comprehension items, drafting an accurate paraphrase of the required information may require careful wording and the use of qualifying expressions. By contrast, it may be relatively easy to write succinct statements that do not correspond to the meaning in the text (i.e., distractors). Test-wise candidates, and canny test preparation coaches, know this, so the advice "if in doubt, go for the longest option" is often given.

The Distractors

Devising plausible distractors is the most difficult part of MC item writing. It is also the most critical, as the choice of distractors is a major factor in determining the degree of difficulty of an item. Consider these two variants of a simple vocabulary item:

Example 1
A chisel is a
A. tool used for cutting wood
B. type of comfortable chair
C. person who cheats at exams

Example 2
A chisel is a tool used for cutting
A. wood
B. paper
C. meat

With Example 1, a test taker who has a vague notion that a chisel is some kind of tool will answer correctly. Example 2 requires more precise lexical knowledge. What makes a distractor plausible, then, may depend on the construct test developers are trying to measure and on the level of ability being targeted.

However, there are some formal principles in distractor design that are applicable to most types of testing needs. For instance, in Example 3 the construct being targeted is the ability to select simple past over present perfect when there is an implied past time reference. It may be tempting to add another distractor, such as "do you buy," to reduce the potential for guessing, but this introduces an additional—lower level—construct (knowledge of present and past question forms), and test takers who understand the context of the situation can easily eliminate this option. Here, two options is the "natural" limit, as it is important to test only one construct at a time in an item (Fulcher, 2014; Spaan, 2007).

Example 3
What a lovely hat! Where __________ it?
A. have you bought
B. did you buy

Reading Comprehension Items

Some aspects of reading comprehension, although testable by MC items, are arguably better tested with other item types. For example, the ability to follow the logical structure of a text can be tested with a sentence- or paragraph re-ordering task. The ability to scan a text for specific information, as when consulting a timetable or financial report, can be tested with short-answer questions.

A construct such as identifying the main idea of a paragraph, however, is less easy to operationalize with a constructed-response task, since it would be challenging to judge whether the test taker's formulation of the main idea is sufficiently accurate, or whether the test taker has really understood the text if their answer is a chunk copied verbatim from the text. With a MC item, however, educators or researchers can offer a paraphrase of the main idea (as the key) and, as distractors a number of statements that bear some relation to the content of the paragraph but that are not the main idea.

Writing a suitable paraphrase to create an item is not necessarily easy, however. The language of the paraphrase needs to be simpler than that of the text (Fulcher, 2014; Spaan, 2007), to avoid assessing comprehension of the question as well as that of the text. Ideally, it should avoid terminology that is in the text (Spaan, 2007). Experienced item writers speak of a need to counter "word spotting," i.e., to foil a test-wise strategy that consists in simply matching words in the item with words in the text. This is not always possible, and attempts to do so can lead to formulations that are convoluted and over-long. In a study of a corpus of TOEFL items, Macmillan (2007) found that instances of lexical repetition between item and text—either simple repetition (the exact same word occurring in both) or complex repetition (two members of the same word family such as *strong* and *strength*)—were quite common. However, such links also existed between the distractors and the text, contributing to their plausibility.

Another important point is to ensure that test takers have to read the text to be able to answer the MC item correctly. When testing comprehension of factual texts, it can be difficult to avoid devising items that can be answered by drawing on world knowledge, common sense or test-wiseness. Of course, "world knowledge" will not be the same for all test takers. For example, many Finnish learners of English would be able to answer the item shown in Example 4 without reading the text.

When devising distractors for comprehension items, a fruitful approach can be to formulate statements that are suggested by phraseology in the text but which do not actually address the question posed by the stem. Another is to formulate statements which one might guess to be true in the light of the topic focus of the text, but which are not true according to the text.

It is best to avoid using absolute qualifiers such as *always* or *never* in distractors. Very often, the meaning expressed in a text concerns what is sometimes, generally or usually the case. It is tempting, then, to use adverbs like *always* and *never* as an easy way of falsifying the meaning in the text in order to create distractors (Frary, 1995; Fulcher, 2014). Test preparation coaches are wise to this and will advise test takers to eliminate options that contain these adverbs.

Example 4 illustrates some of these tips. For instance, the key (option D) is a paraphrase of information given in apposition in the text (*"in keeping with the growing current of cultural nationalism and independence with which he identified"*). It contains a tell-tale complex lexical repetition (nationalism/nationalist), but this is offset by similar links in distractors B and C ("culturally dominant language," "rhythm(s)"). Distractor A is a common-sense expectation but is not stated (and is, as it happens, false).

Example 4

Sibelius wrote pieces for unaccompanied choir throughout his career. In his early examples the words are generally in Swedish, then the culturally dominant language in Finland, but later he gravitated towards Finnish texts, in keeping with the growing current of cultural nationalism and independence with which he identified, and made a point of composing music that is sensitive to the characteristic rhythms of the Finnish language.

Why did Sibelius start writing music to Finnish texts rather than Swedish ones?

Because….

A. Finnish was his first language.
B. Finnish was the culturally dominant language where he lived.
C. He preferred the rhythm of Finnish speech to that of Swedish.
D. He was sympathetic to the Finnish nationalist movement.

Listening Comprehension Items

Similar considerations as above apply to listening comprehension MC items as regards the types of information that can be targeted. However, the test taker's experience in completing MC listening items is different from that in MC reading items. Firstly, the text and the item are delivered via different channels: the auditory and the visual. Test takers have to decode the aural signal and process the written text of the item. Therefore, item developers need to be particularly careful to ensure that the language of the item wording is well within the ability range of the target test taker population to limit the extent to which reading ability is a source of construct-irrelevant variance (Buck, 2001; Spaan, 2007). At lower levels, test developers can address this problem by devising MC items in which the options are presented as pictures, as in Example 5. While expensive to produce, unless you happen to be very good at drawing, they offer a way of reducing reliance on test takers' reading ability to a minimum. (The stem may be recorded orally, using a different voice from the comprehension text; however it is usually printed in the test paper as well.)

Example 5: a graphical multiple-choice item

Audio transcript: Listen to the woman speaking. What activity is she describing?
"I usually play for half an hour when I get home. It's very relaxing after staring at a screen all day, and I'm learning some great tunes!?"

Secondly, the presence of lexical overlap between the required information and the item (the potential for "word spotting") is not necessarily of concern in the way that it is for reading comprehension items; for many purposes the ability to relate the aural signal to the written text is itself part of the listening construct. Indeed, items may be devised expressly to assess this ability, as in Example 6.

Example 6
Audio transcript: "This book costs thirty dollars"
How much does the book cost?
$13 / $30

Thirdly, listening occurs in real time. Listeners cannot scan the text backwards and forwards to locate the required information in the way that readers can with a written text. Therefore, the item stem should indicate clearly what kind of information test takers should listen out for. Additionally, the pacing of the test needs to be carefully considered. Test takers should have time to read the items before they listen, and time to log their answers on the test paper afterwards (Buck, 2001). With a test consisting of short listening texts, each with an associated MC item, the required pauses can be incorporated in the audio track. When several items are associated with a single, longer text, however, the issue of pacing is problematic. Not only do test takers have to cope with the cognitive demands of the item—reading, understanding, eliminating distractors—while processing what they have just heard, they have to simultaneously monitor the continuing aural signal in order to detect the answer to the next item. To mitigate the effects of these cognitive demands, it is good practice to make the wording of such items as brief as possible, and to ensure that the required information is evenly spaced within the text.

Variants of the Multiple-Choice Format

There are many types of test items that do not look like traditional MC items (a stem with a list of options), but that nevertheless require test takers to choose from a selection of possible answers, and so function as MC items. For a thorough treatment of these variants, see Haladyna (2004), Chapters 3 and 6. Below, two examples of the more widely used variants are provided: true/false and MC cloze items.

True/False Items. True/False (T/F) items are effectively MC items with two options only: true and false. The stem is a statement that is either a paraphrase of information in the text or expresses a valid inference from information in the text (if the answer is "true"; if the answer is "false" then the stem is of course a faulty paraphrase of information in the text, or an invalid inference).

A common objection to T/F items is that the probability of answering correctly by random guessing is 50% (e.g., Alderson et al., 1995), which is true of all binary-choice MC items. However, Grosse and Wright (1985) identified an additional problem with T/F items. They found that when they split a T/F test into two subtests, one with all correct answers being "true" and the other with all correct answers being "false," there was a very low correlation between scores on the two tests. They hypothesized that the more able test takers were prone to seeing something wrong with a supposedly "true" statement whereas less able test takers students more readily agree with any printed statement.

A variant of the T/F item type that seeks to reduce the probability of answering correctly by guessing is "True/False/Not given." With items of this type test takers have to decide between three options: the stem agrees with information in the text; the stem contradicts information in the text; or the stem expresses an idea that is not mentioned in the text. With this item type test developers can expect that items for which the key is "not given" will be more difficult than those where the key is "true" or "false," because test takers needs to scan the whole text (or at any rate all of a designated extract) in order to answer conclusively. Moreover, these items are difficult to write as it can be very tricky to distinguish between "false" (the text says that this is not the case) and "not given" (the text does not say that this is the case); similarly, it can be tricky to distinguish between "not given" (the text does not say this) and "true" (the text implies this).

Multiple-Choice Cloze Items. The MC can be combined with the cloze technique—either true cloze (where every *N*th word is deleted) or rational cloze (where the item writer chooses which words to delete). This is often done simply to enable clerical or automated scoring. However, it can have other advantages over open cloze procedures. When a content word is deleted from a text, very often there are a large number of words that could fill the gap.

Example 7: an extract from an open cloze passage
... In the end financial ____________ led me to move to a less ____________ neighbourhood. ...

In Example 7 each gap can take a range of possible answers: *concerns*, *strictures*, *difficulties*... for gap 1; *respectable*, *salubrious*, *interesting*... for gap 2. (Furthermore, the two gaps interact with each other; without further context the answer to gap 1 could be *security* and the answer to gap 2 *shabby*, or any of several negative-connotation adjectives.) This poses a problem for marking, and also makes the item rather easy, as we would have to accept as answers relatively high-frequency, but stylistically deadpan, answers such as *problems* and *expensive*.

By providing options, test developers can constrain the range of possible answers so as to assess knowledge of collocations and the ability to discriminate between near-synonyms—see Example 8.

Example 8: multiple-choice cloze

... In the end financial (1)____________ led me to move to a less (2)____________ neighbourhood. ...

(1) A. stipulations
B. observations
C. consultations
D. considerations

(2) A. prized
B. superior
C. affluent
D. enriched

Instead of providing a set of options for each gap, the answers can also be presented below the text in a "word bank." This is simply a list of the answers in random order with one or more additional items that do not fit in any gap (to make it more difficult to answer the last few gaps by elimination). Effectively, then, all the gaps are provided with the same set of options. The disadvantage of this procedure is that it can be difficult to ensure that each word in the bank will fit in only one of the gaps, and that there is at least one plausible distractor for each gap. For example, if only one of the removed words is a singular verb form, there must be at least one other singular verb form in the bank.

Testing Tips

- Do not give away the answer by making the key noticeably different in length, or type of information, from the distractors.
- Write only as many plausible distractors as you can think of.
- Avoid distractors that can be eliminated easily by applying knowledge of the world, common sense or test-wise strategies.
- When assessing comprehension, try to devise a paraphrase of the required information. Where possible, avoid using the exact wording of the passage.
- When assessing listening comprehension, make sure that the language of the items is well within the expected reading ability range of the target population, or devise graphical MC items.
- Review items carefully to make sure there is only one correct answer, and that all distractors are plausible.
- Trial items with colleagues before you administer them to learners.

Recommended Readings

Haladyna, T. M. (2004). *Developing and validating multiple-choice test items*. Lawrence Erlbaum Associates.

This handbook comprises a comprehensive treatment of the practical and theoretical aspects of MC item development, and of methods of analyzing test responses for the purpose of improving and validating MC test items.

Frary, R. B. (1995). More multiple-choice item writing do's and don'ts. *Practical Assessment Research & Evaluation*, *4*(11), 1–3. https://doi.org/10.7275/djyd-5535

Frary provides a concise summary of basic principles of MC item development.

Fulcher, G. (2014). *Multiple-choice items*. http://languagetesting.info/features/mc/items.html

This feature on Glenn Fulcher's *Language Testing Resources* website (languagetesting.info) comprises a brief introduction and podcast giving an overview of the history of MC items, main issues associated with their use in language assessment, and useful tips for MC item writers.

References

Alderson, J. C. (2000). *Assessing reading*. Cambridge University Press.

Alderson, J. C., Clapham, C., & Wall, D. (1995). *Language test construction and evaluation*. Cambridge University Press.

Alderson, J. C., & Hamp-Lyons, L. (1996). TOEFL preparation courses: A study of washback. *Language Testing*, *13*(3), 280–297. https://doi.org/10.1177/026553229601300304

Buck, G. (2001). *Assessing listening*. Cambridge University Press.

Cheng, H. (2004.). A comparison of multiple-choice and open-ended response formats for the assessment of listening proficiency in English. *Foreign Language Annals*, *37*(4), 544–553. https://doi.org/10.1111/j.1944-9720.2004.tb02421.x

Currie, M., & Chiramanee, T. (2010). The effect of the multiple-choice item format on the measurement of knowledge of language structure. *Language Testing*, *27*(4), 471–491. https://doi.org/10.1177/0265532209356790

Farr, R., Pritchard, R., & Smitten, B. (1990). A description of what happens when an examinee takes a multiple-choice reading comprehension test. *Journal of Educational Measurement*, *27*(3), 209–226. https://doi.org/10.1111/j.1745-3984.1990.tb00744.x

Frary, R. B. (1995). More multiple-choice item writing do's and don'ts. *Practical Assessment Research & Evaluation*, *4*(11), 1–3. https://doi.org/10.7275/djyd-5535

Fulcher, G. (2010). *Practical language testing*. Hodder Education.

Fulcher, G. (2014). *Multiple-choice items*. http://languagetesting.info/features/mc/items.html

Grosse, M. E., & Wright, B. D. (1985). Validity and reliability of true-false tests. *Educational and Psychological Measurement*, *45*(1), 1–13. https://doi.org/10.1177/0013164485451001

Haladyna, T. M. (2004). *Developing and validating multiple-choice test items*. Lawrence Erlbaum Associates.

Haladyna, T. M., & Downing, S. M. (1989). A taxonomy of multiple-choice item-writing rules. *Applied Measurement in Education*, *2*(1), 37. https://doi.org/10.1207/s15324818ame0201_3

Hughes, A. (2003). *Testing for language teachers*. Cambridge University Press.

In'nami, Y., & Koizumi, R. (2009). A meta-analysis of test format effects on reading and listening test performance: Focus on multiple-choice and open-ended formats. *Language Testing*, *26*(2), 219–244. https://doi.org/10.1177/0265532208101006

Lee, H., & Winke, P. (2012). The differences among three-, four-, and five-option-item formats in the context of a high-stakes English-language listening test. *Language Testing*, *30*(1), 99–123. https://doi.org/10.1177/0265532212451235

MacMillan, F. (2007). The role of lexical cohesion in the assessment of EFL reading proficiency. *Arizona Working Papers in SLA & Teaching*, *14*, 75–93. https://journals.uair.arizona.edu/index.php/AZSLAT/article/view/21265/0

Merritt, S. (2006). *Mastering multiple choice*. The Brain Ranch.

Pearson. (2012). *The official guide to PTE Academic*. Pearson Education Limited.

Poundstone, W. (2015). *Rock breaks scissors: A practical guide to outguessing and outwitting almost everybody*. Little Brown and Company.

Purpura, J. E. (2004). *Assessing grammar*. Cambridge University Press.

Read, J. (2000). *Assessing vocabulary*. Cambridge University Press.

Rodriguez, M. C. (2003). Construct equivalence of multiple-choice and constructed-response items: A random effects synthesis of correlations. *Journal of Educational Measurement*, *40*(2), 163–184. https://doi.org/10.1111/j.1745-3984.2003.tb01102.x

Rodriguez, M. C. (2005). Three options are optimal for multiple-choice items: A meta-analysis of 80 years of research. *Educational Measurement: Issues and Practice*, *24*(2), 3–13. https://doi.org/10.1111/j.1745-3992.2005.00006.x

Rupp, A. A., Ferne, T., & Choi, H. (2006). How assessing reading comprehension with multiple-choice questions shapes the construct: A cognitive processing perspective. *Language Testing*, *23*(4), 441–474. https://doi.org/10.1191/0265532206lt337oa

Seinhorst, G. (2008). *Are three options better than four? Investigating the effects of reducing the number of options per item on the quality of a multiple-choice reading test* (Unpublished MA thesis). Lancaster University, Lancaster, UK.
Spaan, M. (2007). Evolution of a test item. *Language Assessment Quarterly*, *4*(3), 279–293. https://doi.org/10.1080/15434300701462937

10
Likert-Type Scale Construction

Aek Phakiti

Background

Second language acquisition (SLA) and language assessment researchers have long been interested in understanding second language (L2) learners' or test-takers' psychological characteristics, including their perceptions (e.g., beliefs, attitudes, self-assessment), cognition (e.g., learning strategies), and affect (e.g., motivation, anxiety), as these are part of, or affect, L2 learning or test performance variation. Likert-type scale questionnaires have been used to investigate these characteristics. The Likert scale was named in 1932 after Rensis Likert, an American psychologist, who developed this type of scale to measure attitudes. The term *Likert-type scale* refers to a discrete intensity of a variable or item (namely a scale) that reflects individual differences, such as "never (0)," "rarely (1)," "sometimes (2)," "usually (3)," and "always (4)."

Items in a Likert-scale questionnaire are "stimuli", and a Likert-type scale is used to represent responses to these stimuli. A Likert-type scale is considered a *closed-response* measurement technique in which participants consider the same issue of interest for different items. Numerical codes attached to an anchor option or a verbal scale descriptor (see Table 10.4) can range from lowest to highest or highest to lowest. The Likert-type scale of an individual item is normally considered an *ordinal* or *rank-order* scale for indicating the intensity or amount of a construct (e.g., "never" = 0 to "always" = 5). An aggregation of multi-items scales, especially with a large sample size, can make the scale a *continuous* or *interval-like* scale.

The scores from Likert-type scale items can be aggregated to form a composite score to represent a value estimate of a construct of interest. For example, in Phakiti et al. (2013), self-efficacy is defined as "an individual's beliefs about their capacity to accomplish a given academic activity or task" (p. 242). Six-point Likert-type scale items were used to measure three sub-components of self-efficacy as presented in Table 10.1. In this table, each participant's responses can be used to form a composite score of the target construct. For example, scores from Items 5, 6 and 7 could be aggregated to form a composite score of academic achievement self-efficacy.

Compared to test scores which are an *interval scale*, the numbers in an ordinal scale do not indicate precisely how much higher or lower one student or test-taker's score is than another. In a test, for example, it can meaningfully be said that Student A gets a score 25% higher than that of Student B. Such statements are not applicable in the case of Likert-type scales. Figure 10.1 demonstrates a Likert-type scale which is used to measure the intensity of a student's agreement with the question.

Table 10.1 Composites of self-efficacy (Phakiti et al., 2013, p. 246)

Construct	*Sub-construct*	*No. of items*	*Items*	*Cronbach's alpha*
Self-efficacy	Academic achievement	3	5, 6, 7	0.78
	Reading and writing	4	8, 9, 10, 11	0.85
	Oral discussion	3	12, 13, 14	0.83

Sample item: When I wrote this academic essay, I made sure I had clear topic sentences in a paragraph.

4-point Likert-type scale:

Strongly disagree (1) Disagree (2) Agree (3) Strongly agree (4)

5-point Likert-type scale:

Strongly disagree (1) Disagree (2) Neutral (3) Agree (4) Strongly disagree (5)

7-point Likert-type scale:

Strongly disagree (1) Somewhat disagree (2) Disagree (3) Neutral (4)

Somewhat agree (5) Agree (6) Strongly agree (7)

Figure 10.1 4-, 5- and 7-point Likert-type scales.

Key Concepts

Measurement: The process of translating observations of a construct of interest (an abstract concept such as motivation and self-regulation) into numbers. Language tests and questionnaires are examples of a procedure that involves measurement.

Likert-type scale: A numeric range of discrete intensity values of a manifest variable to a target construct that can be given differently by participants, students or test-takers (e.g., Never (rate 0) to Always (rate 5)).

Likert scale: An instrument, inventory or questionnaire that includes a collection of Likert-type scale items that measure an abstract concept or construct of interest.

Key Issues

This section first establishes the connection between theory in L2 learning and assessment research and measurement. It will discuss issues related to direct and indirect observations of a construct and inferences made from such observations. Second, it presents the key steps for constructing a Likert-type scale questionnaire.

Theory, Model, Construct, Hypothesis and Measurement

A *theory* is a set of statements about a phenomenon that seeks to explain why it occurs (see VanPatten & Williams, 2015). A good theory should clearly define, explain and exemplify its key constructs. A *model*, however, is developed to explain the key processes involved in the theory. For example, a theory of human memory may have a diagrammatic model that explains how long-term memory interacts with working memory and how each sub-component within each memory type interacts with others in a sequential or parallel manner. A *construct* is an abstract aspect related to a theory. Unlike a physical object, a construct cannot be directly seen, but can only be inferred from observations of behaviours or reflections.

Dörnyei's (2005) theory of L2 motivational self system illustrates the relationships among constructs, hypothesis, and measurement. This motivation theory has three key sub-constructs or domains: (1) ideal L2 self (imagined ideal future self as an L2 user), (2) ought-to L2 self (attributes ones should possess to meet expectations or avoid failures), and (3) L2 learning experience (situational aspects in language processes and personal experiences in language learning or use). For each of these sub-constructs, researchers can develop Likert-type scale items that represent behaviours or perceptions that are theoretically governed by the constructs. They ask study participants to consider the intensity of their responses to relevant statements and map these onto a Likert-type scale.

Figure 10.2 provides a diagram that represents the role of a construct (the Ideal L2 Self) and Likert-type scale items. In this figure, the arrow from the Ideal L2 Self is directed at each item, suggesting that this construct is hypothesised to determine participants' responses to each item. Here, the strength of a participant's vision of his/her Ideal L2 Self is hypothesised to determine his/her responses to each item. A stronger vision will likely manifest itself in a higher value on the response scale.

A *hypothesis* is a statement that predicts a relationship between a construct and observed items or behaviours, as well as among various constructs. A *correlational hypothesis* is used to predict whether two constructs bear any linear relationship to one another, and if they do, to what extent they overlap or can predict each other. A *causal-like hypothesis* is used to determine whether and to what extent one construct can change the nature of another construct.

Measurement in L2 learning or use is often driven by theory. To gain knowledge about a construct, multiple items that measure the same construct are recommended (generally 3 to 5 items), and data from these variables are aggregated to form a composite score to represent the intensity of the construct (see Table 10.1). Nonetheless, in L2 research, not every measurement is

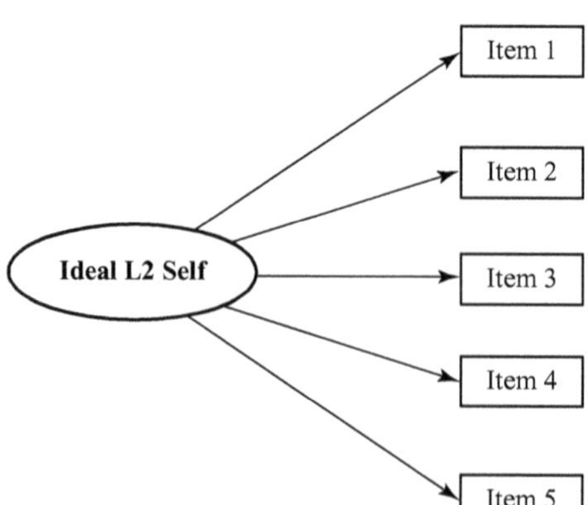

Figure 10.2 Ideal L2 self as an abstract construct.

theoretical (i.e., driven and explained by a theory). *Atheoretical* variables may be associated with L2 learners' preferred time to learn, or to take a test, for example. Here, students' preferences may not be relevant to any particular theory, but a Likert-type scale may still be used.

Stages in Likert-type Scale Construction

Figure 10.3 presents an overview of the key stages in a Likert-type scale construction (see also Phakiti, 2014). The various sections of this chapter will address issues related to these stages.

Purpose and Research Questions. Research purpose and questions determine the kind of research instrument to be used. If, for example, a study aims to understand L2 learners' motivation or test-taking strategies, a Likert-type scale questionnaire will be appropriate. By contrast, if a study aims to measure L2 knowledge, a language test or language elicitation task may be more appropriate.

Target Constructs. Constructs need to be defined and operationalised clearly and with theoretical support. A target construct can be defined and explained through a theory, approach, or model of interest (e.g., reading comprehension, pragmatic skills, motivation, and self-regulation). As noted earlier, atheoretical constructs can also be investigated through Likert-type scale questionnaires.

Review of Existing Questionnaires. During their literature review of existing theories and research, researchers may discover there are existing Likert-type scale questionnaires available for adoption or adaptation. Developing a new questionnaire can be time-consuming and costly, so adapting or adopting an existing questionnaire, especially one that has been used by many

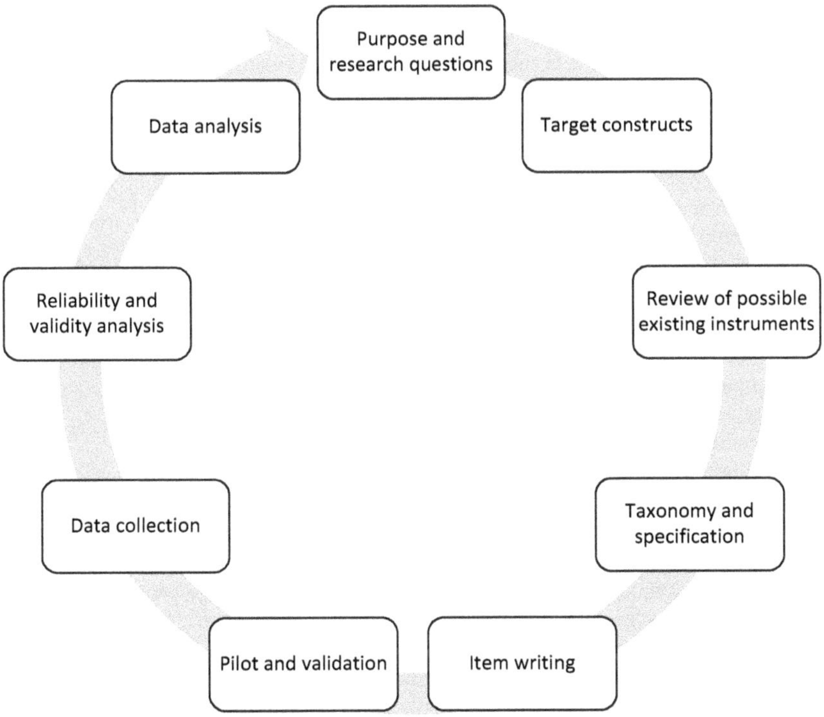

Figure 10.3 Overview of key stages in Likert-type scale construction.

researchers and has validity evidence, can have tangible benefits. Note that if the questionnaire is to be adapted, or used for a different audience, it will need to be subject to further validation.

Published questionnaires are usually included in the appendix or online resources of published articles; alternatively, they may be traced through databases, such as the IRIS Database (Marsden et al., 2016): https://www.iris-database.org/iris/app/home/index.

Taxonomy and Specification. The taxonomy and specification of a Likert-type scale questionnaire is essential for successful research. It is useful to guide researchers not only while they are developing items (discussed next), but also when they analyse their data to answer research questions. It is a written document or blueprint that provides a definition, description, and explanation of the abstract construct(s) to be measured, as well as their manifested behaviours. This document also provides information about, for example, target participants, anchors or verbal scale descriptors (see Table 10.5), the number of points in a Likert-type scale, and the mode of delivery (e.g., paper-based or online). Table 10.2 shows the key aspects of a Likert-type scale taxonomy, and the specifications that should be considered and made available to others. It should be noted that there is no unified structure for a Likert-type scale taxonomy and specification; hence Table 10.2 is only suggestive, and should be considered a working document that can be improved over time.

Table 10.2 Recommended structure of a Likert-type scale taxonomy and specification

Components	*Explanation*
Title	Name of the questionnaire
Developer	Name(s) of the developer
Date	Date of construction/revision
Purposes	What this questionnaire is for; what research project?
Target participants	Who will answer or respond to this questionnaire? (e.g., age, nationalities, L2 proficiency levels, academic discipline; school/undergraduate/postgraduate)
Language use	e.g., English, German, or Chinese; is translation needed?
Construct(s) and its definition	Operational definitions of the constructs as defined by an adopted theory or by the researcher; theoretical framework and references; manifested behaviours for a construct
Items to be used	Observable statements or items of each target construct; the desirable number of items per construct; order of items for different constructs; a summary table of item specifications
Likert-type scale	Expected responses; anchor(s) and point(s) of Likert-type scales e.g., never (1), rarely (2), sometimes (3), often (4), usually (5), or always (6)
Length of the questionnaire	Number of sections including a participant background section; what the actual questionnaire looks like
Estimated amount of time required to complete	Anticipation of time required for participants to complete properly; ethical and practicality considerations may be included
Instructions/ directions	General instructions and section instructions on how to complete the questionnaire
Delivery mode and administration	Paper, online, or both; to be administered before or after an activity; or can be answered any time
Pilot study or validation considerations	Did an expert in the area examine the items or Likert-type scales for feedback or improvement before the main study?; was the questionnaire piloted with some target participants and preliminary data analysis performed?; were interviews with some respondents about their understanding of items conducted?; what were the major changes to the questionnaire after the pilot study?
Reliability and validity	Evidence or considerations of the reliability and validity of the questionnaire; expected and acceptable reliability estimates (e.g., Cronbach's alpha estimates)

Item Writing. Item writing may informally occur during the review of the literature, or the review of existing or similar questionnaires. Items or statements should represent the nature of a target construct and be supported by a theory, approach, or model. Item writing should formally take place after the taxonomy and specification have been completed and checked for feedback. Items should be in line with how a construct is defined. For example, if a construct of interest is "evaluating strategy in writing", which may be defined as "a process of checking whether one's performance is accurate or has addressed a given writing task", strategy items should be related to evaluative behaviours about writing. However, a strategy item, such as "I wrote an outline of how I would structure my essay" cannot be considered to be in line with the definition of the evaluative strategy since this behaviour is more about planning.

In addition to this, researchers may need to decide whether items using *reverse wordings* are needed in their questionnaires (e.g., I *did not check* my essay before I submitted it). Items with reverse wordings allow researchers to observe whether participants read items carefully (items of similar content worded positively or negatively should yield similar information). Table 10.3 exemplifies this. That is, when a negatively worded item is reverse coded, the rated response should be similar to that of the positively worded item. Note that items should not be reverse coded if they are not to be aggregated to form a composite. Also note that in practice, items should not be as close as this in terms of content. It is thought that including negatively reworded items can help reduce *acquiescence bias* (i.e., the tendency for respondents to agree with a statement). Since positively phrased items are recommended for use as they are more comprehensible to respondents, no more than around 10 to 15% of the items should be reverse worded items.

Pilot and Validation. When all the Likert-type scale items have been put together to form a questionnaire, researchers need to review the quality and accuracy of their content, format and language use. These may be reviewed by research topic experts, research methodologists (e.g., questionnaire experts), and language editors. Once feedback has been received, researchers should consider improvements to the questionnaire. Validation may employ *cognitive interviews* with people who have similar characteristics to the target participants. A cognitive interview can help researchers determine whether items are clear, how the scales are interpreted, and whether it is understood what there is to do. The revelation of a lack of clarity or misconceptions arising from cognitive interviews can help researchers revise or delete items. The taxonomy may be updated accordingly.

Data Collection. Prior to data collection, it is important for researchers to seek ethical approval. Different institutes have different ethics protocols (see Sterling & De Costa, 2018). Once approval has been granted, the data collection for the main study may take place. Once data have been collected, researchers should prepare to input the data for statistical analysis.

Reliability and Validity Analysis. Reliability can be described as participants' consistency and accuracy in completing a Likert-type scale questionnaire, whereas validity refers to the appropriate inferences or interpretations and use of their responses to Likert-type scale items. Even if researchers have adopted an existing questionnaire written by a well-regarded researcher who reported a high reliability estimate (e.g., Cronbach's alpha coefficient), or even if they have

Table 10.3 Reverse worded item

No.	*Statement*	*1*	*2*	*3*	*4*	*5*
1.	I checked my essay before I submitted it.					X
2.*	I did not check my essay before I submitted it.	X				

* = reverse worded item

done a pilot study and a comprehensive validation of their Likert-type scale questionnaire before the main study, they are expected to examine the reliability and validity of their data (see also Reliability revisited below). The key reason for this requirement is that the reliability and validity of a questionnaire is affected by a given sample or group of participants, sample sizes, and the time and place at which data collection takes place. Although perceptions and beliefs, for example, can be subjective in nature, it is assumed that reports should be consistent and stable within a reasonable time span (e.g., participants' responses should be similar irrespective of when they answered the questionnaire). Furthermore, items that are designed to tap into the same construct should be correlated to one another.

Establishing the validity of a Likert-type scale questionnaire is less straightforward than addressing its reliability. Apart from the theoretical framework being used, the validity of item responses can be affected by various types of participants' bias (e.g., prestige and self-deception bias), fatigue and motivation. The validity of a Likert-type scale questionnaire may be enhanced through an application of exploratory and/or confirmatory factor analysis (see e.g., Phakiti, 2018a, 2018b). Factor analysis is a statistical approach that allows researchers to establish whether responses to a group of items reflect a common underlying quality or trait. This aids item selection for subsequent analysis. In regard to validity, *consequential validity* (the degree to which the use of the data impacts research participants or society including knowledge building) should not be neglected.

Data Analysis. This stage is important as it produces the results that will allow the main research questions to be answered. Researchers may need to create a composite score to examine the nature of a construct, which may be the average score of the items that measure the construct. The statistical assumptions of an inferential statistical test should be checked before its use (see Roever & Phakiti, 2018). For example, if a research question is related to how different sub-constructs are related to one another, a correlational analysis may be appropriate. If a research question aims to determine a cause-effect or causal-like relationship, a (multiple) regression analysis, a *t*-test, or an analysis of variance (ANOVA) may be performed. The validity of the findings may also be determined by the probability value for the rejection of the null hypothesis (i.e., that there is no relationship). Usually L2 researchers set this probability at .05 or .01 (see e.g., Roever & Phakiti, 2018). However, it is also important for researchers to focus on the statistical effect size as it is related to the strength of any detected relationship.

Recommendations for Practice

This section presents some useful strategies and suggestions for constructing a Likert-type scale questionnaire, as well as an indication of some of its limitations.

Example of Likert-Type Scale Anchors

During the item writing stage, it is useful to consider the anchors to be used with a set of items (e.g., agreement, frequency, trueness, importance, percentages), and the range of the Likert-point scale (e.g., 5-points, 6-points). There are several existing Likert-type scale anchors that can be adopted to suit the nature of any particular target construct. Table 10.4 provides examples of anchors that may be applied in L2 learning and assessment research.

It is important to note that people tend to answer a Likert-type scale question even if they do not know the answer to the question. Therefore, options such as "I don't know" and "Not applicable" should be included. Second, within a given Likert-point scale, the mid-point (e.g., undecided, neutral, neither agree or disagree) may play a role in affecting any finding or inferences made on the basis of participants' responses (see Nadler et al., 2015). Third, the order of the anchors and the appearance of the numerical ratings may lead to differences in participants'

Table 10.4 Sample anchors

Type of perception	*Anchors and assigned values*				
	1	2	3	4	5
Agreement	Strongly disagree	Disagree	Neutral/ undecided	Agree	Strongly agree
Desirability	Very undesirable	Undesirable	Neutral	Desirable	Very desirable
Difficulty	Very easy	Easy	Average	Difficult	Very difficult
Evaluation	Very poor	Poor	Average	Good	Very good
Frequency	Never	Rarely	Often	Usually	Always
Importance	Not at all important	Not important	Neutral	Important	Extremely important
Likelihood	Not at all like me	Not like me	Somewhat like me	Like me	Totally like me
Reflection	Not at all true of me	Not true of me	Somewhat true of me	True of me	Very true of me

Table 10.5 Anchor orders and appearance of numerical ratings in a Likert-type scale

Strongly agree (5)	Agree (4)	Neutral (3)	Disagree (2)	Strongly disagree (1)
Strongly agree (1)	Agree (2)	Neutral (3)	Disagree (4)	Strongly disagree (5)
Strongly disagree (5)	Disagree (4)	Neutral (3)	Agree (2)	Strongly agree (1)
Strongly disagree (1)	Disagree (2)	Neutral (3)	Agree (4)	Strongly agree (5)

responses. Hartley and Betts (2010) investigated the impact of anchor orders and places of numbers of a Likert-type scale assigned to the anchors on the way participants responded. For example, consider the order in Table 10.5. Hartley and Betts found that a Likert-type scale that starts with a positive anchor (e.g., strongly agree), and has the highest point on the left results in higher ratings compared to scales with other orders. Considerations of this nature should be carried out during the validation stage.

Characteristics of Good Likert-Type Scale Items

Well-constructed items (see also Irwing & Hughes, 2018, Table 1.2) should:

1. be complete, error-free sentences. Instructions and items should be grammatically correct and contain no spelling mistakes or inappropriate punctuation marks;
2. use a simple or short sentence structure. Lengthy, complex sentences are not easily understood;
3. use lay language as much as possible. Jargon or specialised terms, slang, colloquial expressions, and/or loaded words should be avoided;
4. use non-threatening, non-offensive language;
5. use mainly positively worded items. A few reverse worded items may be included;

6. avoid double-negative wordings, which can cause misunderstanding (e.g., "Pair-work activity is *not unhelpful*.");
7. avoid double-barrelled items, which include two or more aspects. If an item includes "and", "or", "but" or "because," it is likely to be double-barrelled (e.g., "*Teaching activities and materials* support my learning"). A participant may view teaching activities as supportive, but the materials used as unhelpful, rendering their response to this question meaningless;
8. avoid leading items that cause participants to choose the scale anchor desired by the researcher (e.g., "I *enjoy* taking online self-tests"), or which are likely to be affected by *prestige bias* (i.e., answers that make a person look good, such as "I am studying very hard this semester.").

Reliability Revisited

As discussed above, reliability and validity are important for Likert-type scale data. To establish the reliability of the Likert-type scale data, researchers first examine the descriptive statistics of items (item-level analysis). Descriptive statistics help determine the shape of the data (e.g., normally or non-normally distributed), and whether there are missing data. Reverse worded items should be reverse-coded prior to the reliability analysis being carried out. The concept behind reliability is driven by classical testing theory, which postulates that an observed score equals a true score plus an error. As the amount of error of measurement increases, the consistency of obtaining the same observed score reduces over multiple sittings. Reliability estimates are affected by the number of items, the range of Likert-type scales, and sample sizes (see e.g., Roever & Phakiti, 2018). The concept of test-retest reliability is, however, only aspirational as it is impractical to administer the same questionnaire twice to the same research participants to prove that responses will be the same or similar.

Cronbach's alpha is the most commonly used measure of the reliability of a Likert-type scale questionnaire. It is a measure of internal consistency. If several items are designed to tap into the same construct, the results should be highly correlated. The Cronbach's alpha coefficient (α) ranges from 0 (not at all reliable) to 1 (highly reliable). A coefficient of .70 or higher is viewed as acceptable. In the SPSS (Statistical Package for Social Sciences) programme, there is an option of "scale if item deleted," which allows researchers to investigate whether any particular items drastically reduce the overall reliability. An item that does this can be excluded from further analysis. In practice, researchers are expected to calculate and report both the total reliability and sub-scale estimates. Table 10.6 provides two examples of studies in L2 learning or assessment that employed Likert-type scale instruments.

It should be noted that in Table 10.6, Sardegna et al. (2018) adopted the instrument from Sardegna (2009), and performed exploratory factor analysis leading to a 4-factor structure. In Ertürk and Mumford (2017), no actual reliability coefficient (alpha) was reported for the overall scale of the main data. As discussed below, the reliability of the actual data should always be calculated and reported, as reliability is context-specific (i.e., it depends on the group of participants and the context in which it is administered), and may vary across time and contexts.

A more recent article by McNeish (2018) has questioned the use of Cronbach's alpha as an appropriate measure in social sciences research due to its stringent and unrealistic assumptions, and proposes alternative methods (e.g., omega coefficients, Coefficient *H*, and the greatest lower bound; see McNeish, 2018, for further discussion). In response to McNeish (2018), Raykov and Marcoulides (2019) argue that Cronbach's alpha should not be abandoned.

Furthermore, in recent years, the field of L2 research has seen an increased application of Item Response Theory (IRT) as an alternative to Classical Test Theory (CTT). The basic concept behind CTT is that an observed score is the outcome of the participant's true score and an error, which is treated as a single error term despite there being various sources of errors (e.g., time

Table 10.6 Examples of published Likert-type scale questionnaires in L2 studies

Name of questionnaire	*Construct(s)*	*Sub-constructs*	*Total number of items & sample size*	*Likert-type scales and anchors*	*Internal consistency estimates*
The Strategies for Pronunciation Improvement (SPI) Inventory (Sardegna et al., 2018)	Strategies for pronunciation improvement	3 sub-constructs: Prediction, Production, and Perception	$k = 45$; $N = 704$	5-points; Never (1), Rarely (2), Sometimes (3), Often (4), Always (5)	Prediction ($\alpha = .90$), Production ($\alpha = .94$), and Perception ($\alpha = .89$)
Factors affecting vocabulary test answer selection (Ertürk & Mumford, 2017)	Perceptions of difficulty in acquiring academic vocabulary	No sub-scale	$k = 14$; $N = 588$	5-points; Strongly disagree (1), disagree (2), undecided (3), agree (4), strongly agree (5)	$\alpha = .86$ (based on a pilot study)

and place of data collection, and the characteristics of items and anchors being used). Unlike CTT, IRT helps researchers establish some key characteristics of Likert-type scale items that are independent of participants. That is, IRT pays attention to the properties of individual items (e.g., level of item difficulty and discrimination capacity), rather than the characteristics of scales as a whole as in CTT (see e.g., Bond & Fox, 2007; DeVellis, 2012). For example, IRT can identify whether some items should carry more weight than other items due to the nature of the item content and its discrimination capacity. For instance, in a reading questionnaire, "I underline texts when I read" may have less weighting than "I summarise a text after I complete reading a paragraph." IRT is a valuable analytic tool for researchers analysing Likert-type scale data because it allows researchers to understand that various items cover a spectrum of the same construct and informs them as to whether some items may be excluded, revised, or added.

Caveats of a Likert-Type Scale and Remediation

No research questionnaire is perfect or free from error. A Likert-type scale questionnaire is no exception. First, while it can yield a high reliability estimate, the data may not be meaningful if researchers are not clear or are unknowledgeable about relevant theories. That is, a Likert-type scale questionnaire may not help researchers advance knowledge further if items are poorly constructed, or if item content is randomly selected and underrepresents a target construct. This disadvantage can be addressed through a comprehensive review of the literature, relevant theories, and existing questionnaires. Expert advice and pilot studies can also mitigate this limitation.

Second, like other research techniques (e.g., interviews and think-aloud protocols), researchers rely on participants' accounts and honesty in responding to the questionnaire. Unlike a language test, there are no criteria to judge their responses. Respondents' motivation (or lack thereof) to answer the questionnaire will affect not only the response rate, but also the quality of the responses. Since abstract psychological constructs are internal to the respondents, researchers infer the nature of the construct based on what they have observed. This limitation may be addressed somewhat through clear instructions for the questionnaire, and the researchers' efforts to explain to participants the importance of their responses to the study. If applicable, incentives, such as prize draws, money tokens, or offers of feedback, may encourage participants to answer the questionnaire more carefully and accurately. Explicit acknowledgments of this limitation as a threat to research validity is important in a research report or presentation.

Third, it is important to realise that reading comprehension ability can affect Likert-type scale data. Most Likert-type scale questionnaires require participants to read. Responses that match their true perceptions toward items are affected by how well they understand or comprehend the items. To address this, it is essential for researchers to know who their prospective participants are, so that the level of language use and choices for rating anchors in their questionnaire are appropriate. In some contexts, questionnaire items may be read to participants to make sure they understand them. Other contexts may require a questionnaire to be translated into participants' first language.

Finally, researchers only obtain answers to what they ask participants to respond to. A Likert-type scale questionnaire does not allow researchers to identify emerging themes or unanticipated issues that other techniques (e.g., interviews and observations) can provide. While this is convenient and manageable for a research project, a good understanding of an L2 phenomenon of interest relies on more than a Likert-type scale questionnaire. Therefore, whenever possible, other research techniques should be combined with the use of this kind of questionnaire.

Concluding Remarks

This chapter has presented several key considerations and recommendations for the construction of good Likert-type scale instruments for L2 learning and assessment research. Whilst providing a useful and structured means of collecting data, researchers without a solid conceptual and methodological foundation of Likert-type scales can use a poorly constructed Likert-type scale instrument in their research, thereby producing research findings that are unreliable and invalid. Such findings should be scrutinised as they, if not recognised as such, could contribute to so-called "pseudoscience." The testing tips presented here give some pointers as to how to avoid this pitfall.

Testing Tips

- Plan before writing items (e.g., stages, timeline, costs). Consider what your research questions seek to answer (i.e., conceptualise). Ask whether a Likert-type scale is a suitable method to fulfil your research questions.
- Know the theoretical constructs or aspects you aim to investigate well. This knowledge will influence how you design or create items. Avoid including items that are not relevant to your research questions and limit the use of hypothetical questions (e.g., "what if" items).
- If there is more than one anchor type in a Likert-type scale questionnaire, make sure they are clearly presented before the target items since participants may otherwise use one anchor to answer all items.
- Whenever possible, *translate* the instrument into the participants' most fluent language. A questionnaire should not be used as a means to test your participants' ability to comprehend your instrument.
- Format your Likert-type scale questionnaire to look neat, attractive and professional. This is a *precondition* for valid and reliable data. Check the layout, fonts, structures of items and scales

and accuracy in language use. Instructions should be simple and clear. Present the research aim and ensure consent, confidentiality and anonymity (if applicable).

- Items should be sequenced in a meaningful order, from items dealing with simple issues to items that deal with more complex issues. Similarly, present sections logically, based on the sequence of your research questions.
- Always pilot your instrument before its use. Piloting may reveal any shortcomings of your instrument, such as in the wording of items and responses, formats, lengths, and participants' item comprehension problems. When possible, include expert reviews and cognitive interviews.
- There is no perfect Likert-type scale questionnaire. Each time it is used to collect data, even after several validation studies and collections, a new problem may arise because of the context, group of participants, and time. Remember that a Likert-type scale questionnaire is not the only means to gain knowledge of people's minds.

Recommended Readings

DeVellis, R. F. (2012). *Scale development: Theory and applications* (3rd ed.). SAGE Publications.

This book conceptually and accessibly provides both theoretical and methodological considerations in the development and use of scales for research. It covers topics such as the relationship between theory and measurement, latent variables, reliability, validity, and guidelines for scale development.

Irwing, P., & Hughes, D. J. (2018). Test development. In P. Irwing, T. Booth, & D. J. Hughes (Eds.), *The Wiley handbook of psychometric testing: A multidisciplinary reference on survey, scale and test development*. Wiley & Sons.

Although this chapter is titled "Test development", a large proportion of it focuses on the development of Likert-type item development. This chapter also includes a discussion of stages in an instrument design and its associated psychometric principles.

Johnson, R. L., & Morgan, G. B. (2016). *Survey scales: A guide to development, analysis and reporting*. Guilford Press.

This book provides a step-by-step guide to applications of scales in survey research. Topics in this book include processes in scale development, item-writing guidelines, formatting and reviewing, examining scale quality and data analysis.

References

Bond, T. G., & Fox, C. M. (2007). *Applying the Rasch model: Fundamental measurement in the human sciences* (2nd ed.). Lawrence Erlbaum Associates.

DeVellis, R. F. (2012). *Scale development: Theory and applications* (3rd ed.). SAGE Publications.

Dörnyei, Z. (2005). *The psychology of the language learner: Individual differences in second language acquisition*. Lawrence Erlbaum.

Ertürk, N. O., & Mumford, S. E. (2017). Understanding test-takers' perceptions of difficulty in EAP vocabulary tests: The role of experiential factors. *Language Testing*, *34*(3), 413–433. https://doi.org/10.1177/0265532216673399

Hartley, J., & Betts, L. R. (2010). Four layouts and a finding: The effects of changes in the order of the verbal labels and numerical values on Likert-type scales. *International Journal of Social Research Methodology*, *13*(1), 17–27. https://doi.org/10.1080/13645570802648077

Irwing, P., & Hughes, D. J. (2018). Test development. In P. Irwing, T. Booth, & D. J. Hughes (Eds.), *The Wiley handbook of psychometric testing: A multidisciplinary reference on survey, scale and test development*. John Wiley & Sons.

Likert, R. A. (1932). A technique for the measurement of attitudes. *Archives of Psychology*, *40*, 5–53.

Marsden, E., Mackey, A., & Plonsky, L. (2016). The IRIS repository: Advancing research practice and methodology. In A. Mackey & E. Marsden (Eds.), *Advancing methodology and practice: The IRIS repository of instruments for research into second languages* (pp. 1–21). Routledge.
McNeish, D. (2018). Thanks coefficients alpha: We'll take it from here. *Psychological Methods, 23*(3), 412–433. https://doi.org/10.1037/met0000144
Nadler, J. T., Weston, R., & Voyles, E. C. (2015). Stuck in the middle: The use and interpretation of mid-points in items on questionnaires. *Journal of General Psychology, 142*(2), 71–89. https://doi.org/10.1080/00221309.2014.994590
Phakiti, A. (2014). Questionnaire development and analysis. In A. J. Kunnan (Ed.), *The companion to language assessment* (pp. 1245–1261). John Wiley & Sons.
Phakiti, A. (2018a). Exploratory factor analysis. In A. Phakiti, P. De Costa, L. Plonsky, & S. Starfield (Eds.), *The Palgrave handbook of applied linguistics research methodology* (pp. 423–457). Palgrave.
Phakiti, A. (2018b). Confirmatory factor analysis and structural equation modeling. In A. Phakiti, P. De Costa, L. Plonsky, & S. Starfield (Eds.), *The Palgrave handbook of applied linguistics research methodology* (pp. 459–500). Palgrave.
Phakiti, A., Hirsh, D., & Woodrow, L. (2013). It is not only English: Roles of other learner factors on English language learning and academic learning of ESL international students in Australia. *Journal of Research in International Education, 12*(3), 239–258. https://doi.org/10.1177/1475240913513520
Raykov, T., & Marcoulides, G. A. (2019). Thanks coefficient Alpha, we still need you! *Educational and Psychological Measurement, 79*(1), 200–210. https://doi.org/10.1177/0013164417725127
Roever, R., & Phakiti, A. (2018). *Quantitative methods for second language research: A problem-solving approach*. Routledge.
Sardegna, V. G. (2009). *Improving English stress through pronunciation learning strategies* (Unpublished doctoral dissertation). University of Illinois at Urbana-Champaign.
Sardegna, V. G., Lee, J., & Kusey, C. (2018). Self-efficacy, attitudes, and choice of strategies for English pronunciation learning. *Language Learning, 68*(1), 83–114. https://doi.org/10.1111/lang.12263
Sterling, S., & De Costa, P. (2018). Ethical applied linguistics research. In A. Phakiti, P. De Costa, L. Plonsky, & S. Starfield (Eds.), *The Palgrave handbook of applied linguistics research methodology* (pp. 163–182). Palgrave.
VanPatten, B., & Williams, J. (2015). *Theories in second language acquisition: An introduction* (2nd ed.). Routledge.

11

Pilot Testing

Why and How We Trial

Rita Green

Background

Trialing is an activity which should take place once an instrument such as a set of language test items or a survey questionnaire has been developed whether for SLA research or language assessment purposes. This procedure is variously referred to as *piloting* or *field testing* and some researchers further define it as *pre-trial, main trial or pilot study*. Although much published research refers to trialing as an integral part of research and high-stakes testing, there is little systematic explanation about the necessary steps which should be observed in each part of the procedure.

The aim of trialing is to collect empirical evidence of an instrument's suitability for measuring the targeted attribute, for example, a person's ability to read in English. To do this appropriately, the trial population must reflect the characteristics of the target test population to whom the instrument will be administered. Such attributes as age, gender, geographical location, and ethnic group among others need to be taken into consideration as well as the conditions under which the instrument is trialed. The latter might involve the amount of time provided, the mode of delivery (online versus paper-and-pencil), access to resources such as dictionaries, spell-checkers and so on.

A trial should only take place after a number of crucial stages in the development cycle have been completed including the writing of detailed specifications which outline the construct and how the items are to be developed, as well as describing the procedures for moderation and revision (see Green, 2017, p. 21; also see Green & Fulcher, Chapter 7, this volume).

Key Concepts

Trial: A procedure used to collect empirical evidence of an instrument's suitability for measuring the targeted attribute or construct. [Note that terms such as *pilot* or *field test* are also used.]

Test specifications: A document which describes the intended instrument in detail, and which should be modified until the test design becomes stable. This can take between two and three years.

Item writer guidelines: A document which translates the test specifications into more precise and practical instructions for item writers, to help them produce the intended items and tasks.

Test booklet: A compilation of tasks—whether in paper or online format—representing a (pilot) version of the test, and which is presented to (pilot) test-takers.

Construct: In language testing, this refers to the language knowledge, skills, or abilities which are being targeted, e.g., in a listening test this might include the ability to infer a speaker's attitude, to identify specific information, to understand the main ideas and so on.

Validity: In language testing, a measure of the appropriateness, meaningfulness and usefulness of the inferences drawn, on the basis of test scores, about a test-taker's language ability. [Also see Chapelle, Chapter 2, this volume]

Reliability: In language testing, a measure of accuracy and consistency of measurement.

Key Issues

Why Do We Trial?

Despite all the care which goes into developing an instrument or a set of tasks, it can never be guaranteed to produce valid and reliable results for the target population. It is only when the instrument has been trialed, and the resulting empirical data analyzed, that there can be any evidence to support (or counter) such claims (see Alderson et al., 1995, p. 73).

The empirical evidence which trials produce enables us to obtain a clear picture of how successful the instrument has been in targeting the intended construct and helps us to identify ways of improving its future performance (see Ruel et al., 2016). Very few instruments work perfectly the first time they are trialed, and researchers should be prepared to revise the instrument after the first and even the second trial.

Trialing is generally perceived as part of the quality control that all tests should go through and is widely considered to be a key component of good testing practice (see EALTA, n.d.; ILTA Guidelines, n.d.; Rothgeb, 2008). Trials can range from small scale, what Fulcher (2010, p. 174) refers to as beta prototyping, with perhaps as few as 5 or 6 test-takers, to large-scale trials involving upwards of 300 test-takers. Where numbers are very small (fewer than 30), the data can only be analyzed from a qualitative point of view as any findings could have occurred by chance and might not be repeated with another such population. With larger numbers the findings are likely to be more stable as the "distribution is most likely to approximate a curve of normal distribution" (Fulcher, 2010, p. 180). With larger numbers, both quantitative and qualitative statistics can be collected, for example, the test-takers' responses to a set of tasks, and the respondents' endorsements to a particular questionnaire or survey. The size of a trial might also relate to what is being targeted. For example, where writing or speaking skills are being measured, it often makes sense to initially trial the instrument on a smaller number of test-takers to ascertain that the instructions are clear and that the tasks are capable of generating sufficient language to enable the test-takers to produce a ratable sample.

Despite its crucial importance in determining whether an instrument is suitable for measuring a particular attribute, there are many tests and questionnaires which are simply never trialed. Reasons can include lack of resources, or simply a lack of awareness of the need for instrument piloting and validation. Another common argument put forward is test security. While it is acknowledged that trials must be carried out with the utmost care if the instruments are to be used in future high-stakes situations, numerous project presentations at international language testing conferences have shown that this is feasible (see e.g., Green & Spöttl, 2009, 2011). An important factor in successful trialing is ensuring that the tools are trialed in advance of when they are needed. For example, a trial administered to school leavers in 2025 should be for use in the actual school-leaving exam in 2026 or 2027 at the earliest, thus minimizing any security concerns while simultaneously being able to target the correct test population (in terms of age, ability etc.). Trialing different sets of tasks in different places is another frequently-used solution. Without trialing, the test developer or researcher is quite simply working blind.

Insights That Trials Can Provide

Trials offer many benefits to the test developer or researcher which are explored below

Test Specifications. There should be a direct link between the instrument being trialed and the test specifications, such that it is possible to match every item in a test or questionnaire, or attribute described in a rating scale, to its related construct. For example, one should be able to plot each item in a CEFR (Common European Framework of Reference) B2 test to at least one of the language performance descriptors which make up that level (see Council of Europe, 2001, 2020). Where this cannot be done, there is a relatively high chance that the construct validity of that particular item is questionable. This mismatch often manifests itself in situations where the resulting facility values (see below) are much lower or higher than expected by the researcher. An analysis of the items concerned often reveals that the offending item requires the test-taker to understand something in the text or sound file which does not match the targeted difficulty level, or which is unrelated to the actual construct being targeted.

The actual development of both the test specifications and the item writing guidelines can also benefit from trials. For example, the issue of how much time should be allowed, how many times a sound file should be heard, which particular test methods are appropriate and how many words a particular writing task requires can all be investigated by means of the trial. The resulting data should help to confirm (or refute) decisions taken in the process of developing the specifications and help identify any necessary adjustments (see Bachman & Palmer, 1996, p. 235).

Test Instructions. Unexpected test-taker responses to trialed items and tasks can sometimes be traced back to inadequate or ambiguous instructions. Take for example a reading task based on several short texts in which the test-takers must match the texts with each of the questions. If the instructions fail to include the phrase "You can use a text once only," the test-takers might easily select a text more than once even though this was not the original intention. Another example can be seen in short-answer questions where the researcher has failed to limit the maximum number of words. In this scenario some test-takers may copy complete sentences, thus making it more difficult to determine whether they really did know the answer or were simply guessing. Trialing makes it possible to identify and remove these ambiguities before the test reaches the operational stage thus potentially increasing the validity and reliability of the test scores.

Test Methods. By including a range of different test methods, for example, multiple-choice, short-answer questions, multiple-matching, and true-false-justification items, it is possible for the researcher to analyze how each method is working. To expand, imagine a situation where all the reading tasks are purporting to target one ability level, such as CEFR B2, and where the topics are felt to be equally accessible to the target test population. Using a range of test methods, it can be ascertained which test method the test-takers found the easiest and the most difficult by looking at the item's facility values (see below). When interpreting the findings, care should also be taken to factor in the test-takers' likely familiarity with the particular test method, the varying demands of selected-response versus constructed-response tasks (see e.g., In'nami & Koizumi, 2009) as well as the construct being targeted (inferring propositional meaning versus identifying specific information), since these could also have impacted on the test-takers' performance.

Where more than 10 per cent of the test-takers fail to attempt an answer, this might be interpreted to suggest that the test-takers were less familiar with this method (see Green, 2013). However, this finding could also be due to issues such as ambiguous instructions, insufficient time, the speed of delivery (sound file), the density/difficulty level of the text and/or even issues with the answer key. When analyzing trial data, researchers must be prepared to work through, and systematically eliminate, a wide range of possibilities before being able to identify the most likely reason for a high per cent of unanswered items.

Stakeholder Feedback. Wherever possible, those participating in the trial should be asked to complete a questionnaire to gather insights into their perceptions regarding the instrument being trialed. Where the trial population is large and/or resources are limited, a random selection of the subjects is acceptable provided it is representative of the test population at large. The resulting data can provide insights into task difficulty, the clarity of the instructions, topic accessibility, test method familiarity, and the extent to which the tasks are felt to reflect a good measure of the construct being targeted, for example, listening at CEFR B2 (see Bachman & Palmer, 1996, p. 237). Trials are also a useful resource for feedback to item writers (see Geranpayeh & Taylor, 2013, p. 400).

Recommendations for Practice

Trial Preparation

In order to enhance the possibility of a valid and reliable outcome, there are a range of issues which need to be taken into consideration before a trial can take place.

Identification of the Trial Test Population. This step is crucial. If an inappropriate trial population is selected it will skew both the findings and any subsequent interpretations with likely implications for the validity of the trial and the instrument. The participants must reflect as closely as possible those to whom the instrument will ultimately be given. The trial population should be representative in terms of age, gender, first language (where relevant), ability, geographical location, socio-economical background and ethnic diversity (see Alderson et al., 1995, p. 76). It should also be administered to a sufficient number of test-takers in order to make it feasible to run the required statistical analyses on the resulting data (see below).

Importance of Trial Timing. Timing is vital. If the test-takers are not at the appropriate point in their learning cycle when they take part in the trial, the items and tasks may not perform in the way which the researchers expect. Administering a trial shortly, say two months, before the administration of the operational test is likely to capture higher levels of motivation in the subjects as they can see a real purpose in participating in the trial. Such incentive is likely to result in fewer spoiled papers (due to insincere responses) and unanswered items.

Test-taker incentive is a common challenge which researchers face when organizing a trial; finding ways which encourage subjects to take the exercise sincerely, when it invariably has little or no-stakes for them, is not an easy task. In most circumstances it is also impossible to provide performance feedback to individuals as the items, tasks, and/or scale are usually in the process of being validated thus making it inappropriate to report any findings to the participants.

Selection of Tasks for the Trial. It is important to maximize the opportunities which a trial offers by piloting a wide range of tasks exhibiting different text genres, topics and test methods. This should also help to minimize any possible test method effect or subject bias in terms of gender, geographical location (rural versus urban test populations) and ethnic diversity.

Tasks which have been chosen for the trial should have gone through all the necessary test development stages including peer and expert review (see Green & Fulcher, Chapter 7, this volume). Trialing tasks which are still potentially problematic, for example in terms of the targeted construct, in the hope that they will work, is a very poor use of expensive resources. On the other hand, one of the many advantages of administering a trial is to experiment with new task types to see if they will work. For example, requiring a blog response for the first time in a writing trial, will provide useful insights into whether this is a feasible alternative to add to the range of writing tasks.

Preparation of Trial Booklets. A number of issues need to be taken into account when compiling a test booklet. For example, most test-takers feel some degree of anxiety when sitting a test or taking part in a research study. Although this is likely to be lower in a low or no-stakes situation, it still makes sense to start with a task which is perceived to be slightly easier. In this way, test-taker performance may be less adversely impacted by anxiety, and motivation encouraged. Even when developing a test targeting one difficulty level, for example CEFR B1, it might be argued that some tasks are perceived to be "easier" B1 tasks than others possibly due to the perceived topic accessibility, test method familiarity or the type of construct being targeted.

In order to be able to make claims about a test-takers' ability at a particular level, the trial booklet, like an operational test booklet, must include tasks which reflect a representative sample of the different types of behavior related to that level. This will necessarily vary depending on the difficulty level; compare, for example, what a reader at CEFR A1 can do with one who is at CEFR C1. All tasks should be standardized in terms of their layout and the language used in the instructions so as not to confuse or mislead the test-takers.

Preparation of Key and Rating Scales. In order to expedite the marking of constructed-response items which require test-takers to write an answer, an extensive key should be developed even at the pre-trial stage. It is impossible to predict all the answers that might surface during the trial, particularly for those items which focus on main ideas comprehension as these may be formulated in a number of ways. However, spending time on drafting a list of viable answers will help clarify in the researcher's/test developer's mind how well the construct has been reflected in the item. Simultaneously, a list of non-acceptable answers can be developed. The key for the selected response items such as multiple-choice, multiple-matching, or true-false-not given, while obviously much more straightforward, must be carefully drawn up and verified to ensure there is only one answer (multiple-choice and true-false-not given).

In order to grade any productive tasks such as writing and speaking, a rating scale which reflects the construct outlined in the test specifications must be drafted and trialed. Care must be taken to ensure that the various performance levels are demonstrably different so that they can be used independently of each other. Any ambiguities and/or infelicities which might lead to different interpretations by individual raters must be removed before piloting to optimize the usefulness of the trial.

Role of the Feedback Questionnaire. Questionnaires can be extremely useful in obtaining insights from participants and test administrators, regarding how well the trialed tasks and procedures have worked (see Bachman & Palmer, 1996, pp. 239–245). Piloting feedback questionnaires during the trial makes it possible to check for any ambiguities and to ensure that the questions provide useful information in terms of the research questions being explored. The revised questionnaire can then be used in operational testing.

Depending on the linguistic ability of the participants, some questionnaires will need to be translated into one (or more) of the local languages. Where this happens care must be taken to ensure that the translation is as close as possible to that of the original and that there is no overlap between any Likert scale categories which might lead to reliability issues (see Ruel et al., 2016, p. 113). In addition, some cultures are less familiar with the concept of feedback questionnaires and it may therefore be necessary to explain why they are being given as well as how the resulting data will be used.

Training of Test Administrators and Interlocutors. Those conducting the trial, whether research assistants or test administrators, should receive training before the trial takes place so that they understand the objectives and the procedures which must be followed. This is particularly crucial in those situations where the trial will be administered in a number of different locations. If assistants or test administrators are not consistent in delivering the trial papers or do it in a manner that is not intended by the instrument developers, the resulting data will be meaningless. Detailed guidelines should be drawn up to ensure consistent test administration which reflects that of the proposed live test (see ALTE, 2011, p. 30).

In particular when high-stakes tests are trialed, the administration guidelines should also include a checklist of the materials, equipment, and contingency plans in preparation for the unexpected, for example, a power outage in a remote area. The room arrangements should be checked well before the trial takes place to ensure that there is sufficient light for the test-takers to work in, that the amount of desk space is commensurate with the papers the test-takers will handle and, from a security point of view, that the space between the desks minimizes any possibility of cheating occurring. Where tests or questionnaires are to be delivered online, the quality of the computers and internet providers must be established as well as the number of computers or tablets available. Care must be taken to ensure that external noise (roads, school bells, movement of large numbers of people during breaks if the trial is held in a school) will not impact on participants' performance particularly in such tests which involve listening or speaking.

Guidelines should also be provided regarding how the test paper should be distributed (for example, face down) so as to avoid those at the front of the test room having more time than those at the rear; what information the test-takers need to complete on the test booklet/accompanying papers such as answer sheets; and how the papers will be collected at the end of the test. In addition, the administrators need to be clear about any announcements which should be given during the test, for example, "you now have 30 minutes left." These measures not only help ensure the validity and reliability of the trial, but also act as a trial of the administration procedures themselves in preparation for the operational testing stage.

Training must also be given to interlocutors involved in delivering speaking tests. Their role must be clearly defined (interlocutor versus interlocutor/assessor) and their familiarity with the targeted construct and criteria of assessment determined through training. Detailed guidelines should be drawn up to ensure that the language used by the interlocutor is appropriate in terms of difficulty, and that the same procedure is followed across test administrations (see Fulcher, 2003, pp. 147–155).

Post-Trial Considerations

Marking and Rater Training. The people who will be rating the trial performances must be trained, for example, in terms of what constitutes an acceptable or non-acceptable answer in those items which require the participants to use their own wording (e.g., short-answer questions). The raters should also be aware of what procedure to follow should an unexpected, but apparently feasible, answer appear in the trialed papers. Where multiple raters are involved, the rater who has come across an unexpected response should contact the chief rater and ask about the answer's viability. Where it is deemed acceptable, all other raters must be notified, and asked to review those papers which have already been marked in case the answer has already appeared but been marked as unacceptable. Where it is not accepted as an alternative response, it should be added to the non-acceptable list to save time in the event of it occurring again. This will help establish a more comprehensive answer key for the main administration, as well as helping to review the proposed rating procedures.

Where rating scales are employed in the evaluation of writing and speaking performances, training sessions should be carried out shortly before the trialed performances are graded. The purpose of this session is two-fold. Firstly, the raters need to be (re)familiarized with the demands of the various tasks so as to minimize any individual interpretation over such issues as task fulfilment. Secondly, the raters should be asked to grade a number of performances. This can best be affected by asking the chief rater to identify some potential benchmarks. For example, if the rating scale consists of three levels purporting to reflect a good performance, a minimal pass performance and a fail performance, then performances reflecting those three levels should be identified first. If at all possible, two should be selected for each type of performance as they might differ in particular characteristics. For example, one fail performance could be primarily due to task fulfilment issues, while another could be due to linguistic ones. Using these "benchmark performances" with the group of raters, will help to establish the range of characteristics needed to meet the requirements of each level of the rating scale. It may also help to identify any unforeseen ambiguities in the scale before the raters work on further performances. All of the above recommendations will benefit the validity and reliability of the scores awarded during the trial, and by extension will benefit the conclusions drawn up about the trial as a whole. (For more on rating scales and rater training, see Kuiken & Vedder, Chapter 12; Pill & Smart, Chapter 13, this volume.)

Data Entry. In general, data should be entered at the lowest possible denominator. For example, with tasks such as reading, listening, and language in use, the data should be at the item level. For instance, letters (ABCDE…X) should be entered for the selected-response type tasks and numbers 0/1/9 (incorrect-correct-no answer) for the constructed-response ones. In programs such as IBM SPSS® (Statistical Package for Social Sciences), alphanumeric data can easily be recoded into numerical data (see Green, 2013; Pallant, 2020). Great care must be taken to ensure there are no mistakes during data entry as this will obviously impact on the findings.

Using "9" as the default for "no answers" in constructed-response tasks, and "x" for selected-response ones, is a very useful procedure to follow at the trial stage. A 10 per cent return of "no answers" on a particular item might suggest a problem with the item, the text and/or the sound file and should be investigated further. Such a finding could also be symptomatic of the trial participants not having had sufficient time to complete the items which could mean that either the test-takers or items were not at the targeted level or that insufficient time had been allowed during the pilot. Both scenarios require further analysis by the researchers.

With writing and speaking tasks, data entry should be at the level of the criteria of assessment used in the rating scale where an analytic scale has been employed. For example, when assessing a writing performance, the grades awarded for task fulfilment, organization, range of vocabulary, and grammatical structures should be entered individually. Having data at this level makes it possible to run more analyses (see below) than would be otherwise possible with data which is entered at purely the overall grade level.

Statistical Analyses

Facility Values. The types of statistical analyses which should be run on the collated trial data depend very much on the research questions you want to answer or investigate. Having said this, whether you use a classical statistical package such as IBM SPSS® or a modern/item response theory program such as Winsteps® or Facets® (Linacre, 2019), the first analysis you will probably want to run is one which will tell you about the difficulty level of the items or tasks or, in the case of survey data, how many respondents have endorsed each of the categories. Due to the constraints of this chapter, my comments here will relate purely to running analyses on test data using IBM SPSS®. For insights into how to run basic statistical analyses in Winsteps® and Facets® see Green (2013).

In IBM SPSS®, in order to ascertain the difficulty level of each of the trialed items, select the Analyze menu followed by the option called Frequencies. Running this analysis on both the ABCD data (for example, selected-response multiple-choice items) and the zero/one data (constructed-response type items such as short-answer questions) will reveal a number of useful pieces of information. Firstly, it will reveal the difficulty level or facility value for each item which can be compared to the original test developer's estimate. Secondly, the Frequencies analysis will indicate which options the participants selected, and which ones were ignored or only received a small number of endorsements. For example, in the multiple-choice item in Figure 11.1, it can be seen that very few participants selected options B, C, and D, and that the facility value (option A) was very high at 93 per cent:

	Frequency	Percent
A	95	93.1
B	3	2.9
C	1	1.0
D	3	2.9
Total	102	100.0

Figure 11.1 Frequencies.

In multiple-choice items, all distractors are expected to be endorsed by a certain per cent of the test population otherwise they are considered as not fulfilling their function. Green (2013) cites 7 per cent as the minimum threshold in proficiency test items so in the example above, none of the distractors would be classified as working. In an achievement test, the situation is different as, put simply, the purpose of such tests is to check whether the students have grasped what has been taught. Where this has been successful, the facility values are expected to be high with consequent low distractor values. The third piece of information the Frequencies analysis will provide is the number of unanswered cases associated with each item.

Discrimination. The second analysis you would probably want to run is discrimination in order to check whether the items have separated the stronger participants (in terms of language ability) from the weaker ones in a positive way. This procedure can be found under SCALE in the IBM SPSS® Analyze menu, followed by Reliability Analysis. Figure 11.2, which is based on a 7-item listening task, shows an example of the type of output this analysis produces:

The generally accepted convention is that items with discrimination indices of +.3 and above are felt to be separating the test-takers in a positive way (see the column "Corrected item-total correlation" which provides the point-biserial correlation coefficient).

Internal Consistency. The same SCALE procedure also produces information about the extent to which the items might be considered as "fitting" together that is, targeting the same construct. One of the several types of internal consistency provided by IBM SPSS® is shown in Figure 11.3.

In order to determine whether all the items appear to be measuring the same construct these figures need to be compared with the overall Cronbach's alpha for the task (or questionnaire). In this test, the overall alpha was .768. Where the item's CAID value (Cronbach's Alpha if Item Deleted) is greater than the overall alpha, as is the case in Q3, the item should be reviewed to verify that the construct being targeted is the same as the other items. This is a very useful tool in investigating the construct validity of the instrument under trial.

	Mean	Corrected Item-Total Correlation	N
Q1	.7877	.559	146
Q2	.8356	.430	146
Q3	.7055	.335	146
Q4	.8151	.529	146
Q5	.6096	.460	146
Q6	.8973	.631	146
Q7	.8425	.570	146

Figure 11.2 Discrimination (CITC).

	Mean	Corrected Item-Total Correlation	Cronbach's Alpha if Item Deleted	N
Q1	.7877	.559	.723	146
Q2	.8356	.430	.750	146
Q3	.7055	.335	.775	146
Q4	.8151	.529	.730	146
Q5	.6096	.460	.749	146
Q6	.8973	.631	.720	146
Q7	.8425	.570	.723	146

Figure 11.3 Internal consistency (CAID).

For other statistical analyses which can be used in examining trial data please see such works as Field (2018), Pallant (2020) and Green (2013).

Trialing Tips

- Only trial tasks which conform with your test specifications (construct and performance conditions).
- Include a range of tasks, topics and genres to minimize any possible bias.
- Pay special attention to identifying the test population.
- Develop detailed answer keys (receptive skills) and appropriate rating scales which reflect your construct (productive skills).
- Develop feedback questionnaires to gain insights from stakeholders.
- Develop test administration guidelines and carry-out training of test administrators.
- Train both interlocutors and raters in delivering and grading procedures.

Recommended Readings

Fulcher, G. (2010). *Practical language testing.* Taylor & Francis.

Chapter 6 provides useful insights into the procedures which should be followed before, during, and after the trial administration. The author usefully differentiates between the purposes of a number of different types of trials. The chapter concludes with an explanation of how to calculate the statistics related to item analysis and how the findings should be interpreted.

Green, R. (2013). *Statistical analyses for language testers.* Palgrave MacMillan.

This book provides clear guidelines on how to carry out analyses post-trial. It introduces the reader to two key statistical approaches: classical and modern test theory using the programs IBM SPSS® and Winsteps® & Facets® respectively.

Green, R. (2017). *Designing listening tests: A practical approach.*

Chapter 6 provides an in-depth analysis of the various stages involved in the role trials play in determining whether a listening task works.

References

Alderson, J. C., Clapham, C., & Wall, D. (1995). *Language test construction and evaluation*. Cambridge University Press.
ALTE. (2011). *Manual for language test development and examining*. Council of Europe. https://www.coe.int/en/web/common-european-framework-reference-languages/developing-tests-examining
Bachman, L. F., & Palmer, A. S. (1996). *Language testing in practice*. Oxford University Press.
Council of Europe. (2001). *Common European framework of reference for languages: Learning, teaching and assessment*. Cambridge University Press. https://rm.coe.int/1680459f97
Council of Europe. (2020). Common European framework of reference for languages: Learning, teaching and assessment. Companion Volume. Council of Europe. https://rm.coe.int/common-european-framework-of-reference-for-languages-learning-teaching/16809ea0d4
EALTA. (n.d.). *EALTA guidelines for good practice in language testing and assessment*. http://www.ealta.eu.org/documents/archive/guidelines/English.pdf
Field, A. (2018). *Discovering statistics by using IBM SPSS statistics* (3rd ed.). SAGE Publications.
Fulcher, G. (2003). *Testing second language speaking*. Pearson Education.
Fulcher, G. (2010). *Practical language testing*. Taylor & Francis.
Geranpayeh, A., & Taylor, L. (Eds.). (2013). *Examining listening: Research and practice in assessing second language listening (Studies in language testing)*. Cambridge University Press.
Green, R. (2013). *Statistical analyses for language testers*. Palgrave MacMillan.
Green, R. (2017). *Designing listening tests: A practical approach*. Palgrave MacMillan.
Green, R., & Spöttl, C. (2009, June). *Going national, standardised and live in Austria: Challenges and tensions* [Paper presentation]. European Association for Language Testing and Assessment (EALTA) conference, Turku, Finland.
Green, R., & Spöttl, C. (2011, May). *Building up a pool of standard setting judges: Problems, solutions and insights* [Paper presentation]. European Association for Language Testing and Assessment (EALTA) conference, Siena, Italy.
In'nami, Y., & Koizumi, R. (2009). A meta-analysis of test format effects on reading and listening test performance: Focus on multiple-choice and open-ended formats. *Language Testing*, *26*(2), 219–244. https://doi.org/10.1177/0265532208101006
International Language Testing Association (ILTA). (n.d.). *ILTA guidelines for practice*. https://www.iltaonline.com/page/ITLAGuidelinesforPra
Linacre, J. M. (2019). *Winsteps ® Rasch measurement computer program*. https://www.winsteps.com
Pallant, J. (2020). *SPSS survival manual* (7th ed.). Routledge.
Rothgeb, J. M. (2008). Pilot test. In P. J. Lavrakas (Ed.), *Encyclopedia of survey research methods*. SAGE Publications.
Ruel, E., Wagner, W. E., & Gillespie, B. J. (2016). *The practice of survey research*. SAGE Publications.

12
Scoring Approaches
Scales/Rubrics

Folkert Kuiken & Ineke Vedder

Background

Language learners are often eager to know how proficient they are in speaking or writing a particular language. Also, teachers want to be able to assess accurately and reliably the proficiency level of their learners (Leclerq et al., 2014). Language proficiency can be expressed in simple terms like adequate/inadequate, sufficient/insufficient, pass/fail, etc. Although such terms seem to be straightforward and easy to use, they do not tell us exactly how well learners perform at a particular stage in their acquisition process. For this reason, "simple" ways of arriving at a score for language proficiency have developed into more complex systems for assessing second language (L2) proficiency, such as rubrics or scales, containing various bands or level descriptors.

In our definition of a rating scale, we follow Davies et al. (1999) who characterize a rating scale as "a scale for the description of language proficiency consisting of a series of constructed levels against which a language learner's performance is judged" (p.153). Typically, scales range from zero mastery via partial mastery to full mastery. A proficiency band or level allows some variation, but still, a given level has some characteristics that distinguish it from the level below and the one above. Band descriptors "describe in words performances that illustrate each level of competence defined on the scale" (McNamara, 2000, p. 40).

In the literature rating scales and scoring rubrics are synonymous, with the term rubric being used more often in North American contexts; in what follows we will use the term (rating) scale. As Davies et al. (1999) advocate, scales and descriptors "are not in themselves test instruments and need to be used in conjunction with tests appropriate to the population and test purpose" (pp. 153–154). It is thus important to keep in mind that any score in language assessment is the outcome of an interaction that involves not only the test-taker and the test, but also the prompt or task, the performance itself, the rater, the rating scale, the construct to be measured, and the theory on which the scale is based (Bygate, 2011; Weigle, 2002).

In what follows we discuss which type of scale is suitable for a particular purpose and what the descriptors of a scale should look like. We stress the importance of good-quality rating scales, taking into consideration reliability, validity, and practicality in use of the instrument. We then zoom in on the assessment of speaking and writing viewed from the perspective of second language acquisition (SLA), with a focus on complexity, accuracy, and fluency (CAF). Special attention is paid to the spoken and written performance elicited by means of real-world tasks, on the basis of two studies conducted within the framework of task-based language assessment (TBLA).

Key Concepts

***Rating scale/rubric*:** "[A] series of ascending bands of proficiency" against which language performances are judged. "It may cover the whole conceptual range of learner proficiency, or it may just cover the range of proficiency relevant to the sector or institution concerned" (Council of Europe, 2001, p. 40).

***Rating criteria*:** Aspects of the construct in terms of which a test-taker's performance will be evaluated, e.g., task achievement, linguistic accuracy, organization, fluency, etc.

***Scoring band*:** A level in a rating scale which describes the specific extent to which a language learner can do something in the language and what the linguistic features are of their language use. A rating scale comprises multiple bands.

***Descriptor*:** A statement that stipulates the characteristics of a language performance at a particular band level. A scoring band comprises one or more descriptors per rating criterion.

Key Issues

Several classifications of rating scales have been proposed. The most commonly cited categorization, with respect to type of scoring, is that of holistic versus analytic scales (Hamp-Lyons, 1991; Weigle, 2002). According to the way scales are constructed, so-called intuitive methods can be distinguished from empirical methods (Fulcher, 2003). Other possible distinctions are those between norm-referenced and criterion-referenced scales (Bachman & Palmer, 1996; Luoma, 2004) or between task-dependent and task-independent scales (Brown et al., 2002). Over the years, the advantages and disadvantages of each type, in terms of reliability, validity, and practicality, have been debated.

Holistic Versus Analytic Scales and Scoring Approaches

In essence, the distinction between holistic and analytic scales depends on the question whether a single—holistic—score is given to a task performance, or whether several features of performance are scored separately. Different types of holistic assessment are often distinguished: holistic scoring, primary-trait scoring and multiple-trait scoring. Because the latter partly overlaps with analytic scoring—as demonstrated by Weigle (2002)—in this chapter the two are combined.

Holistic Scoring. In holistic scoring a single score is assigned to a speech or text sample based on the overall impression of the performance. This score is given either impressionistically, or on the basis of a rating scale. An example of holistic scoring is the rating approach used for the TOEFL iBT® Writing Test, with scales that contain one holistic descriptor of the syntactic and rhetorical characteristics at each of six levels of writing proficiency. Figure 12.1 shows the lowest (0) and highest (5) level descriptors of the test's integrated-writing scale.

In the literature numerous advantages of holistic scoring have been mentioned (e.g., Fulcher, 2003; Knoch, 2011): fast and easy to use, and practical for decision-making because it only gives one score. It is flexible in that it allows many different combinations of strengths and weaknesses within a level. There are, however, also some disadvantages linked to holistic scoring (e.g., Bachman & Palmer, 1996). Probably the most important one is that a single score does not allow raters to distinguish between various aspects of speaking or writing, and therefore does not provide useful diagnostic information about a test-taker's speaking or writing ability. Holistic scores are also not always easy to interpret, as raters do not necessarily use the same criteria to arrive at the same judgments. For that reason it may be more difficult to obtain high rater reliability in holistic scoring (Ohta et al., 2018).

0	A response at this level merely copies sentences from the reading, rejects the topic or is otherwise not connected to the topic, is written in a foreign language, consists of keystroke characters, or is blank.
5	A response at this level successfully selects the important information from the lecture and coherently and accurately presents this information in relation to the relevant information presented in the reading. The response is well organized, and occasional language errors that are present do not result in inaccurate or imprecise presentation of content or connections.

Figure 12.1 Level 0 and 5 of TOEFL iBT® test integrated writing rubrics (ETS, 2019).

Primary-Trait Scoring. Similar to holistic scoring, in primary-trait scoring a single score is allocated to a performance, but the scoring procedure is specifically designed for each individual task, or class of tasks, and the rating scale is defined with respect to the specific speaking or writing assignment. Primary-trait scoring includes a description of the task to perform, a statement of the primary-trait (construct) to be measured, a rating scale with level descriptors, samples of performance to illustrate each level, and explanations of why each sample was graded in the way it was (Weigle, 2002). An example of primary-trait scoring can be found in Lloyd-Jones (1977), where students are submitted to a narrative writing task: They receive a picture based on which they have to describe to a good friend what is happening from the perspective of one of the people in the picture. The resulting text is scored on four categories: overall judgment of the performed task, use of dialogue, point of view expressed in the performance, and use of tense.

The advantage of primary-trait scoring is that very careful and explicit statements are made with respect to a specific task. On the negative side, the process of primary-trait scoring is often long and complex, as each task or task type requires the development of a specific rating scale. The score also provides information about the ability of the student to perform that particular task or type of tasks only, rather than tasks in general. This means that the gain in explicitness and a stronger validity are offset against a reduction in the generalizability of the meaning the score provides (Fulcher & Davidson, 2007).

Multiple-Trait and Analytic Scoring. Multiple-trait and analytic scoring have in common that language performance is rated separately on several aspects or criteria. For that reason, as already mentioned, Weigle (2002) does not distinguish between multiple-trait and analytic scoring. Although we agree with Hamp-Lyons (2016) that multiple-trait scoring is not identical to analytic scoring, we follow Weigle's line of reasoning, as differences between the two scoring methods have more to do with procedures for developing and using the scales, rather than with characteristics of the scales themselves. Multiple-trait scoring is, so to say, on the edge of holistic scoring as discussed above and analytic assessment.

In multiple-trait or analytic scoring each score is representative of some performance feature or construct underlying performance. For example, in rating speaking fluency, raters may be asked to provide separate assessments of pausing behavior, repetitions, repairs, and the like. Analytic scales contain a number of criteria, usually three to five (Luoma, 2004, p. 68), each of which have descriptors at the different levels of the scale. For instance, in the ESL Composition Profile (Jacobs et al., 1981) texts are rated on five aspects of writing: content, organization, vocabulary, language use and mechanics, with multiple scoring criteria, each with their own descriptors (see Figure 12.2 for the scoring of content).

Probably the most cited advantage of multiple-trait or analytic scales is that they provide more specific information about learners' language proficiency and are therefore more reliable (see e.g., Hamp-Lyons, 2016). The explicit descriptors provide detailed guidance to raters to evaluate specific strengths and weaknesses of a learner's performance. This leads to more diagnostic

	Score	Descriptors
Content	30-27	EXCELLENT TO VERY GOOD: knowledgeable – substantive – thorough development of thesis – relevant to assigned topic
	26-22	GOOD TO AVERAGE: some knowledge of subject – adequate range – limited development of thesis – mostly relevant to topic, but lacks detail
	21-17	FAIR TO POOR: limited knowledge of subject – little substance – inadequate development of topic
	16-13	VERY POOR: does not show knowledge of subject – non-substantive – not pertinent – OR not enough to evaluate

Figure 12.2 Scoring of content in the ESL composition profile (Jacobs et al., 1981).

information about their abilities. As the scales comprise more detailed descriptors, inexperienced raters can more easily understand and apply the criteria. A drawback of this type of scaling is that it takes longer to evaluate the testees' performances (Weigle, 2002).

Other Possible Distinctions

Rating scales can also be categorized according to the way they are constructed. From that perspective, intuitively developed rating scales are distinguished from empirically based rating scales. Other distinctions concern norm-referenced versus criterion-referenced scales and task-dependent versus task-independent scales.

Intuitively Developed Scales Versus Empirically Based Scales. An intuitively developed scale is designed on the basis of what scale developers consider to be common features at various levels of proficiency. The scale may be developed by either an experienced teacher or language tester, starting with expert judgments, followed by elaboration and refinement by those who use it.

In recent years, several researchers have proposed that scales should be developed based on empirical methods, which can be done in different ways (Fulcher, 2003). For example, the scale may be data-based or data-driven, with bands and descriptors developed on the basis of the features observed by experts in a set of learner data. Another option is an Empirically Based Boundary definition (EBB) scale, where experts divide language samples into better or poorer performances and then develop a sequence of yes/no questions that characterize differences between the performance sets. These questions are then used as scoring guidelines by the raters (e.g., Does the writer display comfort with the use of English? No—Level 1 or below; Yes—Level 2 or 3 ⟶ Can the writer sustain an argument? No—Level 2; Yes—Level 3; see e.g., Ewert & Shin, 2015).

Nowadays, mixed-methods approaches (intuitive—qualitative—quantitative) are increasingly used for the development of rating scales (Green & Hawkey, 2012). For instance, in a study by Chan et al. (2015) on developing a rating tool to assess reading-into-writing skills, methodologies used included a questionnaire, expert panel judgment, group interview, automated textual analysis and analysis of rater reliability.

Norm-Referenced Versus Criterion-Referenced Scales. An issue relevant to scale design is whether the scale should be norm-referenced or criterion-referenced (Bachman & Palmer, 1996; Luoma, 2004). Norm-referenced scales allow comparison of learner performances against each other or against standards set by a norming group. Criterion-referenced scales imply comparison against some external criterion (e.g., the ability to perform a certain job). The latter allow test users to make inferences about how much language ability a test-taker has, rather than how well (s)he performs relative to other individuals (which constitutes norm-referencing).

Task-Dependent Versus Task-Independent Scales. Another distinction between scales is made by Brown et al. (2002) with respect to task-based performance. They distinguish between task-dependent scales—which they consider to be inefficient, as an entire domain of tasks has to be tested one-by-one, and task-independent scales—which estimate the learners' abilities to accomplish similar other tasks. Examples of both types are provided in the section "Recommendations for practice."

No One Best Scale Type. Presented as such, the above-described rating scales all seem to constitute a dichotomy and suggest sharp contrasts. In reality, however, most scales are often positioned on a continuum somewhere in between the two scale extremities. Another important point to note is that the choice for a particular rating scale—whether holistic or analytic, intuitively developed or empirically based, task-dependent or task-independent, norm-referenced or criterion-referenced—depends on the construct to be measured, the purpose for which the scale will be used, and how the score should be reported. In that sense, there is no one best scale type which fits all goals (Turner, 2013).

Scale Levels And Descriptors

Weigle (2002), stressing the importance of the use of explicit levels and scale descriptors, both for teachers, raters and students, lists the following criteria: 1) standardization, i.e., use of descriptors provides the instructor with a standard by which to assess performance efficiently; 2) consistency, i.e., descriptors are valuable for maintaining consistency of standards across different instructors and also within instructors over time; 3) self-assessment, i.e., when students are given scale descriptors in advance, they are aware of the criteria on which they will be judged, resulting in "more productive use of self-assessment" (Covill, 2012).

A particular challenge for scale design, however, is the scarcity of solid theoretical and empirical evidence about language learning/acquisition/development, both in general and with respect to the specific construct that is assessed. This makes it difficult to characterize levels of a proficiency scale in precise, distinctive terms.

Scale Levels. When developing a rating scale, the number of scale levels is an important issue to consider. Rating scales typically contain between three and nine levels. Luoma (2004) argues that the optimum is probably somewhere in the middle: The more levels there are, the more specific the feedback will be, and the easier it will be to show progress; the lower the number of levels, the more consistent the decisions. She therefore envisages four to six levels in a scale.

Ideally, the definition of each level should be independent of the ones above and below it on the scale. However, wordings frequently involve comparative statements, with one level descriptor relative to one or more others. Often, descriptors include quantifiers like *many*, *a few* and *little*, as in Ekiert et al.'s (2018) discourse appropriateness scale, with descriptors ranging from "completely discourse appropriate" to "completely discourse inappropriate." Raters, however, might interpret these quantifiers in different ways, which may result in lower interrater reliability (see Pill & Smart, Chapter 13, this volume).

Scale Descriptors. Referring to Weigle's (2002) earlier mentioned criteria of standardization, consistency and self-assessment, Luoma (2004) listed factors that should to be taken into account when designing descriptors. These are: be brief, be clear, be concrete, be explicit, be usable (practical), and be interpretable and comprehensible independently without reference to other descriptors. Depending on whether the scale is intuitively developed or empirically based, descriptors may be defined on *a priori* grounds, deriving from theoretical notions of what the test is meant to be measuring, or empirically, on the basis of an analysis of data from performances on test tasks. Another important consideration is the way in which performance at the top end of the scale is defined. Particularly in the past, many rating scales made specific reference to the assumed performance of native speakers. This is problematic, however, since performance of native speakers is highly variable, related to educational level, and actually covers a range of positions on the scale (Hulstijn, 2015).

Related Issues

Lately, an increase in the use of integrated scales can be noticed. This goes hand-in-hand with increases in integrated assessments of language skills, particularly reading-into-writing. Research into the development and use of this type of scales has been rare until now, but there are some exceptions (see e.g., Chan et al., 2015; Ewert & Shin, 2015; Fulcher et al., 2011; Ohta et al., 2018).

Another issue which has been given more attention recently is the reliability and validity of scales (see e.g., Turner, 2013). In a study on the validity of L2 writing scales, Becker (2018) concluded that L2 practitioners must make principled and justified decisions about the scoring criteria that they include in scales when assessing students' writing performance. Rater training is crucial in that respect. As has been indicated by, for example, Rezaei and Lovorn (2010), rater training regarding effective scale creation and use will lead to higher reliability and validity (for more on rater training, see Pill & Smart, Chapter 13, this volume).

In order to ensure reliable and valid score inferences, rating scales also need to be regularly monitored and, if necessary, modified. Rating scales often are adopted in different local contexts and therefore need to be systematically reviewed and revised in relation to that context. A good example is the writing section of the Examination for the Certificate of Proficiency in English (ECPE), which has been extensively reviewed by Banerjee et al. (2015), resulting in a completely revised rating scale. Another example is the revision of the above mentioned ESL Composition Profile (Jacobs et al., 1981) by Janssen et al. (2015) for use in placement testing on an English for PhD students program in Colombia. In the latter study the authors made use of multi-faceted Rasch measurement (MFRM), by means of which it is possible to disentangle interactions between the traits of a scale, the consistency of scoring of each rater, and the relative difficulty of each trait, to evaluate the scale's functioning in the new context and to inform scale revisions.

Recommendations for Practice

As demonstrated by the language testing literature discussed above, many studies underline the importance of selecting and developing rating scales in accordance with the construct to be assessed, the intended use, the type of learners, and the L2 proficiency level for which the scale will be employed (e.g., Alderson, 2005; Knoch, 2011). A second recommendation is to empirically try out a rating scale before using it for language testing purposes. Thirdly, (re)validation of an existing rating scale—if used in a different learning context—is crucial, in order to test out its suitability in the new context.

To illustrate these recommendations, we now describe two empirical studies conducted within the framework of TBLA. TBLA aims to investigate how performance may be assessed through linguistic data collected by means of real-world instructional tasks in which the primary focus is on meaning (Ellis & Shintani, 2014). In this type of research various rating instruments have been employed, as shown by the two studies presented below, one by Kuiken and Vedder (2014, 2017, 2018) on the assessment of functional adequacy, the other by Gilabert and Barón (2018) on measurement of cognitive complexity and pragmatic competence.

Assessment of Functional Adequacy

Kuiken and Vedder (2014, 2017, 2018) developed a six-point Likert rating scale for the assessment of functional adequacy. Functional adequacy, as a construct, refers to the appropriateness of the utterances of the speaker/writer within a particular setting and on the basis of a specific target task (e.g., making a phone call to the dentist, taking part in a discussion).

1	2	3	4	5	6
None **of the questions and the requirements of the task have been answered.**	***Some (less than half)*** **of the questions and the requirements of the task have been answered.**	***Approximately half*** **of the questions and requirements of the task have been answered.**	***Most (more than half)*** **of the questions and the requirements of the task have been answered.**	***Almost all*** **the questions and the requirements of the task have been answered.**	***All*** **the questions and the requirements of the task have been answered.**

Figure 12.3 Descriptors of task requirements in the scale for functional adequacy.

Positioned on the continuum holistic-analytic, the rating scale comes closer to the analytic pole. The rating scale is task-independent, and both theoretically and empirically based. Inspired by the conversational maxims of Grice (1975), the following dimensions of the construct are distinguished: task requirements, content, comprehensibility, coherence and cohesion. Task requirements focus on the extent to which the target task is adequately completed, in accordance with genre, register, speech acts, and specific task instructions. Content refers to the adequacy of the number and type of information units in the text. Comprehensibility takes into account the comprehensibility of the text and the amount of effort required from the listener/reader. Coherence and cohesion refer to the adequacy of the utterances of the speaker/writer, in terms of the occurrence of cohesive ties and coherence breaks. An example of the descriptors of the six bands of one of the four scale dimensions (task requirements) is presented in Figure 12.3.

To validate the scale a number of experiments were set up, for oral and written L2 and L1 production and for two different target languages: Dutch L2/L1 and Italian L2/L1 (for a full account, see Kuiken & Vedder, 2014, 2017, 2018). Two training sessions were organized, to familiarize the raters with working with the scale. In order to shed light on raters' employment of the scale and the ways in which they interpreted the different scale dimensions, bands and descriptors, a retrospective panel discussion was organized.

The rating scale has subsequently been tested out for different types of learners and various source and target languages. For instance, it has been tested for the assessment of writing and speaking development of native and non-native speakers of Italian in a research project involving twelve primary and three secondary schools in northern Italy (Pallotti, 2017), and for undergraduate university students of English in Spain (Herraíz Martínez, 2018). The scale has also been tried out with various types of tasks (e.g., decision-making, narrative, instructive, expository and information gap tasks).

What does the development of a scale for the assessment of functional adequacy tell us about the construction of a rating scale in general? First of all, the studies mentioned above—which led to some minor adaptations of the scale descriptors—confirm the importance of piloting and evaluating the reliability, validity, and applicability of the rating tool. Secondly, the results demonstrate that this functional adequacy scale has proven to be a reliable, valid, efficient, and task-independent instrument, which can be employed in different settings, for various task types, and for different source and target languages. Finally, the findings show the necessity of rater training and monitoring of raters over time (see Pill & Smart, Chapter 13, this volume).

Measurement of Cognitive Complexity and Pragmatic Competence

Gilabert and Barón (2018) investigated the relationship between task-complexity and pragmatic competence in the L2 writing of intermediate learners of English as a Foreign Language (EFL). The participants had to write a response to four e-mail messages, at different levels of task complexity. Fifteen expert raters, teachers of EFL, participated in the study.

1 The opening and closing markers are not used.
The adressee is not acknowledged.
The degree of formality is very low and inadequate.
Pragmatic expressions (such as requests and apologies) are awkward and inappropriate.
Mitigation is not used in the pragmatic expressions produced (such as requests or apologies).
6 The use of opening and closing markers is correct for the context.
The addressee is fully acknowledged and is addressed accordingly to his/her position.
The structure of the e-mail follows the expected level of formality.
Pragmatic expressons are fully pragmatically and linguistically appropriate.
Mitigation is always used in pragmatic expressions.

Figure 12.4 Level 1 and 6 of the pragmatics grid in Gilabert and Barón (2018).

In this study, different rating tools were used. All raters first answered a subjective perception questionnaire (nine-point Likert scale) on the required mental effort and perceived difficulty of the different versions of the e-mail task, to obtain a measure of task complexity. The raters also provided qualitative comments to motivate their decisions. For the assessment of pragmatic competence a holistic seven-point Likert scale was employed to rate the pragmatic appropriateness of the learners' e-mail messages.

Different from the analytic and task-independent scale used by Kuiken and Vedder, the two rating scales in Gilabert and Barón included only one scale dimension and are task-dependent. Whereas their task complexity scale was intuitive, their pragmatic rating scale was empirically-based. The scale descriptors, ranging from zero ("pragmatically inappropriate") to six ("fully pragmatically appropriate"), were based on the CEFR (Council of Europe, 2001, 2018) and focused on appropriateness of register, speech act, and politeness of learner output (see Figure 12.4). For a detailed account, the reader is referred to Gilabert and Barón (2018).

A first lesson learnt from this study is that, depending on rating objectives and constructs to be assessed, different rating instruments should be used. A second implication from the study is that expert judgments by experienced teachers can serve as a reliable way to discriminate among different complexity levels: Asking raters to evaluate task complexity is a readily available technique that does not require expensive equipment (eye-trackers, reaction-time software) and may provide valuable insights for performance assessment, task design and language pedagogy.

Testing Tips

- The choice of the type of rating scale should depend on the assessment purpose for which the scale is used, in relation to the construct and rating objectives.
- Scale dimensions of the rating scale should be derived from the construct to be assessed.
- Scale descriptors should be explicit and clear, and relevant to the target language task which the learner has to complete.
- Prior to implementation in research or testing, a scale should be piloted by raters on sample performances representing a range of performance levels, to evaluate the scale's overall quality and practicality.
- Rater training is necessary: Training sessions, panel discussions and practice materials are crucial for raters to become accustomed with working with scoring bands and descriptors.

Recommended Readings

Luoma, S. (2004). *Assessing speaking*. Cambridge University Press.

This book can be recommended, particularly with regard to Chapter 4: Speaking scales (pp. 59–95), which contains many examples of various types of scales.

Weigle, S. (2002). *Assessing writing*. Cambridge University Press.

This book is a good resource for those who need practical advice for designing tasks and scoring procedures for writing tests, especially Chapter 6: Scoring procedures for writing assessment (pp. 108–139).

Crusan, D. (Ed.). (2015). The use of rubrics to assess writing: Issues and challenges [Special issue]. *Assessing Writing, 26*.

This volume bundles a collection of articles looking into the development process, role and uses of rating scales in writing assessment in various contexts.

References

Alderson, J. C. (2005). *Diagnosing foreign language proficiency: The interface between learning and assessment*. Continuum.

Bachman, L. F., & Palmer, A. S. (1996). *Language assessment in practice: Developing language assessments and justifying their use in the real world*. Oxford University Press.

Banerjee, J., Yan, X., Chapman, M., & Elliott, H. (2015). Keeping up with the times: Revising and refreshing a rating scale. *Assessing Writing, 26*, 5–19. https://doi.org/10.1016/j.asw.2015.07.001

Becker, A. (2018). Not to scale? An argument-based inquiry into the validity of an L2 writing scale. *Assessing Writing, 37*, 1–12. https://doi.org/10.1016/j.asw.2018.01.001

Brown, J. D., Hudson, T., Norris, J. M., & Bonk, W. (2002). *An investigation of second language task-based performance assessments*. University of Hawai'i Press.

Bygate, M. (2011). Teaching and testing speaking. In M. H. Long & C. J. Doughty (Eds.), *The handbook of language teaching* (pp. 412–441). Wiley-Blackwell.

Chan, S., Inoue, C., & Taylor, L. (2015). Developing rubrics to assess reading-into-writing skills: A case study. *Assessing Writing, 26*, 20–37. https://doi.org/10.1016/j.asw.2015.07.004

Council of Europe. (2001). *Common European framework of reference for languages: Learning, teaching, assessment*. Cambridge University Press.

Council of Europe. (2018). *Common European framework of reference for languages: Learning, teaching, assessment. Companion volume with new descriptors*. Council of Europe.

Covill, A. (2012). College students' use of a writing rubric: Effect on quality of writing, self-efficacy and writing practices. *The Journal of Writing Assessment, 5*(1), 1–9.

Davies, A., Brown, A., Elder, C., Hill, K., Lumley, T., & McNamara, T. (1999). *Dictionary of language testing*. Cambridge University Press.

Ekiert, M., Lampropoulou, S., Révész, A., & Torgersen, E. (2018). The effects of task type and L2 proficiency on discourse appropriacy in oral task performance. In N. Taguchi & Y. Kim (Eds.), *Task-based approaches to teaching and assessing pragmatics* (pp. 247–263). John Benjamins.

Ellis, R., & Shintani, N. (2014). *Exploring language pedagogy through second language acquisition research*. Routledge.

ETS. (2019). *TOEFL iBT® test independent and integrated writing rubrics*. https://www.ets.org/s/toefl/pdf/toefl_writing_rubrics.pdf

Ewert, D., & Shin, S.-Y. (2015). Examining instructors' conceptualizations and challenges in designing a data-driven rating scale for a reading-to-write task. *Assessing Writing, 26*, 38–50. https://doi.org/10.1016/j.asw.2015.06.001

Fulcher, G. (2003). *Testing second language speaking*. Pearson/Longman.

Fulcher, G., & Davidson, F. (2007). *Language testing and assessment: An advanced resource book*. Routledge.

Fulcher, G., Davidson, F., & Kemp, J. (2011). Effective rating scale development for speaking tests: Performance decision trees. *Language Testing, 28*(1), 5–29. https://doi.org/10.1177/0265532209359514

Gilabert, R., & Barón, J. (2018). Independently measuring cognitive complexity in task design for interlanguage pragmatic development. In N. Taguchi & Y. Kim (Eds.), *Task-based approaches to teaching and assessing pragmatics* (pp. 159–190). John Benjamins.

Green, A., & Hawkey, R. (2012). Marking assessments: Rating scales and rubrics. In C. Coome, P. Davidson, B. O' Sullivan, & S. Stoynoff (Eds.), *The Cambridge guide to second language assessment* (pp. 299–306). Cambridge University Press.

Grice, H. P. (1975). Logic and conversation. In P. Cole & J. L. Morgan (Eds.), *Speech acts* (pp. 41–58). Academic Press.

Hamp-Lyons, L. (1991). *Assessing second language writing in academic contexts*. Ablex.

Hamp-Lyons, L. (2016). Farewell to holistic scoring. Part two: Why build a house with only one brick? *Assessing Writing*, *29*, A1–A5. https://doi.org/10.1016/j.asw.2016.06.006

Herraíz Martinez, A. (2018). *Functional adequacy: The influence of English-medium instruction, English proficiency and previous language learning experience* (Unpublished doctoral dissertation). University Jaume I, Castellón, Spain.

Hulstijn, J. H. (2015). *Language proficiency in native and non-native speakers: Theory and research*. John Benjamins.

Jacobs, H., Zinkgraf, S., Wormuth, D., Hartfiel, V., & Hugley, J. (1981). *Testing ESL composition: A practical approach*. Newbury House.

Janssen, G., Meier, V., & Trace, J. (2015). Building a better rubric: Mixed methods rubric revision. *Assessing Writing*, *26*, 51–66. https://doi.org/10.1016/j.asw.2015.07.002

Knoch, U. (2011). Rating scales for diagnostic assessment of writing: What should they look like and where should the criteria come from? *Assessing Writing*, *16*, 81–96. https://doi.org/10.1016/j.asw.2011.02.003

Kuiken, F., & Vedder, I. (2014). Rating written performance: What do raters do and why? *Language Testing*, *31*(3), 329–348. https://doi.org/10.1177/0265532214526174

Kuiken, F., & Vedder, I. (2017). Functional adequacy in L2 writing: Towards a new rating scale. *Language Testing*, *34*(3), 321–336. https://doi.org/10.1177/0265532216663991

Kuiken, F., & Vedder, I. (2018). Assessing functional adequacy of L2 performance in a task-based approach. In N. Taguchi & Y. Kim (Eds.), *Task-based approaches to teaching and assessing pragmatics* (pp. 265–285). John Benjamins.

Leclercq, P., Edmonds, A., & Hilton, H. (2014). *Measuring L2 proficiency: Perspectives from SLA*. Multilingual Matters.

Lloyd-Jones, R. (1977). Primary trait scoring. In C. R. Cooper & L. Odell (Eds.), *Evaluating writing* (pp. 33–69). National Council of Teachers of English.

Luoma, S. (2004). *Assessing speaking*. Cambridge University Press.

McNamara, T. (2000). *Language testing*. Oxford University Press.

Ohta, R., Plakans, L. M., & Gebril, A. (2018). Integrated writing scores based on holistic and multi-trait scales: A generalizability analysis. *Assessing Writing*, *38*, 21–36. https://doi.org/10.1016/j.asw.2018.08.001

Pallotti, G. (2017). Applying the interlanguage approach to language teaching. *International Review of Applied Linguistics*, *55*(4), 393–412. https://doi.org/10.1515/iral-2017-0145

Rezaei, A. R., & Lovorn, M. (2010). Reliability and validity of rubrics for assessment through writing. *Assessing Writing*, *15*, 18–39. https://doi.org/10.1016/j.asw.2010.01.003

Turner, C. E. (2013). Rating scales for language tests. In C. A. Chapelle (Ed.), *The encyclopedia of applied linguistics*. Blackwell/Wiley. https://doi.org/10.1002/9781405198431.wbeal1045

Weigle, S. (2002). *Assessing writing*. Cambridge University Press.

13

Raters

Behavior and Training

John Pill & Cameron Smart

Background

In second language testing, test developers seek to measure aspects of test-takers' underlying knowledge and skills through their performance on tasks designed for the purpose. In direct tests of writing and speaking, test-taker performances are often extensive, and consequently complex to assess. Test developers therefore generally provide a rating scale to capture aspects of the performance that, in their view, comprise the skill(s) to be measured. Their scale defines in advance these aspects of performance (combined or separated out, holistic or analytic) along with their observable characteristics at different levels of proficiency; it seeks to operationalize the underlying construct, for example, test-takers' ability to write an academic essay. While decisions about what is important and what counts as evidence of different levels of performance are made in advance, they can only be applied during or following each test-taker's performance. A human rater is required to mediate between the established measurement tool—the rating scale—and test-taker performance. Decisions about the quality of performance are termed "subjective," in contrast to "objective" scoring using an answer key applied to the selected-answer responses generally found in reading and listening tests and in discrete-point tests of grammar and vocabulary. However, it should be acknowledged that subjectivity is inherent in all judgments made by humans. Therefore, rather than viewing it as negative—unreliable, unscientific, and to be avoided if possible, it would seem more helpful to see this subjectivity as natural—inevitable, characteristically human (for better or worse), and an anticipated feature to be managed appropriately.

The development and validation of rating scales is considered in Kuiken and Vedder (Chapter 12, this volume). Our focus is the human rater who takes the essential evaluative responsibility in performance assessment. Lumley (2002) stresses the rater's importance:

> The rater, not the scale, lies at the centre of the process. It is the rater who decides:
>
> - which features of the scale to pay attention to;
> - how to arbitrate between the inevitable conflicts in scale wordings; and
> - how to justify her impression of the text in terms of the institutional requirements represented by the scale and rater training.
>
> (p. 267)

Because of our professional backgrounds, our perspective in this chapter is based on experience with raters in language testing. Nevertheless, the importance of raters in second language acquisition (SLA) research is also clear, and immediately discernible through a review of the first paragraph of this chapter substituting "research" for "testing," "participant" for "test-taker," and "researchers" for "test developers." The significance of raters' decisions has been recognized and researched more fully in the context of language testing, but such decisions affect the outcomes of any study involving human assessment of performance, for example, to measure longitudinal change or the attainment of a predetermined standard (for a collection of examples, see Kuiken & Vedder, 2014).

Increasingly, automated measurement using the power of computers is employed in language testing and SLA research. In automated measurement, human judgment is replaced or complemented by the statistical manipulation of sets of quantifiable data extracted automatically from a performance in digital form and taken to represent features of performance as they are conventionally understood. Sophisticated measures are in use and under development (e.g., D. S. McNamara, Crossley, Roscoe, Allen, & Dai, 2015). However, neither human rating nor automated rating can be said to provide the perfect solution for every situation (for a comparison, see Bejar, Williamson, & Mislevy, 2006). Despite technological advances, human raters are unlikely to become redundant in the near future. The practicalities of using automated scoring remain challenging in many contexts. A study might use a commercially available English test that involves automated scoring as a pre- and post-treatment measure of general language proficiency but, if customized delivery or greater analytical detail is sought, human raters will probably be engaged.

This initial section ("Background") shows that language testing and SLA research are similar in how they gather and analyze data, and that human raters remain a customary feature of this process, despite advances in automated scoring. In the next section ("Key Issues"), we provide an overview of published research on raters in language testing. These issues are not generally considered to the same degree in SLA research, which is understandable because rater involvement is mainly to facilitate research studies; raters are taken for granted rather than made the focus of investigation. Nevertheless, we argue that rater behavior should be considered more deeply by SLA researchers because raters' judgments—the outcome of their characteristics and practices—have a direct impact on the quality of research results just as they affect the reliability of test scores.

Key Concepts

***Rater characteristics*:** These can be divided into fixed or fluid characteristics. More fixed characteristics are expertise and background (similarity to other raters and to test-takers/participants) as well as raters' approach to rating and the cognitive processes they use. More fluid characteristics may be physical or psychological (e.g., energy level, alertness, mood, motivation); they may relate to raters' acquaintance with test-takers/participants or to a specific role (e.g., interlocutor-rater, online rater).

***Rater practices*:** The ways raters approach the rating task and the strategies they use. Practices may be intuitive and individual, or instructed and shared by a rating team.

***Rater effects*:** Differences in scoring due to rater characteristics and practices, generally demonstrated using statistical tools. Examples of rater effects include consistency and randomness in scoring, severity/leniency, and bias due to an aspect of the rating situation.

Key Issues

A rater is required to make judgments, usually represented as a set of scores, about written or spoken performances. (In this way, we define rating as different from coding data, which is not considered in this chapter.) The (set of) judgments should be consistent if repeated—on a different day, by a different rater, and so on—with the same score or scores being given to the same performance and to other performances similar in the aspects being judged, and different scores being given to performances different in those aspects. The reliability of the scoring process is supported by using appropriate rating scales. Most pertinent to this chapter, it is also affected by *characteristics* of the raters and their rating *practices*, with any resultant differences in scoring being called rater *effects*, and by their training. We examine these issues in turn.

Rater Characteristics

First, we review characteristics that are more fixed. An expert rater is assumed to do a better job than a non-expert rater, but there are different types of expertise to consider. Studies show that experienced raters are more consistent than novices (e.g., Weigle, 1998). Lim (2011) found that novices rating writing approached levels of consistency and accuracy of experienced raters relatively quickly, particularly with greater volume or frequency of rating, and that raters could maintain levels of rating quality (therefore supporting a claim for the existence of "expert" raters). Through training and experience, some raters become adept at rating and can apply their skills across a range of rating scales on a variety of tests. However, not everyone immediately has the characteristics conventionally required of a rater. For example, rather than giving a score, teachers may be more used to providing formative comments directly to the performer, seeking to improve rather than categorize performance. Training is necessary to establish appropriate rater behavior and thereby develop rating expertise. From our experience, we suggest that some people discover they are temperamentally unsuited to rating, perhaps finding it monotonous or stressful, while others enjoy it, maybe gaining satisfaction from striving to rate consistently.

Aside from expertise in the process of rating, expertise in the domain being rated is also valued. For example, raters with experience teaching academic writing are likely to be able to recognize features of stronger and weaker performance in this area. However, the issue can become complicated: these experts in writing for academic purposes may focus on features of performance different from those that matter to experts in particular disciplines (e.g., engineering or history). There can be more than one perspective on a performance, as Elder (1993) found in her study of the assessment of trainee teachers from non-English-speaking backgrounds teaching mathematics and science through the medium of English. Although the two groups of raters, namely teachers of English as a second language (ESL) and subject-specialist teachers, generally agreed in their broad judgment of communicative effectiveness, differences were noted in how they rated particular features of performance, with the ESL teachers concentrating on language issues while the subject specialists focused on classroom interaction (see Hsieh, 2011).

In contrast to domain expertise, the perspective of "linguistic laypersons" as raters has also been investigated. For example, Sato (2018) found that raters without linguistic training who assessed spoken interaction tended to consider features of performance that are rarely part of rating criteria based on communicative competence models. These included non-verbal behavior, composure and attitude, as well as quality of ideas and relevance to topic. In an experimental study by Duijm, Schoonen and Hulstijn (2018), linguistically trained professional raters and untrained non-professional raters both recognized variation in fluency and accuracy across a set of spoken performances, with the trained raters focusing relatively more on accuracy and the untrained raters on fluency. It is apparent that raters with different expertise (or backgrounds) bring varied perspectives to the rating process.

A team of raters is often selected to have members with similar characteristics; for instance, applicants need a teaching qualification and a sufficiently high score in a recognized test of the language to be rated. Requiring similar backgrounds (outside the scope of legally protected characteristics for employment) is an attempt to reduce variability in scoring among the raters. New raters can be socialized into the established rating behaviors of a group, but it is important to check that rating of the group as a whole remains meaningful and anchored in its context.

Other rater characteristics studied particularly for speaking tests include the language background of raters, and raters' familiarity with features of speech of test-takers, notably accent. Raters' first language is now generally viewed as irrelevant. Instead, a sufficient level of proficiency in the language to be rated, and how to provide evidence of this, must be determined. In the context of a high-stakes test of spoken English in China, Zhang and Elder (2014) found that teacher raters with English as a second language delivered ratings similar to those of teacher raters with English as a first language (who underwent parallel training in using the rating scale), although the two groups approached the rating process somewhat differently. Xi and Mollaun (2011) compared Indian raters' rating of TOEFL iBT test performances by first-language speakers of Hindu and Tamil, on one hand, and of other languages, on the other. They found that rater familiarity with test-taker accents did not affect rating in a context where rater selection and training was rigorous and holistic rating was used. In contrast, another study using the TOEFL iBT speaking test found accent familiarity positively affected the holistic rating of raters with English as their first language for Spanish and Chinese test-takers, but the effect was not significant for Korean test-takers (Winke, Gass, & Myford, 2013). The variation in the findings of these and other studies (e.g., Kim, 2009; Wei & Llosa, 2015; for rater-background effects on writing, Johnson & Lim, 2009) indicates the complexity of this issue: Raters' language background may be "a proxy for a range of other variables which may themselves impact equally powerfully or more powerfully on how language proficiency is viewed and rated" (Zhang & Elder, 2014, p. 320).

We now turn to rater characteristics that are more fluid. Class teachers may act as raters and will therefore know individual test-takers. This is a core element of the test construct in some public secondary school examinations, such as the school-based assessment (SBA) component in the Hong Kong Diploma of Secondary Education, where teachers rate their own students in a speaking exam. It is also part of testing foreign language subjects in the United Kingdom's school system. This familiarity may influence teachers' rating, and they may award scores that relate more to their experience of the test-taker in class (or to an overall impression of the individual) than to test performance. In contexts in which SBA is employed, statistical means or check-marking by external examiners may be used to adjust raters' initial scores and reduce the effect of such bias (Cheung, 2016). Other high-stakes tests also have procedures in place for raters to declare acquaintance with a test-taker, whose performance is then reallocated for rating. As another variable, the rater role changes in different speaking tests. Raters may rate audio or video recordings following the interaction, they may attend and rate as the interaction takes place, or they may facilitate the interaction themselves, as interlocutor and rater (see Brown, 2003, 2012). These roles place different demands on raters. In some speaking tests (e.g., Cambridge English's *B2 First*), two raters are present, one serving as interlocutor and rating on a holistic rating scale, the other focusing exclusively on rating with an analytic scale (Taylor & Galaczi, 2011).

Rater fatigue is one of several physical or physiological factors that might affect rater performance; other examples are hunger, mood, and motivation. Ling, Mollaun, and Xi's (2014) study of TOEFL iBT speaking raters working online at home investigated the effects of a variety of work patterns. They found that, while standards of accuracy and consistency remained high under all conditions, raters working a six-hour day with three two-hour sessions and a change in the task type rated for each session performed better in terms of rating accuracy and consistency than raters working other session patterns in six- and eight-hour days. However, these raters were not the most productive. In a small-scale study of rater fatigue when rating on-screen essays, Drave (2011) found that all raters reported fatigue but that there was no fatigue effect on rating performance.

Rater Practices

In this section, we consider how raters approach their task by reviewing studies of rater practices when rating writing. In exploratory research, Milanovic, Saville, and Shen (1996) proposed a model of marking behavior, and then investigated the actual practices of 16 raters on Cambridge ESL exams using introspective written reports, verbal reports and group interviews. Analysis revealed different "marking approaches," involving whether the script was read once or twice and whether this was done spontaneously or systematically, whether a provisional mark was given during a read-through, and the different speeds and focuses of read-throughs. Cumming, Kantor, and Powers (2002) investigated the decision-making processes of experienced ESL writing raters to establish rating procedures as part of the development of TOEFL iBT. They categorized 27 behaviors into three areas in a proposed rating framework: self-monitoring focus (interpretation and judgment), rhetorical and ideational focus, and language focus. The researchers described rating as "interactive, multifaceted decision making" (Cumming et al., 2002, p. 88).

Lumley's (2005) detailed study of the rating behavior of four writing raters working with an analytic scale demonstrated how a rating scale alone cannot cover all eventualities. Using think-aloud protocols, Lumley found that raters develop personal strategies as they attempt to deal fairly with rating procedures, inevitably creating "tension and indeterminacy" (p. 312). He concluded that adequate rater training, including guidelines to supplement the scale, is necessary to maintain rating quality. A study of the rating of an integrated reading-to-write task (Gebril & Plakans, 2014) indicates the complexity of the rating processes in this context, with raters' focus changing depending on the quality of the performance (a finding shared with Cumming et al., 2002).

Understanding of raters' cognitive processes should be evident in the validity argument for a test, as it is important to demonstrate consistency of raters' mental processing in relation to the test construct and measurement goals (Bejar, 2012). Bejar proposes a descriptive model of the rating process for writing (Figure 13.1). Its division into two phases indicates how the validity of the rating element depends on decisions made in the design phase about, for example, what the rubric (rating scale) measures, how this is exemplified in benchmark (anchor) performances, and how training is managed.

Rater Effects

Rater effects are the consequences of rater characteristics and practices which are observable in ratings. They include: a) consistency and randomness in a rater's scores; b) rater severity (or leniency), where a rater scores consistently lower (or higher) than the rater group overall or than benchmark ratings; c) central tendency and overuse of extremes, where rating tends towards either the middle or the extremes of scales; d) illusory halo (positive) and horns (negative) (Cheung, 2016), where scores for some or all criteria are affected by a rater's view of the performance as a whole or of a particular criterion (e.g., grammatical accuracy); and e) rater bias, where a feature of the assessment situation systematically affects a rater's scoring (Eckes, 2017).

Studies by Eckes show how statistical analysis of raters' scoring patterns using item response modeling and cluster analysis allows classification into rater types. In Eckes (2008), 64 experienced raters were asked to indicate the importance they gave to nine commonly used writing criteria. Analysis indicated six rater types (clusters), which were named after the most (or least) important criterial characteristic for that type: syntax, correctness, structure, fluency, non-fluency and non-argumentation (i.e., raters in the last two clusters saw the criterion as unimportant). Eckes (2012) sought to link these rater types (based on raters' own perceptions) to rater behavior in operational rating. Eckes showed how the importance given by a rater type to a feature of performance is linked to the scores given for that feature by raters of that type. Namely, criteria

Assessment design phase

- Assessment design process identifies evidence of the different levels [of] performance called for
- **Scoring rubrics** are formulated to formalize the relevant gradations of performance
- Items and tasks are created to elicit performance
- Items and tasks are pretested and evaluated; do they elicit the evidence called for?
- If so, collect **benchmark and range-finders** to train raters
- Recruit and train raters using the scoring rubric, benchmark and range finders
- Raters form a **mental scoring rubric** based on the training
- Ideally, as a result of the training all raters will rate equivalently but their background or other factors could lead to **rater effects**

Scoring phase

- Rater reads a work product and forms a **mental response representation**
- Rater compares the **similarity** of resulting representation with mental scoring rubric
- Based on that comparison the rater tentatively assigns the response to a score category
- The score they assign to a specific response depends on
  - The true quality of the response
  - The quality of their mental scoring rubric
  - The quality of the representation they formed for this response
  - The **prior information** they have accumulated during the scoring
  - The state of the rater, e.g., fatigue
  - Environmental conditions
  - The nature of the responses previously scored

Figure 13.1 Descriptive model for the writing rating process (Bejar, 2012, p. 5).

important to a rater type are likely to be rated more severely by that type, and criteria not important to a rater type are likely to be rated more leniently. Eckes (2017) provides an overview of several studies on these rater types.

Knowledge of an individual's rater type could inform monitoring and training to manage rater variability (Eckes, 2008). For instance, raters of the type that does not give attention equally to all criteria should be encouraged towards a more consciously "bottom-up" analytic rating process, perhaps leading to greater consistency. In the following section, we consider the practicalities of rater training, based on the research findings in this section.

Recommendations for Practice

Rater Training

Research set out in the previous section illustrates how variability in rater characteristics is inevitable. It has been suggested (e.g., Moss, 1994; see also Hamp-Lyons, 2007) that the rating process value this variation instead of trying to remove it, and that consensus be sought through discussion and compromise, as when deciding the outcome of a job interview or thesis defense. However, for practical reasons, training is generally the tool used to mitigate rater effects. T. F. McNamara (1996) is realistic about its likely results: "the most appropriate aim of rater training is to make raters internally consistent so as to make statistical modeling of their characteristics possible, but beyond this to accept variability in stable rater characteristics as a fact of life, which must be compensated for in some way" (p. 127). Multi-facet Rasch analysis can be employed in the post-marking phase to produce fair-scores accounting for patterns of rater severity when double rating (or more) is used. In a research study where a sufficient quantity of rating is done to allow for such analysis, this should be the approach taken. Less complex procedures involve taking the average of scores given by two raters, and adjudication by a third rater when two raters' ratings diverge by more than is acceptable. Researchers also need to decide the minimum level of inter- and intra-rater reliability acceptable for their study. For example, a coefficient of .80 or more is often required in high-stakes contexts.

Publicly available information about rater training procedures of major test providers is limited and mostly deals with large-scale training (e.g., for speaking examiner training for some Cambridge examinations, see Taylor & Galaczi, 2011; see also Council of Europe, 2011). While the scale is different from that of typical SLA research studies, we believe that the stages presented indicate a sound general procedure to follow—in both SLA and language testing contexts.

Selection

- Decide the background and expertise raters need to make valid ratings in the context of the study and to be seen by reviewers as doing so. To reduce variability, select raters who are similar in ways that matter.
- Have more than one rater. Otherwise, there is no evidence that ratings are not in some way idiosyncratic, thereby potentially reducing a study's reliability. Raters act as a check on each other's performance; "no one judgment can be said to be definitive" (Lumley & McNamara, 1995, p. 57).

Induction

- Ensure raters understand the study's context, who its participants are, and the purpose of their judgments. Have raters attempt the tasks involved themselves. However, do not share information that might bias ratings, for instance, a study's focus on gender differences in speaking performance.
- Indicate that each rater must meet standards of accuracy to participate.
- Confirm rater availability and access to required tools (e.g., internet access for online rating).

Training

- Ensure raters understand the construct being measured through the rating scales as well as features of performance not for consideration.
- Support reflection on the scope of each analytic criterion and the wording of descriptors to distinguish levels of performance.
- Initially, provide benchmark performances with their ratings to exemplify standards and prompt discussion and internalization of the scales (familiarization).
- Subsequently, give practice in applying the scales to new performances, then supply agreed ratings with supporting commentary (calibration). Provide feedback.
- Discuss procedures for irregular performances (e.g., underlength or illegible writing scripts, memorized or off-topic performances).
- Encourage good rating habits, for example, always returning to the scale as the principal guide for decision-making, developing self-awareness of rating consistency, rating independently of other raters.
- Establish the rating procedures for the study (e.g., timing requirements, presentation of writing scripts online or on paper; for online rating, see Brown & Jaquith, 2012).
- Establish work patterns to promote reliability (e.g., maximum number of performances to rate per session).
- Provide opportunities for raters to ask about the process. Research into online training indicates that raters value such interaction with trainers (e.g., Knoch, Fairbairn, Myford, & Huisman, 2018).

Raters generally undertake these three stages once only. In contrast, the following stages constitute a repeating cycle. If rating occurs intermittently, research indicates that raters need to re-calibrate to maintain required standards (e.g., Lumley & McNamara, 1995).

Standardization

- Set out the required level of agreement with benchmark rating that permits raters to participate in the study.
- Review the use of scales and give practice in applying them to performances; supply agreed ratings with supporting commentary. Provide feedback.
- Have each rater rate further performances independently and check these ratings with benchmarked standards to show that the rater can apply scales accurately (certification).

Monitoring

- Review each rater's performance, both as part of training and during the rating process. For example, run statistical analyses or include benchmark performances alongside performances for routine rating to check raters' consistency (intra- and inter-rater reliability, rater drift from established standards). Provide feedback.
- Have clear remedial (and eventual removal) processes for raters not meeting the required level of agreement to continue rating.

Research studies show that feedback to raters, mentioned several times in the stages of training, is beneficial. For example, Elder, Knoch, Barkhuizen, and von Randow (2005) found that giving individual feedback (drawn from multi-facet Rasch analysis of the ratings of a group of raters) generally had a positive effect on raters' attitudes and consistency. However, they also found that raters became more cautious, reducing the overall discriminatory power of the rating process. The positive effect of providing individual feedback may be in raters' increased awareness of their own behavior, and their subsequent endeavors to improve it, rather than immediately measurable in rating performance (Knoch, Read, & von Randow, 2007).

The procedures of rater training presented above and in Figure 13.1 may seem onerous for SLA researchers, given that raters in this context are but one part of a research method designed and implemented to generate data for analysis and discussion. Raters are only rarely the focus of research itself. Nevertheless, and in conclusion, we hope that this chapter has validated the assertion that the procedures of a research study—in this case, specifically the rating of participant performance by human raters—must themselves be reliable in order to support any claims for the reliability of resulting research findings. From both language testing and SLA perspectives, we note the power of raters to affect test scores and research data through their interpretation of how to apply the measurement tools they use. We acknowledge the inherent tension between procedures for standardization and different stances taken by raters (consciously or otherwise) towards the rating task and what/who they represent when carrying it out.

Testing Tips

- Always involve the judgment of more than one rater.
- Consider the purpose of the rating and select raters who will promote it.
- Provide training to help raters develop their internal consistency.
- Monitor the rating process, comparing scores for the same performances by different raters.

Recommended Readings

Brown, A. (2012). Interlocutor and rater training. In G. Fulcher & F. Davidson (Eds.), *The Routledge handbook of language testing* (pp. 413–425). Routledge. https ://do i.org /10.4 324/9 78020 31812 87.ch 28

A useful overview of issues in rater training.

Eckes, T. (2012). Operational rater types in writing assessment: Linking rater cognition to rater behavior. *Language Assessment Quarterly*, *9*(3), 270–292. https://doi.org/10.1080/15434303.2011.649381

Research seeking to connect rater types based on raters' perceptions of what matters to rating behavior.

Lumley, T. (2005). *Assessing second language writing: The rater's perspective*. Peter Lang.

An influential study showing how writing raters interact with rating scales.

References

Bejar, I. I. (2012). Rater cognition: Implications for validity. *Educational Measurement: Issues and Practice*, *31*(3), 2–9. https://doi.org/10.1111/j.1745-3992.2012.00238.x

Bejar, I. I., Williamson, D. M., & Mislevy, R. J. (2006). Human scoring. In D. M. Williamson, R. J. Mislevy, & I. I. Bejar (Eds.), *Automated scoring of complex tasks in computer-based testing* (pp. 49–81). Lawrence Erlbaum.

Brown, A. (2003). Interviewer variation and the co-construction of speaking proficiency. *Language Testing*, *20*(1), 1–25. https://doi.org/10.1191/0265532203lt242oa

Brown, A. (2012). Interlocutor and rater training. In G. Fulcher & F. Davidson (Eds.), *The Routledge handbook of language testing* (pp. 413–425). Routledge. https://doi.org/10.4324/9780203181287.ch28

Brown, A., & Jaquith, P. (2012). The development and validation of an online rater training and marking system: Promises and pitfalls. In B. O'Sullivan (Ed.), *Language testing: Theories and practices* (pp. 244–261). Palgrave Macmillan.

Cheung, T. K. Y. (2016). *The management of public examinations: 101 questions and answers*. Hong Kong Examinations and Assessment Authority.

Council of Europe. (2011). *Manual for language test development and examining*. Language Policy Division, Council of Europe. https://www.coe.int/en/web/common-european-framework-reference-languages/developing-tests-examining

Cumming, A., Kantor, R., & Powers, D. E. (2002). Decision making while rating ESL/EFL writing tasks: A descriptive framework. *The Modern Language Journal*, *86*(1), 67–96. https://doi.org/10.1111/1540-4781.00137

Drave, N. (2011, November 23–28). *Marker "fatigue" and marking reliability in Hong Kong's Language Proficiency Assessment for Teachers of English (LPATE)*. [Paper presentation]. International Association for Educational Assessment. 37th Annual Conference, Manila, Philippines. https://iaea.info/conference-proceedings/37th-annual-conference-2011/

Duijm, K., Schoonen, R., & Hulstijn, J. H. (2018). Professional and non-professional raters' responsiveness to fluency and accuracy in L2 speech: An experimental approach. *Language Testing*, *35*(4), 501–527. https://doi.org/10.1177/0265532217712553

Eckes, T. (2008). Rater types in writing performance assessments: A classification approach to rater variability. *Language Testing*, *25*(2), 155–185. https://doi.org/10.1177/0265532207086780

Eckes, T. (2012). Operational rater types in writing assessment: Linking rater cognition to rater behavior. *Language Assessment Quarterly*, *9*(3), 270–292. https://doi.org/10.1080/15434303.2011.649381

Eckes, T. (2017). Rater effects: Advances in item response modeling of human ratings—Part I [Guest editorial]. *Psychological Test and Assessment Modeling*, *59*(4), 443–452.

Elder, C. (1993). How do subject specialists construe classroom language proficiency? *Language Testing*, *10*(3), 235–254. https://doi.org/10.1177/026553229301000303

Elder, C., Knoch, U., Barkhuizen, G., & von Randow, J. (2005). Individual feedback to enhance rater training: Does it work? *Language Assessment Quarterly*, *2*(3), 175–196. https://doi.org/10.1207/s15434311laq0203_1

Gebril, A., & Plakans, L. (2014). Assembling validity evidence for assessing academic writing: Rater reactions to integrated tasks. *Assessing Writing*, *21*, 56–73. https://doi.org/10.1016/j.asw.2014.03.002

Hamp-Lyons, L. (2007). Worrying about rating [Editorial]. *Assessing Writing*, *12*(1), 1–9. https://doi.org/10.1016/j.asw.2007.05.002

Hsieh, C.-N. (2011). Rater effects in ITA testing: ESL teachers' versus American undergraduates' judgments of accentedness, comprehensibility and oral proficiency. *Spaan Fellow Working Papers in Second or Foreign Language Assessment*, *9*, 47–74.

Johnson, J. S., & Lim, G. S. (2009). The influence of rater language background on writing performance assessment. *Language Testing*, *26*(4), 485–505. https://doi.org/10.1177/0265532209340186
Kim, Y.-H. (2009). An investigation into native and non-native teachers' judgments of oral English performance: A mixed methods approach. *Language Testing*, *26*(2), 187–217. https://doi.org/10.1177/0265532208101010
Knoch, U., Fairbairn, J., Myford, C., & Huisman, A. (2018). Evaluating the relative effectiveness of online and face-to-face training for new writing raters. *Papers in Language Testing and Assessment*, *7*(1), 61–86.
Knoch, U., Read, J., & von Randow, J. (2007). Re-training writing raters online: How does it compare with face-to-face training? *Assessing Writing*, *12*(1), 26–43. https://doi.org/10.1016/j.asw.2007.04.001
Kuiken, V., & Vedder, I. (Eds.). (2014). Assessing oral and written L2 performance: Raters' decisions, rating procedures and rating scales [Special issue]. *Language Testing*, *31*(3). https://doi.org/10.1177/0265532214526179
Lim, G. S. (2011). The development and maintenance of rating quality in performance writing assessment: A longitudinal study of new and experienced raters. *Language Testing*, *28*(4), 543–560. https://doi.org/10.1177/0265532211406422
Ling, G., Mollaun, P., & Xi, X. (2014). A study on the impact of fatigue on human raters when scoring speaking responses. *Language Testing*, *31*(4), 479–499. https://doi.org/10.1177/0265532214530699
Lumley, T. (2002). Assessment criteria in a large-scale writing test: What do they really mean to the raters? *Language Testing*, *19*(3), 246–276. https://doi.org/10.1191/0265532202lt230oa
Lumley, T. (2005). *Assessing second language writing: The rater's perspective*. Peter Lang.
Lumley, T., & McNamara, T. F. (1995). Rater characteristics and rater bias: Implications for training. *Language Testing*, *12*(1), 54–71. https://doi.org/10.1177/026553229501200104
McNamara, D. S., Crossley, S. A., Roscoe, R. D., Allen, L. K., & Dai, J. (2015). A hierarchical classification approach to automated essay scoring. *Assessing Writing*, *23*, 35–59. https://doi.org/10.1016/j.asw.2014.09.002
McNamara, T. F. (1996). *Measuring second language performance*. Longman.
Milanovic, M., Saville, N., & Shen, S. (1996). A study of the decision-making behaviour of composition markers. In M. Milanovic & N. Saville (Eds.), *Performance testing, cognition and assessment: Selected papers from the 15th Language Testing Colloquium, Cambridge and Arnhem* (pp. 92–114). Cambridge University Press.
Moss, P. (1994). Can there be validity without reliability? *Educational Researcher*, *23*(2), 5–12. https://doi.org/10.3102/0013189X023002005
Sato, T. (2018). The gap between communicative ability measurements: General-purpose English speaking tests and linguistic laypersons' judgments. *Papers in Language Testing and Assessment*, *7*(1), 1–31.
Taylor, L., & Galaczi, E. (2011). Scoring validity. In L. Taylor (Ed.), *Examining speaking: Research and practice in assessing second language speaking* (pp. 171–233). Cambridge University Press.
Wei, J., & Llosa, L. (2015). Investigating differences between American and Indian raters in assessing TOEFL iBT speaking tasks. *Language Assessment Quarterly*, *12*(3), 283–304. https://doi.org/10.1080/15434303.2015.1037446
Weigle, S. C. (1998). Using FACETS to model rater training effects. *Language Testing*, *15*(2), 263–287. https://doi.org/10.1177/026553229801500205
Winke, P., Gass, S., & Myford, C. (2013). Raters' L2 background as a potential source of bias in rating oral performance. *Language Testing*, *30*(2), 231–252. https://doi.org/10.1177/0265532212456968
Xi, X., & Mollaun, P. (2011). Using raters from India to score a large-scale speaking test. *Language Learning*, *61*(4), 1222–1255. https://doi.org/10.1111/j.1467-9922.2011.00667.x
Zhang, Y., & Elder, C. (2014). Investigating native and non-native English-speaking teacher raters' judgements of oral proficiency in the College English Test–Spoken English Test (CET–SET). *Assessment in Education: Principles, Policy & Practice*, *21*(3), 306–325. https://doi.org/10.1080/0969594X.2013.845547

Part III

Measuring Individual Differences

14
Measuring Aptitude

Karen Roehr-Brackin

Background

The conceptualization of aptitude developed by John B. Carroll in the 1950s is still a benchmark for researchers today. Carroll's (1962, 1990) model of aptitude was derived empirically from large-scale factor-analytic studies during which a number of aptitude subtests were administered in order to identify those with the greatest predictive validity. This work resulted in the development of the Modern Language Aptitude Test (MLAT; Carroll & Sapon, 1959; Carroll & Sapon, 2002b) for adult English speakers learning a foreign language through intensive instruction. The MLAT comprises five subtests: Number Learning, Phonetic Script, Spelling Clues (all measuring primarily phonetic coding ability), Words in Sentences (measuring grammatical sensitivity), and Paired Associates (measuring associative memory).[1] Taken together, these subtests provided the greatest predictive power in the least time-consuming fashion, which allowed the test developers to remove other draft subtests, including a language learning task aimed at measuring inductive language learning ability (Stansfield & Reed, 2004).

The MLAT was complemented by the Pimsleur Language Aptitude Battery (PLAB; Pimsleur, 1966) aimed at adolescent English speakers. The PLAB is modeled on the MLAT and includes subtests of sound-symbol association (measuring phonetic coding ability), sound discrimination (measuring phonetic coding ability and associative memory), and language analysis (measuring inductive language learning ability and grammatical sensitivity). In addition, subtests of English vocabulary knowledge and interest in learning a foreign language are included. The test taker's overall academic performance in terms of their grade point average also feeds into the test score. In this sense, the PLAB reflects a broader view of aptitude which includes non-linguistic cognitive ability and motivation.

Key Concepts

***Language learning aptitude*:** A set of cognitive and perceptual abilities that facilitate the language learning process; a specific capacity for learning foreign or second languages (L2s) quickly, successfully, and with ease.

***Phonetic coding ability*:** The ability to code unfamiliar sounds for further processing and retention.

***Grammatical sensitivity*:** The ability to identify the function of words in sentences.
***Inductive language learning ability*:** The ability to infer linguistic patterns from exemplars.
***Associative memory*:** The ability to create and retain form-meaning associations.
***Language-analytic ability*:** The ability to infer linguistic patterns and make generalizations.

Key Issues

Empirical Findings and Theoretical Developments

A much-cited criticism of Carroll's model of aptitude and the MLAT is that the classic conceptualization of the construct and its measurement are a product of their time, so they may have little validity outside that context. Put differently, the MLAT may effectively predict L2 learners' success in intensive language instruction drawing on an audiolingual teaching method, but it may be irrelevant in other learning situations. This issue has been addressed empirically by studies investigating aptitude-treatment interactions (for a concise overview, see Roehr, 2012). Taken together, findings indicate that aptitude as conceptualized in the classic model and measured by the MLAT is relevant in all learning settings, both naturalistic (Abrahamsson & Hyltenstam, 2008; DeKeyser, 2000) and instructed. It is also relevant in the context of different instructional approaches in both the classroom and the laboratory (Ehrman & Oxford, 1995; Erlam, 2005; Robinson, 1997; Wesche, 1981; Yilmaz, 2013). While this line of research has revealed that different components of aptitude may play different roles in different conditions, it has provided convincing evidence that the classic model of aptitude and the MLAT have lasting relevance.

More than 60 empirical studies investigating the role of aptitude in second language acquisition (SLA) have been conducted over the years, and two recent meta-analyses of this research (Li, 2015, 2016) provided an overview of the cumulative results. The first meta-analysis (Li, 2015) focused on the relationship between aptitude and morphosyntactic attainment. A total of 33 primary studies completed between 1959 and 2013 were included, with most studies conducted from 2007 onwards. Aptitude test batteries included the MLAT, translated versions of the MLAT, any test batteries modeled on the MLAT, as well as individual subtests and various combinations of subtests. The criterion variable of morphosyntactic attainment was assessed in different ways in the primary studies, with measures including grammaticality judgments, error correction, reading comprehension and written production. The 33 primary studies contributed 309 effect sizes involving 3,106 learners. The results show an aggregated effect size of .31 with narrow confidence intervals, suggesting a robust effect. In other words, aptitude explains about 10% of the variance in morphosyntactic learning. This is arguably considerable, given that the L2 learning process is influenced by a multitude of learner-internal and learner-external factors.

Li (2015) further reported that aptitude affected high school participants' learning more than it affected university students' learning. The reason for this may be that high school students are less advanced learners, with aptitude playing a greater role at lower levels of proficiency. In addition, university students are a select group who may be more homogeneous and advanced, resulting in weaker or no correlations. The results further suggest that in instructed settings, older learners are less likely to draw on aptitude than younger learners. This may be due to a confound between age and instructional setting, with younger learners more likely to be at high school and at lower levels of proficiency. The mean effect size of aptitude in naturalistic settings was significant, confirming a role for aptitude in both untutored and tutored contexts. In the latter, explicit instruction showed stronger correlations with aptitude than implicit instruction (Li, 2015).

The second meta-analysis to be considered here (Li, 2016) focused on the relationship between aptitude and other individual difference variables, as well as on the relationship between aptitude and SLA in terms of both general proficiency and specific skills. Primary studies conducted up to 2014 were considered, but aptitude-treatment interaction studies included in the meta-analysis above were excluded. The predictor variable was aptitude, and the individual difference factors of motivation, anxiety, intelligence, and working memory (WM) capacity, differentiated into executive WM and phonological short-term memory (PSTM), were treated as covariates. The criterion variable of L2 achievement was subdivided into general proficiency, knowledge of grammar and vocabulary, and the skills of listening, speaking, reading, and writing. The data set consisted of 66 primary studies reporting on results from 109 unique samples, with a sampled population of 13,035 participants.

The results showed a weak relationship between aptitude and motivation. This suggests that the two variables are separate constructs and account for unique variance in L2 learning, as one would expect. Aptitude and anxiety were negatively correlated, indicating that higher-aptitude learners experience less anxiety, whereas lower-aptitude learners experience more anxiety, which is again as expected. Aptitude was correlated at a medium level of strength with intelligence, suggesting partial overlap between the two constructs (see also Sasaki, 1996). Finally, the results revealed a moderate correlation between aptitude and executive WM, and a weak correlation between aptitude and PSTM.

The correlation coefficient of .49 identified for the criterion variable of general L2 proficiency indicated that aptitude was a strong predictor in this case, with about 25% of the variance accounted for. The mean effect size was larger for high-school than for university-level learners, which indicated that traditional aptitude measures may be better predictors at lower levels of proficiency, based on the assumption that high school learners have had less L2 experience than university learners. Alternatively, the correlation for university-level learners may have been attenuated by more homogeneous aptitude scores in that more select population, as already noted above. For general L2 proficiency, phonetic coding ability was a stronger predictor than both language-analytic ability and associative memory, with the latter the weakest predictor. With regard to specific L2 knowledge domains and skills, mostly moderate associations with aptitude were found, except for writing. Unsurprisingly, language-analytic ability was the strongest predictor for grammar knowledge (Li, 2016).

In summary, the findings from the two meta-analyses offer powerful evidence for a significant role of aptitude in both instructed and naturalistic SLA across a range of ages and learning contexts. Measures of aptitude significantly predict L2 attainment in terms of both general proficiency and knowledge of morphosyntax.

From the 1990s onwards, L2 research has been increasingly informed by insights from cognitive psychology. As a consequence, proposals for updating the classic model of aptitude have been put forward. The suggestion that grammatical sensitivity and inductive language learning ability may be subsumed under the label of language-analytic ability (Skehan, 1998, 2002) has been readily accepted, and the notion is now widely used (for a discussion, see Chapter 4 in Roehr-Brackin, 2018). Another important development is the argument that WM capacity should be considered a component of aptitude (Kormos, 2013; Miyake & Friedman, 1998; Sawyer & Ranta, 2001; Wen, 2012; Winke, 2013) in view of the fact that there is now considerable evidence for the predictive power of this construct in L2 learning (for a narrative review, see Juffs & Harrington, 2011; for a meta-analysis, see Linck et al., 2014; for an example of a recent study, see Serafini & Sanz, 2016). Finally, the proposals for a theoretical reconceptualization of aptitude put forward by Peter Skehan and Peter Robinson directly speak to the interface between testing and L2 acquisition research.

Skehan (2002, 2015, 2016) argued that if components of aptitude can be linked to the assumed stages of SLA, then aptitude research can make an important contribution to L2 learning research and theorizing, and vice versa. This is because, ultimately, hypotheses about the nature of aptitude and the content of aptitude tests can be regarded as hypotheses about the nature of L2 learning. For instance, at the initial stage of input processing, WM capacity with a special emphasis on

PSTM and the closely related construct of phonetic coding ability are deemed important. At the next stage, noticing, a degree of analysis is required, so WM would seem to be of relevance again, since the more material one can keep online, the more material there is for noticing to operate on. As connections need to be made between the input and existing knowledge representations, both executive WM and PSTM appear to be relevant. A subsequent stage of pattern identification and generalization primarily draws on language-analytic ability, and so forth.

Concluding his analysis, Skehan (2016) pointed out that earlier stages of the SLA process which are concerned with knowledge construction are quite well represented in classic models of aptitude, the notion of WM, and any associated measures. The focus appears to be above all on explicit and domain-specific (in the sense of language-based) knowledge and processes. By contrast, later stages, which are concerned with gaining control via fast and automatic access to existing knowledge representations, do not necessarily map onto classic aptitude components and their associated measures. The focus is on implicit and domain-general abilities and processes, which are only beginning to be considered in the most recent aptitude research (see below).

Robinson (2001, 2005, 2007) made comparable links between conceptualizations of aptitude and L2 learning with his proposal of four aptitude complexes, which consist of combinations of specific cognitive abilities. Each complex can be related to L2 processing under different instructional conditions and in the context of different task types. The four complexes are aptitude for focus on form via recasts, incidental learning via oral content, incidental learning via written content, and explicit rule learning. Each aptitude complex consists of specific ability factors, and individual learners may differ in the strength of ability factors feeding into the same aptitude complex. For instance, aptitude for focus on form via recasts draws on a learner's ability to notice gaps between their output and an interlocutor's recast. A number of primary cognitive abilities are hypothesized to underlie the ability factors associated with each of the four aptitude complexes. For example, the ability to notice gaps is based on perceptual speed, the ability to recognize patterns, and PSTM.

While these proposals constitute timely and informative contributions to theorizing in the areas of L2 learning and language learning aptitude, they are not concerned with the measurement of aptitude per se. Conversely, other approaches informed by current work in cognitive science have focused on developing new measures of aptitude.

Current Approaches to Measuring Aptitude

The measure designed by Grigorenko et al. (2000) represents an innovation in aptitude test development. The researchers put forward the so-called CANAL-F (cognitive ability for novelty in acquisition of language—foreign) framework, which is based on the assumption that the ability to cope with novelty and ambiguity is central to successful SLA. It is argued that the acquisition of L2 knowledge draws on a number of general cognitive processes, including encoding, comparison, transfer, and combination. The researchers posit that these cognitive processes operate at the lexical, morphological, semantic, and syntactic level. The CANAL-FT simulates an L2 learning situation by gradually introducing the regular and consistent artificial language Ursulu, which reflects various typological characteristics. In the course of the test, Ursulu is presented gradually, embedded within an English-language context. Overall, the CANAL-FT involves both immediate and delayed recall of linguistic material. Test takers are required to learn the meanings of neologisms from context, understand the meaning of passages, engage in paired-associate learning, make inferences about linguistic structures from exemplars, and explicitly learn language rules. Items are presented auditorily or visually, except for the language rules, which are presented in writing only (for sample items, see the appendix of Grigorenko et al., 2000).

The researchers reported on two validation studies. The first study provided evidence for convergent validity with the MLAT and discriminant validity with two tests of general intelligence.

The second study suggested that the CANAL-FT has predictive power that is comparable to that of the MLAT, with participants' performance on the test and their success on a language course as rated by their instructors correlating at around .40 (Grigorenko et al., 2000).

Another important development in the design of aptitude measures is the Hi-LAB (Linck et al., 2013), which was designed to distinguish very successful from ordinarily successful L2 learners and predict achievement in the learning of languages that are particularly challenging from an English speaker's point of view (Doughty, 2019). The researchers proceeded on the assumption that aptitude tests such as the MLAT best predict learning at earlier stages, given that the MLAT was originally piloted with and normed on beginning language learners taking short, intensive language courses. By contrast, less is known about factors predicting high-level achievement over the long term, which was operationally defined as highly proficient performance on standardized language proficiency tests and/or high-level job performance in a single or multiple languages. In theoretical terms, high-level aptitude is described as "a composite of domain-general cognitive abilities and specific perceptual abilities that, together, can support or constrain one's ability to attain high-level proficiency as an adult learner" (Linck et al., 2013, p. 535).

The reported 2013 Hi-LAB validation study compared a high-attainment group to a comparison group of mixed-attainment L2 speakers with various proficiency levels; measures of listening and reading achievement were used, with all participants educated professionals. A battery of 11 cognitive and perceptual tests was administered, comprising a running memory span test, an anti-saccade test, a Stroop test and a task-switching numbers test assessing various aspects of the executive function of WM; a letter span and a non-word span test assessing PSTM; a paired-associates test assessing associative memory; an available long-term memory synonym test assessing retrieval from long-term memory; a serial reaction time test assessing implicit learning ability and processing speed; a test of phonemic discrimination contrasting Hindi and English, and a test of phonemic categorization based on Russian assessing auditory perceptual acuity.

In summary, the results showed that measures of PSTM, implicit learning, and associative memory were robust predictors of high attainment; measures of executive function were marginally predictive for listening, though with a negative coefficient. Overall, the Hi-LAB was better at predicting listening than reading achievement, so it may be advisable to additionally include measures of visual perceptual acuity in any future versions (Doughty, 2019; Linck et al., 2013).

While the Hi-LAB and the CANAL-FT represent a departure from the MLAT, the LLAMA aptitude test battery (Meara, 2005) is strongly influenced by the classic four-component model of aptitude. It is a computer-administered test for adolescent and adult learners comprising four subtests labeled LLAMA B, D, E, and F. All subtests except LLAMA D consist of a study phase whose length is set to a default, but can be adjusted by the researcher, and an untimed test phase; the LLAMA D consists of a presentation phase with fixed timings and a test phase. Testing on LLAMA D, E and F follows a two-way multiple-choice format, with incorrect responses penalized to compensate for guessing.

LLAMA B is a vocabulary learning task assessing associative memory. During the study phase, the participant tries to learn associations between picture stimuli and novel words taken from a Central American language. The test phase tests vocabulary recognition. LLAMA D is a test of phonetic coding and assesses auditory pattern recognition. The participant listens to short stretches of computer-generated sound sequences based on the names of natural objects in a British Columbian indigenous language. In the test phase, the participant must decide whether they have heard a given sound sequence before or not. LLAMA E tests sound-symbol association, similar to the MLAT Phonetic Script subtest. During the study phase, the participant tries to learn associations between a set of consonant-vowel sound strings and their spelling in letters resembling the international phonetic alphabet. In the test phase, the participant must recognize the correct spelling of a given combination of sound strings. Finally, LLAMA F is a test of grammatical inferencing assessing inductive language learning ability. During the study phase, the participant attempts to learn the grammar of a new language by making inferences from short sentences (form) shown in association with pictures they describe (meaning). The test phase requires recognition of grammatically correct vs. grammatically incorrect sentences describing associated pictures.

The LLAMA originated as a project geared at undergraduate students in applied linguistics at the main author's home institution, but has since found its way into empirical SLA and aptitude research, even though the test website alerts researchers to the fact that the LLAMA has not been formally validated. However, in recent years researchers have begun to examine the validity and reliability of the LLAMA battery in more detail. Results to date are mixed, showing both promising findings (Granena, 2013a; Rogers et al., 2016) and identifying shortcomings (Bokander & Bylund, 2020). The research group behind the LLAMA have resumed their work as well (Rogers et al., 2016).

Apart from the MLAT, the LLAMA is the most widely used aptitude test battery in L2 learning research today. The popularity of the LLAMA is at least partly due to the fact that it is independent of a test taker's first language, unlike the English-based CANAL-FT and MLAT, although versions of the MLAT in a small number of other languages do exist. Second, and arguably most importantly, the LLAMA and the associated test manual are freely available to anyone who wishes to use the measure,[2]—quite unlike the Hi-LAB, the CANAL-FT,[3] and the MLAT,[4] which are not accessible to researchers. Therefore, a practical recommendation for researchers who wish to measure aptitude in adolescent or adult learners is to make use of the LLAMA, while bearing in mind that full validation is still ongoing.

Recommendations for Practice

The preceding discussion has highlighted key issues informing language learning aptitude research today by providing an overview of how theorizing and measurement of the construct have developed over the past decades. Aptitude research no longer necessarily relies exclusively on language-based measures as exemplified by the MLAT subtests, but additionally draws on domain-general measures such as tests of executive WM, PSTM, or serial reaction time tasks that assess broader cognitive abilities underlying not only language processing, but also other kinds of information processing. The inclusion of such measures reflects work in cognitive psychology and its application to SLA research. Indeed, Doughty (2019) used the term *cognitive language aptitude* to encapsulate the construct's modernization and larger scope. Moreover, within the construct, the importance of both explicit and implicit knowledge and learning is taken into account (Skehan, 2015, 2016; Wen et al., 2017). The MLAT primarily focuses on the measurement of aptitude for explicit learning, as exemplified by subtests assessing language-analytic ability and associative memory. Even though the relevant subtests are timed, they permit the test taker to work strategically, test hypotheses and make inferences. By contrast, more recent test batteries additionally include tasks that may tap aptitude for implicit learning, as exemplified by the LLAMA D sound recognition subtest and the serial reaction time task on the Hi-LAB (see also Granena, 2013a, 2013b, 2016). These tasks require online processing and do not give the test taker any opportunity to engage in strategy use or conscious reflection. Future research will need to establish what role aptitude components for explicit and implicit learning play at different points in the developmental process and in different learning situations, and how they might interact with other individual difference factors.

A related but as yet unresolved question pertains to the stability or malleability of language learning aptitude. Traditionally, aptitude has been regarded as a relatively stable trait (Carroll, 1981; Sawyer & Ranta, 2001; Skehan, 1998) that does not undergo any major changes once an individual has reached cognitive maturity, regardless of environmental changes or accumulating L2 experience, for instance. More recently, this position has been called into question (Grigorenko et al., 2000; Wen et al., 2017), either directly or indirectly. Indeed, it is entirely conceivable that extensive experience with L2 learning and dedicated training in linguistics, for example, may improve an individual's performance on (certain) measures of aptitude, similar to the argument that targeted WM training may improve performance on (certain) measures of WM (Foster et al., 2017; Morrison & Chein, 2011). Establishing whether and to what extent this is the case for aptitude in cognitively mature learners would require longitudinal research.

In the case of young learners up to around 12 years of age, there is strong evidence that aptitude is dynamic and not at all stable (Roehr-Brackin & Tellier, 2019; Suárez & Muñoz, 2011; Tellier, 2015; Tellier & Roehr-Brackin, 2013). In other words, as children mature, their performance on the same aptitude measure gradually improves. However, aptitude measures can still be used to predict performance or to make links with L2 development, and with explicit and implicit learning (Kiss, 2009; Kiss & Nikolov, 2005; Roehr-Brackin & Tellier, 2019; Tellier & Roehr-Brackin, 2017). As in the case of adults, there is a relatively small choice of instruments available to researchers interested in child SLA. The child version of the MLAT, the MLAT-Elementary (MLAT-E; Carroll & Sapon, 2002a) is commercially available,[5] but like the adult MLAT, is designed for English speakers. Versions in a small number of other languages have been produced, and researchers have attempted to create alternative tests (Miller & Phillips, 1982; Milton & Alexiou, 2006), but none of these have been formally validated or are readily available. The development of a first language-independent aptitude test battery that is suitable for children under the age of 12 thus constitutes another direction for future research.

Testing Tips

- SLA researchers and language testers need not solely use standardized tests of L2 aptitude, such as the MLAT or PLAB, to measure cognitive language aptitude. They can also consider using tests of cognitive ability that measure aptitude components, such as tests of working memory capacity (see Wen, Juffs, and Winke, Chapter 16, this volume) and attentional control (inhibition, updating, or resource allocation tests).
- When reporting the results of aptitude testing, researchers should publish the raw, item-level test data in an open-access, public repository or in a supplementary file so that the data are available for secondary analyses.
- SLA researchers and language testers who measure aptitude as a variable of interest or as a control variable should report the aptitude tests' reliability coefficients, with those values calculated from the study's sample data. This is important because normed reliability information from standardized aptitude tests may be from long ago, when instruction was more memory-dependent, or may be based on a sample of test takers who differ considerably from the study sample.

Recommended Readings

Granena, G., & Long, M. H. (Eds.). (2013). *Sensitive periods, language aptitude, and ultimate L2 attainment*. John Benjamins.

This edited volume considers the role of aptitude in learners of different ages and offers both empirical and theoretical chapters.

Li, S. (2015). The associations between language aptitude and second language grammar acquisition: A meta-analytic review of five decades of research. *Applied Linguistics*, *36*(3), 385–408. https://doi.org/10.1093/applin/amu054

This paper provides a definitive overview of cumulative results arising from empirical research into the role of aptitude in L2 grammar learning.

Wen, Z., Biedroń, A., & Skehan, P. (2017). Foreign language aptitude theory: Yesterday, today and tomorrow. *Language Teaching*, *50*(1), 1–31. https://doi.org/10.1017/S0261444816000276

The authors offer a comprehensive and in-depth review of the history of aptitude research as well as suggestions for future work in the field.

Notes

1 For MLAT sample items, see http://lltf.net/mlat-sample-items/. For a brief overview of other classic tests such as the PLAB, DLAB, VORD, etc. see Chapter 3 in Dörnyei (2005) or Wen et al. (2017).
2 See http://www.lognostics.co.uk/tools/llama/
3 An incomplete version of the CANAL-FT can still be obtained, but the original audio-files are no longer available (Elena Grigorenko, Linda Jarvis, personal communication, July 9, 2018).
4 The MLAT used to be commercially available, but researchers are now barred from purchasing it; for further details, see http://lltf.net/aptitude-tests/language-aptitude-tests/modern-language-aptitude-test-2/
5 See http://lltf.net/aptitude-tests/language-aptitude-tests/mlat-elementary/

References

Abrahamsson, N., & Hyltenstam, K. (2008). The robustness of aptitude effects in near-native second language acquisition. *Studies in Second Language Acquisition*, *30*, 481–509. https://doi.org/10.10170S027226310808073X

Bokander, L., & Bylund, E. (2020). Probing the internal validity of the LLAMA language aptitude tests. *Language Learning*, 70(1), 11–47. https://doi.org/10.1111/lang.12368

Carroll, J. B. (1962). The prediction of success in intensive foreign language training. In R. Glaser (Ed.), *Training research and education* (pp. 87–136). John Wiley & Sons.

Carroll, J. B. (1981). Twenty-five years of research on foreign language aptitude. In K. C. Diller (Ed.), *Individual differences and universals in language learning aptitude* (pp. 83–118). Newbury House.

Carroll, J. B. (1990). Cognitive abilities in foreign language aptitude: Then and now. In T. S. Parry & C. W. Stansfield (Eds.), *Language aptitude reconsidered* (pp. 11–29). Prentice Hall.

Carroll, J. B., & Sapon, S. (1959). *The modern language aptitude test*. Psychological Corporation.

Carroll, J. B., & Sapon, S. M. (2002a). *Modern language aptitude test—Elementary: MLAT-E*. Second Language Testing Foundation.

Carroll, J. B., & Sapon, S. M. (2002b). *Modern language aptitude test: MLAT*. Second Language Testing Inc.

DeKeyser, R. M. (2000). The robustness of critical period effects in second language acquisition. *Studies in Second Language Acquisition*, *22*, 499–533. https://doi.org/10.1017/S0272263100004022

Dörnyei, Z. (2005). *The psychology of the language learner: Individual differences in second language acquisition*. Lawrence Erlbaum Associates.

Doughty, C. J. (2019). Cognitive language aptitude. *Language Learning*, *69*(S2), 101–126. https://doi.org/10.1111/lang.12322

Ehrman, M. E., & Oxford, R. L. (1995). Cognition plus: Correlates of language learning success. *The Modern Language Journal*, *79*(1), 67–89. https://doi.org/10.1111/j.1540-4781.1995.tb05417.x

Erlam, R. (2005). Language aptitude and its relationship to instructional effectiveness in second language acquisition. *Language Teaching Research*, *9*(2), 147–171. https://doi.org/10.1191/1362168805lr161oa

Foster, J. L., Harrison, T. L., Hicks, K. L., Draheim, C., Redick, T., S., & Engle, R. W. (2017). Do the effects of working memory training depend on baseline ability level? *Journal of Experimental Psychology: Learning, Memory, and Cognition*, *43*(11), 1677–1689. https://doi.org/10.1037/xlm0000426

Granena, G. (2013a). Cognitive aptitudes for second language learning and the LLAMA language aptitude test. In G. Granena & M. H. Long (Eds.), *Sensitive periods, language aptitude, and ultimate L2 attainment* (pp. 105–129). John Benjamins.

Granena, G. (2013b). Individual differences in sequence learning ability and second language acquisition in early childhood and adulthood. *Language Learning*, *63*(4), 665–703. https://doi.org/10.1111/lang.12018

Granena, G. (2016). Cognitive aptitudes for implicit and explicit learning and information-processing styles: An individual differences study. *Applied Psycholinguistics*, *37*, 577–600. https://doi.org/10.1017/S0142716415000120

Grigorenko, E. L., Sternberg, R. J., & Ehrman, M. E. (2000). A theory-based approach to the measurement of foreign language learning ability: The Canal-F theory and test. *The Modern Language Journal*, *84*(3), 390–405. https://doi.org/10.1111/0026-7902.00076

Juffs, A., & Harrington, M. (2011). Aspects of working memory in L2 learning. *Language Teaching*, *44*(2), 137–166. https://doi.org/10.1017/S0261444810000509

Kiss, C. (2009). The role of aptitude in young learners' foreign language learning. In M. Nikolov (Ed.), *The age factor and early language learning* (pp. 253–276). Mouton de Gruyter.

Kiss, C., & Nikolov, M. (2005). Developing, piloting, and validating an instrument to measure young learners' aptitude. *Language Learning*, *55*(1), 99–150. https://doi.org/10.1111/j.0023-8333.2005.00291.x

Kormos, J. (2013). New coneptualizations of language aptitude in second language attainment. In G. Granena & M. H. Long (Eds.), *Sensitive periods, language aptitude, and ultimate L2 attainment* (pp. 131–152). John Benjamins.

Li, S. (2015). The associations between language aptitude and second language grammar acquisition: A meta-analytic review of five decades of research. *Applied Linguistics*, *36*(3), 385–408. https://doi.org/10.1093/applin/amu054

Li, S. (2016). The construct validity of language aptitude: A meta-analysis. *Studies in Second Language Acquisition*, *38*(4), 801–842. https://doi.org/10.017/S027226311500042X

Linck, J. A., Hughes, M. M., Campbell, S. G., Silbert, N. H., Tare, M., Jackson, S. R., Smith, B. K., Bunting, M. F., & Doughty, C. (2013). Hi-LAB: A new measure of aptitude for high-level language proficiency. *Language Learning*, *63*(3), 530–566. https://doi.org/10.1111/lang.12011

Linck, J. A., Osthus, P., Koeth, J. T., & Bunting, M. F. (2014). Working memory and second language comprehension and production: A meta-analysis. *Psychonomic Bulletin & Review*, *21*, 861–883. https://doi.org/10.3758/s13423-013-0565-2

Meara, P. (2005). *LLAMA language aptitude tests*. University of Wales Swansea.

Miller, A., & Phillips, D. (1982). Towards a new language aptitude test. *British Journal of Language Teaching*, *20*(2), 97–100.

Milton, J., & Alexiou, T. (2006). Language aptitude development in young learners. In C. Abello-Contesse, R. Chacón-Beltrán, M. D. López-Jiménez, & M. M. Torreblanca-López (Eds.), *Age in L2 acquisition and teaching* (pp. 177–192). Peter Lang.

Miyake, A., & Friedman, N. P. (1998). Individual differences in second language proficiency: Working memory as language aptitude. In A. F. Healy & L. E. Bourne (Eds.), *Foreign language learning: Psycholinguistic studies on training and retention* (pp. 339–364). Lawrence Erlbaum Associates.

Morrison, A. B., & Chein, J. M. (2011). Does working memory training work? The promise and challenges of enhancing cognition by training working memory. *Psychonomic Bulletin & Review*, *18*(1), 46–60. https://doi.org/10.3758/s13423-010-0034-0

Pimsleur, P. (1966). *The Pimsleur language aptitude battery*. Harcourt.

Robinson, P. (1997). Individual differences and the fundamental similarity of implicit and explicit adult second language learning. *Language Learning*, *47*(1), 45–99. https://doi.org/10.1111/0023-8333.21997002

Robinson, P. (2001). Individual differences, cognitive abilities, aptitude complexes and learning conditions in second language acquisition. *Second Language Research*, *17*(4), 368–392. https://doi.org/10.1177/026765830101700405

Robinson, P. (2005). Aptitude and second language acquisition. *Annual Review of Applied Linguistics*, *25*, 46–73. https://doi.org/10.1017/S0267190505000036

Robinson, P. (2007). Aptitudes, abilities, contexts, and practice. In R. M. DeKeyser (Ed.), *Practice in a second language: Perspectives from applied linguistics and cognitive psychology* (pp. 256–286). Cambridge University Press.

Roehr, K. (2012). Aptitude treatment interaction (ATI) research. In P. Robinson (Ed.), *The Routledge encyclopedia of second language acquisition* (pp. 31–35). Routledge.

Roehr-Brackin, K. (2018). *Metalinguistic awareness and second language acquisition*. Routledge.

Roehr-Brackin, K., & Tellier, A. (2019). The role of language-analytic ability in children's instructed second language learning. *Studies in Second Language Acquisition*, 1–21. https://doi.org/10.1017/S0272263119000214

Rogers, V., Meara, P., Aspinall, R., Fallon, L., Goss, T., Keey, E., & Thomas, R. (2016). Testing aptitude: Investigating Meara's (2005) LLAMA tests. *EuroSLA Yearbook*, *16*, 179–210. https://doi.org/10.1075/eurosla.16.07rog

Sasaki, M. (1996). *Second language proficiency, foreign language aptitude, and intelligence*. Peter Lang.

Sawyer, M., & Ranta, L. (2001). Aptitude, individual differences, and instructional design. In P. Robinson (Ed.), *Cognition and second language instruction* (pp. 319–353). Cambridge University Press.
Serafini, E. J., & Sanz, C. (2016). Evidence for the decreasing impact of cognitive ability on second language development as proficiency increases. *Studies in Second Language Acquisition*, *38*, 607–646. https://doi.org/10.1017/S0272263115000327
Skehan, P. (1998). *A cognitive approach to language learning*. Oxford University Press.
Skehan, P. (2002). Theorising and updating aptitude. In P. Robinson (Ed.), *Individual differences and instructed language learning* (pp. 69–94). John Benjamins.
Skehan, P. (2015). Foreign language aptitude and its relationship with grammar: A critical overview. *Applied Linguistics*, *36*(3), 367–384. https://doi.org/10.1093/applin/amu072
Skehan, P. (2016). Foreign language aptitude, acquisitional sequences, and psycholinguistic processes. In G. Granena, D. O. Jackson, & Y. Yilmaz (Eds.), *Cognitive individual differences in second language processing and acquisition* (pp. 17–40). John Benjamins.
Stansfield, C. W., & Reed, D. J. (2004). The story behind the modern language aptitude test: An interview with John B. Carroll (1916–2003). *Language Assessment Quarterly*, *1*(1), 43–56. https://doi.org/10.1207/s15434311laq0101_4
Suárez, M. d. M., & Muñoz, C. (2011). Aptitude, age and cognitive development: The MLAT-E in Spanish and Catalan. *EuroSLA Yearbook*, *11*, 5–29. https://doi.org/10.1075/eurosla.11.03sua
Tellier, A. (2015). *Metalinguistic awareness and foreign language learning in primary school: A classroom study with children aged 8 to 9 years* (Unpublished doctoral dissertation). University of Essex.
Tellier, A., & Roehr-Brackin, K. (2013). The development of language learning aptitude and metalinguistic awareness in primary-school children: A classroom study. *Essex Research Reports in Linguistics*, *62*(1), 1–28. https://www1.essex.ac.uk/linguistics/external/errl/errl62-1.pdf
Tellier, A., & Roehr-Brackin, K. (2017). Raising children's metalinguistic awareness to enhance classroom second language learning. In M. d. P. García Mayo (Ed.), *Learning foreign languages in primary school: Research insights* (pp. 22–48). Multilingual Matters.
Wen, Z. (2012). Working memory and second language learning. *International Journal of Applied Linguistics*, *22*(1), 1–22. https://doi.org/10.1111/j.1473-4192.2011.00290.x
Wen, Z., Biedroń, A., & Skehan, P. (2017). Foreign language aptitude theory: Yesterday, today and tomorrow. *Language Teaching*, *50*(1), 1–31. https://doi.org/10.1017/S0261444816000276
Wesche, M. B. (1981). Language aptitude measures in streaming, matching students with methods, and diagnosis of learning problems. In K. C. Diller (Ed.), *Individual differences and universals in language learning aptitude* (pp. 119–154). Newbury House.
Winke, P. (2013). An investigation into second language aptitude for advanced Chinese language learning. *The Modern Language Journal*, *97*(1), 109–130. https://doi.org/10.1111/j.1540-4781.2013.01428.x
Yilmaz, Y. (2013). Relative effects of explicit and implicit feedback: The role of working memory capacity and language analytic ability. *Applied Linguistics*, *34*(3), 344–368. https://doi.org/10.1093/applin/ams044

15
Measuring Motivation

Janina Iwaniec & Karen J. Dunn

Background

The roots of language learning motivation research can be traced back to bilingual Canada, where in the 1950s, Gardner and Lambert observed that variation in language learning achievement could be more fully explained if, in addition to learners' verbal intelligence and language learning aptitude, a new factor labelled *language learning motivation* was taken into account. Gardner and Lambert (1972) believed that "when the social setting demands it, people master a second language no matter what their aptitude might be" (p. 2). In other words, under certain circumstances, motivation to learn a language is as powerful, if not more powerful, than many or most cognitively based individual differences. Since then, research on language learning motivation has flourished. A large number of theories and constructs outlining motivation's shape and influence on second-language (L2) learning have been proposed. In this chapter, we introduce three of the most influential theories of language learning motivation. We then focus on how motivation is measured, and we overview recent research on motivation, where we stress that current research does not robustly address the complex and dynamic relationship between motivation and achievement. We conclude by providing testing tips for researchers interested in exploring language learning motivation further.

Key Concepts

Extrinsic motivation: Motivation that is underlined by external factors, such as rewards, punishments, or societal expectations.

Ideal L2 self: A future, possible vision of oneself as a successful language user.

Instrumental orientation: Motivation spurred by utilitarian reasons connected with mastery of language learning.

Integrative motive: The first theory of motivation specific to language learning proposed by Gardner (1985).

Integrative orientation: This is the key concept in Gardner's "Integrative Motive," defined as "willingness to be like valued members of the language community" (Gardner & Lambert, 1972, p. 271).

International posture: Motivation to learn a language defined by openness to others and interest in the products of other cultures; strongly associated with the position of English as a dominant language.

Intrinsic motivation: Learner's internal motivation that is key to learning and personal development, accompanied by positive feelings.

L2 motivational self-system: The theory of language learning motivation proposed by Dörnyei in 2005, including three constructs, ideal L2 self, ought-to L2 self, and language learning experience.

Language learning experience: The influence of the immediate language learning environment.

Ought-to L2 self: A future, possible vision of oneself in relation to language learning, shaped by more or less internalised motives of who one "should be."

Self-determination theory: The theory of motivation developed by Deci and Ryan (1985), the key constructs of which include intrinsic and extrinsic motivation.

Key issues

Gardner's Contribution to Language Learning Motivation Research

Robert Gardner is a key figure in early language learning motivation research. His contribution extends to situating motivation in a broader process of language acquisition, as he was the first to propose a comprehensive theory of language learning: the Socio-Educational Model of Second Language Acquisition (Gardner, 1985), a model that positions language learning within a social and cultural milieu. Within this theory, a range of individual learner differences, of which motivation is one, are postulated to affect both linguistic and non-linguistic learning outcomes. In a career spanning more than six decades, Gardner made a vast contribution to the understanding of motivation, including laying foundations on the measurement of motivation in his development of the first instrument for assessing levels of language learning motivation: the Attitude Motivation Test Battery, or ATMB (Gardner, 1985).

A key foundation of Gardner's approach to motivation was to acknowledge that whilst motivation is often referred to in the singular, it encapsulates a range of dispositions. In 1985, Gardner conceptualised motivation as part of a multi-layered construct known as the *integrative motive*. The integrative motive was proposed to consist of three components: integrativeness, attitudes toward the learning situation, and motivation. Each of these facets in turn subsumed further constructs (Gardner, 1985).

Gardner's research concentrated on two broad reasons as to why learners pursue language learning. The integrative orientation saw learners as driven to master the language by a desire to identify with the target language community. Meanwhile, an instrumental orientation stemmed from utilitarian benefits about language learning (Gardner & Lambert, 1972) and incorporated a large number of potential goals, such as getting a promotion, passing an exam, or increasing one's chances on the job market.

In his theory of motivation, Gardner (1972) highlighted the fact that language learning involves not only having a command of linguistic resources, but learning the culture and behaviours associated with the language. With much of his research rooted in the French-Canadian context, the integrative motive was found to be good at explaining differential success in language learning in a bilingual society, where two language communities (the L1 and the L2) live together or in relative proximity to each other. However, in other contexts, the conceptualisation of integrative motive became problematic, as it was not always easy for L2 learners to define a target group or community who spoke the language as an L1 and with whom the L2 learners could identify. This was particularly pertinent for English, which as a global language has many speakers from diverse cultural and geographic backgrounds.

Furthermore, whilst there was a clear case for distinguishing integrative orientation from instrumental orientation in the learning journey of bilingual Francophone or Anglophone Canadians, it is often impossible to make a distinction between integrativeness and instrumentality in the case of English (Dörnyei, 2005; Yashima, 2000). English is a lingua franca in today's world, a global language spoken by 1.5 billion users. As such, English dominates many aspects of modern life such as computer sciences, aviation, the movie industry, and the economy, and is more and more frequently required as a basic skill, rather than something that includes a need for cultural integration. Consequently, Yashima (2000) proposed a new construct, *international posture*, which mirrors the role of English in today's world. International posture includes "interest in foreign or international affairs, willingness to go overseas to study or work, readiness to interact with intercultural partners and [...] a non-ethnocentric attitude toward different cultures" (p. 57).

Whilst the separation between motivational traits described by Gardner may not be relevant for a small number of world languages, it is still applicable for learning languages in some situations. In these cases, the question arises as to what degree of identification the integrative orientation implies. More recently, Dörnyei (2005) distinguished between two versions of integrativeness. The strong one refers to social identification and integration, whereas the weak one incorporates a sense of belonging and interest. It can be argued that the strong form of the integrative motive might not be possible, or even desirable, for every language learner, whereas the weak version might not be sufficient to contribute strongly to effort investment, in particular effort in learning a language in a foreign language context.

Such ongoing discussions bear witness to the fact that Gardner's contribution to language learning motivation research is still germane. In many ways, he paved the way to the explanations and understandings of this construct that are still being explored today.

Self-Determination Theory

Whilst Gardner's work stressed the influence of the social setting in which language learning takes place, Deci and Ryan's (1985) self-determination theory focused on the psychological aspects of an individual learner's motivation. This includes how motivation is related to wellbeing and supports an individual's growth, as well as how motivation can be affected in micro-settings, such as in a language classroom.

Intrinsic motivation is a key concept in self-determination theory. Ryan and Deci (2000) defined it as "an inherent tendency to seek out novelty and challenges, to extend and exercise one's capacities, to explore, and to learn" (p. 70). Intrinsic motivation is accompanied by positive feelings of interest, curiosity, excitement, enjoyment, competence, and self-determination. Intrinsically motivated activity is perceived as an end in itself, meaning that people will carry out an activity that they are intrinsically motivated to do, without the need for other rewards (Ryan & Deci, 2000). The concept of intrinsic motivation is often contrasted against extrinsic motivation, which concerns the performance of an activity for reasons other than inherent satisfaction (Ryan & Deci, 2000), such as to avoid punishment or receive a reward.

Rather than there being two polar opposites between intrinsic and extrinsic motivations, Deci and Ryan (1985) specified that four types of extrinsic motives exist, depending on how internalised they are. This outlined a continuum between extrinsic and intrinsic motivation. The least internalised type is *external regulation*, which is when the action is performed to get a reward or satisfy an external demand. The second type is *introjected regulation*, which "involves taking in a regulation but not fully accepting it as one's own" (Deci & Ryan, 1985, p. 72). The third is *identified regulation*, which is when the goal is valued and recognised as being of personal importance and, finally, *integrated regulation*, when the behaviour is fully consistent with the individual's values and needs. While integrated behaviours are performed for outcomes other than inherent enjoyment, they share many features with intrinsically motivated behaviours (Deci & Ryan, 1985).

Research on the self-determination theory is not limited to language learning motivation but extends to a range of domains, including, among others: human development in families, schools, and societies; psychotherapy; health care; sports; wellness; and pervasive social contexts. Kimberly Noels and colleagues most extensively researched different aspects of the self-determination theory in relation to language learning, including the learning of English, Spanish, and Chinese. One of the key contributions of research into self-determination theory in language learning centres on the provision of a set of clear implications on how teachers can create supportive learning environments (Lamb, 2017). The focus on the individual within this theory means, however, that the social aspect of language learning is largely ignored.

L2 Motivational Self System

In 2005, Zoltán Dörnyei proposed a new theory of language learning motivation, the L2 Motivational Self System, or L2MSS. This theory stressed the role of the language learning environment, but it also included two self-related factors, the *ideal L2 self* and the *ought-to L2 self*. L2MSS was immediately adopted by language learning motivation researchers, perhaps due to its apparent simplicity and a clear link to Gardner's work (see Dörnyei, 2005).

In the context of the L2MSS, the ideal L2 self is an image of oneself as a proficient speaker of an L2. It is a vision of what the learner wants to become in the future. The ought-to L2 self refers to the qualities one should possess, for example one should try to avoid negative consequences that might result from their behaviour. Hence, learners for whom the ought-to L2 self is the main source of motivation tend to study languages because they see it as their duty to do so, or they do it to avoid disappointing others. Alongside these considerations, the model takes into account the *L2 learning experience*, a factor which concerns the influence of the immediate environment on language learning (Dörnyei, 2005). Unlike the two possible selves which capture future visions, this component reflects immediate temporal influences on language learning, for example the role of peer groups, the teacher, or the curriculum.

Dörnyei (2005) proposed that the motivational power of possible selves arises from the discrepancy between what the individual is and what they want to become. The discrepancy between the two states results in the experience of discomfort, which leads to the individual trying to minimise it by diminishing the existing discrepancy. However, the motivational properties of ideal and ought-to L2 selves are dependent on a number of conditions. The learner needs to generate a desired future image that is elaborate, vivid, plausible, but, at the same time, sufficiently different from the current self. Closing the gap requires substantial effort on the part of the learner. Having ideal and ought-to L2 selves that are in harmony with each other is more likely to spur effort investment, although having a strong rebellious self can be also fruitful.

L2MSS has been heavily researched in a large number of contexts (see for example the volume edited by Dörnyei & Ushioda, 2009). Previous empirical studies show that the ideal L2 self and the language learning experience are related to increased behavioural investment in language learning. In contrast, the concept of the ought-to L2 self has been found to be more problematic as it appears to influence motivation variably in different learning contexts. For example, Taguchi et al. (2009), who investigated the motivation of learners from Japan, China, and Iran, found that the ought-to L2 self was related to family influence and the intended effort towards learning English, but this latter relationship was much weaker than in the case of the ideal L2 self. Yet in the context of Hungary, the motivational properties of the ought-to L2 self were limited (Csizér & Kormos, 2009). In some respects, however, the L2MSS has given researchers the tools they need to elucidate these cultural and contextual differences in language learning.

Overall, it can be seen that the key theoretical standpoints from Gardner, Ryan, and Dörnyei have contributed much to teasing apart the many aspects of motivation in the realm of second language learning. Whilst their research spotlights slightly different social or psychological aspects of motivation, the insights can be understood as largely complementary to one another, each helping to build a much richer picture of the language learner. More broadly, the work of these researchers has firmly established L2 motivation as a key element in L2 individual difference research.

How Is Motivation Measured?

Since the days of Gardner, whose work heavily relied on the use of questionnaires and statistical analyses, motivation has been predominantly measured using quantitative methodologies. Although Boo et al. (2015) indicated that studies classified as employing methodologies other than quantitative (qualitative, mixed-methods, and innovative) are on the rise, the quantitative approach still makes up the bulk of investigations in the field. These often take the form of analysing responses to questionnaires consisting of targeted groups of questions designed to assess participants' motivational traits and the intensity of various aspects of motivation.

The first instrument developed to measure language learning motivation was Gardner's Attitude/Motivation Test Battery (ATMB; Gardner, 1985). The scales included in ATMB mirror constructs from the integrative motive discussed above. The ATMB itself contains three types of questions, differing in response format, namely, multiple choice, Likert scale (see Phakiti & Bi, Chapter 10, this volume), and semantic differential assessments (where the participant is asked to provide an evaluation on a scale of two opposite adjectives, for example useful–useless). Although the integrative motive is no longer a dominant framework of language learning motivation, individual scales from the ATMB are still in use, albeit often adapted to a new context.

Researchers interested in assessing language learning motivation in terms of the self-determination theory often draw on items from the Language Learning Orientations Scales (LLOS), which was first validated by Noels and colleagues (Noels et al., 2000). This questionnaire only employs Likert scales as a response format and is much shorter in format compared to the fairly lengthy ATMB. A brief survey can be useful if motivation is one of several constructs researched in a study.

Researchers investigating motivation according to Dörnyei's L2MSS tend to focus on the three key constructs of interest ("ideal L2 self," "ought-to L2 self," and "L2 learning experience"). An example of this is the questionnaire by Taguchi et al. (2009). However, the development of measurement instruments designed to operationalise the L2MSS is still ongoing. One of the criticisms of early questionnaires is that they fail to take into account the fact that the motivational power of the future selves is dependent on a number of conditions. The most basic condition is the existence of a sufficiently elaborate and vivid possible self. The risk of employing a simplified measurement instrument lies in its inability to discriminate between learners who do, and those who do not, have an available future self-image. For the measurement of the future selves to yield reliable results, items should provide the right level of detail to establish that the respondent possesses the vision, that it is elaborate, and they consider it to be plausible.

One of the few scholars who undertook this challenge was Hessel (2015). She developed an 8-item scale of the ideal L2 self. Again in a series of Likert-scale items, learners provide responses intended to capture their level of engagement with their L2 vision, including desirability, accessibility, perceived self-discrepancy, plausibility, and declared effort investment, all of which are the pre-conditions to the motivational power of the ideal L2 self, as specified by Dörnyei (2009). Hessel's results suggested that the frequency of imagining the desired state, the perceived gap between the current and future self, and the desirability of the future vision contributed significantly to explain variance in learners' effort investment. In contrast, perceived plausibility was associated with increased effort investment, but once other conditions were controlled for, its unique contribution was not significant. In this way, Hessel's approach provided a more detailed picture of the web of perceptions that constitute a learner's relationship with their ideal L2 self.

Meanwhile, the motivational role of the ought-to L2 self has been shown to be limited in comparison to the ideal L2 self (Taguchi et al., 2009), and in some context, its role has been found to be questionable (Csizér & Kormos, 2009). Some scholars have attributed these results to the poor reliability and validity of the scales used to measure these constructs. Consequently, a number of revisions have been suggested in the operationalisation of the ought-to L2 self. One of them was Teimouri (2017), who proposed to differentiate between the two aspects of the ought-to L2 self: *own*, which is endorsed by the individual, and *others*, which is imposed by others around. Teimouri (2017) subsequently developed the scales to measure both constructs. His findings indicate that the two aspects of the ought-to L2 self are distinct. The ought-to L2 self/own was found to be strongly related to both the ideal L2 self and the ought-to L2 self/others, whereas the ought-to L2 self/others and the ideal L2 self were not clearly related. Yet, even in this reformulation, the relationship between both aspects of the ought-to L2 self and the measure of effort investment was much weaker than that with the ideal L2 self.

With respect to the *language learning experience*, it is not clear yet that research instruments account adequately for the full range of potential influences that impact the immediate language learning environment, which subsequently is proposed to affect L2 learning. The definition provided by Dörnyei (2005) is broad and implies that there are a large number of potential influences, such as parents, teachers, peers, teaching materials, curriculum, and assessment methods, just to mention a few. To measure this construct appropriately, first the scholar would need to decide on which environmental influences to focus, and then create multiple scales for measurement. Instead, studies up to the current date tend to take a shortcut and employ one scale, which often actually takes a form of language learning attitudes (see Taguchi et al., 2009, as an example).

The development of innovative and more specific or dynamic measures of motivation is one of the main areas in language learning motivation research. Advances in the operationalisation of theoretical concepts coupled with a greater sophisitication in the statistical tools available to researchers has led to an increasingly detailed understanding of language learners' motivation. There is, of course, room to delve further into these relationships and to fine-tune the instruments used. For example, for the most part motivational surveys are cross-sectional by design, in that they capture the motivation of a given group of learners at one point in time. Longitudinal designs are rare, meaning that the full potential for such investigations largely remains, as yet, unexplored. Studies that employ pre- and post-test design as well as randomised control trials are even rarer (Lamb, 2017).

Yet not all motivational studies are quantitative. Recently, the field has experienced a dynamic turn, which is mirrored in the growth of mixed-methods and qualitative studies (see, for example, Rasool & Winke, 2019). In these studies, motivation is a complex phenomenon that is affected by (and affects) a multitude of factors, often in a non-linear way. To research it, scholars often employ a range of innovative as well as standard qualitative methods, for example interviews, multimodal narratives, and journals. To further explore such methodologies, see studies in the volume edited by Dörnyei et al. (2015).

Overview of Recent Research on Language Learning Motivation

Since the introduction of Dörnyei's L2MSS in 2005, there has been a revival of language learning motivation research and a surge in the number of motivation-related publications. In this section, we briefly present the recent research on language learning motivation and also point out areas that are still under-investigated.

Boo et al.'s (2015) review of journal articles and book chapters focusing on L2 motivation and published between 2005 and 2014 shows that much of the recent language learning motivation research draws to a greater or lesser extent on Dörnyei's (2005) theory. In contrast, investigations utilising Gardner's (1985) framework declined, and those looking solely at self-determination theory plateaued. As L2MSS is a relatively new framework, one major strand of research focuses on validating the theory and developing research instruments to measure its constructs, as described in the previous section, an area of research that could use the help of SLA researchers who specialise in assessment. Additionally, a number of studies looked at the relationship between L2MSS and other frameworks.

While language learning motivation is now being investigated in more geographical contexts than ever before, English is by far the most researched language in the field, with seven out of 10 published studies focusing on motivation to learn English (Boo et al., 2015). This imbalance means that motivation to study languages other than English (LOTE) is not fully explored. This is particularly problematic because, as Dörnyei and Al-Hoorie (2017) explained, mobility and migration between countries are bigger than ever before. This means that a lot of individuals are learning languages other than English. As discussed above, the position of English as a *lingua franca* situates it in an almost unique motivational sphere, meaning that the transferability of this research is not always a given. Moreover, it is likely that the dominant role of English is interacting with motivation to learn LOTE and this interaction has not been explored (Dörnyei & Al-Hoorie, 2017).

Language learners attending university are the most researched group in L2 motivation studies (Boo et al., 2015). This reflects the opportunistic side of this research area as scholars tend to have easy access to this particular group of learners. However, as students enrolled in compulsory education constitute the largest group of language learners, there is a need for further investigation involving students at secondary school level. Lamb (2017) observed that encounters that occur in the L2 classroom are crucial in shaping learners' attitudes and motivations. Whilst *motivating* as process is gaining more and more researcher's attention, Lamb (2017) noted most of these studies do not employ very rigorous methodological designs. Moreover, even though the existing evidence suggests an association between teacher's motivation and their students' motivation (Lamb, 2017), there have been only a few attempts to study language-teaching motivation amongst teachers.

Finally, and importantly, although the link between language learning motivation and achievement has been at the core of this field from the beginning, there is still a surprising dearth of quality studies exploring the relationship. Early attempts to measure language proficiency in motivational studies (see Gardner & Lambert, 1972) left a lot to be desired. These studies tended to adopt a range of rather subjective measures, such as self-ratings provided by learners themselves, or grades awarded by teachers. Yet, as this early body of research reported a positive, hence desirable, link between motivation and achievement, there has been little incentive to re-examine it. Since then, few investigations have explored this question. For example only two studies focused on whether the possible L2 selves and language learning experience are associated with proficiency gains (Moskovsky et al., 2016; Saito et al., 2019). The findings of these studies are, to some extent, contradictory. Moskovsky et al. (2016) reported that the ought-to L2 self was not significantly correlated with proficiency and the correlations with the other two L2MSS components were negative. Whilst Saito et al.'s (2019) results also pointed to a negligible role of the ought-to L2 self in explaining oral proficiency gains, they did, however, demonstrate the ideal L2 self to be positively related to proficiency. Considering these discrepancies, it is clear that there is an urgent need for further studies investigating the link between motivation and proficiency. Besides well-defined and carefully measured motivational constructs, it is imperative that future studies incorporate rigorous measures of L2 proficiency. From the language assessment perspective, policy-makers and teachers alike would also benefit from a heightened understanding of how language test performance is affected by differential motivations. Furthermore, the link between motivation and proficiency requires longitudinal investigation. For example, motivation can wax and wane over the course of learning, as can proficiency development. How motivation, as a dynamic, changing construct, can shape and spur learning, which is also a dynamic and changing construct, needs empirical investigation.

Recommendations for Practice

When embarking on a study of language learning motivation, it is important to first establish the underlying theory of motivation that will guide the research, and to have a clear idea of the method that will be employed to analyse the findings. As indicated in the section above on the measurement of motivation, it is generally best practice to provide a good amount of detail on a narrower and more carefully specified range of constructs and the interrelationships between these, than to attempt to cover too much and only provide a superficial picture.

The use of questionnaires is a key method for collecting data on language learning motivation. In formulating a motivational questionnaire, it is relevant to draw on the experiences of previous researchers, but equally important to consider the needs of the specific group of learners who will be responding to the questionnaire. A fairly obvious example is that the role of parental influence will be very different depending on the stage of life learners are at, and accordingly they will react differently to being asked about this.

Carrying out survey or questionnaire-based research is deceptively simple. To undertake a robust study of this nature, however, involves a complex set of procedures in both design and implementation. A good starting point for considering the issues involved is given in the section by Wagner in Mahboob et al. (2016). He introduced some of the key issues in conducting and presenting the findings of survey research, including participant sampling, instruments, administration and data collection, analysis, and writing up.

A good example of a frequently used motivational questionnaire is the one developed by Taguchi et al. (2009). This questionnaire comprises a series of 6-point Likert items, a common response format in language learning motivation research. However, it is worth noting that insights from educational measurement suggest that 7 to 11-point Likert scales promote more robust data dispersal over shorter 4, 5 or 6-point alternatives (Leung, 2011). Hessel's (2015) research into the ideal L2 self is an example of motivational research that employs an 11-point scale. See also Phakiti and Bi, Chapter 10, this volume, for further discussion.

Additionally, when designing a motivational questionnaire, it is best not to plan to rely on a single question to find out about a given concept, as this increases the risk of misinterpretation, bias, and measurement error. Multi-item scales allow one to combine information from responses to several questions targeting the same construct, giving more robust insight into the motivational trait(s) of interest. This is especially important if one is planning to analyse results using exploratory/confirmatory factor analysis (EFA/CFA), or structural equation modelling (SEM). These statistical methods explicitly address the researcher's need to gain insights into constructs, such as motivation, that are not directly observable. Depending on the nature of the research questions, one can take an exploratory or confirmatory approach in analysing the data. EFA can be used to explore whether questions are measures of a single underlying construct or are multidimensional. CFA on the other hand is useful to test whether specified groups of questions are measuring pre-identified constructs. SEM is an extension of CFA which allows researchers to explore relationships between these constructs. For CFA and SEM, it has been suggested that incorporating at least three items per construct will avoid the risk of running into estimation problems (Kline, 2005).

And finally, motivation researchers should consider time carefully within their studies. Looking at motivation on a macro level (measured perhaps once a year) may necessarily render the construct as less dynamic than measuring motivation on a micro level (measured perhaps every ten minutes during a 40 minute, in-class collaborative task). Motivation research must be positioned well within time so that theorists can come to understand better the relationship between motivation and L2 learning, two constructs that are mutually influencing and time dependent.

Testing Tips

- Formulate your research questions bearing in mind existing language learning motivation research within the theoretical framework that you are working with.
- Establish the most appropriate methodological approach for your specific research questions and context: qualitative or quantitative, or mixed methods. Be able to provide clear justification for your selection.
- Plan carefully your choice of participants; for quantitative studies this will involve specifying your sampling strategy.
- Choose or design the research instrument you will need to investigate language learning motivation; be sure to consider the content focus and the impact the response option format will have on your resultant data; see discussion above.
- Ensure you can provide validation evidence for your instrument. If you create your own tool or apply an existing one in a substantially different context, you will need to re-validate it for this purpose (see Révész & Brunfaut, Chapter 3, this volume).
- Make sure that you present the results of relevant descriptive analysis, including reliability analysis (see Green, Chapter 11, this volume, for more information on this).
- Include the interpretation of the results in the discussion section and link your findings explicitly to relevant language learning and motivation literature.

Recommended Readings

Dörnyei, Z., & Ryan, S. (2015). Motivation. In *The psychology of the language learner revisited* (pp. 72–105). Routledge.

This chapter on motivation provides a solid overview of previous theoretical and empirical developments in the field of language learning motivation from its onset. It also gives a detailed discussion of Dörnyei's (2005) L2MSS, as well as other theoretical constructs that have been put forward since then.

Dörnyei, Z., & Taguchi, T. (2010). *Questionnaires in second language research: Construction, administration, and processing* (2nd ed.). Routledge.

This book offers a detailed and easy-to-digest guideline on the use of questionnaires in applied linguistics research, from design, through to data collection, and analysis of the resultant data. The final chapter includes an insightful illustration of how a motivational questionnaire is developed. But beware that their suggestion to use a 6-point Likert-scale runs counter to suggestions from educational measurement to use a larger scale (9 to 11-point), or even different types of innovative scales.

Lamb, M. (2017). The motivational dimension of language teaching. *Language Teaching*, *50*(3), 301–346. https://doi.org/10.1017/s0261444817000088

In this state-of-the-art article, Lamb presents a thorough overview of the current research, focusing on the implications for language teaching. This is the most recent and detailed overview of language learning motivation research.

References

Boo, Z., Dörnyei, Z., & Ryan, S. (2015). L2 motivation research 2005–2014: Understanding a publication surge and a changing landscape. *System*, *55*, 145–157. https://doi.org/10.1016/j.system.2015.10.006

Csizér, K., & Kormos, J. (2009). Learning experiences, selves and motivated learning behaviour: A comparative analysis of structural models for Hungarian secondary and university learners of English. In Z. Dörnyei & E. Ushioda (Eds.), *Motivation, language identity and the L2 self* (pp. 98–119). Multilingual Matters.
Deci, E. L., & Ryan, R. M. (1985). *Intrinsic motivation and self-determination in human behavior*. Plenum Press.
Dörnyei, Z. (2005). *The psychology of the language learner: Individual differences in second language acquisition*. Lawrence Erlbaum Associates.
Dörnyei, Z. (2009). The L2 motivational self system. In Z. Dörnyei & E. Ushioda (Eds.), *Motivation, language identity and the L2 self* (pp. 9–43). Multilingual Matters.
Dörnyei, Z., & Al-Hoorie, A. H. (2017). The motivational foundation of learning languages other than global English: Theoretical issues and research directions. *Modern Language Journal, 101*(3), 455–468. https://doi.org/10.1111/modl.12408
Dörnyei, Z., Macintyre, P. D., & Henry, A. (Eds.). (2015). *Motivational dynamics in language learning*. Multilingual Matters.
Gardner, R. C. (1985). *Social psychology and second language learning: The role of attitudes and motivation*. Edward Arnold Ltd.
Gardner, R. C., & Lambert, W. E. (1972). *Attitudes and motivation in second-language learning*. Newbury House Publishers.
Hessel, G. (2015). From vision to action: Inquiring into the conditions for the motivational capacity of ideal second language selves. *System, 52*, 103–114. https://doi.org/10.1016/j.system.2015.05.008
Kline, R. B. (2005). *Principles and practice of structural equation modeling*. Guilford Press.
Lamb, M. (2017). The motivational dimension of language teaching. *Language Teaching, 50*(3), 301–346. https://doi.org/10.1017/s0261444817000088
Leung, S. O. (2011). A comparison of psychometric properties and normality in 4-, 5-, 6-, and 11-point likert scales. *Journal of Social Service Research, 37*(4), 412–421. https://doi.org/10.1080/01488376.2011.580697
Mahboob, A., Paltridge, B., Phakiti, A., Wagner, E., Starfield, S., Burns, A., Jones, R. H., & De Costa, P. I. (2016). TESOL quarterly research guidelines. *TESOL Quarterly, 50*(1), 42–65. https://doi.org/10.1002/tesq.288
Moskovsky, C., Racheva, S., Assulaimani, T., & Harkins, J. (2016). The L2 motivational self system and L2 achievement: A study of Saudi EFL learners. *The Modern Language Journal, 16*, 1–14. https://doi.org/10.1111/modl.12340
Noels, K. A., Pelletier, L. G., Clément, R., & Vallerand, R. J. (2000). Why are you learning a second language? Motivational orientations and self-determination theory. *Language Learning, 50*(1), 57–85. https://doi.org/10.1111/1467-9922.53223
Rasool, G., & Winke, P. (2019). Undergraduate students' motivation to learn and attitudes towards English in multilingual Pakistan: A look at shifts in English as a world language. *System*, 82, 50–62. https://doi.org/10.1016/j.system.2019.02.015
Ryan, R. M., & Deci, E. L. (2000). Self-determination theory and the facilitation of intrinsic motivation, social development, and well-being. *American Psychologist, 55*(1), 68–78. https://doi.org/10.103711 0003-066X.55.1.68
Saito, K., Dewaele, J., Abe, M., & In'nami, Y. (2019). Motivation, emotion, learning experience and second language comprehensibility development in classroom classroom settings: A cross-sectional and longitudinal study. *Language Learning, 68*(3), 1–35. https://doi.org/10.1111/lang.12297
Taguchi, T., Magid, M., & Papi, M. (2009). The L2 motivational self-system among Japanese, Chinese and Iranian learners of English: A comparative study. In Z. Dörnyei & E. Ushioda (Eds.), *Motivation, language identity and the L2 self* (pp. 66–98). Multilingual Matters.
Teimouri, Y. (2017). L2 selves, emotions, and motivated behaviors. *Studies in Second Language Acquisition, 39*(4), 681–709. https://doi.org/10.1017/S0272263116000243
Yashima, T. (2000). Orientations and motivation in foreign language learning: A study of Japanese college students. *JACET Bulletin, 31*, 121–133. https://kuir.jm.kansai-u.ac.jp/dspace/bitstream/10112/6873/1/KU-1100-20000315-09.pdf

16

Measuring Working Memory

Zhisheng (Edward) Wen, Alan Juffs & Paula Winke

Background

Cognitively oriented second language acquisition (SLA) researchers have long been interested in what it takes to learn a language well, with "well" being able to be defined in myriad ways. As explained by Ortega (2009, pp. 82–83), modern cognitive SLA theories center on *information processing* as a key cognitive mechanism in SLA that may be responsible for successful language learning. Information processing is the mental processes and representation manipulations in the mind that work through input so that it can be used in output, otherwise known as language performance. Information processing happens in the cognitive workspace of *working memory* (WM), which is, unfortunately, limited in its capacity (Conway et al., 2007). The direct corollary of this theory is that "people who have better working memory capacities can learn an L2 more efficiently" (Ortega, p. 90). Another corollary is that people who have better WM capacity may be able to perform better than their peers who have less room (less cognitive workspace capacity) for information processing.

Because WM is central to SLA and second language (L2) performance, researchers have explored the effects of WM on L2 learning domains and bilingual processing extensively (see Juffs & Harrington, 2011; Wen, 2012, 2016; Wen et al., 2015; Wen & Li, 2019). Results have converged on the positive effects of WM on L2 learning processes and outcomes (e.g., see Linck et al., 2014; Grundy & Timmer, 2017 for two meta-analyses of empirical evidence). Specifically, WM has been found to underlie the acquisition and development of L2 vocabulary (e.g., Cheung, 1996; Malone, 2018), L2 collocations and nativelike selections (e.g., Foster et al., 2014), and L2 morpho-syntax or grammar (e.g., O'Grady, 2017), as well as modulate some secondary cognitive processes implicated in L2 interactions and linguistic performance, such as noticing of L2 corrective feedback (e.g., Mackey et al., 2002). Research with child L2 learners has shown that children with higher WM have somewhat more consistent performance across L2 writing-test tasks (Michel et al., 2019). Given the overall positive effects of WM on SLA (with $r = 0.25$ as reported by Linck et al., 2014) and specific L2 processes and products (as reviewed by Leeser & Sunderman, 2016; Wen & Li, 2019), proposals have been made to incorporate WM not just as a key individual difference in SLA, but also as a central component of language aptitude (Doughty, 2019; Wen et al., 2017; Wen, 2016, 2019; Winke, 2013).

More recently, SLA and language testing researchers have investigated the effects of working memory on performance outcomes, with prime investigations focusing on whether various tasks, perhaps inadvertently, assess working memory capacity, especially when young learners or tasks with high complexity are involved (Michel et al., 2019; Zalbidea, 2017). This line of research can inform theoretical and policy debates within language assessment that center on the social consequences of using test results that rely on factors beyond language development or achievement, factors that may be present as byproducts of language test administration, such as timed conditions (see Juffs, 2017, for a discussion on WM as a byproduct that arises from, but may not causally influence, SLA). Results from such inquiries must be found, and then ethically discussed, to understand whether working memory is beneficially or detrimentally part of society's uses of language-test scores, especially when the tests are implemented as part of selection or gate-keeping processes that bestow upward social and economic mobility.

Key Concepts

Working memory: Working memory is the cognitive workspace in the mind, controlled by the central executive (or chief engineer of working memory), that allows humans to simultaneously store and process information in immediate consciousness for a limited duration to allow mental tasks to be completed that lead to learning or the long-term storage of new memories/information.

Central executive: The central executive is the chief engineer or traffic cop of working memory. It has the capacity to focus attention on the various working memory components, and can divide or switch attention accordingly. It is the link between working memory and the long-term memory store.

Phonological loop: The short-term storage space in the mind in which the person can rehearse phonological information.

Visuospatial sketchpad: The short-term storage space in the mind in which the person can manipulate visual and spatial information.

Episodic buffer: A temporary, limited capacity system controlled by the central executive that can bind information from the phonological loop and visuospatial sketchpad and move it to long term memory.

Key Issues

Despite the popularity of WM tests in cognitive science, SLA, and language testing, many measurement and methodological issues remain unresolved. We review them here.

WM-Test Construct Issues

Since the inception of the seminal WM model proposed by the British cognitive psychologists Baddeley and Hitch (1974), the construct of WM has evolved considerably (Baddeley, 2012; Cowan, 2017; Nee & D'Esposito, 2018). How it is measured has evolved as well, making way for a plethora of choices for SLA and language testing researchers who want to measure WM. Theorists have settled that WM has a *limited capacity*, though the source of variation is debated (Conway et al., 2007). The limitations can be manifested in terms of memory span (how much one can remember while processing other information) and memory duration (how long one can store memorized information of varying length or types), which are rather easy targets for measurement, but the limitations can be traded off, complicating the measurement of WM. As described by Miyake and Shah (1999), WM is best conceived as a *primary memory subsystem*, used for learning or manipulating information that consists of multiple components and executive functions. This, in a nutshell, blurs what, exactly, can and should be measured to assess working memory capacity, but points to the notion that multiple measures of various components of working memory together may overall provide a better representation of one's working memory. Like aptitude (see Oberauer et al., 2018; Roehr-Brackin, Chapter 14, this volume), working memory is multi-componential, making its measurement a difficult task.

Looming above the construct issue is a theory question that can drive approaches toward WM research. The question is parallel to the one posed about L2 aptitude: whether working memory can be increased and improved through practice and exercise (Lumsden et al., 2016). Education researchers investigate if an approach to improve learning is to manipulate learning tasks in such a way that they do not rely on one's working memory as much (see Gathercole, 2011). Thus, findings that working memory is important for learning may not be universal if learning can (and perhaps in some educational contexts should) be manipulated to reduce reliance on working memory. Indeed, working memory may be important for certain types of learning in certain conditions, necessitating complex investigations across various domains and learning contexts. SLA researchers have already begun researching the potential beneficial effects of bilingualism on WM (e.g., Calvo et al., 2016; Lukasik et al., 2018). This approach can be extended to investigate how task characteristics and conditions can be designed to overcome WM limitations in mediating task performance (see Skehan, 2015; Wen, 2016; Wen et al., 2017). This is important for the design of test tasks as well: Can they be rendered less dependent on working memory, and if they can, should they be?

WM-Test Selection Issues

Researchers have the difficult task of choosing which WM tests are appropriate for their studies. Working memory tests were first designed as native-language (L1) reading span tasks. One of the most widely used formats of WM test is that of Daneman and Carpenter (1980), in which participants are asked to read aloud increasingly longer sets of sentences (a processing component) and then recall the final words of all the sentences in the set in their original presentation order (a storage component), with the theory that both tasks are modulated by the central executive. For example, at the two-sentence-set level, participants are asked to read aloud the following sentences, and then recall the sentences' final words, usually in order (as cited from and explained by Miyake, 2001, p. 163, numbers added):

(1) Due to his gross inadequacies, his position as director was terminated abruptly.
(2) It is possible, of course, that life did not arise on the earth at all.

Test takers would be presented with two sets of two sentences, then three sets of three sentences, and so on, until the test taker could no longer recall the final words consistently for a set, which would indicate the test takers' WM set size. At first, researchers only recorded test takers' recall of the final words. Later, Waters and Caplan (1996) adjusted the scoring procedures of the reading span task by measuring the response latency and accuracy of sentence judgment (measuring the processing components), and the recall of final words (the storage component). Waters and Caplan laid bare that researchers had decisions to make in terms of what, ultimately, they were measuring, *and* what they were scoring: for example, researchers could (a) drop participants who did not perform at an arbitrarily defined criterion on processing and then use remaining participants' recall scores only as a measure of WM, or (b) use the storage and processing scores, weighted or not, as categorical, ranked, or continuous data, respectively, with the ability to assign partial credit as desired. The same scoring choices and decision trees appeared with other popular tests of WM, such as the Speaking Span Task (Daneman & Green, 1986) and the Operation Span Task (Turner & Engle, 1989; Engle, 2002).

Other popular WM tests had fewer scoring problems because there was less to score. In the standard versions of the non-word repetition span task (e.g., Gathercole et al., 1994; Gathercole, 2006), non-words are formed from a string of letters or sounds that do not exist in the given language but still conform to its phonotactic rules (e.g., acklar and veincort; Cheung, 1996). In most studies using this test, participants were asked to repeat back non-words, interspersed with real words, of increasing length. In SLA, some researchers use real words from another language; e.g., French (2006) used Arabic words for his French-speaking learners of English. Many viewed these tasks as measuring phonological memory, but "there is no real consensus as to what the NRT actually measures" (Coady & Evans, 2008, p. 3). Performance is known to be affected by lexical knowledge; however, the test is often used with young children to test their phonological short-term memory (see Williams, 2012, for a review) because it is cognitively appropriate (it presents a simpler cognitive-load challenge that is friendlier for children).

Similarly, another format that is often favored and administered by neuroscientists, the *n*-back task, can be simple to score. Participants are usually presented with a series of visual or auditory stimuli (such as a series of patterns, pictures, or letters) and are asked to indicate whether each stimulus (let's say a letter) was presented *n* trials previously. That is, in a four-back test, a test taker will click a button after seeing the letter K if K was also presented four trials back. One can think of an *n*-back test with a larger distance back as being more cognitively difficult than one with less distance (see Gajewski et al., 2018). As explained by Linck et al. (2014), intermediary trials within the *n*-back may or may not have *lures*, that is, repeated stimuli in the wrong (non-targeted) position (in our example, a lure for a K would be a K presented three trials back in a four-back test), which can increase the cognitive load, as lures distract. However, a major limitation with the *n*-back task is its lack of construct validity (despite its face validity and its popularity; Kane et al., 2007). In theory, it does not fit the "simple" memory span tasks (e.g., the NRT) exactly, nor the "complex" memory span tasks (e.g., the reading-, operation-span tasks etc.), as Jarrold and Towse (2006) have acknowledged: They noted that one may consider the *n*-back test as lying "somewhere between simple and complex span tasks" (p. 47). Meanwhile, Linck et al. (2014) wrote that the *n*-back with lures may best "predict performance on L2 tasks that specifically rely on... conflict resolution, such as the reading of garden-path sentences that require syntactic reinterpretation at the point of disambiguation" (p. 876). Scores on *n*-back tasks may be a proxy for executive processes in younger test takers, attention and executive processes in middle-aged test takers, but verbal memory and updating in older-aged test takers (Gajewski et al., 2018). Such age-related research and theorizing on the *n*-back task will prove interesting for SLA researchers who are just beginning to investigate how different working memory functions affect different L2 learning domains, and who are just beginning to explore how those parallel or non-parallel effects change over the lifespan.

Meanwhile, researchers in psychology continue to produce new methods for measuring WM, and SLA and language testing researchers interested in measuring WM should stay abreast of psychologists' work. For example, psychologists at the University of Maryland, who partnered with applied linguists and language testers at the same institution (Atkins et al., 2014), developed several online, non-verbal working memory tasks, mostly by creating instruments that tended to correlate well with other, more-well-known tests of working memory. One of their WM tasks is a four-dimensional online spatial game called Shapebuilder that the authors found correlates positively with other complex WM span tasks, but which circumvents some of the traditional problems of previous WM tests, such as the need to administer long tests in lab settings, or the potential interference of one's L1 on score interpretation.

Another source for WM tests from psychology is Engle's Georgia Institute of Technology attention and WM lab (http://englelab.gatech.edu/taskdownloads.html). The lab has several WM tests (including operation span tasks, visual array orientation judgment tasks, etc.) that they have developed and that researchers can download for free, after obtaining lab permission. For example, Zalbidea (2017) used an Engle lab operation span task to measure WM in a study on the effects of WM on task performance, depending on the task's complexity level and mode (speaking versus writing). Other SLA and language testing researchers have taken Engle's WM tests and have downloaded them, and then replaced the English directions and/or sentences/words with translations (there are WM test translations in over 15 languages on the site). Researchers can use these translations, or create new ones and send them back to Engle to put on the website, as done by Gass et al. (2019). Other WM tests also exist on IRIS (https://www.iris-database.org/), and researchers can download them from there as well.

In this short chapter, we are unable to review and explain other types of assessments that measure working memory, or that measure cognitive functioning that is important to working memory, such as the Stroop test, which assesses one's ability to inhibit cognitive interference, something that is important for concentrating attention during WM-dependent tasks (see Lü et al., 2019, who used a Stroop test to measure Chinese college students' executive control when learning L2 English metaphors.) However, we point out that all complex cognitive tests and working memory tests need scoring justification and reliability reports that are specific to the research sample under investigation. As described by Nobre et al. (2013), it is also crucial that researchers provide theoretical arguments or empirical evidence that the components or functions intended to be assessed are actually recruited to perform the measurement tasks. This, in turn, is a request for researchers to be sure that their cognitive tests are valid as measures of the targeted constructs or functions (see Chapelle, Chapter 2, this volume; Révész & Brunfaut, Chapter 3, this volume). Test reliability information from norming or pilot studies can be reported, and often are, but reporting those should not exempt authors from reporting reliability estimates that are based on the study sample (Conway et al., 2005). This can be difficult, however, when using commercial WM tests, especially if the test designers do not provide the researchers with the item-level data necessary for generating a sample's reliability estimate.

WM Measurement Issues

As expertly described by Atkins et al. (2014), many working memory tests are plagued with measurement difficulties of which we believe SLA researchers should be aware. We summarize Atkins et al.'s writing here, and we refer readers to their full text for elaborations on these themes.

First, Atkins et al. explained, many working memory tests available publicly were validated with narrow samples from college campuses, thus the use of their scores from other language-learner samples (e.g., children or adolescents) will need empirical justification (see Gajewski et al., 2018, on WM across the lifespan). We further note that because college students are pre-selected through admissions qualifications and self-selection, WM tests validated on them may not well represent the full range of WM abilities that may exist in populations.

Second, many WM tests were validated for the language or languages of the original administrations. Thus, even though WM tests, such as the Engle Lab tests, have been and can be easily translated, "the translated materials must be validated all over again" (Atkins et al., p. 418). This may be true, as Atkins et al. pointed out, for non-verbal tests of WM as well. For example, "digit span is susceptible to differences between languages in which there are more syllables in the phonological representation for number. Welsh participants show a reduced digit span relative to English that is likely not due to inherent [WM] differences…" (p. 417).

Most importantly, as Atkins et al. noted (p. 418), WM tests often do not meet the American Educational Research Association (AERA), American Psychological Association (APA), and the National Council on Measurement in Education (NCME) (2014) standards for educational and psychological testing, one of which is that psychological tests must have high reliability, with the minimum standard being a reliability coefficient of .75 or higher. As noted by Conway et al. (2005) and others, many WM tests have medium or low reliability, most likely, as viewed by Atkins et al., because "they are prone to ceiling effects and skew" (p. 418). A compounding problem reported by Atkins et al. is that WM researchers will at times apply corrections to render their WM-score distributions more normal, such as done by Kane et al. (2004): Atkins et al. described how Kane et al. replaced outliers' extreme WM scorers with the mean plus or minus 3.5 standard deviations. While this practice may be common, Atkins et al. noted that it would be good if researchers would publish their raw, unadjusted WM-test outcomes so that a test's real and contextualized skewness and kurtosis could be known.

A key resource for SLA researchers concerning WM test measurement issues is the Conway et al. (2005) paper, which reviews scoring options for WM tests and discusses how those scoring choices may affect study outcomes. Their work, as well as work by researchers such as Leeser and Sunderman (2016), who demonstrated empirically that WM's relationship with L2 learning can depend on the "WM task type, scoring method and type of analysis" (Leeser & Sunderman, p. 89), stressed the importance of publicly publishing, as part of Open Science, raw WM test data in public data repositories alongside the SLA articles that have WM as a measure. Secondary researchers or meta-analysis researchers in the future may be able to use the raw data to reanalyze WM test data in standardized ways to extract more comparable, cross-study WM effect sizes.

Higher-Level WM Methodological Issues

SLA researchers have recently begun considering dynamic and developmental factors during the implementation of WM tasks (Jackson, 2020; Sagarra, 2017; Serafini & Sanz, 2016). These obviously include the consideration of participants' age and L2 proficiency and how those affect test takers' cognitive engagement with the tasks in question. For example, among L1 or L2 learners, a simple non-word memory span task may be appropriate for measuring phonological WM among young learners, whereas a complex WM task should be implemented to measure adult learners' WM capacity (Juffs, 2006; Wen, 2016). Meanwhile, it is also possible that the more obvious or significant effects of WM (as witnessed at the beginning and intermediate stages of SLA) can be expected to gradually diminish as participants' L2 proficiency develops (Serafini & Sanz, 2016).

In addition, when researchers choose which WM tests to give, they are choosing to attend to specific aspects of WM theory (see Cai & Dong, 2012; Wen, 2014). As suggested by the findings in Cai and Dong (2012), decisions must be made, in a hierarchical order of weighting, as to (1) the *information types* of the WM measure (verbal versus non-verbal), (2) the *encoding modalities* (listening span task versus reading span task versus speaking span task, etc.), and (3) the *encoding languages* (i.e., whether the test is conducted in participants' L1 or L2). As discussed by Zalbidea (2017), variation in research findings on whether WM influences L2 task performance may be due to the type of WM test used, be it a reading span test, a backward digit span test, or an operation span test, because the tests "differ in the extent to which individuals must process input actively" (p. 347). In this sense, it becomes imperative for SLA researchers to understand well how test selection and test method choices may influence research outcomes. Additionally, as Linck et al. (2014) and Leeser and Sunderman (2016) cautioned, a minor change in research design and methodology may significantly affect the results and analyses in WM–SLA research. Therefore, documentation and debate in WM assessment procedures will be critical for the future development of WM–SLA, and WM-language testing, research.

Recommendations for Practice

We now propose four general principles as guidelines for conceptualizing and measuring WM in future SLA and language testing research. First, a dynamic, developmental, and hierarchical (non-linear) view should be adopted in regards to the construct of WM and in order to apply it in future SLA and language testing studies targeting learners of different ages and L2 proficiency levels (see Jackson, 2020). This is because WM is not argued to be unidimensional: WM, theoretically, is the same as all other cognitive aptitude constructs, multi-componential (Wen, forthcoming). Thus, it is imperative to tease apart the different hierarchical factors (e.g., information type, encoding modality, and encoding language, as outlined by Cai & Dong, 2012) and components that influence the outcomes of WM measures that are utilized in SLA and language testing research.

Second, future research needs to shift from global, subsystem-oriented WM tasks (as in current practice) to more WM-function-oriented assessment procedures. Specifically, these finer-grained WM functions can include *updating*, as measured by the running memory span task (Bunting et al., 2006), *task switching*, and *inhibitory control*, as assessed by other cognitive tests (e.g., Indrarathne & Kormos, 2018; Doughty, 2019).

Third, recent years have witnessed a paradigm shift from a "structural" view to a "functional" view of WM in current cognitive psychology, particularly within neuroscience; thus, it is hoped that more concerted efforts from both applied linguists and cognitive neuroscientists can be directed towards applying state-of-the-art technologies (eye-tracking, event-related potentials, functional magnetic resonance imaging, etc.; see Indrarathne & Kormos, 2018) to pin down the core cognitive mechanisms and executive functions underlying the *maintenance*, *access*, and *control* of the languages residing in the bilingual or multi-lingual brain (Altarriba & Isurin, 2013).

And finally, it is important for SLA and language testing researchers to investigate how applied linguists can best manage WM loads in classroom tasks and in language tests, especially when vulnerable populations are involved (children, low education learners, and those with learning disabilities; e.g., Juffs, 2006). WM is important for learning and performance, but it should not determine who can learn and who can pass which tests.

Testing Tips

- The selection of WM tasks should take into account the participant's age and L2 proficiency level.
- Researchers should be aware that WM-test selection may influence study outcomes, and seek to use multiple WM tests rather than one, with each selection justified by theory.
- Because of the importance of WM for SLA and language testing, researchers should continue to investigate WM not just as a variable of interest, but as a control factor in SLA and testing investigations.
- Researchers should carefully review the work by Conway et al. (2005) and Leeser and Sunderman (2016) to understand how scoring choices may affect the empirical findings of their SLA or language testing research.
- No matter how one scores a WM test, those scoring procedures, and justifications for them, should be documented by the researchers, either in the research, or in a supplementary file.
- As with any empirical study, if not bound by a confidentiality agreement (as is often the case in language testing research), the raw, item-level data from the WM tests should be published in an open-source data repository so that secondary researchers may re-analyze the WM data to explore the results further.

Recommended Readings

Conway, A., Kane, M., Bunting, M., Hambrick, D., Wilhelm, O., & Engel, R. (2005). Working memory span tasks: A methodological review and user's guide. *Psychonomic Bulletin & Review*, *12*, 769–786. https://doi.org/10.3758/BF03196772

The authors present a thorough review of major working memory span tasks in cognitive psychology and discuss how they can be scored and tested for reliability in various ways.

Li, S. (2017). Cognitive differences and ISLA. In S. Loewen & M. Sato (Eds.), *The Routledge handbook of instructed second language learning* (pp. 396–417). Routledge.

Li overviews cognition and cognitive functioning important for instructed second language acquisition as defined under the umbrellas of language aptitude and working memory.

Wen, Z. (2016). *Working memory and second language learning: Towards an integrated approach.* Multilingual Matters.

Wen presents a detailed review of working memory theories, assessment procedures, and empirical studies, providing an integrative perspective on theorizing and measuring working memory in SLA.

References

AERA, APA, & NCME. (2014). *Standards for educational and psychological testing*. American Educational Research Association.

Altarriba, J., & Isurin, L. (2013). *Memory, language, and bilingualism: Theoretical and applied approaches*. Cambridge University Press.

Atkins, S. M., Sprenger, A. M., Colflesh, G. J. H., Briner, T. L., Buchanan, J. B., Chavis, S. E., Chen, S. Y., Iannuzzi, G. L., Kashtelyan, V., Dowling, E., & Harbison, J. I. (2014). Measuring working memory is all fun and games: A four-dimensional spatial game predicts cognitive task performance. *Experimental Psychology*, *61*(6), 417–438. https://doi.org/10.1027/1618-3169/a000262

Baddeley, A. D. (2012). Working memory: Theories, models and controversies. *Annual Review of Psychology*, *63*, 1–30. https://doi.org/10.1146/annurev-psych-120710-100422

Baddeley, A. D., & Hitch, G. (1974). Working memory. In G. A. Bower (Ed.), *The psychology of learning and motivation* (Vol. 8). Academic Press.

Bunting, M. F., Cowan, N., & Saults, J. S. (2006). How does running memory span work? *Quarterly Journal of Experimental Psychology*, *59*, 1691–1700. https://doi.org/10.1080/17470210600848402

Cai, R., & Dong, Y. (2012). Effects of information type, encoding modality, and encoding language on working memory span: Evidence for the hierarchical view (In Chinese). *Foreign Language Teaching and Research*, *44*(3), 376–388.

Calvo, N., Ibáñez, A., & García, A. M. (2016). The impact of bilingualism on working memory: A null effect on the whole may not be so on the parts. *Frontiers in Psychology*, *7*, 265. https://doi.org/10.3389/fpsyg.2016.00265

Cheung, H. (1996). Nonword span as a unique predictor of second-language vocabulary learning. *Developmental Psychology*, *32*(5), 867–873. https://doi.org/10.1037/0012-1649.32.5.867

Coady, J. A., & Evans, J. L. (2008). Uses and interpretations of non-word repetition tasks in children with and without specific language impairments (SLI). *International Journal of Language & Communication Disorders*, *43*(1), 1–40. https://doi.org/10.1080/13682820601116485

Conway, A., Kane, M., Bunting, M., Hambrick, D., Wilhelm, O., & Engel, R. (2005). Working memory span tasks: A methodological review and user's guide. *Psychonomic Bulletin & Review*, *12*, 769–786. https://doi.org/10.3758/BF03196772

Conway, A. R. A., Jarrold, C., Kane, M. J., Miyake, A., & Towse, J. N. (Eds.). (2007). *Variation in working memory*. Oxford University Press.

Cowan, N. (2017). The many faces of working memory and short-term storage. *Psychonomic Bulletin & Review*, *24*, 1158–1170. https://doi.org/10.3758/s13423-016-1191-6

Daneman, M., & Carpenter, P. A. (1980). Individual differences in working memory and reading. *Journal of Verbal Learning and Verbal Behavior*, *19*, 450–466. https://doi.org/10.1016/S0022-5371(80)90312-6

Daneman, M., & Green, I. (1986). Individual differences in comprehending and producing words in context. *Journal of Memory and Language*, *25*, 1–18. https://doi.org/10.1016/0749-596X(86)90018-5

Doughty, C. J. (2019). Cognitive language aptitude. *Language Learning*, *68*, 101–126. https://doi.org/10.1111/lang.12322

Engle, R. W. (2002). Working memory capacity as executive attention. *Current Directions in Psychological Science*, *11*, 19–23. https://doi.org/10.1111/1467-8721.00160

Foster, P., Bolibaugh, C., & Kotula, A. (2014). Knowledge of nativelike selections in an L2: The influence of exposure, memory, age of onset and motivation in foreign language and immersion settings. *Studies in Second Language Acquisition*, *36*(1), 101–132. https://doi.org/10.1017/S0272263113000624

French, L. M. (2006). *Phonological working memory and L2 acquisition: A developmental study of children learning French in Quebec*. Edwin Mellen Press.

Gajewski, P. D., Hanisch, E., Falkenstein, M., Thönes, S., & Wascher, E. (2018). What does the N-back task measure as we get older? Relations between working-memory measures and other cognitive functions across the lifespan. *Frontiers in Psychology*, *9*, 2208. https://doi.org/10.3389/fpsyg.2018.02208

Gass, S., Winke, P., Isbell, D. R., & Ahn, J. (2019). How captions help people learn languages: A working-memory, eye-tracking study. *Language Learning & Technology*, *23*(2), 84–104. https://doi.org/10125/44684

Gathercole, S. (2006). Nonword repetition and word learning: The nature of the relationship. *Applied Psycholinguistics*, *27*(4), 513–543. https://doi.org/10.1017.S0142716406060383

Gathercole, S. (2011). Dr. Susan Gathercole explains working memory. *YouTube*. https://youtu.be/S65D2oazf8M

Gathercole, S. E., Willis, C. S., Baddeley, A., & Emslie, H. (1994). The children's test of nonword repetition: A test of phonological working memory. *Memory*, *2*(2), 103–127. https://doi.org/10.1080/09658219408258940

Grundy, J. G., & Timmer, K. (2017). Bilingualism and working memory capacity: A comprehensive meta-analysis. *Second Language Research*, *33*(3), 325–340. https://doi.org/10.1177/0267658316678286

Indrarathne, B., & Kormos, J. (2018). The role of working memory in processing L2 input: Insights from eye-tracking. *Bilingualism: Language and Cognition*, *21*, 355–374. https://doi.org/10.1017/S1366728917000098

Jackson, D. O. (2020). Working memory and second language development: A complex, dynamic future? *Studies in Second Language Learning and Teaching*, *10*(1), 89–109. https://doi.org/10.14746/ssllt.2020.10.1.5

Jarrold, C., & Towse, J. N. (2006). Individual differences in working memory. *Neuroscience*, *139*(1), 39–50. https://doi.org/10.1016/j.neuroscience.2005.07.002

Juffs, A. (2006). Working memory, second language acquisition and low-educated second language and literacy learners. In I. van de Craats, J. Kuvers, & M. Young-Scholten (Eds.), *LOT occasional papers* (pp. 89–104). Netherlands Graduate School of Linguistics.

Juffs, A. (2017). The importance of grain size in phonology and the possibility that phonological working memory is epiphenomenal. *Applied Psycholinguistics*, *38*(6), 1329–1333. https://doi.org/10.1017/S0142716417000297

Juffs, A., & Harrington, M. (2011). Aspects of working memory in L2 learning. *Language Teaching*, *44*, 137–166. https://doi.org/10.1017/S0261444810000509

Kane, M. J., Conway, A. R. A., Miura, T. K., & Colflesh, G. J. (2007). Working memory, attention control, and the *n*-back task: A question of construct validity. *Journal of Experimental Psychology – Learning Memory and Cognition*, *33*(3), 615–622. https://doi.org/10.1037/0278-7393.33.3.615

Kane, M. J., Hambrick, D. Z., Tuholski, S. W., Wilhelm, O., Payne, T. W., & Engle, R. W. (2004). The generality of working memory capacity: A latent-variable approach to verbal and visuo-spatial memory span and reasoning. *Journal of Experimental Psychology: General*, *133*, 189–217. https://doi.org/10.1037/0096-3445.133.2.189

Leeser, M., & Sunderman, G. (2016). Methodological issues of working memory tasks for L2 processing research. In G. Granena, D. O. Jackson, & Y. Yilmaz (Eds.), *Cognitive individual differences in second language processing and acquisition* (pp. 89–104). John Benjamins.

Linck, J. A., Osthus, P., Koeth, J. T., & Bunting, M. F. (2014). Working memory and second language comprehension and production: A meta-analysis. *Psychonomic Bulletin & Review*, *21*(4), 861–883. https://doi.org/10.3758/s13423-013-0565-2

Lü, J., Liang, L., & Chen, B. (2019). The effect of executive control ability on the comprehension of second language metaphor. *International Journal of Bilingualism*, *23*(1), 87–101. https://doi.org/10.1177/1367006917709096

Lukasik, K. M., Lehtonen, M., Soveri, A., Waris, O., Jylkkä, J., & Laine, M. (2018). Bilingualism and working memory performance: Evidence from a large-scale online study. *PLoS One*, *13*(11), e0205916. https://doi.org/10.1371/journal.pone.0205916

Lumsden, J., Edwards, E. A., Lawrence, N. S., Coyle, D., & Munafò, M. R. (2016). Gamification of cognitive assessment and cognitive training: A systematic review of applications and efficacy. *JMIR Serious Games*, *4*(2), e11. https://doi.org/10.2196/games.588

Mackey, A., Philp, J., Egi, T., Fujii, A., & Tatsumi, T. (2002). Individual differences in working memory, noticing of interactional feedback and L2 development. In P. Robinson (Ed.), *Individual differences and second language instruction* (pp. 181–209). John Benjamins.

Malone, J. (2018). Incidental vocabulary learning in SLA: Effects of frequency, aural enhancement, and working memory. *Studies in Second Language Acquisition*, *40*(3), 651–675. https://doi.org/10.1017/S0272263117000341

Michel, M., Kormos, J., Brunfaut, T., & Ratajczak, M. (2019). The role of working memory in young second language learners' written performances. *Journal of Second Language Writing*, *45*, 31–45. https://doi.org/10.1016/j.jslw.2019.03.002
Miyake, A. (2001). Individual differences in working memory: Introduction to the special section [Special section: Individual differences in working memory]. *Journal of Experimental Psychology: General*, *130*(2), 163–168. https://doi.org/10.1037/0096-3445.130.2.163
Miyake, A., & Shah, P. (1999). *Models of working memory: Mechanisms of active maintenance and executive control*. Cambridge University Press.
Nee, D. E., & D'Esposito, M. (2018). Working memory: An evolving concept. In J. T. Wixted (Ed.), *Stevens' handbook of experimental psychology and cognitive neuroscience* (4th ed.). John Wiley and Sons.
Nobre, A. d. P., Rodrigues, J. d. C., Sbicigo, J. B., Piccolo, L. d. R., Zortea, M., Junior, S. D., & de Salles, J. F. (2013). Tasks for assessment of the episodic buffer: A systematic review. *Psychology & Neuroscience*, *6*(3), 331–343. http://dx.doi.org/10.3922/j.psns.2013.3.10
Oberauer, K., Lewandowsky, S., Awh, E., Brown, G. D., Conway, A., Cowan, N., Donkin, C., Farrell, S., Hitch, G. J., Hurlstone, M. J., & Ma, W. J. (2018). Benchmarks for models of short-term and working memory. *Psychological Bulletin*, *144*(9), 885–958. https://doi.org/10.1037/bul0000153
O'Grady, W. (2017). Working memory and language: From phonology to grammar. *Applied Psycholinguistics*, *38*(6), 1340–1343. https://doi.org/10.1017/S0142716417000327
Ortega, L. (2009). *Understanding second language acquisition*. Hodder Education.
Sagarra, N. (2017). Longitudinal effects of working memory on L2 grammar and reading abilities. *Second Language Research*, *33*(3), 341–363. https://doi.org/10.1177/0267658317690577
Serafini, E. J., & Sanz, C. (2016). Evidence for the decreasing impact of cognitive ability on second language development as proficiency increases. *Studies in Second Language Acquisition*, *38*(4), 607–646. https://doi.org/10.1017/S0272263115000327
Skehan, P. (2015). Limited attention capacity and cognition. In M. Bygate (Ed.), *Domains and directions in the development of TBLT* (pp. 123–155). John Benjamins.
Turner, M. L., & Engle, R. W. (1989). Is working memory task dependent? *Journal of Memory and Language*, *28*, 127–154. https://doi.org/10.1016/0749-596X(89)90040-5
Waters, G. S., & Caplan, D. (1996). The measurement of verbal working memory and its relation to reading comprehension. *Quarterly Journal of Experimental Psychology*, *49A*, 51–74. https://doi.org/10.1080/713755607
Wen, Z. (2012). Working memory and second language learning. *International Journal of Applied Linguistics*, *22*, 1–22. https://doi.org/10.1111/j.1473-4192.2011.00290.x
Wen, Z. (2014). Theorizing and measuring working memory in first and second language research. *Language Teaching*, *47*(2), 173–190. https://doi.org/10.1017/S0261444813000517
Wen, Z. (2016). *Working memory and second language learning: Towards an integrated approach*. Multilingual Matters.
Wen, Z. (2019). Working memory as language aptitude: The phonological/executive model. In Z. Wen, P. Skehan, A. Biedron, S. Li, & R. Sparks (Eds.), *Language aptitude: Advancing theory, testing, research and practice* (pp. 187–214). Routledge.
Wen, Z. (forthcoming). Reflections on language aptitude models and tests. In S. Mercer & T. Gregersen (Eds.), *The Routledge handbook of psychology of language learning and teaching*. Routledge.
Wen, Z., Biedron, A., & Skehan, P. (2017). Foreign language aptitude theory: Yesterday, today and tomorrow. *Language Teaching*, *50*(1), 1–31. https://doi.org/10.1017/S0261444816000276
Wen, Z., & Li, S. (2019). Working memory in L2 learning and processing. In J. W. Schwieter & A. Benati (Eds.), *The Cambridge handbook of language learning* (pp. 365–389). Cambridge University Press.
Wen, Z., Mota, M., & McNeill, M. (2015). *Working memory in second language acquisition and processing*. Multilingual Matters.
Williams, J. N. (2012). Working memory and SLA. In S. Gass & A. Mackey (Eds.), *The Routledge handbook of second language acquisition* (pp. 427–441). Routledge/Taylor & Francis.
Winke, P. (2013). An investigation into second language aptitude for advanced Chinese language learning. *The Modern Language Journal*, *97*(1), 109–130. https://doi.org/10.1111/j.1540-4781.2013.01428.x
Zalbidea, J. (2017). 'One task fits all?' The roles of task complexity, modality, and working memory capacity in L2 performance. *The Modern Language Journal*, *101*(2), 335–352. https://doi.org/10.1111/modl.12389

17
Measuring Anxiety

Liying Cheng & Ying Zheng

Background

Anxiety is a well-documented construct traditionally defined in the educational literature as a cognitive phenomenon that can affect second language performance and achievement (Cassady & Johnson, 2002). Clinical anxiety is related to physiological manifestations, such as increased galvanic skin response and heart rate, dizziness, nausea, and feelings of panic. Anxiety is a construct that has many manifestations and triggers, and is dealt with in many disciplines of research. In second language acquisition (SLA), anxiety is an important construct that influences the cognitive process in learning (Ellis, 2008).

Recognizing language anxiety within the broader context of research on anxiety, MacIntyre (1998) observed that *language-learning anxiety* is a form of situation-specific anxiety. He noted that research on language anxiety should employ measures of anxiety experienced in specific second and foreign language contexts. In this chapter, we use both second and foreign language learning to refer to the learning of a language which is not a first language (henceforth, L2). We use L2 in general, but cite specific terms when quoting previous researchers. Language anxiety is conceived as "the worry and negative emotional reaction aroused when learning or using a second language" (MacIntyre, 1998, p. 27). Similarly, Horwitz et al. (1991) conceptualized *foreign language anxiety* as a "distinct complex of self-perceptions, beliefs, feelings, and behaviors related to classroom language learning arising from the uniqueness of the language learning process" (p. 31).

The relationship between anxiety and assessment may be referred to as *test anxiety*, which is "the set of cognitive, affective, and behavioral reactions that accompany concern over possible negative consequences contingent upon performance in a test or evaluative situation" (Zeidner, 1998, p. 25). Test anxiety is characterized by different cognitive manifestations, such as comparing self-performance to peers, considering the consequences of test failure, low levels of confidence in performance, and excessive worry over tests and evaluation (e.g., In'nami, 2006; Liu & Jackson, 2008; Zheng & Cheng, 2018).

Key Concepts

Anxiety: Anxiety is a feeling of nervousness or unease that affects one's cognitive functioning, attentional control, and coping mechanisms.

Trait anxiety: Trait anxiety is anxiety proneness or a person's tendency to respond to a stressful event in an anxious fashion. It is the stable tendency to experience anxiety across many situations.

State anxiety: State anxiety is unpleasant emotional arousal in face of threatening demands or dangers, which can be measured through methodologies such as think-aloud protocols, retrospective interviewing, heart rate monitoring, or skin conductance indexing of sympathetic nervous system activation or emotional arousal.

Situational anxiety: Situational anxiety is a specific type of anxiety that occurs during a particular situation, oftentimes unfamiliar, that puts a person in an acute state of anxiety.

Test anxiety: Test anxiety is a situational anxiety that manifests itself or is triggered during test taking. It can be triggered by the time pressure of testing, or the stakes of testing, or other test-related situational factors.

Language classroom anxiety: Language classroom anxiety is a situational anxiety that is triggered by varying stimuli in the language classroom, which can be exacerbated by the symptoms of trait anxiety itself.

Key Issues

Empirical studies on measuring anxiety have had a long tradition in SLA and education literature. We will discuss two major dimensions of SLA anxiety research due to their prominence: foreign (or L2) language anxiety, and L2 test-taking anxiety. Another anxiety-related dimension within SLA is willingness to communicate (WTC); and this can be seen as a sub-construct of L2 or foreign language anxiety, or as a construct in its own right that is mediated by anxiety. It of course comes into play, in particular, during the assessment of L2 speaking. We do not directly review it here as it is the focus of Chapter 18 by MacIntyre and Ayers-Glassey, this volume. But we do overview recent research on the links between WTC and L2 learning anxiety.

The empirical studies we review below were conducted in various L2 learning and testing contexts and resulted in many empirically tested measures of anxiety. MacIntyre (2017) provided an overview of anxiety research approaches: the Confounded Approach[1] exploring anxiety and its effect on language learning; the Specialized Approach examining anxiety experiences in specific skill areas of language (situation-specific); and a contextualized Dynamic Approach, in which anxiety is studied in connection with a complex web of language experiences, situating anxiety among a multitude of interacting factors. The empirical studies below should be examined through these approaches.

Foreign Language (or L2) Anxiety

Horwitz et al. (1991) defined a construct of foreign language anxiety to capture the effects of anxiety on foreign language learning specifically. The authors developed the Foreign Language Classroom Anxiety Scale (FLCAS) to measure this situation-specific anxiety in foreign language classroom settings. The FLCAS consists of four major variables: communication apprehension, test anxiety, fear of negative evaluation, and anxiety related to the foreign language class. This self-report instrument triggered an avalanche of similar studies. The results of the early studies on anxiety demonstrated that foreign language anxiety exerts a debilitating role on learning in foreign language classroom contexts.

The results further showed consistently negative relationships with foreign language achievement (e.g., Saito & Samimy, 1996; Salehi & Marefat, 2014). However, researchers pointed out that the FLCAS mostly focused on speaking performance in foreign language class settings and suggested an extension of the construct of foreign language anxiety to other language skill domains such as reading and listening (e.g., Elkhafaifi, 2005; Kim, 2000; Saito, Horwitz & Garza, 1999). Saito et al. (1999) argued for a conceptual distinction between general foreign language anxiety and specific foreign language reading anxiety. They developed the Foreign Language Reading Anxiety Scale (FLRAS) and employed it along with the FLCAS to measure both general foreign language anxiety and specific foreign language reading anxiety of 30 first-semester classes of Spanish, Russian, and Japanese. The results showed whereas general FL anxiety was found to be independent of target language, levels of reading anxiety were found to vary by target language and seem to be related to the specific writing systems. In addition, students' reading anxiety levels increased with their perceptions of the difficulty of reading in their FL, and their grades decreased in conjunction with their levels of reading anxiety and general FL anxiety.

Many SLA researchers have explored the link between L2 anxiety and the construct of willingness to communicate, or WTC (see Chapter 18, this volume). Recently, Khajavy et al. (2017) studied the links among three variables: emotions, classroom environment, and WTC through 1,528 secondary students from 65 different classrooms in Iran. The researchers studied these through latent multilevel analysis. Particularly related to anxiety measurement, six items on a 5-point Likert scale from Khodadady and Khajavy (2013) were used to assess students' anxiety levels while communicating in English. Meanwhile, students' WTC was assessed via seven 5-point Likert scale items from Khajavy et al. (2016). The findings showed that low anxiety was a predictor of high WTC, although that relationship was only found at the personal level; no significant contextual effect was found between these two variables at the classroom level. Another study on WTC and anxiety was done by Denies et al. (2015), who compared WTC in and outside the classroom settings of 1,000 grade-12 students of French as a second language in Flanders, Belgium. The study was the first to establish that the impact of specific variables, especially those of anxiety and integrativeness, differed across classroom and real-life settings. In class, perceived competence served as a dominant predictor of WTC. Outside of class, anxiety served as the dominant predictor of WTC. As the researchers stated, the differences across the two settings indicated that in real communications, anxiety "played a much bigger role, to the point that it seems to overrule part of [students'] integrative motivation" (p. 733).

Test Anxiety

Almost 60 years ago, Sarason (1959) wrote that "we live in a test-conscious, test-giving culture in which the lives of people are in part determined by their test performance" (p. 26). These words continue to resonate to the present day. Such a phenomenon is particularly true in societies that are more test-oriented and test-consuming (Cheng et al., 2014). Due to this role of test performance as a powerful determinant of one's success in education as well as in professional careers, tests have been recognized as a potential source of general anxiety (Zeidner, 2007). In fact, studies across cultural and educational contexts have reported a high degree and prevalence of test-related anxiety among students, substantiating the position of tests as a source of anxiety (Connor, 2001; McDonald, 2001; Putwain, 2007; Segool et al., 2013).

Anxiety that emerges specifically in test situations is referred to as test anxiety. More current research on the construct of test anxiety found consistent findings, i.e., high test-anxious individuals had lower performance than did their low test-anxious counterparts. In addition, test anxiety scores were moderately correlated with general anxiety scores but formed more consistently negative correlations with academic test scores than general anxiety scores did. Test-anxious students are characterized by relatively high sensitivity to potentially anxiety-provoking features inherent in test situations. As a result, when exposed to evaluative situations in general, and test situations in particular, these students tend to exhibit anxiety-related cognitive and affective reactions, such as reduced feelings of self-efficacy, self-derogatory cognitions, negative emotional states, and physiological arousal, which may contribute to test performance decrements.

Test anxiety is widely accepted to be a multi-dimensional construct consisting of two related yet distinct facets: the cognitive facet or *worry*, and the affective facet, or *emotionality*. Of these two facets of test anxiety, the worry component has been shown to be more consistently and strongly related to lower test performance. The worry component is defined as any cognitive expression of concern about one's own performance in impending or anticipated evaluative events (Flett & Blankstein, 1994). The worry component is characterized by fear of failure, task-irrelevant thinking, and negative self-referential cognitions, such as self-blame and self-devaluing thoughts (Eysenck, 1992). These negative self-preoccupations and self-ruminative thoughts act as an extra load on the cognitive system, leading to cognitive deficits during cognitive processes necessary for performance: Attention, memory, and retrieval are reduced.

Although there has been some contradictory evidence in previous empirical studies, it has been repeatedly documented that individuals high in test anxiety may experience decrements in test performance in various evaluation situations. The inverse relationship between test anxiety and test performance and the stronger effects of the worry component have been replicated in more recent empirical studies. Hong (1999) investigated the differential effects of both the worry and emotionality components of test anxiety on undergraduate students' course final examinations using a literal pre-test and post-test test-anxiety scale (in Hong's appendix, p. 447). Although these two components of test anxiety were moderately correlated with each other, only the worry component had a significantly negative effect on students' test performance. Similarly, Chapelle et al. (2005) investigated whether or not undergraduate and graduate students' current cumulative GPAs and general academic achievement significantly differed across low, moderate, and high test-anxious groups. Regardless of the students' gender and study level, students in higher test-anxiety groups had significantly lower GPAs and general academic achievement than did students in lower test-anxiety groups. In addition, both GPAs and general academic achievement were significantly and negatively correlated with total test anxiety scores, worry scores, and emotionality scores. However, the correlations were stronger for the worry scores than for the emotionality scores, further supporting a stronger influence of the cognitive component of test anxiety on test performance.

In addition, Thomas et al. (2017) investigated the debilitative effects of cognitive test anxiety on academic performance of undergraduate students in the United States. Students' cognitive test anxiety was significantly and negatively correlated with their 4-year cumulative GPA. In regression analysis, cognitive test anxiety explained a significant amount of the variance in the students' 4-year cumulative GPAs and also served as a significantly negative predictor of their 4-year cumulative GPAs. These detrimental effects of cognitive test anxiety stayed statistically significant after controlling for previous academic performances (first-year GPAs), suggesting the negative influences of cognitive test anxiety on long-term academic outcomes. In fact, the relationship cannot be a simple cause-effect, but potentially cyclical. In other words, anxiety can be both cause and effect in these situations.

As test performance plays an increasingly important role in various high-stakes decisions, students have reported greater levels of anxiety about high-stakes tests (Abrams et al., 2003; Barksdale-Ladd & Thomas, 2000; Jones & Egley, 2004; Putwain, 2008; Segool et al., 2013; Triplett & Barksdale, 2005). Because of this, researchers have been particularly interested in the extent to which test anxiety influences students' performance on high-stakes tests. Test anxiety has been shown to be moderately negatively correlated with total scores as well as subject scores of various high-stakes accountability tests in the United Kingdom (Putwain, 2008; Putwain et al., 2010) and the United States (Cassady & Johnson, 2002; von der Embse & Witmer, 2014).

In contrast to the abundant research on how test anxiety influences general academic achievement and high-stakes accountability test performance, research on the relationship between test anxiety and test performance in the context of language achievement has been relatively scarce and with inconsistent findings due to the complexity of SLA. For example, researchers have reported both positive and negative correlations between test anxiety and foreign language course grades (Horwitz, 1986). Inconsistent findings are also present in relation to language test performance. Test anxiety did not significantly correlate with test performance in foreign language reading in three recent studies (Amiryousefi & Tavakoli, 2011; Birjandi & Alemi, 2010; Javanbakht & Hadian, 2014) and was not a significant predictor of performance in foreign language listening tests (In'nami, 2006).

In contrast, Cheng et al. (2014) showed a component of test anxiety was a significantly negative predictor of high-stakes language test performance in reading, listening, writing, and speaking. The authors investigated the extent to which motivation and test anxiety affected university student test-takers' performance on three high-stakes English proficiency tests (two in China and one in Canada) across different social and educational contexts. These three tests had contextual differences in intended purposes, test-taker characteristics, and reported subskills. Skill anxiety, a factor of cognitive test anxiety in this study, significantly and negatively predicted performance on all three of the English proficiency tests. Although the degree to which skill anxiety influenced test performance varied across tests, skill anxiety consistently and negatively predicted performance on all of the reported subskills, including reading, listening, writing, and speaking. In addition, Zheng and Cheng (2018) identified three anxiety factors: class anxiety, low test confidence, and test anxiety, each having different predictive powers on language proficiency outcomes.

While understanding the cognitive characteristics of test anxiety is crucial for making valid inferences about test-takers' L2 language ability, social factors arising from varying second language learning conditions within and across contexts can be as important as cognitive factors in understanding test-takers' L2 performance (Fox & Cheng, 2007). Social, educational, and economical factors interact with or determine individuals' cognitive factors. Barkhuizen (2004) argued that social factors, mediated through learner attitudes, affect language learning.

Recommendations for Practice

In high-stakes testing, test anxiety can act as a potential source of construct-irrelevant variance. Contextual differences are claimed to exist in test-takers' test anxiety because socialization and educational practices differ, e.g., parental expectations may put excessive pressure on students to achieve on tests (Bodas & Ollendick, 2005). In addition, levels of test anxiety may vary based on the different stakes and uses of testing systems, i.e., admission, placement, or immigration. Facing the globalization in education, measuring learner and learning anxiety from cross-cultural and educational policy perspectives is equally crucial (Zheng, 2008). Researchers have conducted a series of studies paying significant attention to anxiety-reducing strategies that students, teachers, and curriculum designers can use in and out of class. These studies provide a fuller understanding of measuring anxiety, yet from a different angle.

Kondo and Yang (2004) collected different tactics their participants had used to deal with anxiety and came up with five categories, including preparation, relaxation, positive thinking, peer seeking, and resignation. Also related to students' strategies, Mohammadi et al. (2013) showed that students who equipped themselves with suitable language learning strategies would know how to deal with language anxiety effectively. This was confirmed in a study by Martirossian and Hartoonian (2015), who explored the relationship between foreign language classroom anxiety and self-regulated learning strategies. The data revealed that there was a negative relationship between these two factors: The more strategies students used, the better they could cope with communication apprehension, test anxiety, and fear of negative evaluation. However, as pointed out in these two studies, students may not be aware of these strategies and need guidance in employing the most suitable tactics for themselves. Teachers, therefore, should be aware of their roles in creating a supportive environment where students can be independent in acquiring appropriate strategies when confronting language anxiety (Mohammadi et al., 2013). Alrabai (2015) suggested some teachers' strategies based on his quasi-experimental study of teachers' anxiety-reducing strategies among EFL teachers in Saudi Arabia. Findings indicated that teachers could significantly decrease their students' FLA levels by promoting cooperative learning, showing faith in students' abilities, giving positive feedback, providing students with control over their learning, and involving them in decision-making. Moreover, it was highlighted that teachers should avoid "antagonistic behavior" toward students, including criticizing or overly correcting their errors.

Future Research

With the current internationalization and the increasing use of English as a *lingua franca* (ELF) in SLA, new areas of research have emerged, focusing on the link between anxiety and the use of English as Lingua Franca (ELF) outside class or among learners from different countries. One of the early studies was conducted by Dahlgren et al. (2006), who investigated an intercontinental online MA program with the participation of students from four countries: Sweden, South Africa, Canada, and Australia. The findings showed that the use of ELF resulted in mistake anxiety, i.e., a majority of students were anxious about making typos and other linguistic mistakes when taking part in the web discussions or posting messages. Especially, the mistake anxiety in using ELF was more common among those who were less privileged economically. Wilang and Singhasiri (2017) examined the relationship between ELF anxiety and its effects on intelligibility and comprehensibility through their self-developed Anxiety Scale for Spoken Englishes as a Lingua Franca (ASSELF). Three factors of ELF anxiety among Thai and foreign graduate students in Thailand were identified from the analysis: interlocutor-induced difficulties, language-processing difficulties, and apprehension over interlocutors. Among these three factors, the last one debilitated the intelligibility of international speakers remarkably. The study confirmed a correlational relationship between anxiety and intelligibility and comprehensibility: If the former increased, the latter would decrease.

The relationship between foreign language acquisition (FLA) and bi/multilingualism has also been questioned in relation to anxiety, i.e., whether multiple language learning experiences will help learners of a certain foreign language reduce their foreign language learning anxiety level (Dewaele, 2010). Thompson and Lee (2013) addressed the gap in the current literature by examining the anxiety profiles of low-level multilingual versus high-level multilingual learners of English in Korea. They found that knowledge of a foreign language other than English at an intermediate level had a positive effect in lowering students' FLA anxiety levels. In addition to second/foreign language learners, research on anxiety and multilingualism has also addressed immigrants. This area of research is significantly needed in the sense that SLA/FLA may directly permeate most aspects of their daily lives (Garcia de Blakeley et al., 2017; Sevinç & Backus, 2017).

Moving beyond the Confounded Approach and the Specialized Approach as categorized by McIntyre (2017) in researching anxiety, McIntyre further suggested that researchers need to look at the continuous and integrated nature of anxiety in interaction with multiple individual and social factors. In addition to the traditional cross-sectional approach, longitudinal studies are encouraged to track the dynamic trajectory of anxiety changes over a period of time. This dynamic take on measuring anxiety is timely conceptually, but it also poses methodological challenges in measuring anxiety. Teimouri et al. (2019), through a recent meta-analysis of anxiety, confirmed some of the conclusions McIntyre drew. For example, anxiety is best conceptualized as a negative predictor of language achievement. Most importantly, they proposed that theoretical frameworks are called for wherein cognitive, social, affective, and behavioral components of language anxiety and their subtle interrelationships can be examined and explained in detail.

A comprehensive and robust methodology to capture either anxiety over time at the micro level (before, during, and right after an anxiety triggering event) or anxiety with other factors at the macro level (over a semester or a longer period of time) is a step forward in researching and measuring L2 learning and testing anxiety.

Testing Tips

The research on investigating anxiety in SLA has primarily used questionnaires as the measurement tool. These questionnaires are referred to as anxiety scales. Conducting research of this nature needs to pay attention to the following major aspects.

- **Fitness of the anxiety scales**: In SLA, anxiety can be conceptualized as trait or state. Excellent and oft-used scales of anxiety in SLA and other fields, such as the GAD-7 (see Figure 1 in Spitzer et al., 2006), the Test Anxiety Inventory (or TAI, see Spielberger, 2010; Szafranski et al., 2012), the Test Anxiety Inventory for Children and Adolescents (TAICA, Loew, Lee, Witteborg et al., 2008), and a modified TAI for measuring change in anxiety pre- and post-assessment (in Hong, 1999, p. 447) can be adopted and/or adapted by SLA and language testing researchers to measure baseline/general and situation-specific anxiety levels over time.
- **Beyond equivalence of the anxiety scales**: An increasing number of studies that investigate anxiety in SLA adopt anxiety scales tested in one research context in one language to another context in a different language. Researchers need to ensure the quality of translation goes beyond equivalence to represent the authentic learning and testing contexts. This means researchers need to see the translation process of the anxiety scales as a process of inter-cultural interaction and research, rather than a lexical transfer of meaning (see Alanen & Huhta, Chapter 33, on measuring in multiple languages, this volume).
- **Appropriate choice of factor analyses**: Due to the nature of anxiety research, the choice of factor analyses is essential. Based on our second point above, we recommend that researchers conduct exploratory factor analysis as their first step and pay specific attention to how well certain items function (or not) in their own research context (see McKay & Plonsky, Chapter 44, this volume).
- **Representativeness of sampling**: The representativeness of the sample characteristics is of paramount importance in anxiety research when individuals' learning performance and test scores are used as indicators. Researchers need to include the appropriate demographic information of their participants and profile the participants first before doing further analysis, and report the results accordingly.
- **Measuring the dynamic and complex nature of anxiety**: Instead of traditional cross-sectional examinations of anxiety, one challenging direction for measuring anxiety would be to capture the dynamic nature of anxiety over time in both micro and macro contexts, with a consideration of looking into casual effects with performance as well as with the interaction between other individual differences and affective factors (see e.g., Miller et al., 2018).

Note

1 MacIntyre (2017) called it the Confounded Approach "because the ideas about anxiety and their effect on language learning were adopted from a mixture of various sources without detailed consideration of the meaning of the anxiety concept for language learners" (p. 11).

Recommended Readings

Rachman, S. J. (2020). *Anxiety* (4th ed.). Routledge.

This fourth edition, foundational textbook on anxiety is a must-have book for SLA and language testing researchers conducting research on anxiety. Rachman covers the latest developments in anxiety theory, research, measurement, and therapy.

MacIntyre, P. (2017). An overview of language anxiety research and trends in its development. In C. Gkonou, M. Daubney, & J.-M. Dewaele (Eds.), *New trends into language anxiety* (pp. 11–30). Multilingual Matters.

This overview reviewed the research literature on language anxiety from three broad approaches: the Confounded Approach, the Specialized Approach, and a contextualized Dynamic Approach, reflecting both historical trends and assumptions about the topic.

Cheng, L., Klinger, D., Fox, J., Doe, C., Jin, Y., & Wu, J. (2014). Motivation and test anxiety in test performance across three testing contexts: The CAEL, CET and GEPT. *TESOL Quarterly*, *48*, 300–330. https://doi.org/10.1002/tesq.105

This study examined motivation, test anxiety, and perceptions of test importance and purpose to test-takers across three social and educational contexts.

References

Abrams, L. M., Pedulla, J. J., & Madaus, G. F. (2003). Views from the classroom: Teachers' opinions of statewide testing programs. *Theory into Practice*, *42*(1), 18–29. https://doi.org/10.1207/s15430421tip4201_4

Alrabai, F. (2015). The influence of teachers' anxiety-reducing strategies on learners' foreign language anxiety. *Innovation in Language Learning and Teaching*, *9*(2), 163–190. https://doi.org/10.1080/17501229.2014.890203

Amiryousefi, M., & Tavakoli, M. (2011). The relationship between test anxiety, motivation and MI and the TOEFL iBT reading, listening and writing scores. *Procedia: Social and Behavioral Sciences*, *15*, 210–214. https://doi.org/10.1016/j.sbspro.2011.03.075

Barkhuizen, G. (2004). Social influences on language learning. In A. Davies & C. Elder (Eds.), *The handbook of applied linguistics* (pp. 552–575). Blackwell.

Barksdale-Ladd, M. A., & Thomas, K. F. (2000). What's at stake in high-stakes testing: Teachers and parents speak out. *Journal of Teacher Education*, *51*(5), 384–397. https://doi.org/10.1177/0022487100051005006

Birjandi, P., & Alemi, M. (2010). The impact of test anxiety on test performance among Iranian EFL learners. *Broad Research in Artificial Intelligence and Neuroscience*, *1*(4), 44–58. http://brain.edusoft.ro/index.php/brain/article/view/131

Bodas, J., & Ollendick, T. H. (2005). Test anxiety: A cross-cultural perspective. *Clinical Child & Family Psychology Review*, *8*(1), 65–88. https://doi.org/10.1007/s10567-005-2342-x

Cassady, J. C., & Johnson, R. E. (2002). Cognitive test anxiety and academic performance. *Contemporary Educational Psychology*, *27*(2), 270–295. https://doi.org/10.1006/ceps.2001.1094

Chapell, M. S., Blanding, Z. B., Silverstein, M. E., Takahashi, M., Newman, B., Gubi, A., & McCann, N. (2005). Test anxiety and academic performance in undergraduate and graduate students. *Journal of Educational Psychology*, *97*(2), 268–274. https://doi.org/10.1037/0022-0663.97.2.268

Cheng, L., Klinger, D., Fox, J., Doe, C., Jin, Y., & Wu, J. (2014). Motivation and test anxiety in test performance across three testing contexts: The CAEL, CET and GEPT. *TESOL Quarterly*, *48*(2), 300–330. https://doi.org/10.1002/tesq.105

Connor, M. J. (2001). Pupil stress and standard assessment tasks. *Emotional and Behavioural Difficulties*, *6*(2), 103–111. https://doi.org/10.1080/13632750100507660

Dahlgren, M. A., Larsson, S., & Walters, S. (2006). Making the invisible visible: On participation and communication in a global, web-based master's programme. *Higher Education*, *52*, 69–93. https://doi.org/10.1007/s10734-004-5784-z

Denies, K., Yashima, T., & Janssen, R. (2015). Classroom versus societal willingness to communicate: Investigating French as a second language in Flanders. *The Modern Language Journal*, *99*(4) 718–739. https://doi.org/10.1111/modl.12276

Dewaele, J.-M. (2010). Multilingualism and affordances: Variation in self-perceived communicative competence and communicative anxiety in French L1, L2, L3 and L4. *International Review of Applied Linguistics in Language Teaching*, *48*, 105–112. https://doi.org/10.1515/iral.2010.006

Elkhafaifi, H. (2005). Listening comprehension and anxiety in the Arabic language classroom. *The Modern Language Journal*, *89*(2), 206–222. https://doi.org/10.1111/j.1540-4781.2005.00275.x
Ellis, R. (2008). *The study of second language acquisition* (2nd ed.). Oxford University Press.
Eysenck, M. W. (1992). *Anxiety: The cognitive perspective*. Lawrence Erlbaum Associates.
Flett, G. L., & Blankstein, K. R. (1994). Worry as a component of test anxiety: A multidimensional analysis. In G. C. L. Davey & F. Tallis (Eds.), *Worrying: Perspectives on theory, assessment and treatment* (pp. 135–181). Wiley.
Fox, J., & Cheng, L. (2007). Did we take the same test? Differing accounts of the Ontario Secondary School Literacy Test by first and second language test takers. *Assessment in Education: Principles, Policy & Practice*, *14*(1), 9–26. https://doi.org/10.1080/09695940701272773
Garcia de Blakeley, M., Ford, R., & Casey, L. (2017). Second language anxiety among Latino American immigrants in Australia. *International Journal of Bilingual Education and Bilingualism*, *20*(7), 759–772. https://doi.org/10.1080/13670050.2015.1083533
Hong, E. (1999). Test anxiety, perceived test difficulty, and test performance: Temporal patterns of their effects. *Learning and Individual Differences*, *11*(4), 431–447. https://doi.org/10.1016/S1041-6080(99)80012-0
Horwitz, E. K. (1986). Preliminary evidence for the reliability and validity of a foreign language anxiety scale. *TESOL Quarterly*, (3), 559–562. https://doi.org/10.2307/3586302
Horwitz, M. B., Horwitz, E. K., & Cope, J. (1991). Foreign language classroom anxiety. In E. K. Horwitz & D. J. Young (Eds.), *Language anxiety: From theory and research to classroom implications* (pp. 27–39). Prentice Hall.
In'nami, Y. (2006). The effects of text anxiety on listening performance. *System*, *34*(3), 317–340. https://doi.org/10.1016/j.system.2006.04.005
Javanbakht, N., & Hadian, M. (2014). The effects of test anxiety on learners' reading test performance. *Procedia: Social and Behavioral Sciences*, *98*(6), 775–783. https://doi.org/10.1016/j.sbspro.2014.03.481
Jones, B. D., & Egley, R. J. (2004). Voices from the frontlines: Teachers' perceptions of high-stakes testing. *Education Policy Analysis Archives*, *12*, 1–34. https://doi.org/10.14507/epaa.v12n39.2004
Khajavy, G., MacIntyre, P., & Barabadi, E. (2017). Role of the emotions and classroom environment in willingness to communicate: Applying doubly latent multilevel analysis in second language acquisition research. *Studies in Second Language Acquisition*, *40*(3), 1–20. https://doi.org/10.1017/S0272263117000304
Khajavy, G. H., Ghonsooly, B., Hosseini, A., & Choi, C. W. (2016). Willingness to communicate in English: A microsystem model in the Iranian EFL classroom context. *TESOL Quarterly*, *50*(1), 154–180. https://doi.org/10.1002/tesq.204
Khodadady, E., & Khajavy, G. H. (2013). Exploring the role of anxiety and motivation in foreign language achievement: A structural equation modeling approach. *Porta Linguarum*, *20*(6), 269–286. http://profdoc.um.ac.ir/articles/a/1035999.pdf
Kim, J. H. (2000). *Foreign language listening anxiety: A study of Korean students learning English* (Unpublished doctoral dissertation). University of Texas at Austin.
Kondo, D., & Yang, Y. L. (2004). Strategies for coping with language anxiety: The case of students of English in Japan. *ELT Journal*, *58*(3), 258–265. https://doi.org/10.1093/elt/58.3.258
Liu, M. & Jackson, J. (2008). An exploration of Chinese EFL learners' unwillingness to communicate and foreign language anxiety. *The Modern Language Journal*, *92*(1), 71–86. https://doi.org/10.1111/j.1540-4781.2008.00687.x
Lowe, P. A., Lee, S. W., Wittebort, K. M., Prichard, K. W., Luhr, M. E., Cullinan, C. M., Mildren, B. A., Raad, J. M., Cornelius, R. A., & Janik, M. (2008). The test anxiety inventory for children and adolescents (TAICA). *Journal of Psychoeducational Assessment*, *26*(3), 215–230. https://doi.org/10.1177/0734282907303760
MacIntyre, P. D. (1998). Language anxiety: A review of the research for language teachers. In D. J. Young (Ed.), *Affect in foreign language and second language learning* (pp. 24–45). McGraw-Hill.
MacIntyre, P. D. (2017). An overview of language anxiety research and trends in its development. In C. Gkonou, M. Daubney, & J.-M. Dewaele (Eds.), *New trends into language anxiety* (pp. 11–30). Multilingual Matters.
Martirossian, A., & Hartoonian, A. (2015). Lowering foreign language anxiety through self-regulated learning strategy use. *English Language Teaching*, *8*(12), 209–222. https://doi.org/10.5539/elt.v8n12p209
McDonald, A. S. (2001). The prevalence and effects of test anxiety in school children. *Educational Psychology*, *21*(1), 89–101. https://doi.org/10.1080/01443410020019867
Miller, Z. F., Fox, J. K., Moser, J. S., & Godfroid, A. (2018). Playing with fire: Effects of negative mood induction and working memory on vocabulary learning. *Cognition and Emotion*, *32*(5), 1105–1113. https://doi.org/10.1080/02699931.2017.1362374

Mohammadi, E. G., Biria, R., Koosha, M., & Shahsavari, A. (2013). The relationship between foreign language anxiety and language learning strategies among university students. *Theory and Practice in Language Studies*, *3*(4), 637–646. https://doi.org/10.4304/tpls.3.4.637-646

Putwain, D. W. (2007). Test anxiety in UK schoolchildren: Prevalence and demographic patterns. *British Journal of Educational Psychology*, *77*(3), 579–593. https://doi.org/10.1348/000709906X161704

Putwain, D. W. (2008). Test anxiety and GCSE performance: The effect of gender and socio-economic background. *Educational Psychology in Practice*, *24*(4), 319–334. https://doi.org/10.1080/02667360802488765

Putwain, D. W., Connors, L., & Symes, W. (2010). Do cognitive distortions mediate the test anxiety-examination performance relationship? *Educational Psychology*, *30*(1), 11–26. https://doi.org/10.1080/01443410903328866

Saito, Y., Horwitz, E. K., & Garza, T. J. (1999). Foreign language reading anxiety. *The Modern Language Journal*, *83*(2), 202–218. https://doi.org/10.1111/0026-7902.00016

Saito, Y., & Samimy, K. K. (1996). Foreign language anxiety and language performance: A study of learner anxiety in beginning, intermediate, and advanced-level college students of Japanese. *Foreign Language Annals*, *29*(2), 239–249. https://doi.org/10.1111/j.1944-9720.1996.tb02330.x

Salehi, M., & Marefat, F. (2014). The effects of foreign language anxiety and test anxiety on foreign language test performance. *Theory and Practice in Language Studies*, *4*(5), 931–940. https://doi.org/10.4304/tpls.4.5.931-940

Sarason, I. G. (1959). Intellectual and personality correlates of test anxiety. *Journal of Abnormal and Social Psychology*, (2), 272–275. https://doi.org/10.1037/h0042200

Segool, N. K., Carlson, J. S., Goforth, A. N., von der Embse, N., & Barterian, J. A. (2013). Heightened test anxiety among young children: Elementary school students' anxious responses to high-stakes testing. *Psychology in the Schools*, *50*(5), 489–499. https://doi.org/10.1002/pits.21689

Sevinç, Y., & Backus, A. (2017). Anxiety, language use and linguistic competence in an immigrant context: A vicious circle? *International Journal of Bilingual Education and Bilingualism*, *22*(6), 706–724. https://doi.org/10.1080/13670050.2017.1306021

Spielberger, C. D. (2010). Test anxiety inventory. In *The Corsini encyclopedia of psychology*. Wiley. https://doi.org/10.1002/9780470479216.corpsy0985

Spitzer, R. L., Kroenke, K., & Williams, J. B. W. (2006). A brief measure for assessing generalized anxiety disorder: The GAD-7. *Journal of the American Medical Association Internal Medicine*, *166*(1), 1092–1097. https://doi.org/10.1001/archinte.166.10.1092

Szafranski, D. D., Barrera, T. L., & Norton, P. J. (2012). Test anxiety inventory: 30 years later. *Anxiety, Stress & Coping*, *24*(6), 667–677. https://doi.org/10.1080/10615806.2012.663490

Teimouri, Y., Goetze, J., & Plonsky, L. (2019). Second language anxiety and achievement: A meta-analysis. *Studies in Second Language Acquisition*, *41*(2), 363–387. https://doi.org/10.1017/S0272263118000311

Thomas, C. L., Cassady, J. C., & Heller, M. L. (2017). The influence of emotional intelligence, cognitive test anxiety, and coping strategies on undergraduate academic performance. *Learning and Individual Differences*, *55*, 40–48. https://doi.org/10.1016/j.lindif.2017.03.001

Thompson, A. S., & Lee, J. (2013). Anxiety and EFL: Does multilingualism matter? *International Journal of Bilingual Education and Bilingualism*, *16*(6), 730–749. https://doi.org/10.1080/13670050.2012.713322

Triplett, C. F., & Barksdale, M. A. (2005). Third through sixth graders' perceptions of high-stakes testing. *Journal of Literacy Research*, *37*(2), 237–260. https://doi.org/10.1207/s15548430jlr3702_5

von der Embse, N. P., & Witmer, S. E. (2014). High-stakes accountability: Student anxiety and large-scale testing. *Journal of Applied School Psychology*, *30*(2), 132–156. https://doi.org/10.1080/15377903.2014.888529

Wilang, J. D., & Singhasiri, W. (2017). Out-of-class anxiety in a non-English speaking context and its effects on intelligibility and comprehensibility. *Issues in Educational Research*, *27*(3), 620–638. http://www.iier.org.au/iier27/wilang.pdf

Zeidner, M. (1998). *Test anxiety: The state of the art*. Plenum Press.

Zeidner, M. (2007). Test anxiety in educational contexts: Concepts, findings, and future directions. In P. A. Schutz & R. Pekrun (Eds.), *Emotion in education* (pp. 165–184). Academic Press.

Zheng, Y. (2008). Anxiety and second/foreign language learning revisited. *The Canadian Journal of New Scholars in Education*, *1*(1), 1–12. https://files.eric.ed.gov/fulltext/ED506736.pdf

Zheng, Y., & Cheng, L. (2018). How does anxiety in foreign language classrooms and cognitive tests influence language performance? *Language Testing in Asia*, *8*(1), 1–19. https://doi.org/10.1186/s40468-018-0065-4

18

Measuring Willingness to Communicate

Peter D. MacIntyre & Samantha Ayers-Glassey

Background

Willingness to communicate (WTC) is a well-established concept in the communication literature (McCroskey & Richmond, 1991; Hodis, Bardhan, & Hodis, 2010). It has also been accepted in applied linguistics, particularly as a predictor of success in second language (L2) learning and L2 usage among adults (Gregersen & MacIntyre, 2014; MacIntyre, Clément, Dornyei & Noels, 1998). Defined as the readiness to enter into communication with another person or persons (McCroskey & Baer, 1985), WTC has been viewed as an important variable underlying the interpersonal communication process. WTC has long been theorized to function as a personality trait, showing stable individual differences over time, though variability from one situation to another is certainly to be expected (McCroskey & Richmond, 1991). Several studies have proposed that WTC may be influenced by other personality-based variables such as introversion, self-esteem, anomie, and alienation (Burgoon, 1976; McCroskey & Richmond, 1987). From the beginning, WTC has been studied as a trait-like construct (McCroskey & Richmond, 1991; MacIntyre & Charos, 1996), an approach later supplemented by a more situated, dynamic conceptualization that emphasizes variability and fluctuations of WTC in real time (MacIntyre et al., 1998; MacIntyre et al., 2017; MacIntyre & Legatto, 2011).

Key Concepts

Willingness to Communicate (WTC): The probability that a person will choose to communicate, given the opportunity. That probability can be determined over a long or short period of time.

Trait-like WTC: A stable tendency for some people to speak more than others over a long period of time.

Dynamic (state) WTC: A state of mind or a feeling of being willing to communicate at a particular moment with a particular person (or persons) that can fluctuate a great deal in a short time.

Complex Dynamic Systems: Not a theory itself, but a meta-theoretical approach to studying both variability and stability, with particular emphasis on interactions that help to explain changes in the system being examined. For example, if WTC is studied dynamically, researchers might ask what moment-to-moment changes in emotions, cognition, physiology, interpersonal actions (such as nonverbal feedback), and other factors can help to explain changes in WTC from one moment to the next.

Key Issues

It is a deceptively simple question to ask: Why do some people seek, while others avoid, communication in their second language? Originally, research centered on approaching the question from a trait-like perspective that emphasized stable individual differences. Burgoon (1976) identified a number of sociological and psychological constructs that pointed to a stable predisposition to avoid or devalue oral communication. Burgoon called this construct Unwillingness to Communicate (UnWTC), linking it to anomie, alienation, low self-esteem, introversion, and communication apprehension. McCroskey and Baer (1985) re-oriented the construct in a positive direction, calling it WTC. Studies showed that WTC correlated with the variables identified by Burgoon (see McCroskey & Richmond, 1991), indicated differences across cultures (McCroskey & Richmond, 1990), and predicted who would initiate communication (MacIntyre, Babin, & Clément, 1999).

More recently, researchers have been emphasizing that, although there are general tendencies in communication, WTC fluctuates a lot within a given communication situation. Changes in WTC are produced by a set of interacting, complex dynamic systems (MacIntyre & Legatto, 2011) that integrate psychological, linguistic, educational, and communicative factors in real time. From a research perspective, such factors have typically been studied independently of one another, in part because the key issues for conceptualizing and measuring WTC change depend on the timescale being considered. On the one hand, if attention is drawn to WTC as a stable characteristic that differs among people (with some people typically more willing to speak and others more hesitant), then attention is drawn toward factors such as personality, competence levels, and the regular features of the social or cultural setting. Such factors would be considered relatively stable or time invariant; typically measured only once by the researchers and considered to be relatively constant over time (Long, 2012). On the other hand, if attention is drawn to the strength of feeling willing or unwilling to communicate at a particular moment, then attention is directed toward details of the specific context such as the people in the situation, changes in felt emotions (e.g., anxiety), and feelings of confidence with the conversation topics. These types of factors would be considered time varying, requiring multiple measurements across time, as the results change with changes in the context (Long, 2012). Because WTC can be viewed on multiple timescales, it has the potential to provide an interface among these lines of inquiry and focus attention on a critically important aspect of language learning: why some learners choose to speak and others remain quiet when an opportunity to use the L2 arises.

Research into WTC has adopted several complementary approaches to help understand both long-term stability and short-term fluctuations. Although some authors emphasize the difference between trait-like and dynamic conceptualizations, or quantitative versus qualitative approaches, we believe that the various perspectives can be considered complementary rather than opposites. Trait-like approaches emphasize stability among persons (and differences within a group of people) and dynamic approaches emphasize variability within a person. These perspectives complement each other like two sides of the same coin. In the remainder of this chapter, we will describe five measures of WTC from a trait-like perspective (for details of each measure see Ayers-Glassey & MacIntyre, 2019) and two measures from a dynamic perspective.

Measuring Trait-Like WTC

The most frequently used measure of WTC in the first-language (L1) communication literature is McCroskey and Baer's (1985) 20-item scale. Scale items are based on three types of speakers who have varying degrees of familiarity with the respondent (friends, acquaintances, and strangers) crossed with four communication contexts (dyads, small groups, meetings, and public speaking), yielding 12 core WTC items. The other eight items are considered fillers (e.g., "talk to a secretary"). Responses are recorded on a 0%–100% scale that reflects how willing the respondent would be to talk in each of the situations described in the items. The measurement properties of the scale have been shown to be quite good (McCroskey, 1992, demonstrated an internal reliability estimate of .92) and its correlations with personality factors (such as extraversion) and communication factors (such as anxiety and perceived competence) support its validity in both the L1 and L2 (Gregersen & MacIntyre, 2014). The understanding of WTC afforded by the trait approach has been productive, highlighting the facilitating roles of extraversion and perceived communication competence, as well as the limiting roles of neuroticism and anxiety/communication apprehension (Hodis et al., 2010; McCroskey & Richmond, 1991; MacIntyre & Charos, 1996). In many ways, the WTC scale has accomplished the goals set by its authors: It is a reliable, valid measure of individual differences in the propensity to initiate communication.

Adapting the WTC construct to L2 contexts has been particularly instructive for research on WTC. The original McCroskey scale has been used in several studies (e.g., MacIntyre, Baker, Clément, & Conrod, 2001; MacIntyre, Baker, Clément, & Donovan, 2003). The scale tends to show comparable reliabilities whether referring to an L1 or L2, at least in the context where communicating in either L1 or L2 is a realistic possibility. Over the years, several authors have addressed the need to use items that make more sense in contexts where the respondents might communicate, especially in situations wherein the language being learned is spoken infrequently (Peng, 2013; Weaver, 2005).

One of the first trait-like scales to be developed with the L2 classroom in mind was reported by MacIntyre, Baker, Clément and Conrod (2001). They created two parallel scales, one referring to communicating inside the classroom and the other referring to similar situations of communicating outside the classroom. In addition, the scales featured items tapping WTC in four skill areas: speaking (8 items), writing (8 items), comprehension (6 items), and reading (5 items). Examples of items include talking about your summer vacation, writing a story, listening to instructions, and reading a letter from a pen pal. The reliabilities for each subscale were acceptable, ranging from .81 to .96.

Weaver (2007) also saw the need to contextualize communication in situations encountered by the respondents, but found the MacIntyre et al. (2001) items to be inappropriate for the context in which he was working: learning English in Japan. He undertook the development of a new classroom-oriented scale using the Rasch approach to scale development. Rasch uses a complex approach to modeling measurement processes based on consideration of both item difficulty and respondents' abilities. Weaver's scale contained 34 items tapping into WTC for speaking and writing in the Japanese context. Examples of items included "greet someone in English" and "write a self-introduction in English." Although the scale was developed using sophisticated modeling techniques, it has not been widely used.

More recently, additional WTC scales have been proposed. Ryan (2009) edited items from existing sources to produce an eight-item scale, with each item presented twice, one referring to WTC in Japanese and the other measuring WTC in English. Khatib and Nourzadeh (2015) tested a new 27-item Instructional WTC scale among English-language learners in Iran. The authors suggested that items reflect six dimensions (communicative self-confidence, integrative orientation, situational context of L2 use, topical enticement, learning responsibility, and off-instruction communication), though additional validation work certainly is required. Finally, Mystowska-Wiertelak and Pawlak (2016) developed a scale in the Polish context to measure WTC among advanced learners of English. Items from eight pre-existing scales were combined and modified to be appropriate for the Polish L2 education system, focusing on WTC both in- and outside the classroom, along with six accompanying variables (communication confidence, learner beliefs, classroom environment, international posture, the ideal L2 self, and the ought-to L2 self). The authors concluded by emphasizing the need for further refinement and factor analysis.

The scales described above assess WTC in different contexts and in different skill areas. Their strengths lie in the ability to efficiently and systematically assess WTC within a group. The responses are trait-like in the sense that the scores generated by the scales are assumed to be fairly stable over a short period of time (days or weeks) and they reflect meaningful differences from one person to the next. However, Peng (2007, 2014), Cao (2006, 2011, 2013) and others (e.g., de Saint Léger & Storch, 2009; Khajavy, Ghonsooly, Hosseini Fatemi, & Choi, 2016) have suggested that there are a number of contextual factors that must be considered in discussing WTC, and Kang (2005) has argued that questionnaires are not "insightful enough" to do the job. The standard, self-report measurement strategy employed by the WTC scales reviewed above also limits the sensitivity of the measures to details of individual experiences and nuances of contexts. Whereas these scales can identify how high or low WTC is for a person, they do not directly address the question of *why* one's WTC is high or low, nor how it fluctuates from moment to moment. Research addressing the origins and fluctuations of WTC has taken a variety of approaches; here we will focus on qualitative and dynamic considerations in WTC measurement.

Qualitative Methods

Qualitative studies often use techniques such as interviews and focus groups with very small sample sizes (Maxwell, 2013). Although there are significant issues with this approach—including data comparability across persons, faults in memory, potential for various biases, and limits on generalizability of the findings—there are also advantages, including the depth and richness of responses, the flexibility to alter the course of an interview (to pursue interesting or unexpected comments), and more deeply-probing questions. Qualitative studies of WTC have shed light on several factors or processes which influence WTC.

Qualitative studies of WTC have produced interesting results concerning some of the more subtle processes involved in making people more-or-less willing to communicate. Kang (2005) studied four learners who were videotaped communicating in English (L2). A variety of situational factors were identified and divided into three categories: *security* defined by a lack of anxiety within the specific situation, *excitement* based on emotions in the specific moment, and *responsibility* reflecting "a feeling of obligation or duty to deliver and understand a message, or to make it clear" (p. 285). Cao and Philip (2006) used a combination of measurement approaches, starting with trait-like WTC (McCroskey & Richmond, 1991), supplemented by a classroom observation checklist featuring observable communication behavior (e.g., asking a question, volunteering an answer), and supported by interviews with the eight participants. Cao and Philip (2006) found that contextual factors (e.g., group size), interpersonal factors (e.g., participation of one's interlocutor), and intra-learner factors (e.g., self-confidence) combine to influence WTC.

In a study that attempted to balance the need for qualitative data with the desire for larger sample sizes, MacIntyre, Burns, and Jessome (2011) examined a group of young French immersion students aged 12 to 14. All of them were English speakers learning French, taking almost all of their academic courses in their L2 at an eastern-Canadian public school. Respondents were asked to use structured diaries over six weeks to discuss details of situations in which they were most willing and least willing to communicate. One hundred respondents provided descriptions of 241 situations in which they felt high WTC and 179 situations in which they felt unwilling to communicate. It was somewhat surprising that results revealed no clear difference between situations creating WTC and UnWTC. Results showed that communication incorporates considerable ambivalence because of personal, familial, and social conflicts. The students were equivocal on issues of how welcome error correction might be, whether they enjoyed or felt embarrassed by their special status as immersion students, whether they wanted to speak the L2 outside school, and other issues. Their experiences revealed a great number of subtle interactions to be considered when asking why WTC rises and falls in a given communicative situation. Interactions among subtle features of the learner and relevant factors in the context create a sense of willingness to speak up or remain quiet, an emergent state that has the potential to change very quickly, especially in young adolescence. Perhaps the most striking implication for measuring WTC or UnWTC is that the situations that create WTC are not so different from those associated with UnWTC, at least in the sample at hand.

From a measurement perspective, how does a researcher focus on the sometimes subtle reasons for changes in WTC when trait scales tend to measure the stability of it? Over the past few years, innovative approaches to measuring changes in WTC and other communication variables in real time have been developed. The theoretical foundation of the work lies in complex dynamic systems theory (CDST, see Larsen-Freeman & Cameron, 2008; Lewis, 2011; Thelen & Smith, 1994) which emphasizes the emergent, self-organizing, and non-linear properties of systems with multiple interacting components, such as one human being communicating with another (Fogel, 2006; Lang, 2014).

Dynamic WTC

Communication has ebbs and flows that characterize a process that can change suddenly and in unpredictable ways. The communication process is meaning-oriented, with meaning derived from the interactions among verbal, visual, vocal, contextual, personal, and other cues integrated with an individual's unique history of experiences meeting up with current feelings and thoughts.

The language of a dynamic systems approach and its underlying assumptions are probably unfamiliar to readers in much of the social sciences, and has been summarized elsewhere (Larsen-Freeman, 2015). CDST emphasizes that elements of situations combine in non-linear ways, as when a conversation is altered dramatically by a brief, subtle, non-verbal cue. Because the communication system is open to external influences, it can be unpredictable. For this reason, the emphasis is on the dynamic changes over time, allowing that systems do settle into stable patterns. Further, CDST focuses squarely on processes occurring over different timescales (e.g., language use per-second vs. per-semester) and the highly contextualized nature of the processes. Thus far, CDST studies have been fairly descriptive in their accounts and often do not claim generalizability beyond the local situation.

Taking the dynamic approach leads to new types of research questions, issues that cannot be addressed with typical questionnaire-based studies. In a recent chapter we emphasized that the research questions must change when considered from a CDST perspective (MacIntyre, MacKay, Ross, & Abel, 2018). For example, prior research using the McCroskey (1992) WTC questionnaire addressed research questions such as "what are the correlations among WTC, communication apprehension and perceived competence?" (McCroskey & Richmond, 1991). However, from a dynamic perspective researchers might ask "what happens to WTC as anxiety and perceptions of competence rise and fall during interpersonal communication?" The measurement approaches to answering this second type of question are very different from cross-sectional survey research, and they differ as well from test-retest issues (Hodis et al., 2010). To clarify the nature of measuring dynamic systems, van Dijk, Verspoor and Lowie (2011, p. 62) proposed criteria that can be applied to collecting data addressing CDST questions:

> ...if we really want to know how an individual (or group) develops over time, we need data that is dense (i.e., collected at many regular measurement points), longitudinal (i.e., collected over a longer period of time), and individual (i.e., for one person at a time and not averaged out).

These criteria imply that longitudinal data collected in two or three waves would not likely lead to the amount of information necessary to assess changes over time. According to Singer and Willett (2003), a single wave of data (i.e., cross-sectional) does not tell us much about how or why a change has occurred. A second wave of data would provide only slightly more information; however, it would not be able to inform people about the shape of the change (e.g., linear, non-linear, chunked), rather only what the degree of change was between the two observation times involved. The more data collection points incorporated in a study, the better. Together, a density of data points can provide a more flexible model of change with much less restriction and potential for measurement error. It can be noted also that collecting qualitative data through interviews and focus groups often does not meet van Dijk et al.'s (2011) criteria unless the data collection process explicitly targets change over time. In short, data that best addresses CDST approaches are dense, longitudinal, and individual, and unique methods are necessary to collect such data.

A specific example of a CDST approach to studying communication, the idiodynamic method (MacIntyre, 2012), produces dense, rich data connected to communication events. The method has four steps:

1. A communication event is video-recorded.
2. Immediately after the recording is made, participants use the specially-written idiodynamic software to rate themselves on a variable of interest (e.g., WTC) at a rate of once per second, allowing for ratings to be linked closely in time to communication events. A bit-map graph of the ratings can be printed immediately after watching the video.
3. With the help of a research assistant, the video and graph are reviewed together to isolate meaningful changes in the ratings (peaks and valleys) and the respondent's explanation of what is happening. This interview is also recorded.
4. The videos are transcribed for further analysis.

To date there have been several idiodynamic studies, one with a focus on WTC (MacIntyre & Legatto, 2011) and others that examine anxiety (Gregersen, MacIntyre, & Meza, 2014), the self (Mercer, 2015), and fluency (Wood, 2016), among other topics. An example of an idiodynamic graph showing ratings of approach (scores above 0) and avoidance (scores below 0) is presented in Figure 18.1.

The idiodynamic studies conducted to date have described WTC as strongly connected with processes that are ongoing over a short period of time, such as vocabulary retrieval, emotional reactions, and other factors that change rapidly. A recent study by MacIntyre and Serroul (2015) focused on approach-avoidance motivation for communicating in the L2 across eight specific

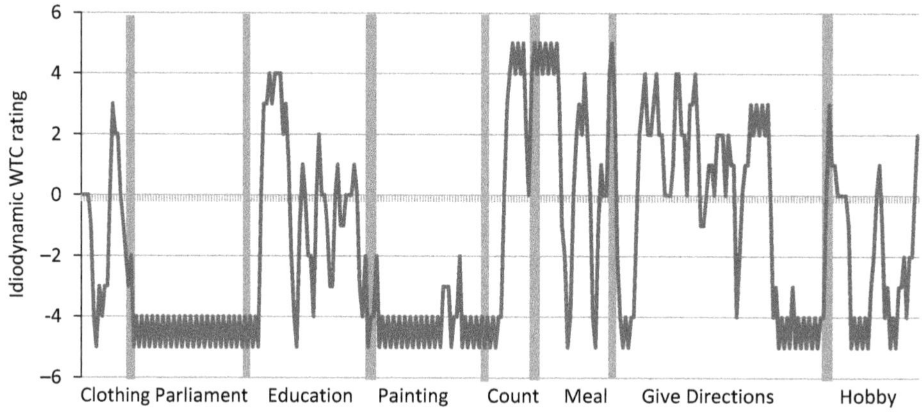

Figure 18.1 An example of idiodynamic WTC ratings.

tasks in a question-and-answer oral interview format (e.g., describe the clothing you are wearing, what is the role of parliament in Canadian government, describe a hobby or interest outside school, and so on). They described WTC as part of "the four horsemen" of interconnected affective reactions: feeling willing to communicate, feeling motivated to talk, rising and falling anxiety, and an ongoing self-evaluation of competence (p. 130). Idiodynamics allow researchers to build accounts of communication that are highly sensitive to time as it unfolds. In doing so they can examine the detailed ways in which communication traits operate in practice as they unfold in real time, generating the dense, individual-level data that CDST requires.

Idiodynamic studies (e.g., Gregersen, MacIntyre, & Meza, 2014) typically are conducted in a controlled setting and lab-based studies can be criticized for creating artificial communication environments; video recording equipment and subsequent interviews are not naturally-occurring parts of interpersonal communication. In one adaptation of the method, Gregersen and MacIntyre (2017) used video recordings as part of a teacher training exercise to gain a complete record of changes in emotion (focusing on anxiety) throughout a practice-teaching exercise. A similar approach might be applicable to other teaching occasions that routinely employ video as part of instructional design.

A more naturalistic measurement method for WTC is based on the notion of experience sampling that has been used to investigate experiences occurring in day-to-day life (Hektner, Schmidt, & Csikszentmihalyi, 2007). Experience sampling requires respondents to report on what they are doing and how they are reacting at fixed or random intervals, in response to a prompt sound (such as a notification sound in a classroom or on a phone app). Recently, a Polish group of researchers have been using this type of method to study WTC in L2 classroom contexts (Mystkowska-Wiertelak & Pawlak, 2016, 2017; Pawlak & Mystkowska-Wiertelak, 2015) where students capture their ratings of WTC in response to a "beep" that occurs several times during a classroom lesson. In the most recent study in this series, Mystkowska-Wiertelak (2016) examined changes in WTC during a semester-long course. The method is flexible and allows for minimal disruption in the naturally-occurring activities of the classroom. Studies of WTC in language classrooms, as learners interact in meaningful ways, have a particular ecological validity about them (Cao & Philip, 2006; Cao, 2011, 2013). There is value in further examining WTC with the experience sampling method.

Recommendations for Practice

There are good reasons for measuring WTC, including that it has been proposed as a valid goal, and perhaps the ultimate goal, of the language learning process (MacIntyre et al., 1998). To what extent WTC affects language testing and the veracity of test scores is an open question. Further, the role of WTC in development from young to older learners has not been assessed in practice. Among young children, an unwillingness to communicate with strangers is an age-appropriate behavior, but it varies widely from child to child. A communicative approach to language learning favors those with higher levels of WTC, and for that reason concerned teachers will consider carefully how WTC is affecting their students. Language teaching practices that are sensitive to variation in WTC among the learners can better account for individual differences to help ensure that testing is not unduly influenced by a willingness or unwillingness to talk. It is especially important to understand this issue with younger learners who may be prematurely streamed out of language learning.

Future innovation in measuring WTC may be on the horizon. Innovations in physiological indices of WTC such as eye-tracking which can measure a learner's visual attention to an interlocutor's eyes or face, could be explored as providing a particularly helpful, non-invasive correlate of WTC. WTC measures can be expanded to skill domains other than speaking, by developing new measures of willingness to write, read, and listen. Additionally, quick, self-assessment strategies, such as structured response grids (Pawlak & Mystkowska-Wiertelak, 2015), thermometer-shaped figures (Macintyre et al., 1999), idiodynamic software (MacIntyre & Legatto, 2011), or even self-assessment manikins (SAMs) used in cognitive psychology to measure arousal could be adopted by SLA researchers to measure WTC dynamics. When language assessment is based on communicative practice, measuring WTC and coming to understand its influence on learners and their test scores is recommended.

Testing Tips

- The communication situations reflected in measures of willingness-to-communicate, especially questionnaires, must make sense to the respondents.
- Decide whether the skill you want to focus on is speaking, writing, comprehension, or reading, and be clear on what "communication" means in the context of any given study.
- Use a timescale appropriate for the research question. If the question is about changes over longer timescales within a group of learners, such as increases in WTC as the result of taking a semester-long language course, then questionnaire measures likely will be appropriate. If the focus is on changes over a short time, methods such as idiodynamics, experience sampling, stimulated recall, diary reflections, etc. may be appropriate.
- It is not necessary to limit a study to only one method; it can be informative to study large groups qualitatively or to use questionnaires as information for case studies.
- To investigate the processes underlying WTC for an individual, it is important to ask participants to respond in their own ways to reflect their understanding of what is happening when they choose to communicate. Asking about WTC in different contexts may be especially helpful in illustrating the thought processes a person experiences when presented with an opportunity to communicate or not.
- In bilingual and multilingual contexts, consider asking about WTC in more than one language to understand the contrast situations where the target language is available

Recommended Readings

McCroskey, J. C. & Richmond, V. P. (1991). Willingness to communicate: A cognitive view. In M. Booth-Butterfield (Ed.), *Communication, Cognition, and Anxiety* (pp. 19–37). SAGE Publications.

This chapter, reprinted from the *Journal of Social Behavior and Personality*, presents the L1 WTC scale and the rationale for its development. WTC varies among native language speakers but WTC in L1 is not simply transferred to learning additional languages.

MacIntyre, P. D. & Legatto, J. J. (2011). A dynamic system approach to willingness to communicate: Developing an idiodynamic method to capture rapidly changing affect. *Applied Linguistics*, *32*(2), 149–171. https://doi.org/10.1093/applin/amq037

The first published study using the idiodynamic method to investigate WTC. The authors show that WTC fluctuates rapidly in response to a variety of communication factors including task demands, emotional reactions such as rising anxiety, and vocabulary retrieval processes.

Mystkowska-Wiertelak, A. & Pawlak, M. (2017). *Willingness to communicate in instructed second language acquisition: A micro and macro perspective*. Multilingual Matters.

A book that describes in detail WTC research being conducted in classrooms. The micro perspective is analogous to a dynamic conceptualization of WTC and the macro perspective to a trait-like perspective.

References

Ayers-Glassey, S., & MacIntyre, P. D. (2019). *Measuring willingness to communicate in first and additional languages: An annotated bibliography* (Unpublished manuscript). Cape Breton University.

Burgoon, J. K. (1976). The unwillingness-to-communicate scale: Development and validation. *Communication Monographs*, *43*(1), 60–69. https://doi.org/10.1080/03637757609375916

Cao, Y. (2006). Exploring dynamism in willingness to communicate: A longitudinal case study. *New Zealand Studies in Applied Linguistics, 12*(2), 1–16.

Cao, Y. (2011). Investigating situational willingness to communicate within second language classrooms from an ecological perspective. *System*, *39*(4), 468–479. https://doi.org/10.1016/j.system.2011.10.016

Cao, Y. (2013). Exploring dynamism in willingness to communicate: A longitudinal case study. *Australian Review of Applied Linguistics*, *36*, 160–176. https://doi.org/10.1075/aral.36.2.03cao

Cao, Y., & Philip, J. (2006). Interactional context and willingness to communicate: A comparison of behavior in whole class, group and dyadic interaction. *System*, *34*(4), 480–493. https://doi.org/10.1016/j.system.2006.05.002

de Saint Léger, D., & Storch, N. (2009). Learners' perceptions and attitudes: Implications for willingness to communicate in an L2 classroom. *System*, *37*(2), 269–285. https://doi.org/10.1016/j.system.2009.01.001

Fogel, A. (2006). Dynamic systems research on inter-individual communication: The transformation of meaning-making. *Journal of Developmental Processes*, *1*, 7–30.

Gregersen, T., & MacIntyre, P. D. (2014). *Capitalizing on language learners' individuality: From premise to practice*. Multilingual Matters.

Gregersen, T., & MacIntyre, P. D. (2017). *Optimizing language learners' nonverbal behavior from tenet to technique*. Multilingual Matters.

Gregersen, T., MacIntyre, P. D., & Meza, M. D. (2014). The motion of emotion: Idiodynamic case studies of learners' foreign language anxiety. *The Modern Language Journal*, *98*, 574–588. https://doi.org/10.1111/modl.12084

Hektner, J. M., Schmidt, J. A., & Csikszentmihalyi, M. (2007). *Experience sampling method: Measuring the quality of everyday life*. SAGE Publications.

Hodis, G. M., Bardhan, N. R., & Hodis, F. A. (2010). Patterns of change in willingness to communicate in public speaking contexts: A latent growth modeling analysis. *Journal of Applied Communication Research*, *38*(3), 248–267. https://doi.org/10.1080/00909882.2010.490840

Kang, S. (2005). Dynamic emergence of situational willingness to communicate in a second language. *System*, *33*(2), 277–292. https://doi.org/10.1016/j.system.2004.10.004

Khajavy, G. H., Ghonsooly, B., Hosseini Fatemi, A., & Choi, C. W. (2016). Willingness to communicate in English: A microsystem model in the Iranian EFL classroom context. *TESOL Quarterly*, *50*, 154–180. https://doi.org/10.1002/tesq.204

Khatib, M., & Nourzadeh, S. (2015). Development and validation of an instructional willingness to communicate questionnaire. *Journal of Multilingual and Multicultural Development*, *36*(3), 266–283. https://doi.org/10.1080/01434632.2014.914523

Lang, A. (2014). Dynamic human-centered communication systems theory. *Information Society*, *30*(1), 60–70. https://doi.org/10.1080/01972243.2013.856364

Larsen-Freeman, D. (2015). Ten 'lessons' from dynamic systems theory: What is on offer. In Z. Dörnyei, P. MacIntyre, & A. Henry (Eds.), *Motivational dynamics in language learning* (pp. 11–19). Multilingual Matters.

Larsen-Freeman, D., & Cameron, L. (2008). *Complex systems and applied linguistics*. Oxford University Press. https://doi.org/10.1111/j.1473-4192.2007.00148.x

Lewis, M. D. (2011). Dynamic systems approaches: Cool enough? Hot enough? *Child Development Perspectives*, *5*, 279–285. https://doi.org/10.1111/j.1750-8606.2011.00190.x

Long, J. D. (2012). *Longitudinal data analysis for the behavioral sciences using R*. SAGE Publications.

MacIntyre, P. D. (2012). The idiodynamic method: A closer look at the dynamics of communication traits. *Communication Research Reports*, *29*(4), 361–367. https://doi.org/10.1080/08824096.2012.723274

MacIntyre, P. D., Babin, P. A., & Clément, R. (1999). Willingness to communicate: Antecedents and consequences. *Communication Quarterly*, *47*, 215–229. https://doi.org/10.1080/01463379909370135

MacIntyre, P. D., Baker, S. C., Clément, R., & Conrod, S. (2001). Willingness to communicate, social support, and language-learning orientations of immersion students. *Studies in Second Language Acquisition*, *23*(3), 369–388. https://doi.org/10.1017/S0272263101003035

MacIntyre, P. D., Baker, S., Clément, R., & Donovan, L. A. (2003). Talking in order to learn: Willingness to communicate and intensive language programs. *Canadian Modern Language Review*, *59*, 589–607. https://doi.org/10.3138/cmlr.59.4.589

MacIntyre, P. D., Burns, C., & Jessome, A. (2011). Ambivalence about communicating in a second language: A qualitative study of French immersion students' willingness to communicate. *The Modern Language Journal, 95*(1), 81–96. https://doi.org/10.1111/j.1540-4781.2010.01141.x

MacIntyre, P. D., & Charos, C. (1996). Personality, attitudes, and affect as predictors of second language communication. *Journal of Language and Social Psychology, 15*(1), 3–26. https://doi.org/10.1177/0261927X960151001

MacIntyre, P. D., Clément, R., Dörnyei, Z., & Noels, K. A. (1998). Conceptualizing willingness to communicate in a L2: A situational model of L2 confidence and affiliation. *The Modern Language Journal, 82*(4), 545–562. https://doi.org/10.1111/j.1540-4781.1998.tb05543.x

MacIntyre, P. D., & Legatto, J. J. (2011). A dynamic system approach to willingness to communicate: Developing an idiodynamic method to capture rapidly changing affect. *Applied Linguistics, 32*(2), 149–171. https://doi.org/10.1093/applin/amq037

MacIntyre, P. D., MacKay, E., Ross, J., & Abel, E. (2017). The emerging need for methods appropriate to study dynamic systems: Individual differences in motivational dynamics. In L. Ortega & Z. Han (Eds.), *Complexity theory and language development: In celebration of Diane Larsen-Freeman* (pp. 97–122). John Benjamins. https://doi.org/10.1075/lllt.48

MacIntyre, P. D., & Serroul, A. (2015). Motivation on a per-second timescale: Examining approach-avoidance motivation during L2 task performance. In Z. Dörnyei, P. D. MacIntyre, & A. Henry (Eds.), *Motivational dynamics in language learning* (pp. 109–138). Multilingual Matters.

Maxwell, J. A. (2013). *Qualitative research design: An interactive approach* (3rd ed.). SAGE Publications.

McCroskey, J. C. (1992). Reliability and validity of the willingness to communicate scale. *Communication Quarterly, 40*(1), 16–25. https://doi.org/10.1080/01463379209369817

McCroskey, J. C., & Baer, J. E. (1985). *Willingness to communicate: The construct and its measurement* [Paper presentation]. Speech Communication Association Annual Convention, Denver, CO, USA.

McCroskey, J. C., & Richmond, V. P. (1987). Willingness to communicate. In J. C. McCroskey & J. A. Daly (Eds.), *Personality and interpersonal communication* (pp. 129–156). SAGE Publications.

McCroskey, J. C., & Richmond, V. P. (1990). Willingness to communicate: Differing cultural perspectives. *Southern Journal of Communication, 56*, 72–77. https://doi.org/10.1080/10417949009372817

McCroskey, J. C., & Richmond, V. P. (1991). Willingness to communicate: A cognitive view. In M. Booth-Butterfield (Ed.), *Communication, cognition, and anxiety* (pp. 19–37). SAGE Publications.

Mercer, S. (2015). Dynamics of the self: A multilevel nested systems approach. In Z. Dörnyei, P. D. MacIntyre, & A. Henry (Eds.), *Motivational dynamics in language learning* (pp. 139–163). Multilingual Matters.

Mystkowska-Wiertelak, A. (2016). Dynamics of classroom WTC: Results of a semester study. *Studies in Second Language Learning and Teaching Department of English Studies (SSLLT), 6*(4), 651–676. https://doi.org/10.14746/ssllt.2016.6.4.5

Mystkowska-Wiertelak, A., & Pawlak, M. (2016). Designing a tool for measuring the interrelationships between L2 WTC and confidence, beliefs, motivation, and context. In M. Pawlak (Ed.), *Classroom-oriented research* (pp. 19–37). Springer.

Mystkowska-Wiertelak, A., & Pawlak, M. (2017). *Willingness to communicate in instructed second language acquisition: A micro and macro perspective*. Multilingual Matters.

Pawlak, M., & Mystkowska-Wiertelak, A. (2015). Investigating the dynamic nature of L2 willingness to communicate. *System, 50*, 1–9. https://doi.org/10.1016/j.system.2015.02.001

Peng, J. (2007). Willingness to communicate in the Chinese EFL classroom: A cultural perspective. In J. Liu (Ed.), *English language teaching in China: New approaches, perspectives, and standards* (pp. 250–269). Continuum.

Peng, J. E. (2013). The challenge of measuring willingness to communicate in ELF contexts. *The Asia-Pacific Education Researcher, 22*(3), 281–290. https://doi.org/10.1007/s40299-012-0053-x

Peng, J. E. (2014). *Willingness to communicate inside the EFL classroom and beyond: An ecological perspective*. Multilingual Matters.

Ryan, S. (2009). Self and identity in L2 motivation in Japan: The ideal L2 self and Japanese learners of English. In Z. Dorynei & E. Ushioda (Eds.), *Motivation, language identity and the L2 self* (pp. 120–143). Multilingual Matters.

Singer, J. D., Willett, J. B., & Willett, J. B. (2003). *Applied longitudinal data analysis: Modeling change and event occurrence*. Oxford University Press.

Thelen, E., & Smith, L. B. (1994). *A dynamic systems approach to the development of cognition and action*. MIT Press.

van Dijk, M., Verspoor, M., & Lowie, W. (2011). Variability and DST. In M. H. Verspoor, K. de Bot, & W. Lowie (Eds.), *A dynamic approach to second language development* (pp. 55–84). John Benjamins Publishing Company.

Weaver, C. (2005). Using the Rasch model to develop a measure of second language learners of willingness to communicate within a language classroom. *Journal of Applied Measurement*, *6*(4), 396–415.
Weaver, C. (2007). Willingness to communicate: A mediating factor in the interaction between learners and tasks. In K. Van den Branden, K. Van Gorp, & M. Verhelst (Eds.), *Tasks in action: Task-based language education from a classroom-based perspective* (pp. 153–187). Cambridge Scholars Press.
Wood, D. (2016). Willingness to communicate and second language speech fluency: An idiodynamic investigation. *System*, *60*, 11–28. https://doi.org/10.1016/j.system.2016.05.003

Part IV

Measuring Language Development

19

Measuring Complexity, Accuracy, and Fluency (CAF)

Gabriele Pallotti

Background

The acquisition and use of a second language have always been seen as multifaceted processes in SLA research. However, it was only in the mid-1990s that the Complexity, Accuracy and Fluency (CAF) triad became established as a standard way of describing the multidimensionality of language performance, in particular after the works of Skehan (1998) and Wolfe-Quintero, Inagaki and Kim (1998).

In the following years, some contributions described how these dimensions vary over time in L2 development. The bulk of research, however, focused on how the three constructs vary according to task's features, testing in particular the predictions of two theoretical models, the Cognition Hypothesis (Robinson, 2015) and the Limited Attentional Capacity Model (Skehan, 1998; 2015). Results, however, are far from being clear and consistent. The main problem lies in the fact that all these studies have used a large variety of measures and operationalizations of both independent variables (task conditions) and dependent variables (CAF measures), often paying little attention to their construct validity (Ellis, 2018; Plonsky & Kim, 2016). Only more recently some critical reviews have aimed to clarify the constructs' theoretical and operational definitions (Bulté & Housen, 2012; Lambert & Kormos, 2014; Norris & Ortega, 2009; Pallotti, 2009, 2015; Skehan & Foster, 2012).

In language testing and assessment, too, the three dimensions of Complexity, Accuracy and Fluency play an important role. Most language tests consider accuracy as one of the dimensions to be assessed, in terms of the presence of errors, while "fluency has been a component of speaking assessment since the Second World War" (Fulcher, 2015, p. 77). Complexity is also often included in performance descriptors and several studies have found a positive correlation between test scores and more complex language use (e.g., Thirakunkovit et al., 2019 and references therein).

Before turning to a presentation of the three dimensions, some general clarifications are in order. The first concerns an asymmetry between the three constructs. Complexity and Fluency have to do with the interlanguage system as such, of which they describe several characteristics in positive terms, such as the presence of some structures, or its delivery rate. Accuracy, on the other hand, implies the comparison with another system, namely the target language, which is conducted in negative terms by counting errors (cases in which certain structures are *not* produced).

A second point concerns modality. Complexity and accuracy may be evaluated in basically the same way in oral and written texts: The most important difference lies in the choice of the reference units, which may be identified in writing by means of punctuation (sentences or T-Units; Hunt, 1965), while in oral production this identification often relies on prosody and intonation (utterances or AS-Units; Foster, Tonkyn, & Wigglesworth, 2000). If written data are collected with keylogging programs, even the fluency of written production can be evaluated in much the same way as in oral speech. In the absence of these direct measures, writing fluency becomes a rather different construct.

In the following pages, I will present the three dimensions, discussing, for each of them, the construct's theoretical definition and possible operationalizations. Since it is not possible to review all the measures, I will list only the most used, which have best withstood criticisms and are, in my opinion, more valid. Validity will be assessed mainly in logical-conceptual terms, as the correspondence of the measure to the construct it intends to measure, and in terms of reliability (constancy of the measure across evaluators). To my knowledge, no studies have explicitly addressed the issue of validating CAF measures, although some factor analyses have shown that the three dimensions are in fact relatively independent (e.g., Koizumi & In'nami, 2014; Norris & Ortega, 2009). Several authors (e.g., Polio & Shea, 2014; Wolfe-Quintero, Inagaki & Kim, 1998) have proposed to evaluate the validity of CAF measures based on their ability to vary over time or in relation to changes in task conditions. However, this approach is questionable, because it assumes what needs to be demonstrated: If a measure does not vary over time, or across tasks, this can simply be a fact, not a problem with the measure's validity. In other words, considering good measures only those varying where we expect variation means assuming that our theories, or expectations, are valid in themselves, which seems to be too strong an assumption in the current state of knowledge. One can speak at most about the *practical usefulness* of a measure in discriminating learners at different levels, or for assessing the effects of different communicative activities (see e.g., Hsieh & Wang, 2019).

Key Concepts

Complexity: The number of elements and their interrelationships in a text or linguistic system. It can be grammatical (i.e., required by the linguistic system) or stylistic (i.e., the result of free choices by language users). May be applied to specific levels of linguistic description: phonology, lexicon, morphosyntax, pragmatics.

Accuracy: The conformity of linguistic performance to target-language norms. May be applied to specific levels of linguistic description: phonology, lexicon, morphosyntax, pragmatics.

Fluency: The extent to which linguistic production is (and/or perceived as) fast and smooth. Three dimensions are usually identified: speed (articulation rate), breakdown (number and length of pauses), repair (number of reformulations, false-starts, etc.). Fluency is generally a holistic measure of language performance.

Key issues

Complexity

Learning a new language consists first of all in building a system of patterns and rules, which becomes increasingly vast and thus more complex. The term *complexity* is commonly used to refer both to a structural dimension (number of elements of a system, intricacy of their relationships), and to a cognitive dimension, as the effort needed to process the whole system or some of its structures. In the interest of terminological transparency, I would recommend reserving the term *complexity* only to the first, structural, sense and to call *difficulty* the second aspect, which is also in line with language testing parlance (Pallotti, 2009, 2015). Therefore, a text containing many "sophisticated" linguistic structures (because they are acquired late, or because they are often produced with errors) should be said to be more "difficult" or "advanced," but not more "complex." Of course, it may be empirically demonstrated that more structurally complex linguistic units tend to be more difficult, and produced at more advanced levels, but this is not a good reason to call these different constructs by the same name.

Lexical Complexity. Assessing lexical complexity from a structural point of view implies calculating the variety of lexemes within a text. Since the type/token ratio (the number of times a lexical item is repeated in a text) is influenced by text length, several alternative measures have been proposed, such as the Guiraud index (types/sq root tokens; which only offers a partial correction), the Standardized Type/Token Ratio (STTR; the calculation of the average lexical diversity within samples of constant length), or MTLD, vocd-D and HD-D (for a review, McCarthy & Jarvis, 2013).

Other measures that have been proposed for assessing complexity, but actually concern difficulty, calculate the proportion of more or less rare words in a text, i.e., those belonging to the first, second, third, etc. band in a frequency ranking. The underlying idea is that if a learner produces rare words, her lexical competence may be deemed to be more advanced than that of one who is limited to a basic lexicon. All this makes sense, but I think it is more appropriate to say that a rare word like *tar* is more difficult or advanced than *car*, rather than saying it is more complex.

Morphological Complexity. The few existing measures of morphological complexity gauge the average diversity of exponents, or morphological processes, in a text. Pallotti (2015; Brezina & Pallotti, 2019) proposed the Morphological Complexity Index (MCI), which calculates the average diversity of inflectional exponents within and between samples of 10 forms randomly extracted from a text. De Clercq and Housen (2019) additionally used the Types/Family (Horst & Collins, 2006) and the Inflectional Diversity (Malvern et al., 2004) measures, that are based on the calculation of the ratio of different inflected word forms per lemma.

Syntactic Complexity. In many studies, "linguistic complexity" has been represented by syntactic complexity alone and operationalized by just one or two measures, such as the average length of units or the subordination ratio; a clear example of construct under-representation (Bulté & Housen, 2012). On the other hand, many studies employed redundant measures, i.e., tapping into the same sub-dimensions of the construct, e.g., subordination ratio together with number of clauses per T-Unit (Norris & Ortega, 2009).

Unlike lexical and morphological complexity measures, which look at the variety of forms, syntactic complexity measures mainly concern the average "depth" of syntactic structures. With a view to simplification, Pallotti (2015) proposed to select only three of the many measures in this area, namely the average number of words per phrase, number of phrases per clause and number of clauses per higher-order syntactic unit (sentence, T-Unit, AS-unit). De Clercq and Housen (2017) have proposed a measure accounting for the variety of syntactic structures, too.

Fluency

Fluency can be seen as an observable characteristic of texts ("utterance fluency"), as a reflection of cognitive processes ("cognitive fluency"), and as the perception of an external observer ("perceived fluency") (Segalowitz, 2010). From a cognitive perspective, fluency is connected to the dimension of "control" of language production processes—that is, with their proceduralization and automatization—and with functions such as planning and monitoring. On a descriptive level, three main dimensions are usually identified: speed, breakdown and repair (Tavakoli & Skehan, 2005).

Speed Fluency. This dimension represents how fast language is produced. It may be measured by counting the number of syllables per unit of time, for example 1 minute (speech rate). However, this measure is spurious, as it confounds articulation speed and the amount of pausing. A better operationalization is articulation rate, that is, the number of syllables per speaking time unit.

Breakdown Fluency. This dimension can be calculated by observing the number and length of pauses or, vice versa, the time in which a speaker produces language over total time (phonation time ratio). If pauses are counted, then a decision must be made as to how long a silence must be in order to be considered as a pause (typical values are around 0.3–0.4 seconds). Another indicator may be the number of words produced between one pause and another, referred to as "words per burst," "mean length of run" or "mean length of utterance." The position of pauses is also important. It has been noted, for example, that native speakers and advanced learners tend to pause between syntactic constituents, mainly to meet conceptual planning needs, while lower-level learners also pause within these constituents, probably to search for words (De Jong, 2016; Tavakoli, 2011).

Repair Fluency. This measure concerns the number of repair phenomena (e.g., self-repetitions, reformulations, hesitations, false starts). It gives an indication of the uncertainty experienced by speakers and of how they may consciously monitor their production.

Most research on fluency has concentrated on oral productions. However, the measures presented above can be applied to writing too, provided one has access to keylogging programs. For instance, Gunnarsson (2012) counted the number of words per burst (i.e., between two relatively long pauses), controlling for participants' L1 typing speed, to avoid confounding linguistic fluency with typing skills. It is also possible to calculate the number of keystrokes per minute, which is equivalent to the phonation time ratio.

In the absence of online data regarding the writing process, assessing fluency in written productions becomes more problematic. A gross indicator may be the number of words/characters per minute, provided that the writing time for each composition is known. If this information is missing, and only the final written product is available, a possible measure may be overall text length.

Most studies discussed fluency in monologic productions. However, some researchers have stressed the importance of considering fluency in dialogues too, which is given not only by the fluency of individual productions, but also by how speakers exchange turns. Peltonen (2017) for instance found that more advanced learners tend to produce fewer and shorter inter-turn pauses and use more other-repetitions to ensure coherence in dialogue. Sato (2014) has shown that, both in objective measurements and in subjective ratings, individual and interactional fluency are distinct constructs.

Accuracy

While fluency and complexity describe the interlanguage system as such and in positive terms (what is there), accuracy describes it in relation to another system, namely the L2, and in negative terms (what is missing, i.e., the number of errors). This calls into question the very idea of interlanguage as an autonomous system, whose logic and regularities should be explained in their own right, and results in the "comparative fallacy" (Bley-Vroman, 1983) of describing a language in terms of another (e.g., describing Spanish by listing its differences with English), or describing something in terms of what it is not (e.g., describing the language of a three-year old by listing the structures she has not mastered yet). An "interlanguage approach" (Pallotti, 2017) to teaching and assessment, on the contrary, consists in understanding the strategies underlying learners' productions and reconstructing their interlanguage as a system. While this attitude is certainly not as widespread as that of counting and weighing errors (the "accuracy" perspective), it may be relevant especially for formative assessment, and, after some training, teachers can apply it in ordinary classroom contexts (Pallotti, 2010; 2017).

From a psycholinguistic point of view, accurate productions may be seen as depending on the degree of conscious monitoring, so that accuracy would be inversely related to fluency, but this would only apply to occasional mistakes, or slips, while systematic errors due to the interlanguage as such could not be corrected by paying greater attention. Therefore, accurate productions may depend on a more proceduralized norm-oriented interlanguage system, and be thus positively related to increased fluency. Furthermore, accuracy must be assessed by referring to a system of "correct" norms, which is not always easy, due to sociolinguistic variation across social and geographical contexts.

Despite these theoretical difficulties, in practice accuracy is often considered to be an important aspect for language tests' end-users (especially in summative evaluation), as well as being frequently assessed in SLA research. Accuracy may be operationalized through global measures, such as the average number of errors per unit (clause, sentence, T-Unit, AS-Unit) or, conversely, by the proportion of error-free units. It remains difficult, however, to define exactly what errors are, especially if lexical, morphological, syntactic, phonological or spelling errors are bundled together; moreover, this index is influenced by the average length of units. To overcome this problem, Foster and Skehan (2012) proposed the measure "maximum length of accurate clause," which consists in listing all the clauses in order of length, establishing a cut-off of accuracy (e.g., 70%) and calculating the maximum length of clauses reaching that accuracy threshold.

Other authors counted grammatical, lexical, spelling, appropriateness errors separately (e.g., Kuiken & Vedder, 2012), or proposed more specific measures, such as the proportion of error-free relative clauses, or verbs, or past-tense verbs (Kormos, 2014). Some have also weighted errors according to their impact on comprehensibility (Foster & Wigglesworth, 2016; Kuiken & Vedder, 2008), or to their concerning more or less complex or advanced structures (Gunnarsson, 2012). However, these measures mix constructs, such as accuracy, on the one hand, and comprehensibility or interlanguage development, on the other, which are logically and, to some extent, empirically different.

The Relevance of CAF for Language Testing

Most tests nowadays are not limited to assessing language proficiency in and for itself, but strive to see it in the context of a larger communicative competence. This points to one of the main limitations of CAF research, which in most cases describes the formal characteristics of linguistic productions with little or no concern for their communicative adequacy. One of the first to raise the issue was Pallotti (2009), for whom "adequacy can be seen both as a separate dimension, theoretically independent from CAF (although it may be empirically found to be related to it), and as a way of interpreting CAF measures themselves" (p. 596).

Some studies have followed the first direction, correlating functional adequacy assessments with CAF measures (e.g., de Jong et al., 2012; Révész, Ekiert, & Torgersen, 2016). However, the second path is probably more fruitful for language assessment. Given that the basic construct of most contemporary tests is linguistic-communicative competence, the measurement of Complexity, Accuracy and Fluency should be interpreted according to this fundamental dimension. Thus, a communicatively oriented test should not only assess whether a production is more or less complex, or fluent, but whether and to what extent such complexity and fluency are appropriate for performing communicative tasks. For instance, there may be target domains where complex linguistic structures (e.g., rare words or long sentences) may be unnecessary, or even harmful, so that the more would not necessarily be the better.

As regards fluency, Fulcher (2015) argues that most studies that assessed it with measures such as speech rate or pause number and length under-represented the construct, limiting themselves to a purely objective account, with low-inference descriptive categories. If the latter were interpreted at all, this was done in terms of underlying cognitive processes, such as "cognitive fluency"

(Segalowitz, 2010). This approach thus neglected the communicative function of pauses, disfluencies, and articulation speed, and their role in the co-construction of meaning among participants, which, in his opinion, are the key aspects in a test, and that only a human rater can adequately assess.

Recommendations for Practice

Mind Your Constructs

Fulcher's criticism raises the fundamental questions: What do we want to measure, and how? Terms like *complex*, *accurate* and *fluent* are regularly used in descriptor scales, but many of them are polysemic, vague and with different meanings in the ordinary language versus technical domains. Therefore, a first contribution of CAF research may be to help test developers and users to be more explicit about these constructs. In practice, many rating scales and test scores will be based on a number of these aspects at the same time, but this should be the result of an intended choice, with a clear awareness of what (sub)dimensions have been bundled together and why.

With regard to **complexity**, one needs to specify whether it regards the lexicon, morphology or syntax, or all of them. The complexity of each of these levels should be interpreted in different ways: Lexical complexity may index the ability to express precise semantic nuances, morphological complexity concerns the command of a wide range of grammatical structures, while syntactic complexity may have to do with grammatical proficiency, too, but also with cultural and individual rhetorical choices—written academic language tends to favor more syntactically complex texts than professional or mundane usages, but even the ideal or standard level of syntactic complexity in academic texts is not the same in different languages; furthermore, there is always an unavoidable degree of individual stylistic preferences. One should also bear in mind the distinction between complexity and difficulty.

Fluency is a multidimensional construct, too, since it results from different aspects such as speech rate, pauses, reformulations, and because it can be interpreted in different ways. Observable phenomena may be seen as indicating increasingly automatic cognitive processes (cognitive fluency), or as more or less functional behaviors for achieving communicative purposes (perceived fluency). Also, several aspects of L2 fluency (especially length of pauses and articulation rate) are correlated to L1 speaking style, which requires great care when comparing candidates using the same absolute measures (de Jong, 2018).

In a purely communicative approach to language testing, **accuracy** should not be very relevant, for the main aim should be to assess whether candidates are able to perform certain communicative activities, regardless of how they use articles or conjugate verbs. Most errors at the intermediate and advanced levels do not affect comprehensibility and thus communicative effectiveness, while problems at lower levels are better characterized, rather than in terms of errors, in terms of a basic interlanguage system, which may not be adequate to clearly express some lexical and grammatical meanings. This is perhaps why most accuracy scales classify errors according to their impact on comprehensibility, although this mixes two theoretically and empirically distinct dimensions. A classification of errors based on their appearance in a developmental sequence may be useful for placing learners in different classes or course levels; however, in this case I would recommend carrying out a comprehensive interlanguage analysis, which goes beyond simply counting and classifying errors, but includes a systematic description of learners' strategies.

Objective Measures and Human Ratings

Once the constructs have been clearly defined, the next decision concerns how they should be assessed. Most SLA studies have employed objective measures, whereas in language testing performance is usually assessed through rating scales used by human judges (see Kuiken & Vedder,

Chapter 12, this volume; Pill & Smart, Chapter 13, this volume). The relationship between objective measures and human ratings can be seen in different ways. It might be argued that they concern different constructs: For example, objective fluency measurements would give an indication of individual cognitive processes, while subjective ratings would assess the social and communicative uses of (dis)fluency phenomena. The question then arises as to whether these different constructs, measured in different ways, are all relevant for the test purposes. On the other hand, one may argue that objective measures and human ratings (should) assess the same constructs, with holistic rating just being a more practical alternative than the meticulous counting of errors, pauses or clauses. In this case, the correlation between objective and subjective evaluation needs to be determined: Most studies have found them to range from fair to good, but rarely very strong (e.g., Brown, Iwashita, & McNamara, 2005).

The analytic study of CAF may be relevant for raters' training, making them aware of subtle distinctions in the constructs they are evaluating. For instance, when assessing complexity, judges seem to pay more attention to general syntactic complexity features, like average length of syntactic constituents or subordination ratio, than to intra-clausal phenomena (Tonkyn, 2012). As regards fluency, measures like articulation rate and length of pauses correlate rather clearly with human ratings, while filled pauses and repairs seem to bear less directly on human perceptions of fluency, possibly because they may have to do more with individual speaking style or task demands (Kormos & Dénes, 2004; Sato, 2014; Tavakoli, Nakatsuhara, & Hunter, 2017).

These results thus show one of the main consequences of CAF research for language assessment. CAF analytic measures are unlikely to be directly used to arrive at a test score, both because calculating them is time-consuming (although automatic scoring is becoming increasingly available for some of them), but also, and more importantly, because human judgment is often necessary to determine the communicative value of these linguistic aspects. Nonetheless, fine-grained CAF analyses may be valuable in various ways to language assessment, for instance to validate constructs and assessment procedures, to develop data-based rating scales or for improving assessors' performance, making them aware of the multidimensionality of many test constructs.

Testing Tips

- Consider whether complexity, accuracy, and fluency are really relevant for the test construct. For instance, a task-based test with a strong communicative orientation may include task completion as the main or only criterion and consider the linguistic characteristics of candidates' production as irrelevant.
- If CAF dimensions are deemed to be part of the construct to be evaluated, the following considerations may apply.
    - **Complexity.** Evaluate the importance of complexity in the target domain. Complex constructions seem to be highly valued in academic contexts, but may not be so in others; in any case, complexity cannot grow indefinitely and beyond a certain level it may hamper functional communication.
    - **Fluency.** Consider the role that individual style and task characteristics have on aspects of fluency. Mechanistic interpretations in terms of "the more, the better" may be problematic.
    - **Accuracy.** Be careful not to confound accuracy with communicative adequacy or interlanguage development.
- CAF dimensions (together with a thorough interlanguage analysis) may be more appropriate for formative than for summative assessment.

Recommended Readings

Brown, A., Iwashita, N., & McNamara, T. (2005). An examination of rater orientations and test-taker performance on English-for-academic-purposes speaking tasks. *ETS Research Report Series, 2005*. https://www.ets.org/Media/Research/pdf/RR-05-05.pdf

A comprehensive report comparing holistic ratings and CAF measures in the validation of oral language tasks and assessment procedures.

de Jong, N. H. (2018). Fluency in second language testing: Insights from different disciplines. *Language Assessment Quarterly*, *15*(3), 237–254. https://doi.org/10.1080/15434303.2018.1477780

An exemplary article showing how research on CAF (in this case, fluency) may be applied in language testing contexts.

Housen, A., Kuiken, F., & Vedder, I. (Eds.). (2012). *Dimensions of L2 performance and proficiency. Complexity, accuracy and fluency in SLA*. John Benjamins.

An influential collection of papers, covering many theoretical and practical issues related to CAF. Some chapters also specifically address the language testing perspective.

References

Bley-Vroman, R. (1983). The comparative fallacy in interlanguage studies: The case of systematicity. *Language Learning*, *33*(1), 1–17. https://doi.org/10.1111/j.1467-1770.1983.tb00983.x

Brezina, V., & Pallotti, G. (2019). Morphological complexity in written L2 texts. *Second Language Research*, *35*(1), 99–119. https://doi.org/10.1177/0267658316643125

Brown, A., Iwashita, N., & McNamara, T. (2005). An examination of rater orientations and test-taker performance on English-for-academic-purposes speaking tasks. *ETS Research Report Series, 2005*. https://www.ets.org/Media/Research/pdf/RR-05-05.pdf

Bulté, B., & Housen, A. (2012). Defining and operationalising L2 complexity. In A. Housen, F. Kuiken, & I. Vedder (Eds.), *Dimensions of L2 performance and proficiency: Complexity, accuracy and fluency in SLA* (pp. 21–46). John Benjamins. https://doi.org/10.1075/lllt.32.02bul

De Clercq, B., & Housen, A. (2017). A cross-linguistic perspective on syntactic complexity in L2 development: Syntactic elaboration and diversity. *The Modern Language Journal*, *101*(2), 315–334. https://doi.org/10.1111/modl.12396

De Clercq, B., & Housen, A. (2019). The development of morphological complexity: A cross-linguistic study of L2 French and English. *Second Language Research*, *35*(1), 71–97. https://doi.org/10.1177/0267658316674506

de Jong, N. H. (2016). Predicting pauses in L1 and L2 speech: The effects of utterance boundaries and word frequency. *International Review of Applied Linguistics in Language Teaching*, *54*(2), 113–132. https://doi.org/10.1515/iral-2016-9993

de Jong, N. H. (2018). Fluency in second language testing: Insights from different disciplines. *Language Assessment Quarterly*, *15*(3), 237–254. https://doi.org/10.1080/15434303.2018.1477780

de Jong, N. H., Steinel, M. P., Florijn, A., Schoonen, R., & Hulstijn, J. H. (2012). The effect of task complexity on functional adequacy, fluency and lexical diversity in speaking performances of native and non-native speakers. In A. Housen, F. Kuiken, & I. Vedder (Eds.), *Dimensions of L2 performance and proficiency: Complexity, accuracy and fluency in SLA* (pp. 121–142). John Benjamins.

Ellis, R. (2018). *Reflections on task-based language teaching*. Oxford University Press.

Foster, P., & Skehan, P. (2012). Complexity, accuracy, fluency and lexis in task-based performance. In A. Housen, F. Kuiken, & I. Vedder (Eds.), *Dimensions of L2 performance and proficiency: Complexity, accuracy and fluency in SLA* (pp. 199–220). John Benjamins. https://doi.org/10.1075/lllt.32.09fos

Foster, P., Tonkyn, A., & Wigglesworth, G. (2000). Measuring spoken language: A unit for all reasons. *Applied Linguistics*, *21*(3), 354–375. https://doi.org/10.1093/applin/21.3.354

Foster, P., & Wigglesworth, G. (2016). Capturing accuracy in second language performance: The case for a weighted clause ratio. *Annual Review of Applied Linguistics*, *36*, 98–116. https://doi.org/10.1017/S0267190515000082

Fulcher, G. (2015). *Re-examining language testing: A philosophical and social inquiry*. Routledge. https://doi.org/10.4324/9781315695518

Gunnarsson, C. (2012). The development of complexity, accuracy and fluency in the written production of L2 French. In A. Housen, F. Kuiken, & I. Vedder (Eds.), *Dimensions of L2 performance and proficiency:*

Complexity, accuracy and fluency in SLA (pp. 247–276). John Benjamins. https://doi.org/10.1075/lllt.32.11gun
Horst, M., & Collins, L. (2006). From faible to strong: How does their vocabulary grow? *Canadian Modern Language Review/Revue canadienne des langues vivantes*, *63*(1), 83–106. https://doi.org/10.3138/cmlr.63.1.83
Hsieh, C.-N., & Wang, Y. (2019). Speaking proficiency of young language students: A discourse-analytic study. *Language Testing*, *36*(1), 27–50. https://doi.org/10.1177/0265532217734240
Hunt, K. W. (1965). *Grammatical structures written at three grade levels*. [Paper presentation]. National Council of Teachers of English, Champaign, IL, United States.
Koizumi, R., & In'nami, Y. (2014). Modeling complexity, accuracy, and fluency of Japanese learners of English: A structural equation modeling approach. *JALT Journal*, *36*(1), 25–46.
Kormos, J. (2014). Differences across modalities of performance. In H. Byrnes & R. Manchón (Eds.), *Task-based language learning: Insights from and for L2 writing* (pp. 193–216). John Benjamins. https://doi.org/10.1075/tblt.7.08kor
Kormos, J., & Dénes, M. (2004). Exploring measures and perceptions of fluency in the speech of second language learners. *System*, *32*(2), 145–164. https://doi.org/10.1016/j.system.2004.01.001
Kuiken, F., & Vedder, I. (2008). Cognitive task complexity and written output in Italian and French as a foreign language. *Journal of Second Language Writing*, *17*(1), 48–60. https://doi.org/10.1016/j.jslw.2007.08.003
Kuiken, F., & Vedder, I. (2012). Syntactic complexity, lexical variation and accuracy as a function of task complexity and proficiency level in L2 writing and speaking. In A. Housen, F. Kuiken, & I. Vedder (Eds.), *Dimensions of L2 performance and proficiency: Complexity, accuracy and fluency in SLA* (pp. 143–170). John Benjamins. https://doi.org/10.1075/lllt.32.07kui
Lambert, C., & Kormos, J. (2014). Complexity, accuracy, and fluency in task-based L2 research: Toward more developmentally based measures of second language acquisition. *Applied Linguistics*, *35*(5), 606–614. https://doi.org/10.1093/applin/amu047
Malvern, D., Richards, B. J., Chipere, N., & Durán, P. (2004). *Lexical diversity and language development: Quantification and assessment*. Palgrave Macmillan. https://doi.org/10.1057/9780230511804
McCarthy, P. M., & Jarvis, S. (2013). From intrinsic to extrinsic issues of lexical diversity assessment. In S. Jarvis & M. Daller (Eds.), *Vocabulary knowledge: Human ratings and automated measures* (pp. 45–78). John Benjamins.
Norris, J. M., & Ortega, L. (2009). Towards an organic approach to investigating CAF in instructed SLA: The case of complexity. *Applied Linguistics*, *30*(4), 555–578. https://doi.org/10.1093/applin/amp044
Pallotti, G. (2009). CAF: Defining, refining and differentiating constructs. *Applied Linguistics*, *30*(4), 590–601. https://doi.org/10.1093/applin/amp045
Pallotti, G. (2010). Doing interlanguage analysis in school contexts. In I. Bartning, M. Martin, & I. Vedder (Eds.), *Communicative proficiency and linguistic development* (pp. 159–190). EuroSLA Monographs.
Pallotti, G. (2015). A simple view of linguistic complexity. *Second Language Research*, *31*(1), 117–134. https://doi.org/10.1177/0267658314536435
Pallotti, G. (2017). Applying the interlanguage approach to language teaching. *International Review of Applied Linguistics in Language Teaching (IRAL)*, *55*(4), 393–412. https://doi.org/doi.org/10.1515/iral-2017-0145
Peltonen, P. (2017). Temporal fluency and problem-solving in interaction: An exploratory study of fluency resources in L2 dialogue. *System*, *70*, 1–13. https://doi.org/10.1016/j.system.2017.08.009
Plonsky, L., & Kim, Y. (2016). Task-based learner production: A substantive and methodological review. *Annual Review of Applied Linguistics*, *36*, 73–97. https://doi.org/10.1017/S0267190516000015
Polio, C., & Shea, M. C. (2014). An investigation into current measures of linguistic accuracy in second language writing research. *Journal of Second Language Writing*, *26*, 10–27. https://doi.org/10.1016/j.jslw.2014.09.003
Révész, A., Ekiert, M., & Torgersen, E. N. (2016). The effects of complexity, accuracy, and fluency on communicative adequacy in oral task performance. *Applied Linguistics*, *37*(6), 828–848. https://doi.org/10.1093/applin/amu069
Robinson, P. (2015). The cognition hypothesis, second language task demands, and the SSARC model of pedagogic task sequencing. In M. Bygate (Ed.), *Domains and directions in the development of TBLT* (pp. 87–121). Benjamins.
Sato, M. (2014). Exploring the construct of interactional oral fluency: Second language acquisition and language testing approaches. *System*, *45*, 79–91. https://doi.org/10.1016/j.system.2014.05.004
Segalowitz, N. (2010). *The cognitive bases of second language fluency*. Routledge.
Skehan, P. (1998). *A cognitive approach to language learning*. Oxford University Press.

Skehan, P. (2015). Limited attentional capacity and cognition: Two hypotheses regarding second language performance on tasks. In M. Bygate (Ed.), *Domains and directions in the development of TBLT* (pp. 123–155). John Benjamins.

Tavakoli, P. (2011). Pausing patterns: differences between L2 learners and native speakers, *ELT Journal*, 65(1), 71–79. https://doi.org/10.1093/elt/ccq020

Tavakoli, P., Nakatsuhara, F., & Hunter, A. M. (2017). Scoring validity of the Aptis speaking test: Investigating fluency across tasks and levels of proficiency. *ARAGs Research Reports Online*, 1–56. https://www.britishcouncil.org/sites/default/files/tavakoli_et_al_layout.pdf

Tavakoli, P., & Skehan, P. (2005). Strategic planning, task structure, and performance testing. In R. Ellis (Ed.), *Planning and task performance in a second language* (pp. 239–273). John Benjamins. https://doi.org/10.1075/lllt.11.15tav

Thirakunkovit, S., Rodríguez-Fuentes, R. A., Park, K., & Staples, S. (2019). A corpus-based analysis of grammatical complexity as a measure of international teaching assistants' oral English proficiency. *English for Specific Purposes*, *53*, 74–89. https://doi.org/10.1016/j.esp.2018.09.002

Tonkyn, A. (2012). Measuring and perceiving changes in oral complexity, accuracy and fluency. In A. Housen, F. Kuiken, & I. Vedder (Eds.), *Dimensions of L2 performance and proficiency: Complexity, accuracy and fluency in SLA* (pp. 221–244). John Benjamins. https://doi.org/10.1075/lllt.32.10ton

Wolfe-Quintero, K., Inagaki, S., & Kim, H. Y. (1998). *Second language development in writing: Measures of fluency, accuracy, & complexity*. University of Hawaii Press.

20

Measuring Vocabulary Development

Benjamin Kremmel & Ana Pellicer-Sánchez

Background

Vocabulary learning is key to successful second language acquisition and use. It has consistently been shown to be among the most important predictors of language ability (Alderson, 2005). Gardner (2013) states that vocabulary is the "fuel of language, without which nothing meaningful can be understood or communicated" (p. 2). Indeed, "[m]any learners see second language acquisition as essentially a matter of learning vocabulary" (Read, 2000, p. 1). As such, assessing learners' vocabulary knowledge or the development thereof appears crucial to both foreign language teachers, as well as many SLA researchers, be it for diagnostic purposes or as a proxy measure for proficiency. However, while testing someone's vocabulary knowledge seems reasonably straightforward at first glance, a number of issues arise upon closer inspection: What is a word? What does knowing a word mean? What is the best way to assess this knowledge? How can we interpret the test scores in a meaningful way?

This chapter addresses these questions and outlines the status quo of the SLA field on them, as practitioners and researchers should consider these questions when designing or selecting a measure of vocabulary knowledge. While many may simply choose to select and use one of the many vocabulary tests that are publicly available and—too often—forget to ask themselves how trustworthy, reliable, and valid these available vocabulary tests are, we aim to critically evaluate some of the existing types of vocabulary tests and point to the general lack of validation evidence surrounding many of these. First, however, we briefly unpack the notions of "vocabulary" and "knowledge" before discussing different operationalizations of these terms for measurement.

Key Concepts

Vocabulary: Although often conceptualized as individual words, vocabulary comprises a range of different types of lexical items, including various types of formulaic sequences. Approaches to defining the construct of vocabulary knowledge can be broadly distinguished into three categories:

- ***Vocabulary breadth***: Quantity, or number of vocabulary items for which at least one meaning sense is known.

- ***Vocabulary depth*:** Quality, or how well a vocabulary item is known, including aspects such as pronunciation, derivation, or collocation knowledge.
- ***Lexical fluency*:** Speed or automaticity of retrieval of vocabulary items.

Key Issues

What Is Vocabulary?

Laufer and Goldstein (2004) maintain that "[v]ocabulary tests are contingent upon the test designer's definition of lexical knowledge" (p. 399). However, Read and Chapelle (2001) argue that the nature of vocabulary as an assessment construct is "ill-defined" (p. 1). Their observation, dating back to 2001, that vocabulary researchers have "given comparatively little attention to defining "vocabulary knowledge" or "vocabulary size" as theoretical constructs" (Read & Chapelle, 2001, p. 7), unfortunately still largely holds true. Indeed, different scholars have used and continue to use a variety of definitions and approaches.

"Vocabulary" has been traditionally equated with individual words. However, there seems to be a consensus among vocabulary researchers today, that formulaic sequences or chunks (e.g., idioms like *spill the beans*, collocations like *heavy rain*) should also be conceptualized as vocabulary items as they are distinct meaning units themselves. Nevertheless, the notion that language use is made up of (prefabricated) multi-word units (Wray, 2002; see also Gries, Paquot, & Yoder, Chapter 21, this volume) is still often ignored in the measurement of vocabulary knowledge with most tests focusing on single words.

In addition, researchers also differ in their conceptualizations of what is involved in *knowing* a word or phrase. Below, we will describe conceptualizations of vocabulary knowledge along three commonly used dimensions: breadth (size), depth, and fluency (automaticity of retrieval). This corresponds to Daller, Milton and Treffers-Daller's (2007) concept of "lexical space" and we will illustrate these constructs using prominent measurement tools and techniques. Table 20.2 indicates where the tests discussed or samples thereof can be accessed.

Measuring Vocabulary Breadth

Vocabulary breadth, often referred to as vocabulary size, is the most prominent and most tested dimension of vocabulary knowledge. Anderson and Freebody (1981) define breadth as "the number of words for which the person knows at least some of the significant aspects of meaning" (p. 92). This could refer to the number of words taught in class, e.g., as part of an achievement test, or the number of words more generally as sampled from a corpus-based frequency list for an overall estimate of vocabulary size or for diagnostic purposes. Nation and Webb (2011) identify three main approaches to assessing vocabulary breadth: "(1) counting the words that someone produces, (2) counting the number of words in a dictionary and testing what proportion of these are known, and (3) sampling from various frequency levels and testing to estimate the amount of vocabulary known at each level" (p. 196). Only a few studies have approached the issue of vocabulary breadth measurement with the second approach, by sampling from dictionaries (an exception is Goulden, Nation and Read (1990), but their resulting test was a self-assessment tool rather than a validated test (Read, 2013)). We now provide a brief overview of the four most prominent types of vocabulary breadth tests, with the first three methods employing approach number three, and the fourth method as one example of approach number one as listed above: (1) Yes/No checklist tests, (2) vocabulary levels tests, (3) the Vocabulary Size Test, and (4) Lexical profiling of learner productions.

Yes/No Checklist Tests. This type of vocabulary test aims at measuring learners' receptive vocabulary size and was first proposed by Meara and Buxton (1987) as an alternative to established multiple-choice tests of L2 vocabulary knowledge. Test takers simply check against a list of lexical items whether they know it (Yes) or not (No).

A percentage of "pseudowords" (Beeckmans et al., 2001), varying in ratio in different studies (Meara, 1992), is generally added to the list to counter learners' overestimation of their vocabulary knowledge. However, this item format has been critiqued for lacking verification of knowledge (Eyckmans, Van de Velde, van Hout, & Boers, 2007). By comparing scores on Yes/No tests to learners' performances on other criterion measures that require demonstration of knowledge (e.g., interviews), research has found that students overestimate (e.g., Pellicer-Sánchez & Schmitt, 2012) or, in rarer cases, underestimate (Stubbe, Stewart, & Pritchard, 2010) their vocabulary knowledge. These tests also operationalize a very simplistic notion of vocabulary knowledge as no multiple word meanings or multiple dimensions of word knowledge are tested (Beeckmans et al., 2001), and they perform unreliably with low-level learners (Meara, 1996).

While incredibly practical to design and administer (see Lemhoefer & Broersma, 2012, for the example of LexTALE), there is no consensus on how to best score and meaningfully interpret responses, despite numerous experiments with different scoring procedures and correction formulae (e.g., Beeckmans et al., 2001; Eyckmans et al., 2007; Pellicer-Sánchez & Schmitt, 2012).

Vocabulary Levels Test (VLT). The Vocabulary Levels Test (VLT) is a diagnostic test that assesses the vocabulary breadth of learners in a multiple matching format. Test takers are presented with six words and corresponding meaning senses of three of these. They are then asked to indicate for each meaning sense which single word it matches. The test therefore assesses form recognition.

There is a fixed number of such clusters of three items for each frequency level from which the target words were sampled. The VLT was initially developed by Nation (1983, 1990) and revised by Schmitt, Schmitt, and Clapham (2001). Since then, different revisions have been launched (see McLean & Kramer, 2015; McLean, Kramer, & Beglar, 2015; Webb, Sasao, & Balance, 2017). In the original and some revised versions, the clusters were sampled in equal amounts with either six or ten clusters from the levels of the 2,000, 3,000, 5,000, and 10,000 most frequent word families and in the 2001 version, the Academic Word List (AWL) (Coxhead, 2000). Newer VLT versions test at increments of 1,000 levels.

Despite the popularity of the VLT in both pedagogy and research, there is surprisingly scarce validation evidence for each of its iterations. Schmitt, Schmitt, and Clapham's (2001) revision and validation provides a detailed account of the rationale, principles, and extensive trialing that guided the test revision and offers a thorough validation study. However, few replication studies corroborate or extend the validation evidence for this version. Some follow-up studies have problematized guessing and item interdependence in the format (e.g., Stewart & White, 2011; Webb, 2008). Also, care needs to be exercised to interpret scores per level and not aggregate scores across levels as a total vocabulary size estimate was not intended by the test designers. For this, the next test may be more appropriate.

Vocabulary Size Test (VST). A different test of vocabulary breadth gaining increasing popularity in second language acquisition (SLA) research is the Vocabulary Size Test (VST) (Nation & Gu, 2007). This multiple-choice test claims to establish a total estimate of written, receptive vocabulary size. Candidates are presented with a target word, a short, non-defining sentence, and four alternative definitions of the word in question, one of which is the key.

The test targets ten or five words per 1,000 frequency band up to the 14,000 or 20,000 most frequent word families of English according to the BNC corpus, depending on the test version. A total vocabulary size estimate is arrived at by multiplying the scores by 100 or 200 respectively, each test item thus representing 100 or 200 word families. However, for the monolingual as well as bilingual versions of the VST, validity evidence is sparse and rather mixed (see Beglar, 2010; Gyllstad, 2012). Gyllstad, Vilkaité, and Schmitt (2015) found that ten items might not be a sufficient sampling rate to represent any level. Instead, they suggest a rate of about 30 items per 1,000 word family frequency level. Even though some iterations of the VST have added an "I don't know" option or even a penalty instruction (Zhang, 2013), proneness to guessing (Gyllstad, Vilkaité, & Schmitt, 2015; Stewart, 2014) and word family-based sampling (Kremmel & Schmitt, 2016) remain serious issues for the interpretability of VST scores.

Lexical Profiling. The previous three test types can be described as discrete and selective in the way they assess vocabulary knowledge. In more integrated, comprehensive and embedded measurement options (Read, 2000), which are particularly useful for measuring productive vocabulary knowledge, learner performances (oral or written) are typically profiled using tools that allow for an analysis of the frequencies of words used in the production. Although this approach could also be used for analyzing the vocabulary depth knowledge, it is primarily used for profiling the range of vocabulary that learners are able to employ. The value of such an approach lies in the contextualization provided for the target items and it thus operationalizes a broader view of vocabulary that includes multi-word phrases, idioms and other formulaic units. However, this embeddedness in a written or spoken performance may be a threat to construct validity if the test result is primarily taken as an indication of a person's lexical knowledge, as more than lexical knowledge could be tested in such tasks (for a detailed overview of different measures of lexical sophistication, richness, and diversity, see Crossley, Salsbury, McNamara, & Jarvis, 2011).

Measuring Vocabulary Depth

Depth of vocabulary knowledge refers to "how well one knows a word" (Qian, 2002, p. 515). Schmitt (2008) argues that depth of knowledge is essential to understand and use a word appropriately. However, Schmitt (2014) also acknowledged that the "diversity of depth conceptualizations makes it extremely difficult to know how to approach depth from a theoretical perspective" (p. 915). Nation (2001) provided probably the most comprehensive and influential model of components of vocabulary knowledge to date (see Table 20.1).

His framework identifies the three categories, form, meaning and use, which are further detailed into subcategories that could be known both receptively and/or productively. Any of these aspects could therefore be considered as referring to aspects of depth of vocabulary knowledge. However, while these categories have been the basis for a number of vocabulary tests, they pose problems in real-world application as they are interrelated and to some extent mutually interdependent.

With vocabulary knowledge being as multifaceted as established, it seems impossible to measure all aspects of this knowledge in just one test. For practical reasons, therefore, most instruments that measure vocabulary depth only focus on one component (Qian & Schedl, 2004). This section exemplifies depth tests by way of the Word Associate Format (WAF) and different measures of the construct collocation knowledge.

Word Associates Format (WAF). The WAF, first developed by Read (1993), is probably the most prominent test of vocabulary depth. It is generally presented in a variation of a multiple-choice format and taps into meaning senses of target words and also aspects of a word's use. The format is based on word association and presents the candidate with six or eight words, half of which are associated with the target word.

The associations, depending on the variation of the format, are primarily semantic and collocational. In its original eight-option format, the options are equally distributed, also visually,

Table 20.1 Nation's (2001, p. 27) framework of vocabulary knowledge

Form	spoken	R	What does the word sound like?
		P	How is the word pronounced?
	written	R	What does the word look like?
		P	How is the word written and spelled?
	word parts	R	What parts are recognizable in this word?
		P	What word parts are needed to express the meaning?
Meaning	form and meaning	R	What meaning does this word form signal?
		P	What word form can be used to express this meaning?
	concept and referents	R	What is included in the concept?
		P	What items can the concept refer to?
	associations	R	What other words does this make us think of?
		P	What other words could we use instead of this one?
Use	grammatical functions	R	In what patterns does the word occur?
		P	In what patterns must we use this word?
	collocations	R	What words or types of words occur with this one?
		P	What words or types of words must we use with this one?
	constraints on use (register, frequency...)	R	Where, when, and how often would we expect to meet this word?
		P	Where, when, and how often can we use this word?

across these two categories of associations and the test taker is instructed to indicate the four correct associations. Schoonen and Verhallen (2008) suggest a six-option format which focuses on sematic relations between the options and the target words. The main issue with this type of test is that "[n]ot every word has the right properties to function as a stimulus word" (Greidanus et al., 2004, p. 203) and that it is unclear how split scores (e.g., 1-2 correct, 1–2 incorrect) should be interpreted (Schmitt, Ng, & Garras, 2011).

Collocation Measures. Collocation knowledge has been described as "one of the most important types of 'contextualized' word knowledge" (Schmitt, 2010, p. 229). It is therefore understandable that the field has seen an increased interest in depth measures featuring this component. Different test formats to capture this knowledge have been recently investigated.

Gyllstad's (2009) COLLEX 5, for example, asks candidates to select the real verb+noun collocation from three options. The 50 test items were controlled for frequency of their components and their strength of association. Gyllstad's alternative format COLLMATCH 3 resembles the checklist Yes/No format in its latest version with all its advantages and shortcomings as discussed above. Candidates simply indicate whether a presented verb+noun combination is a collocation or not. Both tests appear to yield reasonable reliability values and are able to profile clear progressions along proficiency levels. Eyckmans' (2009) Discriminating Collocations Test (DISCO) also follows the principle of a Yes/No format with interspersed non-collocations, but has yet to be demonstrated to yield reliable and valid scores.

These formats that ask test takers to select/supply collocates for the given node have been criticized for giving little or no insight into the candidate's knowledge of the whole collocation. Revier (2009) thus suggested a new format, CONTRIX, which requires candidates to produce whole collocations. The matrix format asks test takers to construct the collocation to fill a sentence gap from potential collocation components. The format provides some context and restricts responses as learners select from a limited number of choices. The 45-item test is balanced for semantic categories, verb constituency, item frequency, and noun-constituent frequency. However, further validation evidence would be necessary.

Measuring Lexical Fluency

The vast majority of vocabulary learning studies have examined improvements in learners' breadth/size and depth of vocabulary knowledge. However, in order not to interrupt the normal flow of communication, learners must have fast, automatic, and easy access to the words they know (Meara, 1996). Fluency of vocabulary knowledge has mainly been conceptualized in terms of accuracy and speed of lexical access. Despite its importance for successful vocabulary use, the measurement of lexical fluency has been somewhat neglected in vocabulary learning research (Schmitt, 2010). This section provides a brief overview of the two main techniques that have been used to measure lexical fluency, i.e., lexical decisions tasks (LDT) (including primed LDT, and self-paced reading tasks) and eye-tracking, as well as other alternative measures of lexical fluency, i.e., *Q_Lex* (Meara & Miralpeix, 2017) and the *Vocabulary Recognition Speed Test* (VORST) (Laufer & Nation, 2001).

Lexical Decision Tasks (LDT). Fluency of vocabulary knowledge has mainly been measured by response times (RTs) to target words in timed lexical decision tasks (LDTs). In this test, learners are presented with strings of letters, either orally or visually, and they have to quickly decide whether those strings are real words or not. While similar in format to the Yes/No tests, a key difference is that Yes/No tests only take into account the number of words known, whereas timed LDTs take into consideration the time it takes learners to decide that they recognize a word or not (Miralpeix & Meara, 2014). LDTs have successfully been integrated in vocabulary learning studies exploring development of lexical fluency (e.g., Elgort, 2011; Pellicer-Sánchez, 2015), but research in this area is still scarce.

Faster response times in LDTs are generally thought to reflect more fluent lexical access. However, researchers have argued for the need to distinguish between qualitative changes in the underlying cognitive mechanisms, which would be an indication of "automatization", and quantitative changes produced by a decrease in RT duration and variability. In order to make this distinction, Segalowitz proposed the calculation of the coefficient of variation (CV) as a measure of response-time variability (Segalowitz & Segalowitz, 1993). However, there is no consensus in the usefulness of the CV as a measure of automaticity (Hulstijn et al., 2009).

LDTs provide a RT measure to individual words presented in isolation. *Self-paced reading tasks*, on the contrary, measure recognition of words presented in context. In self-paced reading tasks, a given text is displayed word-by-word or phrase-by-phrase and participants have to press a button to make the next word or phrase appear. Self-paced reading tasks can therefore be used to measure speed and fluency of word recognition and lexical access of words in context (see Jegerski, 2014, for a review of the self-paced reading method).

Eye-tracking. The more traditional measure of lexical fluency, i.e., LDT, has the main disadvantage of measuring lexical access to words in isolation. Self-paced reading tasks overcome this by allowing researchers to present target items in context. However, participants are required to press a button after reading each word/phrase. Eye tracking, in contrast, allows researchers to examine fluency of lexical access and processing in more naturalistic contexts without the need to perform any button presses. Eye-tracking records the eyes' *fixations*, i.e., when the eyes stop, the *saccades*, i.e., movements between fixations, and the *regressions*, i.e., movements back to earlier parts of the text when reading. Eye-tracking allows researchers to record a wide range of measures of eye movements, which are usually divided into early measures and late measures. In vocabulary studies, early measures (e.g., *first fixation duration, first pass reading time*) reflect earlier stages of automatic lexical access and lexical processing, whereas late measures (e.g., *number of fixations, total reading time*) reflect higher-level processes of lexical integration (Pellicer-Sánchez & Siyanova-Chanturia, 2018) (see Conklin, Pellicer-Sánchez, & Carrol, 2018, for a comprehensive review of eye-movement measures).

Eye-tracking can also be used to examine learners' recognition of words that are presented auditorily. This is traditionally done through the visual-world paradigm, which presents a visual display (objects or static scenes) while participants process words presented in the spoken input. The experimental display usually includes objects that correspond to the words in the auditory input or that are semantically related. Listeners tend to look at the objects that are mentioned or implied, trying to map the spoken with the visual input (for a review see Huettig, Rommers, & Meyer, 2011).

Other Lexical Fluency Measures. The potential difficulty in measuring RTs accurately using standard equipment led Meara and Miralpeix (2017) to suggest an alternative measure of lexical fluency. The *Q_Lex* presents 55 words hidden in a string of letters (e.g., TRRBONAPPLEASHTOVP) and test takers have to identify the hidden word (APPLE in the example). The items are presented on the screen for two seconds, but responses are not timed. The underlying assumption is that the number of words correctly identified can be treated as a measure of accessibility to the whole lexicon. However, considerable work needs to be conducted before Q_Lex is considered a reliable test of lexical accessibility.

Another interesting proposal to measure speed of lexical access is the *Vocabulary Recognition Speed Test* (VORST) by Laufer and Nation (2001). VORST was conceived as a tool to measure word recognition and the association between form and meaning. The VORST is a computerized version of the VLT (Nation, 1990). The main difference with the original VLT is that each item is presented one at a time on a computer screen. The test records the number of correct answers and the response time between the appearance of the test item and the typing of the answer. This measure has rarely been used in vocabulary studies and has not been subject to appropriate validation.

Measuring Vocabulary Development

All of the above measures could, in theory, be used to measure the development of a person's vocabulary knowledge. However, many of the instruments for breadth and depth might lack the granularity to arrive at clear inferences about vocabulary learning gains (Kremmel, 2019). For instance, the VLT or VST will not easily show gains after short learning or intervention periods. The Vocabulary Knowledge Scale (VKS) (Paribakht & Wesche, 1997) is one of the few instruments that follows a more developmental approach. It is essentially a six-point elicitation scale ranging from "I don't remember having seen this word before" to "I can use this word in a sentence," which is complemented by a request to provide a synonym, L1 translation, or sentence. In this way, the scale takes into account the partial, incremental and dynamic process of word knowledge development and combines assessing the form-meaning link as well as some aspects of depth of word knowledge. While the VKS may be more useful than ordinary self-report scales in that the higher stages of the scale also require demonstration of the self-asserted knowledge, the major problem with the VKS, as with all other developmental approaches to vocabulary measurement, is that we do not know enough about the incremental acquisition of vocabulary knowledge in order to decide on the best scale to measure it (Schmitt, 2010). Despite this, the VKS has frequently been used as a research tool in SLA studies (e.g., Bruton, 2009; Golonka et al., 2015) (Table 20.2).

Recommendations for Practice

Validation of Instruments for Measuring Vocabulary Development

As outlined above, there are a number of different assessment tools and formats available, but one of the key issues with the current state of vocabulary knowledge measurement instruments

Table 20.2 Tests discussed in the chapter

Test	*Available at*
Yes/No checklist tests	http://www.lognostics.co.uk/tools/V_YesNo/V_YesNo.htm
Vocabulary Levels Test	https://www.norbertschmitt.co.uk/vocabulary-resources Note that there are also several updated versions, some of which can be found on the lextutor.ca website
Vocabulary Size Test	https://www.victoria.ac.nz/lals/about/staff/Publications/paul-nation/Vocabulary-Size-Test-14000.pdf
Word Associates Test	https://www.lextutor.ca/tests/wat/
COLLEX 5 and COLLMATCH 3	Gyllstad (2009)
DISCO	Eyckmans (2009)
CONTRIX	Revier (2009)

is that of lacking validation evidence. This pertains particularly to measurement tools of vocabulary breadth and depth. These tests have often been designed by vocabulary researchers with the best intentions, but little concern for best practice in language assessment. As language tests, however, it is necessary that vocabulary tests adhere to the principles of validity and reliability, and ideally also authenticity, practicality, and washback (Bachman & Palmer, 1996), and that the validity of claims and interpretations based on their scores are substantiated by theory and evidence. While sometimes multiple studies are carried out on one test or test format, the evidence is hardly ever brought together in a coherent validation argument (Schmitt, Nation, & Kremmel, 2019). Evidence needs to be collected systematically to show the functioning of a measure, and back claims about what scores mean and how they can be interpreted (see Schmitt, Schmitt, & Clapham, 2001, Chapelle, 1994, or Voss, 2012, for examples). Evidence should be gathered in terms of the psychometric qualities of the instrument (e.g., reliability, dimensionality) through statistical procedures such as IRT or correlational studies with other criterion or skills measures, and through qualitative research looking into test taking processes, for instance using think-aloud methodology. These, however, are only examples and a comprehensive validation could require much more depending on the claims being made based on scores, with research methodologies selected based on the required interpretations and arguments to support them. The tool (or tools) to measure vocabulary knowledge and track its development need to be chosen and validated carefully according to the construct of interest, the test purpose, and the interpretations and claims that are intended to be made. Importantly for test development, this validation needs to be done before a test is launched unto the unsuspecting public, teacher, or researcher, and it is unlikely to be covered sufficiently in one publication that can then be re-cited over and over as proof that a particular test or variations thereof are valid. Each new test form, and each new test use, ideally requires new validation evidence, and language assessment researchers are offering the tools and frameworks, such as argument-based approaches, to do so (see e.g., Kane, 2006; Chapelle, 2012, Bachman & Palmer, 2010; Mislevy, Steinberg, & Almond, 2003; see also Révész & Brunfaut, Chapter 3, this volume). We therefore see the future of this as a two-way street: As language testers certainly need to become more knowledgeable about vocabulary acquisition, vocabulary researchers, particularly those creating or using tests, should become more language assessment literate in order to move the field forward (see Harding & Kremmel, Chapter 6, this volume).

Testing Tips

- Determine the purpose of your vocabulary measurement: Why do you want to test vocabulary?
- Define your understanding of "vocabulary": This will impact on your item selection.
- Determine which aspect of vocabulary knowledge you are interested in: breadth, depth, fluency? Choose your instruments accordingly.
- Make sure you are sampling sufficiently and representatively to arrive at robust inferences.
- Pilot and refine your instruments, check their psychometric properties.
- Gather mixed-method validation evidence and present it in a validation argument to support your claims.

Recommended Readings

Read, J. (2000). *Assessing Vocabulary*. Cambridge University Press.

This book is probably still the most comprehensive work on vocabulary assessment to date.

Read, J. (2013). Second language vocabulary assessment. *Language Teaching*, *46*(1), 41–52. https://doi.org/10.1017/S0261444812000377

This article offers a useful overview of key studies and milestones in vocabulary test development and research.

Schmitt, N. (2010). *Researching vocabulary: A vocabulary research manual*. Palgrave Macmillan.

Schmitt's volume is the standard for vocabulary research and contains a substantive section on vocabulary measurement issues.

References

Alderson, J. C. (2005). *Diagnosing foreign language proficiency*. Continuum.

Anderson, R. C., & Freebody, P. (1981). Vocabulary knowledge. In J. T. Guthrie (Ed.), *Comprehension and teaching: Research reviews* (pp. 77–117). International Reading Association.

Bachman, L. F., & Palmer, A. S. (1996). *Language testing in practice*. Oxford University Press.

Bachman, L. F., & Palmer, A. S. (2010). *Language assessment in practice*. Oxford University Press.

Beeckmans, R., Eyckmans, J., Janssens, V., Dufranne, M., & Van de Velde, H. (2001). Examining the Yes/No vocabulary test: Some methodological issues in theory and practice. *Language Testing*, *18*(3), 235–274. https://doi.org/10.1177/026553220101800301

Beglar, D. (2010). A Rasch-based validation of the vocabulary size test. *Language Testing*, *27*(1), 101–118. https://doi.org/10.1177/0265532209340194

Bruton, A. (2009). The vocabulary knowledge scale: A critical analysis. *Language Assessment Quarterly*, *6*(4), 288–297. https://doi.org/10.1080/15434300902801909

Chapelle, C. (1994). Are C-tests valid measures for L2 vocabulary research? *Second Language Research*, *10*, 157–187.

Chapelle, C. (2012). Validity argument for language assessment: The framework is simple. *Language Testing*, *29*(1), 19–27. https://doi.org/10.1177/0265532211417211

Conklin, K., Pellicer-Sánchez, A., & Carrol, G. (2018). *Eye-tracking: A guide for applied linguistics research*. Cambridge University Press.

Coxhead, A. (2000). A new academic word list. *TESOL Quarterly*, *34*(2), 213–238. https://doi.org/10.2307/3587951

Crossley, S. A., Salsbury, T., McNamara, D. S., & Jarvis, S. (2011). Predicting lexical proficiency in language learner tests using computational indices. *Language Testing*, *28*(4), 561–580. https://doi.org/10.1177/0265532210378031

Daller, H., Milton, J., & Treffers-Daller, J. (2007). *Modelling and assessing vocabulary knowledge*. Cambridge University Press.

Elgort, I. (2011). Deliberate learning and vocabulary acquisition in a second language. *Language Learning*, *61*(2), 367–413. https://doi.org/10.1111/j.1467-9922.2010.00613.x

Eyckmans, J. (2009). Towards an assessment of learners' receptive and productive syntagmatic knowledge. In A. Barfield & H. Gyllstad (Eds.), *Researching collocations in another language: Multiple interpretations* (pp. 139–152). Palgrave Macmillan.

Eyckmans, J., Van de Velde, H., van Hout, R., & Boers, F. (2007). Learners' response behaviour in Yes/No vocabulary tests. In H. Daller, J. Milton, & J. Treffers-Daller (Eds.), *Modelling and assessing vocabulary knowledge* (pp. 59–76). Cambridge University Press.

Gardner, D. (2013). *Exploring vocabulary: Language in action*. Routledge.

Golonka, E., Bowles, A., Silbert, N., Kramasz, D., Blake, C., & Buckwalter, T. (2015). The role of context and cognitive effort in vocabulary learning: A study of intermediate-level learners of Arabic. *The Modern Language Journal*, *99*(1), 19–39. https://doi.org/10.1111/modl.12191

Goulden, R., Nation, I. S. P., & Read, J. (1990). How large can a receptive vocabulary be? *Applied Linguistics*, *11*(4), 341–363. https://doi.org/10.1093/applin/11.4.341

Greidanus, T., Bogaards, P., van der Linden, E., Nienhuis, L., & de Wolf, T. (2004). The construction and validation of a depp word knowledge test for advanced learners of French. In P. Bogaards & B. Laufer (Eds.), *Vocabulary in a second language: Selection, acquisition, and testing* (pp. 191–208). John Benjamins.

Gyllstad, H. (2009). Designing and evaluating tests of receptive collocation knowledge: COLLEX and COLLMATCH. In A. Barfield & H. Gyllstad (Eds.), *Researching collocations in another language: Multiple interpretations* (pp. 153–170). Palgrave Macmillan.

Gyllstad, H. (2012, May 31–June 2). *Validating the vocabulary size test: A classical test theory approach*. [Poster presentation]. European Association for Language Testing and Assessment (EALTA) conference, University of Innsbruck, Austria.

Gyllstad, H., Vilkaitė, L., & Schmitt, N. (2015). Assessing vocabulary size through multiple-choice formats: Issues with guessing and sampling rates. *International Journal of Applied Linguistics*, *166*(2), 278–306. https://doi.org/10.1075/itl.166.2.04gyl

Huettig, F., Rommers, J., & Meyer, A. S. (2011). Using the visual world paradigm to study language processing: A review and critical evaluation. *Acta Psychologica*, *137*(2), 151–171. https://doi.org/10.1016/j.actpsy.2010.11.003

Hulstijn, J. H., Van Gelderen, A., & Schoonen, R. (2009). Automatization in second-language acquisition: What does the coefficient of variation tell us? *Applied Psycholinguistics*, *30*(4), 555–582. https://doi.org/10.1017/S0142716409990014

Jegerski, J. (2014). Self-paced reading. In J. Jegerski & B. VanPatten (Eds.), *Research methods in second language psycholinguistics* (pp. 20–49). Routledge.

Kane, M. T. (2006). Validation. In R. L. Brennan (Ed.), *Educational measurement* (pp. 17–64). American Council on Education/Praeger Publishers.

Kremmel, B. (2019). Measuring vocabulary gains. In S. Webb (Ed.), *The Routledge handbook of vocabulary studies* (pp. 406–418). Routledge.

Kremmel, B., & Schmitt, N. (2016). Interpreting vocabulary test scores: What do various item formats tell us about learners' ability to employ words? *Language Assessment Quarterly*, *13*(4), 377–392. https://doi.org/10.1080/15434303.2016.1237516

Laufer, B., & Goldstein, Z. (2004). Testing vocabulary knowledge: Size, strength, and computer adaptiveness. *Language Learning*, *54*(3), 399–436. https://doi.org/10.1111/j.0023-8333.2004.00260.x

Laufer, B., & Nation, P. (2001). Passive vocabulary size and speed of meaning recognition. *EUROSLA Yearbook*, *1*, 7–28.

Lemhoefer, K., & Broersma, M. (2012). Introducing LexTALE: A quick and valid lexical test for advanced learners of English. *Behavior Research Methods*, *44*, 325–343. https://doi.org/10.3758/s13428-011-0146-0

McLean, S., & Kramer, B. (2015). The creation of a new vocabulary levels test. *Shiken*, *19*(2), 1–11.

McLean, S., Kramer, B., & Beglar, D. (2015). The creation and validation of a listening vocabulary levels test. *Language Teaching Research*, *19*(6), 741–760. https://doi.org/10.1177/1362168814567889

Meara, P. (1992). *EFL vocabulary tests*. Lognostics.

Meara, P. (1996). The dimensions of lexical competence. In G. Brown, K. Malmkjaer, & J. Williams (Eds.), *Performance and competence in second language acquisition* (pp. 35–53). Cambridge University Press.

Meara, P., & Buxton, B. (1987). An alternative to multiple choice vocabulary tests. *Language Testing*, *4*(2), 142–154. https://doi.org/10.1177%2F026553228700400202

Meara, P., & Miralpeix, I. (2017). *Tools for researching vocabulary*. Multilingual Matters.
Miralpeix, I., & Meara, P. M. (2014). The written word. In J. Milton & T. Fitzpatrick (Eds.), *Dimensions of vocabulary knowledge* (pp. 30–44). Macmillan.
Mislevy, R. J., Steinberg, L. S., & Almond, R. G. (2003). On the structure of educational assessments. *Measurement: Interdisciplinary Research and Perspectives*, *1*(1), 3–62. http://doi.org/10.1207/S15366359MEA0101_02
Nation, I. S. P. (1983). Testing and teaching vocabulary. Guidelines, *5*(1), 12–25.
Nation, I. S. P. (1990). *Teaching and learning vocabulary*. Heinle and Heinle.
Nation, I. S. P. (2001). *Learning vocabulary in another language*. Cambridge University Press.
Nation, I. S. P., & Gu, P. Y. (2007). *Focus on vocabulary*. NCELTR Publications.
Nation, I. S. P., & Webb, S. (2011). *Researching vocabulary*. Heinle-Cengage ELT.
Paribakht, T. S., & Wesche, M. B. (1997). Vocabulary enhancement activities and reading for meaning in second language vocabulary acquisition. In J. Coady & T. Huckin (Eds.), *Second language vocabulary acquisition* (pp. 174–200). Cambridge University Press.
Pellicer-Sánchez, A. (2015). Developing automaticity and speed of lexical access: The effects of incidental and explicit teaching approaches. *Journal of Spanish Language Teaching*, *2*(2), 126–139. https://doi.org/10.1080/23247797.2015.1104029
Pellicer-Sánchez, A., & Schmitt, N. (2012). Scoring Yes-No vocabulary tests: Reaction time vs. nonword approaches. *Language Testing*, *29*(4), 489–509. https://doi.org/10.1177/0265532212438053
Pellicer-Sánchez, A., & Siyanova-Chanturia, A. (2018). Eye movements in vocabulary research: Current findings and future directions. *International Journal of Applied Linguistics*, *169*(1), 5–29. https://doi.org/10.1075/itl.00004.pel
Qian, D. D. (2002). Investigating the relationship between vocabulary knowledge and academic reading performance: An assessment perspective. *Language Learning*, *52*(3), 513–536. https://doi.org/10.1111/1467-9922.00193
Qian, D. D., & Schedl, M. (2004). Evaluation of an in-depth vocabulary knowledge measure for assessing reading performance. *Language Testing*, *21*(1), 28–52. https://doi.org/10.1191/0265532204lt273oa
Read, J. (1993). The development of a new measure of L2 vocabulary knowledge. *Language Testing*, *10*(3), 355–371. https://doi.org/10.1177%2F026553229301000308
Read, J. (2000). *Assessing vocabulary*. Cambridge University Press.
Read, J. (2013). Second language vocabulary assessment. *Language Teaching*, *46*(1), 41–52. https://doi.org/10.1017/S0261444812000377
Read, J., & Chapelle, C. (2001). A framework for second language vocabulary assessment. *Language Testing*, *18*(1), 1–32. https://doi.org/10.1177/026553220101800101
Revier, R. L. (2009). Evaluating a new test of whole English collocations. In A. Barfield & H. Gyllstad (Eds.), *Researching collocations in another language: Multiple interpretations* (pp. 125–138). Palgrave Macmillan.
Schmitt, N. (2008). Instructed second language vocabulary learning. *Language Teaching Research*, *12*(3), 329–363. https://doi.org/10.1177/1362168808089921
Schmitt, N. (2010). *Researching vocabulary: A vocabulary research manual*. Palgrave Macmillan.
Schmitt, N., Nation, P., & Kremmel, B. (2019). Moving the field of vocabulary assessment forward: The need for more rigorous test development and validation. *Language Teaching*, 1–12. https://doi.org/10.1017/S0261444819000326
Schmitt, N., Ng, J. W. C., & Garras, J. (2011). The word associates format: Validation evidence. *Language Testing*, *28*(1), 105–126. https://doi.org/10.1177/0265532210373605
Schmitt, N., Schmitt, D., & Clapham, C. (2001). Developing and exploring the behaviour of two new versions of the vocabulary levels test. *Language Testing*, *18*(1), 55–88. https://doi.org/10.1177/026553220101800103
Schoonen, R., & Verhallen, M. (2008). The assessment of deep word knowledge in young first and second language learners. *Language Testing*, *25*(2), 211–236. https://doi.org/10.1177/0265532207086782
Segalowitz, N., & Segalowitz, S. (1993). Skilled performance, practice, and the differentiation of speed-up from automatization effects: Evidence from second language word recognition. *Applied Psycholinguistics*, *14*(3), 369–385. https://doi.org/10.1017/S0142716400010845
Stewart, J. (2014). Do multiple-choice options inflate estimates of vocabulary size on the VST? *Language Assessment Quarterly*, *11*(3), 271–282. https://doi.org/10.1080/15434303.2014.922977
Stewart, J., & White, D. (2011). Estimating guessing effects on the vocabulary levels test for differing degrees of word knowledge. *TESOL Quarterly*, *45*(2), 370–380. https://doi.org/10.5054/tq.2011.254523

Stubbe, R., Stewart, J., & Pritchard, T. (2010). Examining the effects of pseudowords in yes/no vocabulary tests for low level learners. *Kyushu Sangyo University Language Education and Research Center Journal*, *5*, 5–23.

Voss, E. (2012). *A validity argument for score meaning of a computer-based ESL academic collocational ability test based on a corpus-driven approach to test design* (Unpublished PhD dissertation). Iowa State University.

Webb, S. (2008). Receptive and productive vocabulary sizes of L2 learners. *Studies in Second Language Acquisition*, *30*(1), 79–95. https://doi.org/10.1017/S0272263108080042

Webb, S., Sasao, Y., & Ballance, O. (2017). The updated vocabulary levels test: Developing and validating two new forms of the VLT. *ITL: International Journal of Applied Linguistics*, *168*(1), 34–70. https://doi.org/10.1075/itl.168.1.02web

Wray, A. (2002). *Formulaic language and the lexicon*. Cambridge University Press.

Zhang, X. (2013). The I don't know option in the vocabulary size test. *TESOL Quarterly*, *47*(4), 790–811. https://doi.org/10.1002/tesq.98

21

Measuring Lexicogrammar

Magali Paquot, Stefan Th. Gries & Monique Yoder

Background

Lexicogrammar is a level of linguistic structure where lexis and grammar are not seen as independent, but rather as mutually dependent. The idea that lexis and grammar are interrelated has been promoted by a number of linguistic theories and approaches. In corpus linguistics, more particularly, empirical investigations of large corpora have shown that lexicogrammatical co-selection phenomena are ubiquitous in language (e.g., verbs such as *arrest*, *elect*, *name*, and *estimate* are twice as frequent in the passive as in the active form; the adjective *mere* is attested only in attributive position; Biber et al., 1999; see also Römer, 2009). The study of lexicogrammatical patterns has also exhibited particular growth with the popularization of usage-based or constructionist/Construction Grammar approaches, in which lexical items and grammatical constructions are considered to not be qualitatively different from each other, but differ only with regard to the degree of abstractness within one unified constructicon (Goldberg, 2006).

Lexis and grammar, however, have traditionally been studied separately in second language acquisition (SLA) and measured as two separate constructs in language testing. Historically, grammar used to be the most central area of linguistic enquiry in SLA (Lardière, 2014) and, only over time, the lexicon has come more at the forefront as well. Today, vocabulary is also largely considered an independent component of language competence that covers all aspects (i.e., form, meaning, and use) of what is involved in knowing a word (see Kremmel & Pellicer-Sánchez, Chapter 20, this volume). Within vocabulary research, much interest has been placed on the learner's development of phraseology or formulaic language (e.g., Schmitt, 2004; Siyanova-Chanturia & Pellicer-Sánchez, 2018), and on how this development relates to notions such as Pawley and Syder's (1983) "native-like selection" or Sinclair's (1991) "idiom principle," according to which "a language user has available to him or her a large number of semi-preconstructed phrases that constitute single choices, even though they might appear to be analysable into segments" (p. 110).

In language testing, the separation between lexis and grammar "can be seen both in models of language ability that are used to inform test development and validation, and in many frequently used rating scales that are used to score performance assessments" (Römer, 2017, p. 477-478). This is certainly the case in international standards for describing language ability and major international language tests (e.g., the writing band descriptors of the International English Language Testing System (IELTS) distinguish between "lexical resource" and "grammatical range and accuracy"). Römer (2017) attributed this separation to the history of the construct of "language proficiency" in language testing, with early language testing researchers prior to the 1970s promoting a skills/component model of language reflective of pedagogical methods rooted in behavioral psychology and structural linguistics, which assumed that language could be subdivided into its separate components. Measurement theory and practice as outlined by Lado's (1961) seminal work on foreign language testing advocated task types that facilitated test reliability over authenticity. Thus, discrete-point task types in which grammar and vocabulary were clearly distinguished and measured as separate constructs that demonstrate learners' knowledge of sentence-level grammar and lexis were the norm in test development for decades. In the 1970s and 1980s, John Oller's theories on the pragmatics of knowledge, beliefs, and expectations of language users in the contexts in which they experience language made way for discourse-based testing procedures known as integrative language tests. Oller (1979) perceived discrete-point and integrative tests to be in contrast, where "discrete items take language skill apart, integrative tests put it back together" (p. 37), and he identified cloze, dictation, oral interviews, and written compositions as integrative language test task types that require access to language meaning through deeper linguistic resources. However, as authenticity (i.e., how a test reflects real-world language tasks) became a criterion of test validity and communicative competence became a component of language proficiency (Canale & Swain, 1980), cloze and dictation tasks fell out of favor. As a result, tasks that emulate what a test-taker will have to do with the language yet measure lexis and grammar indirectly through spoken and written language performances have also gained popularity in both large-scale and classroom-based assessments.

With this development came an increased awareness of the difficulty in assessing vocabulary and grammar independently. Ruegg, Fritz, and Holland (2011), for example, showed that the lexis scores for test-takers' written performances on the Kanda English Proficiency Test (KEPT) were predicted by the scores on the grammar scale much more than range, frequency, or lexical accuracy. Because of the difficulty in distinguishing lexical vs. grammatical competence, they recommended collapsing the scales into a single "lexicogrammar" scale as already done for the speaking section of the KEPT (cf. also Alderson & Kremmel, 2013 for a similar discussion in a study that re-examined the content validation of a grammar test). The controversial issue here is whether it is enough to merge the dimensions of grammar and lexis into one lexicogrammatical dimension to claim that we are now measuring lexicogrammar as defined above. We believe that it is not. However, there is a shortage of research to date on how lexicogrammatical competence can and should be measured in language testing and SLA research. In what follows, we sketch out key issues that should be addressed in future research.

Key Concepts

Lexicogrammar: The lexicogrammatical dimension of language deals with (preferred) co-occurrences between words and their grammatical environments, or between grammatical structures and their lexical environments (cf. Biber, Conrad, & Reppen, 1998, p. 84).

Phraseology: Loosely defined as "the study of the structure, meaning and use of word combinations" (Cowie 1994, p. 3168). From a distributional or frequency-based perspective on phraseology, Gries (2008) defined phraseological units or phraseologisms as co-occurring forms or lemmas of lexical items with other linguistic elements. These elements may be other lexical items, such as deterministic co-occurrences (e.g., *kith and kin* / *strong tea*), or grammatical patterns when these are not grammatical relations (i.e., lexical items combined with grammatical constructions, such as the verb *hem* frequently occurring in the passive form).

> ***Constructions***: Form-meaning pairs that exist at all levels of linguistic representation, forming the core of usage-based theories of second language acquisition. As Goldberg (2006, p. 5) stated:
>
> Any linguistic pattern is recognized as a construction as long as some aspect of its form or function is not strictly predictable from its component parts or from other constructions recognized to exist. In addition, patterns are stored as constructions even if they are fully predictable as long as they occur with sufficient frequency.

Key Issues

Indirect Measurement of Lexicogrammar

By its very nature, lexicogrammar lends itself well to indirect measurement in learners' written and spoken performances, and corpus linguistic techniques provide effective ways to do so. Corpus linguists have long studied the degree to which co-occurrence patterns of linguistic elements help to identify and understand differences of functional characteristics between two or more elements such as active vs. passive or *will* vs. *shall* vs. *going-to* future. A range of theoretical frameworks and techniques is available to explore lexicogrammar in corpora, including Pattern Grammar (Hunston & Francis, 2000), lexical bundles or *n*-gram analysis (Biber, 2007), and phrase-frames (Römer, 2017), but one type of approach that follows squarely from the above statement that lexis and grammar are deeply intertwined is collostructional analysis (Stefanowitsch & Gries, 2003; Gries & Stefanowitsch, 2004a, 2004b). Collostructional studies explore how the co-occurrence patterns of lexical items in/and grammatical constructions help to identify, quantify, and interpret the following kinds of functional characteristics of linguistic elements:

- characteristics of individual constructions in collexeme analysis (Stefanowitsch & Gries, 2003), e.g., what do the verbs occurring in the ditransitive (*give*, *tell*, *show*, ...) reveal about the construction's function(s)?
- differences of two or more constructions in distinctive collexeme analysis (Gries & Stefanowitsch, 2004a), e.g, how do verbs occurring in the ditransitive and the prepositional dative distinguish the two constructions' functions?

While the methods of collostructional analysis mentioned above differ slightly from each other, they are both based on 2×2 co-occurrence frequency tables as represented in Figure 21.1.

	Constr: *x*	Constr: other	Sum		Constr: *x*	Constr: *y*	Sum
Word: *y*	*a*	*b*	*a*+*b*	Word: *w*	*a*	*b*	*a*+*b*
Word: other	*c*	*d*	*c*+*d*	Word: other	*c*	*d*	*c*+*d*
Sum	*a*+*c*	*b*+*d*	*a*+*b*+*c*+*d*	Sum	*a*+*c*	*b*+*d*	*a*+*b*+*c*+*d*

Figure 21.1 Schematic representation of co-occurrence tables for collexeme analysis (left) and distinctive collexeme analysis (right).

For collexeme analyses, one determines for every word $y_{1\text{-}n}$ occurring in a slot of construction *x* its frequency in *x* (*a*), its overall frequency (*a*+*b*), the frequency of the construction in the corpus (*a*+*c*), and the corpus size (*a*+*b*+*c*+*d*) to then compute a statistic that expresses how much y_n "(dis)likes to occur in" *x*. For distinctive collexeme analyses, one determines for every word $w_{1\text{-}n}$ occurring in a slot of either construction *x* or *y* its frequency in *x* (*a*), its frequency in *y* (*b*), and the frequency of each construction in the corpus (*a*+*c* and *b*+*d*) to then compute a statistic that expresses which of the two constructions w_n "(dis)likes to occur in" and how much. Both of these measures are essentially basic association measures that capture the contingency between a word (often a verb) and a construction. For the collexeme analysis of the ditransitive in Stefanowitsch and Gries (2003, p. 229), for example, *a* is the frequency of *give* in the ditransitive (461), *b* is the frequency of *give* elsewhere (699), *c* is the frequency of ditransitives without *give* (497), and *d* is the frequency of all other verbs in all other constructions (137007).

While the initial studies based on these methods involved native-speaker (NS) data only, soon first connections to second and foreign language acquisition/learning appeared, to determine to what degree the constructional preferences that NSs exhibit with certain words are also characteristic of (differently proficient) non-native speakers (NNSs). This approach implies that lexicogrammatical accuracy in learner language cannot simply be reduced to a rule-based binary concept or right vs. wrong: The *standard* of native speakers' usage is nowhere near monolithic, but is instead inherently probabilistic and unpredictable from general rules (see discussion of "nativelike selection" in Pawley & Syder, 1983). Modifying Wulff and Gries's (2011) definition of accuracy slightly, one might define lexicogrammatical accuracy in L2 production as the nativelike selection of constructions (in the above Goldbergian sense of the term) given a certain context, where context can be defined as broadly as necessary. This in turn requires a quantitative/probabilistic perspective to measure the degree of convergence between native and non-native language use and patterning.

One application of collostructional methods to learner data is Ellis, Römer, and O'Donnell (2016). Among other things, they analyzed native speaker corpus data (the British National Corpus) on the use of a variety of verb-argument constructions (VACs) and computed bidirectional measures that reflect the degree to which verbs "like to occur" in constructions and vice versa. These results were then also correlated with learners' verb generation in experimental studies (see below) and, more importantly, with longitudinal corpus data from the European Science Foundation (ESF) project involving learners of English with Italian (four speakers) and Punjabi (three speakers). For three verb-argument constructions—verb-locative, verb-object-locative, and double-object constructions—they found "that NS collexeme strength (Fisher-Yates) is a very strong predictor of NNS language acquisition, as is ΔP (Construction→Word)" (p. 231). Ellis et al. (2016)'s research is also noteworthy for how the authors extended the traditional corpus-linguistic co-occurrence approach involved in collostructional analyses to investigate the effect of entrenchment (as measured by lemma frequencies of the verbs in the constructions), contingency (again measured by ΔP Construction→Word), and semantic prototypicality (as measured by betweenness centrality in the semantic network of all verbs per construction) on VACs in learner language.

Another way to approach lexicogrammatical competence in learner performance is to frame it in terms of lexicogrammatical complexity. This follows from Paquot's (2019) proposal to add the construct of phraseological complexity to the toolbox of interlanguage complexity research on the grounds that traditional measures of syntactic complexity and lexical complexity cannot account for how words naturally combine to form conventional patterns of meaning and use. Building on previous research on complexity, Paquot (2019) distinguished two main dimensions of phraseological complexity, i.e., variety and sophistication (cf. Ortega, 2003), and approached phraseological complexity via relational co-occurrences, i.e., co-occurring words that appear in a specific structural or syntactic relation (e.g., adjective + noun, adverbial modifier + verb, verb +

direct object). Phraseological diversity was operationalized as root type-token ratios. Two methods were tested to measure phraseological sophistication. First, sophisticated word combinations were defined as academic collocations that appear in the *Academic Collocation List* (Ackermann & Chen, 2013). Second, it was approximated with average pointwise mutual information (*MI*) scores as this measure has been shown to bring out word combinations made up of closely associated medium to low-frequency (i.e., advanced or sophisticated) words. Interestingly, the proposed measures of phraseological sophistication have the potential to tap into the (lexicogrammatical) specificities of different registers, tasks, and modalities as they rely on corpus-derived lists of word combinations and their associations (see Paquot, 2019). Results revealed that, unlike traditional measures of syntactic and lexical complexity, measures of phraseological sophistication, and the *MI*-based measures more particularly, distinguish L2 performance at the B2, C1, and C2 levels of the Common European Framework of References (Council of Europe, 2001). This suggests that essential aspects of language development from upper-intermediate to very advanced proficiency levels are situated in the phraseological dimension (see also Paquot, 2018; Paquot, Naets, & Gries, in press).

Paquot's (2019) proposal can be directly applied to measuring lexicogrammatical complexity, which is correspondingly defined here as the range of lexicogrammatical patterns surfacing in language production and their degree of sophistication. Thus, a learner text with a wide range of (target-like) lexicogrammatical patterns and a high proportion of sophisticated patterns will be said to be more complex than one where the same few basic patterns are often repeated. Although there are currently no instruments available to measure lexicogrammatical complexity:

- specialists in vocabulary assessment will already be familiar with the constructs of range and sophistication, and how to measure them;
- recent lexical diversity measures such as the ones discussed in Jarvis and Daller (2013) could be tweaked to work with word combinations, lexicogrammatical patterns, and the like;
- there are already a few general or register-specific frequency-based lists of phrases that could serve as the basis for the measurement of lexicogrammatical sophistication (e.g., Martinez & Schmitt, 2012) but we definitely need more resources—especially lists of sequences that do not have non-compositionality as their main defining criterion—developed for production purposes, and for languages other than English;
- sophistication of lexicogrammatical patterns can also be approached via collostructional analysis (see above), for which Gries provides an R script and its documentation (www.stgries.info/teaching/groningen/index.html).

Note that the corpus techniques described here are largely language independent (except for frequency-based lists) and should also help establish whether the construct is theoretically valid across languages (cf. Rubin et al., in press, for a first study of lexicogrammatical complexity in L2 Dutch). Although they are certainly more computationally expensive than *n*-gram models, they also hold the potential to inform automated assessment.

Direct Measurement of Lexicogrammar

For practicality reasons, language testers and SLA researchers may sometimes want/have to measure lexicogrammatical competence directly. As mentioned above, the lexicogrammatical dimension partly overlaps with phraseology or formulaic language. As a result, any attempt at measuring lexicogrammar directly will typically run into the same issues as encountered in the measurement of formulaic sequences. Among the characteristics identified by Gyllstad and Schmitt (2019) as factors that render the testing of formulaic language highly challenging, the following are particularly relevant when it comes to measuring lexicogrammar:

- *Construct definition and operationalization*: The lexicogrammatical dimension of language entails a range of categories with their own characteristics, e.g., constructions (conventionalized form-meaning pairings that will be identified with statistical association measures), and lexical bundles or phrases (recurring word sequences typically identified with the criteria of frequency and dispersion).
- *The scope of the construct*: There are a very large number of lexicogrammatical items, but lexicogrammar is not rule-based: There is simply no "rule" that the learners should apply to demonstrate good knowledge of the construct. As with vocabulary items, checking learners' knowledge means each lexicogrammatical item would need to be tested separately.

As put by Gyllstad and Schmitt (2019),

> These two factors work against both the identification of the target population and the representative sampling of items from that population. This leaves researchers in a very challenging position, and it is probably next to impossible to develop a definite list of all the existing [lexicogrammatical patterns] in a language, and then to develop a test for these sequences.
>
> (p. 175)

A number of solutions to the above issues are available. Item selection can rely on the combined use of native and learner corpora. Techniques such as collostructional analysis (see above) or *n*-gram extraction can first be used to extract the most typical constructions or lexical bundles in a given register. Learner corpora can then be used to identify lexicogrammatical items which learners "tend not to use (absence) or use infrequently (underuse) or too frequently (overuse) in speech or writing" (Granger, 2015, p. 487), thus potentially informing the selection, description and sequencing of test items (cf. also Granger, 2009). In vocabulary research, Gyllstad and Schmitt (2019) also recommend to "focus on much more constrained, and thus identifiable, subsets of FLs, in order to make the resulting scores more meaningful" (p. 181) and to use adaptive tests "to achieve a better and more focused sampling" (p. 187).

A different approach is adopted in the development of "Language in Use" tests that aim to test lexicogrammar in context, such as the integrative multiple-choice gap-fill, banked gap-fill, word formation gap-fill, and editing tasks that can be found in the Austrian secondary school-leaving examination for foreign languages. As authenticity is central to communicative language testing, the language elements that make up such tests are not selected beforehand but emerge from the texts that are selected for the design of such integrative tasks (Weiler, 2018, p. 65). One obvious advantage of these tasks is that they follow Schmitt and Schmitt's (2020) recommendation:

> But the more test writers wish to measure learners' ability to actually use words in real world situations, the further the tests need to move toward the embedded, comprehensive, and context-dependent ends of the continuums.
>
> (p. 174)

The downside, however, is that this is done at the expense of prototypical use. It is also not clear how scores from these tests would relate to the underlying population of items that make up the lexicogrammar construct (see Gyllstad, 2019, for a similar discussion on the measurement of formulaic language).

In SLA studies using experiments, by contrast, researchers have typically resorted to discrete-point measures to explore foreign language learners' knowledge of a delimited set of conventionalized lexicogrammatical patterns carefully selected from corpus data. Gries and Wulff (2009), for example, made use of a sentence completion task and an acceptability rating task to investigate whether the gerund and infinitival complement constructions in English (*She tried rocking the baby* vs. *She tried to rock the baby*) are also stored as constructions by German foreign language learners of English. Ellis et al. (2016) relied on a range of psycholinguistic experiments to explore the role of VAC frequency, type-token frequency distribution, contingency, and semantic prototypicality upon VAC free-association processing in L2 speakers.

Recommendations for Practice

In rating scales (rubrics), a lexicogrammatical scale should tap into more than just the sum of lexical and grammatical knowledge—it is just a different construct. Unlike Ruegg et al. (2011), and despite our theoretical commitment to the lexis/grammar continuum, we do not think that it is necessarily a good idea to replace the grammar and vocabulary scales by a lexicogrammatical scale in foreign language tests. This is especially true if this is mainly done for lack of agreement between raters on what can be considered lexical as opposed to grammatical.

Apart from them just being different constructs, one of the main practical reasons for maintaining a distinction between grammar, lexis, and lexicogrammar is that the three scales may not be similarly useful at all proficiency levels. Research has shown that unlike traditional measures of syntactic and lexical complexity, measures of phraseological/lexicogrammatical complexity can discriminate between learners' performances across the more advanced proficiency levels (Paquot, 2019; see also Crossley et al., 2012 for a study that reported strong correlations between *n*-gram indices and essay quality). This is because the phraseological and lexicogrammatical dimensions of language develop slowly and remain an area of difficulty even for advanced learners (e.g., Paquot & Granger, 2012). A lexicogrammatical scale will thus probably be particularly relevant at the (upper) intermediate and advanced levels. By contrast, vocabulary and grammatical scales may still remain essential scales to assess beginner and intermediate learners. More research is definitely needed in this area.

However, there will probably not be such a thing as a one-size-fits-all lexicogrammatical test. Lexicogrammatical patterns differ from register to register (e.g., Biber et al., 1999). Their selection is influenced by a variety of linguistic and extra-linguistic factors (including crosslinguistic influence for foreign language learners; e.g., Ellis et al., 2016), which makes lexicogrammar a highly context-dependent phenomenon. As a result, a lexicogrammatical test developed in one specific context will probably not fit many other different contexts. If the fields of language testing and SLA want to assess lexicogrammatical competence reliably and validly, they will likely need to develop tests for different purposes (e.g., tests for learners with different L1 backgrounds, tests for different situational contexts). However, before such developments can occur, there is a need for more research into how lexicogrammatical competence interacts with foreign language proficiency and development across modes, tasks, registers, and other linguistic, contextual, and/or situational characteristics. One approach that will suit these purposes particularly well is the MuPDAR approach (short for Multifactorial Prediction and Deviation Analysis using Regressions; Gries & Deshors, 2014). This technique imputes the choices and/or judgments of the speakers of the reference/standard language from corpus data annotated with regard to many linguistic and contextual characteristics with a first statistical model/classifier, which allows the analyst to then explore non-nativelike choices with a second statistical model/classifier. Wulff and Gries (2015) put forth an application of this protocol to the question of prenominal adjective order by native speakers of English, and Chinese and German learners of English. Their first regression was run on adjective-adjective-noun sequences from the British National Corpus, which were annotated for a variety of predictors governing adjective order from multiple levels of linguistic analysis. That first model was used to impute native speaker choices for the non-native speaker data, which were then compared to the non-native speaker choices to run a second analysis on whether the learners made nativelike choices or not, a protocol that leads to extremely fine-grained results.

While it is probably not realistic to expect language testers to conduct MuPDAR studies to, for example, select valid test items at different proficiency levels, findings of such sophisticated and time-consuming research designs have important implications for the field. They provide empirical evidence in support of Schmitt's (2010) claim that "context-dependent formats will obviously provide a better way of tapping into the 'contextualized' facets of word knowledge like collocation and register" (p.173), but also demonstrate very clearly that context needs to be approached in all its complexity when it comes to test item selection and description. In that sense, it is recommended that, when developing instruments for measuring lexicogrammatical knowledge, language testers and SLA researchers focus as much on authenticity of use as on *prototypical* linguistic context of use, which is likely to differ from one situational context to the next and will best be described based on corpus data.

Testing Tips

- When setting out to measure lexicogrammar, choose and make explicit your choice of construct definition.
- Establish for what purposes you want to test lexicogrammatical competence.
- Identify language elements that make up the construct (e.g., constructions, phrases).
- Determine which dimension (i.e., accuracy, range, or sophistication) of lexicogrammatical knowledge you want to test and develop or choose your instruments accordingly.
- To select and/or describe lexicogrammatical items, use large corpora ideally representing the registers that best correspond to the objectives of your language test or research instrument.
- Make use of the relevant metrics to analyze corpus data and extract/describe lexicogrammatical items: Frequency should never be used as a single criterion and you need to consider dispersion, too. Strength of association is a useful way to operationalize lexicogrammatical sophistication depending on the association measure used.
- Never underestimate the impact of the selected corpus on the selection and description of lexicogrammatical items. Evaluating the reliability of item selection/description in a second corpus is highly recommended.
- Favor context-dependent instruments.
- Pilot and refine your instruments sufficiently—make sure you are tapping into the construct of lexicogrammar and can distinguish it from lexis and grammar if these two constructs are part of your test or research instrument, too.

Recommended Readings

Gyllstad, H. (2019). Measuring knowledge of multiword items. In S. Webb (Ed.), *The Routledge Handbook of Vocabulary Studies* (pp. 387–405). Routledge.

This chapter offers a review of different approaches to the measurement of multiword items from the perspective of vocabulary research.

Kremmel, B., Brunfaut, T., & Alderson, J. C. (2017). Exploring the role of phraseological knowledge in foreign language reading. *Applied Linguistics*, *38*(6), 848–870. https://doi:10.1093/applin/amv070

This study found that measures of phraseological knowledge outperformed traditional syntactic and vocabulary measures in predicting reading comprehension variance.

Paquot, M. (2018). Phraseological competence: A missing component in university entrance language tests? Insights from a study of EFL learners' use of statistical collocations. *Language Assessment Quarterly*, *15*(1), 29–43. https://doi.org/10.1080/15434303.2017.1405421

This article demonstrates with the help of learner corpus data the practical relevance of the phraseological dimension of language for writing assessment in higher education.

References

Ackermann, K., & Chen, Y.-H. (2013). Developing the Academic Collocation List (ACL): A corpus-driven and expert-judged approach. *Journal of English for Academic Purposes*, *12*(4), 235–247. https://doi.org/10.1016/j.jeap.2013.08.002

Alderson, J. C., & Kremmel, B. (2013). Re-examining the content validation of a grammar test: The (im)possibility of distinguishing vocabulary and structural knowledge. *Language Testing*, *30*(4), 535–556. https://doi.org/10.1177/0265532213489568

Biber, D. (2007). Lexical bundles in university spoken and written registers. *English for Specific Purposes*, *3*, 263–286. https://doi.org/10.1016/j.esp.2006.08.003

Biber, D., Conrad, S., & Reppen, R. (1998). *Corpus linguistics: Investigating language structure and use*. Cambridge University Press.

Biber, D., Johansson, S., Leech, G., Conrad, S., & Finegan, E. (1999). *The Longman grammar of spoken and written English*. Longman.

Canale, M., & Swain, M. (1980). Theoretical bases of communicative approaches to second language teaching and testing. *Applied Linguistics*, *1*(1), 1–14. https://doi.org//10.1093/applin/I.1.1

Council of Europe. (2001). *Common European framework of reference for languages: Learning, teaching, assessment*. Cambridge University Press.

Cowie, A. P. (1994). Phraseology. In R. E. Asher (Ed.), *The encyclopaedia of language and linguistics* (pp. 3168–3171). Pergamon.

Crossley, S. A., Cai, Z., & McNamara, D. S. (2012). Syntagmatic, paradigmatic, and automatic n-gram approaches to assessing essay quality. In P. M. McCarthy & G. M. Youngblood (Eds.), *Proceedings of the 25th international Florida artificial intelligence research society (FLAIRS) conference* (pp. 214–219). AAAI Press.

Ellis, N. C., Römer, U., & O'Donnell, M. B. (2016). *Usage-based approaches to language acquisition and processing: Cognitive and corpus investigations of Construction Grammar*. Wiley.

Goldberg, A. (2006). *Constructions at work: The nature of generalization in language*. Oxford University Press.

Granger, S. (2009). The contribution of learner corpora to second language acquisition and foreign language teaching: A critical evaluation. In A. Aijmer (Ed.), *Corpora and langauge teaching* (pp. 13–32). John Benjamins.

Granger, S. (2015). The contribution of learner corpora to reference and instructional materials design. In S. Granger, G. Gilquin, & F. Meunier (Eds.), *The Cambridge Handbook of Learner Corpus Research* (pp.485–510). Cambridge University Press.

Gries, S. T. (2008). Phraseology and linguistic theory: A brief survey. In S. Granger & F. Meunier (Eds.), *Phraseology: An interdisciplinary perspective* (pp. 3–25). John Benjamins.

Gries, S. T., & Deshors, S. C. (2014). Using regressions to explore deviations between corpus data and a standard/target: Two suggestions. *Corpora*, *9*(1), 109–136. https://doi.org/10.3366/cor.2014.0053

Gries, S. T., & Stefanowitsch, A. (2004a). Extending collostructional analysis: A corpus-based perspective on 'alternations'. *International Journal of Corpus Linguistics*, *9*(1), 97–129. https://doi.org/10.1075/ijcl.9.1.06gri

Gries, S. T., & Stefanowitsch, A. (2004b). Co-varying collexemes in the *into*-causative. In M. Achard & S. Kemmer (Eds.), *Language, culture, and mind* (pp. 225–236). CSLI.

Gries, S. T., & Wulff, S. (2009). Psycholinguistic and corpus linguistic evidence for L2 constructions. *Annual Review of Cognitive Linguistics*, *7*, 163–186. https://doi.org/10.1075/arcl.7.07gri

Gyllstad, H. (2019). Measuring knowledge of multiword items. In S. Webb (Ed.), *The Routledge handbook of vocabulary studies* (pp. 387–405). Routledge.

Gyllstad, H., & Schmitt, N. (2019). Testing formulaic language. In A. Siyanova-Chanturia & A. Pellicer-Sánchez (Eds.), *Understanding formulaic language: A second language acquisition perspective* (pp. 174–191). Routledge.

Hunston, S., & Francis, G. (2000). *Pattern grammar: A corpus-driven approach to the lexical grammar of English*. John Benjamins.

Jarvis, S., & Daller, M. (2013). *Vocabulary knowledge: Human ratings and automated measures*. Benjamins.

Lado, R. (1961). *Language testing: The construction and use of foreign language tests*. McGraw-Hill.

Lardière, D. (2014). Linguistic approaches to second language morphosyntax. In S. M. Gass & A. Mackey (Eds.), *The Routledge handbook of second language acquisition* (pp. 163–176). Routledge.

Martinez, R., & Schmitt, N. (2012). A phrasal expressions list. *Applied Linguistics*, *33*(3), 299–320. https://doi.org/10.1093/applin/ams010

Oller, J. (1979). *Language tests at school: A pragmatic approach*. Longman.

Ortega, L. (2003). Syntactic complexity measures and their relationship to L2 proficiency: A research synthesis of college-level L2 writing. *Applied Linguistics*, *24*(4), 492–518. https://doi.org/10.1093/applin/24.4.492

Paquot, M. (2018). Phraseological competence: A missing component in university entrance language tests? Insights from a study of EFL learners' use of statistical collocations. *Language Assessment Quarterly*, *15*(1), 29–43. https://doi.org/10.1080/15434303.2017.1405421

Paquot, M. (2019). The phraseological dimension in interlanguage complexity research. *Second Language Research*, *35*(1), 121–145. https://doi.org/10.1177/0267658317694221

Paquot, M., & Granger, S. (2012). Formulaic language in learner corpora. *Annual Review of Applied Linguistics*, *32*, 130–149. https://doi.org/10.1017/S0267190512000098

Paquot, M., Hubert, N., & Gries, S. T. (in press). Using syntactic co-occurrences to trace phraseological complexity development in learner writing: Verb + object structures in LONGDALE. In B. L. Bruyn & M. Paquot (Eds.), *Second language acquisition and learner corpora*. Cambridge University Press.

Pawley, A., & Syder, F. H. (1983). Two puzzles for linguistic theory: Native-like selection and native-like fluency. In J. C. Richards & R. W. Schmidt (Eds.), *Language and communication* (pp. 191–226). Longman.

Römer, U. (2009). The inseparability of lexis and grammar: Corpus linguistic perspectives. *Annual Review of Cognitive Linguistics*, *7*, 140–162. https://doi.org/10.1075/arcl.7.06rom

Römer, U. (2017). Language assessment and the inseparability of lexis and grammar: Focus on the construct of speaking. *Language Testing*, *34*(4), 477–492. https://doi.org/10.1177/0265532217711431

Rubin, R., Housen, A., & Paquot, M. (in press). Phraseological complexity as an index of L2 Dutch writing proficiency: A partial replication study. In S. Granger (Ed.), *Perspectives on the second language phrasicon: The view from learner corpora*. Multilingual Matters.

Ruegg, R., Fritz, E., & Holland, J. (2011). Rater sensitivity to qualities of lexis in writing. *TESOL Quarterly*, *45*(1), 63–80. https://doi.org/10.5054/tq.2011.240860

Schmitt, N. (2004). *Formulaic sequences: Acquisition, processing, and use*. John Benjamins.

Schmitt, N. (2010). *Researching vocabulary: A vocabulary research manual*. Palgrave Macmillan.

Schmitt, N., & Schmitt, D. (2020). *Vocabulary in language teaching* (2nd ed.). Cambridge University Press.

Sinclair, J. (1991). *Corpus, concordance, collocation*. Oxford University Press.

Siyanova-Chanturia, A., & Pellicer-Sánchez, A. (2018). *Understanding formulaic language: A second language acquisition perspective*. Routledge.

Stefanowitsch, A., & Gries, S. T. (2003). Collostructions: Investigating the interaction between words and constructions. *International Journal of Corpus Linguistics*, *8*(2), 209–243. https://doi.org/10.1075/ijcl.8.2.03ste

Weiler, T. (2018). *Investigating the construct tested through four item types used to assess lexicogrammatical competence in English as a foreign language* (Unpublished doctoral dissertation). Lancaster University, UK.

Wulff, S., & Gries, S. T. (2011). Corpus-driven methods for assessing accuracy in learner production. In P. Robinson (Ed.), *Second language task complexity: Researching the cognition hypothesis of language learning and performance* (pp. 61–87). John Benjamins.

Wulff, S., & Gries, S. T. (2015). Prenominal adjective order preferences in Chinese and German L2 English: A multifactorial corpus study. *Linguistic Approaches to Bilingualism*, *5*(1), 122–150. https://doi.org/10.1075/lab.5.1.05wul

22
Measuring Grammar

Patti Spinner

Background

Methods for assessing grammatical ability have changed a great deal alongside parallel changes in SLA theory and language pedagogy. For many years, language was viewed by most professionals as consisting primarily of grammar and vocabulary. The goal of language study was to understand and acquire the knowledge of these words and structures, often through the use of metalinguistic labels and analysis (e.g., Diller & Walsh, 1981). Language pedagogy followed from this notion; that is, teachers often strove to ensure that students understood grammar and memorized vocabulary words (the grammar-translation approach) (Richards & Rodgers, 2001). Assessment methods followed classroom practice and frequently consisted of translation tasks and discrete-point testing such as multiple-choice questions and fill-in-the-blanks. Consider this example modeled from a 1969 university entrance exam:

(1) "John seems tired."
"Yes, his parents should make him__________more."
a) to sleep
b) sleeps
c) sleep
d) sleeping

Although the item includes a short dialog, the only information necessary to answer correctly is the knowledge that *make* is followed by the bare form of the verb here.

The 1970s through '90s brought significant changes to the way language was viewed. Importantly, form and structure were no longer seen as the primary substance of language; rather, language function was seen as central to a multidimensional linguistic system that includes grammar as one of many components. For example, in systemic-functional linguistics (Halliday, 1994), grammar is only one of many resources that can be used to communicate meanings. The view of grammar itself also expanded. For instance, Larsen-Freeman (1989) pointed out that grammar is multidimensional, consisting not only of forms and structures, but also the meanings these forms and structures express, and the contexts in which grammar is used.

Parallel changes were occurring in the way second language acquisition and pedagogy were viewed. Krashen (1980) argued against the grammar-translation approach, claiming that second languages could be acquired in a similar manner to first languages, that is, through natural exposure to input rather than through an explicit focus on grammar and vocabulary. Thus the use of the target language during instruction became an important feature of the modern classroom. Additionally, interaction with other speakers of a target language was seen as crucial for the development of target language skills and knowledge (e.g., Long, 1996). These ideas were reflected in new approaches to teaching, specifically the communicative approach, which focuses on meaningful and natural communication as a goal of language instruction.

This turn towards communicative teaching and learning led to increased focus on listening and speaking skills, both in the classroom and during language assessment (see Larsen-Freeman, 1989). Listening and speaking skills were assessed with interviews, recorded interactions, and the like. However, despite these changes, for many years grammar assessment remained basically unchanged, in that it primarily consisted of discrete-point testing of grammar rules (Purpura, 2004).

More recently, however, grammar assessment has changed significantly, at least in some areas. Many high-stakes tests have removed separate sections that focused specifically on grammar, instead integrating grammar assessment into speaking and writing tasks. For instance, the speaking portion of the TOEFL (Test of English as a Foreign Language) is rated by a rubric with a section on "language use" that includes an assessment of grammatical accuracy. Importantly, however, the focus is on comprehensibility and communication rather than total control of forms. For instance, even the highest score allows for "systematic errors" as long as they do not obscure meaning. Grammar is measured this way based on the reasoning that performance in various settings, including academic settings, should be measured as directly as possible (Educational Testing Service, n.d.).

The turn away from the separate assessment of grammar has led many researchers and teachers to view discrete-point testing of grammar as old-fashioned at best. In fact, many view it as harmful because of negative washback; that is, if teachers prepare students for grammar assessments by encouraging them to master explicit, metalinguistic knowledge of grammar rather than to develop an implicit knowledge of grammar that can be used in meaningful communication, it will actually impede students' language acquisition.

However, it is probably unwise to consider these types of assessments completely useless or unacceptable (see Jin & Cortazzi, 2011, for a discussion of "negative stereotypes" of older styles of grammar teaching and evaluation). For certain purposes, traditional assessments such as fill-in-the-blanks and sentence combinations can be appropriate. For instance, teachers may find them to be a useful and efficient way to determine whether students have acquired an understanding of basic forms and meanings of grammar (Purpura, 2004). These assessments can be useful for determining whether students are ready to perform particular language tasks or whether they are confused or need further support (for example, in diagnostic assessment contexts). Therefore, when the goal of testing is specific and limited in this way, it can be appropriate to use traditional measures.

On the other hand, older-style assessments of grammar still take place in settings in which they are not completely appropriate. For example, some high-stakes tests of global English ability still use discrete-point measures of grammar, including prescriptive norms such as *who* versus *whom* that are rarely understood (let alone mastered) by native speakers (see e.g., the Test for English Majors (TEM) in China). These tests, which encourage students to focus on metalinguistic knowledge of grammar, may not promote using grammar in a communicative way.

Even if testmakers can agree that assessments should be updated to include an understanding of grammatical ability as a component of communicative competence, issues arise that make it challenging to determine the most reliable, appropriate, and useful ways to assess learners' grammatical ability. To some extent, the difficulty lies in the fact that there is no agreed-upon definition for grammatical ability and no agreed-upon model of second language acquisition. The following section explores how varying views of these issues affect the way grammatical ability might be measured, and how methods are currently being developed for better assessment of grammar.

Key Concepts

***Discrete-point testing*:** In a discrete-point language test, the goal is to test one specific linguistic element, for instance prounouns or past tense marking, at a time. Often these tests involve tasks such as fill-in-the-blanks or multiple-choice questions.

***Metalinguistic knowledge*:** This concerns explicit knowledge about language, such as knowledge of grammar rules, including the ability to explain them. Having metalinguistic knowledge does not entail being able to use that knowledge in a communicative setting.

***Communicative approach*:** An approach to language teaching that focuses on meaningful communication rather than knowledge about grammar or other language elements.

***Explicit knowledge*:** Knowledge that is conscious and can be articulated, for example, knowing that English past tense involves the ending *–ed*.

***Implicit knowledge*:** Knowledge that cannot clearly be articulated. Rather, implicit knowledge may be demonstrated in tasks that tap into levels of knowledge that are unconscious.

***Processability Theory*:** A theory of language acquisition based in Lexical Functional Grammar (Kaplan & Bresnan, 1982) that predicts a sequence of acquisition of a variety of morphosyntactic elements.

***Rapid Profile*:** A tool that can be used to determine a learner's placement on the processability theory scale.

Key Issues

Defining the Construct

The determination of the best assessment method for grammatical ability depends largely on the purpose of the measure. For instance, an assessment to determine learners' explicit knowledge of verb agreement will differ greatly from an assessment to determine which learners might make the best instructors in a college-level physics course. However, for now let us assume that the goal is to measure learners' implicit knowledge of a wide variety of grammatical forms and structures. Let us further assume that the assessment may be used for a variety of purposes, such as to help make determinations of placement in an intensive English program, to provide descriptions of participants in a research study, or to offer feedback for instructors and students about strong and weak areas in a series of language courses. To summarize, the desired test will measure overall grammatical ability for a general purpose.

The crucial question that arises is: What exactly is grammatical ability? Intuitively, most learners will tell you: verb agreement, relative clauses, tense and aspect. In short: forms and structures. Indeed, if forms and structures were all there were to grammar, it would be relatively easy to assess with questions such as the one in (1). But as many researchers have noted, grammar must include meaning, as well. For instance, consider case markers in German. The German preposition *in* (whose meaning overlaps with the English preposition *in*) takes on different meanings when followed by a noun in accusative case versus dative case; that is, *in*+acc indicates directional movement, while *in*+dat indicates non-directional movement.

(2) *Sie ging in den Park.*
She walked in the-acc park
"She walked to the park (a destination)"

Sie ging in dem Park.
She walked in the-dat park
"She walked in the park (a location)."

While knowing the forms of dative and accusative case is necessary to communicate clearly, it is not sufficient. Therefore, meaning must be included in measurements of grammatical ability. This can be accomplished through a variety of methods, including dialogs and short responses. Discrete-point test items can also be used, such as the following (see Purpura, 2014 for further examples):

(3) The girl was chased around the house by the cat.
True or false? The cat chased the girl.

Grammatical ability involves not only meaning but pragmatics, as well. Indeed, in Larsen-Freeman's (1991) and Rea-Dickens's (1991) models of grammar, pragmatic ability is part of grammatical ability. For instance, learners need to know the contexts in which it is appropriate to use certain grammatical forms, such as passive, and when it is more appropriate to use active voice. Indeed, for certain assessment purposes, including pragmatic ability in a grammar assessment may be wholly appropriate. For the purposes of this chapter, however, we will follow Purpura's (2004) view of grammatical knowledge: "Grammatical knowledge is involved when examinees understand or produce utterances that are grammatically precise and contextually meaningful" (p. 89). Note that this definition includes both form and meaning, production and comprehension, accuracy and semantic appropriateness.

Measuring grammatical ability as part of productive tasks, specifically speaking and writing tasks, is generally seen as a good way to include form and meaning as part of assessment, because the focus of these tasks is meaningful communication, and grammar is measured mainly for its contribution to a clear message. Generally, measurements of speech and writing tasks are conducted with rubrics, often including separate scores for grammatical ability in addition to a number of other factors, including content, vocabulary use, or task fulfillment. Grammatical ability is generally rated as involving complexity and accuracy, that is, the production of a variety of grammatical structures (e.g., sentences with dependent clauses) and grammatical accuracy (e.g., correct realization of tense marking). For instance, the IELTS (International English Language Testing System) rubric for writing tasks contains descriptors such as "uses a wide range of structures with full flexibility and accuracy; rare minor errors occur only as 'slips'" for high proficiency test-takers, and "attempts sentence forms but errors in grammar and punctuation predominate and distort the meaning" for low-level test-takers (British Council/idp IELTS Australia/Cambridge Assessment English, n.d.).

While these types of assessment for grammatical ability are an improvement over discrete-point testing for the purposes of high-stakes tests such as the IELTS, there remain both theoretical and practical concerns over their use. From a practical standpoint, there is concern about how the rubrics are used by raters. Interestingly, one of the main concerns is that an evaluation of grammar can "take over" the rest of the scale. That is, raters focus more on grammatical ability than on issues such as content or vocabulary, so that an interview or essay evaluation essentially is a measurement of a learner's grammatical abilities (e.g., Raffaldini, 1988; Savignon, 1985), an undesirable quality for a test that aims to measure a variety of skills.

From an SLA perspective, there are theoretical concerns, as well. First, it is not clear that grammatical accuracy improves in a direct, linear way, as characterized on most rubrics. A straightforward improvement of accuracy is not a feature of any theory of second language acquisition, with the possible partial exception of Skill Acquisition Theory (DeKeyser, 2015). The premise of Skill Acquisition Theory is that explicit grammatical knowledge can become automatized through exposure and practice, perhaps developing into implicit knowledge over time. Following this theory, we might predict a gradual improvement in accuracy as skills become automatized. Even so, the theory allows for different grammatical structures to improve at different rates, and there is nothing in the theory that states that grammatical skills improve in a predictable, linear fashion.

Other SLA theories directly contradict the idea that grammatical accuracy improves predictably. Some researchers note that learners may periodically become less accurate on certain structures as their development progresses. So-called "U-shaped development," in which accuracy increases and then decreases before increasing again, is attested in first language acquisition and proposed to occur in second language acquisition, as well (e.g., Lightbown, 1985). Additionally, supporters of dynamic systems theory (e.g., De Bot, Lowie, & Verspoor, 2007; Larsen-Freeman, 1997) argue that accuracy on forms does not develop in a linear way, and may rise and fall as various factors interact. Another theory, Processability Theory (Pienemann, 1998, 2005), states that while emergence (the first productive uses) of various language phenomena occurs in a certain way, accuracy varies somewhat unpredictably for a variety of reasons.

Still other SLA theories speak to grammatical accuracy only in an indirect manner, with researchers examining learners' performance with the purpose of understanding the operation of the linguistic system with regard to particular structures. For instance, researchers working in a Minimalist framework may examine learners' production or judgment data to determine whether a particular grammatical feature is present or absent. However, these studies do not make predictions for overall accuracy on grammatical structures. Finally, it should be noted that most of these rubric-based assessments focus on production rather than comprehension. Accurate comprehension of grammatical forms is also a crucial part of grammatical ability (VanPatten, 1993).

Despite these issues, it may be possible to include accuracy in a grammar assessment that is based in SLA theory to some extent. Norris (1996) found that learners' accuracy in producing German word order increased in parallel with oral proficiency levels as rated by the ACTFL scale (ACTFL, 1986, Proficiency Guidelines). In fact, at advanced developmental stages, accuracy on word order rules was useful in distinguishing the more advanced levels of oral proficiency from lower levels. Norris attributed these findings to increased processing efficiency in more proficient speakers. These findings are compelling and need to be followed up with further research.

Part of the reason for the disconnect between SLA theories and the methods that are typically used to evaluate learners' grammatical ability is that many SLA theorists strive to describe morphosyntactic development, while many assessment researchers focus on proficiency. Proficiency generally refers to language learners' ability to speak, read, write, or understand a language in real world situations, typically as rated by ability to communicate meaningfully, clearly, and accurately. Development, on the other hand, generally refers to changes that occur in the interlanguage system in response to target language input or other language stimuli. Generally, these changes are understood to be the result of movement towards a more targetlike version of the interlanguage, but the path may be a circuitous one, and may even be destined to fail in particular ways. Because concepts of development and proficiency, while related, refer to fundamentally different perspectives on learner language, it is not clear whether they can both contribute to a single measure of learner language.

The situation may be somewhat different with usage-based approaches to SLA that have been developed in recent years. These approaches take the view that language consists of constructions (e.g., Goldberg, 1995, 2006), which are pairs of form and meaning or function. Constructions do not have a uniform makeup; they can consist of a morpheme such as plural *–s*, or a syntactic frame such as NP Verb NP PP (e.g., *I put the letter in the mailbox*), with labels for component parts depending on the particular constructionist approach. Acquisition takes place as language learners' cognitive mechanisms work to create associations between forms and meanings (that is, constructions) in response to language input (see Ellis & Wulff, 2014 for a summary). The view of grammar from this perspective is notably different than the way it has been discussed in this chapter so far. Grammar is not separate from vocabulary; in fact, lexicon and grammar are inseparable and are better thought of together under the term *lexicogrammar* (see Paquot, Gries, & Yoder, Chapter 21, this volume). With this understanding of grammar, the goal of grammar assessment takes on a new direction.

Towards a Grammar Assessment

Both assessment and SLA researchers have expressed the desire to work together to create better grammar assessment tools (e.g., Chapelle, Chung, Hegelheimer, Pendar, & Xu, 2010; Purpura, 2014; Spinner, 2011). Primarily, the goal has been to explore ways in which development might be incorporated into a proficiency measure. The purpose is to find a way to measure learner development in a way that would be useful for a variety of purposes: decisions regarding placement in intensive English programs, measurement of successful instruction in language programs, division of learners into groups for research purposes, etc. SLA researchers have in fact documented a number of developmental sequences that are attested for learners of English, including sequences for production of questions, modals, word order, and negation. Additionally, proposals have been made regarding developmental orders for forms used to express tense and aspect (e.g., Andersen & Shirai, 1996; Bardovi-Harlig, 2000).

Despite these promising findings, concerns have been raised by Purpura (2004) and others about the extent to which these developmental sequences could be used in language assessment. First, SLA research has focused on a relatively small number of morphosyntactic issues, not enough to provide a comprehensive picture of learners' abilities. Additionally, it is not clear what role instruction might play in affecting developmental sequences. Finally, accuracy is often not measured in these developmental measures, making it more difficult to assess in a traditional way.

A number of attempts have been made to meet these challenges and find ways to incorporate developmental measures into a grammatical assessment. Most of these attempts involve Processability Theory (PT) (Pienemann, 1998, 2005). PT holds particular promise for an assessment measure because it posits a universal hierarchical sequence for language development, regardless of the first language of learners. It has also received substantial empirical support (e.g., Bonilla, 2015; Sakai, 2008). PT predicts the sequence of acquisition for a variety of morphosyntactic elements in any language. For English, predictions are made for elements including third person singular *–s*, questions with auxiliaries, object pronouns, possessives, and more. Crucially, though, it predicts the *emergence* of these forms and structures, not accuracy. Emergence refers to the first times the form or structure is used in a productive (not memorized or chunked) way.

Researchers have taken various approaches to incorporating PT into assessment measures. Pienemann's own measure is the computer-based Rapid Profile (RP) assessment, which takes about 15 minutes. During a RP assessment, a learner and native English-speaking interlocutor engage in conversation and various language tasks designed to elicit the forms and structures in the PT framework (questions, possessives, etc.). During the interaction, a trained observer listens for the relevant forms and structures and enters this information into the system, so that a developmental level for the learner can be determined.

There are a few potential problems with using this system for assessment. First, as noted earlier, it refers to emergence, not accuracy. That is, it is a measure of development rather than proficiency. Second, it is somewhat impractical for use with larger groups. Spinner (2011) attempted to address these issues by using a Rapid Profile-like system with smaller amounts of oral data that learners recorded in response to a few prompts. In that study, she also examined predictions from another theory of grammatical acquisition, Organic Grammar (Vainikka & Young-Scholten, 2006). Results demonstrated that the Rapid Profile order was more successful at accounting for learner production than Organic Grammar, although neither one was able to distinguish between learners at more advanced levels. Spinner noted, however, that the data were not well suited to the task and that further study with improved prompts could produce better results.

Several other researchers have had success with online grammar tests implementing forms and structures from PT along with other morphosyntactic elements, using various item types such as word jumbles or sentence completion tasks. Norris's (2005) test centered on word order measures from PT, such as SVO word order, adverb fronting, and subject-verb inversion in Yes/No questions. Relative clauses were also included to provide further information particularly about advanced learners. Norris created a short computer-based measure and found that even short tests with only 12 items were sufficient to distinguish between different levels of grammatical ability.

Chapelle et al. (2010) also used grammatical elements from PT, in addition to features used by Norris (2005) and other SLA researchers, in the creation of a grammatical assessment tool. Chapelle et al. determined that including a measure of meaning rather than simply form (see Purpura, 2004) was important. For this reason, context was included when possible, such as dialogs or cartoon strips. Some tasks were fairly traditional, such as fill-in-the-blank or word jumble tasks, in addition to a short paragraph writing task that was scored with a rubric. The researchers found that the test results correlated with other measures of grammatical ability and suggested that with some additional items and further development, it could be used to supplement grammatical assessment of learners in a practical way.

Although these studies have suggested promising directions for future grammar assessment, much of the current work in this area looks at grammatical ability not as an independent construct but rather as one of many language features that can distinguish between less or more proficient writing and speaking. Rather than looking towards formal or functional theory of SLA, these approaches tend to be data-driven and compatible with construction grammar and usage-based models of grammatical acquisition. In many of these studies, the goal is to identify a set of lexicogrammatical phrases or grammatical expressions (in addition to other linguistic features) as typical of essays or speech samples from particular proficiency levels. These expressions are then used to conduct evaluations of the samples, and these evaluations are compared with scores from human raters. The most commonly used measures for many years were the so called "CALF" measures, which include grammatical features as part of measures of syntactic complexity, accuracy, lexical complexity, and fluency (Ortega, 2003; Wolfe-Quintero, et al., 1998). With advances in usage-based and corpus-driven research, however, additional measures are being introduced that include a variety of grammatical constructions such as verb-argument constructions, cleft structures, the dative alternation construction, and others (e.g., Kim, 2018). In conducting this research, some have argued that an appropriate way to measure accuracy is to compare L2 and L1 texts in a probabilistic way, rather than considering structures absolutely correct or incorrect (e.g., The Multifactorial Prediction and Deviation Analysis using Regressions [MuPDAR] method of Gries & Deshors, 2014). That is, by comparing language L2 texts to L1 texts, it is possible to see how closely L2 speech or writing approximates L1 norms.

Assessment measures based in the usage-based framework will focus on fundamentally different language phenomena than those that are based in formal linguistic theory. This fact may make it seem that the two approaches are incompatible. However, both of these approaches are valuable for understanding the trajectory of second language acquisition and for forming a clear idea of what constitutes grammatical ability. Because they speak to different aspects of grammatical ability, they both have much to contribute to assessment of grammar moving forward.

Recommendations for Practice

When developing or selecting a grammar assessment tool, whether for language testing or SLA research purposes, first, determine exactly what kind of grammatical knowledge you need to assess. Are you interested in implicit knowledge and how it can be deployed during real-life communication with other speakers of the language? Or do you need to assess how well instruction has succeeded in helping students understand particular grammatical concepts? Is there a particular skill (e.g., interacting with L1 speakers, writing academic prose) that your learners need to master?

Second, regardless of the type of grammatical ability you are trying to assess, incorporate not just form but also meaning into the measure. This can be accomplished by tying grammatical measures into speaking or writing tasks, or by creating test items in which interpretations of particular grammatical structures in context are required. Ideally, meaning should be assessed both on a sentence level (that is, meanings of words and structures in the context of a single sentence), and at a discourse level (that is, interpretations in broader contexts); see Purpura (2014) for exploration of this idea.

Third, include measures of both production and comprehension in the grammatical measure when possible. Many assessments of grammar focus entirely on production by using speaking or writing tasks, but including interpretation and comprehension tasks such as dialogs or picture selection tasks will give a fuller picture of test-takers' ability.

Finally, consider using several different kinds of measures to get a clearer picture of learners' grammatical ability, for instance, an essay that is scored with a rubric plus a more traditional measure—see Chapelle et al. (2010) for an example. Consider also adding a measure of lexicogrammatical ability.

Testing Tips

- Determine exactly what kind of grammatical knowledge you need to assess; then select your assessment tool accordingly. There is no "one size fits all" measure.
- A good measure of grammatical ability will usually measure both form and meaning, not form alone.
- Depending on your goals, it may be valuable to measure grammatical ability in both production (e.g., with speaking tasks) and comprehension (e.g., with listening tasks).
- For a more comprehensive picture of learners' abilities, consider using more than one type of measure, for instance, a measure of lexicogrammatical abilty, an essay scored with a rubric, and a traditional multiple-choice test.

Recommended Readings

Purpura, J. (2004). *Assessing grammar*. Cambridge University Press.

James Purpura's book on the assessment of grammar is probably the most thorough and well-considered work on the topic of grammar assessment. It is still relevant today, along with Purpura's more recent work on the topic (see e.g., Purpura, 2014).

Chapelle, C. A., Chung, Y. R., Hegelheimer, V., Pendar, N., & Xu, J. (2010). Towards a computer-delivered test of productive grammatical ability. *Language Testing*, *27*(4), 443–469.

In this article, the researchers consider an innovative method for evaluating grammatical development that invites further exploration of this topic.

Pienemann, M. (1998). *Language processing and second language development: Processability theory*. John Benjamins.

This book is the definitive reference for Processability Theory and the place to begin to gain an understanding of PT.

References

American Council on the Teaching of Foreign Languages. (1986). *ACTFL proficiency guidelines*. ACTFL.

Andersen, R. W., & Shirai, Y. (1996). The primacy of aspect in first and second language acquisition: The pidgin-creole connection. In W. C. Ritchie & T. K. Bhatia (Eds.), *Handbook of second language acquisition* (pp. 527–570). Academic Press. https://doi.org/10.1016/b978-012589042-7/50018-9

Bardovi-Harlig, K. (2000). *Tense and aspect in second language acquisition: Form, meaning, and use*. Wiley-Blackwell.

Bonilla, C. (2015). From number agreement to the subjunctive: Evidence for processability theory in L2 Spanish. *Second Language Research*, *31*(1), 53–74. https://doi.org/10.1177/0267658314537291

British Council/idp IELTS Australia/Cambridge Assessment English. (n.d.). IELTS writing assessment criteria - Task 1 (public version). https://www.ielts.org/-/media/documents/online-tutorial/writing-assessment-criteria-t1.ashx?la=en

Chapelle, C. A., Chung, Y. R., Hegelheimer, V., Pendar, N., & Xu, J. (2010). Towards a computer-delivered test of productive grammatical ability. *Language Testing*, *27*(4), 443–469. https://doi.org/10.1177/0265532210367633

De Bot, K., Lowie, W., & Verspoor, M. (2007). A dynamic systems theory approach to second language acquisition. *Bilingualism: Language and Cognition*, *10*(1), 7–21. https://doi.org/10.1017/s1366728906002732

DeKeyser, R. M. (2015). Skill acquisition theory. In B. VanPatten & J. Williams (Eds.), *Theories in second language acquisition: An introduction* (2nd ed., pp. 94–112). Routledge.

Diller, K., & Walsh, T. (1981). "Living" and "dead" languages: A neurolinguistic distinction. *Actes Du 5ème Congrès de L'Association Internationale de Linguistique Appliquée*: *Montréal*, *5*, 99.

Educational Testing Service. (n.d). TOEFL. https://www.ets.org/toefl/?WT.ac=etshome_toefl_menu_180417

Ellis, N. C., & Wulff, S. (2014). Usage-based approaches to SLA. In B. VanPatten & J. Williams (Eds.), *Theories in second language acquisition: An introduction* (2nd ed., pp. 75–93). Routledge.

Goldberg, A. E. (1995). *Constructions: A construction grammar approach to argument structure*. University of Chicago Press.

Goldberg, A. E. (2006). *Constructions at work: The nature of generalization in language*. Oxford University Press.

Gries, S. Th., & Deshors, S. C. (2014). Using regressions to explore deviations between interlanguage and native language: Two suggestions. *Corpora*, *9*(1), 109–136. https://doi.org/10.3366/cor.2014.0053

Halliday, M. A. K. (1994). *An introduction to functional grammar* (2nd ed.). Edward Arnold.

Jin, L., & Cortazzi, M. (2011). Re-evaluating traditional approaches in second language teaching and learning. In E. Hinkel (Ed.), *Handbook of research in second language teaching and learning* (Vol. 2, pp. 558–575). Routledge.

Kaplan, R., & Bresnan, J. (1982). Lexical-functional grammar: A formal system for grammatical representation. In J. Bresnan (Ed.), *The mental representation of grammatical relations* (pp. 173–281). MIT Press.

Kim, S. (2018, September 20–22). *Predicting CEFR proficiency level using grammatical criterial features*. [Paper presentation]. American Association for Corpus Linguistics Conference, Atlanta, GA, United States.

Krashen, S. (1980). The input hypothesis. In J. Alatis (Ed.), *Current issues in bilingual education* (pp. 144–158). Georgetown University Press.

Larsen-Freeman, D. (1989). Pedagogical descriptions of language: Grammar. *Annual Review of Applied Linguistics*, *10*, 187–195. https://doi.org/10.1017/s026719050000129x

Larsen-Freeman, D. (1991). Teaching grammar. In M. Celce-Murcia (Ed.), *Teaching English as a second or foreign language* (2nd ed., pp. 279–296). Newbury House.

Larsen-Freeman, D. (1997). Chaos/complexity science and second language acquisition. *Applied Linguistics*, *18*(2), 141–165. https://doi.org/10.1093/applin/18.2.141

Lightbown, P. M. (1985). Great expectations: Second-language acquisition research and classroom teaching. *Applied Linguistics*, *6*(2), 173–189. https://doi.org/10.1093/applin/6.2.173

Long, M. H. (1996). The role of the linguistic environment in second language acquisition. In W. C. Ritchie & T. K. Bhatia (Eds.), *Handbook of second language acquisition* (Vol. 2, pp. 413–468). Academic Press. https://doi.org/10.1016/b978-012589042-7/50015-3
Norris, J. M. (1996). *A validation study of the ACTFL guidelines and the German speaking test* (Unpublished MA thesis). University of Hawai'i at Manoa, Honolulu.
Norris, J. M. (2005). Using developmental sequences to estimate ability with English grammar: Preliminary design and investigation of a web-based test. *University of Hawai'i Second Language Studies*, *24*(1), 24–128.
Ortega, L. (2003). Syntactic complexity measures and their relationship to L2 proficiency: A research synthesis of college-level L2 writing. *Applied Linguistics*, *24*(4), 492–518. https://doi.org/10.1093/applin/24.4.492
Pienemann, M. (1998). *Language processing and second language development: Processability theory*. John Benjamins. https://doi.org/10.1075/sibil.15
Pienemann, M. (2005). Discussing PT. In M. Pienemann (Ed.), *Cross-linguistic aspects of processability theory* (pp. 61–83). John Benjamins. https://doi.org/10.1075/sibil.30.04pie
Purpura, J. (2004). *Assessing grammar*. Cambridge University Press. https://doi.org/10.1017/CBO9780511733086
Purpura, J. (2014). Assessment of grammar. In A. J. Kunnan (Ed.), *Companion to language assessment* (pp. 100–124). Wiley-Blackwell. https://doi.org/10.1002/9781118411360.wbcla147
Raffaldini, T. (1988). The use of situation tests as measures of communicative ability. *Studies in Second Language Acquisition*, *10*(2), 197–216. https://doi.org/10.1017/s0272263100007312
Rea-Dickins, P. (1991). What makes a grammar test communicative? In J. C. Alderson & B. North (Eds.), *Language testing in the 1990s: The communicative legacy* (pp. 112–131). Macmillan.
Richards, J., & Rodgers, T. (2001). *Approaches and methods in language teaching*. Cambridge University Press.
Sakai, H. (2008). An analysis of Japanese university students' oral performance in English using processability theory. *System*, *36*(4), 534–549. https://doi.org/10.1016/j.system.2008.03.002
Savignon, S. J. (1985). Evaluation of communicative competence: The ACTFL provisional proficiency guidelines. *The Modern Language Journal*, *69*(2), 129–134. https://doi.org/10.1111/j.1540-4781.1985.tb01928.x
Spinner, P. (2011). L2 assessment and morphosyntactic development. *Studies in Second Language Acquisition*, *33*(4), 529–561. https://doi.org/10.1017/s0272263111000301
Vainikka, A., & Young-Scholten, M. (2006). The roots of syntax and how they grow: Organic grammar, the basic variety, and processability theory. In S. Unsworth, T. Parodi, A. Sorace, & M. Young-Scholten (Eds.), *Paths of development in L1 and L2 acquisition* (pp. 77–106). John Benjamins. https://doi.org/10.1075/lald.39.05vai
VanPatten, B. (1993). Grammar instruction for the acquisition rich classroom. *Foreign Language Annals*, *26*, 433–450. https://doi.org/10.1111/j.1944-9720.1993.tb01179.x
Wolfe-Quintero, K., Inagaki, S., Kim, H. Y., Kim, H. Y., & Inagaki, S. (1998). *Second language development in writing: Measures of fluency, accuracy, & complexity*. University of Hawai'i Press.

23

Measuring Phonology

Dustin Crowther

Background

The past few years have seen renewed theoretical and pedagogical interest in second language (L2) *pronunciation* in general (Munro & Derwing, 2015), but also an increased emphasis specifically on L2 pronunciation *assessment* (Isaacs & Trofimovich, 2017; Kang & Ginther, 2018). While SLA research has spent significant energy on how specific phonological considerations may impact L2 users' ability to express meaning, language testing has tended to view L2 speaking on a more holistic level, relegating phonological features to only a minimal role (Isaacs & Trofimovich, 2017). As I will endeavor to highlight in this chapter, any disconnect between these two fields is a disservice to those who are most affected: L2 learners.

Eckman (2018) described *phonology* as a subpart of a larger *grammar* system which enables the production and comprehension of utterances. He specifically referred to phonology as "the subpart of a grammar that underlies the pronunciation patterns of the language" (p. 25–26). As such, phonology has often been viewed as an area of study focused on the sound systems of a language (e.g., Derwing & Munro, 2015). In SLA research, this study is operationalized through analysis of an L2 learner's oral utterance, which includes both *segmental* (i.e., vowels, consonants) and *suprasegmental* (i.e., prosodic elements such as word stress, intonation, and rhythm) considerations. For this reason, when referring to L2 learners' holistic oral utterance, with no reference to any specific phonological measure, I utilize *pronunciation*, and when referring to the individual linguistic characteristics of each utterance (i.e., the phonological properties), I refer to *phonology*.

An SLA Perspective

The wealth of SLA research into L2 pronunciation is beyond the scope of the current chapter. For example, I make only passing reference to work on ultimate attainment (e.g., Abrahamsson & Hylstenstam, 2009; Flege, Munro, & MacKay, 1995; Moyer, 1999), though such scholarship has been vitally informative for the stream of research highlighted below. Instead, I emphasize scholarship aligned with Levis (2005), who described two principles that define how researchers, teachers, and learners have viewed L2 pronunciation acquisition and teaching. The first principle is a more traditional view that prioritizes attaining native-like pronunciation in the target language (i.e., the *Nativeness* Principle). The second principle emphasizes that L2 speakers can produce understandable speech while possessing a foreign accent, and that different phonological features have different effects on understandable speech (i.e., the *Intelligibility* Principle). SLA pronunciation scholarship has strongly advocated for an emphasis on intelligibility, primarily based on evidence that attaining accent-free speech is a rare occurrence, even for learners beginning at a young age (e.g., Flege et al., 1995; Moyer, 1999). In much of this research, scholars have focused on three global dimensions: accentedness, comprehensibility, and intelligibility.

While overlap exists between the global dimensions of accentedness, comprehensibility, and intelligibility, they are also partially distinct constructs (Derwing & Munro, 2015). Speech that is (sometimes heavily) accented can be comprehensible and intelligible. Similarly, speech perceived as requiring more effort to comprehend can be understood, just as perceptually easy-to-understand speech may be misunderstood. A great number of scholars have investigated which phonological measures influence L2 speakers' performance within these dimensions, both in isolation (e.g., Field, 2005; Munro & Derwing, 2006) and in relation to each other (e.g., Kang, Rubin, & Pickering, 2010; Trofimovich & Isaacs, 2012). In the latter, an emphasis has been placed on the phonological measures associated with comprehensibility, as it has been argued that despite the use of the term "intelligibility" in rating scales of standardized proficiency tests, it is comprehensibility that is being measured (Harding, 2017). A consistent finding is that while listeners attend to a wide range of linguistic measures (including grammar and lexicon) when assessing comprehensibility, phonologically speaking, both segmental (individual sounds) and suprasegmental (prosody-based) measures are of importance to producing comprehensible speech (e.g., Crowther et al., 2015; Trofimovich & Isaacs, 2012).

A Language Testing Perspective

To begin, Fulcher (2014) defined speaking as "the verbal use of language to communicate with others" (p. 23), and highlighted how this verbal use was defined *not only* by phonological considerations, but *also* fluency, linguistic accuracy, communicative strategies, and communicative competence. Assessing L2 pronunciation as a construct is not the same as assessing L2 speaking. However, an all-inclusive emphasis on speaking has led to phonological considerations being minimized within L2 speaking assessment literature (Isaacs & Trofimovich, 2017).

L2 speaking is assessed for different reasons. Large-scale standardized tests such as IELTS and TOEFL are used to determine L2 English speakers' linguistic preparedness for English-medium academic study (as well as for migration and work purposes; www.ielts.org/). The oral proficiency interviews (OPIs) conducted by ACTFL serve both educational and professional purposes (www.languagetesting.com/). In addition, US universities require international teaching assistants (ITAs) to complete oral proficiency assessments to determine their preparedness to teach undergraduate and graduate coursework (e.g., Choi, 2017). Considering this diversity, it is not surprising that we see a range of criteria within L2 speaking rubrics. For example, the IELTS speaking rubric (www.ielts.org/en-us/ielts-for-organisations/ielts-scoring-in-detail) includes categories for Fluency and Coherence, Lexical Resource, Grammatical Range and Accuracy, and Pronunciation. For comparison purposes, the TOEFL speaking rubrics (www.ets.org/toefl/ibt/scores/understand) emphasize General Description, Delivery, Language Use, and Topic Development, though, unlike IELTS, combine phonological considerations with fluency under the Delivery criterion. The ACTFL proficiency guidelines refer to pronunciation, but do not do so at all levels.

While accepting that language testing has focused more generally on speaking, there is much that can be discussed in regards to how phonological measures have been treated. One key difference between how SLA and language testing treat pronunciation regards the global dimensions discussed previously. Language testing has shown a tendency to conflate accentedness and comprehensibility (Harding, 2017). For example, Ockey and French (2014) devised a "Strength of Accent Scale" as a tool to investigate potential accent effects on TOEFL listening tasks. They describe accent within their framework as:

> the degree to which an individual's speech patterns are perceived to be different from the local variety, and how much this difference is perceived to impact comprehension of listeners who are familiar with the local variety. Therefore, *the strength of an accent indicates the degree to which it is judged to be different than the local variety, and how it is perceived to impact the comprehension of users of the local variety.*
>
> (p. 695, emphasis added)

In another example, Isaacs, Trofimovich, Yu, and Muńoz Chereau (2015) highlighted how accentedness, intelligibility, and comprehensibility had been conflated in the revised-IELTS pronunciation scale. For example, consider this descriptor from Band 8, in which all three constructs are represented: "easy to understand throughout; L1 [first language] accent has minimal effect on intelligibility." However, since several studies have found high correlations between accentedness and comprehensibility ratings (for example, Crowther, Trofimovich, & Isaacs, 2016 found *rs* > .90), the extent to which the two dimensions are truly distinct could be questioned. On the other hand, such correlations have also been shown to vary in strength when considered across individual L2 speakers (Munro & Derwing, 1995).

To delve further into the effects of dimension conflation, Isaacs et al. (2015) conducted a mixed-methods analysis of eight IELTS examiners' rating processes, with a specific interest in the use of the Pronunciation scale. Their quantitative approach enabled them to investigate the influence of phonological measures on test scoring. Their qualitative approach allowed them to analyze the beliefs and experiences of the examiners during the scoring process. They found that phonologic measures such as *Vowel & Consonant Errors*, *Word Stress*, and *Intonation* had weaker associations with both Speaking in general and Pronunciation specifically than did grammatical and lexical measures. Associations with the global dimension of comprehensibility were even weaker. However, as phonological measurement was conducted through the use of semantic differential scales completed by the same IELTS examiners (i.e., highly subjective measures), the actual influence of each phonological measure is questionable. Maybe more important is that the examiners, through pre- and post-assessment questionnaires and focus group interviews, indicated a lack of alignment in what they attended to when conducting their assessments. Examiners seemingly struggled most with Pronunciation; not only did they tend to assign this score last, several referred to difficulties differentiating it from Fluency & Coherence. Others indicated that they referred to the scores they assigned to other categories before scoring Pronunciation. This might explain the stronger associations with grammatical and lexical measures Isaacs et al. found. Finally, different examiners indicated that they attended to different phonological measures when assigning their Pronunciation scores. When Isaacs et al. compared their examiners' assigned scores to IELTS-provided official scores, a number of inconsistent classifications were identified, leading the authors to argue for greater construct precision in scale descriptors.

Key Concepts

Global dimensions of L2 speech (adapted from Derwing & Munro, 2015)

- ***Accentedness*:** How well an L2 speaker can approximate the sounds of a target community.
- ***Comprehensibility*:** How easy or difficult an L2 speaker's utterance is to understand.
- ***Intelligibility*:** Degree of match between an L2 speaker's intended meaning and the listener's accuracy of understanding.

- ***Fluency***: A fourth dimension (see Pallotti, Chapter 19, this volume) which has been treated both as a target on par with the above (e.g., Derwing, Rossiter, Munro, & Thomson, 2004) and also as a predictor of each (e.g., Crowther, Trofimovich, Saito, & Isaacs, 2015).

Key Issues

I now discuss several key considerations that may help bridge SLA and language testing inquiry into L2 pronunciation and also serve to strengthen our scholarly pursuits. These include listener/rater considerations, subjective/objective measures of phonological features, monologic/interactive speech, and the continuing global spread of English.

Listener/Rater

In bridging SLA and language testing scholarship, a key distinction is between listener and rater. *Listener* groups can include nearly anyone, while *rater* groups consist of those with formal training in how to rate speaking test performances (Yan & Ginther, 2018). Listeners are more drawn upon in SLA research to assign scalar ratings for the aforementioned global dimensions. Raters are more characteristic of language testing research.

Both streams of research aim to explore how key variables may impact listeners'/raters' assessment of L2 speech. Considerations of listener variables in SLA-related speech rating can be traced back to the early matched-guise work of Lambert and colleagues (e.g., Lambert, Hodgson, Gardner, & Fillenbaum, 1960), with much contemporary SLA research interested in topics related to L1 familiarity (e.g., Bent & Bradlow, 2003), L1 influence (e.g., Crowther et al., 2015), and native- versus non-native-listener effects (e.g., Crowther et al., 2016). In the field of language testing, discrepancies based on such effects are viewed as threats to validity, and have been the focus of a significant body of literature (e.g., Huang, Alegre, & Eisenberg, 2016; Winke, Gass, & Myford, 2013).

Research investigating speaker and listener effects have primarily focused either on global considerations (SLA) or task performance (language testing), with not much focus given to phonological considerations. Kang (2012), who focused on ITA testing, found that non-native listeners were stricter than native listeners, with suprasegmental measures accounting for substantial variance in speaking scores. Crowther et al. (2015) compared L1 Farsi, Hindi, and Chinese learners of English, and found that while segmental accuracy was a strong predictor of accentedness across speaking groups (*r*s > .90), it was less consistent as a predictor for comprehensibility (*r*s = .57–71). In general, L1 Chinese speakers demonstrated stronger associations across phonological measures. Such variation is intriguing, as all three groups reported statistically similar IELTS and TOEFL scores. Comparing native- to non-native-English listeners' assessments of accentedness and comprehensibility, Crowther et al. (2016) found minimal quantitative differences in terms of both global measures and associated phonological measures. There has been less emphasis on how phonological measures might influence raters, with Isaacs et al. (2015, discussed above) being the most substantial.

Subjective/Objective Measuring of Phonological Features

There is a substantial body of literature that discusses the different phonological measures that may influence listeners' and raters' assessment of L2 pronunciation. For example, Trofimovich and Isaacs (2012) identified 19 measures—five phonological, six fluency-based, and seven grammatical/lexical/discourse measures. Kang et al. (2010) included 29 measures, 21 of which were phonological (the remaining were fluency-based). The difference in quantity is due to a difference in specificity. For example, where Trofimovich and Isaacs featured intonation as a single measure, Kang et al. referred to 18 different measures. I draw upon these two studies to illustrate an important point in phonological coding, one that links directly back to a concern of Lado (1961): How objectively can we assess L2 speakers' performance on such phonological measures?

To code their 19 measures, Trofimovich and Isaacs (2012) drew upon trained coders' native speaker intuitions (e.g., is an intonation contour correct based on how you would produce it?). Acknowledging the subjectivity of this approach, the authors were encouraged by high intercoder agreement (> .85). Taking this a step further, Saito, Trofimovich, and Isaacs's (2017) use of semantic differential scales indicated that listeners' subjective assessment of specific phonological measures aligned closely with the coding procedure described above (both studies drew upon the same speech samples). This approach subsequently served as the basis for Crowther et al. (2015), in which the same listeners assessed both global (accentedness, comprehensibility) and linguistic (phonology, fluency, lexicon, grammar) measures.

To code their range of measures, Kang et al. (2010) utilized *spectrograms*, *frequency or pitch of fundamental formant*, and *intensity*, as determined through computer-assisted analysis. Such an approach falls in line with the increasing use of automated speech recognition (ASR). Littman, Strik, and Lim (2018) described the goal of a standard ASR system as being "to determine which spoken words are present in a given speech (audio) signal" (p. 295). Interested readers are referred to Litman et al. and Van Moere and Suzuki (2018) for more in depth descriptions, but, in short, an ASR system consists of a language model (probabilities of words and sequences of words) and acoustic models (how the sounds of a language are pronounced) which build on input consisting of a lexicon and a large corpus of audio files (Litman et al., 2018). ASR then uses these models to identify what is said in a given speech sample. Such procedures help to eliminate the potential listener/rater effects highlighted above, and can even allow for more automated analysis of segmental and intonational measures of speech. This, in turn, gives a sense of objectiveness in coding. Of concern is that some measures (specifically frequency- and time-based) are more easily addressed through ASR than others (prosody), primarily due to difficulty in identifying an appropriate standard (e.g., based on a regional dialect) for the model input (Isaacs, 2018). Perhaps even more concerning is an incidental emphasis on accentedness rather than intelligibility. Specifically, phonological errors are determined via comparison to a pre-established norm, without consideration that some phonological errors will be more detrimental to intelligible communication than others (Isaacs, 2018).

A final thought regarding the subjective/objective measurement divide comes from Derwing and Munro (2015). L2 speech "simply cannot be measured without recourse to listeners" (p. 9). Derwing and Munro highlighted how listeners/raters consider contextual factors that acoustic coding cannot, a process which may allow listeners/raters to accommodate deviations from a specified norm. The semantic differential scales used in Saito et al. (2017) and Isaacs et al. (2015) may be one initial way to account for such listener/rater accommodation, but more empirical research in both SLA and language testing is needed in this regard.

Monologic/Interactive Speech

Within SLA, much of the above research focused on monologic speech (e.g., picture narrative). However, it is currently unclear how appropriate scalar ratings are to scoring L2 speech in interactive contexts. Specifically, monologic speech allows listeners to attend to a single speaker, which in turn allows for the isolation of which phonological measures are associated with these same listeners' scalar ratings. The presence of an additional speaker during interaction would require the listener to now split their focus while assigning scalar ratings, which could lead to the perception of Speaker A influencing the perception of Speaker B. More commonly, interaction-orientated studies rely on different methodological tools than discussed above, primarily (a method of) discourse analysis (e.g., Jenkins, 2000) and stimulated recall (e.g., Kennedy, Guénette, Murphy, & Allard, 2015). Generally, these studies have indicated that phonology-based communicative breakdowns are more frequently the result of segmental rather than suprasegmental errors (e.g., Kennedy et al., 2015; Loewen & Isbell, 2017). If a communicative breakdown is the direct result of a loss of meaning, Loewen and Isbell (2017) proposed that intelligibility, rather than comprehensibility, may be a more relevant construct for interactive speech. Elaborating off their interpretation, it may be that while suprasegmental measures may create difficulty in understanding an utterance (i.e., comprehensibility), they are less likely to impact the accuracy of understanding (i.e., intelligibility). This potential interpretation, of course, needs more focused empirical investigation.

Compared to SLA-oriented research, paired and group assessment appears to receive far less focus in standardized testing, with one exception being the collaborative task included within the Cambridge First Certificate of English's battery of speaking tests (see Galaczi, 2008, for an overview). Rather, much existing research focuses on oral proficiency interviews (OPIs), an examiner-candidate interaction format employed by ACTFL. While OPIs involve some degree of interactivity, they are still primarily learner-centered, as demonstrated by the existence of both person- and computer-moderated OPIs (e.g., Thompson, Cox, & Knapp, 2016). While interactive variety can indeed exist within such testing (e.g., Plough & Bogart, 2008), the role that the learner takes differs greatly than if they were to interact with a fellow learner. In considering paired assessment at the classroom level, researchers have emphasized individual, discourse, and task variables, with examples including group member personality (Ockey, 2009, 2011), interlocutor proficiency (e.g., Davis, 2009), interactional competence (May, 2011), and planning time (Nitta & Nakatsuhara, 2014). However, as might be expected given the emphasis on L2 speaking in language testing, research that has considered paired/group assessment has focused less on phonological considerations compared to SLA research. Pursuing the role of phonology in interaction, (e.g., communicative breakdowns; phonological accommodation) would appear to be a significant matter for both SLA and language testing research (Isaacs, 2018).

The Global Role of English(es)

We now see increased discussion of how *Global Englishes* might inform language testing, highlighted by both the benefits and complexities of such inclusion (e.g., Brown, 2014). Given the undeniable global use of English (Low & Pakir, 2018), we have begun to see research which tests the effects of different varieties of English on listening comprehension (e.g., Kang, Thomson, & Moran, 2018) and speech perception (e.g., Kang & Moran, 2014). Global Englishes scholars advocate for an emphasis on intelligible speech without adherence to any specific native-norm. However, despite Jenkins' (2000) influential, but debateable (e.g., Munro & Derwing, 2006; Isaacs, 2018), Lingua Franca Core, much recent emphasis has been on which communicative strategies and interactive techniques (e.g., borrowing, code-switching) allow for mutual intelligibility in multilingual and multicultural interaction (MacKenzie, 2014). If Intelligibility is viewed as co-constructed meaning by individuals at a given time and in a given context (Nelson, 1982), then Global Englishes insight may actually be more applicable to testing L2 speaking than specifically L2 pronunciation, which may be inseparable from users' repertoire of communicative strategies for pre-empting and repairing communicative breakdowns.

Recommendations for Practice

Despite differences in how SLA and language testing both treat and attend to L2 pronunciation, there are also clear avenues of alignment and collaboration. A key recognition is that phonological measures of L2 speech are a contributor to communicative success. While they should be analyzed in conjunction with non-phonological considerations (e.g., fluency, grammar, lexicon), they cannot be overlooked when assessing L2 speaking. However, as previously referenced, different means of assessing specific phonological measures have been employed, some based on subjective intuition (e.g., Trofimovich & Isaacs, 2012), others on acoustic analysis (e.g., Kang et al., 2010). To highlight this variation in measurement procedures, I below provide examples drawn from SLA-orientated studies. The phonological measures included are commonly considered to impact listeners' comprehension of an L2 utterance and for each I have included an intuition-based (first example provided) and acoustic-based (second example provided) approach.

Segments

- "on hearing each token, the listeners clicked a phonetic symbol on a computer screen that corresponded to the closest English vowel" (Munro & Derwing, 2008, p. 486; measured accuracy of vowel production in minimal pairs such as "pet" and "pat")
- "each vowel token was isolated, and first and second formant (F1 and F2, respectively) measurements were taken from the midpoint of each production using a script in Praat... The F1 provides information regarding the vowel's production along the height dimension, whereas the F2 provides information regarding the production along a front-back dimension" (Solon, Long, & Gurzynski-Weiss, 2017, p. 359; elicited speech from L2 Spanish learners and native Spanish speakers for comparison)

Word Stress

- "total number of instances of misplaced or missing primary stress in polysyllabic words divided by the total number of polysyllabic words produced" (Trofimovich & Isaacs, 2012, p. 908; drew on coders' native speaker intuition)
- "The acoustic measurements included fundamental frequency (FO), vowel and syllable duration, and intensity of the accent-bearing elements" (Nguyen & Ingram, 2005, p. 313; compared how native and non-native speakers differentiated between stressed and unstressed elements in English words)

Intonation

- "number of correct pitch patterns at the end of phrases over the total number of instances where pitch patterns are expected, as signaled by preboundary lengthening" (Trofimovich & Isaacs, 2012, p. 908)
- "measuring the F0 of the same lexical item presented initially as new information and thus appearing in following instances as given information" (Kang et al., 2010, p. 558; note that this was only one of 12 intonation-orientated measures included)

Rhythm

- "the difference in stress (emphasis) between content and function (grammatical) words" (Crowther et al., 2015, p. 823–824; listeners used semantic differential scales to assign ratings)
- "Each sentence was segmented into vocalic sequences (*V*) and consonantal clusters (*C*) intervals and syllables (*S*)... We calculated the rhythm measures on vocalic sequences (*nPVI-V*, *VarcoV*), consonantal clusters (*nPVI-C* and *VarcoC*), and syllables (*nPVI-S* and *VarcoS*), as well as mean syllable durations (*meanS*) for each sentence from each speaker" (Ordin &

Polyanskaya, 2015, p. 537; used PRAAT to analyze acquisition of English speech rate by French and German learners)

With the above range of coding techniques in mind, I once again echo Lado (1961) in questioning whether any one truly objective, valid approach towards measuring learners' phonological performance exists. While the acoustic-based techniques described provide a means to accurately measure their specific phonologic property, they remain only one of many possible techniques. Any application to language testing would require three key considerations:

1. which phonological measure(s) to assess, ideally drawn from those deemed to impact intelligibility;
2. a theoretical decision on which specific coding technique to use to ensure consistency across testtakers; and
3. a standard to be compared against (a complex challenge given the proliferation of variation within languages such as Arabic, English, and Chinese).

Drawing on the discussion throughout this chapter, I conclude with brief tips for both SLA researchers and language testers to help better understand the relationship between L2 pronunciation and speaking assessment.

Testing Tips

For SLA Researchers

- Be aware that phonological measures account for only a subset of variance in listeners' assessment of L2 comprehensibility. If the primary goal of L2 speaking is to produce understandable utterances, then consideration must be given to additional variables such as grammar, lexicon, and discourse (not to mention interactional considerations, such as turn-taking and negotiation).
- Carefully select subjective and/or objective coding procedures, with an understanding of their limitations. While subjective measures are susceptible to listener/rater variation, objective measures cannot account for listeners' potential accommodation strategies for determining meaning.

For Language Testers

- Whereas SLA researchers must be aware that phonological measures form only a subset of L2 speaking ability, language testers need be aware that the same measures still need attention when assessing L2 speech.
- Care must be given to scale/rubric construction to ensure clarity of constructs. Descriptors should emphasize comprehensibility/intelligibility over accentedness, with a focus on phonological measures deemed to promote/hinder understandable speech.

Recommended Readings

Derwing, T. M., & Munro, M. J. (2015). *Pronunciation fundamentals: Evidence-based perspectives for L2 teaching and research*. John Benjamins.

This book provides a highly accessible, detailed overview of historical and contemporary research into L2 pronunciation, and how findings can and should inform ongoing research and pedagogical practices.

Isaacs, T., & Trofimovich, P. (Eds). (2017). *Second language pronunciation assessment: Interdisciplinary perspectives*. Multilingual Matters.

This volume draws on insights of a range of SLA and language testing scholars to consider how L2 pronunciation assessment might be informed by testing and social considerations, classroom practice, and insights gained from other language skills.

Kang, O., & Ginther, A. (Eds.). (2018). *Assessment in second language pronunciation*. Routledge.

This volume covers a range of topics relevant to L2 pronunciation assessment, including issues of validity, scale usage, and listener/rater distinctions. It also includes multiple chapters on technology usage in L2 speech assessment.

References

Abrahamsson, N., & Hyltenstam, K. (2009). Age of onset and nativelikeness in a second language: Listener perception versus linguistic scrutiny. *Language learning*, *59*(2), 249–306. https://doi.org/10.1111/j.1467-9922.2009.00507.x

Bent, T., & Bradlow, A. (2003). The interlanguage speech intelligibility benefit. *The Journal of the Acoustical Society of America*, *114*(3), 1600–1610. https://doi.org/10.1121/1.1603234

Brown, J. D. (2014). The future of world Englishes in language testing. *Language Assessment Quarterly*, *11*(1), 5–26. https://doi.org/10.1080/15434303.2013.869817

Choi, I. (2017). Empirical profiles of academic oral English proficiency from an international teaching assistant screening test. *Language Testing*, *34*(1), 49–82. https://doi.org/10.1177/0265532215601881

Crowther, D., Trofimovich, P., & Isaacs, T. (2016). Linguistic dimensions of second language accent and comprehensibility: Nonnative listeners' perspectives. *Journal of Second Language Pronunciation*, *2*(2), 160–182. https://doi.org/10.1075/jslp.2.2.02cro

Crowther, D., Trofimovich, P., Saito, K., & Isaacs, T. (2015). Second language comprehensibility revisited: Investing the effects of learner background. *TESOL Quarterly*, *49*(4), 814–837. https://doi.org/10.1002/tesq.203

Davis, L. (2009). The influence of interlocutor proficiency in a paired oral assessment. *Language Testing*, *26*(3), 367–396. https://doi.org/10.1177/0265532209104667

Derwing, T. M., & Munro, M. J. (2015). *Pronunciation fundamentals: Evidence-based perspectives for L2 teaching and research*. John Benjamins.

Derwing, T. M., Rossiter, M. J., Munro, M. J., & Thomson, R. I. (2004). Second language fluency: Judgments on different tasks. *Language Learning*, *54*(4), 655–679. https://doi.org/10.1111/j.1467-9922.2004.00282.x

Eckman, F. R. (2018). Theoretical L2 phonology. In O. Kang, R. I. Thomson, & J. M. Murphy (Eds.), *The Routledge handbook of contemporary English pronunciation* (pp. 25–38). Routledge.

Field, J. (2005). Intelligibility and the listener: The role of lexical stress. *TESOL Quarterly*, *39*(3), 399–423. https://doi.org/10.2307/3588487

Flege, J. E., Munro, M. J., & MacKay, I. R. A. (1995). Effects of age of second-language learning on the production of English consonants. *Speech Communication*, *16*(1), 1–26. https://doi.org/10.1016/0167-6393(94)00044-B

Fulcher, G. (2014). *Testing second language speaking*. Routledge.

Galaczi, E. D. (2008). Peer–peer interaction in a speaking test: The case of the First Certificate in English examination. *Language Assessment Quarterly*, *5*(2), 89–119. https://doi.org/10.1080/15434300801934702

Harding, L. (2017). What do raters need in a pronunciation scale? The users' view. In T. Isaacs & P. Trofimovich (Eds.), *Second language pronunciation assessment* (pp. 12–34). Multilingual Matters.

Huang, B., Alegre, A., & Eisenberg, A. (2016). A cross-linguistic investigation on the effects of raters' accent familiarity on speaking assessment. *Language Assessment Quarterly*, *13*(1), 25–41. https://doi.org/10.1080/15434303.2015.1134540

Isaacs, T. (2018). Shifting sands in second language pronunciation teaching and assessment research and practice. *Language Assessment Quarterly*, *15*(3), 273–293. https://doi.org/10.1080/15434303.2018.1472264

Isaacs, F, & Trofimovich, P. (Eds.). (2017). *Second language pronunciation assessment*. Multilingual Matters.
Isaacs, T., Trofimovich, P., Yu, G., & Muńoz Chereau, B. (2015). Examining the linguistic aspects of speech that most efficiently discriminate between upper levels of the revised IELTS pronunciation scale. IELTS Research Reports Series, *4*, 1–48. https://www.ielts.org/-/media/research-reports/ielts_online_rr_2015-4.ashx
Jenkins, J. (2000). *The phonology of English as an international language*. Oxford University Press.
Kang, O. (2012). Impact of rater characteristics and prosodic features of speaker accentedness on ratings of international teaching assistants' oral performance. *Language Assessment Quarterly*, *9*(3), 249–269. https://doi.org/10.1080/1543403.2011.642631
Kang, O., & Ginther, A. (Eds.). (2018). *Assessment in second language pronunciation*. Routledge.
Kang, O., & Moran, M. (2014). Functional loads of pronunciation features in nonnative speakers' oral assessment. *TESOL Quarterly*, *48*(1), 176–187. https://doi.org/10.1002/tesq.152
Kang, O., Rubin, D., & Pickering, L. (2010). Suprasegmental measures of accentedness and judgments of language learner proficiency in oral English. *The Modern Language Journal*, *94*(4), 554–566. https://doi.org/10.1111/j.1540-4781.2010.01091.x
Kang, O., Thomson, R. I., & Moran, M. (2018). Empirical approaches to measuring the intelligibility of different varieties of English in predicting listener comprehension. *Language Learning*, *68*(1), 115–146. https://doi.org/10.1111/lang/12270
Kennedy, S., Guénette, D., Murphy, J., & Allard, S. (2015). Le rôle de la prononciation dans l'intercompréhension entre locuteurs de français lingua franca [The role of pronunciation in comprehension between speakers of French as a lingua franca]. *Canadian Modern Language Review*, *71*(1), 1–25. https://doi.org/10.3138/cmlr.2139
Lado, R. (1961). *Language testing: The construction and use of foreign language tests*. Longman.
Lambert, W. E., Hodgson, R. C., Gardner, R. C., & Fillenhaum, S. (1960). Evaluational reactions to spoken languages. *Journal of Abnormal and Social Psychology*, *60*(1), 44–51. https://doi.org/10.1037/h0044430
Levis, J. M. (2005). Changing contexts and shifting paradigms in pronunciation teaching. *TESOL Quarterly*, *39*(3), 369–377. https://doi.org/10.2307/3588485
Litman, D., Strik, H., & Lim, G. S. (2018). Speech technologies and the assessment of second language speaking: Approaches, challenges, and opportunities. *Language Assessment Quarterly*, *15*(3), 294–309. https://doi.org/10.1080/15434303.2018.1472265
Loewen, S., & Isbell, D. (2017). Pronunciation in face-to-face and audio-only synchronous computer-mediated learner interactions. *Studies in Second Language Acquisition*, *39*(2), 225–256. https://doi.org/10.1017/S0272263116000449
Low, E. L., & Pakir, A. (2018). *World Englishes: Rethinking paradigms*. Routledge.
MacKenzie, I. (2014). *English as a lingua franca: Theorizing and teaching English*. Routledge.
May, L. (2011). Interactional competence in a paired speaking test: Features salient to raters. *Language Assessment Quarterly*, *8*(2), 127–145. https://doi.org/10.1080/15434303.2011.565845
Moyer, A. (1999). Ultimate attainment in L2 phonology: The critical factors of age, motivation, and instruction. *Studies in Second Language Acquisition*, *21*(1), 81–108. https://doi.org/10.1017/S0272263199001035
Munro, M. J., & Derwing, T. M. (1995). Foreign accent, comprehensibility, and intelligibility in the speech of second language learners. *Language Learning*, *45*(1), 73–97. https://doi.org/10.1111/j.1467-1770.1995.tb00963.x
Munro, M. J., & Derwing, T. M. (2006). The functional load principle in ESL pronunciation instruction: An exploratory study. *System*, *34*(4), 520–531. https://doi.org/10.1016/j.system.2006.09.004
Munro, M. J., & Derwing, T. M. (2008). Segmental acquisition in adult ESL learners: A longitudinal study of vowel production. *Language Learning*, *58*(3), 479–502. https://doi.org/10.1111/j.1467-9922.2008.00448.x
Munro, M. J., & Derwing, T. M. (2015). A prospectus for pronunciation research in the 21st century: A point of view. *Journal of Second Language Pronunciation*, *1*(1), 11–42. https://doi.org/10.1075/jslp.1.1.01mun
Nelson, C. L. (1982). Intelligibility and nonnative varieties of English. In B. B. Kachru (Ed.), *The other tongue: English across cultures* (pp. 58–73). University of Illinois Press.
Nguyen, T. T. A., & Ingram, J. (2005). Vietnamese acquisition of English word stress. *TESOL Quarterly*, *39*(2), 309–319. https://doi.org/10.2307/3588314
Nitta, R., & Nakatsuhara, F. (2014). A multifaceted approach to investigating pre-task planning effects on paired oral test performance. *Language Testing*, *31*(2), 147–175. https://doi.org/10.1177/0265532213514401

Ockey, G. (2011). Self-consciousness and assertiveness as explanatory variables in of L2 oral ability: A latent variable approach. *Language Learning*, *61*(3), 968–989. https://doi.org/10.1111/j.1467-9922.2010.00625.x

Ockey, G. J. (2009). The effects of group members/ personalities on a test taker's L2 group oral discussion test scores. *Language Testing*, *26*(2), 161–186. https://doi.org/10.1177/0265532208101005

Ockey, G. J., & French, R. (2014). From one to multiple accents on a test of L2 listening comprehension. *Applied Linguistics*, *37*(5), 693–715. https://doi.org/10.1093/applin/amu060

Ordin, M., & Polyanskaya, L. (2015). Acquisition of speech rhythm in a second language by learners with rhythmically different native languages. *The Journal of the Acoustical Society of America*, *138*(2), 533–544. https://doi.org/10.1121/1.4923359

Plough, I. C., & Bogart, P. S. (2008). Perceptions of examiner behavior modulate power relations in oral performance testing. *Language Assessment Quarterly*, *5*(3), 195–217. https://doi.org/10.1080/15434300802229375

Saito, K., Trofimovich, P., & Isaacs, T. (2017). Using listener judgments to investigate linguistic influences on L2 comprehensibility and accentedness: A validation and generalization study. *Applied Linguistics*, *38*(4), 439–462. https://doi.org/10.1093/applin/amv047

Solon, M., Long, A. Y., & Gurzynski-Weiss, L. (2017). Task complexity, language-related episodes, and production of L2 Spanish vowels. *Studies in Second Language Acquisition*, *39*(2), 347–380. https://doi.org/10.1017/S0272263116000425

Thompson, G. L., Cox, T. L., & Knapp, N. (2016). Comparing the OPI and the OPIc: The effect of test method on oral proficiency scores and student preference. *Foreign Language Annals*, *49*(1), 75–92. https://doi.org/10.1111/flan.12178

Trofimovich, P., & Isaacs, T. (2012). Disentangling accent from comprehensibility. *Bilingualism: Language and Cognition*, *15*(4), 905–916. https://doi.org/10.1017/S1366728912000168

Van Moere, A., & Suzuki, M. (2018). Using speech processing technology in assessing pronunciation. In O. Kang & A. Ginther (Eds.), *Assessment in second language pronunciation* (pp. 137–152). Routledge.

Winke, P., Gass, S., & Myford, C. (2013). Raters' L2 background as a potential source of bias in rating oral performance. *Language Testing*, *30*(2), 231–252. https://doi.org/10.1177/0265532212456968

Yan, X., & Ginther, A. (2018). Listeners and raters: Similarities and differences in evaluation of accented speech. In O. Kang & A. Ginther (Eds.), *Assessment in second language pronunciation* (pp. 67–88). Routledge.

24
Measuring L2 Pragmatics

Veronika Timpe-Laughlin & Soo Jung Youn

Background

Crystal (1997) described pragmatics as "the study of language from the point of view of users, especially of the choices they make, the constraints they encounter in using language in social interaction, and the effects their use of language has on other participants in the act of communication" (p. 301). Accordingly, second language (L2) pragmatic competence constitutes the ability to use the target language in a given sociocultural context relative to different interlocutors. Thus, pragmatics is concerned with the complex interplay between linguistic forms, social actions, and meaning in language use contexts or how interlocutors deploy form-function-context mappings to achieve specific communicative goals (Taguchi & Roever, 2017).

Pragmatics is a key component of communicative language ability (Timpe-Laughlin, Wain, & Schmidgall, 2015) that has spurred a "flurry of research" (Roever, 2006, p. 229) in both SLA and language testing. SLA researchers have investigated the development of L2 pragmatics, focusing in particular on developmental trajectories, cross-linguistic transfer, and learning processes (Bardovi-Harlig, 2012; Kasper & Rose, 2002). By contrast, research concerned with the assessment of L2 pragmatics has generally focused on the feasibility of assessing social language use. Although both strands of research focus on slightly different aspects, they are both concerned with how to define the nature of pragmatic ability, how to elicit pragmatic behaviors using suitable instruments, and how to measure the development of L2 pragmatics.

Overall, measuring L2 pragmatics provides valuable insights into L2 learners' pragmatic knowledge and abilities to perform communicative actions using the target language. These insights into L2 pragmatic development can then be used by teachers, students, and potential employers to aid instruction and learning or the selection of candidates for specific tasks. Additionally, SLA researchers may benefit from theoretical and practical developments in L2 pragmatics assessment insofar as the insights may help to (a) select suitable instruments to elicit pragmatic behaviors for the purpose of exploring learning and (b) lend support to determine what constitutes more or less effective use of language in context. Hence, if we aim to understand how L2 learners learn and use their linguistic repertoire to generate meaning and carry out communicative acts when interacting with different interlocutors in diverse communicative contexts, assessing pragmatics is key.

L2 Pragmatic Competence: From a Rationalist Speech Act Perspective to a Discursive View

Early conceptualizations of pragmatics are mostly rooted in three rationalist, philosophical theories: speech act theory (Searle, 1976), politeness theory (Brown & Levinson, 1987), and Grice's (1975) theory of conversational implicature. Searle (1976) coined the term *speech act* which denotes various types of communicative actions (e.g., request, refusal, apology) that have become the fundamental unit of analysis in traditional L2 pragmatics research. When analyzing speech acts, researchers mainly draw upon three contextual variables derived from politeness theory—power difference between a speaker and a hearer, social distance, and imposition— to examine how speakers intentionally select linguistic means to encode speech acts in a given communicative context. Grice's (1975) theory of conversational implicature focused on understanding or inferring non-literal meaning in utterances using contextual information. Together, these theories underpin the traditional and rationalist approach to pragmatics. Accordingly, learners' knowledge of linguistic conventions, their abilities to infer implied meaning, and use pragmatic strategies appropriate to the pragmatic intention have been emphasized heavily in pragmatics research.

Informed by these philosophical theories, L2 pragmatics features prominently in earlier models of communicative competence (e.g., Bachman & Palmer, 1996; Canale & Swain, 1980), which primarily depict pragmatic competence as consisting of two dimensions: functional and sociolinguistic knowledge. Functional knowledge or pragmalinguistics (Leech, 1983) is concerned with learners' understanding of appropriate linguistic tools to achieve various communicative functions. It refers to the linguistic means necessary to achieve pragmatic meaning and comprehend speakers' intentions. Sociolinguistic knowledge or sociopragmatics (Leech, 1983) refers to learners' understanding of contextual variables such as social norms, conventions, and rules that influence appropriate language use and interpretation in various contexts. In sum, this rationalist view of pragmatics focuses predominantly on the goal a speaker hopes to achieve with a particular speech act (i.e., illocutionary force) and the linguistic forms they select to realize it.

However, critics of the rationalist pragmatics view have argued that such theories risk underrepresenting how L2 learners jointly organize their turns while employing interactional resources to accomplish pragmatic actions (Kasper, 2006; Roever, 2011). Conversation Analysis-based studies have documented how learners' ability to organize turns and utilize linguistic resources for pragmatic actions develop over time (Al-Gahtani & Roever, 2012; Pekarek-Doehler & Berger, 2018), and critics have argued for a discursive approach to speech act pragmatics grounded in Conversation Analysis (CA). This approach aligns with more recent frameworks of communicative competence such as Celce-Murcia's (2007) model of communicative competence, which explicitly defines varying components of pragmatic competence in spoken interaction, including learners' *conversational knowledge* of conventional turn-taking systems and *actional competence* of accomplishing various speech acts. The discursive approach to pragmatics therefore broadens the rationalist construct definition by including learners' abilities to accomplish pragmatic meaning and actions in jointly organized sequences using diverse interactional and linguistic resources (Kasper & Ross, 2013).

Both rationalist and discursive approaches to pragmatics play key roles in how the construct has been defined and operationalized for the purposes of assessment. The rationalist tradition tends to focus on the ability to employ pragmatic strategies and linguistic resources to accomplish speech acts, specifying appropriate language for certain situations. The discursive approach focuses on the ability to organize pragmatic resources across turns in interaction, thus suggesting an assessment approach in which speakers collaborate to accomplish communicative goals. Depending on the L2 pragmatic dimensions to be assessed, one needs to carefully orient to the existing pragmatic theories as a basis of construct definition.

Key Concepts

***Pragmatic competence*:** The ability to *use* language appropriately (from a cultural and social perspective) in different situations relative to different interlocutors in order to achieve specific communicative goals.

***Interactional competence*:** The ability to successfully utilize knowledge about participation patterns, turn-taking, register, and pragmatics when co-constructing meaning in a communicative exchange with interlocutors.

***Speech acts*:** Expressions that present information and serve a certain communicative function such as requests or apologies.

***Discourse completion tasks (DCT)*:** Means of eliciting certain speech acts. Traditionally, DCTs tend to include the description of a situation (i.e., the prompt), an utterance made by a putative interlocutor, and a space for test-takers to write what they would say in that specific situation.

***Role-play*:** A type of performance assessment oftentimes used to elicit specific pragmatic phenomena in talk-in-interaction. When engaging in a role-play, test-takers act out a specific part and scenario with one or more interlocutors.

Key Issues

The short history of the field of L2 pragmatics assessment can be broadly categorized into three phases (Roever, Fraser, & Elder, 2014): (1) the sociopragmatic phase, focusing on assessing speech acts in a cross-cultural perspective, (2) the pragmalinguistic phase, focusing on assessing additional sub-components of the larger L2 pragmatics construct (e.g., implicatures and routine formulae), and (3) the interaction phase, focusing on assessing discursive pragmatics by means of interactive, performance-based measures. Accordingly, L2 pragmatics assessments have progressed from primarily discrete-skills measures to more discursive, performance-based assessments, aiming to elicit pragmatic phenomena in talk-in-interaction.

Sociopragmatics, Speech Acts, and Discourse Completion Tasks

Influenced by interlanguage pragmatics research and rationalist theories, early L2 pragmatics measures focused predominantly on the assessment of speech acts in cross-cultural settings. In line with politeness theory (Brown & Levinson, 1987) and the theory of speech acts (Searle, 1976), researchers who developed the first L2 pragmatics assessments in the 1990s tended to view test-takers as individual, rational actors who use their linguistic repertoire in order to achieve a particular intended communicative goal (Kasper, 2006; Youn & Bogorevich, 2019). It was assumed that speakers would first decide what communicative act to carry out, and then use their available linguistic resources to realize the speech act. Kasper (2006) referred to this conceptualization as the "intention-plus-convention model" (p. X), arguing that "speakers first determine the illocutionary force, propositional content, and politeness they intend to convey and then proceed to 'realize' these pragmatic intentions by selecting appropriate 'conventions of means' and 'conventions of form'" (p. 295f.).

Against this backdrop, most of the early L2 pragmatics assessments were based on discourse completion tasks (DCTs) in order to measure L2 learners' sociopragmatic competence (see Figure 24.1 for a sample written DCT). Hudson, Detmer, and Brown (1992, 1995) developed the first large-scale cross-cultural pragmatics assessment battery to measure Japanese ESL learners' sociopragmatic abilities in using the speech acts of request, refusal, and apology. It included three types of DCTs: 24 paper-and-pencil *written DCTs* that required test-takers to write down

Situation: You want to apply for a job in a small office. You want to get an application form. You go to the office and see the office manager sitting behind a desk.

You:

____

____

____

Figure 24.1 A sample written DCT (Hudson, Detmer, & Brown, 1995, p. 89).

what they would say in reaction to certain prompts, 24 paper-and-pencil *multiple choice DCTs* (MCDCTs) in which respondents were asked to mark the appropriate utterance for a given situation among three answer options, and 24 *oral DCTs* in which examinees' verbal reaction to certain prompts were audio-recorded. Additionally, Hudson et al. turned eight DCT situations into role-plays to be acted out with trained interlocutors that aimed to elicit the three targeted speech acts. Consistent with the underpinning rationalist theories, test-takers' DCT responses and role-play performances were evaluated by trained native speaker raters, using a 5-point scale ranging from "very unsatisfactory" to "completely appropriate" to evaluate responses across different criteria, including the ability to use the correct speech act, formulaic expressions, amount of information, degree of formality, directness, and politeness. They reported reasonable results with reliabilities ranging from .75 for the role-plays to .86 for the written DCTs (see Brown, 2008). Only the MCDCTs showed lower reliabilities—a finding that was also observable across several spin-off studies that investigated L2 learners' pragmatic competence in different language learning contexts (e.g., Brown & Ahn, 2011; Liu, 2007; Tada, 2005; Timpe, 2013; Yamashita, 1996; Yoshitake, 1997). A potential reason for the relatively low reliability of MCDCTs could be the challenge to write distractors that are clearly unacceptable, but still plausible.

Overall, Hudson, Detmer, and Brown were able to produce a test battery with good psychometric qualities. In this sense the tests "worked" as assessment tools. However, the standard for a "correct" response relied on the intuitions of native speakers who were rating the role-play performances and DCT responses. Thus, the DCTs were used as a measure of pragmatic knowledge and ability to realize a targeted speech act in "*the* correct way"—an approach reflective of the rationalist tradition.

The use and popularity of DCTs in the sociopragmatics-oriented, speech act focused assessments following Hudson et al. (1995) is not surprising as DCTs have a number of advantages. They allow test developers to systematically implement context variables such as differences between interlocutors with regard to power, distance, and imposition. They are fairly easy to administer large-scale, tend to be rather efficient with regard to scoring, and are thus rather practical elicitation devices. However, while they may capture test-takers' offline knowledge of semantic formulae, they are "far from faithful emulations of actual conversation" (Roever, 2014, p. 127). Responses are not constructed under the pressure of real time communication and test-takers therefore oftentimes respond in a way they think they would respond in that situation, which is not necessarily how they actually respond in real-life interactions (Golato, 2003).

Also, many studies utilized native speaker (NS) judgments to gauge appropriateness—an aspect that is highly critical insofar as "judgments of what is and what is not appropriate differ widely among NSs and are probably more a function of personality and social background variables than of language knowledge" (McNamara & Roever, 2006, p. 57). In sum, although these early assessments constituted an important first step toward measuring L2 pragmatics, they focused heavily on only a small part of the larger construct, while neglecting pragmatic dimensions such as pragmalinguistics, implicatures, and extended discursive interaction.

Jack is talking to his housemate Sarah about another housemate, Frank.

Jack: 'Do you know where Frank is, Sarah?'

Sarah: 'Well, I heard music from his room earlier.'

What does Sarah probably mean?

1. **Frank forgot to turn the music off.**
2. **Frank's loud music bothers Sarah.**
3. **Frank is probably in his room.**
4. **Sarah doesn't know where Frank is.**

Figure 24.2 Sample of a multiple-choice implicature comprehension item (Roever, 2006, p. 238).

Pragmalinguistics and Technology

In response to these relatively narrow, sociopragmatics-oriented construct representations, a stronger focus on the pragmalinguistic dimension began to emerge coupled with further advances in technology. Roever (2006) developed a web-based test battery that operationalized further construct dimensions in three distinct test sections. The first section aimed at assessing the comprehension of implicatures via computer-scored multiple-choice items (Figure 24.2), the second section targeted comprehension of routine formulae, also assessed via computer-scored multiple-choice items, and the third part consisted of rater-scored DCTs with rejoinders that assessed the production of requests, apologies, and refusals (for a discussion see Roever, Fraser, & Elder, 2014). Supposedly, Roever's assessment was also culturally agnostic in the sense that the test was not designed for a specific cross-cultural context. Administering the assessment battery to 335 EFL and ESL learners in Germany, Australia, and Japan, Roever (2011) reported relatively high reliability estimates for the different sections, ranging between .71 (routine section) and .89 (speech act part). Also, factor analysis showed distinct factors for the three sections, providing evidence that these skills represented separate aspects of the construct of pragmalinguistic ability (Roever, Fraser & Elder, 2014).

Still operating within the speech act tradition, Roever and similar studies (e.g., Itomitsu, 2009) broadened the scope of L2 pragmatics assessment, shifting it from a narrower focus on speech acts, politeness, and appropriateness to a more pragmalinguistic orientation with a conventionality-correctness focus. While this was an important next step as they added a stronger focus on reception, their operationalization underrepresented a key component: context. Their items were limited with regard to relationships between interlocutors and the co-constructed nature of pragmatics in talk-in-interaction (Roever, Fraser, & Elder, 2014)—aspects that drive current work in the third phase of L2 pragmatics assessment.

Discursive Pragmatics and Interaction

To develop a more comprehensive construct representation, recent L2 pragmatics assessment studies have drawn upon CA in order to inform their test instruments and scoring procedures (Kasper & Ross, 2013; Roever & Kasper, 2018), thus aiming to account for the co-constructed, sequential unfolding of pragmatic meaning across multiple turns in real-life conversations. Criticizing the lack of correspondence between pragmatic phenomena elicited via DCTs and empirical real-life talk-in-interaction data, Walters (2007, 2009) developed a test battery that was informed by CA findings. First, Walters (2007) examined how pragmatic actions, such as compliments, are accomplished turn-by-turn by interlocutors, focusing on turn organizations of compliments and evaluations. Then, he used directed 10–15 minute role-plays to assess 27 NSs of English and 42 ESL learners in the United States with regard to three pragmatic actions: evaluation responses, compliment responses, and pre-sequence responses. Additionally, he used two CA-trained raters to evaluate these phenomena using a 4-point rubric. He attained very low interrater agreement estimates of .2 for the role-plays which makes reliable inferences questionable. However, despite the reliability issues, Walters' (2007, 2009) approach was innovative and critical insofar as it showed how CA could be used to inform test design and scoring procedures in L2 pragmatics assessment.

In recent years, researchers and test developers have further refined Walters' (2007) original approach, applying it to the measurement of L2 pragmatics in extended discourse (Grabowski, 2009; Youn, 2015). For example, Youn (2015) incorporated an interactional focus that was rooted in discursive pragmatics (Kasper, 2006) and interactional competence (Hall & Pekarek Doehler, 2011). Based on a thorough task-based needs analysis of interactions in a university setting (Youn, 2018), Youn developed different role-plays: two requests and a refusal to a person of a higher status, and a negotiation of meaning with a peer. Administering the role-plays to 102 ESL learners with different L1s and ESL proficiency levels, Youn analyzed the performance data qualitatively using CA and quantitatively deploying multifaceted Rasch measurement. She identified performance markers for learners at different levels of proficiency which she then used to inform the design of her scoring rubrics that included five rating criteria on a three-point scale: turn organization, engagement with interaction, sensitivity to situation, content delivery, and language use. Especially the first two criteria provided insights into how test-takers deployed pragmatic actions in conversations.

The discursive approach to assessing L2 pragmatics has certainly led to higher levels of authenticity and construct representation by measuring pragmatics as a jointly constructed phenomenon in more interactive formats that resemble real-life conversations. Most of the studies have focused on spoken interaction, however, with pragmatics phenomena in L2 writing largely absent. Also, most tests and assessments in this tradition have used role-plays to operationalize and approximate authentic talk-in-interaction. However, role-plays tend to be time- and resource-intensive with regard to administration and scoring. Furthermore, these assessments have oftentimes been conducted in the context of research studies and thus low-stakes contexts, so it remains questionable what inferences and claims can be made relative to learners' real-world performances.

Recommendations for Practice

In order to choose or develop an appropriate pragmatics measure, it may help to take into account a key question: *What is the intended use of the pragmatics assessment?* Establishing the goal or purpose of a pragmatics assessment will determine *what* is supposed to be measured, *why* it is measured, *who* will take the test, and *how* the test-based information is supposed to be utilized. While these questions (see also Testing tips) need to be answered for any assessment (see Norris (2012) for a detailed discussion), there are certain aspects that should be taken into account in particular when measuring L2 learner's ability to make connections between linguistic forms, communicative functions, and the given context.

Which Pragmatics Features Should Be Included?

The construct of pragmatics is complex to say the least. It includes phenomena as different as speech acts, routine formulae, reactive tokens, politeness markers, speech styles, address forms, discourse strategies, and hedging (see Taguchi & Kim, 2018). Therefore, it is impractical, if not impossible, to cover the entire construct in any individual assessment. Researchers or test developers have to select features of the construct that are of interest for their specific context or purpose. For example, if the goal of an assessment is to find out if a learner in a university setting can ask a professor in a polite and appropriate way for an extension of a term paper, feedback on a report, or a letter of recommendation, requests would be the phenomenon that should constitute the focus of the pragmatics assessment. By contrast, if the goal is to identify a customer service representative who can write polite emails that reassure worried clients, then the pragmatic focus may need to be placed on features such as salutations, tone, and genre (i.e., how to write an "assurance" email). Investigation of the target language use (TLU) context (through observations, corpora, or research studies) can help determine which pragmatic features to focus on in an assessment.

DCTs or Role-Plays?

Most of the studies reviewed above utilized DCTs or role-plays to elicit pragmatic phenomena. However, it is important to keep in mind the relative advantages and limitations of DCTs and role-plays. For example, if the goal is to test learners' offline pragmatic *knowledge*, DCTs may constitute a valuable elicitation device. By contrast, if the goal is to evaluate online pragmatic *performance*, how a learner produces or comprehends pragmatic meaning in interaction, then role-plays will provide stronger evidence of the ability to use pragmatic knowledge in actual communication. And conversely, cognitive demands during interaction may obscure learners' knowledge of pragmatic forms.

For example, Safont (2004) examined the effect of explicit instruction on L2 request acquisition using DCTs and role-plays. She reported that post-test results from written DCT data revealed more noticeable changes in learners' request strategies, compared to the strategies elicited from role-plays. More processing demand required in role-plays than DCTs might explain the different outcomes. This does not necessarily indicate the advantage of DCTs over role-plays; instead, it shows that students may have the pragmatic knowledge to write down a request but may not be able to use this knowledge in real time. When researchers examine the instructional effect on L2 pragmatics, DCTs may provide insights into learners' knowledge, while role-plays might be appropriate as outcome measures when pragmatic targets of interest require *performance* and online processing in interactive discourse.

How to Establish Benchmark Criteria?

Pragmatic norms (i.e., what is and what is not appropriate) can vary from one context to the next and even among speakers in the same situation. Therefore, appropriateness can be described as a "moving target" and test developers or researchers should follow certain steps to establish a benchmark or norm. First, they need to determine what kinds of behavior need to be elicited or observed in order to draw inferences about learners' pragmatic ability in a certain context, as mentioned earlier. Observations, corpora, or analyses of discourse also provide insights into what stronger and weaker performance "looks like" for that specific situation. Analyses of language use also lead to decisions regarding whether test-takers' performances will be evaluated against a native speaker norm, a certain target language variety, or an intercultural context in which the L2 is used as a *lingua franca*. In short, the assessment of L2 pragmatics hinges upon the context of language use.

Once appropriate criteria are established, they will need to be comprised in a scoring rubric that raters can use to evaluate performances consistently. Therefore, scoring rubrics should include relevant descriptors and performance examples to describe the given criterion in a concrete, concise, and clear way. Additionally, raters should receive thorough training to ensure that they attend to the relevant criteria and apply the rubric consistently. Otherwise, raters might simply fall back onto their own potentially inappropriate intuitions.

Finally, test-takers' subjectivity and identity tend to be another source of variability. Research has found that sometimes individuals deliberately diverge from the target pragmatic norms in order to highlight their own cultural identity (e.g., Hassall, 2015). Hence, pragmatic choices are interconnected with individuals' (cultural) values and goals. To not penalize an L2 learner who makes an informed decision in the creation of a unique identity and diverges from target pragmatic behavior, it may make sense in some contexts to give test-takers an opportunity to justify why they adopted a particular register, strategy, or response style by building into the assessment a feedback component that minimizes potential bias and allows test-takers to verbalize their reasons, thus showing meta-pragmatic awareness.

In sum, researchers and test developers should consider taking four main steps when developing a pragmatics assessment. First, identify the intended use of the pragmatics assessment as the main driver for assessment development that will determine (a) the reference context about which inferences are to be made, (b) the construct focus, and (c) the test design. Second, it is important to feature in any pragmatics assessment task a well-defined communicative context or situation with an audience/interlocutor and a clear communicative goal. Then, the language used in the reference context should be examined through observations or empirical analyses to determine criteria and levels of performance that can be used in a scoring rubric. Finally, it is critical to train raters in applying the rubric in a consistent way.

Testing Tips

Five guiding questions relevant to L2 pragmatics assessment that may aid test developers and stakeholders in selecting and/or creating an L2 pragmatics measure:

- ***What is the purpose of the pragmatics assessment?***

It is important to consider the reason *why* an L2 pragmatics assessment is needed because different uses and purposes for measuring L2 pragmatics may require different approaches to implementing pragmatic assessments.

- ***Which features of L2 pragmatics should be measured by the assessment?***

Given the complexity of the nature of L2 pragmatics, test developers have to select the specific aspects of knowledge or performance that are of interest for their chosen context. Choices have to be made which will inevitably result in some aspects of the pragmatics construct not being included the assessment (Roever, 2011).

- ***How should pragmatic features be elicited?***

As a general rule of thumb, DCTs should be used for eliciting aspects of pragmatic knowledge, while role-plays may be better suited to elicit pragmatic performance in interaction. In any way, it is critical to contextualize the scenario presented to students in order to adequately allow for form-function-context mapping.

- ***What is the standard used for evaluation?***

One of the most challenging issues is to establish a benchmark or norm against which test-taker performances can be evaluated, given the variability in pragmatic norms across speech communities and communicative situations (Roever, 2014; Timpe-Laughlin et al., 2015; Timpe-Laughlin, 2018). To establish a benchmark or norm, test developers need analyses of performances in language use contexts to understand what good performance "looks like" for that specific situation and how L2 learners at different levels of pragmatic ability may realize the pragmatic feature.

- ***How will pragmatics assessment impact test-takers?***

When creating an assessment it is important to consider the potential positive and negative impacts that the assessment may have (Norris, 2012), and strive to maximize positive impact (e.g., increased implementation of pragmatics in L2 instruction) while minimizing potential negative impact (e.g., teaching pragmatics by means of DCTs to prepare students for the assessment).

Recommended Readings

Cohen, A. (2018). *Learning pragmatics from native and nonnative language teachers.* Multilingual Matters.

The chapter on "The assessment of pragmatics" focuses on measuring pragmatics in the context of the L2 classroom. Although primarily rooted in the rationalist speech act tradition, it provides a number of useful examples of different activities (mainly DCTs) and how they can be implemented in the context of research and learning-oriented assessments.

Taguchi, N., & Roever, C. (2017). *Second language pragmatics*. Oxford University Press.

Taguchi and Roever offer a state-of-the-art overview of current research issues and practices of L2 pragmatics, describe methods to assess L2 pragmatics from the rationalist and discursive approaches, and propose future research directions for L2 pragmatics in English as a lingua franca.

Roever, C., & Kasper, G. (2018). Speaking in turns and sequences: Interactional competence as a target construct in testing speaking. *Language Testing*, *35*, 331–355. https://doi.org/10.1177%2F0265532218758128

This article presents an argument for integrating situational and social context of language use in speaking assessment. It illustrates how the discursive approach to interactional data contributes to the production of validity evidence.

References

Al-Gahtani, S., & Roever, C. (2012). Proficiency and sequential organization of L2 requests. *Applied Linguistics*, *33*(1), 42–65. https://doi.org/10.1093/applin/amr031

Bachman, L. F., & Palmer, A. S. (1996). *Language testing in practice: Designing and developing useful language tests*. Oxford University Press.

Bardovi-Harlig, K. (2012). Formulas, routines, and conventional expressions in pragmatics research. *Annual Review of Applied Linguistics*, *32*, 206–227. https://doi.org/10.1017/S0267190512000086

Brown, J. D. (2008). Raters, functions, item types and the dependability of L2 pragmatics tests. In E. Alcón Soler & A. Martínez-Flor (Eds.), *Investigating pragmatics in foreign language learning, teaching and testing* (pp. 224–248). Multilingual Matters.

Brown, J. D., & Ahn, R. C. (2011). Variables that affect the dependability of L2 pragmatics tests. *Journal of Pragmatics*, *43*(1), 198–217.

Brown, P., & Levinson, S. C. (1987). *Politeness: Some universals in language usage*. Cambridge University Press.

Canale, M., & Swain, M. (1980). Theoretical aspects of communicative approaches to second language teaching and testing. *Applied Linguistics*, *1*, 1–47. https://doi.org/10.1093/applin/I.1.1

Celce-Murcia, M. (2007). Rethinking the role of communicative competence in language teaching. In E. Alcón Soler & M. P. Safont Jordà (Eds.), *Intercultural language use and language learning* (pp. 41–57). Springer.

Crystal, D. (Ed.). (1997). *The Cambridge encyclopedia of language*. Cambridge University Press.

Golato, A. (2003). Studying compliment responses: A comparison of DCTs and recordings of naturally occurring talk. *Applied Linguistics, 21*, 90–121. https://doi.org/10.1093/applin/24.1.90
Grabowski, K. C. (2009). *Investigating the construct validity of a test designed to measure grammatical and pragmatic knowledge in the context of speaking* (Unpublished PhD dissertation). Columbia University, NY.
Grice, H. P. (1975). Logic and conversation. In P. Cole & J. Morgan (Eds.), *Syntax and semantics* (pp. 41–58). Academic Press.
Hall, J. K., & Pekarek Doehler, S. (2011). L2 interactional competence and development. In J. K. Hall, J. Hellermann, & S. Pekarek Doehler (Eds.), *L2 interactional competence and development* (pp. 1–15). Multilingual Matters.
Hassall, T. (2015). Individual variation in L2 study-abroad outcomes: A case study from Indonesian pragmatics. *Multilingua – Journal of Cross-Cultural and Interlanguage Communication, 34*, 33–59. https://doi.org/10.1515/mult-2013-0050
Hudson, T. D., Detmer, E., & Brown, J. D. (1992). *A framework for testing cross-cultural pragmatics* (Technical Report #2). University of Hawai'i, Second Language Teaching and Curriculum Center.
Hudson, T. D., Detmer, E., & Brown, J. D. (1995). *Developing prototype measures of cross-cultural pragmatics* (Technical Report #7). University of Hawai'i, Second Language Teaching and Curriculum Center.
Itomitsu, M. (2009). *Developing a test of pragmatics of Japanese as a foreign language* (Unpublished doctoral dissertation). Ohio State University, Columbus, OH.
Kasper, G. (2006). Speech acts in interaction: Towards discursive pragmatics. In K. Bardovi-Harlig, C. Félix-Brasdefer, & A. S. Omar (Eds.), *Pragmatics and language learning* (Vol. 11, pp. 281–314). Second Language Teaching and Curriculum Center, University of Hawai'i.
Kasper, G., & Rose, K. R. (2002). *Pragmatic development in a second language*. Blackwell.
Kasper, G., & Ross, S. (2013). Assessing second language pragmatics: An overview and introductions. In S. Ross & G. Kasper (Eds.), *Assessing second language pragmatics* (pp. 1–40). Palgrave Macmillan.
Leech, G. (1983). *Principles of pragmatics*. Longman.
Liu, J. (2007). Developing a pragmatics test for Chinese EFL learners. *Language Testing, 24*, 391–415. https://doi.org/10.1177%2F0265532207077206
McNamara, T. F., & Roever, C. (2006). *Language testing: The social dimension*. Blackwell.
Norris, J. M. (2012). Purposeful language assessment: Selecting the right alternative test. *English Teaching Forum, 3*, 41–45.
Pekarek Doehler, S., & Berger, E. (2018). L2 interactional competence as increased ability for context-sensitive conduct: A longitudinal study of story-openings. *Applied Linguistics, 39*, 555–578. https://doi.org/10.1093/applin/amw021
Roever, C. (2006). Validation of a web-based test of ESL pragmalinguistics. *Language Testing, 23*, 229–256. https://doi.org/10.1191/0265532206lt329oa
Roever, C. (2011). Testing of second language pragmatics: Past and future. *Language Testing, 28*, 463–481. https://doi.org/10.1177/0265532210394633
Roever, C. (2014). Assessing pragmatics. In A. J. Kunnan (Ed.), *The companion to language assessment* (pp. 125–139). John Wiley & Sons.
Roever, C., Fraser, C., & Elder, C. (2014). *Testing ESL sociopragmatics: Development and validation of a web-based test battery*. Peter Lang.
Roever, C., & Kasper, G. (2018). Speaking in turns and sequences: Interactional competence as a target construct in testing speaking. *Language Testing, 35*, 331–355. https://doi.org/10.1177/0265532218758128
Safont, M. P. (2004). An analysis of EAP learners' pragmatic production: A focus on request forms. *Ibérica, 8*, 23–39.
Searle, J. (1976). A classification of illocutionary acts. *Language in Society, 5*, 1–23.
Tada, M. (2005). *Assessment of ESL pragmatic production and perception using video prompts* (Unpublished doctoral dissertation). Temple University, Philadelphia, PA.
Taguchi, N., & Kim, Y. (2018). Task-based approaches to teaching and assessing pragmatics: An overview. In N. Taguchi & Y. Kim (Eds.), *Task-based approaches to teaching and assessing pragmatics* (pp. 1–24). John Benjamins. https://doi.org/10.1075/tblt.10.01tag
Taguchi, N., & Roever, C. (2017). *Second language pragmatics*. Oxford University Press.
Timpe, V. (2013). *Assessing intercultural language learning: The dependence of receptive sociopragmatic competence and discourse competence on learning opportunities and input*. Peter Lang.
Timpe-Laughlin, V. (2018). Pragmatics in task-based language assessment: Opportunities and challenges. In N. Taguchi & Y. Kim (Eds.), *Task-based approaches to teaching and assessing pragmatics* (pp. 287–304). John Benjamins. https://doi.org/10.1075/tblt.10.12tim

Timpe-Laughlin, V., Wain, J., & Schmidgall, J. (2015). *Defining and operationalizing the construct of pragmatic competence: Review and recommendations* (Research Report No. RR-15-06). Educational Testing Service.
Walters, F. S. (2007). A conversation-analytic hermeneutic rating protocol to assess L2 oral pragmatic competence. *Language Testing, 24*, 155–183. https://doi.org/10.1177/0265532207076362
Walters, F. S. (2009). A conversation analysis-informed test of L2 aural pragmatic comprehension. *TESOL Quarterly, 43*, 29–54. https://doi.org/10.1002/j.1545-7249.2009.tb00226.x
Yamashita, S. (1996). *Six measures of JSL pragmatics*. University of Hawai'i at Mānoa, National Foreign Languages Resource Center.
Yoshitake, S. (1997). *Interlanguage competence of Japanese students of English: A multi-test framework evaluation* (Unpublished doctoral dissertation). Columbia Pacific University, San Rafael, CA.
Youn, S. J. (2015). Validity argument for assessing L2 pragmatics in interaction using mixed methods. *Language Testing, 32*, 199–225. https://doi.org/10.1177/0265532214557113
Youn, S. J. (2018). Task-based needs analysis of L2 pragmatics in an EAP context. *Journal of English for Academic Purposes, 36*, 86–98.
Youn, S. J., & Bogorevich, V. (2019). Assessment in L2 pragmatics. In N. Taguchi (Ed.), *Routledge handbook of SLA and pragmatics* (pp. 308–321). Routledge.

25
Measuring L2 Reading

Eun Hee Jeon & Junko Yamashita

Background

Reading is a complex process which involves a coordination of multiple subcomponents (Grabe, 2012; Grabe & Stoller, 2019). Early measurement practices of reading primarily focused on simply assessing how well the reading skill functions without much concern for theoretical grounding (Hannon & Daneman, 2001). Since the 1970s, however, reading research has predominantly followed a multi-component approach, which assumes that reading comprehension draws from various knowledge (e.g., phonological, orthographical, lexical, or syntactic knowledge) and processing components (e.g., working memory, attention), and individual variation within each component must be examined to understand individual differences in reading comprehension. This theory-driven, multi-component approach substantially advanced our understanding of reading and contributed to the development and use of comprehensive reading test batteries, both by commercial test developers and researchers. For example, the TOEFL PBT—a regularly used standardized reading test among L2 reading researchers—includes vocabulary and grammar components built within the test. One drawback of administering comprehensive test batteries encompassing various reading components, however, is their lack of practicality; long testing sessions are taxing on test-takers and costly. To strike a balance between theoretical soundness and practicality, researchers have made some creative attempts. The Diagnostic Assessment of Reading Comprehension (DARC; see below) is, for example, a result of such efforts.

In the history of L2 reading measurement, the development of TOEFL 2000 (Internet Based TOEFL) materialized more modern thinking about reading comprehension processes and reading assessment. Enright et al. (2000) brought together three theoretical perspectives—the processing perspective, the task perspective, and the reader purpose perspective. Much in line with Second Language Acquisition (SLA) research on automaticity and skill development (DeKeyser, 2001), the processing perspective contends that the reader's processing efficiency of components such as decoding, word recognition, syntactic parsing, and working memory are the key factors of individual reading ability difference. The task perspective reflects more traditionally popular research interests within L2 testing, namely, the effects of text or task variables, and sees them as sources of individual variation in test performance. Lastly, the reader purpose perspective introduces Carver's (1997) work on different modes of reading depending on the reader's purpose (e.g., reading for general comprehension, reading to learn). Additionally, the idea of reading multiple texts to build an intertextual model was included in the framework, given its significant presence in academic reading (Goldman, 1997). This new framework introduced some important changes in TOEFL 2000. The task- and the reader-purpose perspectives, for example, led to the inclusion of more varied text and task types as well as more challenging reading tasks such as reading to learn or reading to integrate information. Compared to the reading subtest of the previous TOEFL, which mostly focused on reading to locate discrete information and reading for basic comprehension, these changes contributed to increasing the construct validity of TOEFL 2000 as a test of academic English proficiency and rendered the test more discriminating by raising the ceiling of the test scores (Enright et al., 2000).

Another important standardized test for assessing L2-English proficiency for educational purposes is IELTS (International English Language Testing System). Currently, IELTS has two modules: Academic and General Training. The former is for studies at the tertiary level or professional registration, and the latter for studies at the secondary level, non-academic training, or immigration. Accordingly, input texts in the reading test are different across the modules, with relatively longer texts on academic topics in Academic Reading and shorter texts on topics pertinent to everyday life and work-related issues in General Training Reading. However, both modules evaluate a similar set of reading achievements (e.g., reading for main ideas/details; understanding implied meanings; recognizing writer's opinions/purposes), and their scores are reported on the same 9-band scale (IELTS information for candidates, retrieved from www.ielts.org, August 24, 2018). Recent validation studies of IELTS reading tests examine whether test-taking processes adequately embody literacy activities in the target domains (e.g., Moore, Morton, Hall, & Wallis, 2015) and cognitive processes in a reading model by Khalifa and Weir (2009) (e.g., Bax, 2013). IELTS employs multiple item formats on any one passage (Alderson, 2000). Although this means extra care must be paid to ensure the test's reliability (Davis, 2008), including diverse item formats raises IELTS' ecological validity as different test-takers normally respond to text in different ways.

Historically, the typical study in SLA involved older L2 learners and this trend was also true of L2 reading and reading assessment research. However, there has been a rapidly growing body of research with young bilingual readers. Due to the historically strong presence of young immigrants and French-English bilingual children in the school system, the US and Canada have well-established research programs on bilingual literacy development (e.g., Carlisle et al., 1999; Chen et al., 2012), and now, with increasing influx of economic immigrants and refugees from conflict regions to the Nordic and Western European countries, biliteracy research is also growing fast in Europe. Compared to participants of L2 reading studies who are typically at least college age or older, participants of bilingual reading studies are younger, with ages ranging from Pre-Kindergarten to adolescence. They also differ from older L2 readers in that they are developing literacy skills in their L1 and L2 simultaneously, therefore, their L1 literacy skills vary more widely than among older L2 readers.

Bilingual reading studies are often borne out of the concern that language minority children lag behind their monolingual peers on standardized reading tests. Menken (2008) reported that English Language Learner (ELL) children score 20 to 50 points lower than their monolingual English-speaking children on standardized reading tests. Similarly, the US National Assessment of Educational Progress reported that ELL children scored 36 points lower than their English monolingual peers on the fourth-grade national reading assessment in 2010. As reading comprehension is fundamental to academic achievement, the use of well-designed reading tests to accurately assess students' reading abilities and to inform instruction is paramount. Researchers have pointed out, however, that existing assessment practices have not been without problems in respect to language minority children. In the following sections, we discuss these problems and suggest future directions.

Key Concepts

Reading: Of the many definitions of L2 reading available, we find Shiotsu's (2010) definition aptly captures the consensus within the field and is also in line with our componential approach to reading comprehension; Shiotsu (2010) defined "reading as a complex cognitive process that the individual is involved in while engaged with a written text" (p. 4).

Automaticity: For linguistic or cognitive processes to operate with accuracy and speed while consuming little to no cognitive resources, they must become automatic. Processes that have acquired automaticity are stable, ballistic (uncontrollable), and not subject to introspection. For the success of reading comprehension, acquiring automaticity in lower-level processes is important because this releases attentional resources for higher-level processes that are necessary to achieve comprehension.

Biliteracy: This refers to having reading and writing skills in two languages. It is important to note that bilingualism and biliteracy are distinctly different concepts because bilingualism does not guarantee biliteracy.

Key Issues

What a test measures and whether it measures what test developers intend to test (construct validity) is of a central concern in the measurement of reading abilities. Although test validation research until today has provided valuable insights, validation is an on-going process. Readers will see that the validity question underlies many key issues we discuss below.

Our current understanding of the measurement of reading comprehension can be summarized as follows. First, no single test can measure reading comprehension in its entirety. Conversely, a test of sufficient quality can measure some aspects of reading comprehension. Thus, oftentimes we need different tests to measure different aspects of reading comprehension. Second, even the same test (or the same test item/task) can measure different things for different readers because different readers may utilize different reading components as they respond to a test item. For instance, in order to answer a question about the meaning of a word in a context, some readers may simply use their vocabulary knowledge while others may guess its meaning from the context. Third, in practice, researchers are not always consistent in how they operationalize the same or similar constructs or what construct they aim to measure using the same test. In sum, there is no one perfect test, and a vast number of tests and test tasks have been used. Thus, we must make sometimes difficult decisions when we choose our reading tests. To provide an overview of how reading researchers have made such decisions when using tests of reading comprehension, we conducted a comprehensive review of 87 studies involving a L2 reading comprehension measure. All studies were published in journals of applied linguistics or related fields or in edited volumes. These studies were retrieved through a systematic search of 4 electronic databases and 29 journals. The earliest publication date of a journal searched was 1916 (first issue of *The Modern Language Journal*) and the search cut-off date was May 2017. Although these studies varied in their purposes, all of them followed the multi-componential approach to reading comprehension and adopted one or more measures of passage-level reading comprehension. Due to space limitations, the list of references appearing in Tables 25.1, 25.2 and 25.3 is provided in the following open access data repository (Jeon, 2020).

Use of Standardized Reading Tests

The summary in Tables 25.1 and 25.2 represent two different orientations of reading research mentioned above. Table 25.1 includes studies involving college-age or older L2 readers with

Table 25.1 Standardized reading tests used in L2 studies

Test Names	*Studies*
Adult Basic Learning Examination (MCQ)	Bernhardt & Kamil (1995)
College English Test (MCQ)	Shiotsu & Weir (2007)
Defense Language Proficiency Test (MCQ)	Winke (2013)
Gates MacGinities Reading Tests (CQ)	Li & Kirby (2015)
General Tests of English Language Proficiency (CQ)	Jeon (2011)
Graduate Record Examination (MCQ)	Zhang (2012)
Nelson-Denny Reading Test (MCTQ)	Erçtin & Alptekin (2013); Morrison (2004); Nassaji & Geva (1999)
Stanford Diagnostic Reading Measure (MCQ)	August (2006)
TESTCan (MCQ, Cloze)	Morrison (2004)
Test of English as a Foreign Language (Paper Based Test) (MCQ)	Choi et al. (2003); Harrington & Sawyer (1992); Irvine et al. (1974); Jiang et al. (2011); Kato (2009); Koda (1998); Olmez (2016); Shang (2010); Tsai et al. (2010); Yamashita & Shiotsu (2017)
Test of English Majors (Band 8) (MCQ)	Zhang (2012)

solid L1 literacy skills. Table 25.2, on the other hand, includes studies involving younger readers who are developing L1 and L2 literacy simultaneously in second or foreign language settings.

In both tables, the test item types appear in parentheses after the test name. Table 25.1 shows that the most commonly used standardized reading test among the L2 reading studies we reviewed is the reading comprehension section of TOEFL-PBT (10 studies), followed by the Nelson-Denny Reading Test (3 studies). In terms of the test item format, multiple-choice questions (MCQ) were by far the most popular choice. The popularity of MCQ by these mostly commercial, standardized tests may be attributed to the cost of test development and scoring procedures (Francis et al., 2005).

As can be seen in Table 25.2, among the bilingual reading studies, the Woodcock Language Proficiency Battery (WLPB), the Gates MacGinities-Reading Tests (GMRT), and the Gray Oral Reading Test (GORT) were the three most commonly used tests, appearing in eight, five, and three studies, respectively. As for the test item format, MCQ was again clearly the most popular choice, although a few tests also used cloze or gap-filling items alongside MCQ.

Research has shown that different standardized reading tests, despite their common use of certain item types (primarily MCQ and cloze), tap into different cognitive abilities, and, therefore, cannot be considered interchangeable. Although not involving L2, Keenan, Betjemann, and Olson (2008) is an important study that compared the GORT, the Qualitative Reading Inventory (QRI), the Woodcock-Johnson Passage Comprehension subtest (WJPC), and the Reading Comprehension test of the Peabody Individual Achievement Test (PIAT), the first two of which are also commonly used by L2 reading researchers. The results showed that the four tests were only moderately correlated, indicating that they were measuring different skills. The regression analysis results showed that decoding accounted for the most variance in PIAT and WJPC while listening comprehension accounted for the most variance in the GORT and QRI. The authors explained that this is because PIAT and WJPC both have short passages and involve cloze items which can be affected by word-level processing skills. The authors further noted that GORT and

Table 25.2 Standardized reading tests used in bilingual reading studies

Test Names	*Studies*
California Achievement Test (MCQ)	Carlisle et al. (1999)
Ein Leseverständnistest für Elementarschüler (MCQ)	Limbird et al. (2014)
Gates MacGinities Reading Tests (MCQ)	Crosson & Lesaux (2010); Jia et al. (2014); Kieffer & Lesaux (2008); Leider et al. (2013); Mancilla-Martinez & Lesaux (2010)
Gray Oral Reading Test (MCQ)	Grant et al. (2012); Jared et al.(2011); Pae & Sevick (2011)
Peabody Individual Achievement Test-Revised (MCQ)	Lam et al. (2012); Pasquarella et al. (2011)
Stanford Achievement Test (MCQ)	Baker et al. (2012); Kim (2012)
Tests Diagnostique de Lecture pour les Classes d'Immersion	Noonan et al. (1997)
Test of Sentence Reading Efficiency and Comprehension (Sentence verification)	Leider et al. (2013)
Wide Range Achievement Test–Expanded Edition (MCQ)	Wang et al. (2006)
Woodcock Language Proficiency Battery (MCQ)	August et al. (2006); Francis et al. (2006); Goodwin et al. (2015); Gottaro & Mueller (2009); Grant et al. (2012); Kieffer & Lesaux (2008); Mancilla-Martinez & Lesaux (2010); Proctor et al. (2005)
Woodcock-Munoz Language Survey (MCQ)	Leider et al. (2013); Swanson et al. (2011)
Woodcock-Johnson Psycho-Educational Battery-Revised (Gap-filling)	Lindsey et al. (2003)
Woodcock Language Proficiency Battery-Passage Comprehension subtest (Cloze)	Goodwin et al. (2015)
Woodcock Reading Mastery Tests (MCQ, Cloze)	Kim (2012); Rydland et al. (2012)

QRI scores are strongly predicted by the test-takers' listening comprehension abilities because the test questions are read to the test-takers.

A review of reading tests used in bilingual reading research reveals that most of them were standardized tests normed on monolingual readers. While it is now widely agreed that bilingual competence cannot be measured against monolingual standards (Cook, 1997), the use of these L1 reading tests on young bilingual readers may have been tolerated for practical reasons. As noted earlier, one key motivation of bilingual reading research is to ensure bilingual children's academic success in mainstream education settings populated by their monolingual peers. Notwithstanding the qualitative differences from their monolingual peers, the practical realities for bilingual readers are still the mainstream classrooms where they are expected to meet the milestones laid out for their monolingual peers and where they are assessed using monolingual standards. Whether these practical demands justify the indiscriminate use of L1 reading tests on bilingual readers or the lack of validation studies of such tests with bilingual children, however, must be critically examined. At a fundamental level, the interpretation of a norm-referenced test score is only meaningful and appropriate if the test-taker is from the norming population. Interpreting a bilingual child's score against the mismatching monolingual norm, therefore, is problematic as it can lead to misleading information about the child's reading abilities and furthermore, when fallen into untrained hands, risks stigmatizing bilingual readers as poor readers, and worse, poor learners. These concerns clearly call for validation studies of frequently used standardized reading tests with bilingual readers. Such validation studies would allow interpreting bilingual children's test scores appropriately and make it possible to compare how the same test functions differently (if at all) when assessing monolingual and bilingual readers (see also Brown & Bhatia, Chapter 37; Kormos & Taylor, Chapter 39, this volume).

Use of Researcher-Made Reading Tests

Table 25.3 summarizes the researcher-made reading tests used in L2 and bilingual (indicated by an asterisk) reading studies. We included both fixed-ratio (indicated by "F") and gap-filling (indicated by "G"; also known as random- and rational-deletion, respectively) cloze procedures in the category of "cloze." It is evident that, compared to those of standardized reading tests, the item types of researcher-made reading tests are much more diverse, featuring 17 different types of test items.

Among constructed response item types, written or oral recall tasks in L1 or L2 were the most common. Oral recall was used in two studies involving younger readers, while written recall tests were used in studies with older L2 readers. We suspect that this trend reflects the fact that younger readers typically do not yet have the writing skills suitable for written recall tasks either in their L1 or L2. For older L2 readers, far more studies used written recall in the readers' L1 than in L2. This decision probably reflects researchers' caution to avoid the effects of L2 writing proficiency as an extraneous variable (Lee, 1986).

The second most common item type was the cloze item for which both fixed-ratio and gap-filling procedures have been employed. The construct validity of cloze tests, especially whether they measure global-level comprehension, was once a hot topic in L2 testing research. While the debate remains open, Bachman (1985) provided a balanced insight; cloze tests generally contain various items that require different levels of linguistic and cognitive processing. Therefore, cloze tests can measure global-level text comprehension. However, fixed-ratio cloze tests, as they allow little control over item selection, are likely to include more items testing local-level comprehension or lexicogrammatical knowledge rather than global-level comprehension. Given this, a researcher who is interested in using a cloze test to measure global and local comprehension as well as lexicogrammatical knowledge is advised to use the gap-filling test rather than the fixed-ratio test. Further caution may also be necessary as there is a possibility that readers with different reading abilities tend to use different processes to answer questions as demonstrated by McCray and Brunfaut (2018) using banked gap-filling test items.

As for the selected-response item types, MCQ was again a popular choice for researcher-made reading tests. This trend underscores the popularity of the multiple-choice item type in reading research despite difficulties involved in writing good distractors and the threat of guessing by test-takers.

Components of Higher-Level Comprehension Processes

One critical purpose of componential approaches to reading is to identify variables causing reading ability differences and to inform teaching. To achieve this goal, we need information (test scores) on each component. Reading research has made greater advances in addressing lower-level components, with our understanding of higher-level components being left far behind, partly due to the lack of well-researched assessment tools for components of higher-level comprehension. A relatively new measure of reading comprehension called the DARC may have potential for filling this gap.

Table 25.3 In-house reading test item types used in L2 reading studies and bilingual reading studies

Test Item Types	*Studies*
Constructed response	
Written recall	Fontanini & Tomitch (2009); Haynes & Carr (1990)
Written recall in reader's L1	Barnett (1988); Brantmeier & Vanderplank (2008); Brisbois (1995); Chun & Payne (2004); Horiba (2012); Khaldieh (2001); Pulido & Hambrick (2008)
Oral recall (retell)	*Hoover & Gough (1990); *Lefrancois & Armand (2003)
Cloze (F=fixed ratio, G=gap-filling)	Bensoussan & Ramraz (1984, G); Carson et al. (1990, F); Harrington & Sawyer (1992, F); Koda (1992, F); Koda (1998, F); Tsai et al. (2010, G); Yamashita & Shiotsu (2017, G)
Summary completion	Walter (2004)
Open-ended questions	*Lefrancois & Armand (2003); *Siu & Ho (2015)
Short answer questions	Harsch & Hartig (2016); Koda (1992); *Li et al. (2012)
Sentence completion	Brantmeier & Vanderplank (2008)
Selected response	
Multiple choice	Alptekin & Erçtin (2009 made); Brantmeier & Vanderplank (2008); *Cheung et al. (2007); Chun & Payne (2004); *Edele & Stanat (2016); Fecteau (1999); Fontanini & Tomitch (2009); Harsch & Hartig (2016); Hawas (1990); Henning et al. (1981); Koda (1998); Larson (1983); Lee & Schallert (2014); *Lefrancois & Armand (2003); *Li et al. (2012); Mecartty (2000); Oh (2016); Park (2001); Payne et al. (2009); Rai et al. (2015); Sang et al. (1986); Shiotsu & Weir (2007);Shiotsu (2010); *Siu & Ho (2015); Van Gelderen et al. (2004)
Multiple choice cloze	Bensoussan & Ramraz (1984, G)
Forced choice cloze	*Geva & Ryan (1993, F)
T/F questions	*Edele & Stanat (2016)
Matching	Harsch & Hartig (2016)
Sentence verification tests	*Royer & Carlo (1991)
Summary completion test	Walter (2004)
Overall evaluation of the text	Olmez (2016)
Completing diagrams or tables	Harsch & Hartig (2016)

DARC was originally developed and validated for L1-English university students (Hannon & Daneman, 2001; Potts & Peterson, 1985), and also applied to the L1-Spanish ELL population in the elementary grades (e.g., August, Francis, Hsu, & Snow, 2006). It was designed to measure four components of higher-level comprehension processes: text memory, text inferencing, accessing background knowledge, and knowledge integration. The basic form of the DARC is as follows: Readers read a brief passage that describes relations among several entities (e.g., A is larger than B), some of which are pseudowords (making new information that readers learn from the text) and the rest are real words (providing clues to background knowledge that readers access in the process of comprehension). After reading the passage, readers answer questions that are designed to test the four components using a dichotomous answer format (true/false or yes/no). For the DARC to achieve its purpose, researchers must ensure that the linguistic level of the DARC is within the test-takers' language and print processing abilities so that the scores are not, or only minimally, affected by lower-level processes, and also that cognitive challenges are developmentally appropriate, considering factors such as age and culture. Extant research has lent support to the DARC's construct validity. For example, the DARC was less strongly related to word reading (August et al., 2006) and lower-level skills such as decoding or oral fluency (Francis et al., 2005) than standardized reading comprehension tests that were compared against DARC in those studies.

In Hannon and Daneman's (2001) study, the DARC was administered in about 30 minutes and predicted a substantial amount of variance in the Nelson-Denny test, displaying a much greater predictive power than vocabulary or memory scores. The researchers accordingly argued that the DARC would offer an efficient testing option in place of a large reading test battery. Albeit a valid argument, we must note that the participants of this study were L1-university students for whom reading variance was likely to be explained by higher-level processes. While evidence for validity, reliability, and practicality of the DARC has started emerging with young bilingual readers as well, continued research is necessary to ensure these findings are generalizable.

Recommendations for Practice

In our pursuit of construct validity, the first and foremost recommendation is to remain vigilant and specific about the purpose of measurement in a given context, and select or create tests that satisfy the purpose. From cognitive and developmental perspectives, it is critical to consider characteristics of test-takers, because sources of individual differences developmentally change. For instance, decoding is fundamental for young and novice readers, whereas inferencing is generally more important for older and more advanced readers.

Another important consideration concerns the social contexts of testing. For instance, L2 academic language tests such as TOEFL and IELTS assess reading comprehension abilities necessary in tertiary education in English speaking contexts. If the purpose of measurement is within the scope of these tests, items from these well-researched tests may be suitable. Although using measurement tools that are in popular use has some advantages, measurement purposes should always be given priority. This is well-illustrated by Alptekin and Erçetin's (2009) case. Despite common use of a recall task in previous studies, they chose not to use it because taking the input passage away during testing was not suitable for their specific purposes. For bilingual literacy researchers, with the apparent advantage of the availability of numerous standardized tests (although these may be unsuitable for bilingual populations—as discussed above), information from studies that compared multiple standardized tests is useful when researchers make decisions on their measurement tools (e.g., August et al., 2006; Keenan et al., 2008).

L2 researchers often have to make their own tests as demonstrated by the variety of tests in Table 25.3. Preparing a useful reading comprehension test is thus one of the critical phases of L2 studies, consuming much of the research time. A recommendation to L2 researchers is to draw on past research efforts and utilize test items from earlier studies (with evidence of adequate functioning) as much as possible, because making a test is not as easy as it might seem for novices. Researchers can select items from available tests, combine them to make their own set of items, conduct a pilot study to examine their quality, revise them where necessary, and repeat this process until satisfactory quality is achieved (see also Green & Fulcher, Chapter 7, this volume). This process still requires substantial commitment but may be much more efficient when compared to making a new test completely from scratch. Communication with the original test owners (either a person or a testing institution) and fulfilment of any requirement is a necessary research skill. As pointed out above, it is important to note that researchers are not always consistent in how they operationalize the construct of a test. We must make decisions about test items based on theory and the purpose of the research. Needless to say, evidence of the quality provided by a test about a given population of test-takers must be presented, whether the test is developed by researchers or adopted from an external source.

A final important recommendation is to use multiple item types wherever feasible, not only to increase our capacity of measurement (note that a single test measures only part of the construct) but also to mitigate largely unpredictable effects from various sources (e.g., test formats or background knowledge). If we use a more advanced statistical method such as structural equation modeling that can control for measurement errors, multiple measures increase precision of measurement (Francis et al., 2005). However, testing is a highly practical endeavor. We must find a pragmatic compromise between theoretical soundness, psychometric requirements, and feasibility constraints. Researchers need to make informed decisions on the construct of reading comprehension they measure in light of their purposes. Even under practical constraints, researchers can increase variations in measurement by including multiple input texts, text genres, and test formats. Any small efforts for expanding the variety of testing methods are encouraged for more refined measurement of reading comprehension.

Testing Tips

- Ensure that questions cannot be answered without comprehending the reading passage.
- Keep a balance among different types of questions (e.g., factual, inferential, gist, details).
- Wherever possible, include multiple test item types (e.g., MCQ, short answer, summary).
- Choose text genre (e.g., narrative, information, argumentative) according to your purpose or suitability for the target test-takers.
- Use test passages that are understandable based on general world knowledge (i.e., not biased in terms of cultural or technical background).
- Avoid test passages that may arouse strong emotions among test-takers.
- Stay updated on test validation research findings.
- When interpreting a norm-referenced test score, ensure that the test-taker belongs to the norming population.

Recommended Readings

Alderson, J. C. (2000). *Assessing reading*. Cambridge University Press.

This book provides an overview of the nature of L2 reading and offers practical advice on designing, developing, and using tests of reading comprehension through examples of actual test items.

Grabe, W. (2009). *Reading in a second language: Moving from theory to practice*. Cambridge University Press.

This book is a comprehensive overview of L2 reading research and its implications to practitioners. It also includes a chapter which discusses tests and test task types in relation with the purpose of testing.

Koda, K. (2005). *Insights into second language reading*. Cambridge University Press.

This book synthesizes a remarkable array of research findings and provides a conceptual foundation for researching L2 reading. Part III brings theory into practice and covers assessment and instruction of reading.

References

Alderson, J. C. (2000). *Assessing reading*. Cambridge University Press.

Alptekin, C., & Erçetin, G. (2009). Assessing the relationship of working memory to L2 reading: Does the nature of comprehension process and reading span task make a difference? *System*, *37*(4), 627–639. https://doi.org/10.1016/j.system.2009.09.007

August, D., Francis, D. J., Hsu, H.-Y. A., & Snow, C. E. (2006). Assessing reading comprehension in bilinguals. *The Elementary School Journal*, *107*(2), 221–238. https://doi.org/10.1086/510656

Bachman, L. F. (1985). Performance on cloze tests with fixed-ratio and rational deletions. *TESOL Quarterly*, *19*(3), 535–556. https://doi.org/10.2307/3586277

Bax, S. (2013). The cognitive processing of candidates during reading tests: Evidence from eye-tracking. *Language Testing*, *30*(4), 441–465. https://doi.org/10.1177/0265532212473244

Carlisle, J. F., Beeman, M., Davis, L. H., & Spharim, G. (1999). Relationship of metalinguistic capabilities and reading achievement for children who are becoming bilingual. *Applied Psycholinguistics*, *20*(4), 459–478.

Carver, R. (1997). Reading for one second, one minute, or one year from the perspective of Rauding theory. *Scientific Studies of Reading*, *1*(1), 3–43. https://doi.org/10.1207/s1532799xssr0101_2

Chen, X., Ramirez, G., Luo, Y. C., Geva, E., & Ku, Y. (2012). Comparing vocabulary development in Spanish- and Chinese-speaking ELLs: The effects of metalinguistic and sociocultural factors. *Reading and Writing*, *25*(8), 1991–2020. https://doi.org/10.1007/s11145-011-9318-7

Cook, V. (1997). Monolingual bias in second language acquisition research. *Revista Canaria de Estudios Ingleses*, *34*, 35–50.

Davies, A. (2008). *Assessing academic English: Testing English proficiency 1950–1989: The IELTS solution*. Cambridge University Press.

DeKeyser, R. (2001). Automaticity and automatization. In P. Robinson (Ed.), *Cognition and second language instruction* (pp. 125–151). Cambridge University Press.

Enright, M. K., Grabe, W., Koda, K., Mosenthal, P., Mulcahy-Ernt, P., & Schedl, M. A. (2000). *TOEFL 2000 reading framework: A working paper* (TOEFL Monograph No. MS-17). Educational Testing Service. https://www.ets.org/Media/Research/pdf/RM-00-04.pdf

Francis, D. J., Fletcher, J. M., Catts, H. W., & Tomblin, J. B. (2005). Dimensions affecting the assessment of reading comprehension. In S. G. Paris & S. A. Stahl (Eds.), *Center for improvement of early reading achievement (CIERA): Children's reading comprehension and assessment* (pp. 369–394). Lawrence Erlbaum Associates.

Goldman, S. R. (1997). Learning from text: Reflections on the past and suggestions for the future. *Discourse Processes*, *23*(3), 357–398. https://doi.org/10.1080/01638539709544997

Grabe, W. (2012). *Reading in a second languages*. Cambridge University Press.

Grabe, W., & Stoller, F. L. (2019). *Teaching and researching reading* (3rd ed.). Taylor and Francis. https://doi.org/10.4324/9781315726274

Hannon, B., & Daneman, M. (2001). A new tool for measuring and understanding individual differences in the component processes of reading comprehension. *Journal of Educational Psychology*, *93*(1), 103–128. https://doi.org/10.1037/0022-0663.93.1.103

Jeon, E. H. (2020). *References: Tabled studies* (IRIS 937960; Version V1) [Data set]. IRIS. https://www.iris-database.org/iris/app/home/detail?id=york:937960

Keenan, J. M., Betjemann, R. S., & Olson, R. K. (2008). Reading comprehension tests vary in the skills they assess: Differential dependence on decoding and oral comprehension. *Scientific Studies of Reading*, *12*(3), 281–300. https://doi.org/10.1080/10888430802132279

Khalifa, H., & Weir, C. J. (2009). *Examining reading: Research and practice in assessing second language reading*. Cambridge University Press.

Lee, J. F. (1986). On the use of the recall task to measure L2 reading comprehension. *Studies in Second Language Acquisition*, *8*(2), 201–212. https://doi.org/10.1017/s0272263100006082

McCray, G., & Brunfaut, T. (2018). Investigating the construct measured by banked gap-fill items: Evidence from eye-tracking. *Language Testing*, *35*(1), 51–73. https://doi.org/10.1177/0265532216677105

Menken, K. (2008). *English learners left behind: Standardized testing as language policy*. Multilingual Matters LTD.

Moore, T., Morton, J., Hall, D., & Wallis, C. (2015). Literacy practices in the professional workplace: Implications for the IELTS reading and writing tests. IELTS Research Reports Online Series, *1*, 1–46. https://www.ielts.org/-/media/research-reports/ielts_online_rr_2015-1.ashx?_ga=2.209062098.1706296377.1588867167-512909769.1588867167

Potts, G. R., & Peterson, S. B. (1985). Incorporation versus compartmentalization in memory for discourse. *Journal of Memory and Language*, *24*(1), 107–118. https://doi.org/10.1016/0749-596X(85)90018-X

Shiotsu, T. (2010). *Components of L2 reading: Linguistic and processing factors in the reading test performances of Japanese EFL learners. Studies in language testing* (Vol. 32). Cambridge University Press.

26
Measuring L2 Listening

Aaron Olaf Batty

Background

Listening occupies a peculiar place among the language skills, in that, while it is the first skill humans develop in their first language (L1) and is the means by which they acquire it, it received very little research or pedagogical attention in the second language (L2) until well into the second half of the 20th century (Taylor & Geranpayeh, 2011). It has occupied a rather low priority in Second Language Acquisition (SLA) research, and is often argued to be the hardest language skill to test (Field, 2013). Nonetheless, its importance to second language acquisition is undeniable, and listening tasks have featured on large-scale language tests since the early 1900s at the latest (Taylor & Geranpayeh, 2011). This chapter will attempt to de-mystify the processes of listening, review some of the recent listening acquisition and assessment literature, and give some practical guidance on developing one's own instruments to measure L2 listening.

The Listening Process

One commonality between the various definitions of listening in the literature is their conception of listening primarily as a process. The descriptions of this process are based largely on the findings of cognitive psychology research on attention and memory from the 1950s through the 1980s (Field, 2013). Early conceptions of the process included the *bottom-up* and *top-down* approaches to making sense of auditory information—bottom-up being the process of building a mental representation of meaning from the words understood in the input, and top-down being the use of other information (e.g., background knowledge, context, nonverbal cues, etc.) to make sense of the linguistic input. Although the bottom-up process was favored by listening researchers in the early years, it was replaced by the top-down process, and then understood to occur simultaneously in the interactive model (Flowerdew & Miller, 2010). In recent years, however, there has been a move away from these terms (if not the general concepts) in favor of more detailed processing models. One influential model is that popularized by Field (2013) which separates the processes involved in making sense of spoken language into two broad categories: *decoding* and *meaning-building*.

Decoding. The first step to processing is phonological decoding, in which the auditory stream is parsed into L2 phonemes. This is a task much more fraught than it may first appear. The first challenge is due to neurological commitment to one's L1 phonemic system, which hinders later ability to even perceive L2 phonemes (Zhang, Kuhl, Imada, Kotani, & Tohkura, 2005). Additionally, true speech production includes many variations of phonemes (due to weak or reduced forms, regional or personal variation, and others) of which the listener must be aware to be able to assemble them into syllables, words, and lexical chunks. This is again challenged by the fact that in connected speech, word boundaries are often indistinct and there are often striking differences between words' citation forms and how they are pronounced in the real world (Field, 2013).

After identifying the words in the auditory stream, they must be arranged into syntax. This happens probabilistically, based on the listener's familiarity with the language. An experienced listener has a keen sense of words that are likely to appear together, and can therefore predict chunks before and as they happen, facilitating syntactic decoding (Field, 2009). It is this level of automaticity that separates lower-level L2 listeners from higher-level listeners. Even if a lower-level listener knows every word in an uttered sentence, and is familiar with the syntactic structures, he or she may lack the experience, and therefore automaticity, necessary to assemble them in real time, based on accurate prediction.

Meaning-building. Once the auditory stream has been parsed into words and syntax, the listener uses other information to interpret the input and to build a mental representation of the meaning. This can include nonverbal signals, knowledge about the world (including cultural/pragmatic expectations), or what the speaker has said up to that point—all of which is information that one uses to build meaning while listening in the L1 as well (Field, 2009). However, the listening process is not thought to be unidirectional, from decoding to meaning building. Rather, listeners, whether they be working in the L1 or L2, employ all of these simultaneously, continuously monitoring their understanding (Imhof, 2010) based on the entire range of information available, all the way from the phoneme through to overarching cultural values. Deficiencies in any of these can degrade or even destroy the listener's comprehension of the speaker's message (Field, 2013).

A Brief History of L2 Listening Research and Assessment

Within the field of communication studies, scholarly research into listening may go back as far as the late 1800s (Bodie, Janusik, & Välikoski, 2008); in the field of SLA, however, it is much more recent. Although listening instruction featured in British language programs from the late 1960s (Field, 2009), it was not until the late 1970s with the advent of communicative language teaching that it began to play a larger role in L2 language instruction (Taylor, 2013). It was the early 1990s, however, when listening finally "took off" as a common topic of SLA research, and since then research has followed a wide variety of strands, including psychometric measurement, discourse analysis, listener strategies, and listening for specific purposes such as lecture listening and note-taking (Flowerdew & Miller, 2010).

The history of second language listening assessment (at least as far as English as an L2 is concerned) is remarkably long, with listening seemingly making its debut in 1913 on Cambridge University's Certificate of Proficiency in English (CPE), which featured a *thirty-minute* dictation task (Weir, 2013). From the 1920s at least, but certainly by the middle of the last century, "objective," discrete-point listening tests came to dominate L2 listening assessment, as the audio-lingual approach to language pedagogy took hold (Weir & Vidaković, 2013). These tasks, often operationalized via multiple-choice items, focused on such skills as phonemic discrimination, paraphrasing, and choosing appropriate responses to questions posed aurally (Buck, 2001). With the increasing availability of tape recorders in the 1960s and 1970s, listening tasks expanded their scope beyond such relatively prosaic language skills. A notable example is the Test of English as a Foreign Language (TOEFL), established in 1964 by the Educational Testing Service (ETS), which kept the discrete-point questions of its predecessors, but moved its focus to comprehension of short recorded clips of single speakers' speech. A similar format was adopted by the Cambridge tests in the years following (Taylor & Geranpayeh, 2011).

With the rise of communicative language teaching in the classroom in the 1980s came increased interest in attempting to better contextualize listening tasks on tests in order to more closely simulate authenticity. This can be seen in the development of the International English Language Testing System (IELTS) in 1989, which featured monologues and dialogues from social settings, conversations and lectures mimicking those that examinees may encounter when studying in an English-speaking country, and a range of formality and accents (Taylor & Weir, 2012). With its "TOEFL 2000" revision initiative in the early 2000s, ETS also sought to "focus on language use in context, not on decontextualized skills such as phoneme recognition and comprehension of single sentence utterances" and provide examinees "an opportunity to demonstrate their ability to comprehend coherent, appropriate, and meaningful messages" (Bejar, Douglas, Jamieson, Nissan, & Turner, 2000, p. 5).

As we enter the third decade of the 21st century, this move toward greater approximation of the target language use (TLU) domain (Bachman & Palmer, 1996) continues, with assessment researchers increasingly turning their sights toward more authentic tasks featuring unscripted speech, a wider range of accents, the use of visual information, and even integrating listening assessment into writing and/or oral tasks (Ockey & Wagner, 2018). In recent years, large-scale tests have begun to follow suit, the Pearson PTE tests, the TOEFL iBT, and Trinity College London's Integrated Skills in English (ISE) tests being only a few examples of tests incorporating some or all of these features.

Key Concept

***Listening*:** No single agreed-upon definition of listening has been adopted among either L1 or L2 listening researchers. However, the International Listening Association, an organization formed primarily to research L1 listening and communication, drafted an official definition for their organization in 1995:

> Listening is the process of receiving, constructing meaning from, and responding to spoken and/or nonverbal messages.
>
> ("An ILA definition of listening," 1995, p. 4).

Although broader than one usually finds within the fields of SLA or L2 assessment, each component of this definition can be found somewhere in these fields' literature, as this chapter will illustrate.

Key Issues

There has been a sustained, concerted effort in the L2 listening assessment field to tie assessment methods more closely to the findings of listening assessment research following a model of test validation concerned with *cognitive validity*—the degree to which a test elicits the same cognitive processes a listener would use in real-world L2 listening. As such, much listening assessment research of late has investigated the extent to which various tests and assessment methods link to the models of comprehension suggested by psycholinguistic and acquisition research. This section reviews some of the major topics of SLA listening research in recent years, and illustrates their links to L2 assessment practice and research.

Phonological Processing

There has been a great deal of psycholinguistic research interest in the processes involved in L2 listening in recent years. One challenge facing L2 listeners is that foreign phonemes must be perceived through the acquired phonemic system of the L1 shortly after the first year of life. The difficulty of this is only exacerbated by normal variability between speakers, speech rates, and phonetic context (Rost, 2016). Given the difficulty of phonological decoding for L2 listeners, one would expect that higher phonological complexity would be associated with more difficult tests. Révész and Brunfaut (2013) investigated this assumption (among others), but found that it was, in fact, a poor predictor of test difficulty with their sample and instrument.

One challenge of phonological decoding for the L2 listener is the fact that natural, connected speech, wherein speakers use reduced or weak forms in order to speak more quickly and efficiently, differs greatly from words spoken in isolation. This problem has also been a popular topic of SLA research, especially with regard to the efficacy of instruction. This interest is shared by recent assessment researchers as well, with assessment scholars advocating for more "authentic," or even unscripted, material in L2 listening tests (Wagner, 2014) to enhance tests' cognitive validity. Brown and Kondo-Brown (2006) explored this topic in detail, reviewing several methods of testing recognition of reduced forms, advocating that they play a bigger part in classroom-based testing. More recently, Wagner and Toth (2014) compared the results of two versions of a listening test, one using an unscripted conversation, and another using a scripted recreation of the same conversation, finding that the unscripted version was more difficult. These findings highlight the difficulty L2 listeners have in phonologically decoding natural speech, but also the importance of its use in assessment.

Another topic closely associated with the phonological features of input and its impact on L2 listening is that of accent, which has been an important topic among language researchers in the past few years. Not surprisingly, research into listening to unfamiliar L2 accents finds that they negatively impact comprehension and lower scores on listening tests featuring them (Ockey, Papageorgiou, & French, 2016). In the case of English tests, however, English's status as the de facto lingua franca ensures that L2 listeners will encounter not only various L1 varieties of it, but many accented L2 varieties as well. For this reason, there has been a growing call in the assessment literature for English tests to include regional and L2 accents in their listening material (Ockey & Wagner, 2018). This is not without complications, however. Field (2013) cautions that it may be unfair to include accents that test-takers are unlikely to have ever heard, particularly in foreign language learning contexts, and Harding (2012) raises further issues based on his finding that sharing an L1 with the L2 speaker featured on a listening test may unfairly facilitate comprehension.

Skills

Ever since Richards (1983) proposed his oft-cited list of "micro-skills" necessary for L2 listening comprehension, researchers have sought to explain L2 listening in terms of a set of skills. These may be described, as Richards does, in terms of abilities, e.g., "ability to recognize vocabulary used in core conversational topics" (p. 228), or as components of language ability, e.g., "vocabulary," as in Andringa et al. (2012). They may also be addressed by examining test characteristics which correspond to a particular listening skill or component. Although the skills approach has given way somewhat to the process model discussed above (Field, 2009), it still enjoys attention, especially among listening assessment researchers and teachers.

In their research into the impact of subskills on listening comprehension, Andringa et al. (2012) found that the best predictors were, not surprisingly, linguistic knowledge (vocabulary, grammar, and segmentation accuracy) and general reasoning ability. The importance of L2 vocabulary knowledge was similarly demonstrated by Vandergrift and Baker (2015), who suggest that, like reading, L2 listening may require a threshold vocabulary level, below which the percentage of words that are unknown becomes too large to be guessed based on the surrounding known words. This finding was also in line with the findings of the Révész and Brunfaut (2013) study discussed previously, which found that lexical and discourse complexity had the greatest effect on listening test difficulty. Cheng and Matthews (2018) also found scores on an auditory dictation vocabulary test to be highly predictive of scores on a large-scale listening test. Although the bulk of these studies approach the question of listening subskills from the perspective of assessment, they offer insight into acquisition as well, clearly demonstrating the importance of lexical processing in L2 listening.

Strategies

Over the past several decades, listening comprehension strategies have been a major line of SLA listening research. Research into listening strategies has resulted in numerous taxonomies of behaviors that learners employ to facilitate learning or comprehension of their L2s, but the most oft-cited classification of strategies is based on O'Malley and Chamot (1990), which breaks learning strategies into three categories: *metacognitive strategies*—actively and consciously monitoring one's learning, e.g., planning for a learning task, checking one's understanding, identifying problems in comprehension; *cognitive strategies*—doing things with the incoming information in real time, e.g., summarizing to oneself, taking notes, making predictions; and, finally, *social and affective strategies*—working with others to enhance learning, e.g., asking the speaker for clarification or working with other learners. More recently, it is metacognitive strategies which have enjoyed the most attention, especially in relation to acquisition (e.g., Vandergrift & Goh, 2011).

With respect to testing, learning strategies are not well-researched, but the role of communicative strategies is of great importance to assessment. Field (2013) acknowledges the importance of communicative strategy use in test-taking, as any strategy a listener would have at his or her disposal "in the wild" is part of that listener's listening proficiency, and should be reflected in scores. A recent study by Kök (2018) investigated the impact of strategy use on IELTS listening scores. It was found that increased strategy use was positively correlated with greater listening proficiency, and that those participants with high metacognitive strategy use performed significantly better than those using more cognitive strategies, illustrating the link between acquisition and assessment.

Non-verbal and Visual Cues

When the International Listening Association met in 1995 to define listening (see the "Key Concept" box above), the source of the most disagreement was whether to consider nonverbal communication to be a part of listening. Non-verbal behavior ultimately won out, and it is easy to see why: Most of the time, when we are listening to people speak, we can see them as well, picking up cues from their facial expressions and other body language. We can also glean additional information from the setting, such as a classroom or a café or an office. All of these sources of information operate as a "co-text" to the verbal signals (Rost, 2016, p. 42) and help us shape our expectations and improve our interpretations of what is heard. In fact, some research has found that up to 66% of the meaning in a social situation is encoded in the visual channel, and is particularly useful for revealing the speaker's attitudes, emotions, personality, and interpersonal relations (Burgoon, Guerrero, & Floyd, 2016).

There has, however, been remarkably little research into the impact of nonverbal and other visual information on language acquisition, and what does exist is more relevant to assessment. Research on this topic has explored the comparative difficulty of audio- and video- based listening tests, with varied results (Ockey & Wagner, 2018). Other research has explored test-takers' perceptions of video on listening tests (e.g., Cubilo & Winke, 2013); amount of time spent viewing the video (e.g., Wagner, 2010); comparing the effect of video on different text types, proficiencies (Batty, 2015), and item type (Batty, 2018); and employing eye-tracking methodology to explore test-takers' use of nonverbal communicative cues (Batty, 2020) or other visuals such as presentation slides (Suvorov, 2015). From a theoretical standpoint, most would agree that the inclusion of video on L2 listening tests enhances validity, because it elicits the processes test-takers can be expected to use in real-world communication (Field, 2013; Ockey & Wagner, 2018), although some concerns about the usefulness of the measures resulting from such tests remain (Batty, 2018).

Recommendations for Practice

Taylor and Geranpayeh (2011) described language testing as "the art of the possible" (p. 94), and nowhere is this more true than when testing listening—whether for research or assessment purposes. The multidimensional and interactive nature of listening makes measurement difficult from a theoretical standpoint, but at least as much so from a practical standpoint. Whereas in principle a reading test can technically be constructed with little more than a word processing program, listening tests typically require the use of audio recording and editing equipment at least, performers (of some kind), and delivery technology (ranging from an MP3 player and a set of speakers to network audio streaming software). The addition of any other input or output (e.g., visuals, writing/speaking) may increase theoretical validity, but will do so at the cost of time/money. Finally, the higher the stakes and the larger the scale of the assessment, the more important the statistical reliability of results becomes, which may limit the test designer's choice of tasks to somewhat conservative, discrete-point test tasks, rather than more novel, integrative and/or interactive ones. Tasks that would be risky choices for a high-stakes test may prove to be useful and interesting in language classes and research. Every choice made in developing a listening test represents trade-offs between theory and practice, validity and reliability, benefit and cost. Choosing the right task for one's purpose relies upon balancing considerations of the TLU domain, intended score use, and real-world practicality. There are myriad test tasks designed to measure different aspects of the listening process, ranging from highly-focused, discrete-point items testing recognition or comprehension, through highly integrated, interactive tasks measuring everything from listening through speaking and communicative competence. The list below is by no means intended to be comprehensive, but should serve as a basic introduction.

Discrete Tasks

Discrete tasks aim to measure a single point with a single item, be it the correct recognition of a phoneme, an appropriate paraphrase of a stimulus, identifying a detail from a conversation, or making an unambiguous inference from what is heard. These task types all suffer some threats to their validity (as all tasks do). Selecting from only two options introduces a large guessing rate. Multiple-choice questions usually require test-takers to expend cognitive effort in discerning small differences in the propositional content of the answer options, which would not be necessary in real-world circumstances. Gap fills require the test-taker to simultaneously listen, read a sentence or text containing the gap, and write down the missing word(s), which is also unlikely in real-world listening (Field, 2013). However, these types of items are also relatively easy to write, usually easy to mark (as the answers are unambiguous), and—if well-written—make for statistically reliable tests. Examples are:

- *Phonemic pairs*: Test-takers must choose or write the word they hear, e.g., "truck" vs. "track."
- *Listening for prosody*: Test-takers hear a sentence featuring intonation or stress that differentiates it from a phonologically-similar, but semantically-different sentence (e.g., "can" and "can't" in fast speech), and must indicate which they heard.
- *Identifying reduced forms*: Test-takers hear a sentence with a phonologically- or lexically-reduced form (e.g., "Give'm an inch and he will take a mile") and must indicate or write what word has been reduced (e.g., Ito, 2006).

- *Multiple-choice comprehension*: This is probably the most common item format for listening tests, wherein a question about the stimulus is followed by several possible answers from which the test-taker must choose the most appropriate. It can be tailored to explicit, factual information, or implicit interpretations (as long as they are unambiguous). For lower-level or younger test-takers, the options can be replaced with pictures if the content is of a concrete, imageable nature.
- *Gap-fill or short constructed response*: The required response can range in length from one word through a sentence or two; however, the longer the response, the more difficult it is to mark (e.g., Does spelling count? Does grammar count?).

Integrative Tasks

Integrative tasks aim to incorporate a combination of language skills in an attempt to more closely model real-world language use. Although this would normally be associated with improved validity, in some cases the tasks can be somewhat contrived. In all cases, though, it is often unclear what skill is being measured, limiting these tasks' usefulness for diagnostic purposes. The difficulty of creating these tasks can range from being rather straightforward to quite involved, possibly requiring the creation of a rating rubric. Marking these tasks is another drawback, as the test-taker response is largely unconstrained, and some subjectivity in marking is virtually assured to present itself. A short list of example tasks is below.

- *Dictation*: In this task, the test-taker must transcribe part or the whole of a sentence or longer passage he or she hears. Depending on length, it can engage everything from phonological through discourse-level knowledge.
- *Listen and repeat*: Similar to dictation, the test-taker must immediately repeat what he or she has heard, which can be taxing on working memory and requires a high degree of automaticity in language processing (e.g., Van Moere, 2012).
- *Listen-to-write / listen-to-speak*: Test-takers listen to a stimulus (e.g., a short lecture) and write or speak a summary or a response. These integrated tasks likely tap into the constructs of writing or speaking at least as much as that of listening.

Interactive Tasks

Although these are arguably a special type of integrative task, the involvement of one or more interlocutors adds yet another dimension, as it allows communicative competence to play a part. In such tasks, "while-listening" behavior can also be examined (e.g., backchanneling, body language to indicate comprehension, recasts), and also what Field (2009) calls "repair strategies" (actions such as requesting clarification or repetition). Just as with the integrated tasks immediately above, the central challenge associated with these tasks is the impossibility of separating listening proficiency from other factors such as communicative competence. Examples include:

- *Interviews*: Test-takers sit for an interview with a rater. These can include recorded listening material or simply listening to the interviewer (e.g., Nakatsuhara, 2012).
- *Paired or group oral discussions*: Two or more test-takers discuss a topic and are rated by a rater who does not participate (e.g., Van Moere, 2006).
- *Information-gap*: Test-takers listen to material and explain it to another test-taker or rater to complete a task (e.g., Batty & Stewart, 2016).

Testing Tips

- *Keep your test purpose in mind*: Make sure that whatever you can capture about listening in the TLU domain—be it authentic or pseudo-spontaneous speech, technical vocabulary, accents, etc.—is included.
- *Keep your test purpose in mind (again!)*: Resist the urge to incorporate more non-listening factors (e.g., writing/speaking, nonverbal information) in your test than you have a solid theoretical justification for doing so, and a clear purpose for any information resulting from them. Every test development decision incurs a theoretical and/or practical cost. Make the best choices possible for *your* test.
- *Performances matter*: If your listening test will include recorded content, in order to best match the TLU domain, endeavor to find performers who can deliver that content in a realistic fashion. These people can be found in community theatre troupes, university theatre departments, or even talent agencies. At the same time, always consider how the test items relate to the delivery, and whether specific guidance needs to be given to the performers to ensure that the items operate as intended.

Recommended Readings

Rost, M. (2016). *Teaching and researching listening* (3rd ed.). Taylor and Francis.

This is the third edition of Michael Rost's oft-cited overview of listening, which covers both the L1 and L2 contexts, but also L2 listening instruction and assessment. It is comprehensive and is an excellent jumping-off point for deeper reading on the topic.

Green, R. (2017). *Designing listening tests*. Palgrave Macmillan.

Rita Green provides a comprehensive look at every step and every consideration in the creation of listening tests, from the theoretical construct through test specifications, item and passage writing, validation, and score reporting. It is the most complete handbook to the practical development of L2 listening tests available.

Ockey, G. J., & Wagner, E. (2018). *Assessing L2 listening: Moving towards authenticity*. John Benjamins.

This volume reviews the most recent trends and developments in the field of L2 listening assessment, with sections on the use of authentic texts, the inclusion of various accents in listening passages, the use of audio-visual texts, and interactive tests of listening. In addition to overviews by the authors, each topic includes new empirical research by active researchers in the field.

References

Andringa, S., Olsthoorn, N., van Beuningen, C., Schoonen, R., & Hulstijn, J. (2012). Determinants of success in native and non-native listening comprehension: An individual differences approach. *Language Learning*, *62*(2), 49–78. https://doi.org/10.1111/j.1467-9922.2012.00706.x

Bachman, L. F., & Palmer, A. S. (1996). Test usefulness: Qualities of language tests. In *Language testing in practice: Designing and developing useful language tests* (pp. 17–42). Oxford University Press.

Batty, A. O. (2015). A comparison of video- and audio-mediated listening tests with many-facet Rasch modeling and differential distractor functioning. *Language Testing*, *32*(1), 3–20. https://doi.org/10.1177/0265532214531254

Batty, A. O. (2018). Investigating the impact of nonverbal communication cues on listening item types. In E. Wagner & G. J. Ockey (Eds.), *Assessing L2 listening: Moving towards authenticity* (pp. 161–175). John Benjamins.

Batty, A. O. (2020). An eye-tracking study of attention to visual cues in L2 listening tests. *Language Testing*. Advance online publication. https://doi.org/10.1177/0265532220951504

Batty, A. O., & Stewart, J. (2016). Theoretical underpinnings of an objective test of communicative competence in Japan. In V. Aryadoust & J. Fox (Eds.), *Trends in language assessment research and practice: The view from the Middle East and the Pacific Rim* (pp. 387–413). Cambridge Scholars Publishing.

Bejar, I. I., Douglas, D., Jamieson, J., Nissan, S., & Turner, J. (2000). *TOEFL 2000 listening framework: A working paper* (Working Paper No. RM-00-07) (p. 60). Educational Testing Service. https://www.ets.org/Media/Research/pdf/RM-00-07.pdf

Bodie, G. D., Janusik, L. A., & Välikoski, T.-R. (2008). *Priorities of listening research: Four interrelated initiatives. A white paper sponsored by the research committee of the International Listening Association.* International Listening Association. https://listen.org/resources/Documents/White_Paper_PrioritiesResearch.pdf

Brown, J. D., & Kondo-Brown, K. (2006). Testing reduced forms. In J. D. Brown & K. Kondo-Brown (Eds.), *Perspectives on teaching connected speech to second language speakers* (pp. 247–264). University of Hawaii Press.

Buck, G. (2001). *Assessing listening.* Cambridge University Press.

Burgoon, J. K., Guerrero, L. K., & Floyd, K. (2016). *Nonverbal communication.* Routledge.

Cheng, J., & Matthews, J. (2018). The relationship between three measures of L2 vocabulary knowledge and L2 listening and reading. *Language Testing, 35*(1), 3–25. https://doi.org/10.1177/0265532216676851

Cubilo, J., & Winke, P. (2013). Redefining the L2 listening construct within an integrated writing task: Considering the impacts of visual-cue interpretation and note-taking. *Language Assessment Quarterly, 10*(4), 371–397. https://doi.org/10.1080/15434303.2013.824972

Field, J. (2009). *Listening in the language classroom.* Cambridge University Press.

Field, J. (2013). Cognitive validity. In A. Geranpayeh & L. Taylor (Eds.), *Examining listening: Research and practice in assessing second language listening* (pp. 77–151). Cambridge University Press.

Flowerdew, J., & Miller, L. (2010). Listening in a second language. In A. D. Wolvin (Ed.), *Listening and human communication in the 21st century* (pp. 158–177). Wiley-Blackwell.

Harding, L. (2012). Accent, listening assessment and the potential for a shared-L1 advantage: A DIF perspective. *Language Testing, 29*(2), 163–180. https://doi.org/10.1177/0265532211421161

ILA. (1995). An ILA definition of listening. *The Listening Post, 53*, 4. https://listen.org/resources/Documents/53_Apr_95.pdf

Imhof, M. (2010). What's going on in the mind of a listener? The cognitive psychology of listening. In A. D. Wolvin (Ed.), *Listening and human communication in the 21st century* (pp. 97–126). Wiley-Blackwell.

Ito, Y. (2006). The comprehension of English reduced forms by second language learners and its effect on input-intake process. In J. D. Brown & K. Kondo-Brown (Eds.), *Perspectives on teaching connected speech to second language speakers* (pp. 67–81). University of Hawaii Press.

Kök, İ. (2018). Relationship between listening comprehension strategy use and listening comprehension proficiency. *International Journal of Listening, 32*(3), 163–179. https://doi.org/10.1080/10904018.2016.1276457

Nakatsuhara, F. (2012). The relationship between test takers' listening proficiency and their performance on the IELTS speaking test. In L. Taylor & C. J. Weir (Eds.), IELTS collected papers 2: *Research in reading and listening assessment* (pp. 519–573). Cambridge University Press.

Ockey, G. J., Papageorgiou, S., & French, R. (2016). Effects of strength of accent on an L2 interactive lecture listening comprehension test. *International Journal of Listening, 30*(1–2), 84–98. https://doi.org/10.1080/10904018.2015.1056877

Ockey, G. J., & Wagner, E. (2018). *Assessing L2 listening: Moving towards authenticity.* John Benjamins.

O'Malley, J. M., & Chamot, A. U. (1990). *Learning strategies in second language acquisition.* Cambridge University Press.

Révész, A., & Brunfaut, T. (2013). Text characteristics of task input and difficulty in second language listening comprehension. *Studies in Second Language Acquisition, 35*(1), 31–65. https://doi.org/10.1017/S0272263112000678

Richards, J. C. (1983). Listening comprehension: Approach, design, procedure. *TESOL Quarterly, 17*(2), 219–240. https://doi.org/10.2307/3586651

Rost, M. (2016). *Teaching and researching listening* (3rd ed.). Taylor and Francis.

Suvorov, R. (2015). The use of eye tracking in research on video-based second language (L2) listening assessment: A comparison of context videos and content videos. *Language Testing, 32*(4), 463–483. https://doi.org/10.1177/0265532214562099

Taylor, L. (2013). Introduction. In A. Geranpayeh & L. Taylor (Eds.), *Examining listening: Research and practice in assessing second language listening* (pp. 1–35). Cambridge University Press.

Taylor, L., & Geranpayeh, A. (2011). Assessing listening for academic purposes: Defining and operationalising the test construct. *Journal of English for Academic Purposes*, *10*(2), 89–101. https://doi.org/10.1016/j.jeap.2011.03.002
Taylor, L., & Weir, C. J. (2012). Introduction. In L. Taylor & C. J. Weir (Eds.), *IELTS collected* papers 2*: Research in reading and listening assessment* (pp. 1–33). Cambridge University Press.
Van Moere, A. (2006). Validity evidence in a university group oral test. *Language Testing*, *23*(4), 411–440. https://doi.org/10.1191/0265532206lt336oa
Van Moere, A. (2012). A psycholinguistic approach to oral language assessment. *Language Testing*, *29*(3), 325–344. https://doi.org/10.1177/0265532211424478
Vandergrift, L., & Baker, S. (2015). Learner variables in second language listening comprehension: An exploratory path analysis. *Language Learning*, *65*(2), 390–416. https://doi.org/10.1111/lang.12105
Vandergrift, L., & Goh, C. (2011). *Teaching and learning second language listening: Metacognition in action*. Routledge.
Wagner, E. (2010). Test-takers' interaction with an L2 video listening test. *System*, *38*(2), 280–291. https://doi.org/10.1016/j.system.2010.01.003
Wagner, E. (2014). Using unscripted spoken texts in the teaching of second language listening. *TESOL Journal*, *5*(2), 288–311. https://doi.org/10.1002/tesj.120
Wagner, E., & Toth, P. D. (2014). Teaching and testing L2 Spanish listening using scripted vs. unscripted texts. *Foreign Language Annals*, *47*(3), 404–422. https://doi.org/10.1111/flan.12091
Weir, C. J. (2013). An overview of the influences on English language testing in the United Kingdom 1913–2012. In C. J. Weir, I. Vidaković, & E. D. Galaczi (Eds.), *Measured constructs: A history of Cambridge English examinations, 1913–2012* (pp. 1–102). Cambridge University Press.
Weir, C. J., & Vidaković, I. (2013). The measurement of listening ability 1913–2012. In C. J. Weir, I. Vidaković, & E. D. Galaczi (Eds.), *Measured constructs: A history of Cambridge English examinations, 1913–2012* (pp. 347–426). Cambridge University Press.
Zhang, Y., Kuhl, P. K., Imada, T., Kotani, M., & Tohkura, Y. (2005). Effects of language experience: Neural commitment to language-specific auditory patterns. *NeuroImage*, *26*(3), 703–720. https://doi.org/10.1016/j.neuroimage.2005.02.040

27

Measuring L2 Speaking

Fumiyo Nakatsuhara, Chihiro Inoue & Nahal Khabbazbashi

Background

Most language educators would agree that direct assessments of speaking are resource-intensive, logistically-complex endeavours, and most will have seen pragmatic decisions made to compromise the ways in which speaking is assessed due to practical constraints in resource-limited contexts (Vidaković & Galaczi, 2013). The status of speaking ability in second language (L2) teaching and learning can, however, be traced back to the late 19th century in Europe, which saw the rise of the *direct method* and the *oral method* with a primary emphasis on oral fluency (e.g., Palmer, 1921) and the *Reform Movement* in language education (e.g., Sweet, 1899), which stressed the importance of spoken language with particular focus on phonetics. The core role of speaking in L2 teaching was reflected in the testing approach adopted in the Cambridge Certificate of Proficiency in English (CPE) launched in 1913. The original CPE test (1913–45) assessed knowledge of phonetics in addition to a 1-hour speaking component, which involved dictation, read-aloud, and conversation tasks in an examiner-candidate direct speaking format. The test initially targeted English teacher trainees, and is one of the earliest examples of a speaking construct included in L2 proficiency tests (Vidaković & Galaczi, 2013).

What paved the way for a dramatic shift in L2 speaking assessment practices in the mid-20th century was the experience of the World Wars, which highlighted a shortage of military personnel proficient in speaking a foreign language. In the US, the increased interest in enhancing speaking skills led to the development of the US Foreign Service Institute (FSI) Oral Proficiency Interview (OPI) introduced in 1952. The OPI test was noteworthy in the history of oral assessment on two accounts: Firstly, its original holistic scale included performance descriptors defining features of distinct levels of proficiency and secondly, its revised scale incorporated analytic components (accent, comprehension, fluency, grammar, and vocabulary). Therefore, it made a significant step towards defining a multi-faceted speaking construct and to assessing it reliably (Fulcher, 2003). The FSI OPI test and its rating scale gave rise to subsequent oral assessment initiatives in the US in the 1960s to 1980s, including the Interagency Language Roundtable speaking test, and the American Council for the Teaching of Foreign Languages (ACTFL) OPI. In the UK, it was also during the 1970s when the University of Cambridge Local Examinations Syndicate (UCLES) started denoting performance descriptors to standardise ratings by their oral examiners. As such, "the 1960s to 1980s … saw a growth in the explicit description of performance in assessment scales, and by extension, in the explicit definition of the test construct via the scales" (Vidaković & Galaczi, 2013, p. 268).

It should be noted that the rating scales and performance descriptors developed at the time were not informed by empirical research but were rather based on expert intuition (Fulcher, 2003). If we look back at the early days of SLA research in the 1970s, it appears that the field did not place much prominence on speaking ability per se and speaking was predominantly viewed as one of the modes that reflected learners' underlying *interlanguage* system (e.g., Corder, 1971). As such, there was little research that shed light on the nature or acquisition of speaking ability and thus language testing (LT) researchers had to rely primarily on intuitive expert judgement—rather than empirical evidence—for speaking scale construction.

However, developments in psycholinguistic research provided SLA and LT researchers with a useful framework to understand the nature of speaking. Levelt's (1989) cognitive processing model for speaking remains, to this day, one of the most influential models of L1 speech production, serving as a basis for subsequent L2 speaking models developed in both SLA and LT (e.g., de Bot, 1992; Field, 2011). The wide acceptance of Levelt's model provided a shared theoretical background and helped strengthen the relationship between the two fields.

The growth of speaking research in SLA was tremendous in the 1990s. Following Skehan's (1989) L2 proficiency framework, SLA researchers devised analytical measures for Complexity, Accuracy, and Fluency (CAF) that can usefully quantify L2 speaking performance and reliably predict L2 speaking proficiency (e.g., Révész, Ekiert, & Torgersen, 2016; Skehan, 2009; Pallotti, Chapter 19, this volume). In the field of LT, the 1990s saw various new approaches to inform rating scale construction and validation, one of which was an empirical analysis of candidates' speech output (e.g., Fulcher, 1996). The development of CAF measures in SLA was timely, contributing to systematic micro-analyses of candidates' speech samples elicited in speaking tests (e.g., Brown, 2006; Iwashita, Brown, McNamara, & O'Hagan, 2008; Tavakoli, Nakatsuhara, & Hunter, 2017), and in turn enhancing our understanding of the speaking construct.

Another body of literature to which both SLA and LT research mutually contributed is the examination of the componential structures of L2 speaking proficiency. This is a key line of research for further understanding of the speaking construct and involves an analysis of the extent to which and in what ways holistic, global ratings of speaking proficiency are related to subjective or objective measures of analytical features of speech (e.g., de Jong, Steinel, Florijn, Schoonen, & Hulstijn, 2012; Iwashita et al., 2008; McNamara, 1990). To date, probably the most comprehensive study of this kind is de Jong et al.'s (2012) Structural Equation Modelling study, which provided evidence for a multidimensional view of L2 oral proficiency consisting of linguistic knowledge (vocabulary and grammar), processing skills (lexical retrieval and sentence building), as well as pronunciation skills (speech sounds, word stress, and intonation). The significance of linguistic knowledge and processing skills, which explained over three-quarters of the variance in communicative success in speaking in their study, also supports a prominent place for those components in an L2 proficiency model and sheds new light upon earlier models of L2 proficiency, such as Canale and Swain's (1980) and Bachman and Palmer's (1996).

At present, the speaking construct measured in tests is becoming more diversified than ever. On the one hand, expansion of the construct is observed in interactive speaking tests tapping into *interactional competence* (e.g., Galaczi & Taylor, 2018; Galaczi & Taylor, Chapter 32, this volume), and in interactive and integrated oral test tasks tapping into interactive listening (e.g., Ockey & Wagner, 2018). In these tests, speaking is seen both as a cognitive and a social, interactional trait, resonating Long's (1996) Interactional Hypothesis. On the other hand, we see a narrowing of the speaking construct in semi-direct and automated speaking assessments that are essentially underpinned by a psycholinguistic construct, tapping into *processing competence* (Van Moere, 2012), i.e., the efficiency with which learners process language. These contrasting views of the speaking construct will be revisited throughout this chapter; for example, in terms of how they are represented in test methods or task design. We will also touch on the ways in which technology-mediated speaking tests have started to offer solutions to cover both ends of the construct definition continuum. Here, it is important to note that we do not find the diversification of the measured construct in LT problematic. Our view is aligned with that of Van Moere (2012, p. 340); "a complementary approach to communicative and psycholinguistic testing will undoubtedly lead to stronger and fairer assessments," and it can offer learners and test users a wide range of choices to select the spoken test that best fits their purposes.

Key Concepts

Levelt's (1989) model of speaking: This model assumes that separate cognitive processes are responsible for different aspects of speech production. It comprises three main systems: Conceptualiser, Formulator and Articulator. For L2 learners, incomplete L2 knowledge and lack of automaticity are thought to affect the Formulator, and Articulator, resulting in less accurate and fluent speech. This model is key when we explore the cognitive validity of speaking tasks (Field, 2011).

Processing competence: The operational definition of processing competence is efficiency of processing language (Van Moere, 2012). It is thought to be a stable and measurable construct that underlies language proficiency, and automated speaking assessment has great potential for tapping into aspects of this construct.

Interactional competence: It is "the ability to co-construct interaction in a purposeful and meaningful way, taking into account sociocultural and pragmatic dimensions of the speech situation and event" (Galaczi & Taylor, 2018, p. 226), which is most appropriately assessed through paired and group oral discussion formats.

Key Issues

Speaking Tasks

Research that involves speaking skills requires using speech elicitation tasks. In both LT and SLA, various types of monologic and dialogic/group oral tasks have been used based on evolving theories, views of the speaking construct (Block, 2003), and practical demands. While the focus and purpose of research and tests may be different, there are overlaps in the task types used in the two fields of study (de Jong, 2018) and they share similar rationales for employing one task type over another.

Monologic Tasks. Monologic tasks in SLA seem to have been primarily used for studying learners' language competence and cognitive processing. While mechanical tasks such as read-aloud and sentence repetition have been used to investigate learners' interlanguage grammar and degrees of automaticity in processing language (Mackey & Gass, 2005), picture description tasks (with a single picture, a few contrastive pictures, or those in a sequence) that elicit an extended monologue have frequently been used in task-based language teaching (TBLT) research. TBLT aims to examine the effects of manipulating task complexity and task conditions on learner output in order to justify and assist in the pedagogic use of tasks by determining how certain task characteristics affect L2 performance. The two major theories behind TBLT are the Cognition Hypothesis (Robinson, 2001) and the Trade-off Hypothesis (Skehan, 1996), both of which assume that tasks with certain characteristics will impose varying processing loads, which may then direct the attention of L2 learners to different aspects of language use (see Pallotti, Chapter 19; Van den Branden, Chapter 30, this volume).

In LT, among monologic tasks, mechanical tasks such as read-aloud and sentence repetition can be found in semi-direct or fully automated tests (e.g., PTE Academic, Versant). Echoing the rationale for using such mechanical tasks in SLA, these tasks tap into the processing speed and short-term memory capacity of learners, and are considered indicative of learners' facility with the language (Van Moere, 2012) rather than their ability to deal with the direct interactional demands of face-to-face exchanges. These tasks, while limiting interpretations of test scores, lend themselves particularly well to automated testing approaches, which is discussed in more detail below, as they can increase the robustness of pronunciation and fluency scoring algorithms in automated systems (e.g., Xi, Higgins, Zechner, & Williamson, 2012).

Picture description tasks that elicit extended monologues are also common in LT, although their focus is more general than in SLA; they are not so much for finding out about learners' processing and its effects on L2 performance, but for making an evaluative judgement on their speaking proficiency by assessing the ability to describe, compare/contrast, or discuss the picture(s) using the language as expected by the test designers in terms of the lexis, grammar, speed, etc.

Dialogic/Group Tasks. In SLA, following the rise of the Interaction Hypothesis (Long, 1996) and the Output Hypothesis (Swain, 1985), dialogic/group tasks have been used for interaction-based research (Mackey & Gass, 2005). This type of task features information-gaps between the paired/grouped learners, and examples include role play, picture comparison and sequencing, instruction, and story-retelling. Using such tasks, SLA researchers have explored the relationship between the types of input, interaction, and feedback, as well as the effects of these factors on learning; for example, the effects of using recasts on learning particular morphosyntactic features as compared to other methods of error correction (e.g., Sato & Loewen, 2018).

Similarly, in LT research and practice, dialogic/group oral tasks are used to tap into learners' interactional competence (Galaczi & Taylor, Chapter 32, this volume). For instance, all Cambridge General English exams now include a paired task where two test-takers have a discussion based on a visual prompt. While a range of LT tasks are available, such as information-gap, ranking, free discussion, and discussion based on a reading text, the focus of LT tasks is again more general than that in SLA. By using these tasks, language testers seek to collect evidence to evaluate how well learners can use various types of language functions (e.g., informational, interactional, and interaction management functions; O'Sullivan, Weir, & Saville, 2002) and how effectively they can communicate with others using their interactional resources, rather than to analyse the extent to which certain morphosyntactic features have been acquired.

The implementation of dialogic/group oral tests is generally considered resource-intensive; however, thanks to recent advances in technology, we have now started to see the emergence of another strand of research addressing the practical challenges of conducting face-to-face speaking tests while emphasising the importance of including interactional competence as part of the speaking construct. For example, Nakatsuhara, Inoue, Berry, and Galaczi (2017a; 2017b) and Berry, Nakatsuhara, Inoue, and Galaczi (2018) explored the use of video-conferencing technology in delivering the IELTS Speaking Test as a solution for addressing the practical and resource-heavy challenges of conducting face-to-face speaking tests. Also, Ockey, Gu, and Keehner (2017) examined the potential of web-based virtual environments (VEs) as platforms for the delivery and assessment of speaking and communication in real time. The option to simulate real-world environments (e.g., a library or a university) within the assessment setting and immersing learners within these settings are viewed as one of the strengths of VEs in visually reflecting the target language use domain. Such a solution not only encourages interaction but has great potential for authentic task-based language learning bringing together SLA and LT.

Scoring Speaking

As well as elicitation tasks, the scoring of the elicited performance is another major factor that contributes to the validity argument in L2 speaking tests. While Chapters 12 and 13 in this volume discuss rating approaches and issues related to rater behaviour and rater training in depth, here we draw our attention to an inter-disciplinary review of research on fluency; de Jong (2018 p. 239) notes a lack of objective criteria for measuring fluency in LT as evidenced in the assessment scales of large-scale exams such as IELTS, TOEFL iBT, and ACTFL OPI where the use of vague descriptors may "leave room for subjective interpretation of fluency" by raters. This is in contrast with SLA approaches that predominantly use objective measures of fluency such as speech rate and mean length of runs in fluency research (de Jong, 2018). The issue of subjective interpretation of assessment scales is also touched on in Isaac's (2018) state-of the-art article on L2 pronunciation.

At the same time, advancements in speech science, automatic speech recognition, and deep neural networking technologies have enabled technology-based forms of testing speaking, and have paved the way for further broadening of the speaking construct by eliciting spontaneous speech and including linguistic features related to lexical use, syntactic complexity, topical coherence, and progression of ideas (Zechner et al., 2015). However, as noted by Chen et al. (2018), in addition to the challenges of speech recognition and associated word error rates, the most problematic areas for an automated system to tackle are those related to the scoring of content, discourse, and topic development. These are higher-level features of speech which are more complex to assess and require a multi-level understanding of speech and communication.

Recommendations for Practice

Speaking Tasks

We have discussed above that although the rationales for selecting certain task types are largely shared between SLA and LT, the research focus appears narrower and more specific in SLA than in LT. This is because the goals of the two fields of study are different. SLA researchers seek "to understand universal, individual and social forces that influence what gets acquired, how fast, and how well, by different people under different learning circumstances" (Ortega, 2009, p. 10). Fundamentally, SLA researchers are more interested in investigating variability as evidenced by numerous studies on the effects of individual and contextual factors on L2 learning, such as age, L1, motivation, cognitive styles, types and amount of input, and types and complexity of tasks.

In contrast, language testers are more interested in the stability of L2 measurement and the generalisability of test results (Alderson, 2010). While individual and contextual variables that influence performance and test results are indeed of interest and the effects of some variables such as planning time, interlocutor/rater characteristics and topics have been extensively researched and usefully applied to testing (e.g., Khabbazbashi, 2017; O'Sullivan, 2008; Wigglesworth & Elder, 2010; Winke, Gass, & Myford, 2013), it is neither possible nor fair for tests—at least for large-scale proficiency tests—to cater for all possible sources of variability. The L2 performance has to be elicited through (a set of) the same or parallel tasks and evaluated using the same rating criteria, and the resultant bands of scores or levels need to clearly differentiate among different levels of ability. Otherwise, meaningful and fair comparisons among test-takers cannot be made. Therefore, tasks, rating scales, and levels used in LT may appear more general or less individualised than those commonly used in SLA research.

As Alderson (2010) notes, in SLA research, the validity and reliability of the instruments do not seem to have been sufficiently reported. For example, in TBLT, picture-based narrative tasks are frequently used as speech elicitation tools to allow for comparisons of L2 performance across different task manipulations. In order for the results of these studies to be credible, the tasks used in a study must be parallel prior to any manipulation (Inoue, 2013). Otherwise, any differences observed in performances are potentially confounded with inherent differences between the tasks, and counterbalancing the order of task presentation cannot sufficiently address this issue. Although more task-based studies nowadays publish the actual tasks used or reveal the source of where the tasks were obtained (e.g., Foster & Tavakoli, 2009; Yuan & Ellis, 2003), only a few provide empirical research evidence of the parallelness of tasks beforehand (Inoue, 2013; Weir & Wu, 2006).

In LT, it is always recommended that test tasks are developed based on test specifications, which control the complexity of the prompts and expected performance in terms of the levels of vocabulary, grammar, functions, discourse type, etc. (Taylor, 2011; Weir, 2005). Parallel versions of the tasks are created and piloted, so as to ensure the performances from different administrations can be meaningfully compared (see Suzuki & Koizumi, Chapter 43, this volume). This practice in LT seems quite relevant to SLA, contributing to enhancing the confidence in and generalisability of valuable findings of SLA speaking research.

Scoring Speaking

An alternative suggestion to subjective, rater-based scoring approaches is the use of more objective measures facilitated by technology and automated approaches to assessing speaking (e.g., Bernstein, Van Moere, & Cheng, 2010). Notwithstanding that these have their own limitations, they can address some of the concerns raised about subjectivity in assessment and bridge the distance between the fields of SLA and LT. At the same time, while automated assessment solutions can detect hundreds of features in speech, it is important for LT researchers to draw on results of SLA studies to incorporate, in the scoring algorithms, those features which are shown to be valid measures of the construct of interest. For example, whereas fluency features of speech rate and pausing are commonly used in automated assessment systems (Chen et al., 2018), several studies in SLA have pointed to the importance of the *location* of pauses as exerting more influence on listeners' perceptions of fluency than the frequency of pauses (e.g., Tavakoli, 2011).

Automated scoring systems rely heavily on constrained and monologic task types. A possible negative impact is therefore an excessive preoccupation with monologic speech in learning contexts at the expense of more interactive tasks and co-constructed dialogues. Another critical issue—closely related to the narrow test construct—is the increased likelihood of candidates displaying abnormal test behaviours or applying strategies in an attempt to cheat or fool automated systems. As a promising solution for retaining the wide construct coverage while making the best use of automated scoring systems, we would like to echo the suggestions by Khabbazbashi and Galaczi (2016), Isaacs (2018), and Lim (2018), and argue for a complementary human-machine approach to assessing speaking with raters focusing on aspects of speech that are too complex for automatic evaluation, and machines measuring relevant features of speech that can be automatically derived and which have been shown to be reliable predictors of oral proficiency.

Feedback

Amongst the criticisms levelled at LT researchers in Shohamy (2000) was a lack of sensitivity to learners and candidates in terms of their individual learning needs. Since then, the field of LT has come a long way in increasing recognition of the importance of learning-oriented approaches to assessment (LOA) and promoting learning by creating a synergy between instruction, assessment, and learning (e.g., Jones & Saville, 2016). Technology has great potential in facilitating this synergy by providing timely and individualised feedback which, according to SLA theories, can promote L2 development (Gass & Mackey, 2015). For example, Franco et al. (2010) designed a toolkit that can score the pronunciation of non-native speakers and provide explicit diagnostic feedback at the phone level for specific pronunciation mistakes; a functionality which can greatly assist teachers in L2 learning contexts where providing individualised support may be practically unfeasible. Morton, Gunson, and Jack (2012) designed a spoken dialogue system where success on the task was defined, not as score targets, but as completing a real-world activity such as buying train tickets through interacting with a series of conversational agents in a web environment. The limitations in automatic speech recognition of this system were countered by the provision of "implicit" feedback such as recasts, repetitions, reformulations, and hints when the system encountered errors in learners' utterance or where learners failed to provide a response. While technical challenges remain in automating spoken interactions and the provision of feedback (Litman, Strik, & Lim, 2018), these examples and the surge of research on educational games, spoken dialogue systems, and whole tutoring systems demonstrate the usefulness of technology in bringing together learning and assessment in innovative ways. Moreover, this integration of learning and assessment and the capacity for systems to collect and track language use data over extended periods of time can greatly advance our understanding of the process of language acquisition and provide exciting avenues for joint research between the fields of SLA and LT.

Testing Tips

- When selecting or designing speaking test tasks, always ask: Where can the construct we wish to measure be located in the cognitive-social construct spectrum of speaking assessments? Are we prioritising, for example, automaticity (speed of processing language), or is our focus more on interactional effectiveness?
- Your answers to these types of questions will help you choose appropriate speaking task formats and scoring methods, and provide you with a selection of available technologies.
- Technologies in delivering and scoring speaking tests and offering individualised feedback are highly useful, as long as we are fully aware of their pros and cons in relation to the construct we wish to measure.

Recommended Readings

Fulcher, G. (2003). *Testing second language speaking*. Longman/Pearson Education.

This book, although written some time ago, provides a thorough guide into designing and implementing speaking tests, as well as useful and critical summaries of research in L2 speaking assessment.

Lim, G. (Ed.). (2018). Conceptualizing and operationalizing speaking assessment for a new century [Special issue], *Language Assessment Quarterly*, *15*(3). https://doi.org/10.1080/15434303.2018.1482493

The articles in this special issue consider important aspects of the speaking construct such as interactional competence, collocational competence, fluency, and pronunciation and whether and to what extent they have been assessed while reflecting on the potential role of technology in enhancing assessment practices.

Taylor, L. (2011). *Examining speaking: Research and practice in assessing second language speaking*. UCLES/Cambridge University Press.

This edited volume presents a review of relevant literature on the assessment of speaking and provides a systematic framework for validating speaking tests.

References

Alderson, J. C. (2010). Language testing-informed SLA? SLA-informed language testing? In I. Bartning, M. Martin, & I. Vedder (Eds.), *Communicative proficiency and linguistic development: Intersections between SLA and language testing research* (pp. 239–248). EUROSLA.

Bachman, L. F., & Palmer, A. S. (1996). *Language testing in practice*. Oxford University Press.
Bernstein, J., Van Moere, A., & Cheng, J. (2010). Validating automated speaking tests. *Language Testing, 27*(3), 355–377. https://doi.org/10.1177/0265532210364404
Berry, V., Nakatsuhara, F., Inoue, C., & Galaczi, E. (2018). Exploring the use of video-conferencing technology to deliver the IELTS speaking test: Phase 3 technical trial. IELTS Partnership Research Papers, *2018*/1. http://www.ielts.org/-/media/research-reports/ielts-research-partner-paper-4.ashx
Block, D. (2003). *Social turn in second language acquisition*. Georgetown University Press.
Brown, A. (2006). Candidate discourse in the revised IELTS speaking test. *IELTS Research Reports, 6*, 71–89. http://www.ielts.org/-/media/research-reports/ielts_rr_volume06_report3.ashx
Canale, M., & Swain, M. (1980). Theoretical bases of communicative approaches to second language teaching and testing. *Applied Linguistics, 1*, 1–47. https://doi.org/10.1093/applin/I.1.1
Chen, L., Zechner, K., Yoon, S., Evanini, K., Wang, X., Loukina, A., Tao, J., Davis, L., Lee, C. M., Ma, M., & Mundkowsky, R. (2018). Automated scoring of nonnative speech using the SpeechRater SM v. 5.0 engine. *ETS Research Report Series*. https://doi.org/10.1002/ets2.12198
Corder, S. P. (1971). Idiosyncratic dialects and error analysis. *International Review of Applied Linguistics, 9*, 147–159. https://doi.org/10.1515/iral.1971.9.2.147
De Bot, K. (1992). A bilingual production model: Levelt's 'Speaking' model adapted. *Applied Linguistics, 13*(1),1–24. https://doi.org/10.1093/applin/13.1.1
De Jong, N. (2018). Fluency in second language testing: Insights from different disciplines. *Language Assessment Quarterly, 15*(3), 237–254. https://doi.org/10.1080/15434303.2018.1477780
De Jong, N., Steinel, M., Florijn, A., Schoonen, R., & Hulstijn, J. (2012). Facets of speaking proficiency. *Studies in Second Language Acquisition, 34*(1), 5–34. https://doi.org/10.1017/S0272263111000489
Field, J. (2011). Cognitive validity. In L. Taylor (Ed.), *Examining speaking: Research and practice in assessing second language speaking* (pp. 65–111). UCLES/Cambridge University Press.
Foster, P., & Tavakoli, P. (2009). Native speakers and task performance: Comparing effects on complexity, fluency and lexical diversity. *Language Learning, 59*(4), 866–896. https://doi.org/10.1111/j.1467-9922.2009.00528.x
Franco, H., Bratt, H., Rossier, R. Rao Gadde, V., Shriberg, E., Abrash, V., & Precoda, K. (2010). EduSpeak: A speech recognition and pronunciation scoring toolkit for computer-aided language learning applications. *Language Testing, 27*(3), 401–418. https://doi.org/10.1177/0265532210364408
Fulcher, G. (1996). Does thick description lead to smart tests? A data-based approach to rating scale construction. *Language Testing, 13*(2), 208–238. https://doi.org/10.1177/026553229601300205
Fulcher, G. (2003). *Testing second language speaking*. Longman.
Galaczi, E., & Taylor, L. (2018). Interactional competence: Conceptualisations, operationalisations, and outstanding questions. *Language Assessment Quarterly, 15*(3), 219–236. https://doi.org/10.1080/15434303.2018.1453816
Gass, S. M., & Mackey, A. (2015). Input, interaction, and output in second language acquisition. In *Theories in second language acquisition: An introduction* (2nd ed., pp. 180–206). Routledge.
Inoue, C. (2013). *Task equivalence in speaking tests: Investigating the difficulty of two spoken narrative tasks*. Peter Lang.
Isaacs, T. (2018). Shifting sands in second language pronunciation teaching and assessment research and practice. *Language Assessment Quarterly, 15*(3), 273–293. https://doi.org/10.1080/15434303.2018.1472264
Iwashita, N., Brown, A., McNamara, T., & O'Hagan, S. (2008). Assessed levels of second language speaking proficiency: How distinct? *Applied Linguistics, 29*(1), 24–29. https://doi.org/10.1093/applin/amm017
Jones, N., & Saville, N. (2016). *Learning oriented assessment: A systemic approach*. UCLES/Cambridge University Press.
Khabbazbashi, N. (2017). Topic and background knowledge effects on performance in speaking assessment. *Language Testing, 34*(1), 23–48. https://doi.org/10.1177/0265532215595666
Khabbazbashi, N., & Galaczi, E. (2016, May 5–8). *Technology and the 'what' of automated speaking tests*. [SIG paper presentation]. European Association of Language Testing and Assessment (EALTA), Valencia, Spain.
Levelt, W. J. M. (1989). *Speaking*. MIT Press.
Lim, G. S. (2018). Conceptualizing and operationalizing second language speaking assessment: Updating the construct for a new century. *Language Assessment Quarterly, 15*(3), 215–218. https://doi.org/10.1080/15434303.2018.1482493
Litman, D., Strik, H., & Lim, G. S. (2018). Speech technologies and the assessment of second language speaking: Approaches, challenges, and opportunities. *Language Assessment Quarterly, 15*(3), 294–309. https://doi.org/10.1080/15434303.2018.1472265

Long, M. H. (1996). The role of the linguistic environment in second language acquisition. In W. Ritchie & T. Bhatia (Eds.), *Handbook of second language acquisition* (pp. 413–468). Academic Press.
Mackey, A., & Gass, S. M. (2005). *Second language research: Methodology and design*. Lawrence Erlbaum Associates.
McNamara, T. F. (1990). Item response theory and the validation of an ESP test for health professionals. *Language Testing*, *7*(1), 52–76. https://doi.org/10.1177/026553229000700105
Morton, H., Gunson, N., & Jack, M. (2012). Interactive language learning through speech-enabled virtual scenarios. *Advances in Human-Computer Interaction*, *2012*, 1–14. https://doi.org/10.1155/2012/389523
Nakatsuhara, F., Inoue, C., Berry, V., & Galaczi, E. (2017a). Exploring the use of video-conferencing technology in the assessment of spoken language: A mixed-methods study. *Language Assessment Quarterly*, *14*(1), 1–18. https://doi.org/10.1080/15434303.2016.1263637
Nakatsuhara, F., Inoue, C., Berry, V., & Galaczi, E. (2017b). Exploring performance across two delivery modes for the IELTS speaking test: Face-to-face and video-conferencing delivery (phase 2). IELTS Research Reports Online Series, *2017*/3, 1–74. http://www.ielts.org/-/media/research-reports/ielts-research-partner-paper-3.ashx
Ockey, G., & Wagner, E. (2018). An overview of interactive listening as part of the construct of interactive and integrated oral test tasks. In G. Ockey & E. Wagner (Eds.), *Assessing L2 listening: Moving towards authenticity* (pp. 179–192). John Benjamins.
Ockey, G. J., Gu, L., & Keehner, M. (2017). Web-based virtual environments for facilitating assessment of L2 oral communication ability. *Language Assessment Quarterly*, *14*(4), 346–359. https://doi.org/10.1080/15434303.2017.1400036
Ortega, L. (2009). *Understanding second language acquisition*. Routledge.
O'Sullivan, B. (2008). *Modelling performance in tests of spoken language*. Peter Lang.
O'Sullivan, B., Weir, C. J., & Saville, N. (2002). Using observation checklists to validate speaking-test tasks. *Language Testing*, *19*(1), 33–56. https://doi.org/10.1191/0265532202lt219oa
Palmer, H. E. (1921). *The oral method of teaching languages*. Heffers.
Révész, A., Ekiert, M., & Torgersen, E. (2016). The effects of complexity, accuracy, and fluency on communicative adequacy in oral task performance. *Applied Linguistics*, *37*(6), 828–848. https://doi.org/10.1093/applin/amu069
Robinson, P. (2001). Task complexity, task difficulty, and task production: Exploring interactions in a componential framework. *Applied Linguistics*, *22*(1), 27–57. https://doi.org/10.1093/applin/22.1.27
Sato, M., & Loewen, S. (2018). Metacognitive instruction enhances the effectiveness of corrective feedback: Variable effects of feedback types and linguistic targets. *Language Learning*, *68*(2), 507–545. https://doi.org/10.1111/lang.12283
Shohamy, E. (2000). The relationship between language testing and second language acquisition, revisited. *System*, *28*(4), 541–533. https://doi.org/10.1016/S0346-251X(00)00037-3
Skehan, P. (1989). *Individual differences in second language learning*. Edward Arnold.
Skehan, P. (1996). A framework for the implementation of task based instruction. *Applied Linguistics*, *17*(1), 38–62. https://doi.org/10.1093/applin/17.1.38
Skehan, P. (2009). Modelling second language performance: Integrating complexity, accuracy, fluency and lexis. *Applied Linguistics*, *30*(4), 510–532. https://doi.org/10.1093/applin/amp047
Swain, M. (1985). Communicative competence: Some roles of comprehensible input and comprehensible output in its development. In S. M. Gass & C. G. Madden (Eds.), *Input in second language acquisition* (pp. 235–253). Newbury House.
Sweet, H. (1899). *The practical study of languages*. Dent.
Tavakoli, P. (2011). Pausing patterns: Differences between L2 learners and native speakers. *ELT Journal*, *65*(1), 71–79. https://doi.org/10.1093/elt/ccq020
Tavakoli, P., Nakatsuhara, F., & Hunter, A. M. (2017). Scoring validity of the Aptis speaking test: Investigating fluency across tasks and levels of proficiency. *ARAGs Research Reports Online*, AR-G/2017/7, 1–56. http://www.britishcouncil.org/sites/default/files/tavakoli_et_al_layout.pdf
Taylor, L. (2011). *Examining speaking: Research and practice in assessing second language speaking*. UCLES/Cambridge University Press.
Van Moere, A. (2012). A psycholinguistic approach to oral language assessment. *Language Testing*, *29*(3), 325–344. https://doi.org/10.1177/0265532211424478
Vidaković, I., & Galaczi, E. G. (2013). The measurement of speaking ability 1913–2012. In C. J. Weir, I. Vidaković, & E. D. Galaczi (Eds.), *Measured constructs: A history of Cambridge English language examinations 1913–2012* (pp. 257–346). UCLES/Cambridge University Press.
Weir, C. J. (2005). *Language testing and validation: An evidence-based approach*. Palgrave Macmillan.

Weir, C. J., & Wu, J. R. W. (2006). Establishing test form and individual task comparability: A case study of a semi-direct speaking test. *Language Testing*, *23*(2), 167–197. https://doi.org/10.1191/02655322061t326oa
Wigglesworth, G., & Elder, C. (2010). An investigation of the effectiveness and validity of planning time in speaking test tasks. *Language Assessment Quarterly*, *7*(1), 1–24. https://doi.org/10.1080/15434300903031779
Winke, P., Gass, S., & Myford, C. (2013). Raters' L2 background as a potential source of bias in rating oral performance. *Language Testing*, *30*(2), 231–252. https://doi.org/10.1177/0265532212456968
Xi, X., Higgins, D., Zechner, K., & Williamson, D. (2012). A comparison of two scoring methods for an automated speech scoring system. *Language Testing*, *29*(3), 371–394. https://doi.org/10.1177/0265532211425673
Yuan, F., & Ellis, R. (2003). The effects of pre-task planning and online planning on fluency, complexity and accuracy in L2 monologic oral production. *Applied Linguistics*, *24*(1), 1–27. https://doi.org/10.1016/j.sbspro.2011.11.445
Zechner, K., Chen, L., Davis, L., Evanini, K., Lee, C. M., Leong, C. W., Wang, X., & Yoon, S. (2015). Automated scoring of speaking tasks in the test of English-for-Teaching (TEFT™). *ETS Research Report Series*, 2015(2), 1–17. https://doi.org/10.1002/ets2.12080

28

Measuring L2 Writing

Hyung-Jo Yoon & J. Dylan Burton

Background

Today, few in education would downplay the importance of writing in second language (L2) learning and assessment, but the reality is that writing assessment as an academic discipline has not had a long history (Behizadeh & Engelhard, 2011). Early efforts in standardized L2 writing assessment began in the early 20th century with a divide between British-European and American assessment philosophies (Hamp-Lyons, 2001). Cambridge University introduced the Proficiency Exam of English in 1913 with a direct test of writing, while the American system favored objective, psychometric methods of measurement and followed proposals by Hillegas (1912) to move to a separation of form and content. Multiple-choice testing of writing skills thus dominated the American paradigm well into the 1970s (Hamp-Lyons, 2001). There was, nonetheless, a gradual return to the direct assessment of writing following the communicative language movement (Canale & Swain, 1980; Hymes, 1972), leading educators to acknowledge that "the best way to test people's writing ability is to get them to write" (Hughes, 2003, p. 83). At the same time, research on reliable scoring methods for the direct measurement of essays has endeavored to make large-scale writing assessment more feasible. Continuing this trend, the 21st century has been marked by a search for authentic direct tests with more reliable scoring systems, leading to increased interest in automated scoring systems. These systems promise precision and accuracy, while alleviating the burden on educators to score stacks of essays by hand.

The field of applied linguistics has been marked by differential approaches to the measurement of L2 writing ability. A large body of SLA research, for example, includes studies where task variables and conditions were manipulated in order to observe their effects on language development and acquisition. In these cases, the ability manifested through writing has often been measured using discrete linguistic features, such as complexity, accuracy, and fluency (see Pallotti, Chapter 19, this volume). Nonetheless, the act of writing is a complex, recursive process, and writing proficiency is multifaceted (Norris & Manchón, 2012), including a range of features beyond CAF measures. Fully representing the construct of L2 writing ability has been one of the main foci of language testers, as inferences about writing ability require information about adequacy and communicative competence as well as linguistic measures (Pallotti, 2009) to build stronger validity arguments. Essential as well is the construction of sound, reliable instruments, since interpretable and generalizable scores are vital to making valid inferences about language ability or development.

In this chapter, we will explore some of the key issues that SLA and language testing researchers may face when assessing L2 writing. Of prime importance is a discussion of the construct to be measured, as different purposes and uses for assessments will determine the breadth of the L2 writing ability that should be defined. Following this, we will discuss the essential characteristics of tasks designed to target that construct, including type, complexity, and mode. We will also elaborate on the scoring mechanism that will provide users with information about the L2 writer. Essential to those working with cognitive-interactional approaches is a discussion of the types of feedback available, in particular computer-automated feedback. Finally, we will end with recommendations for practice for those seeking to design and implement writing assessment into their research studies.

Key Concepts

L2 Writing Ability: The complex processing of form and meaning to produce written language. L2 writing is differentiated from L1 writing ability by the inclusion of language proficiency, resulting in differences in automaticity and accuracy of form as well as varying familiarity with sociocultural and pragmatic norms.

Functional Adequacy: The degree of success a learner exhibits on completing communicative writing tasks. Functional adequacy may include content-related features such as task achievement and discourse organization.

Task: The instrument used to elicit performances from learners. Writing tasks are often short, sentence-level instructions but can also take the form of an integrated text or audio-based input combined with a written text.

Delivery Mode: The physical format of the test prompt and the learners' response. It generally involves the use of pen/pencil and paper or computer-based systems, while tablet, mobile phone, and other options are available.

Automated Essay Scoring: Computer systems that provide scores or subscores for distinct areas of written performance.

Feedback: Human or computer-generated commentary on the quality or discrete aspects of a performance.

Key Issues

Construct Definition

Writing, like speaking, is a complex psychological process nested in a rich sociocultural context. L2 writing ability differs from first language writing ability by the addition of facets such as familiarity with writing systems and target language proficiency (Weigle, 2002). As such, any construct definition must include socio-cognitive elements as well as those of language proficiency. A number of issues must be taken into account when defining what is to be measured, which has resulted in a number of shifting models of writing ability.

Multiple models of writing have been proposed with a focus on writers' cognitive processes during writing (e.g., Hayes, 1996, 2012; Hayes & Flower, 1980). The original model in Hayes and Flower (1980) emphasized the interactive roles of writers' long-term and working memory for the act of composition. With long-term memory factors such as task schemas and genre knowledge remaining as crucial components, Hayes (1996, 2012) has updated his models by adding motivational and affective components (goals and attitudes), as well as immediate writing settings (collaborators and critics, and transcribing technology) and external source use (Leijten, Waes, Schriver, & Hayes, 2013).

Models of L2 writing proficiency often fall within the scope of models of general language proficiency. An early model of writing proficiency proposed by Grabe and Kaplan (1996) included linguistic knowledge (e.g., written codes, phonology, vocabulary, syntax), discourse knowledge (e.g., cohesion, structuring, topics, genre, inferencing), and sociolinguistic knowledge (e.g., functional knowledge, register), as well as rich sociocultural elements of participants, settings, tasks, and topics. General language models proposed by Bachman and Palmer (1996) and Douglas (2000) additionally included metacognitive elements associated with strategic competence (e.g., goal setting, self-assessment, planning). The Common European Framework of Reference Companion Volume (Council of Europe, 2018) is perhaps one of the most complete descriptions to date of language (and also writing) proficiency, covering a wide range of linguistic and socio-cognitive aspects of language use. More on models of language proficiency can be found in Harsch and Malone (Chapter 4, this volume).

In terms of the validity of writing assessments, it is vital to ensure adequate construct coverage taking into account models of processing and language proficiency. Pallotti (2009) argued that one way of doing so is to include a focus on functional adequacy as a key component of any writing task along with linguistic features such as CAF. Functional adequacy here refers to the unfolding of communication and the measurement of its success in context, a feature that Kuiken and Vedder (2017) noted is unfortunately often disregarded in L2 writing studies despite being part of the construct of most current high stakes writing assessments. These authors proposed a framework for measuring functional adequacy, which took into account aspects of task achievement, discourse structure, and an awareness of audience.

Tasks

Tasks in writing assessment are critical to the elicitation of performances that tie the intended construct to outcomes which can be measured consistently. Cumming, Kantor, Powers, Santos, and Taylor (2000) proposed a framework to identify "a set of writing task characteristics and variables believed to account for variance in test performance, an accompanying research agenda, and criteria for a better test" (p. 1). Weir (2005) likewise proposed a socio-cognitive framework for test validation, which took into account a greater range of contextual factors not only for task design but also for scoring and test use. Since these proposals, there have been a large number of empirical studies by SLA researchers that attempted to explicate the relationship between writing task features and learners' language use (e.g., Kormos, 2011; Ong & Zhang, 2010; Révész, Kourtali, & Mazgutova, 2017), and this endeavor is still underway (see Johnson, 2017 for a review). Here we will consider three key task variables: task type, task complexity, and delivery mode.

Task Type. Cumming et al. (2000) offered a comprehensive perspective on writing that considers its communicative functions, task demands, and social influences. Following their conceptual framework, writing began to be viewed as a communicative act, and writing researchers have sought to identify sources of writing task difficulty and score variance. Writing tasks may introduce variability in test-takers' use of writing skills and linguistic repertoires (e.g., Hamp-Lyons & Mathias, 1994; Jeong, 2017; Way, Joiner, & Seaman, 2000; Yoon, 2018), as they may include a range of discourse modes, genres, or topics, on which test-takers may not all perform equally. The statistical analysis of Bouwer, Béguin, Sanders, and van den Bergh (2015), for example, indicated that task type accounted for 11% of the variance in children's writing scores. Way et al. (2000) examined L2 essay scores of descriptive, narrative, and expository tasks, finding that L2 writers tended to perform weaker on expository tasks than descriptive writing. Hamp-Lyons and Mathias (1994) and Jeong (2017), however, found contradictory results. Taking L2 proficiency into account, Jeong (2017) observed that high- and low-level writers performed differently depending on task type. The choice of task may thus introduce unfair bias into tests if learners have not developed the cognitive skills or background knowledge required to perform at their true ability.

Task types may also include different formats, such as writing-only or integrated tasks. While writing-only tasks generally include a short text-based prompt and primarily ask the learner to write from their own experience or knowledge, integrated tasks require the learner to first read and/or listen to input and then synthesize this information in their writing. Much research has been conducted on integrated writing tasks as they have become more prevalent in both high-stakes and classroom settings (Plakans, 2008, 2012). While there is evidence for increased authenticity particularly in academic settings, there are potential difficulties in disentangling the underlying construct of integrated writing tasks (Knoch & Sitajalabhorn, 2013) as well as scoring them (Shin & Ewert, 2014).

Task Complexity. SLA researchers have explored task variables through a lens different from that of writing researchers. Attending to the task internal concept of *task complexity*, SLA researchers manipulate the structure and design of writing tasks to adjust the level of cognitive demands imposed by the tasks. Specifically, they have examined several different task variables that are known to influence task complexity, defined as "attentional, memory, reasoning, and other information processing demands imposed by the structure of the task on the language learner" (Robinson, 2001, p. 29). Based on the task variables proposed by the Triadic Componential Framework (Robinson, 2001, 2005), scholars have explored how linguistic features for writing task completion vary as a result of manipulating task variables such as *number of elements* (e.g., Frear & Bitchener, 2015; Kuiken & Vedder, 2008) and *reasoning demands* (e.g., Kormos, 2011; Ong & Zhang, 2010; Révész et al., 2017).

The manipulation of these variables theoretically leads to a change in task complexity along resource-directing dimensions (e.g., adding more elements will result in the learner's greater use of their cognitive resources for successful task completion), and SLA researchers have tested this conceptual hypothesis that a writing task with greater cognitive complexity would allow a writer to formulate more developed, complex language (Robinson, 2001, 2005). For example, Ong and Zhang (2010) and Révész et al. (2017) examined the effect of reasoning demand manipulation (tasks with idea support considered cognitively less demanding) on learners' written language features. Ong and Zhang found a significant increase in lexical diversity elicited by a more complex task, but Révész et al. did not find a clear pattern of cognitive demand effects on lexical diversity. Using picture narrative tasks manipulated in terms of cognitive demands (story plot provision), Kormos (2011) found that a more complex task led to increased lexical sophistication but no change in lexical diversity. These mixed findings demonstrate that it is difficult to predict patterns of linguistic changes in relation to task demand manipulations in written discourse, possibly due to task-internal and learner factors (e.g., topic familiarity, genre awareness, and language background).

Delivery Mode. A final issue of importance is the delivery of L2 writing tasks via traditional pencil-and-paper or increasingly common computer-based modes. Though past studies showed contradictory findings (e.g., Breland, Lee, & Murake, 2005; Li, 2006), a range of recent studies have considered the comparability of paper and computer-based tasks in terms of score equivalence and cognitive processes (Chan, Bax, & Weir, 2018), essay quality and writer preference (Brunfaut, Harding, & Batty, 2018; Kim, Bowles, Yan, & Chung, 2018), and scores and essay characteristics (Barkaoui & Knouzi, 2018). These studies have concluded that overall there are no consistent effects of delivery mode on scores or performances, but that writers tend to prefer computer-based writing. The mode of delivery, however, can have notable restraints in contexts with limited access to technology or computer training, as learner variables such as computer familiarity, age, and L2 proficiency have been found to moderate delivery mode effects (e.g., Chen, White, McCloskey, Soroui, & Chun, 2011; Jin & Yan, 2017; Wolfe & Manalo, 2004).

Scoring

Apart from discourse analytic, empirical measures of written performance, overall writing quality is generally scored in one of two ways: with human raters using scoring rubrics or with automated essay scoring (AES) systems. Scoring rubrics operationalize the test construct through the wording of the trait descriptors, which may be *holistic*, with all traits clustered within one scoring category, or *analytic*, with various traits scored separately (e.g., grammar, vocabulary, mechanics, etc.). While the purpose of the test will dictate which type of rubric (holistic or analytic) and score criteria to use, holistic rubrics may serve more practical purposes due to ease and quickness of use, although in general research supports the use of analytic scoring rubrics as scores tend to be more reliable and less idiosyncratic. Nonetheless, care must be taken to guard against construct underrepresentation (see Banerjee, Yan, Chapman, & Elliott, 2015), and raters must be adequately trained and monitored (Weigle, 2002). More information on designing rubrics can be found in Kuiken and Vedder (Chapter 12, this volume), and a 2015 special issue of *Assessing Writing* (Crusan, 2015). More information on rater training can be found in Pill and Smart (Chapter 13, this volume).

AES Systems. In recent years AES systems have arisen to target the needs of faster and more reliable rating (Xi, 2010). These systems often use a synthesis of pattern recognition and statistical models as a means to analyze linguistic features and produce an overall holistic score. Researchers have shown concern about the use of scores generated by automated systems (e.g., Condon, 2013; Herrington & Moran, 2001), but others have also offered empirical evidence that automated systems could generate scores comparable to human rater scores (e.g., Attali & Burstein, 2006; Enright & Quinlan, 2010). Based on research findings, there is a growing consensus that AES is of great use at least for performance assessments that have a primary focus on linguistic competence rather than functional adequacy (Weigle, 2013).

Feedback

An area closely aligned with scoring is that of feedback given to learners about their writing. While high-stakes testing systems rarely provide qualitative feedback on performances, a major element of formative assessment is the provision of feedback in order to foster language growth. The importance of feedback on writing has been emphasized by cognitive-interactionists in SLA for decades (Loewen & Sato, 2018), and is thus a key construct in formative assessment (Davidson & Leung, 2009). Nevertheless, there is conflicting evidence of whether it indeed aids acquisition, though error-focused feedback may prove useful for identifying problematic areas of production (Ferris, 2006; Hyland & Hyland, 2006).

With the rise of AES systems, there has been a concurrent rise in automated writing evaluation (AWE) systems designed for classroom-use rather than high-stakes decision-making. Two examples of AWE systems include Criterion (Casal, 2016) and WriteToLearn (Liu & Kunnan, 2016), both of which return feedback on a range of traits. Traits may include syntactic complexity, accuracy, mechanics, organization (sentence and paragraph level), style, and even content relevance and development. Research has shown that this type of feedback can be positive for learners (Wang, Shang, & Briody, 2013), though perhaps somewhat limited in scope (Hoang & Kunnan, 2016; Shermis & Burnstein, 2013) or with unobservable improvements in writing (Huang & Renandya, 2020). Nonetheless, the potential of AWE systems for SLA research is nearly limitless as these systems can quickly and reliably provide empirical data about language use and textual features.

Recommendations for Practice

Decisions to implement writing assessments in SLA research or classroom testing must begin with two main questions. First, consider the purpose of the assessment and how scores will be used. Beginning with this question will lead to task design targeting the linguistic or functional information necessary. For example, if the intended use of the assessment is to compare the development of fluency after an intervention, it will be necessary to write tasks that elicit a sufficient amount of writing such that short answers would only indicate lower levels of fluency. Likewise, if test scores are to determine overall growth in proficiency, it will likely be necessary to include tasks that target a range of higher-level organizational and pragmatic features. On the other hand, if changes to the process of writing are of interest, it will be necessary to gather data from a larger range of tasks over time, and this may include written artifacts and classroom observations. The intended use should drive the choice and number of tasks that are used.

The second key question related to use is how the writing samples elicited will be evaluated. Similar to the first question above, this answer should be driven by the data to be gathered. In the example with fluency measures above, word counts and possibly writing time should be collected. In the case of measuring L2 proficiency through writing, however, the choice of evaluation criteria will be markedly different. The multi-faceted nature of proficiency will likely involve the use of analytic scoring rubrics with evaluations not only on language (syntax, lexis, and mechanics, for example) but discourse organization and content features. In the case of process development, qualitative discourse analytic methods may be more appropriate. The evaluation criteria should reflect back on the targeted construct and intended uses.

When designing tasks, it is important to note that one task can rarely elicit enough information for any purpose. While it is impractical to test learners on the full range of text types and pragmatic functions, care must be taken to elicit as many samples of writing as is practical in a given situation. This will produce a greater picture of learners' L2 writing ability. Furthermore, it is also important to embed tasks with sufficient contextual cues and a high level of specificity. In all cases, the writer should take as primary importance the act of communicating, but the task should be specific enough to elicit the information required by the research at hand. Thus, carefully consider the range of discourse modes and topics, whether the task should be fully contextualized as integrated or not, and the delivery mode. Likewise, given that the writers' L2 proficiency is a key element of L2 writing ability, task complexity must be considered so as not to create tasks that are too easy or too difficult for learners, as the data gathered from these tasks may not be a valid reflection of the writers' true ability.

In terms of scoring, the test purpose and evaluation criteria should inform how samples of writing are quantified or qualified. While objective linguistic measures (e.g., counts of errors for accuracy) may seem to be more straightforward, the definitions of these measures and rater agreement on them are often contentious (Pallotti, 2009). In addition, these may not indicate communicative effectiveness, which requires subjective rating through the use of rubrics. In the case of holistic and analytic rubrics, as discussed in Kuiken and Vedder (Chapter 12, this volume), one of the most important issues is to write descriptors that differentiate between performances at different levels. The criteria for these must be described clearly and ideally *without* the use of vague adverbs (always/sometimes/rarely) whenever possible. Rating scales and rubrics should be extensively piloted, raters should be trained and monitored, and statistical information regarding reliability and agreement should be provided. If learners will be given scores used in a study, ensure that these are meaningful and clear. If AES systems are to be used, ensure that there is a clear understanding of what each system is capable of testing and the type of information they will provide. Many AES systems are proprietary, however, and may be impossible to use in research. An alternative may be text analysis tools such as Coh-Metrix (http://cohmetrix.com), the suite of tools on www.linguisticanalysistools.org/, or Lu's Syntactic Complexity Analyzer (https://aihaiyang.com/software) which are freely available online (see Polio & Yoon, 2018 for the reliability and validity of these tools).

Finally, a key recommendation in designing writing tasks and scoring written performances is to limit threats of construct-irrelevant variance. This type of variance can occur when non-construct-related features have an effect on scores. For example, if clear and straightforward instructions are not provided, or if learners are not given the chance to practice or see example activities, they may be confused during the execution of your tasks. Unfamiliarity can result in performances that do not indicate the learners' true writing ability. Likewise, if raters have not been properly trained using the scoring criteria, they may use these idiosyncratically or rely on their own internal criteria (Lumley, 2002). These types of bias, collectively called rater effects, can also skew inferences from score meaning.

Testing Tips

- Carefully identify the purpose and intended use of your writing test data, and use these to create tasks and evaluation criteria that target the writing skills you wish to measure.
- Create authentic, context-rich writing tasks that are appropriate for your audience in terms of complexity and difficulty. For practical advice on good writing prompt design, see Chapter 5 in Weigle (2002).
- When possible, employ various task types and genres for writing assessment to tap into different aspects of writing proficiency and language ability.
- Ensure that your scoring procedures are clear, detailed, fair, and free from bias.

Recommended Readings

Polio, C., & Friedman, D. A. (2017). *Understanding, evaluating, and conducting second language writing research*. Routledge.

This book provides a detailed explanation and examples of L2 writing research approaches.

Shaw, S. D., & Weir, C. J. (2007). *Examining writing: Research and practice in assessing second language writing (Studies in Language Testing 26)*. Cambridge University Press.

This book offers a summary of research on writing and writing assessment, as well as a discussion of test validation factors.

Weigle, S. (2002). *Assessing Writing*. Cambridge University Press.

Although nearly 20 years old, this book is perhaps the most complete overview of writing assessment. It thoroughly covers construct definition, task development, and scoring.

References

Attali, Y., & Burstein, J. (2006). Automated essay scoring with e-rater v. 2.0. *Journal of Technology, Learning, and Assessment*, *4*, 1–30. https://ejournals.bc.edu/index.php/jtla/article/view/1650

Bachman, L. F., & Palmer, A. S. (1996). *Language testing in practice*. Oxford University Press.

Banerjee, J., Yan, X., Chapman, M., & Elliott, H. (2015). Keeping up with the times: Revising and refreshing a rating scale. *Assessing Writing*, *26*, 5–19. https://doi.org/10.1016/j.asw.2015.07.001

Barkaoui, K., & Knouzi, I. (2018). The effects of writing mode and computer ability on L2 test-takers' essay characteristics and scores. *Assessing Writing*, *36*, 19–31. https://doi.org/10.1016/j.asw.2018.02.005

Behizadeh, N., & Engelhard, G. (2011). Historical view of the influences of measurement and writing theories on the practice of writing assessment in the United States. *Assessing Writing*, *16*(3), 189–211. https://doi.org/10.1016/j.asw.2011.03.001

Bouwer, R., Béguin, A., Sanders, T., & van den Bergh, H. (2015). Effect of genre on the generalizability of writing scores. *Language Testing*, *31*(1), 83–100. https://doi.org/10.1177/0265532214542994

Breland, H., Lee, Y., & Muraki, E. (2005). Comparability of TOEFL CBT essay prompts: Response-mode analyses. *Educational and Psychological Measurement*, *65*, 577–595. https://doi.org/10.1177/0013164404272504

Brunfaut, T., Harding, L., & Batty, A. O. (2018). Going online: The effect of mode of delivery on performances and perceptions on an English L2 writing test suite. *Assessing Writing*, *36*, 3–18. https://doi.org/10.1016/j.asw.2018.02.003
Canale, M., & Swain, M. (1980). Theoretical bases of communicative approaches to second language teaching and testing. *Applied Linguistics*, *1*(1), 1–47. https://doi.org/10.1093/applin/I.1.1
Casal, J. E. (2016). Criterion online writing evaluation. *CALICO Journal*, *33*(1), 146–155. https://doi.org//10.1558/cj.v33i1.27801
Chan, S., Bax, S., & Weir, C. (2018). Researching the comparability of paper-based and computer-based delivery in a high-stakes writing test. *Assessing Writing*, *36*, 32–48. https://doi.org/10.1016/j.asw.2018.03.008
Chen, J., White, S., McCloskey, M., Soroui, J., & Chun, Y. (2011). Effects of computer versus paper administration of an adult functional writing assessment. *Assessing Writing*, *16*, 49–71. https://doi.org/10.1016/j.asw.2010.11.001
Condon, W. (2013). Large-scale assessment, locally-developed measures, and automated scoring of essays: Fishing for red herrings? *Assessing Writing*, *18*, 100–108. https://doi.org/10.1016/j.asw.2012.11.001
Council of Europe. (2018). *Common European framework of reference for languages: Learning, teaching, assessment: Companion volume with new descriptors*. Council of Europe. https://rm.coe.int/cefr-companion-volume-with-new-descriptors-2018/1680787989
Crusan, D. (Ed.). (2015). The use of rubrics to assess writing: Issues and challenges [special issue]. *Assessing Writing*, *26*, 1–82.
Cumming, A., Kantor, R., Powers, D., Santos, T., & Taylor, C. (2000). *TOEFL 2000 writing framework: A working paper. TOEFL monograph series 18*. Educational Testing Service.
Davidson, C., & Leung, C. (2009). Current issues in English language teacher-based assessment. *TESOL Quarterly*, *43*(3), 519–523. https://doi.org/10.1002/j.1545-7249.2009.tb00242.x
Douglas, D. (2000). *Assessing languages for special purposes*. Cambridge University Press.
Enright, M. K., & Quinlan, T. (2010). Complementing human judgment of essays written by English language learners with e-rater® scoring. *Language Testing*, *27*, 317–334. https://doi.org/10.1177/0265532210363144
Ferris, D. (2006). Does error feedback help student writers? New evidence on the short- and long-term effects of written error correction. In K. Hyland & F. Hyland (Eds.), *Feedback in second language writing: Contexts and issues* (pp. 81–104). Cambridge University Press.
Frear, M. W., & Bitchener, J. (2015). The effects of cognitive task complexity on writing complexity. *Journal of Second Language Writing*, *30*, 45–57. https://doi.org/10.1016/j.jslw.2015.08.009
Grabe, W., & Kaplan, R. B. (1996). *Theory and practice of writing: An applied linguistic perspective*. Longman.
Hamp-Lyons, L. (2001). Fourth generation writing assessment. In T. Silva & P. K. Matusda (Eds.), *On second language writing assessment* (pp. 117–127). Erlbaum.
Hamp-Lyons, L., & Mathias, S. P. (1994). Examining expert judgments of task difficulty on essay tests. *Journal of Second Language Writing*, *3*, 49–68. https://doi.org/10.1016/1060-3743(94)90005-1
Hayes, J. R. (1996). A new framework for understanding cognition and affect in writing. In C. M. Levy & S. Randall (Eds.), *The science of writing: Theories, methods, individual differences, and applications* (pp. 1–27). Erlbaum.
Hayes, J. R. (2012). Modeling and remodeling writing. *Written Communication*, *29*, 369–388. https://doi.org/10.1177/0741088312451260
Hayes, J. R., & Flower, L. S. (1980). Identifying the organization of writing processes. In L. W. Gregg & E. R. Steinberg (Eds.), *Cognitive processes in writing* (pp. 3–30). Erlbaum.
Herrington, A., & Moran, C. (2001). What happens when machines read our students' writing? *College English*, *63*, 480–499. https://doi.org/10.2307/378891
Hillegas, M. B. (1912). Scale for the measurement of quality in English composition by young people. Teachers College Record, *13*, 1–54.
Hoang, G. T. L., & Kunnan, A. J. (2016). Automated essay evaluation for English language learners: A case study of my access. *Language Assessment Quarterly*, *13*, 359–376. https://doi.org/10.1080/15434303.2016.1230121
Huang, S., & Renandya, W. A. (2020). Exploring the integration of automated feedback among lower-proficiency EFL learners. *Innovation in Language Learning and Teaching*, *14*(1), 15–26. https://doi.org/10.1080/17501229.2018.1471083
Hughes, A. (2003). *Testing for language teachers* (2nd ed.). Cambridge University Press.
Hyland, K., & Hyland, F. (2006). Feedback on second language students writing. *Language Teaching*, *39*, 83–101. https://doi.org/10.1017/S0261444806003399

Hymes, D. (1972). On communicative competence. In J. Pride & J. Holmes (Eds.), *Sociolinguistics: Selected readings* (pp. 269–293). Penguin.
Jeong, H. (2017). Narrative and expository genre effects on students, raters, and performance criteria. *Assessing Writing*, *31*, 113–125. https://doi.org/10.1016/j.asw.2016.08.006
Jin, Y., & Yan, M. (2017). Computer literacy and the construct validity of a high-stakes computer-based writing assessment. *Language Assessment Quarterly*, *14*(2), 101–119. https://doi.org/10.1080/15434303.2016.1261293
Johnson, M. D. (2017). Cognitive task complexity and L2 written syntactic complexity, accuracy, lexical complexity, and fluency: A research synthesis and meta-analysis. *Journal of Second Language Writing*, *37*, 13–38. https://doi.org/10.1016/j.jslw.2017.06.001
Kim, H. R., Bowles, M., Yan, X., & Chung, S. J. (2018). Examining the comparability between paper- and computer-based versions of an integrated writing placement test. *Assessing Writing*, *36*, 49–62. https://doi.org/10.1016/j.asw.2018.03.006
Knoch, U., & Sitajalabhorn, W. (2013). A closer look at integrated writing tasks: Towards a more focused definition for assessment purposes. *Assessing Writing*, *18*(3), 300–308. https://doi.org/10.1016/j.asw.2013.09.003
Kormos, J. (2011). Task complexity and linguistic and discourse features of narrative writing performance. *Journal of Second Language Writing*, *20*, 148–161. https://doi.org/10.1016/j.jslw.2011.02.001
Kuiken, F., & Vedder, I. (2008). Cognitive task complexity and written output in Italian and French as a foreign language. *Journal of Second Language Writing*, *17*, 48–60. https://doi.org/10.1016/j.jslw.2007.08.003
Kuiken, F., & Vedder, I. (2017). Functional adequacy in L2 writing: Towards a new rating scale. *Language Testing*, *34*(3), 321–336. https://doi.org/10.1177/0265532216663991
Leijten, M., Waes, L. V., Schriver, K., & Hayes, J. R. (2013). Writing in the workplace: Constructing documents using multiple digital sources. *Journal of Writing Research*, *5*, 285–337. https://doi.org/10.17239/jowr-2014.05.03.3
Li, J. (2006). The mediation of technology in ESL writing and its implications for writing assessment. *Assessing Writing*, *11*(1), 5–21. https://doi.org/10.1016/j.asw.2005.09.001
Liu, S., & Kunnan, A. J. (2016). Investigating the application of automated writing evaluation to Chinese undergraduate English majors: A case study of WriteToLearn. *CALICO Journal*, *33*(1), 71–91. https://doi.org/10.1558/cj.v33i1.26380
Loewen, S., & Sato, M. (2018). Interaction and instructed second language acquisition. *Language Teaching*, *51*(3), 285–329. https://doi.org/ 10.1017/S0261444818000125
Lumley, T. (2002). Assessment criteria in a large-scale writing test: What do they really mean to the raters? *Language Testing*, *19*(3), 246–276. https://doi.org/10.1191/0265532202lt230oa
Norris, J., & Manchón, R. M. (2012). Investigating L2 writing development from multiple perspectives: Issues in theory and research. In R. M. Manchón (Ed.), *L2 writing development: Multiple perspectives* (pp. 221–244). de Gruyter Mouton. https://doi.org/10.1515/9781934078303.221
Ong, J., & Zhang, L. J. (2010). Effects of task complexity on the fluency and lexical complexity in EFL students' argumentative writing. *Journal of Second Language Writing*, *19*, 218–233. https://doi.org/10.1016/j.jslw.2010.10.003
Pallotti, G. (2009). CAF: Defining, refining, and differentiating constructs. *Applied Linguistics*, *30*(4), 590–601. https://doi.org/10.1093/applin/amp045
Plakans, L. (2008). Comparing composing processes in writing-only and reading-to-write test tasks. *Assessing Writing*, *13*(2), 111–129. https://doi.org/10.1016/j.asw.2008.07.001
Plakans, L. (2012). Writing integrated items. In G. Fulcher & F. Davidson (Eds.), *The Routledge handbook of language testing* (pp. 602–632). Routledge.
Polio, C., & Yoon, H-J. (2018). The reliability and validity of automated tools for examining variation in syntactic complexity across genres. *International Journal of Applied Linguistics*, *28*, 165–188. https://doi.org/10.1111/ijal.12200
Révész, A., Kourtali, N., & Mazgutova, D. (2017). Effects of task complexity on L2 writing behaviors and linguistic complexity. *Language Learning*, *67*(1), 208–241. https://doi.org/10.1111/lang.12205
Robinson, P. (2001). Task complexity, task difficulty, and task production: Exploring interactions in a componential framework. *Applied Linguistics*, *22*(1), 27–57. https://doi.org/10.1093/applin/22.1.27
Robinson, P. (2005). Cognitive complexity and task sequencing: Studies in a componential framework for second language task design. *International Review of Applied Linguistics*, *43*(1), 1–32. https://doi.org/10.1515/iral.2005.43.1.1
Shermis, M. D., & Burstein, J. (2013). *Handbook of automated essay evaluation: Current applications and new directions*. Routledge.

Shin, S. Y., & Ewert, D. (2014). What accounts for integrated reading-to-write task scores? *Language Testing*, *32*(2), 259–281. https://doi.org/10.1177/0265532214560257

Wang, Y. J., Shang, H. F., & Briody, P. (2013). Exploring the impact of using automated writing evaluation in English as a foreign language university students' writing. *Computer Assisted Language Learning*, *26*(3), 234–257. https://doi.org/10.1080/09588221.2012.655300

Way, D. P., Joiner, E. G., & Seaman, M. A. (2000). Writing in the secondary foreign language classroom: The effects of prompts and tasks on novice learners of French. *Modern Language Journal*, *84*(2), 171–184. https://doi.org/10.1111/0026-7902.00060

Weigle, S. C. (2002). *Assessing writing*. Cambridge University Press. https://doi.org/10.1017/CBO9780511732997

Weigle, S. C. (2013). English language learners and automated scoring of essays: Critical considerations. *Assessing Writing*, *18*, 85–99. https://doi.org/10.1016/j.asw.2012.10.006

Weir, C. (2005). *Language testing and evaluation: An evidence-based approach*. Palgrave Macmillan. https://doi.org/ 10.1057/9780230514577

Wolfe, E. W., & Manalo, J. R. (2004). Composition medium comparability in a direct writing assessment of non-native English speakers. *Language Learning and Technology*, *8*, 53–65. https://doi.org/10125/25229

Xi, X. (2010). Automated scoring and feedback systems: Where are we and where are we headed? *Language Testing*, *27*(3), 291–300. https://doi.org/10.1177/0265532210364643

Yoon, H.-J. (2018). The development of ESL writing quality and lexical proficiency: Suggestions for assessing writing achievement. *Language Assessment Quarterly*, *15*(4), 387–405. https://doi.org/10.1080/15434303.2018.1536756

29

Measuring Implicit and Explicit Learning and Knowledge

Daniel R. Isbell & John Rogers

Background

The terms *implicit* and *explicit* have become widely used in second language acquisition (SLA) (Ellis, 2005; Norris & Ortega, 2000). These terms are used to describe types of language learning processes and linguistic knowledge, which we focus on in this chapter, as well as learning conditions and instructional techniques (e.g., explicit and implicit corrective feedback; Ellis, Loewen, & Erlam, 2006). In language testing, the application of these labels has been most prominent in aptitude tests (see Roehr-Brackin, Chapter 14, this volume). Although the terms implicit and explicit have propagated widely, they have not always been used consistently.

Understanding the differences between implicit/explicit learning and knowledge is crucially important. In Norris and Ortega's (2000) influential meta-analysis of second language (L2) instruction, greater learning effects were found for explicitly-oriented instructional treatments. Norris and Ortega qualified this finding, noting that "the measurement of change induced by instruction is typically carried out on instruments that seem to favor more explicit types of treatments by calling on explicit memory-based performance" (p. 483). To better understand and compare the effects of implicit and explicit learning, it is important to measure outcomes beyond explicit knowledge.

Our aims in this chapter are two-fold. First, we define and disambiguate key concepts related to implicit and explicit L2 learning. Second, we provide an overview of key issues in implicit/explicit learning research and the measurement of implicit/explicit knowledge. We conclude the chapter with recommendations for practice.

First languages (L1s) are thought to be acquired through implicit processes and result in a linguistic system largely composed of *implicit knowledge*, i.e., unconscious, in nature (see Key Concepts). When an L1 English speaker needs to express that an event happened in the past, the addition of the *-ed* morpheme to regular verbs requires no conscious thought. Implicit knowledge is contrasted with *explicit knowledge*, i.e., conscious knowledge, such as metalinguistic knowledge that is taught and learned inside classrooms, for example, descriptions of the different functions of verb tense and aspect used in connection with past events. *Implicit learning* occurs when knowledge is gained or developed by the learner as an unintentional byproduct of processing language for comprehension or communication. For L1 learners, it is commonly assumed that most language acquisition involves implicit learning. *Explicit learning* involves deliberate attention to linguistic form and a conscious attempt by the learner to make sense of patterns or rules. *Awareness* (or lack thereof) is the key feature that distinguishes between implicit/explicit learning and knowledge: Implicit learning and knowledge are characterized by a lack of awareness, whereas explicit learning and knowledge are associated with awareness during the learning process (Williams, 2009).

It is important to emphasize a few points here. The first is that learning is a process that yields knowledge as a product (see e.g., Leow, 2015a). The type of learning process and the product of learning, although interrelated, are not isomorphic. Second, a distinction must be made between learning processes and learning conditions. Learning processes are internal to the learner. Researchers create *learning conditions* that may promote or favor a learning process (or balance of processes), but they ultimately are unable to control which and to what degree learning processes actually occur. Learning conditions (or treatments) are often characterized as implicit/explicit, but these characterizations should be examined carefully. Often, *incidental* and *intentional learning conditions* are more appropriate descriptors, as these terms make fewer assumptions about learner-internal processes.

Further, some researchers have attempted to differentiate instructional techniques such as corrective feedback along implicit (e.g., recasts) and explicit (e.g., metalinguistic feedback) lines (Ellis et al., 2006), but such distinctions also do not necessarily reflect learner-internal processes. In the case of corrective feedback, the goal is to help learners notice (Schmidt, 1995, i.e., become aware of) an error in their production and elicit a corrected form, and as such even "implicit" feedback will invoke explicit learning processes. In such cases, we recommend researchers adopt different terminology, such as *direct* (or *deductive*) and *indirect* (or *inductive*) (e.g., for metalinguistic feedback and recasts, respectively), to characterize instructional approaches and techniques and avoid inappropriate conflation with learners' mental processes.

The distinction between implicit/explicit learning and knowledge is central to many cognitive-interactionist theories of SLA and holds direct relevance for the language classroom. Commonly referred to as the *interface debate*, these theories are concerned with the degree that explicit learning and/or knowledge can facilitate the development of implicit knowledge: Implicit knowledge is the ultimate goal of language learners, given that implicit knowledge is associated with spontaneous, fluent, and effective production (Ellis, 2005; Long, 2017). Depending on one's theoretical framework, implicit and explicit learning processes are not mutually exclusive. In other words, learners can utilize both processes simultaneously. Finally, while a process may lead toward a particular product, it is not guaranteed. It is possible to develop either implicit knowledge, explicit knowledge, or both as a result of either implicit or explicit learning processes (see Paradis, 2009; Suzuki & DeKeyser, 2017 for discussions). Most classroom L2 instruction is largely explicit in nature (Leow, 2015b). Thus, the degree to which explicit learning processes and explicit knowledge can lead to the development of implicit knowledge is what researchers in the subdomain of instructed SLA (ISLA) investigate. They wish to better understand the classroom conditions resulting in the best outcomes for learners, i.e., the development of implicit knowledge (Long, 2017).

Language testers also have good reason to be concerned with the distinctions among implicit/explicit learning and knowledge. For one, the interpretability of any test is strengthened by a detailed understanding of what is being measured, such as the degree to which item/task responses draw on implicit versus explicit linguistic knowledge. Furthermore, as much operational proficiency testing has shifted from context-unspecified, discrete-point items to the use of tasks that approximate real-world language use, test formats that favor careful application of explicit (meta)linguistic knowledge have seen less use. It thus behooves language testers to understand and think carefully about implicit/explicit learning and knowledge.

Key Concepts

***Implicit knowledge*:** Unconscious knowledge; typically cannot be verbalized or otherwise intentionally retrieved.

***Explicit knowledge*:** Conscious knowledge; typically can be verbalized and/or intentionally retrieved.

***Implicit learning*:** The internal process of learning without awareness of what is being learned, typically in incidental conditions, and resulting primarily in implicit knowledge.

***Explicit learning*:** The internal process of learning with awareness of what is being learned, typically intentionally, resulting primarily in explicit knowledge.

***Awareness*:** Subjective experience of cognitive content or external stimulus (Tomlin & Villa, 1994); knowing that something is present or existent in a given moment.

***Intentional learning*:** Learning that occurs with intent.

***Incidental learning*:** Learning that occurs without any intent to learn.

***Learning conditions*:** Features of the external environment and instructional materials/linguistic input which influence learning processes and outcomes.

Key Issues

Although it is possible to distinctly define implicit/explicit knowledge and learning, it can be difficult to maintain the distinctions among these constructs in practice. Below, we review key issues in capturing implicit and explicit learning, methods of testing implicit/explicit knowledge, domain definition, and technical quality of tests.

Capturing Implicit and Explicit Learning

Learning conditions for research on implicit learning present considerable challenges. First is the matter of whether the learning conditions actually invoke implicit learning mechanisms, and second is whether or not explicit learning mechanisms are simultaneously deployed. Keeping in mind that implicit learning occurs without awareness, examining implicit learning poses methodological challenges due to the fact that many common experimental features could potentially raise learners' awareness. For example, participants being generally aware that they are involved in a language learning study can arguably jeopardize the entire enterprise. To mitigate this concern, researchers often employ orienting tasks which are designed to draw participants' conscious attention toward specific aspects of the stimuli (Leow & Zamora, 2017) and away from targeted linguistic structures. Such orientation tasks might take the form of informing participants that they are learning to play a game (Morgan-Short et al., 2012).

Even when the purpose of an intervention is masked and there is no metalinguistic information given about language forms, it may still be possible for explicit learning mechanisms to be invoked. For example, conditions involving output may lead learners to notice gaps in their grammatical knowledge (Swain, 2005), triggering explicit learning processes. Thus, many studies examining implicit learning favor input-only treatments (e.g., Godfroid, 2016; Hamrick & Rebuschat, 2014; Rebuschat & Williams, 2012). Nonetheless, several studies have shown that some participants engage in explicit learning strategies even under input-only implicit learning conditions (e.g., Robinson, 2005; Rogers, 2019), suggesting that learning conditions may influence, but not guarantee, the type of mental processes employed by learners. Given these challenges, researchers should not assume a direct relationship between study participants' cognitive processes and learning condition manipulations. To substantiate any claims as to the conscious status of learning, concurrent measures of awareness (e.g., think-aloud protocols; Leow, 2015a, b) should be utilized.

Methods of Testing Implicit and Explicit Knowledge

Researchers have developed several methods to determine whether knowledge is implicit or explicit. These methods can be grouped into three broad categories: verbal reports, subjective measures of awareness, and direct methods (see Rebuschat, 2013 for an overview).

In verbal reports, participants are asked at the end of the experiment to verbalize any rules or regularities they might have noticed during the experiment. Knowledge is typically considered implicit if participants can demonstrate knowledge (e.g., performance on a grammaticality judgment test, GJT) but cannot verbalize the underlying rule guiding their performance (Rebuschat & Williams, 2012; Robinson, 1997). The results of verbal reports can be used to group participants dichotomously as being "aware" or "unaware" of the underlying rule system (e.g., Williams, 2005) or along a continuum (Brooks & Kempe, 2013). There are several well-known challenges to interpreting a lack of verbalization in retrospective verbal reports as indicative of implicit knowledge (Shanks & St. John, 1994). For instance, participants may not disclose information for many reasons, such as lacking the meta-language needed to describe linguistic rules or regularities (Hamrick & Sachs, 2018).

A second method of establishing the conscious status of knowledge is the use of subjective measures of awareness. Subjective measures are utilized on an item-by-item basis during the testing phase of an experiment, for example, alongside a grammaticality judgment test (see e.g., Rebuschat & Williams, 2012). There are two main types of subjective measures: source attributions and confidence ratings. Source attributions involve participant identification of the basis of their grammaticality decision (for example, guessing, intuition, memory, or rule knowledge). Knowledge can be considered implicit if the performance is significantly above chance levels when participants are basing their decisions on intuition and/or guessing (Dienes et al., 1995). A confidence rating is when participants are asked to indicate their level of confidence for each decision they make during the testing phase (e.g., judging the grammaticality of a sentence). Dienes et al. (1995) held that knowledge can be considered unconscious if there is no statistically significant relationship between the level of confidence and performance.

Like retrospective verbal reports, there are reservations regarding the interpretation of subjective measures of awareness. The interpretation of "intuition" to reflect L1-like implicit knowledge (Dienes, 2008; Rebuschat & Williams, 2012) has been challenged by questions of whether L2 learners can develop such intuition following a minimal amount of exposure in a single laboratory training session (Leow & Hama, 2013). Alternatively, Serafini (2013; see also Rogers, 2017) suggested that the data from source attributions might be best interpreted in terms of degrees of explicitness rather than necessarily reflecting implicit or explicit knowledge as binary alternatives. Namely, when using guess, intuition, memory, or rule as the possible attributions, guess and intuition would reflect no awareness or a relatively low level of it, whereas memory or rule might reflect a higher level of awareness.

Another method of determining whether knowledge is implicit or explicit in nature is through direct and, increasingly, indirect tests. The best-known examples of direct tests were featured in Ellis (2005); Ellis concluded that untimed GJTs and metalinguistic knowledge tests are better measures of explicit knowledge, whereas timed GJTs, elicited imitation tasks, and oral narration tasks draw primarily upon implicit knowledge. Other SLA researchers (e.g., Leung & Williams, 2011) have drawn upon serial reaction time methodology and utilized reaction time measurements as indirect measures of implicit knowledge.

Although direct and indirect tests have been argued to be more sensitive than verbal reports in disentangling implicit and explicit knowledge (Shanks & St. John, 1994), these tests are not without limitations. To illustrate, untimed GJTs are argued to reflect explicit knowledge, and timed GJTs are argued to reflect implicit knowledge (Ellis, 2005). This distinction is predicated on arguments that implicit knowledge is more available for rapid, automatic processing, whereas explicit knowledge is available for slower, more controlled processing. As illustrated by recent research, there are several potential problems with this interpretation. For example, responses to a timed GJT, argued to reflect implicit knowledge, could be contaminated by *automatized explicit knowledge* (AEK), i.e., "conscious linguistic knowledge including different levels of automatization." (Suzuki, 2017, p. 1230, see also DeKeyser, 2017; Vafaee et al., 2017). In other words, it is unclear whether any measure, direct or indirect, solely reflects implicit or explicit knowledge.

Operationalization of Constructs

One challenge in the use of direct and indirect tests as measures of implicit/explicit knowledge lies in interpreting the meaning of scores, in particular the degree that any single measure taps into either implicit or explicit knowledge. However, theory-based criteria for operationalizing measures of implicit and explicit knowledge can support score interpretations. According to Ellis (2005, p. 152), measures of implicit knowledge draw on intuition, have time pressure, focus primarily on meaning, seek consistency in learner responses, should elicit confident responses, do not require metalinguistic knowledge, and tend to favor targets of early learning. Measures of explicit knowledge, on the other hand, draw on knowledge of rules, lack time pressure, focus primarily on linguistic form, may be more variable in learner responses, are likely to elicit unconfident responses, benefit from metalinguistic knowledge, and tend to favor targets of later learning.

While these criteria have been influential, all aspects of operationalizing implicit and explicit linguistic knowledge have not been settled. DeKeyser (2017) proposed that L2 learners, particularly adults with a great deal of training and exposure, rely on highly efficient access to AEK, which features the conscious status of traditional explicit knowledge with speed of access that is nearly indistinguishable from implicit knowledge. Similarly, a measure that requires a primary focus on meaning cannot exclude the application of explicit linguistic knowledge, as learners may have the time and cognitive resources to engage, simultaneously, in meaning-focused comprehension *and* activation of explicit knowledge to analyze forms in the input (DeKeyser, 2017; Suzuki, 2017; Suzuki & DeKeyser, 2015, 2017).

Numerous measures have been used to assess implicit and explicit L2 knowledge. While an exhaustive review is beyond the scope of this chapter, Table 29.1 summarizes commonly used measures, and provides information on the task features and type(s) of L2 knowledge that the measures are thought to assess.

Despite some issues with measurement precision (see e.g., Suzuki, 2017), there seems to be a consensus that indirect measures utilizing RTs (e.g., WM, SPR in Table 29.1) tap into implicit linguistic knowledge and, provided that some level of implicit knowledge is present, do not draw on explicit knowledge to any considerable degree. L1 speakers show consistent and considerable differences in RTs on grammatical and ungrammatical trials in WMT and SPR measures; L2 speakers with greater length of residence in TL environments also tend to show this pattern (Suzuki, 2017; Suzuki & DeKeyser, 2015). For other measures of implicit knowledge, there is still some contention over what is being measured. One factor potentially muddying the waters is modality. Confirming previous findings, Shiu et al. (2018) found that learners scored lower on aural GJTs (timed and untimed) compared to written GJTs. Do aural and written GJTs tap into the same underlying knowledge? Or do aural GJTs, with fleeting stimuli and greater real-time processing constraints, provide a better window into implicit knowledge? There are not yet clear answers, but Kim and Nam (2016) collected some preliminary evidence to suggest that timed, aural GJTs are superior for measuring implicit knowledge. Another issue is speededness. Ellis (2005) argued that T-GJTs are measures of implicit knowledge due to speeded response

Table 29.1 Commonly used measures of implicit and explicit L2 knowledge

Measure	*Prototypical Task Description*	*Construct*
Word Monitoring (WM)	Before listening to a stimulus, learners are shown a word to monitor. While listening, learners must press a button as soon as they hear the monitor word. Grammatical targets precede the monitor word; RTs after monitor words are expected to be slower when preceded by a grammatical violation. After listening, learners must answer a comprehension question related to the stimulus (focus on meaning).	Implicit Knowledge
Self-Paced Reading (SPR)	Learners press a button to show the next word in a stimulus sentence; only one word (or short phrase) is visible at a time. Learners are expected to slow down when reading a word if it contains a grammatical violation (critical region) and/or the word immediately follows a grammatical violation (spillover region). Learners are told to read quickly, and excessively slow reading times are eliminated post-hoc. After reading the sentence, learners answer a comprehension question related to the stimulus (focus on meaning).	Implicit Knowledge
Elicited Imitation (EI)	Learners listen to a statement and then indicate their agreement (focus on meaning). Next, learners repeat the sentence. For statements with grammatical mistakes, learners are expected to correct them when repeating.	Implicit Knowledge (Ellis, 2005)/Explicit Knowledge (Spada, Shiu, & Tomita, 2015)
Oral Narrative	Learners are presented with visuals and/or text depicting a coherent narrative, usually more than one time. This exposure phase has (generous) time limits. Then, learners retell the narrative. Learner responses are coded for correct suppliances of target grammatical forms in obligatory contexts.	Implicit Knowledge (Spada et al., 2015; Suzuki & DeKeyser, 2015)
Timed Grammaticality Judgment Task (T-GJT)	A stimulus is presented, aurally or visually. Within a time limit, learners must read the stimulus and judge its grammatical acceptability.	Implicit Knowledge
Untimed Grammaticality Judgment Task (Un-GJT)	A stimulus is presented, aurally or visually. Without time limit, learners must read the stimulus and decide whether it is grammatical or not.	Explicit Knowledge
Metalinguistic Knowledge Test (MKT)	A stimulus containing an error is presented to the learner. Learners typically do three things: 1) indicate the error (e.g., by underlining it), 2) correct the error, and 3) provide an explanation of the violation/correction. No time limit is imposed.	Explicit Knowledge

conditions. However, Vafaee et al. (2017) and Suzuki and DeKeyser (2015, 2017) claimed that T-GJTs are reflective of (automatized) explicit knowledge. Finally, untimed GJTs (especially in the written modality) and tests of metalinguistic knowledge are largely agreed on as primarily activating explicit knowledge in L2 learners.

In summary, measuring explicit L2 knowledge is relatively straightforward, and there is broad consensus on the construct validity of several explicit knowledge measures. On the other hand, implicit measures require careful consideration given the technical and theoretical challenges in the operationalization of implicit L2 knowledge.

Domain Definition

Beyond specifying a type (e.g., implicit) and subdomain of linguistic knowledge (e.g., morphosyntax) to be targeted, direct and indirect tests require further elaboration on the scope of the domain being measured, i.e., how features/items are selected to adequately represent the targeted construct. As Chapelle (Chapter 2, this volume) points out, clear description of and rationale for domains are necessary for appropriate interpretation of test scores.

When examining implicit/explicit learning, defining the domain is relatively straightforward: what learners were taught or exposed to. This may be a single morphosyntactic feature (e.g., case marking in Rogers et al., 2016) or a small set of lexical items (e.g., 27 items in Hamrick & Rebuschat, 2014). Inferences related to implicit/explicit knowledge based on these measures are delimited by the context of the experiment and scope of the domain, though findings may subsequently be used to support broader theoretical claims about the process and product of learning.

Domain definition is less straightforward when researchers desire to measure implicit/explicit knowledge of a linguistic subdomain more broadly, as the degree to which results can be extrapolated beyond the specific linguistic features and items included in a test requires some thought (i.e., language-as-fixed-effect fallacy, Clark, 1973). Consider Ellis (2005), Suzuki (2017), and Spada et al. (2015), who all sought to measure implicit grammatical knowledge. The instruments in these studies were created based on substantially different domain definitions, which were reflected in the design of the tests: Ellis included 17 English features representing both early and late acquisition that are commonly introduced at various stages in instruction, Suzuki sampled three features of Japanese commonly introduced in introductory language courses, and Spada et al. selected just one English grammar structure. These choices have ramifications on the interpretation of individual test scores and the larger conclusions to be drawn about methods for eliciting implicit knowledge. Domain definitions affect not only the design of tests, but also bear on claims related to the extrapolation of scores to contexts beyond the laboratory.

Technical Quality of Tests

In research, the technical quality of tests is often reduced to a reliability index. However, under the hood of reliability indices are the qualities of individual items/tasks and evaluation of responses. One way of addressing technical quality at the item level for measures of implicit knowledge is to collect data from native speakers and revise or remove items that have unexpected response patterns (e.g., Suzuki, 2017). Unfortunately, examining native speaker data is not always possible or relevant (e.g., in the case of artificial language paradigms), and it appears rare for researchers to conduct (or report) more detailed technical analysis of items based on their larger datasets (but see Vafaee et al., 2017). This is an area where item analysis techniques common in language assessment could be fruitfully applied. Given that many studies of implicit/explicit knowledge and learning do report instrument reliability (but not all, see McKay & Plonsky, Chapter 44, this volume), most often as Cronbach's alpha, conducting basic item analyses should require little additional effort: Most software used for reliability calculations provide item difficulty and discrimination statistics by default. Researchers could use this information to make appropriate instrument revisions (i.e., item revisions or deletions) and increase instrument reliability, which is sometimes modest for measures of implicit/explicit knowledge (e.g., $\alpha = .65$ for the WMT in Vafaee et al., 2017). Such efforts would benefit the quality of score interpretations and have ripple effects in research replications and instrument sharing.

Recommendations for Practice

Implicit knowledge is currently privileged in both SLA and ISLA theory. This construct is likewise important for language testing. Test designers must consider whether tests and tasks they design are assessing implicit or explicit knowledge, or both. In some cases, it may be desirable to test explicit learning. If teaching intentionally focused on explicit linguistic knowledge and was designed to invoke mainly explicit learning mechanisms, an achievement test focusing on explicit knowledge is suitable for making inferences of student achievement. On the other hand, given the challenges involved in tapping implicit L2 knowledge even in tightly-controlled laboratory settings, testers should be cautious regarding claims about implicit/explicit knowledge based on proficiency test scores. Furthermore, claims about the degree to which any assessment reflects implicit or explicit learning can only be made when learning contexts are thoughtfully and thoroughly considered.

In sum, the measurement of implicit and explicit learning is a difficult task with much room for refinement. However, this challenge should not deter researchers from continuing to push forward in this exciting and important area of SLA, nor should it discourage language testers from engaging meaningfully with these important constructs that underlie L2 ability and real-world performance. In consideration of the key issues discussed above, we make the following testing tips for SLA researchers and language testers interested in implicit/explicit knowledge when investigating learning and choosing or developing tests.

Testing Tips

Measuring Implicit/Explicit Learning

- Carefully design instructional treatments to elicit desired learning processes and consider more extended treatments.
- Utilize concurrent measures (e.g., think-aloud protocols) to draw inferences about learning processes and retrospective measures (e.g., verbal reports, subjective measures) to support inferences about the product of learning.
- Triangulation of several measures is highly recommended (Rebuschat, Hamrick, Riestenberg, Sachs, & Ziegler, 2015), especially for investigating implicit learning.
- Investigating awareness via verbal reports and/or subjective measures is helpful, but it is not the final word on the quality of knowledge gained (or not gained). It is possible for linguistic knowledge of two different types to co-exist, and implicit/explicit knowledge are not necessarily absolutes. Some researchers (e.g., Rebuschat & Williams, 2012; Rogers et al., 2016) have interpreted subjective reports of awareness as indicative of knowledge being partially implicit in nature.

Measuring Implicit/Explicit Knowledge

- Define test domains in detail and in relation to the desired interpretations of learners' knowledge. Features of test tasks, which relate closely to the type of knowledge (e.g., implicit/explicit) activated, and the sampling of features/items from the target subdomain are both key in interpretation of scores.
- Conduct detailed item analyses to assure the technical quality of instruments. Removing or revising items with undesirable qualities is recommended.
- Automatized explicit knowledge blurs the line of the classic implicit/explicit distinction and deserves consideration; an opportunity exists to design indirect tests focused on automaticity (i.e., speed) of responses to further the investigation of a potential implicit/AEK distinction.

Recommended Readings

Ellis, R., Loewen, S., Elder, C., Reinders, H., Erlam, R., & Philp, J. (2009). *Implicit and explicit knowledge in second language learning, testing, and teaching*. Multilingual Matters.

This book provides an overview of implicit and explicit knowledge and showcases the relevance of the two constructs in several aspects of L2 research and practice.

Leow, R. (2015a). *Explicit learning in the L2 classroom: A student-centered approach*. Routledge.

Leow focuses on instructed L2 learning, bringing theory and research to bear on what happens in language classrooms.

Rebuschat, P. (Ed.). (2015). *Implicit and explicit learning of languages*. John Benjamins.

This volume provides a wide range of perspectives on implicit and explicit language learning alongside in-depth discussions of relevant research methodology.

References

Brooks, P. J., & Kempe, V. (2013). Individual differences in adult foreign language learning: The mediating effect of metalinguistic awareness. *Memory & Cognition*, *41*(2), 281–296. https://doi.org/10.3758/s13421-012-0262-9

Clark, H. H. (1973). The language-as-fixed-effect fallacy: A critique of language statistics in psychological research. *Journal of Verbal Learning and Verbal Behavior*, *12*(4), 335–359. https://doi.org/10.1016/S0022-5371(73)80014-3

DeKeyser, R. M. (2017). Knowledge and skill in ISLA. In S. Loewen & M. Sato (Eds.), *The Routledge handbook of instructed second language acquisition* (pp. 15–32). Routledge.

Dienes, Z. (2008). Subjective measures of unconscious knowledge. *Progress in Brain Research*, *168*, 49–64. https://doi.org/10.1016/S0079-6123(07)68005-4

Dienes, Z., Altmann, G., Kwan, L., & Goode, A. (1995). Unconscious knowledge of artificial grammars is applied strategically. *Journal of Experimental Psychology*, *21*(5), 1322–1338. https://doi.org/10.1037/0278-7393.21.5.1322

Ellis, R. (2005). Measuring implicit and explicit knowledge of a second language: A psychometric study. *Studies in Second Language Acquisition*, *27*(2), 141–172. https://doi.org/10.1017/S0272263105050096

Ellis, R., Loewen, S., & Erlam, R. (2006). Implicit and explicit corrective feedback and the acquisition of L2 grammar. *Studies in Second Language Acquisition*, *28*(2), 339–368. https://doi.org/10.1017/S0272263106060141

Godfroid, A. (2016). The effects of implicit instruction on implicit and explicit knowledge development. *Studies in Second Language Acquisition*, *38*, 177–215. https://doi.org/10.1017/S0272263115000388

Hamrick, P., & Rebuschat, P. (2014). Frequency effects, learning conditions, and the development of implicit and explicit lexical knowledge. In J. Connor-Linton & L. W. Amoroso (Eds.), *Measured language: Quantitative studies of acquisition, assessment, and variation* (pp. 125–139). Georgetown University Press.

Hamrick, P., & Sachs, R. (2018). Establishing evidence of learning in experiments employing artificial linguistic systems. *Studies in Second Language Acquisition*, *40*(1), 153–169. https://doi.org/10.1017/S0272263116000474

Kim, J., & Nam, H. (2016). Measures of implicit knowledge revisited: Processing modes, time pressure, and modality. *Studies in Second Language Acquisition*, *39*(3), 431–457. https://doi.org/10.1017/S0272263115000510

Leow, R. P. (2015b). Implicit learning in SLA: Of processes and products. In P. Rebuschat (Ed.), *Implicit and explicit learning of languages* (pp. 47–66). John Benjamins.

Leow, R. P., & Hama, M. K. (2013). Implicit learning in SLA and the issue of internal validity: A response to Leung and Williams' "The implicit learning of mappings between forms and contextually derived meanings." *Studies in Second Language Acquisition*, *35*(3), 545–557. https://doi.org/10.1017/S027226311300003X

Leow, R. P., & Zamora, C. C. (2017). Intentional and incidental learning. In S. Loewen & M. Sato (Eds.), *Routledge handbook of instructed second language acquisition* (pp. 33–49). Routledge.

Leung, J. H. C., & Williams, J. N. (2011). The implicit learning of mappings between forms and contextually derived meanings. *Studies in Second Language Acquisition*, *33*(1), 33–55. https://doi.org/10.1017/S0272263110000525

Long, M. H. (2017). Instructed second language acquisition (ISLA): Geopolitics, methodological issues, and some major research questions. *Instructed Second Language Acquisition*, *1*(1), 7–44. https://doi.org/10.1558/isla.33314
Morgan-Short, K., Steinhauer, K., Sanz, C., & Ullman, M. T. (2012). Explicit and implicit second language training differentially affect the achievement of native-like brain activation patterns. *Journal of Cognitive Neuroscience*, *24*(4), 933–947. https://doi.org/10.1162/jocn_a_00119
Norris, J. M., & Ortega, L. (2000). Effectiveness of L2 instruction: A research synthesis and quantitative meta-analysis. *Language Learning*, *50*(3), 417–528. https://doi.org/10.1111/0023-8333.00136
Paradis, M. (2009). *Declarative and procedural determinants of second languages*. John Benjamins.
Rebuschat, P. (2013). Measuring implicit and explicit knowledge in second language research. *Language Learning*, *63*(3), 595–626. https://doi.org/10.1111/lang.12010
Rebuschat, P., Hamrick, P., Riestenberg, K., Sachs, R., & Ziegler, N. (2015). Triangulating measures of awareness: A contribution to the debate on learning without awareness. *Studies in Second Language Acquisition*, *37*(2), 299–334. https://doi.org/10.1017/S0272263115000145
Rebuschat, P., & Williams, J. N. (2012). Implicit and explicit knowledge in second language acquisition. *Applied Psycholinguistics*, *33*(4), 829–856. https://doi.org/10.1017/S0142716411000580
Robinson, P. (1997). Individual differences and the fundamental similarity of implicit and explicit adult second language learning. *Language Learning*, *47*(1), 45–99. https://doi.org/10.1111/0023-8333.21997002
Robinson, P. (2005). Cognitive abilities, chunk-strength, and frequency effects in implicit artificial grammar and incidental L2 learning: Replications of Reber, Walkenfeld, and Hernstadt (1991) and Knowlton and Squire (1996) and their relevance for SLA. *Studies in Second Language Acquisition*, *27*(2), 235–268. https://doi.org/10.1017/S0272263105050126
Rogers, J. (2017). Awareness and learning under incidental learning conditions. *Language Awareness*, *26*(2), 113–133. https://doi.org/10.1080/09658416.2017.1287711
Rogers, J. (2019). Levels of awareness, depth of processing, and the learning of L2 case markings. In R. P. Leow (Ed.), *The Routledge handbook of second language research in classroom learning* (pp. 76–89). Routledge.
Rogers, J., Révész, A., & Rebuschat, P. (2016). Implicit and explicit knowledge of inflectional morphology. *Applied Psycholinguistics*, *37*(4), 781–812. https://doi.org/10.1017/S0142716415000247
Schmidt, R. (1995). Consciousness and foreign language learning: A tutorial on the role of attention and awareness in learning. In R. Schmidt, (Ed.), *Attention and awareness in foreign language learning* (Technical Report #9) (pp. 1–63). University of Hawai'i, Second Language Teaching & Curriculum Center.
Serafini, E. J. (2013). *Cognitive and psychosocial factors in the long-term development of implicit and explicit second language knowledge in adult learners of Spanish at increasing proficiency* (Unpublished doctoral dissertation). Georgetown University.
Shanks, D. R., & St. John, M. F. (1994). Characteristics of dissociable human learning systems. *Behavioral and Brain Sciences*, *17*(3), 367–395. https://doi.org/10.1017/S0140525X00035032
Shiu, L.-J., Yalçin, S., & Spada, N. (2018). Exploring second language learners' grammaticality judgment performance in relation to task design features. *System*, *72*, 215–225. https://doi.org/10.1016/j.system.2017.12.004
Spada, N., Shiu, J. L.-J., & Tomita, Y. (2015). Validating an elicited imitation task as a measure of implicit knowledge: Comparisons with other validation studies. *Language Learning*, *65*(3), 723–751. https://doi.org/10.1111/lang.12129
Suzuki, Y. (2017). Validity of new measures of implicit knowledge: Distinguishing implicit knowledge from automatized explicit knowledge. *Applied Psycholinguistics*, *38*(5), 1229–1261. https://doi.org/10.1017/S014271641700011X
Suzuki, Y., & DeKeyser, R. (2015). Comparing elicited imitation and word monitoring as measures of implicit knowledge. *Language Learning*, *65*(4), 860–895. https://doi.org/10.1111/lang.12138
Suzuki, Y., & DeKeyser, R. (2017). The interface of explicit and implicit knowledge in a second language: Insights from individual differences in cognitive aptitudes. *Language Learning*, *67*(4), 747–790. https://doi.org/10.1111/lang.12241
Swain, M. (2005). The output hypothesis: Theory and research. In E. Hinkel (Ed.), *Handbook of research in second language teaching and learning* (pp. 471–483). Lawrence Erlbaum Associates.
Tomlin, R. S., & Villa, V. (1994). Attention in cognitive science and second language acquisition. *Studies in Second Language Acquisition*, *16*(2), 183–203. https://doi.org/10.1017/S0272263100012870

Vafaee, P., Suzuki, Y., & Kachinske, I. (2017). Validating grammaticality judgment tests: Evidence from two new psycholinguistic measures. *Studies in Second Language Acquisition*, *39*(1), 59–95. https://doi.org/10.1017/S0272263115000455

Williams, J. N. (2005). Learning without awareness. *Studies in Second Language Acquisition*, *27*(2), 269–304. https://doi.org/10.1017/S0272263105050138

Williams, J. N. (2009). Implicit learning in second language acquisition. In W. C. Ritchie & T. K. Bhatia (Eds.), *The new handbook of second language acquisition* (pp. 319–353). Emerald Group.

30
Measuring Task-Based Performance

Kris Van den Branden

Background

One of the main reasons why people take the effort to attend second language courses is to develop the ability to use the target language: Their main aim is to learn and exchange meaningful messages with a view to reaching personal goals. Since the 1980s, the term "task" has been used in the field of applied linguistics, and in the literature on second and foreign language education, is used to define any goal-oriented activity that involves the meaningful use of language. Today, in the curricula of most language courses organized around the world, whether in compulsory education, higher education, or in other educational contexts, students' ability to perform tasks which involve the comprehension and/or production of meaningful messages is prioritized.

In the 1980s, the basic principles of task-based language assessment (TBLA) were positioned as an integral part of a task-based approach to language teaching (TBLT). In TBLT, *task*, rather than text, grammar rules or lexis, is taken as the main unit of analysis for the description of curriculum goals, the organization of classroom activity, and the assessment of learners' performance and development (cf. Candlin, 1987; Long, 1985; Van den Branden, Bygate, & Norris, 2009). Over the past three decades, various definitions of "task" have been proposed, but most definitions closely resemble the one formulated by Bygate, Skehan, and Swain (2001, p. 11):

> A task is an activity which requires learners to use language, with emphasis on meaning, to attain an objective.

In this definition, the "use" of language relates to either the production or comprehension of meaningful messages, or both. The "objective" may take the shape of a linguistic product, such as when students have to write a recipe or fill out a form, but will often be of a non-linguistic nature (e.g., getting the cooking done or reaching a certain destination).

In a task-based approach, the target tasks that constitute the goals of the curriculum are typically derived from an analysis of L2 learners' needs, so the goals stem from the analysis of the tasks they are expected to complete outside the L2 classroom and the concomitant use of language that they are expected to make while trying to do so. Many target tasks involve the integrated use of different skills and linguistic elements (e.g., words, grammar rules). For instance, to write a letter of complaint to a company that sent a wrong invoice, the language user will have to read and interpret the invoice and write a letter while using appropriate vocabulary, following grammar rules, and respecting genre conventions, amongst other things.

Following this line of reasoning, task-based language assessment (TBLA) aims to measure whether students are able to successfully perform relevant tasks up to criterion. From a TBLT perspective, TBLA mainly serves the purpose of determining the extent to which the goals of the task-based curriculum were reached. However, over the past thirty years, TBLA has not only drawn the attention of those interested in evaluating the effects of TBLT or monitoring the progress of L2 learners enrolled in a task-based program, but has been put to a wide range of other uses and been applied in a host of other domains (Norris, 2016). Amongst others, TBLA has been used:

- by governments and professional bodies to determine whether applicants have gained relevant language skills that are associated with gaining citizenship or integrating in society;
- by employers to determine whether candidates have the language skills to perform particular jobs;
- by schools, universities, colleges, and other educational institutions to determine whether students have acquired the minimally required level of language competence to pursue particular studies;
- by teachers who do not aim to adopt a task-based approach, but are interested nevertheless in determining their students' competence to perform functional, communicative tasks, either for summative purposes (i.e., determining whether students can perform particular tasks at the end of an instructional unit) or formative purposes (e.g., providing their students with feedback).

What all the above-mentioned uses have in common is that the assessment primarily focuses on the communicative use of language. This, then, is in line with the credo issued by Mendelsohn in 1989:

> I believe that the goal of testing today … is to see what someone *can do* with the language.
> (p. 96; italics in original)

In this respect, Norris (2016) defined TBLA as "the elicitation and evaluation of language (across all modalities) for expressing and interpreting meaning, within a well-defined communicative context (and audience), for a clear purpose, toward a valued goal or outcome" (pp. 232). The use of tasks for assessment purposes has been further enhanced by the fact that a growing number of influential frameworks and policy papers in which standards for language competence are described (e.g., the Common European Framework of Reference, the Canadian Language Benchmarks) also take tasks as their main unit of analysis.

As much as any other type of assessment, TBLA aims to meet quality standards related to the validity, reliability, and efficiency of the measurement involved. Below, I will describe the main challenges that TBLA faces in this regard.

Key Concepts

Task: In the literature on task-based language teaching (TBLT), tasks are usually defined as the things that people do with a certain goal in mind, and which involve, or even necessitate, the meaningful use of language.

Task-Based Language Assessment (TBLA): A wide variety of methods and procedures that can be used to assess the extent to which language learners are able to perform particular tasks, involving the receptive and/or productive use of the target language, up to criterion.

Key Issues

What Is Supposed to Be Measured?

As mentioned above, from a task-based perspective, assessment tasks should be derived from a thorough analysis of the tasks that candidates are expected to perform in relevant situations and domains. So, for instance in the Canadian CELBAN task-based language test (https://www.celbancentre.ca), which is used to prepare candidates for nursing and assesses whether they have the English language skills required for that profession, candidates need to show, amongst other tasks, that they are able to fill out a medical clinical assessment form on the basis of oral information provided about a patient. Assessment tasks like those aim to elicit and simulate authentic language use in real-life situations that are deemed essential.

However, as Van den Branden (2019) wrote:

> very often in education, assessment is primarily dictated by (a) what can be easily tested, (b) the instruments that are available, and/or (c) the instruments that are mandated from above. Unfortunately, (a), (b), and (c) regularly co-occur: What is mandated from above, for instance by national governments in the shape of centralized and standardized exams, predominantly contains the kind of test items that can be easily administered and corrected in a uniform way across a large population of learners.
>
> (p. 82)

With regard to measuring language performance, discrete-point grammar and vocabulary tests are easier to design, administer, and correct than full-blown task-based assessments. However, tests measuring students' vocabulary size or their mastery of specific grammar rules in the target language through the use of discrete-point items only indirectly relate to the students' actual competence to perform communicative, goal-oriented tasks. This indirect relationship needs to be determined through quantitative empirical research before discrete-point tests can be reliably used as a short-cut to true task-based assessments. Furthermore, the indirect assessments also need to be validated as socially appropriate, fair, and adequately representing the measurement construct. This kind of validation is perhaps done best through additional qualitative (introspective or retrospective) research with the test stakeholders themselves. (For more on test validity, see Chapelle, Chapter 2, this volume.)

The validity issue in measuring task-based performance is further complicated by the fact that, over the past three decades, terms such as *task* and *meaning* have been given a wide range of interpretations, to the extent that virtually anything that students are invited to do with the target language has been called a task. For instance, students who are asked in a language test to select the right word out of ten given vocabulary items and fill them out in the blanks of ten, equally given, sentences have been claimed to use language (yes, indeed, they have to use the words), to primarily focus on meaning (yes, they have to consider the meaning of the sentences), and to try and reach an objective (i.e., getting the items right). Those types of items tend to be particularly popular in standardized, centralized exams and tests that need to be administered to a large population of students because they are easy to administer and correct, and also because for many teachers, policy makers, and language users, they tend to have a relatively high degree of face validity when it comes to measuring language competence. However, this can hardly be called a full-blown, communicative task.

Even if truly communicative and relevant tasks are used in the assessment, a key question that needs to be answered is whether the validity of the task-based assessment is primarily determined by the use of language that the task involves or by the objective that needs to be attained. Long (2015) provided the example of following street directions: If students who take a language test in which they are to follow written street directions reach their destination despite missing particular linguistic information in the input, should they pass? In a similar vein, if students are tested on their ability to order tickets, do they pass if they get their tickets, even though they produced a number of linguistic errors and were downright impolite?

There is no simple answer to those questions. Depending on the purposes of the assessment and the profile of the learners, different answers will be possible. One way to approach this issue is to gradually raise the *linguistic* demands on the basis of the students' actual, expected, or required level of language proficiency. For instance, the Common European Framework of Reference contains a range of can-do statements, describing what learners at six consecutive levels of language development are expected to be able to do with the target language. The expected quality of their output is described in terms of complexity, accuracy, lexical variety, sociolinguistic appropriateness, fluency, and a range of other dimensions, and the same applies to the complexity of the input (i.e., the oral and written messages) that learners are expected to interpret and understand. Conceptually, frameworks like the CEFR adopt a largely linear trajectory of development across the different stages, with the various dimensions of language proficiency following a joint, reasonably predictable, and steadily incremental path. However, research into task performance by basic, intermediate, and advanced second language learners provides strong indications that for tasks at any level of proficiency, students' performance with regard to one particular dimension of language does not automatically imply similar performance with regard to other dimensions. Skehan's Limited Attention Capacity Model (Skehan, 2014) even predicts that students' ambition to perform a task well in terms of complexity or fluency, for instance, is likely to come at the cost of a potentially weaker performance with regard to accuracy. Students at lower and intermediate levels of language proficiency in particular will find it hard to perform at the same level for all dimensions at the same time. This actually raises the question if, and to what extent, students should be given some degree of autonomy on the particular aspects of performance that they prefer to focus on. Suppose two students at low-intermediate level perform an assessment task up to criterion (i.e., they reach their goal), but one student prefers to focus on fluency and hence, speaks relatively fluently while making more grammatical errors, and the second prefers to make slightly fewer grammatical errors at the expense of fluency, do they deserve the same mark?

Rating Scales

Such tricky issues are usually addressed in TBLA by adopting expert judgment approaches or designing rating scales, or a combination of both (Brindley, 1994/2009). Expert judges can be drawn from the domain in which the language tasks are typically performed (e.g., employers, job recruiters, principals…), but if they are not available, teachers, task designers or applied linguists are typically asked to do the job. This, however, is not entirely unproblematic, particularly with judges who do not keep their finger on the pulse of authentic language use in the target domain. In an effort to raise interrater reliability, expert judges are often asked to design, or work with analytic rating scales that describe which aspects of the performance will be evaluated or rated.

The latter is illustrated in the example below, which was taken from a battery of task-based tests called CNaVT (http://cnavt.org/) that are used for the certification of learners of Dutch as a foreign language, designed by a team of university-based test developers at the University of Leuven. The task is part of an official exam for foreign students who aim to show they have acquired the Dutch language skills to enroll as a student in a Dutch-medium university. Figure

30.1 describes the task and the assessment criteria that are used to measure the quality of students' performance.

The example in Figure 30.1 illustrates that the mere identification of rating criteria does not entirely answer key questions like who will pass the test or which grades students should be given. Judges will have to determine which specific success criteria will be used to determine the cut-off point between pass and fail, and how the actual performance by a student will be related to the criteria (e.g., what score a student gets if she fails to answer three out of the five comprehension questions). Rating scales allow judges to relate different cut-off points, scores, and success criteria to different levels of language proficiency.

CONTEXT

You are studying pharmacy at the University of Leuven. For the course "Health in the 21st century" guest lectures will be organized. Students are invited to suggest topics for those guest lectures. You have heard an interview on the radio about medicine residues in soil water. You decide to suggest that this topic be included in the list of guest lectures.

TASK

Listen to the audio fragment (an interview with an expert about medicinal residues in soil water). You will hear the fragment once. You are allowed to take notes while listening. Afterwards write a text with your proposal and your arguments. You are asked to write a coherent text of minimally 180 words. If you use far fewer words, your text will not be evaluated on all the relevant criteria. Your text should include: (a) a short description of the goal of your text; (b) the introduction of the topic, including a clear description of the societal problem introduced in the interview, its causes, and two possible solutions to the problems; (c) three arguments that you use to support your proposal to include this topic in the series of guest lectures and that can convince the reader that this topic is relevant for all pharmacy students; (d) a final conclusion. Your text must be comprehensible for readers who have not heard the interview.

RUBRICS

Content

1. The student explicitly describes the goal of the letter.
2. The student introduces the topic of the presentation in terms of (a) a societal problem, and (b) its possible causes.
3. The student explicitly describes two possible solutions to the problem.
4. The students proposes explicitly to include this presentation in the lecture series
5. The students provides three arguments for including the presentation in the lecture series.
6. The students formulates a conclusion.

Form

1. The appropriate and varied use of relevant vocabulary is evaluated with the use of a five-point scale.
2. The correct use of grammar rules is evaluated with the use of a detailed five-point scale.
3. The cohesion of the text (in terms of the logical, orderly and effective organization of the information) is evaluated with the use of a detailed five-point scale.
4. Spelling: the accuracy of the spelling is evaluated with the use of a detailed five-point scale.

Figure 30.1 Example of a task-based test and its rating scales.

However, the use and development of rating scales tends to be associated with a range of tough decisions, most of which have to do with the fact that the criteria are often too general, vague, or imprecise (e.g., what exactly is "appropriate vocabulary" for a given task?) (Brindley, 1994/2009; Norris, 2009). Another challenge has to do with the fact that depending on the nature of the task, different weights can be assigned to different aspects of performance. For instance, in tasks involving informal conversation with friends or familiar peers, accuracy can be deemed less important than in tasks involving high-stakes communication with superiors or interlocutors the speaker does not know. Thirdly, raters should avoid being stricter and more demanding for second language learners than for native speakers performing the same task, but then again, how strict should they be? Deygers (2017) provided the example of a task-based language test that international students must pass to be allowed to enroll at a Flemish university if they aspire to attend a Dutch-medium program. A substantial proportion of the native speakers (all of whom are automatically allowed to enroll on the basis of having obtained a degree of secondary education in a Flemish Dutch-medium school) failed to pass the test (see also Deygers, Van den Branden, & Van Gorp, 2017).

This issue is further complicated by the fact that the available research on task complexity has produced inconclusive results and leaves many questions unanswered as to what exactly makes some tasks more difficult than others, and how exactly task features can be matched to particular levels of language proficiency (for overviews, see Skehan, 2014; Robinson, 2011). What is clear, though, is that a wide range of task variables impact on the complexity of tasks, and hence, on the difficulty that students experience to perform the task to criterion. For receptive tasks, this includes, amongst others, (a) time pressure (associated with task performance); (b) the extent to which the student is familiar with the task and has relevant prior knowledge; (c) whether the content of the text refers to the here and now and to concrete phenomena or instead to more abstract content; (d) the number of reasoning steps and the type of reasoning involved; (e) the structure of the text; (f) the number of information bits that need to be interpreted; (g) the length of the text; and (h) the type of vocabulary and syntactic structures involved. For productive tasks, this includes, amongst others, (a) planning time (allowed or not before task performance); (b) time pressure, (c) the extent to which the student is familiar with the task and has relevant prior knowledge; (d) the number of reasoning steps and the type of reasoning involved; (e) the number of contributions that are needed; (f) the type of solution to the task; (g) the number of participants involved; (h) the flow of the information (one-way or two-way?); and (i) the level of anxiety raised by the testing situation.

All this may leave teachers and testers wondering what exactly is tested in a so-called task-based measurement, and to what extent the candidate's performance can be extrapolated to the performance of other, more or less similar tasks (Norris, 2009). One way to deal with that uncertainty is to work with norm-referenced evaluation, which takes the comparison of different candidates performing the same assessment task as the basis for grading and judging. In that case, the performance of a representative sample of learners is taken as an indication of what can reasonably be expected in terms of excellent and/or average task performance. Another way to reduce uncertainty and to raise the reliability of the evaluation is to raise the number of observations, measurements, and raters. Interestingly, this solution has also been suggested when it comes to using tasks for purposes associated with *formative* assessment.

Formative Task-Based Assessment

Whereas summative assessment aims to measure, at the end of an instructional unit, whether students have developed the competence to perform certain tasks at a particular level, the main purpose of formative assessment is to foster and support the students' progress. A crucial ingredient of formative assessment is the provision of feedback. There is ample research (e.g., Hattie, 2009; Hattie & Timperley, 2007; Mackey & Goo, 2007) that has shown that feedback has potentially strong positive effects on (language) learning, especially when it is provided in a timely manner (i.e., preferably when the student can make use of it, so during the task performance), if it is clear and easy to interpret, if it relates to the quality of task-performance rather than to the personality of the language user, and if it contains information that can help the student to improve task performance. For this purpose, not only the linguistic product, but also the process of task performance will need to be observed and evaluated.

Van Gorp and Deygers (2014) gave the example of a task-based syllabus for primary education in which students' performance of reading tasks is closely monitored by the teacher, peers and the students themselves on the basis of a carefully worked-out assessment framework. It should be noted that the reading tasks the pupils are expected to perform are not tests or assessment tasks, but the regular classroom-based tasks in the syllabus that are primarily meant to foster their reading development. In other words, task-based assessment is tightly embedded within language teaching. Teachers are encouraged to observe individual students while they are performing a series of reading tasks, to ask students to think aloud while doing so, and to support them on the basis of their observations. In this type of formative assessment, a focus on particular linguistic items (e.g., words, grammar rules, spelling rules, or the pronunciation of certain sounds), or even the use of discrete-point tests serves a primarily diagnostic purpose: They are intended to enrich the picture that the teachers compose of the quality of task performance, the aspects of the tasks for which the performance can be improved, and student development across consecutive task performances. If more than one teacher is involved in the integrated teaching and assessment, different views and evaluations can be shared, exchanged, and complemented.

Taking multiple observations, and the judgment of different raters, into account raises the chance that:

a) the resulting measurement more strongly reflects students' language proficiency, particularly when the range of observations also includes the evaluation of tasks performed in authentic conditions;
b) the negative effect of test anxiety on a particular task performance is mitigated;
c) judges can tease out which particular task features increase or decrease task difficulty for specific leaners (and how they can be addressed);
d) judges can empirically verify whether the evaluation of students' performance of particular types of tasks can be extrapolated to other task types;
e) judges cannot only measure performance, but also growth across varied task performances spread over time. From a task-based perspective, this implies for instance that judges can observe whether students who performed simplified versions of certain target tasks in an early stage gradually develop the competence to meet the demands raised by more complex and more authentic tasks.

Furthermore, if students are given insight in the criteria for successful task performance, they can self-assess their own performance and assess those of their peers, which, in turn, can result in peer feedback. In this way, students can be empowered to monitor and self-regulate their own task performance. In formative assessment, criteria for success can partly be fine-tuned to the current proficiency level of individual learners, so as to tailor task-related challenges (and opportunities to learn) to learners' zone of proximal development.

The Washback Effect of Task-Based Measurement

Research into the implementation of TBLT (e.g., Van den Branden, 2016; Adams & Newton, 2009) amply shows that there are many different reasons why second language teachers are reluctant to work with tasks or to adopt a full-blown task-based or communicative approach in their classrooms. For instance, teachers may lack confidence, expertise, and experience with regard to those approaches; they may not have adequate syllabi at their disposal, feel obstructed by large classroom sizes, experience, or feel obliged to properly prepare their students for largely form-based national exams.

As for the latter, task-based tests and exams have a potentially strong impact on language education and teacher-based language assessment. For one, task-based tests (for instance those designed by professional test designers) are likely to act as models for teachers, which they can use as a source of inspiration for their own teacher-designed measurement instruments. Secondly, task-based tests and exams, particularly those with high stakes, are likely to push teachers to devote more time and attention to the development of communicative skills in their classrooms. Thirdly, task-based tests can help teachers gain more insight in the defining features of tasks and the difference between discrete-point tests and exercises on the one hand, and task-based measurements on the other.

Ultimately, in formative types of assessment, learning, teaching, and assessment blend into each other. In a similar vein, the learner, the teacher, and the judge lose their separate, distinct identities. The learner who self-assesses their task performance becomes their own judge and teacher; same for students who provide their peers with feedback on the basis of task-based assessment. And the teacher becomes as much a learner as the students: By learning more about the way in which students handle tasks, the obstacles they meet when trying to reach task goals and the things that go well, teachers can flexibly adapt their own interventions, and their evaluation of what is going on, to the dynamics of student task engagement.

Recommendations for Practice

The use of tasks for measuring language performance has grown substantially over the past three decades in a varied range of educational and societal contexts, and will continue to do so, in view of the primary importance that is attached to communicative language use in a wide range of curricula and societal domains across the world.

Test designers, be they researchers or educators, should focus on measuring task-based performance because such assessments require, possibly, the least amount of inferencing: Student achievement or ability to use the language (that is, communicate) in authentic tasks (or close simulations to them) can be most directly observed through TBLA. Even when standardized, form-based assessments dominate the majority of language teaching done within a specific language learning program, TBLA has its place. TBLA can serve as diagnostic assessment, be used for as part of placement testing, and can and should be used to understand if students have learned from their performances of tasks in class. Additionally, TBLA should be used because teaching and assessing tasks that involve the comprehension and/or production of meaningful messages may spur motivation for students to continue learning beyond the language program at hand, and success in language learning is often dependent on the continuation of learning.

As described by Galaczi and Taylor in Chapter 32 of this volume, task designers should take advantage of the students' classroom and available learning contexts to have students perform tasks in a variety of speaker configurations, such as in pairs and groups. In this way, task-based work and measurement will help promote the development of the language classroom as a community of practice. As described by Yoon and Burton in Chapter 28 of this volume, tasks should be varied such that over time, students are assessed through a wide range of higher-level and lower-level organizational and pragmatic features. The key is not to assess performance through one task, but rather through many, which will lead to a more robust and meaningful picture of what students can do.

In terms of scoring, researchers and educators can log various criteria on which tasks for the students can be assessed. These criteria can be divided across task-completion and language ability domains, and should be scrutinized to make sure they are age and proficiency-level appropriate. SLA researchers should have task performance rated by more than one rater. The raters should be trained on the criteria, and inter-rater reliability should be estimated, with the researchers providing detailed information on how the non-agreed-upon ratings were adjudicated, either through consensus discussions, or by bringing in an additional rater or raters. Research has shown that individuals' task-performance scores vary more across tasks than across raters, thus educators and SLA researchers should expect a certain amount of score-variation across tasks, as that is human nature: Some people are better at certain tasks than others. Thus one could consider TBLA as being able to well capture the true, multi-dimensional human variation that exists in real-life communication skills.

Testing Tips for SLA/TBLT Researchers

- Select and design assessment tasks that represent the kinds of tasks that students have to be able to perform outside the classroom.
- Design assessment tasks that students can only perform up to criterion if they make appropriate use of the target language; make sure that students' prior, extralinguistic knowledge about the topic at hand does not unduly influence test results (if necessary, provide all students with essential prior knowledge before embarking on the test).
- Include a sufficient amount of items/tasks, and a variety of items/tasks, to enhance reliability. Only include question and item types that students are familiar with.
- Write up clear and detailed instructions for the test-takers, and inform them on the criteria they have to meet.
- For open items, design detailed scoring rubrics relating to relevant dimensions of task performance (e.g., complexity, sociolinguistic appropriateness, clarity, fluency, accuracy of the language use); adapt the choice of relevant dimensions to task type, task goals, and learners' level of proficiency.

Testing Tips for Teachers and Program Leaders

- Select and design a variety of assessment tasks that represent the kinds of tasks that students have to be able to perform outside the classroom.
- Be transparent about the criteria that will be used to evaluate the students' performances. Give students insight into the criteria they have to meet.
- Combine summative with formative assessment and provide ample feedback that helps the students to learn from the assessment.
- Integrate peer assessment and self-assessment in the language classroom.
- Use the results of the assessment to think about enhancing the quality of teaching.

Recommended Readings

Brindley, G. (2009). Task-centred language assessment in language learning. The promise and the challenge. In K. Van den Branden, M. Bygate, & J. Norris (Eds.), *Task-based language teaching: A reader* (pp. 435–454). John Benjamins. (Reprinted from *Language and Learning. Papers presented at the Annual International Language in Education Conference (Hong Kong, 1993)*, pp. 73–94, by N. Bird, (Ed.), 1994.)

This is an excellent introduction to the basic principles of task-based language assessment and some of its main challenges.

Norris, J. M. (2016). Current uses of task-based language assessment. *Annual Review of Applied Linguistics*, 36, 230–244. https://doi.org/10.1017/S0267190516000027

This article provides a fine overview of the varied uses to which TBLA can be put.

Van Gorp, K. & Deygers, B. (2014). Task-based language assessment. In A. Kunnan (Ed.), *The Companion to Language Assessment. Volume II Approaches and Development* (pp. 578–593). Wiley-Blackwell.

For those interested in the implementation of task-based language assessment in compulsory education, this article provides an outline of basic principles and contains a number of telling examples.

References

Adams, R., & Newton, J. (2009). TBLT in Asia: Opportunities and constraints. *Asian Journal of English Language Teaching*, *19*, 1–17.

Brindley, G. (2009). Task-centred language assessment in language learning: The promise and the challenge. In K. Van den Branden, M. Bygate, & J. Norris (Eds.), *Task-based language teaching: A reader* (pp. 435–454). John Benjamins. (Reprinted from *Language and learning*. Papers presented at the annual international language in education conference (Hong Kong, 1993), pp. 73–94, by N. Bird (Ed.), 1994.)

Bygate, M., Skehan, P., & Swain, M. (2001). Introduction. In M. Bygate, P. Skehan, & M. Swain (Eds.), *Researching pedagogic tasks: Second language learning, teaching and testing* (pp. 1–20). Pearson Education Limited.

Candlin, C. N. (1987). Towards task-based language learning. In C. N. Candlin & D. Murphy (Eds.), *Lancaster practical papers in English language education*: *Vol. 7. Language learning tasks* (pp. 5–22). Prentice Hall.

Deygers, B. (2017). *Assessing high-stakes assumptions. A longitudinal mixed-methods study of university entrance language tests, and of the policy that relies on them* (Unpublished doctoral dissertation). University of Leuven.

Deygers, B., Van den Branden, K., & Van Gorp, K. (2017). University entrance language tests: A matter of justice. *Language Testing*, *35*(4), 449–476. https://doi.org/10.1177/0265532217706196

Hattie, J. (2009). *Visible learning: A synthesis of over 800 meta-analyses relating to achievement*. Routledge.

Hattie, J., & Timperley, H. (2007). The power of feedback. *Review of Educational Research*, *77*(1), 81–112. https://doi.org/10.3102/003465430298487

Long, M. (1985). A role for instruction in second language acquisition: Task-based language teaching. In K. Hyltenstam & M. Pienemann (Eds.), *Modelling and assessing second language acquisition* (pp. 77–79). Multilingual Matters.

Long, M. (2015). *Second language acquisition and task-based language teaching*. Wiley-Blackwell.

Mackey, A., & Goo, J. (2007). Interaction research in SLA: A meta-analysis and research synthesis. In A. Mackey (Ed.), *Conversational interaction in second language acquisition: A series of empirical studies* (pp. 407–453). Oxford University Press.

Mendelsohn, D. (1989). Testing should reflect teaching. *TESL Canada Journal*, *7*(1), 95–108. https://doi.org/10.18806/tesl.v7i1.563

Norris, J. (2009). Task-based teaching and testing. In M. Long & C. Doughty (Eds.), *The handbook of language teaching* (pp. 578–594). Wiley-Blackwell.

Norris, J. (2016). Current uses of task-based language assessment. *Annual Review of Applied Linguistics*, *36*, 230–244. https://doi.org/10.1017/S0267190516000027

Robinson, P. (2011). *Second language task complexity: Researching the cognition hypothesis of language learning and performance*. John Benjamins.

Skehan, P. (2014). *Processing perspectives on task performance*. John Benjamins Publishing.

Van den Branden, K. (2016). The role of the teacher in task-based language teaching. *Annual Review of Applied Linguistics*, *36*, 164–181. https://doi.org/10.1017/S0267190515000070

Van den Branden, K. (2019). *Rethinking education and renewing energy for learning: Research, principles and practice*. Routledge.

Van den Branden, K., Bygate, M., & Norris, J. (2009). *Task-based language teaching: A reader*. John Benjamins.

Van Gorp, K., & Deygers, B. (2014). Task-based language assessment. In A. Kunnan (Ed.), *The companion to language assessment. Volume II approaches and development* (pp. 578–593). Wiley-Blackwell.

31
Measuring Literary Competences in SLA

Amos Paran, Carol Spöttl, Ulla Ratheiser & Kathrin Eberharter

Background

Examining the role of literature in learning a second or foreign language (SL or FL) reveals various competing narratives (Paran, 2006). Learning a SL or FL has always been strongly connected with studying the literature of that language, either as an end (learning a language to be able to read its literature) or as a means (using literature to learn a language) (Ahrens, 2012; Maley 2001). Literature therefore also formed an important part of FL examinations, such as the first versions of the Cambridge Proficiency Exam (Weir, Vidaković & Galaczi, 2013; the exam is now known as C2 Proficiency) (Weir, Vidaković, & Galaczi, 2013). On the other hand, the role of literature in FL curricula has varied across history and in different world regions, and there exist divergent narratives about this role depending both on context and on research approach. Even the relationship between the role of literature in FL learning and Communicative Language Teaching (CLT) is contested: Weir (2013) suggested that literature declined with the advent of CLT; Carter (2007) identified a prior decline, claiming that CLT made it easier and more acceptable to incorporate literary texts into ELT; and Alter and Ratheiser (2019) presented yet another view, suggesting that the marginalisation of literature coincided with the publication of the Common European Framework of Reference for Languages (CEFR) (Council of Europe, 2001).

In the third decade of the 21st century, however, literature has maintained its position or indeed made a comeback as a compulsory element of FL education worldwide, including, for example, in Hong Kong (Tsang & Paran, 2020), Israel (see below), and the Netherlands (Bloemert, Paran, Jansen, & van de Grift, 2019). Possibly the strongest sign of this is the inclusion of literature in the recent *Companion Volume to the CEFR* (Council of Europe, 2018), where three new scales relate explicitly to reading and experiencing literature (see below). This contrasts with the original CEFR, where literature was sidelined through tentative language and hedging statements, such as: "It is much to be hoped that teachers of literature at all levels may find many sections of the Framework relevant to their concerns" (Council of Europe, 2001, p. 56).

Literature intersects with FL and language testing in three ways. One is using literary texts in reading comprehension tests (e.g., Fecteau, 1999; Nishihara, 2015), where the literary text is merely another type of input for testing comprehension. The second is using literary texts in tests where candidates explore a theme through a combination of non-fiction and literary extracts.

The third is focusing on literary knowledge and literary competences of SL/FL learners. In this chapter we focus on the two latter areas.

Key Concepts

***Literary knowledge*:** knowledge of or about a literary text. This can be based on memory and/or public knowledge and can sometimes be acquired without having read the text itself.

***Literary skills*:** individual skills/techniques that readers have acquired and that will help them read, analyse, and understand a given literary text.

***Literary competence*:** the ability to draw meaning from a literary text by identifying the skills required for the analysis of the text, by applying them accordingly, and by being aware of what can be gained by applying these skills.

***Literary literacy*:** the readers' ability to thoroughly engage with a literary text, relying on the skills and competences acquired, so as to meaningfully integrate the reading experience into a broader, non-classroom related, extra-literary context.

Key Issues

Assessment Approaches to Literature in Language Learning

Interestingly, Bachman's (1990) model of language competence, highly influential in language testing, referred to the imaginative function of language, including a wide range of activities—from telling jokes to reading novels to going to the theatre—but without addressing how to test it. Carter and Long (1990) presented the first overview of testing literature in language teaching, identifying three common question types (Paraphrase and Context; Describe and Discuss; and Evaluate and Discuss) and suggested that such questions result in what Short and Candlin (1986) called "flight from the text" (p. 29); candidates can often answer questions without having read the literary work, instead reading a crib, summary, or translation. As a remedy, Carter and Long (1990) suggested a language-based approach to teaching literature, with tests focusing on the language of the text and how it achieves meaning. Importantly, they suggested that in such tests learners should have access to the text; they would then not be tested on memory but on their sensitivity to specific language phenomena in the text. Carter and Long (1990) thus pointed out an important construct weakness in literature tests. However, they did not present a model of literary competence or specify the construct being tested.

Spiro (1991), on the other hand, did identify literary competences, starting from a model specifying the competences involved in different types of engagement with literature, such as literary criticism, creative writing, or appreciative reading. She then defined literary skills (used almost interchangeably with literary competence) and presented common task types in testing literature, distinguishing between exams precluding contact with the text (in a typology similar to Carter & Long, 1990), and those where such contact is required. She provided a list of task types and then presented the stages of writing a test, from identifying target competences to planning the overall shape of the test. Spiro (1991) thus provided an example of moving from theoretical discussions of literary and linguistic competences to the practicalities of an EFL literature test. Other models of literary competence in EFL settings have been highly specific, with Burwitz-Melzer (2007) providing a model for upper secondary school level, and Diehr and Surkamp (2015) focusing on lower secondary school.

Paran's (2010) overview of issues arising when assessing literature in EFL contexts, articulated six dilemmas:

1. To test or not to test?
2. Testing language or testing literature?
3. Testing knowledge or testing skills?
4. Testing private appreciation of literature or testing public knowledge about/of literature?
5. Authentic/genuine tasks or pedagogic tasks?
6. Should examiners require metalanguage?

(Paran, 2010, pp. 144–153, *passim*)

A re-examination of these dilemmas suggests grouping them as three challenges:

Challenge 1: Where literature is taught in an SLA context, a policy decision needs to be made whether to test it (Dilemma 1).
Challenge 2: If the policy decision is to test literature, the construct being tested and the model underlying it need to be specified (Dilemmas 2, 3, 4 and 6).
Challenge 3: Once the construct is defined, tests, tasks, and item types need to be devised to operationalise different aspects of the model underlying the construct (Dilemma 5).

Educational systems have responded to these challenges in various ways. Because of the paucity of published scholarship in this area, we now present three specific cases which illustrate different approaches to assessing literature in language teaching. Within each case, the policy decision that was made was to test literature; thus with these three cases, we showcase ways the educational system in question has addressed the various challenges.

Case Studies of Assessing Literature in SLA

Case Study 1 – The Israeli Matriculation Exam: Literature and Critical Thinking. The history of the Israeli EFL literature exam exemplifies how system requirements and external factors may override pedagogic or testing considerations (Paran, 2017). Over the years, literature has been tested through short essay writing in a separate section of the Israeli EFL matriculation exam; short essay writing examined internally by the teacher; and as part of the oral exam, a compromise solution reached when implementing a revision of the oral exam (Shohamy, Reves, & Bejarano, 1986) ran into practical difficulties. The 1998 revision included both a literature part, in which students were tested on the literature they had studied in the last two years of secondary school, and a part in which the students reported on their extensive reading. One change offered greater latitude in terms of choice, leading to teachers consciously choosing shorter, easier pieces in order to help their learners succeed in the exam (Ferman 2004), a narrowing of the literature selected that constitutes a washback effect illustrating the unintended consequences of exam reform. The most recent version of the EFL matriculation exam provides a fair amount of flexibility (State of Israel, Ministry of Education 2017), with literature tested in two parts: a reading log examined internally by the school, and a specific module in the centrally constructed and administered nationwide written exam, in which students are examined on the very small number of works on the syllabus. The exam currently includes three parts: the first two present questions of the types discussed by Carter and Long (1990). However, the exam introduces an additional construct: thinking skills. Candidates are asked to answer a question about a literary text using **one** of a set of thinking skills (listed in an appendix to the exam) and explaining why they chose that specific skill. For example, in a question on Robert Frost's *The Road Not Taken*, candidates are asked what the speaker in the poem thinks they will feel about their decision in the future, and to explain their answer choosing one thinking skill from among comparing and contrasting, distinguishing different perspectives, explaining cause and effect, problem solving, inferring, and explaining patterns. The third part of the exam asks candidates to read a statement about a different work and relate the two by discussing, for example, how relevant the statement is for understanding the literary text (State of Israel, Ministry of Education, 2012).

The thinking skills questions and the questions asking students to relate statements about the work to the piece itself reflect a very specific pedagogical sequence for teaching literary works suggested (in effect, prescribed) by the Ministry of Education. The exam has had a strong washback effect on teaching as well as on coursebooks, all of which structure teaching the small number of pieces read along a seven-part sequence imposed by the ministry, focusing on the types of questions described above (Paran, 2017).

Case Study 2 – The International Baccalaureate Diploma Programme: Creative Response and Critical Comment.[1] A different approach is demonstrated by the assessment of FL literature within the International Baccalaureate Diploma Programme (IB DP), a programme delivered worldwide leading to a school leaving qualification. IB DP students are required to study and be assessed in a "Language B" (the IB DP term for what would normally be called L2) at one of two levels. At the higher level, Language B courses require learners to study at least two longer works (i.e., novels or plays) over the two years of the programme, and to be assessed on their reading. The focus is on enjoyment of the literary work, engagement with it, and on literature as a vehicle for language learning. The assessment accounts for 20% of the final Language B mark, and requires learners to produce a short creative piece of 500–600 words based on one of the literary works they have read, accompanied by a 150-word rationale. The assignment is written during school hours, under the teacher's supervision, within a suggested time of three to four hours (often in more than one sitting). Four sets of criteria are employed in marking the assignment: Language (effectiveness and accuracy; 8 marks available); Content (appreciation of the literary work, and the skill of task planning; 10 marks), Format (adherence to genre conventions and their appropriateness; 4 marks); and Rationale (clarity and convincingness of the rationale; 3 marks).

The tasks suggested for this assessment include writing a new ending, an interview with a character, or a diary entry by one of the characters, showing an appreciation of literary pedagogy in L2 contexts (e.g., Carter & Long, 1991; Collie & Slater, 1987), rooted within a reader response framework (e.g., Rosenblatt, 1978). This has also had various washback effects; Duncan and Paran (2017) found that teachers chose works geared towards the assessment; teachers in large classes, especially, stressed the importance of choosing works with many characters to ensure learners have a choice of assignment options.

Case Study 3 – France: Testing Literature Orally. A third approach appears in the French school leaving exam, the *Baccalauréat* (see Gauthier, 2018, for a general description). Literature in EFL appears in different guises, most prominently in the programme known as *Littérature étrangère en langue étrangère* (LELE, Foreign literature in a foreign language). This is a separate strand in the curriculum during the last two years of secondary education for students who choose literature as one of their specialisations. Literature is tested in the oral part of the *Baccalauréat*, following the regular oral exam, and this part of the exam lasts 10 minutes (see Bellhouse, 2018 for a description of the oral component of the EFL *Baccalauréat*). Learners choose two themes from those studied. For each theme, they construct a dossier which includes two extracts from the works studied, as well as additional texts they have chosen (e.g., excerpts from critical works, adaptations, illustrations, etc.) that they consider relevant to understanding and evaluating their chosen extracts. Before the exam, the learner is told which of the two dossiers they will present, and then has 10 minutes to prepare for the whole exam (including LELE). Once the general oral exam is over, the learner presents their LELE dossier for five minutes, followed by five minutes of discussion, initiated by the examiner. The learner is marked on four aspects of their performance: Presentation of the dossier; Level of literary reading; Literary context and environment; and Oral expression. Each area is awarded between 0 and 5 points. To achieve the highest level, examinees are required to provide a rich and exact description of the theme of the texts presented and provide a full and well-argued explanation of their choice. They must include an aesthetic appreciation and a personal critique of the works (Presentation of the dossier); provide a nuanced explanation of the meaning and the importance of the texts, including being able to use appropriate literary analysis methods, and show understanding of implied meanings (Literary reading); place the texts within a literary environment (Literary context); and do this in a clear manner, using rich, diverse, and exact lexis, with complex grammar and well-developed interaction.

Assessing Literature in SLA

These three case studies represent educational systems that include literature in their EFL testing programme (Challenge 1 above), illustrating a variety of assessment issues concerning the construct; test design and assessment criteria; and washback. Our discussion thus next addresses Challenges 2 and 3.

Challenge 2: If the policy decision is to test literature, the construct being tested and the model underlying it need to be specified.

Measuring literary competences in SLA raises issues surrounding both validity and reliability. Issues of construct validity are impacted by such policy factors as whether the syllabus views literature as a vehicle for language acquisition or an educational aim in itself, or by content factors such as the extent to which the literary competences measured can be agreed upon and clearly defined. The construct issue arising from the Israeli case centres on the explicit inclusion of thinking skills and the resulting construct irrelevance in a literature exam (the importance of these skills notwithstanding). Likewise, the IB approach of assessing literature through creative writing raises potential issues of construct irrelevance. A further issue is the danger of construct under-representation, where the curriculum only includes a small number of set pieces (Israel), or where students are only assessed on a small number of pieces (IB). This presents two challenges to reliable test results: the danger of candidates memorising set responses, and the negative washback of only teaching the set pieces and nothing beyond. In the French example this threat of memorisation is offset through interviewer probes following the candidate's prepared presentation. Another construct issue is the language in which the exam is taken; in the three cases we presented above, the exam is taken in the L2, but there have been cases in the past where FL literature exams and indeed teaching were conducted in the L1 (for example, in the Netherlands; see Bloemert et al., 2019; Wolthuis, Bloemert, Tammenga-Helmantel, & Paran, 2019). All these issues must be addressed in order to maximise the validity of the exam.

Challenge 3: Once the construct is defined, tests, tasks, and item types need to be devised to operationalise different aspects of the model underlying the construct.

The three case studies illustrated how one can test literary competences in different modalities (written or oral), performance skills (receptive skills vs. productive skills), and different test formats (short answer format vs. essay; individual long turn vs. interview format).

Issues of assessment criteria arise in all exams; in our case studies, these criteria appear more distinct and equally weighted with the French *Baccalauréat* in comparison to the IB, which, however, illustrates an alternative to the one-off writing test. The assessment criteria provided, though, highlight a number of assessment issues. How much can literary competence and planning competence be rated with only one criterion? And what is the role of language competence in the rationale that students have to write? It appears as if both constructs—language as well as literary competences—are only represented in parts in such an assessment arrangement.

In all cases, however, it is important to consider whether the model underpinning the scale is clearly defined and adequately graded for different levels of performance. The use of assessment criteria has to ensure fair and reliable procedures. This can be achieved through extensive and iterative rater training, provision of benchmarked performances, and recording performances to permit double rating for borderline cases.

Washback

Washback is well-documented in language assessment, including in literature teaching in FL (Duncan & Paran, 2017; Ferman, 2004). The Israeli case study above illustrated the washback from a narrowly prescribed curriculum and a narrowly defined pedagogical approach. On the other hand, the IB case study illustrated a fairly open assessment task and an open approach to writing the assignment that could lead to positive washback and a pedagogical emphasis on the process of writing rather than only on the final product. The French case study also suggested the possibility of positive washback through balancing teacher choice with student choice. A key issue, therefore, in assessing literary competences is the selection of models underpinning both teaching *and* assessment to provide a robust construct for measurement purposes as well as a valid basis for classroom teaching practices.

Modelling Literary Competence and the CEFR Framework

Two recent developments enable us to suggest a systematic approach to assessing literature in SLA. One is a model which clusters related competences into a theoretical model of literary competences (Alter & Ratheiser, 2019); the other is the new scales relating to literature in the *Companion Volume with New Descriptors* (Council of Europe 2018) to the CEFR.

Literary Competence: The Innsbruck Model. Alter and Ratheiser (2019) presented a model charting the competences they considered essential for comprehensive literary literacy in an EFL context, though applicable to other SLA environments and mostly also to L1 users (Figure 31.1). Importantly, this model is rooted in a general linguistic competence of English and a reading competence alike, both of which develop throughout the learning process.

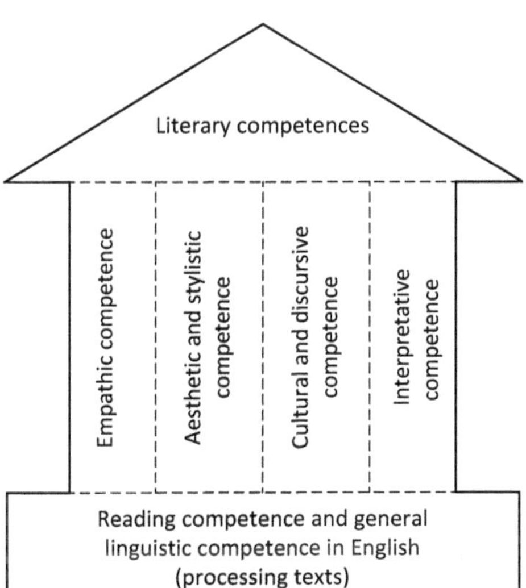

Figure 31.1 The Innsbruck model of literary competences.

The first component, *Empathic competence*, refers to the ability to relate to a text and its characters on an emotional level and is vital for all reading contexts, both for reading for pleasure and for reading in educational settings. Arguably, this is the *sine qua non* for any engagement with creative texts. *Aesthetic and stylistic competence* refer to the appreciation of the qualities of the text as a literary artefact; Aesthetic competence is an individual response (with the ensuing difficulties for objective assessment), whereas Stylistic competence refers to the ability to analyse stylistic features (which can arguably be objectively measured). The third pillar in the model is *Cultural and discursive competence*, namely the ability to identify cultural markers and discourses at work in a specific text. In the sense that literature can open a window into other lives, cultures, or eras, this competence is also considered essential. Finally, *Interpretative competence* allows readers to make sense of and attribute meaning to the results of their analysis of the literary text.

This approach is based on the belief in the interrelatedness of the individual competences. Though the different competences can be targeted separately in teaching, ideally educators will aim at developing all competences simultaneously in their students. Not only can (and should) they be fostered from early on, but working with creative texts along with the competence model will also provide a feasible tool for measuring the progress the learners make. And it is specifically by splitting literary competence into these subcategories that we can measure or assess progress more meaningfully.

Literature in the Companion Volume to the CEFR (2018). The competences in the model in Figure 31.1 have equivalents in the *Companion Volume with New Descriptors* (Council of Europe, 2018) to the CEFR, which include three scales concerned with literature and literary response: *Reading as a leisure activity*; *Expressing a personal response to creative texts (including literature)*; and *Analysis and criticism of creative texts (including literature)*. These scales provide practitioners with the basis for assessing the development of selected literary competences within the language curriculum. Many of the "can do" statements of these new scales, particularly the latter two, have corollaries in the competences outlined in the Innsbruck model. The *Companion* introduced level descriptions that are key features for operationalising the construct by providing the basis for test specifications, potential sources for task design, and specific "can do" statements for rating scale development.

Linking the CEFR with the Innsbruck Model. The four competences in the Innsbruck Model can be easily linked to these new CEFR scales and level descriptors, as illustrated in Table 31.1. Importantly, this involves assessing literary competences within all four modes of language competence (reading, listening, speaking, and writing), as the literary experience involves reading various text types, listening to radio plays and theatre performances, and talking and writing to friends and other audiences about these experiences.

Combining the Innsbruck model and the CEFR offers a step towards addressing Challenge 2 above. Instead of having to deal with language competence and literary knowledge on separate scales, the new CEFR scales enable educators to measure aspects of literary competence *and* language competence at the same time, viewing them as intertwined instead of as discrete entities. Furthermore, this approach gives practitioners some flexibility as the scales describe competency levels in terms of engagement and interpretation (*Expressing a personal response to creative texts)* as well as analysis and evaluation (*Analysis and criticism of creative texts)*. Importantly, the level descriptors for personal response include not only canonical literary works but also songs and films, highlighting the broad definition of creative texts that literature teachers can adopt. Finally, as Table 31.1 indicates, the new CEFR scales reject the myth that literature is only for more advanced learners and explicitly signal that even early stage learners can deal with appropriately chosen literary texts and carry out language tasks connected to them.

Table 31.1 Literary competences and the new companion descriptors: selected examples at different proficiency levels

CEFR Level	*Companion Scale*	*Level Descriptor*	*IBK Competence Model*
C1	*Expressing a personal response to creative texts*	"Can give his/her personal interpretation of the development of a plot, the characters and the themes in a story, novel, film or play."	Interpretative competence
B2	*Analysis and criticism of creative texts*	"Can evaluate the way the work encourages identification with characters, giving examples."	Stylistic competence Aesthetic competence
B1	*Expressing a personal response to a creative text*	"Can describe the emotions he/she experienced at a certain point in a story, e.g., the point(s) in a story when he/she became anxious for a character, and explain why."	Empathic competence
A2	*Analysis and criticism of creative texts*	"Can identify and briefly describe, in basic formulaic language, the key themes and characters in short, simple narratives [...]"	Stylistic competence
A1	*Expressing a personal response to a creative text*	"Can use simple words and phrases to say how a work made him/her feel."	Empathic competence Aesthetic competence

Test Item Format. For both receptive and productive language use, key issues arise for classroom practitioners and test providers. With receptive skills, conceptualising valid item formats is one such challenge. The reading construct targeted in a language exam often focuses on reading for main ideas or reading for specific detail or information. These types of reading exams use closed item formats such as multiple choice or multiple matching and/or open formats such as short answer questions. The issue here is twofold. First, to what extent is the reading construct the same in measuring literary competence? And second, to what extent do these test formats lend themselves to the measurement of literary competences? Beach (2014) pointed out that closed item types assume a definite correct answer, an assumption incompatible with modern reader response theory. Short answer formats and a wider understanding of what kind of answer is accepted for a question might be one way to meet this challenge, particularly in classroom-based assessment.

The following questions, related to the Innsbruck model, provide a starting point for task design:

- *Empathic competence*: Why do we feel sorry for the character?
- *Aesthetic competence*: Comment on the use of blue and grey for a cloud in the illustration.
- *Cultural and discursive competence*: How are gender, minorities, or generational issues presented in this text?
- *Interpretative competence*: What effect does the text have on the reader? How does it achieve this effect?

For the productive modes which lend themselves more readily to assessing literary response, close attention needs to be paid to the reliability of scoring. The assessment criteria need to incorporate features of the literary competences to be measured. Even if provided with an assessment rubric, raters might tend to pay more attention to mechanics and language than the quality of the content of the response (Rezaei & Lovorn, 2010).

Recommendations for Practice

At the beginning of this chapter we discussed the resurgence of literature in SLA environments. This resurgence notwithstanding, assessment in literature in language education is an emergent area which merits and requires additional work. As our case studies demonstrated, high-stakes literature exams in different educational systems have taken widely divergent roads; we have also referred to a number of different models of literary competence. Through focusing on one model of literary competences (the Innsbruck model, see Figure 31.1) we demonstrated possible options for literature becoming an integral part of the construct in assessment practices. In our view, this could strengthen the position of literature, ensuring that it appears as a discipline in its own right within SLA, rather than being merely subservient to language teaching. We provide the following recommendations below for those interested in assessing literary competences.

Select a Well-Defined Model for the Construct

We have focused above on one model of literary competences (Alter & Ratheiser, 2019), though we have also mentioned others. A major challenge for the field is to ensure that assessments are based on a clear model of assessing literature in SLA. The first step in developing a research agenda in this area is to reach a commonly agreed model of literary competence in FL learning.

Teach and Assess Literature at All Levels of Language Learning

All four competences in the Figure 31.1 model can be used in low-level assessment situations; for example, graphic novels appropriate to the learner population can be used to design speaking or writing tasks around describing the visuals, stating, for example, how the characters are represented in the story, or how these visuals make the learner feel.

Use a Variety of Texts Appropriately

Many genres, including less canonical ones, can be used for testing. Thus, for example, graphic novels work for all levels of learners; fairy tales and fables offer familiar themes and characters on which to build, relieving the pressure of language competence and allowing candidates to focus on literary competences.

Validate Tasks and Test Items

We have pointed out above a number of issues of validity and reliability arising from measuring literary competences in SLA. All tasks and test items should be validated empirically to minimise the risks we have discussed (see Chapelle, Chapter 2, this volume; Révész & Brunfaut, Chapter 3, this volume), especially since literature is often tested in high-stakes school leaving exams.

Testing Tips

- Some language functions are equivalent or identical to literary competences: e.g., "evaluate," "compare and contrast," "describe." Use these functions to ensure that you make use of the common ground between the two disciplines.

- Target a variety of literary competences within one assessment task by using more than one language function: e.g., describe the scene, explain how the text made you feel, and compare and contrast the two characters.
- Ensure that questions require spontaneous responses rather than responses that can be prepared and memorised.
- Consider weighting the different rating criteria equally in rating scales and try to ensure raters are sufficiently trained in applying these criteria.
- Where possible, trial assessment tasks with similar test-taker populations.

Note

1 The IB Language B assessment changed with the 2020 administration of the exam. The assessment described in this section was current at the time of writing and refers to the exam as it was presented in the previous curriculum.

Recommended Readings

Hall, G. (2015). *Literature in language education* (2nd ed.). Palgrave Macmillan.

Though not directly concerned with assessment, this comprehensive overview of pedagogical and research issues in literature in language education should serve as a starting point for testers in this area.

Paran, A., & Sercu, L. (Eds.) (2010). *Testing the untestable in language education*. Multilingual Matters.

The literature section of this volume includes three papers about testing literature which have been influential in setting the agenda for literature in language testing in the past decade.

Spiro, J. (1991). Assessing literature: Four papers. In C. Brumfit (Ed.), *Assessment in literature teaching* (pp. 16–83). Macmillan.

This is still the most comprehensive and detailed treatment of testing literature in an EFL context. In four sections (Language Teaching and The Literature Test: Laying the Foundations; Defining Literary Skills; Measuring Literary Skills; and Writing the Literature Test) Spiro looks at the way in which testers can move from defining literary competences to the nitty-gritty of constructing items for literature assessment in a FL.

References

Ahrens, R. (2012). Teaching literature: Introduction. In M. Eisenmann & T. Summer (Eds.), *Basic issues in EFL-teaching and learning* (pp. 181–190). Winter.

Alter, G., & Ratheiser, U. (2019). A new model of literary competences and the revised CEFR descriptors. *ELT Journal*, *73*(4), 377–386. https://doi.org/10.1093/elt/ccz024

Bachman, L. F. (1990). *Fundamental considerations in language testing*. Oxford University Press.

Beach, R. (2014). Assessing responses to literature. In J. Kunnan (Ed.), *The companion to language assessment. Vol 1: Abilities, contexts and learners* (pp. 83–99). John Wiley & Sons. https://doi.org/10.1002/9781118411360.wbcla017

Bellhouse, G. (2018). Are teachers given sufficient tools as examiners in high-stakes language testing? A study of the new foreign language speaking component of the French Baccalauréat. In D. Xerri & P. Vella Briffa (Eds.), *Teacher involvement in high-stakes language testing* (pp. 85–103). Springer. https://doi.org/10.1007/978-3-319-77177-9_6

Bloemert, J., Paran, A., Jansen, E., & van de Grift, W. (2019). Students' perspective on the benefits of EFL literature education. *The Language Learning Journal*, *47*(3), 371–384. https://doi.org/10.1080/09571736.2017.1298149

Burwitz-Melzer, E. (2007). Ein Lesekompetenzmodell für den fremdsprachlichen Literaturunterricht. In L. Bredella & W. Hallet (Eds.), *Literaturunterricht, Kompetenzen und Bildung* (pp. 127–157). WVT.

Carter, R. (2007). Literature and language teaching 1986–2006: A review. *International Journal of Applied Linguistics*, *17*(1), 4–13. https://doi.org/10.1111/j.1473-4192.2007.00130.x
Carter, R., & Long, M. N. (1990). Testing literature in EFL classes: Tradition and innovation. *ELT Journal*, *44*(3), 215–221. https://doi.org/10.1093/elt/44.3.215
Carter, R., & Long, M. N. (1991). *Teaching literature*. Longman.
Collie, J., & Slater, S. (1987). *Literature in the language classroom*. Cambridge University Press.
Council of Europe. (2001). *Common European framework of reference for languages: Learning, teaching, assessment*. Cambridge University Press.
Council of Europe. (2018). *Common European framework of reference for languages: Learning, teaching, assessment. Companion volume with new descriptors*. Council of Europe.
Diehr, B., & Surkamp, C. (2015). Die Entwicklung literaturbezogener Kompetenzen in der Sekundarstufe I: Modellierung, Abschlussprofil und Evaluation. In W. Hallet, C. Surkamp, & U. Krämer (Eds.), *Literaturkompetenzen Englisch. Modellierung – Curriculum – Unterrichtsbeispiele* (pp. 21–40). Klett/Kallmeyer.
Duncan, S., & Paran, A. (2017). *The effectiveness of literature on acquisition of language skills and intercultural understanding in the high school context*. International Baccalaureate Organisation. http://www.ibo.org/contentassets/1fcefe0df17448bebe6781ea0396adff/effect-of-literature-on-language-acquisition-final-report.pdf
Fecteau, M. L. (1999). First- and second-language reading comprehension of literary texts. *The Modern Language Journal*, *83*(4), 475–493. https://doi.org/10.1111/0026-7902.00036
Ferman, I. (2004). The washback of an EFL national oral matriculation test to teaching and learning. In L. Cheng, Y. Watanabe, with A. Curtis (Eds.), *Washback in language testing: Research contexts and methods* (pp. 191–210). Lawrence Erlbaum Associates.
Gauthier, R.-F. (2018). Standard setting in France: The Baccalauréat. In J.-A. Baird, T. Isaacs, D. Opposs, & L. Gray (Eds.), *Examination standards: How measures and meanings differ around the world* (pp. 119–127). UCL IoE Press.
Maley, A. (2001). Literature in the language classroom. In R. Carter & D. Nunan (Eds.), *The Cambridge guide to teaching English to speakers of other languages* (pp. 180–185). Cambridge University Press.
Nishihara, T. (2015). Achievement tests for literary reading in general EFL reading courses. In M. Teranishi, Y. Saito, & K. Wales (Eds.), *Literature and language learning in the EFL classroom* (pp. 115–130). Palgrave Macmillan.
Paran, A. (2006). The stories of literature and language teaching. In A. Paran (Ed.), *Literature in language teaching and learning* (pp. 1–10). TESOL.
Paran, A. (2010). Between Scylla and Charybdis: The dilemmas of testing language and literature. In A. Paran & L. Sercu (Eds.), *Testing the untestable in language education* (pp. 143–164). Multilingual Matters.
Paran, A. (2017, July 23–28). *Literature textbooks in the Israeli EFL context: The interaction of innovation and washback.* [Paper presentation]. International Association of Applied Linguistics (AILA) World Congress, Rio de Janeiro, Brazil.
Rezaei, A. R., & Lovorn, M. (2010). Reliability and validity of rubrics for assessment through writing. *Assessing Writing*, *51*(1), 18–39. https://doi.org/10.1016/j.asw.2010.01.003
Rosenblatt, L. (1978). *The reader, the text, the poem: The transactional theory of the literary work*. Southern Illinois University Press.
Shohamy, E., Reves, T., & Bejarano, Y. (1986). Introducing a new comprehensive test of oral proficiency. *ELT Journal*, *43*(3), 212–220. https://doi.org/10.1093/elt/40.3.212
Short, M. H., & Candlin, C. N. (1986). Teaching study skills for English literature. In C. J. Brumfit & R. A. Carter (Eds.), *Literature and language teaching* (pp. 89–109). Oxford University Press.
Spiro, J. (1991). Assessing literature: Four papers. In C. Brumfit (Ed.), *Assessment in literature teaching* (pp. 16–83). Macmillan.
State of Israel, Ministry of Education. (2012). *English Bagrut exam winter 2012*. Module F.
State of Israel, Ministry of Education. (2017). Integrating higher-order thinking skills (HOTS) with the teaching of literature. In *The teacher's handbook: Requirements section*. http://meyda.education.gov.il/files/Mazkirut_Pedagogit/English/LitReq18.pdf
Tsang, A., & Paran, A. (2020). *Learners' views of literature in ESL education: Curricular and assessment perspectives in a Confucian heritage culture* (Manuscript submitted for publication).
Weir, C. (2013). An overview of the influences on English language testing in the United Kingdom 1913–2012. In C. Weir, I. Vidaković, & E. D. Galaczi (Eds.), *Measured constructs: A history of Cambridge English language examinations* 1913–2012. 1–102. UCLES/Cambridge University Press.

Weir, C., Vidaković, I., & Galaczi, E. D. (2013). *Measured constructs: A history of Cambridge English language examinations 1913–2012*. UCLES/Cambridge University Press.
Wolthuis, F., Bloemert, J., Tammenga-Helmantel, M., & Paran, A. (2019). A curriculum in transition: TL/L1 use in Dutch EFL literature lessons. *Language, Culture and Curriculum*. https://doi.org/10.1080/07908318.2019.1697279

32

Measuring Interactional Competence

Evelina D. Galaczi & Lynda B. Taylor

Background

The term *interaction* typically refers to the spoken interaction that takes place between two or more interlocutors, such as informal conversations and formal interviews. Interaction may be *face-to-face* when the participants share the same physical environment, or it may be mediated by technology in telephone or online contexts. Whatever the medium, such interaction is dynamic and co-constructed by those involved, not necessarily in a linear or predictable manner. It is reciprocal, and participants are both pro-active and re-active, simultaneously processing input as listeners and constructing their own output as speakers, while drawing upon a wide range of linguistic and paralinguistic knowledge and skills. Interaction is thus strongly shaped by diverse cognitive and contextual factors. From a cognitive psychology perspective, human beings seem "designed for dialogue rather than monologue" (Garrod & Pickering, 2004, p. 8), and from a sociological perspective, interaction can be seen as the "primordial site of sociality" (Schegloff, 1986, p. 112). Not surprisingly, acquiring competence in spoken interaction—*interactional competence* (IC)—whether as a native (L1) or second/foreign language (L2) speaker, is a complex and lengthy process.

IC in L2 language education has assumed greater importance in recent decades as applied linguists' understanding of the complex nature of speaking ability has developed. This has been reflected in communicative approaches to language teaching and learning. Speaking tests have consequently evolved to elicit and measure aspects of IC, such as in the introduction of paired/group formats beyond just the individual test interview and the use of video-conferencing.

Our understanding of how IC develops and how it can be measured has been shaped by various pedagogical and socio-political developments over the past century. The focus on IC has its roots in the 1880s when the Direct Method (with its emphasis on oral fluency) and the Reform Movement (with its focus on phonetics and pronunciation) began to take their place alongside the Grammar-Translation Method, which had until then dominated second language pedagogy. The new priority given to oral skills paved the way for a change of focus in L2 assessment in the early 20th century, with the testing of spoken interaction alongside traditional reading and writing. This shift was reflected in the introduction of tests that included a significant conversational component. The Certificate of Proficiency in English introduced in 1913 by UCLES (now Cambridge Assessment English) is a notable example (Weir, Vidaković, & Galaczi, 2013).

The second half of the 20th century saw significant developments in applied linguistics concerning the complex nature of both L1 and L2 speech. Hymes's (1974) ethnography of communication highlighted the central role of speech events, speech acts and context-specific factors in shaping conversation. Halliday (1975) emphasised the fundamentally functional aspect of language use, while van Dijk (1977) revealed the interrelationship between discourse and context. These influential shifts in thinking paved the way for later models of communicative competence (Canale & Swain, 1980; Canale, 1983). From a second language acquisition (SLA) perspective, Kramsch (1986) was among the first to make use of the term *interactional competence* in her discussion of the "dynamic process of communication" (p. 368). Long's (1996) Interaction Hypothesis proposed that interaction can foster acquisition through the need to engage in the negotiation of meaning. Social interaction and the development of IC can thus become a primary source of acquisition and learning (Ellis, 2005).

The 1980s and 1990s saw a growing awareness of the interactional nature of spoken language ability among applied linguists, SLA researchers, and assessment specialists alike. Bachman (1990) and Bachman and Palmer (1996) broadened the focus on communicative competence specifically for L2 assessment purposes, going beyond grammatical competence to considerations of sociolinguistic, discourse and strategic competence. Methodological advances in Conversation Analysis and Corpus Linguistics further contributed to a broader and more nuanced understanding of IC (Lazaraton, 2002). This awareness of the dynamic and reciprocal nature of spoken interaction has challenged some established notions of communicative competence and brought into contrast *psychological* conceptualisations of competence residing *within* an individual and *social* conceptualisations of competence manifested through co-constructed interaction *between* individuals (McNamara, 1997; McNamara & Roever, 2006). As Chalhoub-Deville argued, "individual ability and contextual facets interact in ways that change them both" (2003, p. 369). Chalhoub-Deville (2003) and Young (1998; 2008) appealed for a more comprehensive construct of speaking ability encompassing elements such as awareness of the roles of the individuals in the interaction and the context, as well as interactional resources (e.g., appropriate use of speech acts, managing turn-taking, repairing conversation breakdown, and the ability to use non-verbal behaviours effectively (Young, 2008)). As such, the interlocutors and the host of variables they bring to the interactional event become part of the construct of L2 interaction for language teaching, learning and assessment purposes (Galaczi & Taylor, 2018). Table 32.1 summarises these variables.

Research in applied linguistics has thus highlighted the importance of IC in second language acquisition. However, understanding the role of IC in language development requires more precise instruments for its measurement, raising important issues for construct definition and operationalisation in L2 assessment. We will now briefly explore some of the more challenging questions and their implications for assessing IC.

Table 32.1 Key features of interactional competence (adapted from Galaczi & Taylor, 2018)

Turn Management • Starting • Maintaining • Ending • Pausing/Latching/Interrupting	**Non-Verbal Behaviour** • Eye Contact • Facial Expression • Laughter • Posture	**Interactive Listening** • Backchanneling • Comprehension checks • Continuers
Topic Management • Initiating • Extending • Shifting • Closing	**Breakdown Repair** • Joint Utterance Creation • Self/Other • Recasts	

Key Concepts

Interactional competence: The ability to co-construct interaction in a meaningful way, taking into account contextual factors in the speech situation and event. This ability is supported by linguistic and non-linguistic resources that speakers and listeners leverage, such as *turn-taking management, topic management, interactive listening* and *non-verbal behaviours.*

Turn-taking management: A way of organising conversation, where participants alternate and one speaker speaks at a time. Speakers construct turns which are related to previous turns, and distribute turns to other speakers by using linguistic or non-linguistic cues. Overlapping talk (through interruptions or "latched" turns) and silence between turns is generally avoided.

Topic management: Topics in interaction are guided by the principle of relevance, and develop through "moves," such as topic initiation, topic development, topic closure.

Interactive listening: Listeners use verbal and non-verbal means to signal that they are following the interaction. Verbal means include backchannels, e.g., "yeah" and comprehension confirmations, e.g., "Exactly!"; non-verbal cues include nodding and gaze.

Non-verbal behaviours: Elements of interaction which are not verbal and which transmit meaning, e.g., eye contact, pitch range, gestures, silence.

Interlocutor effect: The influence of the interlocutors' socio-cultural identity and personal characteristics on the interaction generated in a test, e.g., gender or personality.

Key Issues

We will focus on three issues which we see as fundamental to measuring IC: the tension between authenticity and reliability; the effect of interlocutor variables on discourse and scores; and the role of non-verbal behaviours. Before we start our discussion, we include an example of an IC task and IC assessment scales, as a practical illustration of operationalising IC (Figure 32.1 and Table 32.2).

Authenticity and Reliability in Interactional Tests: An Uneasy Partnership

The rich IC construct can be conceptualised both as a *validity asset* due to the authenticity of interactional test tasks and a *validity threat* due to challenges of standardisation. The tension between these two aspects of validity is a difficult—but not unsolvable!—aspect of interactional competence.

Interactional competence is elicited through tasks which allow unscripted interaction during which test-takers co-construct interactional turns; participants are prompted to both lead the unfolding interaction and respond to their interlocutor's talk (e.g., as in the task in Figure 32.1). This is typically achieved with tasks involving at least two human interlocutors in an individual, paired, or group test format (as opposed to computer-delivered prompts). The wide range of features that can be elicited through these tasks (see Table 32.1) can be measured in a number of ways, including rating scales (e.g., Table 32.2) or functional analysis and quantification of elicited speech functions (e.g., Nakatsuhara, Inoue, Berry, & Galaczi, 2017).

While interview tests have been shown to have features of natural conversation (Ross & Berwick, 1992), they may also lack some of these features due to their pre-specified system of turn taking (Johnson & Tyler, 1998; Lazaraton, 1992; Malone, 2003; Young & Milanovic, 1992). There are, therefore, some caveats about the authenticity of the individual test format in relation to natural conversation. Considering these caveats, paired and group tasks are generally considered as more suitable for measuring IC. Compared to individual speaking tasks,

Part 3

Interlocutor Now, I'd like you to talk about something together for about two minutes.
(3 minutes for groups of three).

I'd like you to imagine that a town wants more tourists to visit. Here are some ideas they're thinking about and a question for you to discuss. First you have some time to look at the task.

*Place **Part 3** booklet, open at **Task 21**, in front of the candidates. Allow 15 seconds.*

Now, talk to each other about **why these ideas would attract more tourists to the town.**

Candidates *2 minutes (3 minutes for groups of three)* ....

Interlocutor Thank you.

Now you have about a minute to decide **which idea would be best for the town.**

Candidates *1 minute (for pairs and groups of three)* ....

Thank you. (Can I have the booklet, please?) *Retrieve **Part 3** booklet.*

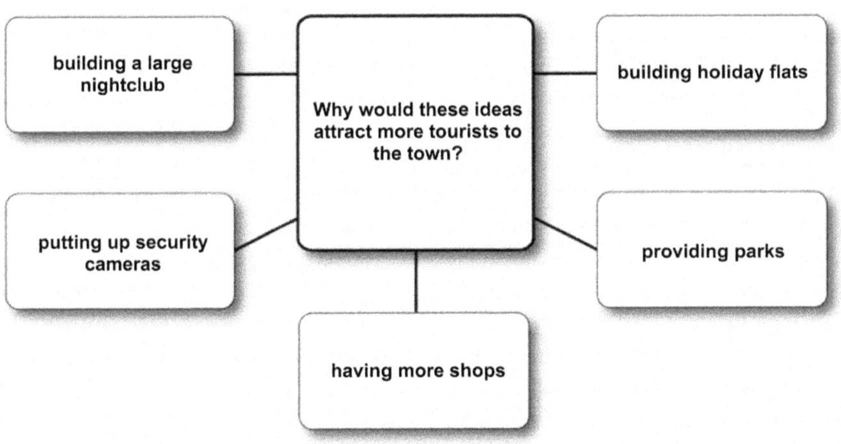

Figure 32.1 Example of an interactional paired task at CEFR level B2 (https://www.cambridgeenglish.org/exams-and-tests/first/exam-format/)

paired/group tasks have been shown to result in more symmetrical interaction patterns (Brooks, 2009; Galaczi, 2008; Kormos, 1999), to elicit a broader range of speech functions (Brooks, 2009; O'Sullivan, Weir, & Saville, 2002), and to provide more opportunities for test-takers to display turn-taking management, topic initiation/expansion/closure, and interactive listening (Brooks, 2009; Ducasse & Brown, 2009; Galaczi, 2014; Gan, Davison, & Hamp-Lyons, 2009; Kormos, 1999; May, 2009; Ross 2017, 2018). The interaction generated in paired/group assessment tasks has also been seen as mirroring good practice in communicative classrooms through promoting interaction opportunities (East, 2016), which are central to developing L2 language proficiency, both from a cognitive perspective (e.g., Interaction Hypothesis: Long, 1996) and a socio-cultural perspective (e.g., Sociocultural Theory: Vygotsky, 1978). There is, therefore,

Table 32.2. Example of an assessment scale used to evaluate IC at CEFR level B2

CEFR Level B2	*IC description*
Band 5	• Initiates and responds appropriately, linking contributions to those of other speakers. • Maintains and develops the interaction and negotiates towards an outcome.
Band 3	• Initiates and responds appropriately. • Maintains and develops the interaction and negotiates towards an outcome with very little support.
Band 1	• Initiates and responds appropriately. • Keeps the interaction going with very little promoting and support.

Source: https://www.cambridgeenglish.org/images/168619-assessing-speaking-performance-at-level-b2.pdf

a solid body of evidence supporting the authenticity and positive impact on learning of paired/group assessment tasks.

That authenticity, however, comes at a price and has implications for the reliability of interactional tests. Co-constructed interaction is complex and variable; it is dynamically shaped by interlocutors and speech situations and is more difficult to predict or control than the talk generated in controlled question-response tasks. Language variability in paired/group tests has been investigated in a number of studies (Lazaraton, 1996; Roever & Kasper 2018). In a now seminal study, Brown (2003) reported that a test-taker came across as a "willing and responsive interlocutor" (p. 1) and was given a higher score when interviewed by an examiner who used more explicit questioning techniques, regularly provided feedback and showed interest in what the test-taker was saying; the same test-taker was perceived as "unforthcoming and uncooperative" (p. 1) and had a lower score when interviewed by an examiner who used implicit closed questions and echoed the test-taker's speech. Test variability is also seen in higher differences in examiner severity in group tests compared to individual tests (e.g., Bonk & Ockey, 2003).

A fundamental issue emerges: If test developers prioritise task authenticity and a broader language construct, then reliability becomes problematic; if they prioritise test reliability, then interaction tasks may be accorded less importance resulting in a narrowed test construct. This presents a key challenge for test developers and applied linguistics researchers: How can the construct of IC be measured without compromising reliability? Clearly, test developers and linguists have a responsibility to design tests which are both valid and reliable for their purpose, and there are a number of ways to balance the competing needs of authenticity and reliability in IC tests. The first is related to *construct definition* and the need to explicitly define the test construct as an interactional construct. Secondly, *test design* plays a key role. Using a range of task types which provide different interactional contexts taps into a broad construct and minimises possible shortcomings of certain task types. For example, an interactional test could have a paired format and include several tasks: a question-and-answer interview task between an examiner and a test-taker, a paired discussion task between test-takers, or a group discussion task between test-takers and the examiner. Third, the *scoring model* is important. This could take the form of assessment scales which include IC alongside other key aspects of the interactional construct, such as grammar, vocabulary, discourse organisation, fluency, and pronunciation. Finally, rigorous *examiner training* in delivering and scoring an IC test would minimise the threat to test reliability.

It is also important to briefly address the issue of interactional tests for young learners. With the role of English in socio-economic advancement, learners and takers of English have become younger. Are interactional tests appropriate for such learners? In exploring this question, Field (2018) noted that first children need to acquire L1 turn-taking conventions, and advised that tasks tapping into L2 IC "should be accorded reduced importance" (2018, p. 146). He made a similar argument regarding the ability to accommodate one's speech, an important marker of interactional competence, noting that young learners "are not generally sensitive to the forms of expression associated with style (i.e., indicators of formality and politeness) and do not master them fully until around the age of 12" (p. 146). The implication is that certain formative, academically oriented, or formally registered interactional tasks may be too complex for learners below 12 to engage in; if interactional tests are used, the individual, interview-like format may be more appropriate to measure certain aspects of speech ability. An interview-like test provides a degree of control and scaffolding which the examiner can offer when managing the interaction. Paired or group-oral exams with children under 12 must be evaluated with criteria that are age-appropriate and reasonable given the children's cognitive-development level. Alternatively, multiple observations (recorded through observation checklists) of a child's interaction in the classroom or on the playground can be used to measure their competence. Young children may not need to be directly tested to gain information on their interactional competence (Becker, 2015), because observations, which may have more construct validity in the child-testing context, can be gathered and documented instead.

The Interlocutor Effect in Interactional Tests: A Threat to Validity?

The key take-away message from the previous section was that a broad interactional construct is essential for SLA and assessment practices, but interactional tests can also introduce variability which is a validity issue. In this section we will focus on one of the main sources of such variability, the *interlocutor effect* (O'Sullivan, 2002), which refers to the influence of the interlocutors' socio-cultural identity and personal characteristics on the discourse generated in a test.

The influence of interlocutors on one another in interaction is a fundamental sociolinguistics principle, with research unequivocally indicating that interlocutor characteristics affect interaction and that individuals accommodate their speech based on their interlocutor (Beebe, 1980). Humans are all, so to speak, linguistic chameleons, in order to be successful in interaction. It is not surprising, therefore, that the interlocutor effect plays a role in interactional tests. It has been found to be present in both individual and paired/group tests, but is potentially more pronounced in the latter. A range of interlocutor variables have been reported to affect interaction (e.g., test-takers' acquaintanceship, gender, extroversion, talkativeness, cultural background, and language proficiency) (Berry, 1993; Chambers, Galaczi, & Gilbert, 2012; Davis, 2009; O'Sullivan, 2002; Nakatsuhara, 2013; Ockey, 2009). For example, Nakatsuhara (2013) found that in a group test the extroversion level of test-takers influenced test performance. Focusing on another variable, acquaintanceship, O'Sullivan (2002) reported that test-takers achieved higher test scores when working with a friend. Crucially, in both these studies (chosen here as typical illustrations of the interlocutor effect) the results were not clear-cut. In Nakatsuhara's (2013) investigation, both an extroversion effect and a task type effect were found: Introverts performed better in structured tasks, extroverts were better in open-ended tasks. In O'Sullivan's (2002) investigation, in addition to the influence of acquaintanceship, the author speculated that gender of the interlocutor played a role, as well as cultural identity. The key insight to emerge from this literature is that despite the influence of the interlocutor on the co-constructed interaction in a speaking test, the *magnitude* or *direction* of that influence is less clear and not directly predictable (Brown & McNamara, 2004).

Since the interlocutor effect can be a validity threat, it is important to consider what test developers should do about it. The most fundamental question relates to defining the *test construct*. If the test aims to tap into an interactional construct, then the variability inherent in tests becomes part of the construct. That variability has to be minimised, but is, crucially, *not* seen as construct-irrelevant variance. Such a view entails a re-conceptualisation of variability from undesirable and associated with error to an essential aspect of IC (Deville & Chalhoub-Deville, 2006). Swain (cited in Fox, 2004) provided useful insights: The variability associated with conversational partners "happens in the real world," she argued, and so "they are things that we should be interested in testing" (p. 240). An implication is that the *test design* needs careful consideration. Tasks need to be designed in a way that entails some control over "uncontrollable variables and unknown effects associated with these variables" (Van Moere, 2006, p. 414). For example, a range of task types need to be used, or the use of paired/group formations in multi-level tests versus level-based tests needs to be given due consideration, since the interlocutor effect in a multi-level test would be potentially more pronounced due to the possibility of matching test-takers at different ability levels.

Non-Verbal Communication: Complexity in Measurement

Non-verbal aspects of communication and their role in the assessment of IC have been either directly or peripherally addressed in a growing body of literature (Ducasse & Brown, 2009; Gan & Davison, 2011; Jenkins & Parra, 2003; May, 2011; Roever & Kasper, 2018; Vo, 2019). Jenkins and Parra's (2003) investigation of Spanish- and Chinese-speaking International Teaching Assistants in a U.S. university has provided a useful systematic analysis of verbal, non-verbal, and paralinguistic behaviours, categorising the latter two categories into kinesic features (e.g., eye contact, smiling), paralinguistic features (e.g., pitch range, rhythm), and non-verbal turn taking (e.g., nodding, silences between turns). The authors found that their participants' non-verbal behaviour played a role in their scores: Participants with high proficiency passed the test regardless of their non-verbal behaviour, and, importantly, so did participants with lower proficiency who could employ effective non-verbal behaviour. Extending the discussion further, Roever and Kasper (2018) argued that non-verbal aspects of interaction are not simply coping strategies when language knowledge is deficient but are, in fact, *integral aspects* of successful interactions. Two other recent studies (Nakatsuhara, May, Lam, & Galaczi, 2018; Vo, 2019) have also confirmed that non-verbal behaviours are viewed by raters as part of the IC construct. Nakatsuhara et al. (2018) produced an extensive list of IC features which raters and teachers attend to, which included non-verbal behaviours. Vo (2019) found that body language (alongside verbal aspects of interaction) was a strong predictor of variance in IC scores. These recent findings are in line with earlier research in the field which views verbal and non-verbal aspects of communication to be integrated in communication (Kendon, 1990). Consensus is developing, therefore, that non-verbal behaviour is an essential aspect of interaction, and yet it is typically not captured systematically in assessment scales and test construct definitions. Why not?

One barrier is that non-verbal interactive behaviour is not part of robust theoretical conceptualisations of IC (Plough, Banerjee, & Iwashita, 2018). A further barrier is that many non-verbal behaviours have been documented to be culture- and language-specific and therefore potentially unfair to test. A further challenge is the relationship between non-verbal behaviour and proficiency level, which is not well understood. There are some tentative steps in this area, with studies indicating that speakers with higher scores generally use more active non-verbal behaviours (Banerjee & Plough, 2016). Complex demands on examiners in evaluating the effectiveness and appropriateness of non-verbal behaviour presents a further challenge (Plough et al., 2018). Finally, the practical constraint of audio—and not video—recordings of interactional tests for post-test marking completely removes the non-verbal aspects of the test interaction. Promising developments regarding this constraint involve the use of video-conferencing technology in interactional tests, which provide video-recorded test samples (Nakatsuhara, Berry, Inoue, & Galaczi, 2017).

Despite these complexities in incorporating non-verbal behaviours in the test construct, there are several initial steps which could be taken in assessment. One is to give such behaviours some prominence in assessment scales, and to reflect that in examiner training. It is also important that non-verbal behaviours should inform language learning and form part of the development of IC

(Nakatsuhara et al., 2018), even if these behaviours are currently only minimally captured in assessment criteria.

Recommendations for Practice

As discussed above, interactional speaking tests are complex events which involve multiple factors, some of which may be difficult to control. Further complicating the issue, the factors interact, which additionally creates complications in producing a score. The list below presents a number of recommendations which could support the design of interactional speaking tests. Due to space limitations, only the most essential considerations are listed; more in-depth overviews of test design in interactional speaking tests can be found in McNamara (1996), Galaczi and ffrench (2011), Taylor and Galaczi (2011); Timpe-Laughlin and Youn, Chapter 24, this volume; and Nakatsuhara, Inoue, & Khabbazbashi, Chapter 27, this volume.

- Tasks need to provide test-takers/learners with the opportunity to initiate and manage the interaction themselves and collaborate in constructing a shared discourse. Such tasks could involve discussing a question/topic, a role play with the test-takers taking on different roles, or an information gap task.
- Both paired and group formats are valuable in eliciting interaction, but when using the group format, it is important to keep the size of the groups limited to about 3 or 4 in order to give all learners/test-takers the chance to contribute to the interaction, and to make the observation of their interactional behaviour manageable for the observers (whether researchers or examiners).
- Interaction is a highly complex cognitive activity and learners at lower levels (e.g., CEFR A1–B1) need interactional support through visual or verbal prompts. Providing specific prompts will also make the interaction generated more predictable and less prone to unexpected responses, which will in turn make it easier to score or analyse reliably.
- The interactional competence (IC) assessment scale used needs to have empirical and theoretical support and include a range of IC aspects, including turn-taking management, topic development, interactive listening, and (if this is a research focus) non-verbal behaviours. It also needs to be scalable (capable of differentiating levels of performance quality).

Testing Tips

- Consult the literature to gain a solid understanding of what interactional competence entails, and outline for yourself which aspects of interactional competence you want to assess.
- Create a scoring chart or rubric that will guide your scoring. Ensure that the scoring criteria accurately and comprehensively represent the construct of interactional competence you want to assess.
- Pre-determine how the scoring categories will be weighted, but consider the scoring guide or rubric and category weights to be a version (1.0; 2.0) that is to be adjusted over time and improved. It will get better through iterative use-and-validation processes.
- Share the scoring categories or rubric with the test-takers ahead of time, so they know what they will be tested on. Doing so will also help them understand what you value as part of interactional competence.
- Use tasks which allow and stimulate genuine, naturalistic interaction.

- Consider whether to use a paired or group format. Take into account what kind of interactional features each format may particularly elicit, while keeping in mind practicalities.
- To adequately measure interactional competence, give test-takers as many opportunities to interact with various interlocutors on as many different tasks as possible. Each task performed gives one snapshot of a learner's interactional competence; multiple measurements with multiple interlocutors on multiple tasks will estimate true performance-ability better.
- Use verbal or visual task prompts to focus the task and provide scaffolding.
- Interview or survey your test-takers post testing to ensure that they feel they were tested adequately and well on their interactional competence. Their feedback can guide your test-revision processes.

Recommended Reading

Galaczi, E., & Taylor, L. (2018). Interactional competence: Conceptualisations, operationalisations, and outstanding questions. *Language Assessment Quarterly*, *15*(3), 219–236. http://doi.org/10.1080/15434303.2018.1453816

This article reviews emerging theoretical perspectives on the construct of interactional competence, describing how it can be operationalised in assessment practice and highlighting some of the challenges of ensuring broad and rich construct representation.

Plough, I., Banerjee, J., & Iwashita, N. (Eds.) (2018). Special issue on interactional competence. *Language Testing*, *35*(3). https://journals.sagepub.com/toc/ltja/35/3

This guest-edited issue contains several papers that focus on the construct of interactional competence, examining data from a variety of contexts, languages and proficiency levels to better understand the construct and how this can inform test design and research.

Young, R. F. (2008). *Language and interaction: An advanced resource book*. Routledge.

This book offers a useful and comprehensive presentation of all the major research themes, questions, and studies in the field of language as social interaction.

References

Bachman, L. (1990). *Fundamental considerations in language testing*. Oxford University Press.

Bachman, L., & Palmer, A. (1996). *Language testing in practice*. Oxford University Press.

Banerjee, J., & Plough, I. (2016, June 20–24). *Behavior in speaking tests: A preliminary model of interaction* [Paper presentation]. Language Testing Research Colloquium (LTRC), Palermo, Italy.

Becker, C. (2015). Assessments and portfolios. In J. Bland (Ed.), *Teaching English to young learners: Critical issues in language teaching with 3–12 year olds* (pp. 261–278). Bloomsbury.

Beebe, L. M. (1980). Sociolinguistic variation and style shifting in second language acquisition. *Language Learning*, *30*(2), 433–445. http://doi.org/10.1111/j.1467-1770.1980.tb00327.x

Berry, V. (1993). Personality characteristics as a potential source of language test bias. In A. Huhta, K. Sajavaara, & S. Takala (Eds.), *Language testing: New openings* (pp. 115–124). Institute for Educational Research, University of Jyväskylä.

Bonk, W. J., & Ockey, G. J. (2003). A many-facet Rasch analysis of the second language group oral discussion task. *Language Testing*, *20*(1), 89–110. http://doi.org/10.1191/0265532203lt245oa

Brooks, L. (2009). Interacting in pairs in a test of oral proficiency: Co-constructing a better performance. *Language Testing*, *26*(3), 341–366. http://doi.org/10.1177/0265532209104666

Brown, A. (2003). Interviewer variation and the co-construction of speaking proficiency. *Language Testing*, *20*(1), 1–25. http://doi.org/10.1191/0265532203lt242oa

Brown, A., & McNamara, T. (2004). "The devil is in the detail": Researching gender issues in language assessment. *TESOL Quarterly*, *38*(3), 524–538. http://doi.org/10.2307/3588353

Canale, M. (1983). From communicative competence to communicative language pedagogy. In J. C. Richards & R. W. Schmidt (Eds.), *Language and communication* (pp. 2–27). Longman.

Canale, M., & Swain, M. (1980). Theoretical bases of communicative approaches to second language teaching and testing. *Applied Linguistics*, *1*(1), 1–47. http://doi.org/10.1093/applin/I.1.1

Chalhoub-Deville, M. (2003). Second language interaction: Current perspectives and future trends. *Language Testing*, *20*(4), 369–383. http://doi.org/10.1191/0265532203lt264oa

Chambers, L., Galaczi, E. D., & Gilbert, S. (2012). Test-taker familiarity in speaking test performance: Does it make a difference? *Research Notes*, *49*, 33–40.

Davis, L. (2009). The influence of interlocutor proficiency in a paired oral assessment. *Language Testing*, *26*(3), 367–396. http://doi.org/10.1177/0265532209104667

Deville, C., & Chalhoub-Deville, M. (2006). Perspectives on inference and generalizability in applied linguistics. In M. Chalhoub-Deville, C. Deville, & P. Duff (Eds.), *Inferences and generalizability in applied linguistics* (pp. 9–16). John Benjamins.

Ducasse, A. M., & Brown, A. (2009). Assessing paired orals: Raters' orientation to interaction. *Language Testing*, *26*(3), 423–443. http://doi.org/10.1177/0265532209104669

East, M. (2016). *Assessing foreign language students' spoken proficiency*. Springer.

Ellis, R. (2005). Principles of instructed language learning. *System*, *33*, 209–224. http://doi.org/10.1016/j.system.2004.12.006

Field, J. (2018). Cognitive validity of tests of listening and speaking designed for young learners. In S. Papp & S. Rixon (Eds.), *Examining young learners: Research and practice in assessing the English of school-age learners. Studies in Language Testing* (Vol. 47, pp. 128–200). UCLES/Cambridge University Press.

Fox, J. (2004). Biasing for the best in language testing and learning: An interview with Merrill Swain. *Language Assessment Quarterly*, *1*(4), 235–251. http://doi.org/10.1207/s15434311laq0104_3

Galaczi, E. D. (2008). Peer-peer interaction in a speaking test: The case of the first certificate in English examination. *Language Assessment Quarterly*, *5*(2), 89–119. http://doi.org/10.1080/15434300801934702

Galaczi, E. D. (2014). Interactional competence across proficiency levels: How do learners manage interaction in paired speaking tests? *Applied Linguistics*, *35*(5), 553–574. http://doi.org/10.1093/applin/amt017

Galaczi, E. D., & ffrench, A. (2011). Context validity of Cambridge ESOL speaking tests. In L. Taylor (Ed.), *Examining speaking: Research and practice in assessing second language speaking. Studies in Language Testing* (Vol. 30, pp. 112–170). UCLES/Cambridge University Press.

Galaczi, E. D., & Taylor, L. (2018). Interactional competence: Conceptualisations, operationalisations, and outstanding questions. *Language Assessment Quarterly*, *15*(3), 219–236. http://doi.org/10.1080/15434303.2018.1453816

Gan, Z., & Davison, C. (2011). Gestural behavior in group oral assessment: A case study of higher- and lower-scoring students. *International Journal of Applied Linguistics*, *21*(1), 94–120. http://doi.org/10.1111/j.1473-4192.2010.00264.x

Gan, Z., Davison, C., & Hamp-Lyons, L. (2009). Topic negotiation in peer group oral assessment situations: A conversation analytic approach. *Applied Linguistics*, *30*(3), 315–334. http://doi.org/10.1093/applin/amn035

Garrod, S., & Pickering, J. M. (2004). Why is conversation so easy? *Trends in Cognitive Sciences*, *8*(1), 8–11. http://doi.org/10.1016/j.tics.2003.10.016

Halliday, M. A. K. (1975). *Learning how to mean*. Edward Arnold.

He, A., & Young, R. (1998). Language proficiency interviews: A discourse approach. In R. E. Young & A. He (Eds.), *Talking and testing: Discourse approaches to the assessment of oral proficiency* (pp. 1–24). John Benjamins.

Hymes, D. (1974). *Foundations in sociolinguistics: An ethnographic approach*. University of Pennsylvania Press.

Jenkins, S., & Parra, I. (2003). Multiple layers of meaning in an oral proficiency test: The complementary roles of nonverbal, paralinguistic, and verbal behaviors in assessment decisions. *The Modern Language Journal*, *87*(1), 90–107. http://doi.org/10.1111/1540-4781.00180

Johnson, M., & Tyler, A. (1998). Re-analyzing the OPI: How much does it look like natural conversation? In R. Young & A. He (Eds.), *Talking and testing: Discourse approaches to the assessment of oral proficiency* (pp. 27–51). John Benjamins.

Kendon, A. (1990). *Conducting interaction: Patterns of behaviour in focused encounters*. Cambridge University Press.

Kormos, J. (1999). Simulating conversations in oral-proficiency assessment: A conversation analysis of role plays and non-scripted interviews in language exams. *Language Testing*, *16*(2), 163–188. http://doi.org/10.1177/026553229901600203

Kramsch, C. (1986). From language proficiency to interactional competence. *The Modern Language Journal*, *70*(4), 366–372. http://doi.org/10.2307/326815

Lazaraton, A. (1992). The structural organization of a language interview: A conversation analytic perspective. *System*, *20*(3), 373–386. http://doi.org/10.1016/0346-251X(92)90047-7
Lazaraton, A. (1996). Interlocutor support in oral proficiency interviews: The case of CASE. *Language Testing*, *13*(2), 151–172. http://doi.org/10.1177/026553229601300202
Lazaraton, A. (2002). *A qualitative approach to the validation of oral language tests. Studies in Language Testing* (Vol. 14). UCLES/Cambridge University Press.
Long, M. (1996). The role of the linguistic environment in second language acquisition. In W. Ritchie & T. Bhatia (Eds.), *Handbook of second language acquisition* (pp. 413–468). Academic Press.
Malone, M. E. (2003). Research on the oral proficiency interview: Analysis, synthesis, and future directions. *Foreign Language Annals*, *36*(4), 491–497. http://doi.org/10.1111/j.1944–9720.2003.tb02138.x
May, L. (2009). Co-constructed interaction in a paired speaking test: The rater's perspective. *Language Testing*, *26*(3), 397–421. http://doi.org/10.1177/0265532209104668
May, L. (2011). Interactional competence in a paired speaking test: Features salient to raters. *Language Assessment Quarterly*, *8*(2), 127–145. http://doi.org/10.1080/15434303.2011.565845
McNamara, T. (1996). *Measuring second language performance*. Addison Wesley Longman.
McNamara, T. (1997). 'Interaction' in second language performance assessment: Whose performance? *Applied Linguistics*, *18*(4), 446–466. http://doi.org/10.1093/applin/18.4.446
McNamara, T., & Roever, C. (2006). *Language testing: The social dimension*. Blackwell.
Nakatsuhara, F. (2013). *The co-construction of conversation in group oral tests*. Peter Lang.
Nakatsuhara, F., Berry, V., Inoue, C., & Galaczi, E. D. (2017). Exploring the use of video-conferencing technology in the assessment of spoken language: A mixed-methods study. *Language Assessment Quarterly*, *14*(1), 1–18. http://doi.org/10.1080/15434303.2016.1263637
Nakatsuhara, F., May, L., Lam, D., & Galaczi, E. D. (2018). Learning oriented feedback in the development and assessment of interactional competence. *Research Notes*, *70*. https://www.cambridgeenglish.org/Images/517543-research-notes-70.pdf
Ockey, G. J. (2009). The effects of group members' personalities on a test taker's L2 group oral discussion test scores. *Language Testing*, *26*(2), 161–186. http://doi.org/10.1177/0265532208101005
O'Sullivan, B. (2002). Learner acquaintanceship and oral proficiency pair-task performance. *Language Testing*, *19*(3), 277–295. http://doi.org/10.1191/0265532202lt205oa
O'Sullivan, B., Weir, C., & Saville, N. (2002). Using observation checklists to validate speaking-test tasks. *Language Testing*, *19*(1), 33–56. http://doi.org/10.1191/0265532202lt219oa
Plough, I., Banerjee, J., & Iwashita, N. (2018). Interactional competence: Genie out of the bottle. *Language Testing*, *35*(3), 427–445. http://doi.org/10.1177/0265532218772325
Roever, C., & Kasper, G. (2018). Speaking in turns and sequences: Interactional competence as a target construct in testing speaking. *Language Testing*, *35*(3), 331–355. http://doi.org/10.1177/0265532218758128
Ross, S. (2017). *Interviewing for language proficiency: Interaction and interpretation*. Palgrave Macmillan.
Ross, S. (2018). Listener response as a facet of interactional competence. *Language Testing*, *35*(3), 357–375. http://doi.org/10.1177/0265532218758125
Ross, S., & Berwick, R. (1992). The discourse of accommodation in oral proficiency interviews. *Studies in Second Language Acquisition*, *14*(2), 159–176. http://doi.org/10.1017/S0272263100010809
Schegloff, E. (1986). The routine as achievement. *Human Studies*, *9*(2), 111–151. http://www.jstor.org/stable/20008964
Taylor, L., & Galaczi, E. D. (2011). Scoring validity. In L. Taylor (Ed.), *Examining speaking: Research and practice in assessing second language speaking. Studies in Language Testing* (Vol. 30, pp. 171–233). UCLES/Cambridge University Press.
van Dijk, T. A. (1977). *Text and context: Explorations in the semantics and pragmatics of discourse*. Longman.
Van Moere, A. (2006). Validity evidence in a university group oral test. *Language Testing*, *23*(4), 411–440. http://doi.org/10.1191/0265532206lt336oa
Vo, S. T. (2019). *Effects of task types on interactional competence in oral communication assessment* (Unpublished doctoral dissertation). Iowa State University, United States.
Vygotsky, L. S. (1978). *Mind in society: The development of higher psychological processes*. Harvard University Press.
Weir, C. J., Vidaković, I., & Galaczi, D. E. (2013). *Measured constructs: A history of Cambridge English language examinations 1913–2012. Studies in Language Testing* (Vol. 37). UCLES/Cambridge University Press.
Young, R. F. (2008). *Language and interaction: An advanced resource book*. Routledge.
Young, R. F., & Milanovic, M. (1992). Discourse variation in oral proficiency interviews. *Studies in Second Language Acquisition*, *14*(4), 403–424. http://doi.org/10.1017/S0272263100011207

33

Measuring Across Languages and in Multiple Languages

Riikka Alanen & Ari Huhta

Background

Measurement of language skills across languages takes place for the same reasons as the assessment of individual languages in general does. Assessment can grossly be divided into three basic purposes: (1) assessment of individual learners for selection or educational purposes; (2) assessment for program evaluation; and (3) assessment for research purposes (Brown, 2013). The first category includes tests used for gatekeeping purposes, viz., for admitting persons to institutions or professions. It also includes achievement (or summative) assessment, which provides an overall evaluation of the learner's achievement of educational objectives. Assessments for educational purposes can also measure gains or growth (through the use of repeated assessments) within individual learners. Organizations providing such assessments in multiple languages include both national and international examination providers. Examples from the United States include the American Council on the Teaching of Foreign Languages (ACTFL) Proficiency Tests (https://www.languagetesting.com/) and the Defense Language Proficiency Test at the Defense Language Institute (see https://www.dliflc.edu/resources/dlpt-guides/). In Europe, some members of the Association of Language Testers in Europe, such as the European Consortium for the Certificate of Attainment in Modern Languages (ECL; https://eclexam.eu/the-ecl-consortium/) and the Finnish National Certificates (https://www.oph.fi/en/national-certificates-language-proficiency-yki), use multilingual examinations. In addition, many educational institutions, such as the University of Florida (Foreign Language Proficiency Examinations; https://teachingcenter.ufl.edu/testing/flpe/) and the Brigham Young University (Foreign Language Achievement Testing Services; https://info.flats.byu.edu/), test across languages (see Winke & Gass, 2019, for a study on the equivalence of admission or achievement standards across languages). The first category also covers formative and diagnostic assessments, for example, DIALANG (https://dialangweb.lancaster.ac.uk/), an online diagnostic system (Alderson, 2005) covering, currently, 14 test languages and 18 feedback languages.

The second major purpose of assessment is program evaluation. The tests used for this purpose can be very similar to gatekeeping/achievement tests, but here they are used to investigate the outcomes of educational systems, curricula, or programs. Local evaluations are carried out at the regional, state, or national level by independent organizations or educational authorities. Most international evaluations focus on L1 literacy, such as PISA (Program for International Student Assessment by the Organization for Economic Co-operation and Development, OECD; www.oecd.org/pisa/) and PIRLS (Progress in International Reading Literacy Study; https://www.iea.nl/

studies/iea/pirls) by the International Association for the Evaluation of Educational Achievement, IEA (see also Gorman, Purves, and Degenhart, 1988, on L1 writing). A rare example of an international evaluation of foreign languages (FL) was the European Survey of Language Competences (ESLC; European Commission, 2013) which covered reading, listening, and writing. Examples of studies on local multilingual FL evaluations include those carried out in the United States by Davin, Rempert, and Hammerand (2014) on speaking, reading, and writing, Bernhardt, Molitoris, Romeo, Lin, and Valderrama (2015) on writing, and Isbell, Winke, and Gass (2019) on speaking.

The third purpose of assessment involves assessment for research purposes. This is obviously one of the main purposes for which SLA researchers use assessment instruments. These instruments can be further divided into those used to control for context variables (e.g., participants' test scores can be used to divide them into less or more advanced learners) and those used to measure L2 development, at varying levels of granularity (e.g., speaking in general vs specific aspects of speaking such as pronunciation). Using comparable measures across languages is important, as it makes it easier to generalize and synthesize findings on different FLs. Good examples of such measures are the cloze-test (e.g., Tremblay, 2011), C-test (e.g., Babaii & Ansary, 2013) and the Elicited Imitation Test (EIT) developed by Ortega and colleagues (Ortega, Iwashita, Norris, & Rabie, 2002; Kim, Tracy-Ventura, & Jung, 2016).

In addition to tests developed specifically for research purposes, SLA researchers often use language tests originally designed for other purposes such as gatekeeping or achievement. Since these tests are not designed to provide detailed information about test-takers' language skills, but rather measure overall proficiency, they are most likely used to divide learners into broad proficiency groups. Gatekeeping or achievement tests have also been used as dependent variables in longitudinal studies on the development of L2 proficiency, even though they are not sensitive to small changes in learners' language skills. Consequently, there needs to be a substantial amount of time between the administration of such tests, as perhaps demonstrated in prior research (e.g., 13–14 weeks in a study using the ACTFL Simulated Oral Interview (SOPI) by Di Silvio, Diao, and Donovan, 2016; 6 months in a study using the TOEFL Junior by Gu, Lockwood, and Powers, 2015; or more than a year in a study with the ACTFL OPIc by Isbell et al., 2019).

Many examinations used for establishing learners' proficiency levels are not part of multilingual testing systems (e.g., TOEFL family of examinations and IELTS only measure English). There are, however, multilingual assessment systems that have been used as part of investigations of L2 development in more than one language. Isbell et al. (2019) employed Chinese, French, Russian, and Spanish versions of the ACTFL OPIc test to investigate the tests' abilities to track the development of learners' speaking skills on the ACTFL scale. For their part, Alderson, Haapakangas, Huhta, Nieminen, and Ullakonoja (2015) used DIALANG reading tests to determine learners' levels in English and Finnish on the Common European Framework of Reference (CEFR; see Council of Europe, 2001) scale.

Tests used for program evaluation can also be used when researchers need a reliable measure across languages. Researchers and educators who conduct studies on educational achievement often struggle with cross-linguistic comparability and can, therefore, work to provide solutions to such problems. For example, Alderson et al. (2015) used retired Finnish PISA reading items to measure teenage participants' L1 Finnish reading ability, one of the explanatory variables in their study of teenage Finnish-speaking English learners' English reading and writing, because the Finnish PISA reading items were the best available measures of that skill for the relevant age range.

A small but increasing number of SLA studies use CEFR-based or ACTFL-based scales to assess the learners' performances across languages. For example, Huhta, Alanen, Tarnanen, Martin, and Hirvelä (2014) investigated development in L2 English and L2 Finnish. The papers in Winke and Gass (2019) compared learning across multiple languages at US universities. In recent years, the emergence of the dimensions of complexity, accuracy, and fluency (CAF) in

SLA research has made it easier to establish links between L2 proficiency scales, criteria, and SLA. Such criteria can be applied with a varying degree of systematicity in the measurement of L2 performance (see e.g., Pallotti, 2009; Housen, Kuiken, & Vedder, 2012). The longitudinal research project LANGSNAP (Mitchell, Tracy-Ventura, & McManus, 2017), for example, followed Anglophone students' development of L2 French and L2 Spanish during study abroad by using multiple measures, including elicited imitation and oral interviews. More research is needed in this area, e.g., the relationship between global measures of proficiency such as the EIT and CAF (see e.g., Ortega et al., 2002; Wu & Ortega, 2013; Huensch & Tracy-Ventura, 2017; De Jong, 2018).

There are a much larger number of SLA studies that seek to compare L2 development across multiple languages by using learner performance in a single task or task type as a measure of various aspects of L2 development. Elicited imitation has recently attracted interest for its use as a measure of implicit L2 grammatical knowledge (e.g., Ortega et al., 2002; Wu & Ortega, 2013; Spada, Shiu, & Tomita, 2015; Kim, Tracy-Ventura, & Jung, 2016). A recent review (Yan, Maeda, Lv, & Ginther, 2016) has also found evidence in support for the use of elicited imitation as a measure of L2 proficiency. Story retelling (the Frog Story is probably the best-known example, see Mayer, 1969) is also a task that has been used in a number of studies (e.g., Berman 1988; Berman & Slobin, 1994; see also Sanchez & Jarvis, 2008). The cloze test and C-test are yet another type of task widely used as a measure of L2 proficiency in different languages (see, e.g., Dörnyei & Katona, 1992; Babaii & Ansary, 2001; Tremblay, 2011).

Approaches to ensuring comparability of assessments in multiple languages can be divided into at least three partly overlapping types:

1. translating or adapting the assessment instruments
2. designing the assessments based on the same blueprint (shared test specifications and item writing guidelines)
3. linking the assessments to a general framework and proficiency scale (e.g., CEFR or ACTFL)

We will next describe these approaches and the ways in which they have been applied in assessment and illustrate them with examples. At the same time, we will discuss the advantages and disadvantages that have been identified in each type of approach.

Key Concepts

Test translation: Translating tests by using concepts, words, and expressions that are equivalent across languages.

Test adaptation: Goes beyond translation; includes activities such as deciding whether the construct can be measured across languages by the test, and further modification of the test content for linguistic and cultural comparability.

Test specifications: A document that defines, and illustrates with examples, the constructs and sub-constructs to be assessed, the texts, and other input materials and task types to be used in a particular test. It also defines the purpose(s) and intended test-taker population(s) of the test.

Key Issues

The main issue in measuring across languages is to ensure that the language assessments are comparable and that the outcomes mean the same for each language; thus, *test equivalency* is a key issue. Different language versions should be comparable as far as the underlying construct is concerned (Clark, 2013), or even to the degree that the scores for different language versions are comparable to each other (see, e.g., Sireci & Berberoglu, 2000; Sireci & Allalouf, 2003). To put it simply, equivalency in the context of L2 assessment means ensuring that different language versions of the same tests measure the same thing; that is, they share the same construct, and are not unduly influenced by construct-irrelevant variance (Clark, 2013).

There are three main approaches to increasing the comparability of language assessments across languages: translation/adaptation; same design; and same scales and framework.

Translation/adaptation

Description. Translating assessment content across languages is, in principle, the most comprehensive method to ensuring comparability of the assessments. This typically involves designing the assessment instruments for one language and then translating them to all other languages (Arffman, 2010). However, translation often involves the adaptation of tests, e.g., including the matter of deciding to what extent the construct can be measured across languages, and modifying test content to suit the target culture. Such approaches mean that the different versions are automatically based on the same test specifications, and that there is little or, possibly, no variation in test content and task types across test versions.

Advantages. Test translation and test adaptation used in international program evaluations such as the PISA and PIRLS studies have had the advantage of being relatively valid and reliable since their development follows standardized procedures honed over years or decades. In PIRLS, which evaluates reading in the language of education among 4th graders (for example, German reading in most German schools), the assessment tasks, questionnaires, and other materials are translated from the English originals (Martin, Mullis, & Hooper, 2017). In the PISA, all tasks are translated from (mainly) English into all the other languages, both in science and mathematics but also in reading literacy in the language(s) of education of the participating countries (Grisay, de Jong, Gebhardt, Berezner, & Halleux-Monseu, 2007). A number of methods are used in adapting content tests such as PISA across languages, including forward and back translations (see Clark, 2013). Forward translation involves straightforward translation of the source text into the target language, whereas in back translation, the target text is translated one more time back into the source language to further evaluate the quality of the translation.

Disadvantages. The main disadvantage lies in the equivalency of translations, an issue which has considerable impacts on the assessments of language abilities. In her analysis of English source texts and their Finnish-language translations from the PISA reading test, Arffman (2010) noted that there is no reliable way to compare text difficulty across languages. In her study, she relied on a detailed analysis of various structural and semantic features of the PISA texts to determine non-equivalencies of difficulty, including language-specific differences in, e.g., grammar, meaning, and in the choices made and strategies used by the translators, all of which having been found problematic in previous studies. She also identified language-specific differences in writing-systems such as the way English and Finnish writers use commas. Her thorough analysis showed the difficulty of reaching complete equivalency across languages, even when using translations of the highest quality.

Although test translations are commonly used in psychological testing (e.g., psycholinguistic, intelligence, and personality tests; for an overview, see Hambleton, Merenda, & Spielberger, 2005; for an example, see the downloadable, translated working memory tests at the Georgia Institute of Technology Attention and Working Memory lab (https://englelab.gatech.edu/translatedtasks.html), test translations are seldom used in L2 proficiency and achievement testing. Rare published examples of this approach in foreign language testing include Clark's (1965) study, in which Spanish achievement tests of reading and listening were successfully translated into Brazilian Portuguese. In contrast, test translation between unrelated languages can be problematic. Rosenbluth (1976) showed that some items in a test for young learners that involved matching verbal instructions with pictures were considerably more difficult when translated from English to Navajo because of the impossibility of using equally simple syntax in both languages to express the same content.

Same design approaches

Description. The second major approach to ensuring cross-language comparability is to construct the assessments using the same design principles, viz., by following the same test specifications and item writing guidelines. Test specifications define the constructs to be assessed, and the materials and task types to be used (e.g., Davidson & Lynch, 2002); item writing guidelines, if separate from test specifications, define in detail the item and task types to be used. This is probably a rather common approach in assessment systems that cover different languages and specifically want their tests to be as comparable as possible, typically for proficiency (gatekeeping) and achievement purposes. Examples include the ACTFL examinations (e.g., as reviewed by Isbell & Winke, 2019), DIALANG tests (Alderson, 2005), and European examinations such as the ECL and the Finnish National Certificates. DIALANG relied on common test specifications to construct tests for 14 languages in five areas of proficiency (Alderson, 2005); ACTFL test development across multiple languages took a similar approach. DIALANG was somewhat unusual as it also used translation across the different languages: the self-assessment instruments ("can do" statements), task instructions, and feedback were all translated from English into the other languages (recent additions have increased the number of such languages from 14 to 18).

Advantages. Shared test specifications underlying test development obviously increase the comparability of the tests. Therefore, several national and international studies of educational achievement (program evaluations) have used this approach when it has not been considered possible to translate the tests. The European ESLC (European Commission, 2013), which covered the five most commonly taught FLs at the end of compulsory education in EU countries, based test design on joint test specifications. Student and teacher questionnaires were, however, translated from the English originals.

Many of the tests and program evaluations described above also rely on the third approach, using a common framework and scale. For example, both DIALANG and the ESLC study not only used the CEFR scale as their construct definition and scale of language proficiency and as the tool to report the outcomes of assessments, but also drew on the horizontal dimension of the CEFR—inventories of language functions, tasks, texts and activities—to design test content.

Disadvantages. The main issue with the common test specifications approach is that specifications vary in terms of their generality. The more general they are, the more differences there will be between test versions both within and between languages. Even very detailed and normative specifications leave some room for variation. For example, the DIALANG test specifications were rather general in that they did not dictate the proportions of different task types and task content areas that every test version across languages must adhere to (Alderson, 2005). Therefore, there is variation in the proportions of particular CEFR content categories, sub-skills, and task types that are represented in each DIALANG language version. Comparability between languages was pursued by both gathering empirical data about the tasks through piloting and by linking the tests (and, thus, languages) at a more general level via CEFR levels (Alderson, 2005).

Common Framework and Same Scale

Description. The third approach to attempting to create comparable assessments across languages relies on a common overall framework and, importantly, on a common scale that defines degrees of language proficiency. Proficiency in these scales is typically defined with respect to what the language users can do in a particular language. That is, they define functional competence. The best known examples of these are the CEFR (Council of Europe, 2001) that was created in Europe but is also used in several countries in Asia, the Middle East and South America, and the US-based ACTFL scale (ACTFL, 2012; Terry, 2016), which has its origins in the Foreign Service Institute/Interagency Language Roundtable (FSI/ILR) scale (Herzog, n.d.). The Australian Second Language Proficiency Rating (ASLPR; Ingram, 1990), later known as the International Second Language Proficiency Rating, and the Canadian Language Benchmarks (CLB, e.g., Fox & Courchêne, 2005) are further examples of such scales. (See Harsch & Malone, Chapter 4, this volume for more information on proficiency frameworks and scales.) A framework and a scale overlap to some degree as both contain definitions of language skills and use of language. Here, language testing specialists use framework as the broader term: A framework in this context contains one or more scales that define degrees of proficiency while it also includes other information about language proficiency. The clearest example of this is the CEFR, which is an extensive document that contains not only dozens of scales but also descriptions of a great number of competences, contexts, functions, texts, and activities involved in learning and using a language. To some degree, the ACTFL, ASLPR, and CLB are also combinations of scales and broader framework-type definitions and illustrations of L2 proficiency, even if they might not explicitly be called frameworks.

Advantages. Relating assessments to the same framework and scale gives them a certain degree of comparability. Importantly, the frameworks listed above are widely known and used, which increases the interpretability of the assessment results that are reported with reference to them and their scales. Particularly the CEFR and ACTFL have been used in multilingual assessment contexts as they offer an approach that helps to communicate the meaning of the results to different audiences, including politicians and other decision makers, as well as the general public.

Disadvantages. Using a common framework and scale is a less controlled way to try to achieve comparability across languages since assessments are not based on common test specifications and may differ considerably in their content and methods, and even in the constructs measured. For example, *reading* or *speaking* may not be defined and operationalized in the same way in different measurements. One reading test may focus on understanding the main point and the writer's stance in a text, and use the summary as the main task type, whereas another test may measure more narrowly defined sub-skills of reading and rely on multiple-choice questions. Both measure reading and both can be linked with a scale such as the CEFR scale, but it is difficult to ascertain exactly how comparable they are. Furthermore, these frameworks may not include guidance on how to create comparable tests or to relate tests with the framework and its scales. This is the case with the CEFR, for example. The ACTFL framework is somewhat different in this respect, at least when it comes to speaking, since standardized procedures have been developed for designing Oral Proficiency Interviews that operationalize the ACTFL speaking scale in a comparable way across different languages (see ACTFL, 2012; Isbell & Winke, 2019).

A range of procedures are used to align assessments with each other and with general frameworks and their scales. For example, the detailed manual developed by the Council of Europe to guide alignment with the CEFR gives a good overview of the procedures involved in such work (Council of Europe, 2009). One approach often used in relating assessments with a common scale is *standard setting*. It is a procedure that involves experts making judgments about the difficulty of test items/tasks with respect to the scale levels or about the ability of language learners, again with respect to the scale (see Cizek & Bunch, 2007). Standard setting has been applied in several multilingual assessment contexts, including DIALANG (Alderson, 2005), the ESLC (Verhelst, 2009), and in the design of a multilingual set of speaking benchmarks of CEFR levels (Breton, Lepage, & North, 2008; see also Jones, 2009, on issues in multilingual standard setting and Kaftandjieva, 2007, on issues in aligning the contents of assessments). Young and Tong's (2016) article on scaling is another good source for procedures on aligning assessment with a common scale. Standard setting and scaling procedures are, thus, promising ways to increase the comparability of tests by relating test scores in different languages to the same broader framework and scale.

Recommendations for Practice

In this chapter, we reviewed three main approaches to measuring language abilities in and across multiple languages. While there is no single best approach, we close by offering testers and SLA researchers suggestions specific to each approach.

Translation/Adaptation Approach

International testing systems such as PISA and PIRLS employ the most thorough system in that test content is translated into all the languages included. The second edition of the *ITC Guidelines for Translating and Adapting Tests* (2018) includes the most complete guidelines to date on how to proceed if one wishes to translate tests from one language into another. The guidelines include pre-conditions on test development, administration, scoring and interpretation, and documentation. In SLA research, the EIT (Ortega et al., 2002) has been translated into a number of languages, while instruments such as the Frog Story that largely rely on non-linguistic input already employ an approach that could be categorized as task or content translation. That is, the task instructions are typically given in the learners' L1, and if the instructions are the same across languages, these tasks can be considered equivalent, assuming that the pictures and other non-linguistic material in the input is interpreted in the same way across languages and cultures.

Same Design Approach

Comparability of tests in different languages is approached by developing tests concurrently by using (1) the same assessment framework, test specifications, and item writing guidelines; and (2) the same standard setting procedures, ratings scales, and test score analysis procedures. Tests are developed in the target language as opposed to translations. Existing SLA research instruments such as elicited imitation and the C-test may be seen to represent this approach to some extent. They are both based on a very precisely defined blueprint for construction and administration. For example, in the design of C-tests, the end half of every other word is deleted. Obviously, the content and some features of the design may still vary across different operationalizations of the elicited imitation test or C-test, but the same can be said for any test designed from identical test specifications.

Same Scale and Framework Approach

The most general approach to achieve comparability across languages in assessment uses the same framework, and particularly the same scale, as the basis of comparability. Internationally, the most widely used scale is the CEFR 6-point scale, but other such scales may be desirable, especially when measuring development in less-studied populations, such as young children (the 6-point WIDA scale, https://wida.wisc.edu/, is promising), or when the language-learning system or context is distanced from CEFR's European learning models (for example, China's Standards of English Language Ability, http://cse.neea.edu.cn/, are promising). If a framework-based approach is chosen, researchers are well advised to follow recommended procedures for linking their instruments to the scale (see, e.g., Council of Europe, 2009) or using pre-existing instruments that have already been linked to the scale, such as retired forms of major international language examinations.

Testing Tips

Test translation/adaptation

- Use tests within the existing research literature (e.g., ACTFL, PISA).
- If you translate yourself, use guidelines (e.g., ITC Guidelines for Translating and Adapting Tests).

Same design

- Develop tests in the target language(s), but make sure that you use the same assessment framework, same test specifications, and same item writing guidelines across the languages.
- Make sure that your standard setting and rating scales are the same, and that the way you analyze test scores are the same.

Same scales and framework

- To compare ratings across languages, use an established assessment framework with procedures in place to link tests to the scales or vice versa (e.g., CEFR or ACTFL).

Recommended Readings

Arffman, I. (2010). The equivalency of translations in international reading literacy studies. *Scandinavian Journal of Educational Research*, *54*(1), 37–59. https://doi.org/10.1080/00313830903488460

Arffman's study highlights the problematic issue of equivalency in translation. The article offers a highly relevant source of useful procedures and potential pitfalls based on an empirical study of the PISA reading test.

Clark, M. (2013). Assessment across languages. In C. A. Chapelle (Ed.) *The encyclopedia of applied linguistics*. https://doi.org/10.1002/9781405198431.wbeal0039

Clark's chapter addresses some of the issues relevant to assessment across languages, including test adaptation. The chapter discusses the most widely used scales to assess language ability across languages (e.g., FSI/ISL, ACTFL, and CEFR).

Solano-Flores, G., & Chía, M. (2017). Validation of score meaning in multiple language versions of tests. In K. Ercikan & J. W. Pellegrino (Eds.), *Validation of score meaning for the next generation of assessments* (pp. 127–137). Taylor & Francis.

The authors outline methods for validating multilingual assessments by ways of examining test-taker response processes.

References

Alderson, J. C. (2005). *Diagnosing foreign language proficiency: The interface between learning and assessment*. Continuum.
Alderson, J. C., Haapakangas, E.-L., Huhta, A., Nieminen, L., & Ullakonoja, R. (2015). *The diagnosis of reading in a second or foreign language*. Routledge.
American Council on the Teaching of Foreign Languages (ACTFL). (2012). *ACTFL proficiency guidelines 2012*. American Council on the Teaching of Foreign Languages. https://www.actfl.org/publications/guidelines-and-manuals/actfl-proficiency-guidelines-2012
Arffman, I. (2010). The equivalency of translations in international reading literacy studies. *Scandinavian Journal of Educational Research*, *54*(1), 37–59. https://doi.org/10.1080/00313830903488460
Babaii, E., & Ansary, H. (2001). The C-test: A valid operationalization of reduced redundancy principle? *System*, *29*(2), 209–219. https://doi.org/10.1016/S0346-251X(01)00012-4

Berman, R. (1988). On the ability to relate events in narrative. *Discourse Processes, 11*(4), 469–497. https://doi.org/10.1080/01638538809544714

Berman, R., & Slobin, D. (Eds.). (1994). *Relating events in narratives: A crosslinguistic developmental study*. Lawrence Erlbaum Associates.

Bernhardt, E., Molitoris, J., Romeo, K., Lin, N., & Valderrama, P. (2015). Designing and sustaining a foreign language writing proficiency assessment program at the postsecondary level. *Foreign Language Annals, 48*(3), 329–349. https://doi.org/10.1111/flan.12153

Breton, G., Lepage, S., & North, B. (2008). *Cross-language benchmarking seminar to calibrate examples of spoken production in English, French, German, Italian and Spanish with regard to the six levels of the Common European Framework of Reference for Languages (CEFR)*. CIEP & Council of Europe. https://rm.coe.int/168045a0cd

Brown, A. (2013). Uses of language assessments. In C. A. Chapelle (Ed.), *The encyclopedia of applied linguistics*. Blackwell. https://doi.org/10.1002/9781405198431.wbeal1237

Cizek, G. J., & Bunch, M. B. (2007). *Standard setting*. SAGE Publications. https://doi.org/10.4135/9781412985918

Clark, J. (1965). Item-by-item parallel achievement tests for different foreign languages. *Journal of Educational Measurement, 2*(1), 77–83. https://doi.org/10.1111/j.1745-3984.1965.tb00394.x

Clark, M. (2013). Assessment across languages. In C. A. Chapelle (Ed.), *The encyclopedia of applied linguistics*. Blackwell. https://doi.org/10.1002/9781405198431.wbeal0039

Council of Europe. (2001). *Common European framework of reference for languages: Learning, teaching, assessment (CEFR)*. Cambridge University Press. https://rm.coe.int/1680459f97

Council of Europe. (2009). *Relating language examinations to the Common European framework of reference for languages: Learning, teaching, assessment (CEFR). A Manual*. Council of Europe Language Policy Division. https://rm.coe.int/1680667a2d

Davidson, F., & Lynch, B. (2002). *Testcraft: A teacher's guide to writing and using language test specifications*. Yale University Press.

Davin, K., Rempert, T., & Hammerand, A. (2014). Converting data to knowledge: One district's experience using large-scale proficiency assessment. *Foreign Language Annals, 47*(2), 241–260. https://doi.org/10.1111/flan.12081

De Jong, N. H. (2018). Fluency in second language testing: Insights from different disciplines. *Language Assessment Quarterly, 15*(3), 237–254. https://doi.org/10.1080/15434303.2018.1477780

Di Silvio, F., Diao, W., & Donovan, A. (2016). The development of L2 fluency during study abroad: A cross-language study. *The Modern Language Journal, 100*(3), 610–624. https://doi.org/10.1111/modl.12343

Dörnyei, Z., & Katona, L. (1992). Validation of the C-test amongst Hungarian EFL learners. *Language Testing, 9*(2), 187–206. https://doi.org/10.1177/026553229200900206

European Commission. (2013). First European survey on language competences. A final report. European Union. https://op.europa.eu/en/publication-detail/-/publication/42ea89dc-373a-4d4f-aa27-9903852cd2e4/language-en/format-PDF/source-119658026

Fox, J., & Courchêne, R. (2005). The Canadian language benchmarks (CLB): A critical appraisal. *Contact, 31*(2), 7–28.

Gorman, T., Purves, A., & Degenhart, R. (1988). *IEA study of written composition*. Pergamon Press.

Grisay, A., de Jong, J., Gebhardt, E., Berezner, A., & Halleux-Monseur, B. (2007). Translation equivalence across PISA countries. *Journal of Applied Measurement, 8*(3), 249–66.

Gu, L., Lockwood, J., & Powers, D. E. (2015). *Evaluating the TOEFL Junior standard test as a measure of progress for young English language learners* (Research Report No. RR-15–22). Educational Testing Service. https://doi.org/10.1002/ets2.12064

Hambleton, R., Merenda, P., & Spielberger, C. (Eds.). (2005). *Adapting educational and psychological tests for cross-cultural assessment*. Lawrence Erlbaum Associates.

Herzog, M. (n.d.) *An overview of the history of the ILR Language proficiency skill level descriptions and scale*. https://govtilr.org/Skills/IRL%20Scale%20History.htm

Housen, A., Kuiken, F., & Vedder, I. (2012). *Dimensions of L2 performance and proficiency: Complexity, accuracy and fluency in SLA*. Benjamins.

Huensch, A., & Tracy-Ventura, N. (2017). Understanding second language fluency behavior: The effects of individual differences in first language fluency, cross-linguistic differences, and proficiency over time. *Applied Psycholinguistics, 38*(4), 755–785. https://doi.org/10.1017/S0142716416000424

Huhta, A., Alanen, R., Tarnanen, M., Martin, M., & Hirvelä, T. (2014). Assessing learners' writing skills in a SLA study: Validating the rating process across tasks, scales and languages. *Language Testing, 31*(3), 307–328. https://doi.org/10.1177/0265532214526176

Ingram, D. (1990). The Australian second language proficiency ratings (ASLPR). *AILA Review, 7*, 46–61.

International Testing Commission. (2018). ITC guidelines for translating and adapting tests (2nd ed.). *International Journal of Testing*, *18*(2), 101–134. https://doi.org/10.1080/15305058.2017.1398166
Isbell, D., & Winke, P. (2019). ACTFL oral proficiency interview – Computer (OPIc). *Language Testing*, *36*(3), 467–477. https://doi.org/10.1177/0265532219828253
Isbell, D., Winke, P., & Gass, S. (2019). Using the ACTFL OPIc to assess proficiency and monitor progress in a tertiary foreign languages program. *Language Testing*, *36*(3), 439–465. https://doi.org/10.1177/0265532218798139
Jones, N. (2009). A comparative approach to constructing a multilingual proficiency framework: Constraining the role of standard-setting. In N. Figueras & J. Noijons (Eds.), *Linking to the CEFR levels: Research perspectives* (pp. 35–44). Cito, Council of Europe & EALTA. http://www.ealta.eu.org/documents/resources/Research_Colloquium_report.pdf
Kaftandjieva, F. (2007). Quantifying the quality of linkage between language examinations and the CEF. In C. Carlsen & E. Moe (Eds.), *A human touch to language testing* (pp. 33–43). Novus Press.
Kim, Y., Tracy-Ventura, N., & Jung, Y. (2016). A measure of proficiency or short-term memory? Validation of an elicited imitation test for SLA research. *The Modern Language Journal*, *100*(3), 655–673. https://doi.org/10.1111/modl.12346
Martin, M., Mullis, I., & Hooper, M. (Eds.). (2017). *Methods and procedures in PIRLS 2016*. https://timssandpirls.bc.edu/publications/pirls/2016-methods.html
Mayer, M. (1969). *Frog, where are you?* Dial Press.
Mitchell, R., Tracy-Ventura, N., & McManus, K. (2017). *Anglophone students abroad: Identity, social relationships, and language learning*. Routledge.
Ortega, L., Iwashita, N., Norris, J. M., & Rabie, S. (2002, October 3–6). *An investigation of elicited imitation tasks in crosslinguistic SLA research*. [Paper presentation]. Second Language Research Forum, Toronto, Canada.
Pallotti, G. (2009). CAF: Defining, refining, and differentiating constructs. *Applied Linguistics*, *30*(4), 590–601. https://doi.org/10.1093/applin/amp045
Rosenbluth, A. (1976). The feasibility of test translation between unrelated languages English to Navajo. *TESOL Quarterly*, *10*(1), 33–43. https://doi.org/10.2307/3585937
Sanchez, L., & Jarvis, S. (2008). The use of picture stories in the investigation of cross-linguistic influence. *TESOL Quarterly*, *42*(2), 329–333. https://www.jstor.org/stable/40264460
Sireci, S. G., & Allalouf, A. (2003). Appraising item equivalence across multiple languages and cultures. *Language Testing*, *20*(2), 148–166. https://doi.org/10.1191/0265532203lt249oa
Sireci, S. G., & Berberoglu, G. (2000). Using bilingual respondents to evaluate translated-adapted Items. *Applied Measurement in Education*, *13*(3), 229–248. http://doi.org/10.1207/S15324818AME1303_1
Spada, N., Shiu, L.-J., & Tomita, Y. (2015). Validating an elicited imitation task as a measure of implicit knowledge: Comparisons with other validation studies. *Language Learning*, *65*(3), 723–751. https://doi.org/10.1111/lang.12129
Terry, R. (2016). *A history of ACTFL*. American Council on the Teaching of Foreign Languages.
Tremblay, A. (2011). Proficiency assessment standards in second language acquisition research: "Clozing" the gap. *Studies in Second Language Acquisition*, *33*(3), 339–372. https://doi.org/10.1017/S0272263111000015
Verhelst, N. (2009). Linking multilingual survey results to the Common European framework of reference. In N. Figueras & J. Noijons (Eds.), *Linking to the CEFR levels: Research perspectives* (pp. 45–58). Cito, Council of Europe & EALTA. http://www.ealta.eu.org/documents/resources/Research_Colloquium_report.pdf
Winke, P., & Gass, S. M. (Eds.). (2019). *Foreign language proficiency in higher education*. Springer. https://doi.org/10.1007/978-3-030-01006-5
Wu, S.-L., & Ortega, L. (2013). Measuring global oral proficiency in SLA research: A new elicited imitation test of L2 Chinese. *Foreign Language Annals*, *46*(4), 680–704. https://doi.org/10.1111/flan.12063
Yan, X., Maeda, Y., Lv, J., & Ginther, A. (2016). Elicited imitation as a measure of second language proficiency: A narrative review and meta-analysis. *Language Testing*, *33*(4), 497–528. https://doi.org/10.1177/0265532215594643
Young, M., & Tong, Y. (2016). Vertical scales. In S. Lane, M. R. Raymond, & T. M. Haladyna (Eds.), *Handbook of test development* (pp. 450–466). Routledge. https://doi.org/10.4324/9780203102961

34

Measuring Intercultural Competence

Gila A. Schauer

Background

In recent years, globalization as well as political and environmental developments have led to an increased interest in intercultural competence. This can be seen in documents on intercultural competence published by organizations such as the United Nations Educational, Scientific and Cultural Organization (UNESCO), the Council of Europe (CoE), and the American Council on the Teaching of Foreign Languages (ACTFL). All three recommend that specific steps be taken to promote intercultural competence. With regard to education, UNESCO (2013) recommended that "intercultural competences [be incorporated] in all levels of formal, informal and non-formal education systems to facilitate learning of intercultural competences and [to] gain flexibility in interactions with cultural others" (p. 27). Focusing on the European Union, Huber and Reynolds (2014, p. 7), argued that:

> [t]he ability to understand one another across and beyond all types of cultural barriers is a fundamental prerequisite for making our diverse democratic societies work. As current events continue to show, there is an urgent need for a concerted effort to develop the necessary attitudes, skills and knowledge that contribute to intercultural competence in the everyday practice of teaching and learning, so that future generations may be equipped to participate in an increasingly global and complex environment.

Thus, there seems to be a general consensus that intercultural competence (IC) is important and should be taught at various levels, even though it is not always quite clear what intercultural competence is. Before addressing different conceptualizations of intercultural competence in more detail, I first discuss concepts and models regarding culture and communicative competence that provide the foundations of IC from a language teaching, learning, and assessment point of view.

Culture

Culture has been defined in many different ways. One well-known conceptualization of culture refers to a *small c* and *big C* view. Secru (2000) wrote "wheareas *small c* culture is commonly understood as referring to phenomena of everyday life, popular cultural products and human behavior, [...] [*b]ig C Culture* is conceived as manifesting itself in ideas, values, history, institutions, literature, philosophy and artistic products" (p. 28). Thus, a distinction is made between culture encoded in everyday life actions, and something that can be viewed as high culture. For example, everyday life actions can be represented by the use of specific language features such as conventionalized expressions when someone sneezes (*Bless you* in English or *Gesundheit* in German) or cultural products accessible to many (e.g., items of clothing showing regional affiliation, such as the *Fischerhemd*, a special kind of durable striped long-sleeved shirt worn in coastal regions of Germany). Meanwhile, high culture may be represented by "products of the arts, philosophy and science that have been held in great esteem by society and deemed to require sophisticated (i.e., cultured) understanding" (Bashford, 2007, p. 1). Another aspect of high culture are the more hidden elements that refer to values that are connected to the core of any society or community, aspects that are difficult to learn and equally difficult to teach.

Addressing the link between culture and an individual's first language(s) and subsequent behavior, Gudykunst and Kim (2003) argued that an individual's language use is closely tied to their socialization into their native culture(s) and language(s). They wrote that because children "learn the language, rules and norms of [their] cultures by a very early age (between 5 and 10 years old), [...] [individuals] generally are unaware of how culture influences [their] behavior in general and [their] communication in particular" (p. 4). This means that individuals are likely to consider the cultural and language norms they encounter in their childhood to be the default. Since a young child's socialization into a culture is often accompanied by very direct instructions on what to do and what not to do (e.g., "Say thank you to the nice lady!" "Use your indoor voice, please!"), individuals that are only exposed to one culture may consider any deviations from the norms that they are familiar with to be indicative of incorrect or inappropriate behavior or poor socialization, rather than characteristic features of different cultural norms. This is one of the reasons why awareness raising about different cultures is essential. The relationship between culture, language, and an individual's ability to function in society and partake in social encounters in diverse contexts is described by McConachy (2018), who wrote, "[c]ulture helps individuals recognize the speech events which help constitute social life and the implicit and explicit norms which relate to these events and the individuals who take part in them. [...] [It] gives individuals a sense of what is expected behavior given the sociocultural context in which language is used" (p. 13).

Thus, knowledge of a culture and language would enable second or foreign language (henceforth L2) learners of German to identify *Grüß Gott* [*Greet God*] as a regional greeting in parts of Southern Germany and Austria that is responded to by repeating the same greeting or any other greeting that fits the context, and is neither a sign of grandeur on the speaker's part or encouragement to attend a religious event. Comprehending the utterance as a greeting and being able to contextualize it as conventional expression directed at interlocutors from all backgrounds can put L2 learners at ease. With cultural instruction, learners of German can come to understand that the greeting stems from that regional culture's historical link to Christianity, but that speakers do not assume shared religious affiliation. This example shows, however, that the notion of culture needs to be more fine-grained than simply equating culture with national culture (cf. also Liddicoat & Scarino, 2013). While knowledge of aspects of national culture, such as the meaning of the red poppy attached to many people's lapels in Britain in November as a sign of remembrance for and gratitude to British soldiers, are important for newcomers into a society, the same applies to more regional aspects of culture, such as the greeting *Grüß Gott* in certain parts of Germany, or the greeting *Ay up me duck* [*hello, my [honorific]*, cf. also Scott, 2017] that is used in Nottinghamshire.

Communicative Competence

In one of the earliest papers on communicative competence, Savignon (1976) conceptualized communicative competence as

> a way of describing what it is a native speaker knows which enables him [or her] to interact effectively with other native speakers. [...] The native speaker knows not only how to say

> something but what to say and when to say it. The linguistic features of an exchange are embedded in cultural context which includes the role of the speaker in a particular context, the role of the other participants and a host of non-verbal communication cues such as distance, posture, gestures, facial expressions.
>
> (p. 4)

In her view, culture and communicative competence are clearly linked. In the following years, several frameworks for communicative competence were proposed and two major perspectives evolved, one that looked at communicative competence from a language teaching perspective (e.g., Canale & Swain 1980; Celce-Murcia, Dörnyei, & Thurrell 1995), and one that was very much influenced by assessment concerns (e.g., Bachman & Palmer 1982; Bachman 1990; Bachman & Palmer 2010). Bachman and Palmer's (2010) model is illustrated in Figure 34.1.

Bachman and Palmer's (2010) model is based on empirical research (Bachman & Palmer 1982; Bachman 1990) and Canale and Swain's (1980) model of communicative competence. Bachman and Palmer's (1982) original conceptualization led to the revised model with the somewhat unwieldy name "ability to use language communicatively" (Bachman & Palmer, 2010, p. 43). The model in Figure 34.1 consists of two main components: language competence, and strategic competence. While the former focuses on aspects of language knowledge (e.g., vocabulary, rhetorical organization, manipulative language use, dialects, varieties, cultural references, and figures of speech), the latter addresses what "can be thought of as higher-order metacognitive strategies that provide a management function in language use, as well as in other cognitive activities" (p. 48). Coming back to my earlier example of different regional greetings in in Nottinghamshire and parts of German speaking countries, knowledge of these regional forms would be included in the pragmatic knowledge component of Bachman and Palmer's (2010) model under knowledge of dialects and varieties.

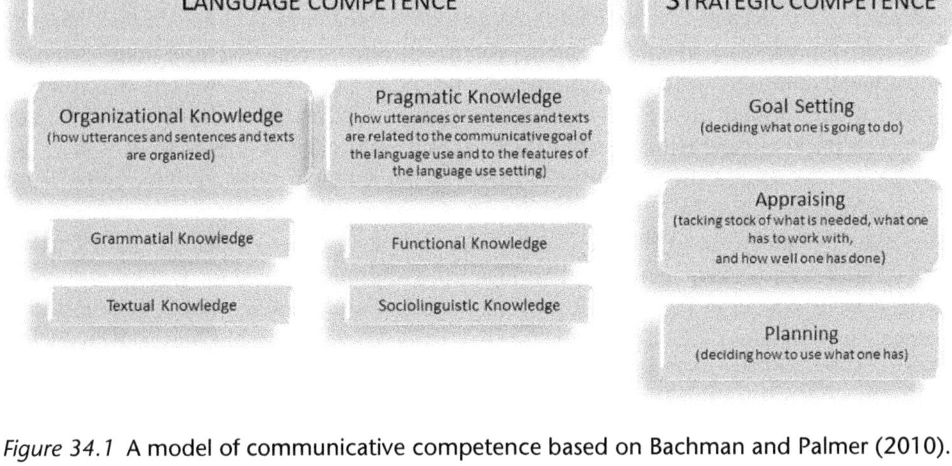

Figure 34.1 A model of communicative competence based on Bachman and Palmer (2010).

Intercultural Competence

As Wolf and Borzikowsky (2018) noted, "[a]s yet, researchers on ICC [Intercultural Competence] have found no consensus how ICC is to define. [...] There seems to be wide agreement that ICC, in its broadest sense, is a heterogeneous construct involving multiple dimensions, which are necessary to interact with people from other cultures adequately and effectively" (p. 489).

This view is supported by Spitzberg and Chignon (2009) who found more than 300 components that are related to intercultural competence in their overview study. These recent evaluations of the field of intercultural competence show that it is extremely complex. While some models of intercultural competence completely disregard or place very little emphasis on an individual's foreign language competence (e.g., Deardorff 2006; Gudykunst 1998), others (e.g., Byram 1997, 2009; Fantini 2019) focus on an individual's L2 skills as well as a wide range of other skills, mind-sets, and characteristics. I concentrate on Byram's and Fantini's models, as they are particularly relevant for SLA.

Central to Byram's (1997, 2009) model is his distinction between *intercultural competence* and *intercultural communicative competence*. He defined intercultural competence as follows: "Individuals have the ability to interact *in their own language* [emphasis added] with people from another country and culture, drawing upon their knowledge about intercultural communication, their attitudes of interest in otherness, and their skills in interpreting, relating and discovering, i.e., of overcoming and enjoying intercultural contact" (Byram, 1997, p. 70). In contrast, intercultural communicative competence is defined by Byram (1997) as:

> [the] abil[ity] to interact with people from another country and culture *in a foreign language* [emphasis added]. [Individuals who have this competence] are able to negotiate a mode of communication and interaction which is satisfactory to themselves and the other and they are able to act as mediator between people of different cultural origins. Their knowledge of another culture is linked to their language competence through their ability to use language appropriately—sociolinguistic and discourse competence—and their awareness of the specific meanings, values and connotations of the language.
>
> (p. 71)

Thus, the main distinction between intercultural competence and intercultural communicative competence that Byram proposed centers on whether an interlocutor uses their first language (L1) or their L2. This is also shown in a schematic illustration he developed (Figure 34.2).

Like Byram, Fantini (e.g., 2009, 2019) has been an influential figure in the field of intercultural competence for decades. He defined "intercultural competence [...] as complex abilities that are required to perform effectively and appropriately when interacting with others who are linguistically and culturally different from oneself" (2009, p. 458). The notions of effective and appropriate communication are central to the field of pragmatics and thus also to one of the key components of Bachman and Palmer's (2010) model of communicative competence.

In his 2019 publication, Fantini proposed a model of intercultural communicative competence which is presented in Figure 34.3. The use of terminology here also shows that he has moved on from intercultural competence in 2009 to intercultural communicative competence in 2019, as the definitions provided for the latter term in 2019 is identical to the one provided for the former in 2009.

Fantini's (2019) model in Figure 34.3 shows a holistic view of intercultural communicative competence which inludes proficiency in the L2, as well as several skills, abilities, and characteristics that are similar to Byram (2009). What is particulary interesting in Fantini's conceptualization, however, is that it explicitly refers to a process; that is, it emphasizes that the acquisition of intercultural communicative competence is not something that can be achieved quickly. The

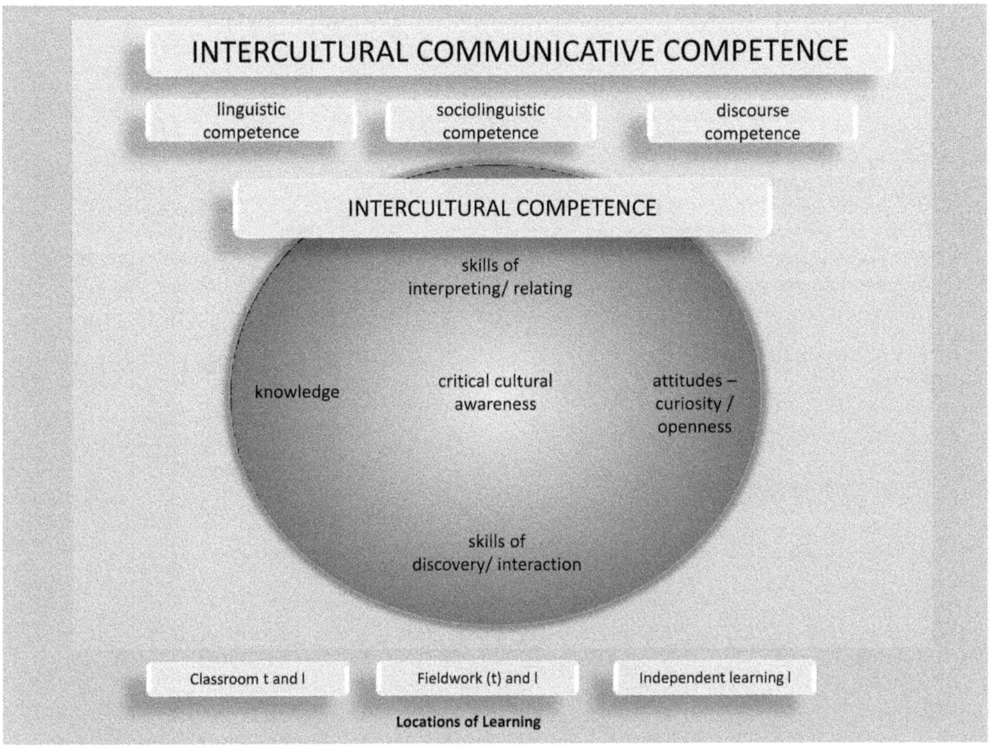

Figure 34.2 Byram's (2009) model of intercultural (communicative) competence.

process view that is proposed here can, for example, also be found in Deardorff's (2006) process model. Highlighting the process involved in acquiring intercultural competence is of key importance with regard to assessment, as it shows that single-moment tests are not a good choice when assessing intercultural competence (Figure 34.4).

Key Concepts

***Collaborative tasks*:** This involves the collaboration between different learner groups in two countries who are typically native speakers of the language the other group is learning.

***Ethnography*:** This is a research method that can be applied in intercultural learning. It involves the close observation and analysis of a group or community and (aspects of) their life. Ethnographers typically become immersed in the target group and its activities and record the observed actions which are subsequently analysed and reflected on.

***Interlanguage pragmatics*:** This is a field of applied linguistics that researches L2 learners' ability to comprehend the target language (including conventionalized expressions), as well as L2 learners' ability to produce language that is contextually appropriate and enables them to successfully and effectively achieve their communicative aims.

***Study abroad*:** This refers to individuals enrolled in higher education programs who live and study in a foreign country for a specific period of time and complete (part of) the requirements of their degree program in the foreign country.

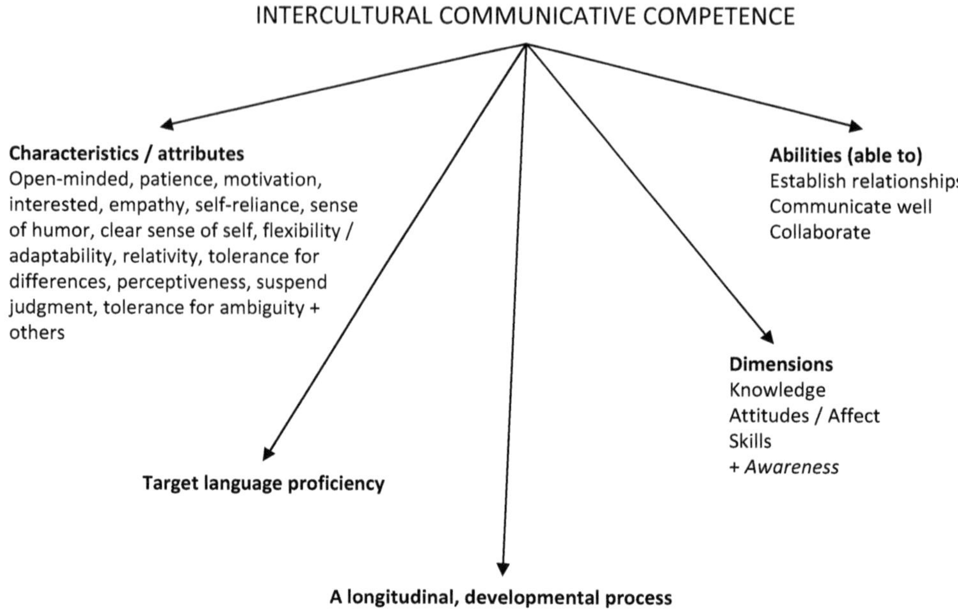

Figure 34.3 Fantini's (2019) model of intercultural communicative competence.

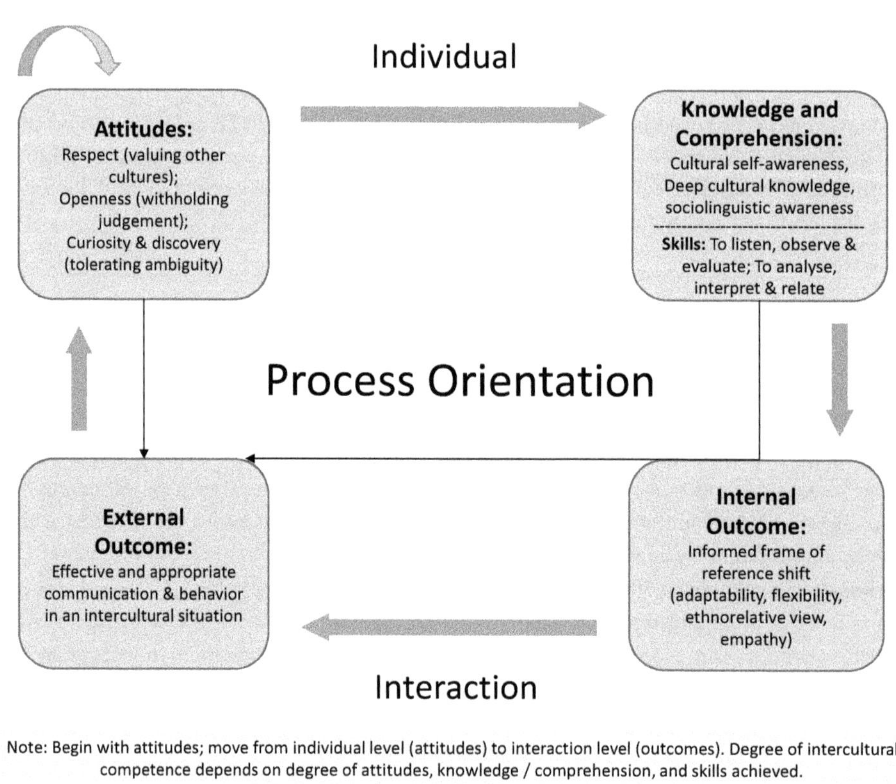

Figure 34.4 Deardorff's (2006) process model of intercultural communicative competence.

Key Issues

The fact that intercultural competence is featured in an edited volume entitled "Testing the Untestable in Language Education" (Paran & Secru, 2010) indicates that measuring IC is not going to be an easy or straightforward endeavor. If we consider the sheer number of competences, skills, and mind-sets that are included in IC frameworks, it becomes clear that trying to assess all of them or even a large number of them will be difficult and time consuming. In the following, I will first address problem areas and then offer some suggestions on how these problems could be addressed.

Liddicoat and Scarino (2010) noted that:

> [i]ntercultural competence in the context of language education imposes a number of challenges for assessment. In part, the difficulty lies in the diverse understandings of the construct to be assessed [...], assessment approaches may elicit only part of the overall construct, considering this to reflect the whole. Byram et al. (2002) argued that while assessing facts or knowledge and understanding about facts is relatively straightforward, any assessment of knowledge will not capture what it means to be intercultural (Liddicoat 2002, 2005; Liddicoat et al 2003).
>
> (p. 52)

The first issue that they refer to relates to the large number of models of intercultural competence available. When intercultural competence is included in foreign language curricula, it is often not accompanied by a detailed definition or a reference to a particular model that teachers can refer to. This means that the concept of intercultural competence often remains vague. In addition, this vagueness means that in countries that also have other foreign language lesson components related to culture, such as *Landeskunde* [*area studies/cultural studies*] in Germany that overlap with intercultural competence in some respects (cf. Oakley, 2003), educators may find it rather difficult to determine what they should be focusing on when they are assessing L2 learners' IC. Here a combination of different assessment methods that address a wide range of aspects may help. Wagner, Perugini and Byram (2018) recommended different intercultural competence projects for different learner populations (ranging from primary school learners to university students) and suggested that educators tap into a diverse range of learners' output via presentations, interviews, self-reports, blog entries, and portfolios.

Another key problem in the area of measuring intercultural assessment is that it is not always clear what the aim of the assessment can—or is supposed—to be, as Liddicoat and Scarino (2010) pointed out when addressing the assessment of facts or knowledge versus *being* intercultural. While it is relatively easy to assess L2 learners' pragmatic ability to correctly produce a response to an expression of gratitude (e.g., *You're welcome* in English or *Bitte schön* in German), how can some of the non-language cultural understanding skills be assessed, such as someone's sense of humour in the L2 or curiosity to learn L2 culture? Is it even ethical to do so?

A further issue raised by Sercu (2010, p. 18) concerns the fact that "many of the assessment techniques proposed are actually also teaching techniques aimed at enhancing learners' culture-specific and/or culture general awareness." This would explain why in many publications that clearly address components of intercultural competence (e.g., McConachy, 2018; Morgan & Cain, 2000) assessment is not mentioned. Instead, the focus is on the learning process and progress of the L2 learners. A related shift towards a view of assessment that sees a close link with personal growth, language teaching, and the assessor as facilitator in the L2 learners' development was described by Glisan, Uribe and Adair-Hauck (2007). In their discussion on authentic performance-based dynamic assessments, they wrote that "performance-based, authentic assessments hold promise as alternative approaches that may bring about a closer connection between instruction and assessment [...] The concept of feedback as a tool for connecting instruction and assessment is at the foundation of dynamic assessment [...]" (pp. 42–43).

Thus, if assessment of intercultural competence is seen as a process-oriented, performance-based dynamic evaluation of L2 learners' engagement with the target language and target culture, this will result in a broader range of assessment options. However, there is still at least one other issue that is potentially problematic, and this is the intercultural competence of the individuals who are assessing the learners. Ryan and Sercu (2005) wrote:

> [f]oreign language teachers are expected to have (near-)native competence in the foreign language they teach. [...] With respect to teachers' familiarity with the foreign cultures associated with the foreign languages they teach, few will state that teachers need a (near-) native knowledge of these target cultures. Yet, if teachers are to pass on culture-specific and culture-general knowledge to their pupils, prepare their pupils for intercultural contact situations and help them to better understand their own cultural identity, they will need a thorough understanding of the target cultures as well as of their own culture, next to some understanding of foreign cultures in general.
>
> (p. 39)

Ryan and Sercu (2005) explained that teachers in their international study responded that "one of the reasons [...] for not getting round to culture teaching more often is that they feel they are not sufficiently familiar with the cultures associated with the language they teach to be able to teach about them" (pp. 39-40). This is a problem that relates to pre-service teacher training (i.e., the content of degree programs that qualify individuals to teach) as well as to in-service teacher development and of course also to teacher's own motivation to update themselves about developments in the cultures that correspond to the foreign languages they are teaching.

The best assessment approach and the best and most detailed account of the model of intercultural competence chosen will not be of great help to L2 learners if their teachers cannot support them in their intercultural learning because they themselves lack the necessary knowledge and may not know to which sources to turn. With regard to teacher education, this means that degree program developers should ask themselves whether (a) they have put sufficient emphasis on intercultural issues in their degree programs, (b) students will be taught how to independently research intercultural issues and be given guidance on trustworthy sources, and (c) they can encourage students to study abroad, or even make study abroad a compulsory course component.

Recommendations for Practice

There are a number of issues that individuals tasked with assessing intercultural competence will need to consider and then resolve for their own purposes and within their contexts. Hopefully they will do so with thorough documentation so that others learning about their work understand the steps and decisions they made in the process of assessing intercultural competence. In my view, three important issues that need to be addressed with regard to assessing intercultural competence in foreign language education are:

1) Comprehensiveness
2) Assessment formats and techniques
3) Real-life transfer

Regarding 1, the big question is whether it is possible to assess all the components (irrespective of ethical concerns that I mentioned above) that are included in any of the intercultural competence models in a fair and reliable way that is in line with good practice in a typical foreign language education setting. The answer is likely going to be *no* for most, if not all, compulsory education settings and *potentially yes* for higher education settings that include study abroad components. Researchers investigating intercultural teaching in primary and secondary school contexts (e.g., Despoteris & Anada 2018; Morgan & Cain 2000) have shown that dynamic-process-oriented assessment on intercultural learning can take place in schools. However, the studies also showed that not all elements of intercultural competence could be addressed, as most investigations focused more on the intercultural competence components in Byram's (1997) framework and less on the L2. On the other side of the coin, we have studies on interlanguage pragmatics that try to address a range of language and culture related areas predominantly in the higher education context (e.g., Barron 2003, Schauer 2009), but do not tend to discuss Byram's intercultural competence skills in great detail.

The only comprehensive intercultural study that covered a wide range of language and non-language related intercultural competence components was the *Ealing Project* (Roberts et al., 2001) which consisted of a minimum of two ethnographic projects, the necessity to engage with members of the target culture during study abroad, and detailed written reports. However, this approach necessitated a special degree program structure and involved dynamic process-oriented assessment over the period of more than two years and was conducted with high proficiency L2 learners.

Individuals tasked with assessing L2 learners' intercultural competence should carefully consider what aspects of intercultural competence can feasibly be focused on in their context. This is in-line with Deardorff's (2009) view that "since assessing the whole of intercultural competence can be a daunting task, it is recommended to prioritize specific aspects of [it]" (p. 481).

However, from an SLA perspective, it is essential that if FL teachers assess intercultural competence, the assessment should not only involve Byram's (2009) intercultural competence components, nor should it only focus on pragmatic competence. Instead, those tasked with assessing intercultural competence in FL education contexts should attempt to combine aspects of both. The Ealing Project is probably the gold standard in intercultural training and assessment. However, it is also very likely to be completely unfeasible for most teaching contexts. Fantini (2009) argued for "combinations of assessment types, formats, and strategies [...] [which] coupled with processes that [...] include the learner in the evaluative process (through self-evaluation, reflection, and feedback), result in better and more varied indicators of progress and of attainment of learning objectives"(p. 464). He suggested assessment techniques such as group discussions, presentations, questionnaires, role-plays, field-tasks, as well as activities that could form part of portfolios for measuring intercultural competence. Based on the review of the literature in the field, the important points to consider with regard to the assessment techniques are (a) that they are age and proficiency-level appropriate, (b) that a process approach is chosen that gives L2 learners the opportunity for personal development, (c) that, if possible, the assessment should be dynamic and involve a range of assessment formats.

The final point relates to whether classroom-based intercultural teaching and testing can provide insights into L2 learners' ability to interact effectively and appropriately with members of the target culture, or indeed with other L2 speakers of the target language. This is an essential point, as intercultural training would not fulfil its aims if individuals were not able to communicate with representatives of other cultures after training. One way of addressing this issue is to try and ensure that intercultural training includes an interactive component with members of the other culture. This could mean school partnership programs that involve the exchange of written correspondence, interactions via internet communication programs and social media, and work on joint tasks. In higher education, it could mean collaborative tasks involving students from different institutions, or again study abroad sojourns for which tasks and/or subsequent reflective reports need to be completed by the L2 learners (e.g., Winke & Teng, 2010).

Assessing intercultural competence is a complex and time-consuming endeavor. However, engaging with intercultural issues can also be a very rewarding experience, not just for L2 learners, but also for educators. Acquiring intercultural skills, such as discovery and interpretation, can lead to personal growth and equip learners with the means to better understand and interact with others in their current and future life-contexts. Knowing how to communicate appropriately and effectively in a foreign language and being sensitive to the communication and decision-making styles of individuals from other cultures can only be to everyone's advantage.

Testing Tips

- ***Use composite scores.*** Researchers intending to assess intercultural competence ought to do so through a composite score of multiple and diverse tasks (e.g., role-plays, presentations, questionnaires, participation in tasks, interactions in group discussion).
- ***Include interactive tasks with individuals from other cultures.*** To obtain better insights into an individual's intercultural awareness and sensitivity, real life situations involving encounters with individuals from different cultures should be included. By experiencing authentic intercultural encounters individuals will be able to put their theoretical knowledge into practice. These experiences can highlight areas that individuals can already do well and thus result in increased confidence in intercultural encounters and can also pinpoint areas in which individuals need to obtain more knowledge or adjust their views to improve their IC. Thus, the *washback* of this type of assessment has multiple benefits.
- ***Be aware of limitations.*** Researchers ought to be aware that any assessment of intercultural competence is an estimate only because IC is a highly *latent trait*, i.e., it is something that cannot be directly observed. Consequently, intercultural competence cannot be assessed *comprehensively*. Any assessment of an individual's IC can only provide a glimpse or rough estimate of aspects of L2 learners' intercultural competence. It is essential that researchers acknowledge and accept that. This also means that no high-stakes or even low-stakes decisions about students based on their intercultural competence scores or estimates can or should be made.

Recommended Readings

Deardorff, D. K. (Eds.). (2009). *The Sage handbook of intercultural competence*. SAGE Publications.

This book includes a number of very different perspectives on intercultural competence and contains chapters by a range of well-known scholars in intercultural competence representing different disciplines and approaches.

Spencer-Oatey, H. and P. Franklin (2009). *Intercultural interaction: A multidisciplinary approach to intercultural communication*. Palgrave.

This book provides an overview of different conceptualizations of intercultural interactions and reviews intercultural competence assessment instruments that are used in non-language focused disciplines.

Wagner, M., Perugini, D. C., & Byram, M. (Eds.). (2018). *Teaching intercultural competence across the age range: From theory to practice*. Multilingual Matters.

This book contains several classroom studies on IC that range from primary to higher education contexts.

References

Bachman, L. F. (1990). *Fundamental considerations in language testing*. Oxford University Press.

Bachman, L. F., & Palmer, A. S. (1982). The construct validation of some components of communicative proficiency. *TESOL Quarterly*, *16*(4). 449–465. https://doi.org/10.2307/3586464

Bachman, L. F., & Palmer, A. S. (2010). *Language assessment in practice: Developing language assessments and justifying their use in the real world*. Oxford University Press.

Barron, A. (2003). *Acquisition in interlanguage pragmatics: Learning how to do things with words in a study abroad context*. John Benjamins.

Bashford, C. (2007). *The pursuit of high culture*. Boydell.

Byram, M. (1997). *Teaching and assessing intercultural communicative competence*. Multilingual Matters.

Byram, M. (2009). Intercultural speaker and the pedagogy of foreign language education. In D. Deardorff (Ed.), *The SAGE handbook of intercultural competence* (pp. 321–332). SAGE Publications.

Canale, M., & Swain, M. (1980). Theoretical bases of communicative approaches to second language teaching and testing. *Applied Linguistics*, *1*(1), 1–47. https://doi.org/10.1093/applin/I.1.1

Celce-Murcia, M., Dörnyei, Z., & Thurrell, S. (1995). Communicative competence: A pedagogically motivated model with content specifications. *Issues in Applied Linguistics*, *6*(2), 5–35. https://escholarship.org/uc/item/2928w4zj

Deardorff, D. K. (2006). Identification and assessment of intercultural competence as a student outcome of internationalization. *Journal of Studies in International Education*, *10*(3), 241–266. https://doi.org/10.1177/1028315306287002

Deardorff, D. K. (2009). Implementing intercultural competence assessment. In D. K. Deardorff (Ed.), *The Sage handbook of intercultural competence* (pp. 477–491). SAGE Publications.

Despoteris, J., & Ananda, K. (2018). Intercultural competence: Reflecting on daily routines. In M. Wagner, D. C. Perugini, & M. Byram (Eds.), *Teaching intercultural competence across the age range: From theory to practice* (pp. 80–93). Multilingual Matters.

Fantini, A. E. (2009). Assessing intercultural competence: Issues and tools. In D. K. Deardorff (Ed.), *The Sage handbook of intercultural competence* (pp. 456–476). SAGE Publications.

Fantini, A. E. (2019). *Intercultural communicative competence in educational exchange: A multinational perspective*. Routledge.

Glisan, E. W., Uribe, D., & Adair-Hauck, B. (2007). Research on integrated performance assessment at the post-secondary level: Student performance across the modes of communication. *Canadian Modern Language Review*, *64*(1), 39–67. https://doi.org/10.3138/cmlr.64.1.039

Gudykunst, W. B. (1998). Applying anxiety/uncertainty management (AUM) theory to intercultural adjustment training. *International Journal of Intercultural Relations*, *22*(2), 227–250. https://doi.org/10.1016/S0147-1767(98)00005-4

Gudykunst, W. B., & Kim, Y. Y. (2003). *Communicating with strangers: An approach to intercultural communication*. McGraw-Hill.

Huber, J., & Reynolds, C. (2014). *Developing intercultural competence through education*. Council of Europe.

Liddicoat, A. J., & Scarino, A. (2010). Eliciting the intercultural in foreign language education at school. In A. Paran & L. Sercu (Eds.), *Testing the untestable in language education* (pp. 52–76). Multilingual Matters.

Liddicoat, A. J., & Scarino, A. (2013). *Intercultural language teaching and learning*. Wiley-Blackwell.

McConachy, T. (2018). *Developing intercultural perspectives on language use*. Multilingual Matters.

Morgan, C., & Cain, A. (2000). *Foreign language and culture learning from a dialogic perspective*. Multilingual Matters.

Oakley, C. (2003). Landeskunde? Area studies? Landeswissenschaft. In M. Legutke & M. Schocker-von Ditfurth (Eds.), *Kommunikativer Fremdsprachenunterricht: Rückblick nach vorn* (pp. 267–274). Narr.

Paran, A., & Sercu, L. (Eds.). (2010). *Testing the untestable in language education*. Multilingual Matters.

Roberts, C., Byram, M., Barro, A., Jordan, S., & Street, B. (2001). *Language learners as ethnographers*. Multilingual Matters.

Ryan, P., & Sercu, L. (2005). Familiarity and contacts with foreign cultures. In L. Sercu (Ed.), *Foreign language teachers and intercultural competence* (pp. 39–49). Multilingual Matters.

Savignon, S. J. (1976). *Communicative competence: Theory and classroom practice*. https://files.eric.ed.gov/fulltext/ED135245.pdf

Schauer, G. A. (2009). *Interlanguage pragmatic development: The study abroad context*. Continuum/Bloomsbury.

Scott, A. (2017). *One kiss or two? The art and science of saying hello*. Duckworth.

Sercu, L. (2000). *Acquiring intercultural communicative competence from textbooks: The case of Flemish adolescent pupils learning German*. Leuven University Press.

Sercu, L. (2010). Assessing intercultural competence: More questions than answers. In A. Paran & L. Sercu (Eds.), *Testing the untestable in language education* (pp. 17–34). Multilingual Matters.

Spitzberg, B. H., & Chignon, G. (2009). Conceptualizing intercultural competence. In D. Deardorff (Ed.), *The Sage handbook of intercultural competence* (pp. 2–52). SAGE Publications.

UNESCO. (2013). *Intercultural competence: Conceptional and operational framework*. UNESCO. https://en.unesco.org/interculturaldialogue/resources/132

Wagner, M., Perugini, D. C., & Byram, M. (Eds.). (2018). *Teaching intercultural competence across the age range: From theory to practice*. Multilingual Matters.

Winke, P., & Teng, C. (2010). Using task-based pragmatics tutorials while studying abroad in China. *Intercultural Pragmatics*, *7*(2), 363–399. https://doi.org/10.1515/iprg.2010.016

Wolf, F., & Borzikowsky, C. (2018). Intercultural competence by international experiences? An investigation of the impact of educational stays abroad on intercultural competence and its facets. *Journal of Cross-Cultural Psychology*, *49*(3), 488–514. https://doi.org/10.1177/0022022118754721

35

Assessing and Evaluating Language Learning Beyond the Classroom

Hayo Reinders & Kathleen M. Bailey

Background

By definition, learning beyond the classroom (LBC) takes place in settings other than a traditional classroom and involves less-direct teaching. Interest in LBC dates back to the late 1970s with the development of theories of learner autonomy (Holec, 1981; Tassinari, 2010; see also Tassinari, 2016, in the recommended readings at the end of this chapter) and self-directed learning (Knowles, 1975; Sheerin, 1997), which value and investigate the learner as an active, self-determinant agent in the learning process. Developments in technology have had an important impetus on research in LBC as more opportunities have become available to learners to locate their own resources (materials, peers, native speakers), either to replace or to complement classroom learning. Reinders and Benson (2017, drawing on Benson 2011) clarified some of the distinctions in LBC by proposing four dimensions or continua, along which it can vary (see Table 35.1).

The first, *location*, relates to the physical or virtual space in which learning takes place. Traditionally, learning is viewed as occurring within the four walls of the language classroom, although correspondence education has been available for at least 300 years. The advent of technology has released the classroom from its physical restraints, with both blended (i.e., partly face-to-face and partly online) and fully online forms of distance learning becoming possible. However, many other locations are available, from the home, to the community, to study abroad, as well as intermediate spaces such as self-access or independent learning centres.

The second dimension is the degree of *formality* involved in the learning, or the degree to which learning is linked to formal qualifications. Naturalistic learning involves, in its extreme form, no formal education at all (although in practice many learners do participate in some formal learning as well).

The third dimension is *pedagogy*, or the degree to which teaching is involved. Language advising sessions exemplify learning in which no subject matter is taught (learners are supported in directing their own learning), but which are usually offered in formal contexts within schools or universities.

Finally, *control* refers to who makes decisions about the learning. A self-directed learner may study from a book that simply replaces the teacher's voice and provides all instruction, structure, and feedback to be found in a regular classroom.

Table 35.1 Key dimensions and terms

Dimensions of LBC	*Terms*
Location: Where and when learning takes place	*Out of class, after-class, extra curricular, self-access, out-of-school, distance*
Formality: The degree to which learning is linked to educational qualifications or structured by educational instutitions	*Informal, non-formal, naturalistic*
Pedagogy: The degree to which teaching is involved	*Non-instructed, self-instructed*
Control: How decisions are distributed between the learner and others	*Autonomous, independent, self-regulated*

Source: Reinders & Benson, 2017

These four dimensions interrelate to create a unique tapestry of possible learning configurations, each of which benefits from its own form of observation and measurement. For example, a MOOC (massive online open course) environment offers a virtual space that may be formal, non-formal, or something in between, that involves both direct teaching and self-directed learning, and in which decisions relating to content and structure are usually made by the instructor(s) (Jitpaisarnwattana & Reinders, 2018). In this case, language learning outcomes are not the only interesting aspect of the learning process; so is the learners' ability to manage their own learning, create (virtual) collaborations with other learners, and self-motivate. Clearly, a range of approaches and instruments would be beneficial in a situation like this, the combination of which is likely to differ from assessment in a classroom-based course.

The terminology covered by LBC is broad and each term has its own history. A full description of this vocabulary is beyond the scope of this chapter (but see Benson, 2011). However, the terms share some characteristics that are relevant in a discussion of measurement and evaluation. In short, the last few decades (from the 1970s onwards) have seen a development towards greater learner-centredness, greater understanding of the socio-cultural aspects of learning, greater understanding of the L2 *learners* (including the ways in which they shape their own learning), and the learning ecologies available to them. These developments have led to a greater interest in the individual experience of learning and how the learners' opportunities, constraints, aspirations and beliefs shape the *what*, the *how*, and the *why* of learning.

Research areas such as "L2 identity" (Ushioda & Dörnyei, 2009), "learners' stories" (Benson & Nunan, 2004), and "the psychology of the language learner" (Dörnyei & Ryan, 2015) are some examples of emerging fields, which place great importance on the *whole* learner as a person, not just the role someone plays inside the classroom.

All of these developments have implications for measurement and evaluation of individual learners' progress. If individual learners are the primary focus of applied linguists' interest, then shouldn't those learners play active roles in the evaluation, as it is only the learners who know what was aimed for, and thus what was achieved? And if educators value the learners, then shouldn't educators attempt to document all aspects of those learners' lives that impinge upon their learning?

Key Concepts

***Learning beyond the classroom (LBC)*:** A catch-all term describing different types of learning that are less formal and more learner-directed than most forms of teacher-guided instruction.

Learner autonomy: The capacity for language learners to act as independent learners, think critically about language and learning outcomes, take responsibility for their language growth, and evaluate their own progress.
Self-directed learning: A humanistic method of learning where language learners develop the skills to make their own decisions about how to accomplish their learning goals.

Key Issues

As the title of this chapter suggests, we are considering how LBC can be *assessed* and *evaluated*. These two terms, as well as *assessment* and *testing*, demand some scrutiny in this context, even though they are widely used.

Historically, in educational research, *measurement* has referred to quantifying a skillset or knowledge base, often through the use of tests. That is, a numerical value from a known scale is assigned to a performance. Tests have been described as comprising stimulus materials, (mental) tasks posed to the learners, the learners' (physical) response, and scoring criteria (Wesche, 1983). Tests are normally done to someone (learners) by someone else (teachers or programme administrator) or by some group in power (testing agencies, ministries of education, state or provincial governments). In LBC situations, however, unless people are referring to course-based homework or distance courses, there may be no tests involved, and indeed, no need for tests to be involved. Thus *measurement* in its traditional meaning may not be relevant to this discussion.

However, the concepts of assessment and evaluation may be relevant to LBC contexts:

> [Assessment] refers to a variety of ways of collecting information on a language learner's ability or achievement. Although testing and assessment are often used interchangeably, the latter is an umbrella term encompassing measurement instruments administered on a one-off basis such as tests, as well as qualitative methods of monitoring and recording student learning, such as observation, simulations, and project work.
>
> (Brindley, 2001, p. 137)

That is, assessment can include testing but it can also involve more qualitative approaches to evaluation, as in peer-assessment and self-assessment (see Cox & Dewey, Chapter 36, this volume).

Assessment is distinguished from evaluation in this context, which is concerned with "the overall language programme, not just with what individual students have learnt" (Brindley, 2001, p. 137). Genesee (2001) adds that evaluation in TESOL "is a process of collecting, analyzing, and interpreting information about teaching and learning in order to make informed decisions that enhance student achievement and the success of educational programmes" (2001, p. 144). *Evaluation* typically refers to assigning a value to the performance of a skill set or to evidence of a knowledge base. A contrast is often made between *formative evaluation* (while learning or a project is ongoing) and *summative evaluation* (at the end of a project or a period of learning).

Thus, with its focus on programmes (rather than individuals), *evaluation* in its broad meaning may or may not be relevant to discussions of LBC, unless LBC is done as a component of a language programme. For example, an English as a Foreign Language (EFL) programme in Hong Kong requires students to attend the university's self-access centre for an hour per week. The resources there range from traditional grammar and vocabulary exercises to listening materials and small rooms for viewing films. So, unless the students have been given specific tutorial recommendations by their teacher, they may pursue whatever English activities interest them in the self-access centre. Their work there is documented in terms of participation, but it is not formally evaluated.

In a related discussion, Everhard (2018) noted that "the complexities of the relationship between assessment and autonomy in language learning, instead of being addressed, seem to have been quite consistently avoided in the autonomy literature, making research in this area a difficult and often perplexing undertaking" (p. 6). While we are discussing the measurement of learning here, rather than the measurement of autonomy, it seems that Everhard's statement applies very well to the measurement of LBC.

There has been some discussion of learner-directed assessment (e.g., Ekbatani & Pierson, 2000), but it has not focused on assessing LBC. For example, Bachman (2000) noted that there is a need for "appropriate assessment procedures in which learners are not only test-takers but also active participants in the assessment process" (p. ix).

Recommendations for Practice

Unlike classroom practice, LBC is opaque in terms of the types of activities in which L2 learners engage. Most learners do not record what they do beyond the classroom, unless instructed by their teachers (e.g., with diaries, see Sundqvist, 2011; with dialogue journals, see Chiesa & Bailey, 2015; Chiesa, Damerow, & Bailey, 2013). In addition, few learners know how to benefit from any reflection they might produce (e.g., in the form of diaries). The development of learner autonomy is, for example, a key focus in language advising sessions and self-access support (see Reinders, 2012). In other words, the aim is to help language learners become more aware and critical. A true reflection of progress in these areas would therefore have to be demonstrated explicitly, and in these terms, by the language learner. The first decision to be made then is what to measure and evaluate. This choice will determine what data are gathered.

A number of tools are available to language learners, teachers, and researchers for capturing LBC. Some of these have been around for a long time and are at least somewhat familiar to practitioners (such as learning diaries). Others are more recent and may be less familiar, such as narrative descriptions of personal learning histories. Yet others are more experimental in that they rely on technological advances and prompt a rethinking of how learning processes can be captured, such as educational data mining. We first describe the available instruments and tools, before considering how the data they generate might be interpreted, either by teachers/researchers or by learners themselves.

Observations can be useful in supporting LBC. The term *observation* here refers to both the process of watching and listening to learners as well as the resulting records of such efforts. These include observations of classroom learning involving skills for LBC (e.g., strategy development and use) and of classroom-directed learning beyond the classroom (e.g., homework, projects). In terms of the former, the website of the Research Institute for Learner Autonomy Education (RILAE, n.d.), located at Kanda University in Tokyo, provides access to a collection of instruments for determining learning strategy use, learning styles, culture learning strategies, and so on. Homework activities can be documented in a learning log (a list of what was done) kept by the learners themselves or by parents of young learners (for a comprehensive list of instruments, visit https://kuis.kandagaigo.ac.jp/rilae/instruments/).

In discussing LBC, it is important to remember that many environments for such learning are available within formal settings. Study groups, writing centres, language advising sessions, language cafes, and study abroad are some examples. Perhaps the most common is the self-access centre, provided to facilitate and support increasingly learner-directed learning by providing learning materials (activities such as movie clubs and discussion groups), as well as the necessary guidance. Self-access centres function as bridges between learning within and beyond the classroom. Learning in such spaces is sometimes recorded electronically (Reinders, 2006) and tools are made available for learners to plan, document, and reflect on their learning, with learning plans, learning records, portfolios and various self- and peer-assessment instruments being the most common. In many countries, use of self-access facilities is mandatory, and students are given credit for having participated in the centre's activities. These records are potentially open to researchers to investigate learning in such spaces.

LBC can also be documented through introspective journals or diaries. Such data include language learners' thoughts and affective responses: "processes that are not otherwise easily accessible or open to investigation and can thus provide useful information to language teachers, learners, and researchers" (Curtis & Bailey, 2009, p. 70). The analysis of such data has been collectively termed *the diary studies*, which are accounts of "second language experience as recorded in a first-person journal" (Curtis & Bailey, 2009, p. 68), and which are analysed qualitatively and/or quantitatively by either the diarist or by another researcher (as in Sundqvist, 2011).

In recent years, some researchers have become interested in capturing students' personal learning histories. For example, Benson and Nunan (2002) included studies of identity, autonomy, motivation, and socio-cultural contexts. These editors also produced a volume of autobiographical and biographical studies, dealing with learner diversity, autonomy, affect and emotion, and distance learning (Benson & Nunan, 2004). Unlike the diary studies, which tend to be both introspective and retrospective, the language learner histories are largely retrospective and cover longer periods of time.

Retrospection about and documentation of one's language learning history can lead to increased self-awareness. For example, in one of the earliest published diary studies, Bailey (1983) documented becoming aware through keeping a journal of her university French class experience that she was very competitive with her classmates, a fact she had been completely unaware of previously.

Researchers have also asked language learners to fill out self-report questionnaires (Pérez-Vidal & Juan-Garau, 2011; Kalaja, Alanen, Palviainen, & Dufva, 2011) or fill out language logs (Martinsen, Baker, Dewey, Brown, & Johnson, 2010) to gather qualitative and quantitative data on the learners' self-regulatory behaviour and the outside-of-class activities that they use to learn language. For example, Pérez-Vidal and Juan-Garau used a self-report questionnaire to monitor outside of class learning in study abroad contexts. They found that when study abroad students involved themselves more in learning outside of class (listening to media, speaking more often with native speakers, etc.), they significantly outperformed their study abroad peers who did not involve themselves in such activities (with gains measured by pre- and post- study abroad speaking tests). Martinsen et al. (2010) had Spanish language learners who were either studying abroad in Spain or participating in a Spanish immersion programme at Brigham Young University fill out a daily chart on 20 different outside-of-class learning activities. For each day, the students recorded the number of minutes that they spent engaged in Spanish in each activity, such as eating breakfast, talking to friends/roommates, watching TV, and doing email (the log is in Appendix B in their paper). The groups differed on their Spanish language use amounts outside of class (abroad students spent more time speaking in Spanish outside of class, while immersion students spent more time speaking Spanish inside of class), but the differences did not align with performance-test differences. Martinsen et al. speculated that the study was too short (the students keep the logs for only one week) to show differences. A promising result of the study was that the abroad students who were participating in a service learning component used Spanish outside of class much more than other groups, which promoted Martinsen et al. to ask for more research on how service learning affects language use and language gains in university-level language programmes.

Another method for documenting learning outside of the classroom was introduced by Freed, Dewey, Segalowitz, and Halter (2004). They introduced a survey called "The Language Contact Profile" to document, among other things, language learners' use of language "in the field" (p. 349). In their 2004 article, they presented two versions of their survey, which are meant to be used as pre- and post-tests. Another version of the survey appeared in Baker-Smemoe, Cundick, Evans, Henrichsen, and Dewey's (2012) research on the relationship between reported out-of-class English language use and English proficiency gains. Dewey (2017) reviewed a number of studies that have used "The Language Contact Profile," which he called the LCP, and discussed that while the LCP has been useful, "language logs and social network surveys have gone beyond the LCP and provided valuable additional insights into how learners report spending their time and who they spend that time" with (p. 56). Indeed, newer research has shown that measures of personality, social networks (size, dispersion, density, etc.), and intercultural sensitivity (measured by the Intercultural Development Inventory developed by Hammer, Bennett, & Wiseman, 2003) can predict who, during study abroad, may be poised to learn more of the language while abroad (see Baker-Smemoe, Dewey, Brown, & Martinsen, 2014). Researchers should avail themselves of this prior work and build upon it.

Additionally, portfolios have been used as learning and assessment tools in language teaching contexts since the early 1990s (see e.g., Hirvela & Pierson, 2000 for an overview). Portfolios are collections of learners' work over time. They are typically used to document progress, for instance, by including multiple subsequent drafts of written projects. Presumably much writing is done outside the environs of the formal classroom setting. Thus, portfolios may be used for assessing LBC. Hirvela and Pierson noted that this view of assessment entails two beliefs: that "learners are capable of meaningfully measuring their own learning, and that a viable form of self-assessment exists, especially in such complex domains as language learning" (p. 105). Indeed, the learners' deep engagement in creating portfolios involves selection and reflection as well as production, which leads to a feeling of ownership, a feeling which "is enhanced by the fact that the portfolio experience is not a brief, one-shot presentation" of the learner's work (Hirvela & Pierson, 2000, p. 109). Compared to assessment via testing, "portfolios represent a fundamentally different approach to language assessment, one which enlarges and reshapes the whole notion of language assessment" (Hirvela & Pierson, 2000, p. 107). Portfolios can be either paper-based or digitally stored. In LBC contexts, language learners' portfolios could include diary entries, photographs of learners' interacting with target language speakers, and recordings of oral interactions.

Another useful tool that can be applied in LBC contexts is the "Europass: The Language Passport," which utilises the Common European Framework of Reference categories as the basis for self-assessment. It can be created on line and is part of a system that includes the learners' curriculum vitae and three other documents produced by authorities (a record of mobility throughout European countries, a diploma supplement for learners who studied in formal higher education contexts, and a certificate supplement, issued to people who completed vocational or other training programmes). The Europass website (https://europa.eu/europass/en) provides many helpful tools, so that most language learners (probably of secondary school ages and above) should be able to use this package of tools independently.

Recent technological developments enable the collection of learning data beyond the classroom. The term *reality mining* describes attempts to capture *everything* related to a particular domain or pursuit (Eagle & Green, 2016). For example, all of a learner's interaction with an online platform can be recorded and analysed, from logins, to time on various tasks, to the number and length of forum posts and so on. Various sensors (such as those built into smartphones) can record additional information (e.g., locations visited and time spoken and in what language) and specialised hardware devices, such as the Kapture (a wristwatch-like device that captures audio continuously, can complement this.

A more established field is that of educational data mining/learning analytics, which is "the measurement, collection, analysis and reporting of data about learners and their contexts, for purposes of understanding and optimising learning and the environments in which it occurs" (Siemens & Gašević, 2012, p. 1). A common form is the analysis of data from learning management systems, although other data sources are being used, such as library usage, attendance records, test scores, biographical data, etc. Learner data can identify individual learners who may struggle (e.g., those who do not log on or complete their work), areas of the curriculum that are problematic (e.g., those that many students cannot complete), or data that reveal differences between groups of learners or between teachers. Learning analytics draw on large datasets to help identify patterns that may otherwise be difficult to observe, and to make predictions about future learning and future cohorts. It can be used to support LBC in two ways: Learning that takes place outside the classroom could be captured (and investigated for its impact on and/or relation to classroom learning), and data can be made available for learners to allow them to inspect and make decisions based on their own learning data (Thomas, Reinders, & Gelan, 2017), thus potentially increasing their agency and their capacity for LBC.

Analysing How

Once a record of LBC exists, it can be analysed for the purposes set in step 1 (see Table 35.1). The quality of LBC can of course only be established in relation to its intended outcomes. For instance, a young learner who is encouraged for the first time to carry out a small-group project in the community as part of a school-based course may be observed for her ability to work collaboratively. University students partaking in a language advising session may be asked to critically reflect on the reasons for her (lack of) progress. Suggestions for measurement and evaluation therefore must be able to accommodate a wide range of different manifestations of LBC.

We therefore propose an array of options based on a framework for LBC developed by Reinders (forthcoming). The framework starts from the viewpoint of a learning ecology, comprised of (overlapping) in-class and beyond-class learning opportunities (see Figure 35.1).

If considering data obtained in a formal classroom setting, iterative four levels or stages of development towards LBC are observed: from initial *encouragement* (usually by a teacher) to considering opportunities beyond the classroom, to active *preparation* (e.g., through strategy instruction), to the provision of *support* during LBC (for example in the form of [online] guidance and feedback), and learning fully beyond the classroom being independently and personally *involved* in one's own learning by engaging in learning tasks (with or without links back to a classroom).

For each of these four dimensions, the distinction between them and how they each foster LBC as discussed above, and how people can gather evidence of learning from them can be considered in terms of the four steps':

Location: In what physical space(s) did learning take place?
Formality: To what extent is the learning linked to qualifications?
Pedagogy: To what extent is instruction involved?
Control: How much choice do the learners exert?

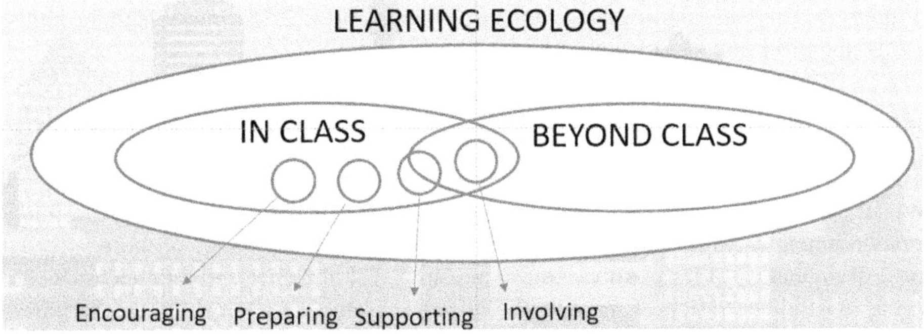

Figure 35.1 Learning ecology.

A graphing of LBC types and their characteristics (the types in Figure 35.1 and in the four characteristics above it) can provide a fine-grained observation on the nature of the learning and its development. A multi-dimensional approach may give useful insights, such as the realisation that learner A, who exclusively and slavishly follows the instructions in her self-study materials, may be less autonomous, and makes fewer individual choices than learner B, who shows evidence of initiative and control within the classroom.

A further layer of analysis to be applied relates to the affordances of LBC. An *affordance* is the "relationship between an organism and a particular feature of its environment" (van Lier, 2000, p. 252). While an affordance allows action, it neither triggers nor causes that action: "What becomes an affordance depends on what the organism does, what it wants, and what is useful for it" (van Lier, 2000, p. 252). Thus, the term refers to *potential* benefits to learning. For example, a laptop may provide a source of authentic listening material for one learner (podcasts or YouTube videos) but an opportunity to play solitaire to another.

An important consideration in evaluating LBC is to determine to what extent a learner has been able to draw on such affordances, such as watching films in the target language, for language learning. Although LBC offers a wide range of possible affordances, a number of them have been identified in the literature as particularly relevant (Reinders, forthcoming).

For instructors an important question is to what extent LBC enables connections to be made to the classroom. Especially with inexperienced learners, or those at the "encouraging," "preparing," or "supporting" stages of their development, such links have been shown to be vital in ensuring long-term success (Gardner, 2006). For example, are learners able to draw on their experiences outside of class to help them be more successful in class? Teachers should note the following:

- In LBC learners tend to interact mainly with their own local environment, but can then bring that back into the classroom or online communities to link to the wider, global environment. The combination of the two can give rise to opportunities to create meaningful connections that can support learning in a wide range of contexts.
- LBC involves more opportunities for bite-sized learning. LBC enables learners to pick up easily where they left off, and to use downtime that would otherwise go unused. These short bursts of learning can then be connected with prior and subsequent learning at a later stage.
- LBC is uniquely personal but also allows social connections to be brought into the learning experiences that are difficult to achieve in a classroom. For instance, in online games, learners can interact with people from many different countries, cultures, and first-language backgrounds.
- Finally, there are pedagogical principles that underpin the provision of opportunities for LBC. A detailed description of these is beyond the scope of this chapter, but in summary, LBC has strong links with the development of learner autonomy because learners have the opportunity to make decisions related to their development of 21st-century learning skills, such as negotiation, collaboration, and leadership.

All of these affordances can be used to evaluate the nature of the ecology (either provided, for example by an instructor, or experienced outside of formal education, as in naturalistic learning), as well as the type and rate of learners' development. Clearly, further detail may need to be added. For example, if the primary interest is in determining learner autonomy, it is not enough to simply ask if the environment provided opportunities and if learners took advantage of these potential affordances. An evaluation of the quality of the nature and level of the learner's autonomy would require further operationalisation of the relevant component elements. Put together, the framework of LBC comprises the above elements, and can be used as a guide towards developing analytical questions regarding LBC.

Testing Tips

Ask learners to record their experiences in language learning diaries. The diary entries provide a form of self-report data in which the language learners comments on their progress. These data are not *measurement* in the strict sense of the term, but can be used for evaluative purposes.

Have learners create a portfolio with samples of their learning beyond the classroom, with the samples demonstrating out-of-class work over time to document progress. The portfolio can include samples of written L2 work and audio recordings of the learner's L2 interaction, as well as testimonials from others about the learner's abilities.

Explore past measures (surveys, questionnaires) and newer ones that have been used to measure learning beyond the classroom, and adopt them and/or adapt them for your uses.

Be creative and innovative, and explore new methods and technologies to document learning beyond the classroom.

Recommended Readings

Benson, P., & Reinders, H. (2011). *Beyond the language classroom*. Palgrave Macmillan.

This edited volume provides an overview of the topic of learning beyond the classroom in a range of different contexts, from early childhood to adult learning. It covers both research and practice-based perspectives.

Everhard, C., & Murphy, L. (2015). *Assessment and autonomy in language learning*. Palgrave Macmillan.

Although specific to the topic of autonomy, many of the ideas discussed in this edited volume are highly relevant to the evaluation and assessment of learning beyond the classroom in general. Several chapters problematise assessment of autonomy and others provide examples of ways in which evaluation, observation, and description of autonomy have been attempted.

Tassinari, M. G. (2016). Assessment for learning; Assessment for autonomy. In A. C. Gitskaki & C. Coombe (Eds.), *Current issues in language evaluation, assessment and testing* (pp. 118–136). Cambridge Scholar Publishing.

This chapter describes integrating assessment of autonomy into classroom teaching practices and illustrates some of the common challenges as well as options available to researchers and practitioners.

References

Bachman, L. R. (2000). Learner-directed assessment in ESL. In G. Ekbatani & H. Pierson (Eds.), *Learner-directed assessment in ESL* (pp. ix–xii). Lawrence Erlbaum Associates.

Baker-Smemoe, W., Cundick, D. K., Evans, N., Henrichsen, L., & Dewey, D. P. (2012). Relationship between reported out-of-class English use and proficiency gains in English. *Applied Language Learning, 22* (1–2), 21–46. https://www.dliflc.edu/wp-content/uploads/2014/04/ALL_v_22.pdf

Baker-Smemoe, W., Dewey, D. P., Brown, J., & Martinsen, R. A. (2014). Variables affecting L2 gains during study abroad. *Foreign Language Annals, 47*(3), 464–486. https://doi.org/10.1111/flan.12093

Benson, P. (2011). *Learner autonomy*. Longman. https://doi.org/10.1002/tesq.134

Benson, P., & Nunan, D. (2002). *The experience of language learning*. The English Centre, University of Hong Kong.

Benson, P., & Nunan, D. (2004). *Learners' stories: Differences and diversity in language learning*. Cambridge University Press.

Brindley, G. (2001). Assessment. In R. Carter & D. Nunan (Eds.), *The Cambridge guide to teaching English to speakers of other languages* (pp. 137–143). Cambridge University Press.

Chiesa, D., Damerow, R. M., & Bailey, K. M. (2013). The use of dialogue journals with university EFL students: A sociocultural perspective. *The Asian Journal of English Language and Pedagogy, 6*, 1–46.

Chiesa, D. L., & Bailey, K. M. (2015). Dialogue journals: Learning for a lifetime. In D. Nunan & J. C. Richards (Eds.), *Language learning beyond the classroom* (pp. 53–62). Routledge. https://doi.org/10.4324/9781315883472

Curtis, A., & Bailey, K. M. (2009). Diary studies. *On CUE Journal*, *3*(1), 67–85. https://jaltcue.org/files/OnCUE/OCJ3-1articles/OCJ3-1-Curtis-Bailey-pp67-85.pdf

Dewey, D. P. (2017). Measuring social interaction during study abroad: Quantitative methods and challenges. *System*, *71*, 49–59. https://doi.org/10.1016/j.system.2017.09.026

Dörnyei, Z., & Ryan, S. (2015). *The psychology of the language learner revisited.* Routledge. https://doi.org/10.4324/9781315779553

Dörnyei, Z., & Ushioda, E. (Eds.). (2009). *Motivation, language identity and the L2 self* (Vol. 36). Multilingual Matters.

Eagle, N., & Greene, K. (2016). *Reality mining: Using big data to engineer a better world.* MIT Press.

Ekbatani, G., & Pierson, H. (2000). *Learner-directed assessment in ESL.* Lawrence Erlbaum Associates. https://doi.org/10.4324/9781410605283

Europass. (n.d.). *What is the language passport?* https://europass.cedefop.europa.eu/europass-support-centre/language-passport/what-language-passport

Everhard, C. J. (2018). Re-exploring the relationship between autonomy and assessment in language learning: A literature overview. *Relay Journal*, 1(1), 6–20. https://kuis.kandagaigo.ac.jp/relayjournal/issues/jan18/everhard/

Freed, B. F., Dewey, D. P., Segalowitz, N., & Halter, R. (2004). The language contact profile. *Studies in Second Language Acquisition*, *26*, 349–356. https://doi.org/10.1017/S027226310426209X

Gardner, D. (2006). *Learner autonomy 10: Integration and support.* Authentik.

Genesee, F. (2001). Evaluation. In R. Carter & D. Nunan (Eds.), *The Cambridge guide to teaching English to speakers of other languages* (pp. 144–150). Cambridge University Press. https://doi.org/10.1017/CBO9780511667206.022

Hammer, M. R., Bennett, M. J., & Wiseman, R. (2003). Measuring intercultural sensitivity: The intercultural development inventory. *International Journal of Intercultural Relations*, *27*, 421–443. https://doi.org/10.1016/S0147-1767(03)00032-4

Hirvela, A., & Pierson, H. (2000). Portfolios: Vehicles for authentic self-assessment. In G. Ekbatani & H. Pierson (Eds.), *Learner-directed assessment in ESL* (pp. 105–126). Lawrence Erlbaum Associates.

Holec, H. (1981). *Autonomy and foreign language learning.* Pergamon (Original work published 1979).

Jitpaisarnwattana, N., & Reinders, H. (2018). Language MOOCs: What teachers should know. *Modern English Teacher*, *27*(2), 46–49.

Kalaja, P., Alanen, R., Palviainen, Å., & Dufva, H. (2011). From milk cartons to English roommates: Context and agency in L2 learning beyond the classroom. In P. Benson & H. Reinders (Eds.), *Beyond the language classroom* (pp. 47–58). Palgrave Macmillan. https://doi.org/10.1057/9780230306790_5

Knowles, M. S. (1975). *Self-directed learning: A guide for learners and teachers.* Association Press. https://doi.org/10.1177/105960117700200220

Martinsen, R. A., Baker, W., Dewey, D., Brown, J., & Johnson, C. (2010). Exploring diverse settings for language acquisition and use: Comparing study abroad, service learning abroad, and foreign language housing. *Applied Language Learning*, *20*(1–2), 45–66. https://www.dliflc.edu/wp-content/uploads/2014/04/ALL20c.pdf

Pérez-Vidal, C., & Juan-Garau, M. (2011). The effect of context and input conditions on oral and written development: A study abroad perspective. *International Review of Applied Linguistics*, *49*, 157–185. https://doi.org/10.1515/iral.2011.008

Reinders, H. (2006). Supporting self-directed learning through an electronic learning environment. In T. Lamb & H. Reinders (Eds.), *Supporting independent learning: Issues and interventions* (pp. 219–238). Peter Lang. https://doi.org/10.1.1.509.2763

Reinders, H. (2012). Language advising in context: Towards pedagogical and institutional integration. In J. Mynard & L. Carson (Eds.), *Advising in language learning: Dialogue, tools and context* (pp. 170–184). Longman.

Reinders, H., & Benson, P. (2017). Research agenda: Language learning beyond the classroom. *Language Teaching*, *50*(4), 561–578. https://doi.org/10.1017/S0261444817000192

RILAE: Research Institute for Learner Autonomy Education. (n.d.). *Instruments.* https://kuis.kandagaigo.ac.jp/rilae/instruments/

Sheerin, S. (1997). An exploration of the relationship between self-access and independent learning. In P. Benson & P. Voller (Eds.), *Autonomy and independence in language learning* (pp. 54–65). Longman.

Siemens, G., & Gasevic, D. (2012). Guest editorial: Learning and knowledge analytics. *Educational Technology & Society*, *15*(3), 1–2. https://www.j-ets.net/ETS/journals/15_3/1.pdf

Sundqvist, P. (2011). A possible path to progress: Out-of-school English language learners in Sweden. In P. Benson & H. Reinders (Eds.), *Beyond the language classroom* (pp. 106–118). Palgrave Macmillan. https://doi.org/10.1057/9780230306

Tassinari, M. G. (2010). *Autonomes Fremdsprachenlernen: Komponenten, Kompetenzen, Strategien*. Peter Lang.

Tassinari, M. G. (2016). Assessment for learning; Assessment for autonomy. In A. C. Gitskaki & C. Coombe (Eds.), *Current issues in language evaluation, assessment and testing* (pp. 118–136). Cambridge Scholar Publishing.

Thomas, M., Reinders, H., & Gelan, A. (2017). Learning analytics in online language learning: Challenges and future directions. In K. Hyland & L. Wong, L. (Eds.), *Faces of English* (pp. 197–212). Routledge. https://doi.org/10.4324/9781315205618

Ushioda, E., & Dörnyei, Z. (2009). Motivation, language identities and the L2 self: A theoretical overview. In Z. Dörnyei & E. Ushioda (Eds.), *Motivation, language identity and the L2 self* (pp. 1–8). Multilingual Matters. https://doi.org/10.1.1.671.4710

van Lier, L. (2000). From input to affordance: Social-interactive learning from an ecological perspective. In J. P. Lantolf (Ed.), *Sociocultural theory and second language learning* (pp. 245–259). Oxford University Press.

Wesche, M. B. (1983). Communicative testing in a second language. *The Modern Language Journal*, *67*(1), 41–55. https://doi.org/10.2307/326692

36

Measuring Language Development Through Self-Assessment

Troy L. Cox & Dan P. Dewey

Background

Talk to any cyclist or runner, and they can name instances when the universe seems to conspire against them with headwinds that hinder their progress. It is easy to identify and often blame external forces for causing us to fail. Conversely, we often attribute success to our own ability, being blissfully unaware of the tailwinds that assist us. This blindness to headwind/tailwind asymmetry (Davidai & Gilovich, 2016) in viewing one's own performance is not limited solely to endurance athletes but can be found in other areas of self-assessment. Performance rarely occurs in a vacuum. There are typically external forces that nudge people toward success or failure. Novices, unaware of a tailwind, will often overestimate their ability, believing perhaps they are "quick learners" or "naturally talented." Experts, on the other hand, who are accustomed to the winds that have helped and hindered them in the past, are likely to be more accurate in perceiving their ability level, and many even underestimate their level of skill. In this chapter, we review foreign and second language self-assessment and note theories in SLA that support its use. We review recent empirical studies on the use of Can-Do statements in self-assessment, and comment on future self-assessment research and theory.

Key Concepts

Agency: "The view that language learners play an active rather than a passive role in language learning by self-regulation and making choices in their production of target forms" (Gass & Mackey, 2012, p. 590). Learners can formatively and actively make choices to improve their L2 learning through regular self-assessment.

Zone of proximal development (ZPD): "The difference between what an individual or group can accomplish alone versus what they can do with mediation. It is the mechanism of psychological development" (Gass & Mackey, 2012, p. 598). Self-assessment with statements indicating a range of levels of performance (e.g., Can-Dos) can inform learners regarding where they might currently be and where they might progress to with assistance from others.

Ideal L2 self: "The L2-specific facet of one's ideal self, that is, the possible future self one desires to become." (Gass & Mackey, 2012, p. 593). Through self-assessment, a learner can determine gaps between what she is capable of doing and what she desires to be capable of doing in the future.

Key Issues

Self-assessment promotes learner self-awareness, self-regulation, self-efficacy and goal setting (Belgrad, 2013; Schunk & Zimmerman, 2001), which have been shown to be important in SLA research (Ortega, 2014). Learners can exercise agency by actively using self-assessment to monitor their progress, establish goals, and engage in activities that can move them to the next level. Self-assessment can serve as a mediating tool "to plan, carry out, talk through, think through, and evaluate activity" (Donato, 2016, p. 42) both by teachers providing scaffolding and learners working within the zone of proximal development (ZPD) to achieve higher levels of proficiency. By comparing their own self-evaluations with standards depicted in self-assessments, learners might better notice the gaps between their abilities and those standards (Schmidt & Frota, 1986). In short, self-assessment is a valuable tool for the learner from a number of SLA perspectives.

In terms of instruction and evaluation, there are a number of benefits of self-assessment. First, given that items can be easily created and learner-scored, it is a practical measure that gives the learner a voice in assessment processes and eliminates concerns over matters such as test security and cheating (LeBlanc & Painchaud, 1985; Strong-Krause, 2000). Moreover, self-assessment has been commended as being more global in nature because it takes into account overall abilities as students know them rather than being based on a small sample gathered through traditional testing (Upshur, 1975).

Self-assessment has been considered for a variety of purposes, including measurement of second language (L2) proficiency (Blanche, 1990), writing (Liang, 2014; Sullivan & Lindgren, 2002), reading (Brantmeier, 2005), speaking (Babii, Taghaddomi, & Pashmforoosh, 2016; de Saint Léger, 2009), and listening comprehension (Blanche & Merino, 1989; Strong-Krause, 2000). It has been used for achievement and diagnostic testing purposes in L1 and L2 assessment (Alderson, 2005; Iver, 1987; Miraglia, 1995) and relatively extensively for placement purposes in L2 programs (Engelhardt & Pfingsthorn, 2013; LeBlanc & Painchaud, 1985; Strong-Krause, 2000; Summers, Cox, McMurry, & Dewey, 2018).

The term self-assessment is often taken to be self-defining, which may be why few studies researching it attempt to define it. LeBlanc and Painchaud (1985) wrote that self-assessment "is not self-grading" and "is not an informal exercise based loosely on a student's intuition" (p. 674). This highlights that learner and teacher motives, their education regarding what is being assessed, and guidance on interpreting and using rating-scale results are important considerations. Overall, although self-assessment has been used for a variety of purposes, as Andrade and Du (2007) pointed out, it is perhaps best viewed as "a process of formative assessment during which students reflect on and evaluate the quality of their work and their learning, judge the degree to which they reflect explicitly stated goals or criteria, identify strengths and weaknesses in their work, and revise accordingly… Put simply, we see self-assessment as feedback for oneself from oneself" (Andrade & Du, 2007, p. 160; cf. Hattie & Timperley, 2007).

Regarding accurate self-perceptions, it is important to note that the characteristics of individual test-takers must also be considered. The cultural backgrounds of learners can have an influence on how they respond to self-assessments (Coombe, 1992; Strong-Krause, 2000). For example, Strong-Krause (2000) found that in comparison to non-Asian participants, "Japanese and Korean speakers tended to underestimate their language abilities in [listening, speaking and writing]" (p. 60). Promotion of modesty and group accomplishment over individual accomplishment might result in lower estimates of one's own abilities. Proficiency level may also come into play; self-estimates may be more accurate at higher levels (Heilenman, 1990; Ma & Winke, 2019;

Strong-Krause, 2000). The Dunning-Kruger effect (Kruger & Dunning, 1999), seen in studies across numerous fields, is when those less proficient tend to largely over-estimate their own abilities, whereas top performers tend to be more accurate or even underestimate. Relatedly, the more experience learners have with a task, the more likely they are to accurately self-assess those abilities (Ma & Winke, 2019; Ross, 1998).

Our Recent Self-Assessment Studies

Over five years, we have conducted three different studies with five different self-assessment instruments linked to the ACTFL 2012 Can-Do statements that examine self-assessment and how well-calibrated speakers are with their ability in their second language. Table 36.1 details the studies by skill area, native language of participants, the second language they were learning, and the instrument used. For this chapter, we will focus on the creation of the self-assessment instruments and operationalization of the Can-Do statements within those assessments.

When designing our self-assessment instruments, we followed the Wilson (2004) constructing measures model, an iterative process in which a construct with different hypothesized levels of traits were defined. Items were then written based on those levels and assembled into an

Table 36.1 Summary of can-do instrument studies

Study	*Skill Area*	*L1*	*L2*	*Instrument*	*Internal Reliability*	*Correlations with OPIs/Test Scores*
Brown, Dewey, & Cox (2014)	Speaking	English N = 36	Russian	Self-Retrospective (Then-Now) Statements ACFTL 2012 Can-Do Subheadings	*Then Statements* Rasch Person Reliability = .96	*Then Statements* with OPIRho = .27
					Now Statements Rasch Person Reliability = .96	*Now Statements* with OPI Rho = .21
Nielson, Dewey, & Cox (2016)	Speaking	English N = 28	Spanish	ACFTL 2012 Verbatim Can-Do Statements with No Video Exemplars	*No Video* Rasch Person Reliability = .83	*No Video* with OPI Rho = .38
		N = 24		ACFTL 2012 Verbatim Can-Do Statements with Video Exemplars	*Video* Rasch Person Reliability = .91	*Video* with OPIRho = .40
Summers, Cox, McMurry, & Dewey (2018)	Speaking & Writing	Various N = 97	English	Speaking Examples based on ACFTL 2012 Can-Do Statements	*Speaking* Rasch Person Reliability = .91	*Speaking* with Speaking LAT*r* = .44
				Writing Examples based on ACFTL 2012 Can-Do Statements	*Writing* Rasch Person Reliability = .95	*Writing* with Writing LAT*r* = .45

instrument (e.g., survey or test) that was administered to the population of interest. The participant responses were then scored and converted to objective measures using Rasch Item Response Theory (IRT). Since Rasch IRT is both person- and item- independent, items that did not align with the construct provided evidence that either (1) the hypothesized construct needed revision or (2) the item was poorly constructed. Revisions were then made, and the process was repeated. One advantage of using this measurement model is that since the item is analyzed (as opposed to the test), it allows for surveys to be adaptive, i.e., not every item needs to be seen by every respondent. Measurement models that are based on classical test theory are person- and item-dependent and lose some of the flexibility that adaptive testing affords.

A prerequisite to using the Wilson (2004) model is to select a hypothesized unidimensional construct of the trait being measured. For languages, there are a number of scales that could be used as the basis for creating a self-assessment instrument, including the Interagency Language Roundtable (ILR), Common European Framework of Reference (CEFR), the Canadian Language Benchmark (CLB), and the American Council on the Teaching of Foreign Languages (ACTFL) Proficiency Guidelines (2012). CEFR has the European Language Portfolio that has been designed for learners to be engaged in autonomous learning (www.coe.int/en/web/portfolio/aim-of-an-elp)—a framework that has been coupled with DIALANG, an exemplary self-administered diagnostic system including self-assessment: https://dialangweb.lancaster.ac.uk/setals). We chose to use the ACTFL scale as our framework for two reasons: 1) each of the five major levels describes a confluence of Function, Accuracy, Content/context and Text type (e.g., FACTs) expectations; 2) the research was conducted in an American/US setting. When the FACTs are aligned, then language learners can monitor what they can consistently do at one level and note when breakdown occurs at the next level. Sublevels represent individual performance of the major level criteria. The Council of State Supervisors for Languages (NCSSFL-) ACTFL Can-Do statements were written to allow learners to judge their performance against the guidelines. Thus, this criterion-referenced linear scale functions well as a construct upon which to write items.

The Brown, Dewey, and Cox (2014) instrument, the *Self-Retrospective (Then-Now) Statements with ACFTL 2012 Can-Do Subheadings*, was used to measure the self-perceived proficiency development of L1 English students participating in a Russian Study Abroad/Internship experience. The instrument consisted of the 36 subheadings from the ACFTL 2012 Can-Do Statements that spanned Intermediate High (IH) to Distinguished (D), and participants responded to a five-category scale that ranged from 1, "Could not do this even with extensive preparation," to 5, "Could do this without any preparation." Participants were asked to answer all the questions (as opposed to select items in adaptive formats) in a self-retrospective manner by indicating what they could do *prior* to their language learning experience (Then) and what they could do *afterward* (Now).

The Nielson, Dewey, and Cox (2016) instrument used the *ACFTL 2012 Verbatim Can-Do Statements* to measure the L2 Spanish abilities of L1 English students who had recently graduated with a major, minor, or certificate in Spanish. This instrument consisted of 21 items with three items at each sublevel ranging from Intermediate Low (IL) to Superior (S). The selected subheadings were similar to the Brown et al. (2014) instrument, but expanded to include examples. For instance, with the Intermediate High subheading above on exchanging information related to mutual interest, an additional five examples were listed including *I can ask for and provide information about a hobby or lifestyle such as bicycling, vegetarianism, video games and sports*; *I can ask for and provide descriptions of places I know and also places I would like to visit*; and *I can talk about my family history*. Thus, there were more detailed examples to which the speaker could reference. This instrument also used a five-category scale, but the statements ranged from 1, "Not at all," to 5, "Quite easily." The statements were administered adaptively in that learners would only see higher pro ficiency statements if they felt they could easily accomplish the lower proficiency statements. There were two versions of this instrument. One consisted solely of the statements with the examples as described thus far. The other included video examples of Spanish speakers who were rated at the different sublevels and were performing tasks aligning with their assessed levels. Thus, with the above example of Intermediate High, there would be a short 45-second clip of a speaker giving a fluent, detailed description or narration of an area of interest that was paragraph length, but which had issues with accuracy that hindered full comprehension, a profile quite typical of that level.

The Summers et al. (2018) instruments, *Speaking and Writing Examples based on ACFTL 2012 Can-Do Statements*, were used to measure the English of students from a variety of language backgrounds (e.g., Spanish, Chinese, Portuguese, etc.). With this 45-item instrument, five topics were introduced (e.g., family, work, education, technology, and food), and then statements were developed that addressed those topics along the continuum of the proficiency scale. For example, for the topic of family, there were nine statements that spanned from Novice Mid: *I can name the members of my family*; to Superior: *I can debate the position of government-sponsored daycare programs in a public forum such as a Parent-Teacher Association meeting*. The intent of keeping the topic constant was to measure how functional ability changed across the different proficiency levels without the influence of topic knowledge. Thus, the students saw a group of statements that increased in difficulty and were presented with either lower level statements (Novice Mid to Intermediate Mid) or higher-level statements (Intermediate High to Superior). This instrument also used a five-category scale; and, the statements ranged from 1, "Strongly Disagree," to 5, "Strongly Agree." The statements were administered adaptively in that learners would only see higher proficiency statement groups if they felt they could easily accomplish the lower proficiency statement group. The respondents answered three of the topic areas before ending.

All five instruments linked to the Can-Do statements were highly reliable (see Table 36.1). Therefore, the L2 learners were stable in their level of self-assessment. Furthermore, perceived difficulty of the tasks aligned with the hypothesized difficulty based on the ACTFL Guidelines. Thus, L2 learners were more likely to feel confident in performing statements that aligned with the lower levels (e.g., greetings, responding to simple questions, etc.) than they were statements aligned at the higher levels (e.g., discussing an abstract topic), and this alignment was higher the more detailed the items were.

The five-point rating scales of these different instruments functioned well. The use of scales in society is pervasive (e.g., reviews of movies, hotels, and sellers), and it is important to analyze how well the scale functions as designed. That is, the categories must be mutually exclusive and easy enough that raters can distinguish between different levels of performance. For instance, a movie review rating scale with many categories, such as Rotten Tomatoes (https://www.rottentomatoes.com/) that presents ratings on a scale of 1 to 100 allows fine nuance in awarding a rating, but it might be difficult to articulate the difference between close ratings such as 14 and 18. The difference between an 85 and a 30, however, would be easier to understand. Dichotomous scales such as thumbs up or thumbs down, are easy for raters to use and for consumers to understand, but such scales force raters to combine truly outstanding movies with simply good movies, and mediocre movies with truly terrible ones. Thus, rating scale diagnostics allow test designers to investigate how well the raters can use the scale that has been provided and what, if any, improvements to the scale can be made. When determining the optimum number of categories, it is good practice to remember that categories can be collapsed if necessary, but if too few options are presented, it is impossible to divide them after the fact. In all three instruments, the least-selected categories were 1 and 2 confirming Heilenman's (1990) caution that respondents tend to overestimate their ability.

However, despite being reliable, having alignment between the proficiency guidelines and empirical item statistics and having the categories function well, there is still not enough evidence to show that the self-assessments have predictive validity on a speaker's language ability.

The correlations ranged from .21 to .45, indicating that only 4% to 20% of the variance in proficiency can be determined through self-assessment. The correlations were higher when the instruments contained more detailed descriptions of what the learners were self-assessing. If learners explicitly learn how to use the Can-Do statements with opportunities to receive calibration feedback, it is likely the alignment between their self-assessment and actual ability would increase. Furthermore, just using the more detailed descriptors in a Can-Do instrument can provide valuable information regarding L2 learners' perceptions of their ability, and these perceptions could be used in low stakes assessment situations such as placement and selection of leveled test forms (see Ma & Winke, 2019).

Finally, our studies confirmed the findings of Tigchelaar et al. (2017) that many of the ACTFL 2012 Can-Do statements did not align with their intended difficulties, especially when statements were written for a sublevel. The major levels have unique criteria: If the FACTs are aligned, then there is evidence of success or failure. The sublevels describe performance of the major level criteria, and thus it is more difficult for item writers to create items. In 2017, ACTFL published revised Can-Do guidelines, so perhaps the difficulties in item alignment with the construct will be lessened.

Recommendations for Practice

Whether using self-assessment for formative, placement, achievement, or other purposes, a number of research-based guidelines for practice ought to be followed. First, use and interpretation of any self-assessment and results ought to be based on the intended purposes (Oscarson, 1997). For example, learners who are informed that their self-assessment results will be used for grading purposes are likely to inflate their results, whereas students knowing their results will be used for placement may underestimate their results if they don't desire to be in an overly challenging class or overestimate their results if they desire to be in a higher level. "In the final analysis, the measurement used to ascertain second language competency depends on the purpose to which it will be put as well as the effect it has on teaching and learning" (Heilenman, 1990, p. 190). If used well, Heilenman suggested, self-assessment has the ability to put the learner "firmly in the centre of the picture" (p. 194).

Regarding the design of self-assessments, developers should note several important points. First, learners are more aware of areas of difficulty than of areas of ease (Bachman & Palmer, 1989); therefore, scales utilizing difficulty level may be more appropriate than those utilizing confidence levels or scales based on capacity (I can, I cannot, etc.). Some suggested self-assessments be administered in the subjects' native languages (e.g., Oscarson, 1997), but researchers (e.g., Roever & Powers, 2005) found no response difference between the L2 and L1, with the caveat that the learners in the study had higher proficiency. Generally, specific and focused tasks providing sufficient detail for learners to envision a scenario are better than shorter, vague or overly abstract statements (Pierce, Swain, & Hart, 1993; Strong-Krause, 2000; Tigchelaar, Bowles, Winke, & Gass, 2017). As is common in survey research, "negatively-worded questions should be used with great care if at all" (Heilenman, 1990, p. 193). Heilenman also noted that "in general, making criteria known and giving learners access to records (i.e., video tapes) of their performance will improve accuracy of self-assessment" (p. 195). Similarly, Strong-Krause (2000) suggested having learners listen to audio recordings requiring the levels of comprehension being assessed and using samples demonstrative of levels being described in other modes as well (see Luoma & Tarnane, 2003 for an example involving L2 writing). Regarding the scale used, Heilenman (1990) indicated it might be good to compress ratings at the higher end (i.e., have more ratings at the positive end) in order to compensate for learners' tendencies to overestimate. This would be most relevant for lower-level learners. Finally, accuracy may vary depending on the skill being assessed. For example, Strong-Krause (2000) noted, "Self-ratings for reading comprehension should probably be avoided. … students have difficulty assessing their comprehension of what they read" (p. 60).

This gives rise to a design recommendation: create items that are closely related to learners' actual experiences, situations they would encounter as users of the language (Heilenman, 1990; Oscarson, 2013; Tigchelaar et al., 2017). Students' frames of reference are typically limited to their own classroom experiences, whereas test constructors often create items that would require in-country immersion experiences to understand and manage (Heilenman, 1990). Relatedly, even prior to an in-country experience, learners are more likely to give higher estimates of their abilities to accomplish higher-level tasks; immediately after such an experience, the ratings will be more modest and accurate, since learners have attempted and struggled with many more of the scenarios they are rating. For this reason, we have recommended retrospective ratings of what one could do at the beginning (Then) and what they could do at the end (Now) to more accurately capture gains during study abroad than a traditional pre-post design (Brown, Dewey, & Cox, 2014). Finally, it is important to note that the more learners practice self-assessment, the more accurate they will be.

As mentioned earlier, self-assessment rarely occurs devoid of external headwinds and tailwinds, making it important to carefully consider when it is appropriate to use them. As many SLA journals have mandated proficiency be reported by means other than class-level, self-assessment could be used to identify outliers or in conjunction with other measures to triangulate proficiency, and could be especially valuable when linked to an external scale such as ACTFL or CEFR. Noticing when the winds are present, however, is a beneficial skill in and of itself. Detecting the tailwind can keep the athlete humble and make them push themselves to exceed the aid the wind is providing. Recognizing the headwinds can make the athlete work harder, knowing that gains more likely occur when resistance is present. Either way, if the language learner is attuned to the winds, they can use the feedback to make improvements.

Testing Tips

- Self-assessments should NOT be used as the sole proxy for language proficiency in SLA studies.
- Self-assessments should be used when SLA researchers are interested in someone's perception of their ability or when they need low-stakes proficiency information.
- Self-assessment items should describe tasks learners have experience attempting.
- Use difficulty levels rather than confidence levels for scales to increase accuracy.
- Train learners to use the instrument and give calibrative feedback to improve accuracy (see the online DIALANG system for an example of how this might be done automatically: https://dialangweb.lancaster.ac.uk/setals).
- To produce more reliable results, include sufficient items using Can-Do statements spanning a range of difficulties.
- When determining how many categories to use in a self-assessment rating scale, it is safer to include more categories than fewer.
- When deciding to administer self-assessments, remember that timing and experience can affect learners' interpretations and ratings—the closer to one's actual attempt, the more accurate the rating is likely to be.
- Have learners view their attempts at tasks and listen to or view their own performance and justify ratings to increase accuracy. Observing others attempt tasks can also help.
- As with any measurement instrument, use statistics (test, item, factor analysis, reliability, etc.) to verify the instrument is functioning as intended and make revisions as necessary.

Recommended Readings

ACTFL. (2017). 2017 *NCSSFL-ACTFL can-do statements*. http://www.actfl.org/global_statements

This site contains an overview of how the Can-Do statements align with the proficiency guidelines and gives examples of tasks in which there is alignment of function, accuracy, content/context, and text type.

Brown, N. A., Dewey, D. P., & Cox, T. L. (2014). Assessing the validity of can-do statements in retrospective (then-now) self-assessment. *Foreign Language Annals*, *47*(2), 261–285. https://doi.org/10.1111/flan.12082

This article provides a summary of the relationship between time of self-assessment and illustrates potential difficulties in using statements that are not detailed enough. It also shows a way in which a Rasch analysis can be conducted.

Summers, M., Cox, T. L., McMurry, B. L., & Dewey, D. P. (2019). Investigating the use of the ACTFL Can-Do Statements in a self-assessment for student placement in an intensive English program. *System*, *80*, 269–287. https://doi.org/10.1016/j.system.2018.12.012

This article provides an illustration in which statements at different levels are seen concurrently and can act as anchors as people rate their own abilities.

References

ACTFL. (2012). *ACTFL proficiency guidelines 2012*. https://www.actfl.org/publications/guidelines-and-manuals/actfl-proficiency-guidelines-2012

Alderson, J. C. (2005). *Diagnosing foreign language proficiency: The interface between learning and assessment*. Bloomsbury. https://doi.org/10.5040/9781474212151

Andrade, H., & Du, Y. (2007). Student responses to criteria-referenced self-assessment. *Assessment and Evaluation in Higher Education*, *32*(2), 159–181. https://doi.org/10.1080/02602930600801928

Babaii, E., Taghaddomi, S., & Pashmforoosh, R. (2016). Speaking self-assessment: Mismatches between learners' and teachers' criteria. *Language Testing*, *33*(3), 411–437. https://doi.org/10.1177/0265532215590847

Bachman, L. F., & Palmer, A. S. (1989). The construct validation of self-ratings of communicative language ability. *Language Testing*, *6*(1), 14–29. https://doi.org/10.1177/026553228900600104

Belgrad, S. (2013). Portfolios and e-portfolios: Student reflection, self-assessment, and goal setting in the learning process. In J. H. McMillan (Ed.), *Sage handbook of research on classroom assessment* (pp. 331–346). SAGE Publications. https://doi.org/10.4135/9781452218649.n19

Blanche, P. (1990). Using standardized achievement and oral proficiency tests for self-assessment purposes: The DLIFLC study. *Language Testing*, *7*(2), 202–229. https://doi.org/10.1177/2F026553229000700205

Blanche, P., & Merino, B. (1989). Self-assessment of foreign language skills: Implications for teachers and researchers. *Language Learning*, *39*(3), 313–340. https://doi.org/10.1111/j.1467-1770.1989.tb00595.x

Brantmeier, C. (2005). Nonlinguistic variables in advanced L2 reading: Learner's self-assessment and enjoyment. *Foreign Language Annals*, *38*(4), 493–503. https://doi.org/10.1111/j.1944-9720.2005.tb02516.x

Brown, N. A., Dewey, D. P., & Cox, T. L. (2014). Assessing the validity of can-do statements in retrospective (then-now) self-assessment. *Foreign Language Annals*, *47*(2), 261–285. https://doi.org/10.1111/flan.12082

Coombe, C. A. (1992). The relationship between self-assessment ratings of functional literacy skills and basic English skills test results in adult refugee ESL learners [Unpublished doctoral dissertation]. The Ohio State University.

Davidai, S., & Gilovich, T. (2016). The headwinds/tailwinds asymmetry: An availability bias in assessments of barriers and blessings. *Journal of Personality and Social Psychology*, *111*(6), 835–851. https://doi.org/10.1037/pspa0000066

de Saint Léger, D. (2009). Self-assessment of speaking skills and participation in a foreign language class. *Foreign Language Annals*, *42*(1), 158–178. https://doi.org/10.1111/j.1944-9720.2009.01013.x

Donato, R. (2016). Sociocultural theory and content-based foreign language instruction: Theoretical insights on the challenge of integration. In L. Cammarata (Ed.), *Content-based foreign language teaching* (pp. 39–64). Routledge. https://doi.org/10.4324/9780203850497

Engelhardt, M., & Pfingsthorn, J. (2013). Self-assessment and placement tests: A worthwhile combination? *Language Learning in Higher Education*, *2*(1), 75–89. https://doi.org/10.1515/cercles-2012-0005

Gass, S. M., & Mackey, A. (Eds.). (2012). *The Routledge handbook of second language acquisition.* Routledge. https://doi.org/10.4324/9780203808184
Hattie, J., & Timperley, H. (2007). The power of feedback. *Review of Educational Research, 77*(1), 81–112. https://doi.org/10.3102/003465430298487
Heilenman, K. L. (1990). Self-assessment of second language ability: The role of response effects. *Language Testing, 7*(2), 174–201. https://doi.org/10.1177/026553229000700204
Iver, D. M. (1987). Classroom factors and student characteristics predicting students' use of achievement standards during ability self-assessment. *Child Development, 58*(5), 1258–1271. https://doi.org/10.2307/1130619
Kruger, J. M., & Dunning, D. (1999). Unskilled and unaware of it: How difficulties in recognizing one's own incompetence lead to inflated self-assessments. *Journal of Personality and Social Psychology, 77*, 1121–1134. https://doi.org/10.1037//0022-3514.77.6.1121
LeBlanc, R., & Painchaud, G. (1985). Self-assessment as a second language placement instrument. *TESOL Quarterly, 19*(4), 673–687. https://doi.org/10.2307/3586670
Liang, J. (2014). Toward a three-step pedagogy for fostering self-assessment in a second language writing classroom. *CATESOL Journal, 26*(1), 100–119. http://files.eric.ed.gov/fulltext/EJ1111888.pdf
Luoma, S., & Tarnanen, M. (2003). Creating a self-rating instrument for second language writing: From idea to implementation. *Language Testing 20*, 440–465. https://doi.org/10.1191/0265532203lt267oa
Ma, W., & Winke, P. (2019). Self-assessment: How reliable is it in assessing oral proficiency over time? *Foreign Language Annals, 52*(1), 66–86. https://doi.org/10.1111/flan.12379
Miraglia, E. (1995). A self-diagnostic assessment in the basic writing course. *Journal of Basic Writing, 14*(2), 48–67. https://wac.colostate.edu/docs/jbw/v14n2/miraglia.pdf
Nielson, J., Dewey, D. P., & Cox, T. (2016, March 11–13). *Second-language self-assessment: The influence of video demonstrations on their accuracy.* [Paper presentation]. Georgetown University Roundtable in Linguistics (GURT): Useful Assessment and Evaluation and Evaluation in Language Education, Georgetown University, Washington, DC, United States.
Ortega, L. (2014). *Understanding second language acquisition.* Routledge. https://doi.org/10.4324/9780203777282
Oscarson, M. (1997). Self-assessment of foreign and second language proficiency. *Encyclopedia of language and education*, 7, 175–187.
Oscarson, M. (2013). Self-assessment in the classroom. In A. J. Kunnan (Ed.), *The companion to language assessment* (pp. 712–729). Wiley-Blackwell. https://doi.org/10.1002/9781118411360.wbcla046
Pierce, B. N., Swain, M., & Hart, D. (1993). Self-assessment in two French immersion programs. *Applied Linguistics, 14*(1), 25–42. https://doi.org/10.1093/applin/14.1.25
Roever, C., & Powers, D. E. (2005). *Effects of language of administration on a self-assessment of language skills.* Educational Testing Service. https://www.ets.org/Media/Research/pdf/RM-04-06.pdf
Ross, S. (1998). Self-assessment in second language testing: A meta-analysis and analysis of experiential factors. *Language Testing, 15*(1), 1–20. https://doi.org/10.1177/026553229801500101
Schmidt, R., & Frota, S. N. (1986). Developing basic conversational ability in a second language: A case study of an adult learner of Portuguese. In R. R. Day (Ed.), *Talking to learn: Conversation in second language acquisition* (pp. 237–326). Newbury House.
Schunk, D. H., & Zimmerman, B. J. (2001). *Self-regulated learning and academic achievement: Theoretical perspectives.* Lawrence Erlbaum Associates. https://doi.org/10.4324/9781410601032
Strong-Krause, D. (2000). Exploring the effectiveness of self-assessment strategies in ESL placement. In G. Ekbatani & H. Pierson (Eds.), *Learner-directed assessment in ESL* (pp. 49–73). Lawrence Erlbaum Associates. https://doi.org/10.4324/9781410605283
Sullivan, K., & Lindgren, E. (2002). Self-assessment in autonomous computer-aided second language writing. *ELT Journal, 56*(3), 258–266. https://doi.org/10.1093/elt/56.3.258
Summers, M., Cox, T. L., McMurry, B. L., & Dewey, D. P. (2019). Investigating the use of the ACTFL Can-Do Statements in a self-assessment for student placement in an intensive English program. *System, 80*, 269–287. https://doi.org/10.1016/j.system.2018.12.012
Tigchelaar, M., Bowles, R. P., Winke, P., & Gass, S. (2017). Assessing the validity of ACTFL Can-Do statements for spoken proficiency: A Rasch analysis. *Foreign Language Annals, 50*(3), 584–600. https://doi.org/10.1111/flan.12286
Upshur, J. (1975). Objective evaluation of oral proficiency in the ESOL classroom. In G. Ekbatani & H. Pierson (Eds.), *Learner-directed assessment in ESL* (p. 49). Lawrence Erlbaum Associates. https://doi.org/10.4324/9781410605283
Wilson, M. (2004). *Constructing measures: An item response modeling approach.* Routledge. https://www.routledge.com/Constructing-Measures-An-Item-Response-Modeling-Approach-1st-Edition/Wilson/p/book/9780805847857

Part V

Testing Specific Populations

37

Testing Bi/Multilingual Learners

Amanda Brown & Tej K. Bhatia

Background

This chapter discusses the (second) language assessment of bi- and multilingual individuals. Behind this seemingly simple title lies multi-layered complexity, with varied definitions of central terms, the dynamic influences of a range of associated variables such as age and individual differences (mentioned briefly here and covered in more depth in other chapters and in the recommended reading), diverse testing contexts and purposes, and a lack of empirically supported testing practices. While acknowledging crucial differences between bilingualism and multilingualism, we use the terms largely interchangeably here to emphasize their similarities and their divergence from monolingualism. In this chapter, we begin with definitions of key constructs as well as outlining the populations relevant to the chapter theme and some of the linguistic differences between bi/multilinguals and monolinguals that complicate the construction of assessment benchmarks. We then discuss the implications of these complexities for assessment practices, closing with tips for testing.

Key Concepts

***(Functional) monolingualism*:** Exposure to only one language (L1) from birth. Possible prior exposure to second languages (L2) but no regular study/use of and limited competence in those languages.

***Early, simultaneous versus late, sequential, consecutive bi/multilingualism*:** Acquisition of two or more L1s from birth, often yielding "native-like" proficiency in each, versus acquisition of an L2 after the L1, generally after the age of four or five.

***Balanced versus unbalanced bi/multilingualism*:** Equal versus unequal proficiency in two or more languages, in general or specific areas (e.g., literacy).

***Plurilingualism*:** Defined by the Council of Europe as multilingualism at the level of the individual, with languages of equal status and competence.

***Multicompetence*:** An individual's knowledge of more than one language.

***Codemixing/Codeswitching*:** The mixing of multiple languages within discourse, both at intra- and inter-sentential levels.

***Translanguaging*:** The discursive practices that emerge in interactions among bi/multilinguals, and specifically the pedagogical techniques used in the education of "emergent bilinguals."

Key Issues

Bi/Multilinguals and the Language(s) Being Assessed

Discussion of language assessment among bi/multilinguals is highly complex, revolving initially around the fundamental issues of determining the languages that should properly be examined in a language assessment, crucially depending on its purpose, and understanding their status in an individual's linguistic repertoire, all of which we reference in the notation "(second) language assessment of bi/multilinguals." From the limited glossary of key concepts, it is apparent that by some definitions, an individual repertoire may not even be considered bi- or multilingual. Here we adopt a maximally inclusive perspective, illustrated by the following distinct contexts and populations considered relevant to the chapter theme:

(1) At the most basic level and under traditional definitions of bi/multilingualism, e.g., simultaneous or early and balanced bi/multilingualism, *language testing of a bi/multilingual learner* would imply the testing of one, both, or all of a bi/multilingual's L1(s) in discrete or combined fashion. In this context, a bilingual acquiring Spanish and English from birth could undergo testing in Spanish, English, or both. Similarly, a multilingual being raised in an English-speaking community with one Spanish-speaking parent and one Polish-speaking parent could undergo testing in any or all of those languages.

(2) Under the same definition and conditions of bi/multilingualism as in (1), with two or more languages acquired from birth, *language testing of a bi/multilingual learner* might involve L2 assessment, i.e., the testing of any language acquired after the L1(s), e.g., a third, fourth, *nth* language. Thus, the early Spanish-English bilingual or Spanish-Polish-English tri/multilingual acquiring Mandarin-Chinese at school would be assessed for L2 competency in Mandarin, though their competence in Spanish, English, and/or Polish discretely or in combination might well be of interest, too.

(3) Under an alternative definition of bi/multilingualism, where the acquisition of an additional language at any stage of proficiency may define an individual as bi- or multilingual (see e.g., Edwards, 2013), the environment outlined in (2) automatically becomes elevated to one of multilingualism. By this alternative definition, from the outset, any individual acquiring an L2 after their L1(s) should be seen as a bi- or multilingual speaker. Thus, all L2 assessment becomes language assessment in a bi- or multilingual context. Here *testing multilingual learners* might involve the individual who acquired Spanish and English from birth and added Mandarin at school being assessed in Mandarin as the L2 and potentially also English and/or Spanish as part of the multilingual repertoire. In parallel, *testing bilingual learners* might involve initially monolingual English speakers who then acquired Spanish at some point in their lives and to any proficiency level being assessed in L2 Spanish and potentially also L1 English.

The relevance of the populations above arises from the lack of a single definition of bi/multilingualism and the resulting ambiguity of "language testing." In some research and professional literature, "bilingualism" refers to one end of the proficiency continuum with "second language acquisition" at the other end, whereas elsewhere, the terms are employed interchangeably. Such blended usages of "bi/multilingual" and "second language learner/user," though confusing, genuinely reflect the complexities involved and appropriately broaden the scope of linguistic profiles that should be considered relevant to this chapter. The term "multicompetent," referring to anyone who is not monolingual, is an inclusive alternative that eliminates ambiguity (for recent coverage, see Cook & Wei, 2016). From the chapter title, readers might predict a focus on (1) above, seeing (2) and particularly the latter example in (3) as unexceptional, representative of more "typical" L2 assessment contexts, and hence the focus of other chapters in this volume. However, research from a multicompetence perspective, which has contributed much to our understanding of the unique characteristics of the bi/multilingual system and extended Bley-Vroman's (1983) notion of the comparative fallacy with respect to the monolingual benchmark, demonstrates that the (second) language assessment of bi/multilinguals is rarely if ever unexceptional. We turn to these insights next.

The Monolingual Native Speaker Benchmark

On theoretical principle, many have questioned the legitimacy of the "native speaker standard" against which language performance is often still measured (e.g., Cook, 1999; Davies, 2003, 2011; Firth & Wagner, 1997). This holds for all L2 assessment since the prescriptive preeminence of a single variety ignores the legitimacy of language variation, and comparison of L2 users to native speakers falls foul of Bley-Vroman's (1983) "comparative fallacy," considered inappropriate and unjust because L2 learners/users by definition can never be "native speakers" of those languages. However, the native speaker standard is particularly problematic in the context of bi/multilingualism when those native speakers are simultaneously envisioned as monolingual since a growing body of research from a multicompetence perspective has revealed qualitative and quantitative differences between multicompetent and monolingual systems. Multicompetence impacts language performance in multifaceted and dynamic ways (see below and papers in e.g., Alonso, 2016; Cook, 2003; Cook & Bassetti, 2011; Golden, Jarvis, & Tenfjord, 2017; Jarvis & Pavlenko, 2008), which can vary by individual and over time, interface with sociopsychological features (e.g., Bhatia, 2017; Wang 2008), and are compounded exponentially the more languages an individual knows (e.g., Bhatia & Ritchie, 2016; Cenoz, Hufeisen, & Jessner, 2001; De Angelis, 2015; De Angelis, Jessner, & Kresic, 2015; Rothman, Amaro, & De Bot, 2013). Such findings support the now legendary statement that "bilinguals are not two monolinguals in one" (Grosjean, 1989, 2010) and motivate the need for multicompetent assessment norms.

A strong case for monolingual native speakers of a single target language constituting a profile far removed from, unattainable for, and in some sense irrelevant to multicompetent language learners and users has been argued in a number of recent publications on both language and general education (e.g., Cruz-Ferreira, 2010; Flores & Schissel, 2014; May, 2014; Shohamy, 2011; Shohamy & Menken, 2015). However, with descriptions of the multicompetent norm still in infancy and the continued existence of invalid and unreliable assessment practices (Lopez, Turkan, & Guzman-Orth, 2017), bilingual children in particular can be labeled as low-achieving (Hopewell & Escamilla, 2014) and are overrepresented in special education programs (Sanchez et al., 2013).

The Multicompetent Norm and Implications for Language Assessment

The assessment of L1 competence, multicompetent or otherwise, is not typically considered an area of interest by L2 testers, teachers, or learners. Indeed, from a functional perspective, self-identification as bi/multilingual generally connotes simultaneous, early acquisition of two or more languages (Edwards, 2013). Such individuals may not, for example, in professional or academic settings, be formally assessed for language competence in any of their L1s. High or at least sufficient proficiency in each language may be implied and simply taken at face value or confirmed through informal measures such as brief interviews. However, research on multicompetent L1(s) has offered critical insights to inform (second) language assessment particularly in bi/multilingual contexts, which warrant consideration along with the assessment purpose.

Language testers should be aware of mixed research findings on the earliest stages of bi/multilingual language development (see discussion in e.g., Serratrice, 2013). Differential rates of growth may be observed for example in the lexicon, often a function of language input and use (e.g., Bialystok, Luk, Peets, & Yang, 2010), with a possible "deficit" in each language potentially until school age (e.g., Hoff, 2018), but a potential surplus in the languages combined (e.g., Pearson, 1998) in comparison to monolingual peers. Thus, in principle, if information about overall lexical knowledge is sought, assessment should include all known languages, potentially using normed measures. However, scores by language should not be benchmarked against those from monolingual peers and consequently viewed from a deficit perspective, but rather against multicompetent norms.

In adulthood, bi/multilinguals may perform more slowly than monolinguals in tasks of word recognition and object naming in and across languages (e.g., Van Gelderen, Schoonen, & de Glopper, 2003), especially with false cognates, and may more frequently experience tip-of-the-tongue states (see Branzi, Calabria, & Costa, 2018, for an overview), though interlingual cognates may be recognized faster (e.g., Dijkstra & van Heuven, 2018). Since sufficient empirical evidence demonstrating the impact of such phenomena on real-time communication is lacking, testers should be aware of their potential place in the multicompetent norm and be cautious when assessing behaviors that involve the speed of word recognition and retrieval as an underlying construct, such as in measures of speaking fluency.

Language switching or mixing, at inter- and intra-sentential levels, is a prominent and widely attested feature often of fully developed and highly proficient multicompetent discourse. Codeswitching/mixing comprises intricate linguistic practices dependent on social and psychological factors such as the participants involved, interactional context, conversational topic, discourse function, and processing economy (e.g., Gardner-Chloros, 2009), with differences detected in bilingual versus multilingual codeswitching/mixing (e.g., Stavans & Swisher, 2006). Similarly, the burgeoning term, "translanguaging," defined among the Key Concepts above, describes individuals' recruitment of their full linguistic repertoire to fulfill interactional objectives, particularly in educational settings, where translingual pedagogies explicitly encourage codeswitching/mixing (see e.g., García & Wei, 2014).

Language mixing can produce constructions that would be rendered ungrammatical by monolingual users of the source languages. Bhatia's research, for example, has focused on two salient aspects of the capacity of the bilingual brain/mind, namely its ability to maintain both language separation on one hand and language integration on the other, which result in a qualitatively distinct language mixing. This research has revealed various facets of bilingual creativity as manifested in grammatical and semantic innovations. For example, in an English-Hindi code-mixed verb phrase, an English verb, e.g., *choose*, is accompanied by a dummy verb, e.g., *karnaa* "to do," forming novel constructions such as *saarii choose kare-gii* "will-do choose a sari," which obeys the innovative rules of the mixed English-Hindi grammar, but is neither permitted by the monolingual Hindi nor English grammars (Bhatia, 1989; Bhatia & Ritchie, 2016).

Parallel research within the framework of crosslinguistic influence, particularly examining the effects of an L2 on the L1, has provided further support for the unique nature of multicompetent systems (see papers in e.g., Alonso, 2016; Cook, 2003; Cook & Bassetti, 2011; Golden et al., 2017; Jarvis & Pavlenko, 2008), including a growing body of work explicitly on the L3 and *Ln* in multilingual contexts (e.g., Cenoz et al., 2001; De Angelis, 2015). In a series of studies eliciting descriptions of motion, Brown and colleagues have shown that, even with only an intermediate level of L2 English, multicompetent Japanese speakers may alter their depiction of trajectories in comparison to monolingual Japanese speakers, using distinctive construction types, marking specific aspects of the event, and adjusting syntactic and non-verbal patterns of information packaging (e.g., Brown, 2010, 2015; Brown & Gullberg, 2008, 2011, 2013), although the extent to which such patterns are detectable in interaction or assessment remains to be determined.

In sum, empirical research on codeswitching/mixing and crosslinguistic influence provides considerable insights for language assessment. Importantly, the differences revealed among mono/bi/multilingual systems vary in prominence. While codeswitching may be relatively obvious, other features are more subtle and their functional impact in real-time communication, questionable. Indeed, the small but significant mono/bilingual differences in speed of word recognition found in Van Gelderen et al. (2003) were found not to impact general reading skills. For benchmarking purposes, in a multicompetent norm, language mixing should be considered typical, potentially manifested by different degrees of visibility, in different ways, to different levels of acceptability, and at different language proficiencies. For language testers, the variables underlying codeswitching/mixing should be considered during test construction with a view to intentionally prompting either a multilingual or monolingual mode (Grosjean, 1989) depending on the instructional background and assessment purpose. While codeswitching may be considered contextually appropriate/inappropriate (see e.g., Berthele, 2012), those advocating translingual pedagogies consider the only valid assessments to be those that also permit translanguaging, and recent developments in the Common European Framework of Reference explicitly target plurilingual (and pluricultural) competence (see below). Testers should be aware of the variation in the acceptability of known unique constructions arising from multicompetent systems, which may be considered ungrammatical in monolingual varieties, and sensitive to the possibility of mixed constructions that have not yet been described.

Recommendations for Practice

The problematizing of the monolingual L1 target has demonstrated that its application as a benchmark in multicompetent language assessment may yield an unjust and inaccurate picture of possible deficiency (e.g., Shohamy, 2011; although note research documenting the superiority of multilinguals in the acquisition of additional languages: Bartolotti & Marian, 2017; De Angelis, Jessner, & Kresic, 2015). These concerns have gained traction in recent years, and mention of the "native speaker" has been limited in the current CEFR descriptors, with only one mention in the Global Scale, two in the Self-Assessment Grid, and none in the Qualitative Common Reference Levels. At the same time, language assessment professionals, teachers, and users/learners themselves recognize the need for a meaningful target to which teaching and learning can aspire and against which language performance can be measured (Davies, 2003). As Cruz-Ferreira (2010) notes, "there can be no assessment if there is nothing to assess against" (p 8).

At the heart of constructing recommendations for practice in the (second) language assessment of bi/multilingual populations lies the need for a reconceptualization of the "norm" as a "multicompetent norm." In this reconceptualization, awareness of variation—at language, community, and individual levels—is key. While efforts in this domain are only slowly emerging and (second) language assessment among bi/multilinguals is a field in relative infancy (Lopez, Turkan, & Guzman-Orth, 2017), some have addressed socio-linguistic/-pragmatic variation. Under Valdman's (2003) "pedagogical norm" framework, multiple native speaker norms are systematically introduced in classrooms, based on linguistic reality, sociopsychological perceptions of appropriacy, and learnability. For example, of the many options for question formation in French, Valdman recommends introducing a subset, beginning with the easiest, *fronting*, but soon replacing that with the less stigmatized *est-ce que* and *inversion* constructions. Cruz-Ferreira (2010) has drawn parallels between such monolingual speaker variation, where multiple varieties are recruited alternately by communicative purpose, and the multiple varieties of multiple languages that bi/multilingual speakers manipulate for similar reasons. Contributions to the same volume describe different contexts of bi/multilingualism, including across ages, languages, and discourse genres, and propose specific multilingual norms. In associated pedagogical initiatives, securing authentic texts illustrating multicompetent performance is critical (e.g., see Sharma & Bhatia, 2014, for a Hindi language text). Alternatively, from the perspective of World Englishes, Canagarajah's (2006) suggestion is to shift focus from individual language varieties to the language user's pragmatic abilities to perform communicative functions across varieties.

This charges test creators to determine appropriate communicative functions for a given assessment purpose and construct contexts that would permit or require the use of different varieties.

Published resources dealing with assessment of general education in bi/multilingual contexts (e.g., De Backer, Van Avermaet, & Slembrouck, 2017) should be distinguished from those dealing specifically with language (e.g., Marian, Blumenfeld, & Kaushanskaya, 2007; Silva-Corvalán & Treffers-Daller, 2016), which generally target the bi/multilingual L1 as opposed to a later-learned L2, L3, *Ln*. In these arenas, practitioners can consult guidelines for applying a multilingual lens to interpreting standardized test results (De Angelis, 2014), for acknowledging language variation (Sandilos et al., 2015), and for the validity of parental and self-report data (e.g., Marian et al., 2007). Some publications offer test creators broader coverage, e.g., papers in Gathercole (2013), with treatment of linguistic, cognitive, and academic skills across ages to adulthood, including a/typical development, in both bi/multilingual and second language learners/users. Gathercole and colleagues discuss, for example, issues associated with inclusion/exclusion in assessment measures of cognates, also noted above, commonly present in translated tests, which are likely to influence performance, albeit differentially depending on factors such as input conditions and language dominance. Thus, test creators should examine assessment materials for the presence of interlingual cognates and either remove or maintain them depending on the assessment purpose.

Important recent developments have responded to the call for assessment of translanguaging or plurilingualism (e.g., Piccardo, 2013; Shohamy, 2011). FREPA—A Framework of Reference for Pluralistic Approaches to Languages and Cultures (Cadelier et al. 2012) and the CEFR Companion Volume with New Descriptors (Council of Europe, 2018), for example, specifically include descriptions of plurilingual (and cultural) competence, defined as the ability to switch from one language to another in comprehension and production, across skill domains. However noteworthy these initiatives, perceived difficulties in implementation still dominated discussion at the 2018 Ottawa Translanguaging Conference since the definition of plurilingualism emphasizes the dynamism of the multi-linguistic system of an individual, which diminishes the potential for generalizable benchmarking.

Overall, assessors should be aware that entirely balanced bi/multilingualism is rare and individuals will typically, naturally, and be reasonably expected to display the competencies necessitated by their environment, self-evident in bilingual typologies (e.g., receptive versus productive, bilingual versus biliterate; see e.g., Bhatia, 2018; Edwards, 2013; Silva-Corvalán & Treffers-Daller, 2016). Thus, proficiency in one language may be biased towards matters of family, while for professional purposes, functionality may be superior in another language. These competencies should also be expected to vary by individual and change over time (Herdina & Jessner, 2002). Thus, the multicompetent system will be dynamic over the lifespan, eluding an "end state" (Rothman et al., 2013). Though assessment measures may legitimately look for parallel cross-language competency in at least some domains at specific times (e.g., see Seal of Biliteracy, adopted in many US states for high school graduation: https://sealofbiliteracy.org/), entirely comparable proficiency in all domains across all languages at all times is not the norm (Grosjean, 1989) and should thus not normally be targeted in assessments.

To conclude, this chapter has discussed the (second) language assessment of bi/multilinguals, outlining definitional complexities, problems with monolingual L1 targets, differences between monolinguals and multicompetent bi/multilinguals, and associated recommendations for practice. Space constraints prevented examination of intersecting variables such as age and language-related impairments, where diagnoses in bi/multilingual populations becomes more challenging (see e.g., Hsieh & Chapman, Chapter 38; Kormos & Taylor, Chapter 39, this volume; McLeod & Verdon, 2017). Much theoretical and empirical work has contributed to the legitimization and characterization of the multicompetent language user. Consequently, groundbreaking attempts to articulate "bi/multilingual norms" and capture plurilingual competencies have begun to emerge in the field of language assessment. However, a single assessment will never prove valid for all bi/multilingual contexts and thus much more work is needed before sufficient and appropriate benchmarks are in place for the language assessment of every multicompetent language user.

Testing Tips

- In all (second) language assessments of bi/multilinguals, prioritize ecological validity, where tests may strive to idealize performance but also reflect communicative realities. Thus test administrators will incorporate language variation and multiple norms, from monolingual and bi/multilingual, multicompetent, and plurilingual discourse. In this process, stakeholders should consult available corpora, solicit judgments, reflect on prior teaching experiences, and build their own assessment response corpora within and across individuals over time to address Valdman's (2003) concepts of "linguistic reality," i.e., how proficient speakers use constructions; perceptions of "appropriacy," i.e., how proficient speakers think constructions should be used; and "learnability," i.e., how easy specific constructions are to learn.
- For more impromptu assessments or when logistical constraints prevent the above, at the very least attempt to benchmark multicompetent language users against those with similar linguistic profiles, for example, comparing developing against developed bilinguals along targeted dimensions. This is especially important if assessments of plurilingual competence are sought, for which language assessors and assessment materials should explicitly incorporate cross-language features, e.g., cognates, engage in language switching/mixing practices, and incorporate holistic scoring using multilingual indices (Gorter & Cenoz, 2017; Schissel, et al., 2018). Here caution in interpreting comparisons is still necessary since factors such as language input, use, and dynamic changes over time would likely render "perfect" benchmarking matches unattainable.
- In the theoretically undesirable but conventional event that competence in only one language of a bi/multilingual's repertoire is in focus, assessment materials should incorporate lexical and structural features unique to that language, e.g., not known cognates, false or otherwise, across languages. Similarly, during assessment, activation of "monolingual mode" (Grosjean, 1989), a state without interactional need for the non-target language(s), is advised. Thus, assessors might delay revealing their own multicompetent status by refraining from language switching/mixing.
- Finally, teachers, testers and indeed language users themselves will likely, and appropriately, be most concerned with the extent to which individuals are functional in specific areas—related to the core construct of assessment validity. Thus, in ensuring that language assessments provide valid representations of specific performance goals, benchmarking should be less normative and more criterion referenced, detailing the dimensions along which task performance would be deemed successful. For example, assessments of academic language might focus on describing levels of reading and synthesizing a range of academic level texts, comprehending extended monologues, and constructing written contributions of differing lengths and genres that are acceptable for a specific and defined purpose, potentially within and across languages.

Recommended Readings

Bhatia, T. K., & Ritchie, W. C. (2013). *The handbook of bilingualism and multilingualism.* Blackwell Publishing Ltd.

This edited volume offers an interdisciplinary primer in central issues associated with bi/multi/plurilingualism, and addresses assessment specifically in chapters related to education and second language acquisition.

Cruz-Ferreira, M. (2010). *Multilingual norms*. Peter Lang.

This edited volume offers an overview of many of the themes discussed here as well as a collection of empirical studies on a broad range of multilingual contexts around the world, including adult and child speakers of different languages and analyses of a variety of linguistic and interactional features that may contribute to the construction of multilingual norms for assessment.

Gathercole, V. C. M. (2013). *Solutions for the assessment of bilinguals*. Multilingual Matters.

This edited volume specifically addresses language assessment in multilingual populations of adults and children, including in atypical development.

References

Alonso, R. A. (2016). *Crosslinguistic influence in second language acquisition*. Multilingual Matters.

Bartolotti, J., & Marian, V. (2017). Bilinguals' existing languages benefit vocabulary learning in a third language. *Language Learning*, *67*(1), 110–140. https://doi.org/10.1111/lang.12200

Berthele, R. (2012). The influence of code-mixing and speaker information on perception and assessment of foreign language proficiency: An experimental study. *International Journal of Bilingualism*, *16*(4), 453–466. https://doi.org/10.1177/1367006911429514

Bhatia, T. K. (1989). Bilinguals' creativity and syntactic theory: Evidence for emerging grammar. *World Englishes*, *8*(3), 265–276. https://doi.org/10.1111/j.1467-971X.1989.tb00668.x

Bhatia, T. K. (2017). Bilingualism and multilingualism from a socio-psychological perspective. *Oxford research encyclopedia in linguistics*. Oxford University Press. https://doi.org/10.1093/acrefore/9780199384655.013.82

Bhatia, T. K. (2018). Bilingualism and multilingualism: Conceptual and methodological issues and challenges. In A. Phakiti, P. De Costa, L. Plonsky, & S. Starfield (Eds.), *The Palgrave handbook of applied linguistics research methodology* (pp. 671–701). Palgrave Macmillan.

Bhatia, T. K., & Ritchie, W. C. (2016). Multilingual language mixing and creativity. *Languages*, *1*(6), 1–14. https://doi.org/10.3390/languages1010006

Bialystok, E., Luk, G., Peets, K., & Yang, S. (2010). Receptive vocabulary differences in monolingual and bilingual children. *Bilingualism: Language and Cognition*, *13*(4), 525–531. https://doi.org/10.1017/S1366728909990423

Bley-Vroman, R. (1983). The comparative fallacy in interlanguage studies: The case of systematicity. *Language Learning*, *33*(1), 1–17. https://doi.org/10.1111/j.1467-1770.1983.tb00983.x

Branzi, F. M., Calabria, M., & Costa, A. (2018). The bilingual language "control system": On the origin of the "hard problem". In S. A. Rueschemeyer & M. G. Gaskell (Eds.), *The Oxford handbook of psycholinguistics* (pp. 118–143). Oxford University Press.

Brown, A. (2010). Gesture viewpoint in Japanese and English: Cross-linguistic interactions between two languages in one speaker. In M. Gullberg & K. de Bot (Eds.), *Gestures in language development* (pp. 113–134). John Benjamins. https://doi.org/10.1075/bct.28.08bro

Brown, A. (2015). Universal development and L1–L2 convergence in bilingual construal of manner in speech and gesture in Mandarin, Japanese, and English. *The Modern Language Journal*, *99*(s1), 66–82. https://doi.org/10.1111/j.1540-4781.2015.12179.x

Brown, A., & Gullberg, M. (2008). Bidirectional crosslinguistic influence in L1–L2 encoding of Manner in speech and gesture: A study of Japanese speakers of English. *Studies in Second Language Acquisition*, *30*(2), 225–251. https://doi.org/10.1017/S0272263108080327

Brown, A., & Gullberg, M. (2011). Bidirectional cross-linguistic influence in event conceptualization? Expressions of path among Japanese learners of English. *Bilingualism: Language and Cognition*, *14*(1), 79–94. https://doi.org/10.1017/S1366728910000064

Brown, A., & Gullberg, M. (2013). L1–L2 convergence in clausal packaging in Japanese and English. *Bilingualism: Language and Cognition*, *16*(3), 477–494. https://doi.org/10.1017/S1366728912000491

Canagarajah, S. (2006). Changing communicative needs, revised assessment objectives: Testing English as an international language. *Language Assessment Quarterly*, *3*(3), 229–242. https://doi.org/ /10.1207/s15434311laq0303_1

Candelier, M., Camilleri Grima, A., Castellotti, A., de Pietro, J. F., Lőrincz, I. Meißner, F. J., Schröder-Sura, A., Noguerol, A., & Molinié, M. (2012). *FREPA: A framework of reference for pluralistic approaches to languages and cultures: Competences and resources*. Council of Europe.

Cenoz, J., Hufeisen, B., & Jessner, U. E. (2001). *Cross-linguistic influence in third language acquisition*. Multilingual Matters.
Cook, V. (1999). Going beyond the native speaker in language teaching. *TESOL Quarterly*, *33*(2), 185–209. https://doi.org/10.2307/3587717
Cook, V. (2003). *Effects of the second language on the first*. Multilingual Matters.
Cook, V., & Bassetti, B. (2011). *Language and bilingual cognition*. Psychology Press.
Cook, V., & Wei, L. (2016). *The Cambridge handbook of linguistic multi-competence*. Cambridge University Press.
Council of Europe. (2018). *Common European framework of reference for languages: Companion volume with new descriptors*. Council of Europe. https://rm.coe.int/cefr-companion-volume-with-new-descriptors-2018/1680787989
Cruz-Ferreira, M. (2010). *Multilingual norms*. Peter Lang.
Davies, A. (2003). *The native speaker: Myth and reality*. Multilingual Matters.
Davies, A. (2011). Does language testing need the native speaker? *Language Assessment Quarterly*, *8*(3), 291–308. https://doi.org/10.1080/15434303.2011.570827
De Angelis, G. (2014). A multilingual approach to analysing standardized test results: Immigrant primary school children and the role of languages spoken in a bi-/multilingual community. *Intercultural Education*, *25*(1), 14–28. https://doi.org/10.1080/14675986.2014.883167
De Angelis, G. (2015). English L3 learning in a multilingual context: the role of parental education and L2 exposure within the living community. *International Journal of Multilingualism*, *12*(4), 435–452. https://doi.org/10.1080/14790718.2015.1071017
De Angelis, G., Jessner, U., & Kresic, M. (2015). *Crosslinguistic influence and crosslinguistic interaction in multilingual language learning*. Bloomsbury.
De Backer, F., Van Avermaet, P., & Slembrouck, S. (2017). Schools as laboratories for exploring multilingual assessment policies and practices. *Language and Education*, *31*(3), 217–230. https://doi.org/10.1080/09500782.2016.1261896
Dijkstra, T., & van Heuven, W. (2018). Visual word recognition in multilinguals. In S. A. Rueschemeyer & M. G. Gaskell (Eds.), *The Oxford handbook of psycholinguistics* (pp. 118–143). Oxford University Press.
Edwards, J. (2013). Bilingualism and multilingualism: Some central concepts. In T. K. Bhatia & W. C. Ritchie (Eds.), *The handbook of bilingualism and multilingualism* (pp. 5–25). Wiley Blackwell. https://doi.org/10.1002/9781118332382.ch1
Firth, A., & Wagner, J. (1997). On discourse, communication, and (some) fundamental concepts in SLA research. *The Modern Language Journal*, *81*(3), 285–300. https://doi.org/10.1111/j.1540-4781.1997.tb05480.x
Flores, N., & Schissel, J. L. (2014). Dynamic bilingualism as the norm: Envisioning a heteroglossic approach to standards-based reform. *TESOL Quarterly*, *48*(3), 454–479. https://doi.org/10.1002/tesq.182
García, O., & Wei, L. (2014). *Translanguaging: Language, bilingualism, and education*. Palgrave Macmillan.
Gardner-Chloros, P. (2009). *Codeswitching*. Cambridge University Press.
Gathercole, V. C. M. (2013). *Solutions for the assessment of bilinguals*. Multilingual Matters.
Golden, A., Jarvis, S., & Tenfjord, K. (2017). *Crosslinguistic influence and distinctive patterns of language learning: Findings and insights from a learner corpus*. Multilingual Matters.
Gorter, D., & Cenoz, J. (2017). Language education policy and multilingual assessment. *Language and Education*, *31*(3), 231–248. https://doi.org/10.1080/09500782.2016.1261892
Grosjean, F. (1989). Neurolinguists, beware! The bilingual is not two monolinguals in one person. *Brain and Language*, *36*(1), 3–15. https://doi.org/10.1016/0093-934X(89)90048-5
Grosjean, F. (2010). *Bilingual: Life and reality*. Harvard University Press.
Herdina, P., & Jessner, U. (2002). *A dynamic model of multilingualism: Perspectives of change in psycholinguistics*. Multilingual Matters.
Hoff, E. (2018). Bilingual development in children of immigrant families. *Child Development Perspectives*, *12*(2), 80–86. https://doi.org/10.1111/cdep.12262
Hopewell, S., & Escamilla, K. (2014). Struggling reader or emerging biliterate student? Reevaluating the criteria for labeling emerging bilingual students as low achieving. *Journal of Literacy Research*, *46*(1), 68–89. https://doi.org/10.1177/1086296X13504869
Jarvis, S., & Pavlenko, A. (2008). *Cross-linguistic influence in language and cognition*. Routledge.
Lopez, A. A., Turkan, S., & Guzman-Orth, D. (2017). Assessing multilingual competence. In E. Shohamy, I. G. Or, & S. May (Eds.), *Language testing and assessment: Encyclopedia of language and education* (3rd ed., pp. 99–102). Springer. https://doi.org/10.1007/978-3-319-02261-1_6
Marian, V., Blumenfeld, H. K., & Kaushanskaya, M. (2007). The Language Experience and Proficiency Questionnaire (LEAP-Q): Assessing language profiles in bilinguals and multilinguals. *Journal of Speech, Language, and Hearing Research*, *50*(4), 940–967. https://doi.org/10.1044/1092-4388(2007/067)

May, S. (Ed.). (2014). *The multilingual turn: Implications for SLA, TESOL and bilingual education*. Routledge.
McLeod, S., Verdon, S., & The International Expert Panel on Multilingual Children's Speech. (2017). Tutorial: Speech assessment for multilingual children who do not speak the same language(s) as the speech-language pathologist. *American Journal of Speech-Language Pathology*, *26*(3), 691–708. https://doi.org/10.1044/2017_AJSLP-15-0161
Pearson, B. (1998). Assessing lexical development in bilingual babies and toddlers. *International Journal of Bilingualism*, *2*(3), 347–372. https://doi.org/10.1177/136700699800200305
Piccardo, E. (2013). Plurilingualism and curriculum design: Toward a synergic vision. *TESOL Quarterly*, *47*(3), 600–614. https://doi.org/10.1002/tesq.110
Rothman, J., Amaro, J., & De Bot, K. (2013). Third language acquisition. In J. Herschensohn & M. Young-Scholten (Eds.), *The Cambridge handbook of second language acquisition* (pp. 372–393). Cambridge University Press. https://doi.org/10.1017/CBO9781139051729.023
Sanchez, S. V., Rodriquez, B. J., Soto-Huerta, M. E., Villarreal, F. C., Guerra, N. S., & Flores, B. B. (2013). A case for multidimensional bilingual assessment. *Language Assessment Quarterly*, *10*(2), 160–177. https://doi.org/10.1080/15434303.2013.769544
Sandilos, L. E., Lewis, K., Komaroff, E., Hammer, C., S., Scarpino, S. E., & Lopez, L. (2015). Analysis of bilingual children's performance on the English and Spanish versions of the Woodcock-Muñoz Language Survey-R (WMLS-R). *Language Assessment Quarterly*, *12*(4), 386–408. https://doi.org/10.1080/15434303.2015.1100198
Schissel, J. L., Leung, C., López-Gopar, M., & Davis, J. R. (2018). Multilingual learners in language assessment: Assessment design for linguistically diverse communities. *Language and Education*, *32*(2), 167–182. https://doi.org/10.1080/09500782.2018.1429463
Serratrice, L. (2013). The bilingual child. In T. K. Bhatia & W. C. Ritchie (Eds.), *The handbook of bilingualism and multilingualism* (pp. 87–108). Wiley Blackwell. https://doi.org/10.1002/9781118332382.ch4
Sharma, N., & Bhatia, T. K. (2014). *The Routledge intermediate Hindi reader*. Routledge.
Shohamy, E. (2011). Assessing multilingual competencies: Adopting construct valid assessment policies. *The Modern Language Journal*, *95*(3), 418–429. https://doi.org/10.1111/j.1540-4781.2011.01210.x
Shohamy, E., & Menken, K. (2015). Language assessment: Past to present misuses and future possibilities. In W. E. Wright, S. Boun, & O. García (Eds.), *The handbook of bilingual and multilingual education*. Wiley Blackwell. https://doi.org/10.1002/9781118533406.ch15
Silva-Corvalán, C., & Treffers-Daller, J. (2016). *Language dominance in bilinguals: Issues of measurement and operationalization*. Cambridge University Press.
Stavans, A., & Swisher, V. (2006). Language switching as a window on trilingual acquisition. *International Journal of Multilingualism*, *3*(3), 193–220. https://doi.org/10.2167/ijm020.0
Valdman, A. (2003). The acquisition of sociostylistic and sociopragmatic variation by instructed second language learners. In C. Blythe (Ed.), *The sociolinguistics of foreign language classrooms* (pp. 57–78). Heinle.
Van Gelderen, A., Schoonen, R., & de Glopper, K. (2003). Roles of linguistic knowledge, metacognitive knowledge and processing speed in L3, L2 and L1 reading comprehension: A structural equation modeling approach. *International Journal of Bilingualism*, *7*(1), 7–25. https://doi.org/10.1177/13670069030070010201
Wang, X. (2008). *Growing up with three languages*. Multilingual Matters.

38

Testing the L2 of Young Learners

Ching-Ni Hsieh & Mark Chapman

Background

Child second language acquisition (SLA) literature suggests that differences in language developmental patterns exist between children and adults (Oliver & Azkarai, 2017; Philp, Borowczyk, & Mackey, 2017). The distinctive child language acquisition trajectory can be attributed to age and associated differences in cognitive abilities, social and emotional development, and first language (L1) literacy. Young language learners (YLLs) are cognitively and socio-emotionally less mature than adult second language (L2) learners; in addition, while they also have prior knowledge of their L1, as adult L2 learners do, a child's L1 knowledge may be less developed when they first start learning the L2 than their adult peers. These characteristics result in different language developmental patterns for various aspects of the L2, including phonological, lexical, and morphosyntactic acquisition (Lakshmanan, 2009).

In this chapter we will review studies inquiring into assessing the L2 of YLLs and offer best practices concerning the testing of this population. We primarily focus on children learning English as a second- or foreign-language, although we review studies that have implications for children learning other languages. We collectively refer to these learners as YLLs in this chapter.

Key Concepts

***Young language learners (YLLs)*:** Children aged between five and 14 years old who are learning English either in a second- or foreign-language-learning context (ESL or ELF). The age range approximates the period of time during which YLLs attend elementary and middle schools in many countries.

***Cognitive abilities*:** The skills and mechanism of how individuals learn, remember, reason, and pay attention. Core cognitive abilities influencing YLL language acquisition include attention, memory capacity, and speed of information processing.

***Literacy skills*:** The skills that an individual needs for reading and writing. Some early literacy skills that are important for children's later reading and writing include phonological awareness (i.e., awareness of sounds), print knowledge (i.e., understanding of the forms and functions of written language), vocabulary, and story comprehension or narrative skills.

***Scaffolding*:** Tools that teachers provide to learners to help them carry out some tasks that are challenging based on their level of language development; such as providing models, sentence frames, and key words.

Key Issues

Recent research on YLL assessments and child SLA has explored topics in (1) linguistic developments or progressions (Bailey, 2017; Bailey, Blackstock-Bernstein, Ryan, & Pitsoulakis, 2016; Bailey & Heritage, 2014; Hsieh & Wang, 2019), (2) cognitive processes required of assessment tasks (Gu & So, 2017; Lee & Winke, 2018; Winke et al., 2018), (3) relationships between cognitive abilities and language outcomes (Blom, 2019; Verhagen & Leseman, 2016), (4) validation of large-scale YLL assessments (Hsieh, 2016; Papp & Walczak, 2016; Papp, Rixon, Saville, & Weir, 2018; So, 2014), (5) testing practices and washback effects in local or regional contexts (Butler, 2009; Cheng & Curtis, 2004; Chik & Besser, 2011), and (6) alternative assessments, such as self-assessment (Butler & Lee, 2010), and peer-assessment (Hung, 2018). The studies reviewed below highlight some of the recent empirical work, research trends, and methodologies that can further applied linguists' understanding of assessing YLLs.

The analysis of linguistic developmental paths to an L2 in young children can help test developers and researchers define constructs, answer theoretical questions focused around assessing language proficiency, and inform the development of rating scales. Situated within the context of US grade-level classrooms, Bailey and her colleagues applied a corpus-driven approach to examining language developmental trajectories of YLLs with the goal of informing formative assessment research and practices (Bailey, 2017; Bailey & Heritage, 2014; Bailey et al., 2016). The researchers collected K–6 grade students' oral and written performances on two types of explanatory discourse (procedural explanations and justifications) and compiled a language corpus as part of the *Dynamic Language Learning Progressions* (DLLPs) project to capture and describe the progressions of language abilities of young learners (Bailey et al., 2016). Using a subset of the DLLPs data, Bailey (2017) found marked differences in the use of complex sentences between English learner kindergarteners and their English monolingual or proficient learner counterparts. However, very little difference in coherence and cohesion was found for the third grader language groups (i.e., L1 or L2 speakers). The observed progressions of language features in Bailey's studies can provide applied linguists and language educators a set of empirically-validated descriptions of how the studied linguistic features typically develop, and under which conditions. These clearly-defined progressions can also assist in the development of rating scales for assessing YLLs.

An important piece of validity evidence needed to support YLL assessments pertains to the cognitive processes required to complete language tasks and the extent to which these processes are in keeping with theoretical expectations (Cho & So, 2014; Winke et al., 2018). Winke et al. (2018) interviewed native-speaking children and L2 learners of English ages seven to nine to understand the children's thought processes while they responded to two standardized English reading and writing tests: the Young Learners Tests of English, Bronze and Silver, administered by Cambridge Michigan Language Assessments. The researchers found that some of the native-speaking children's incorrect responses were impacted by construct-irrelevant variables such as lack of assessment literacy or age-related cognitive functioning. Winke et al. (2018) suggested that pilot-testing of large-scale YLL assessments should include a sample of children who are proficient in the target language (e.g., native-speaking children) who are at the same developmental levels of the target population to ensure the cognitive validity of the test.

Children's learning of an L2 is supported by cognitive abilities such as attention, working memory, and information-processing. Recent research in child SLA has seen a growing interest in the use of cognitive measures to examine the associations between cognitive abilities and language outcomes among YLLs (Blom, 2019; Verhagen & Leseman, 2016). In a longitudinal study, Blom (2019) found that working memory and attention predicted vocabulary knowledge in the majority language (Dutch) among immigrant children who lived in the Netherlands and spoke Turkish or Tarifit as the home, minority language. The researchers used the Dutch version of the Peabody Picture Vocabulary Test (PPVT) to measure receptive vocabulary knowledge of the participants. The PPVT (Dunn & Dunn, 2007) is a standardized vocabulary test that asks test-takers to listen to a target word and choose a correct matching referent out of four pictures and is commonly used to measure children's receptive vocabulary knowledge.

Validations of large-scale YLL assessments are important processes to provide empirical evidence to back the claims made about test-score uses. In an attempt to provide content validity evidence to support a standardized YLL EFL assessment, *TOEFL Primary*®, Hsieh (2016) compared the content of the listening and reading sections of the test, with the core communication goals and the enabling language knowledge, skills, and abilities (KSAs) represented in various EFL curricula. Employing teacher judgments to determine the degree of match between the test content and the relevance and importance of the KSAs assessed for successful classroom performance, the researcher found a high level of content alignment. However, the results also revealed that teacher judgments of the content relevance were impacted by teachers' perceptions of the appropriateness of the task types and the topics of the assessment tasks. This finding implied that the choice of appropriate task types and topics for YLL assessments should be made with YLLs' age and life experience in mind. Topics that are familiar and accessible to YLLs and that do not require culture-specific knowledge are particularly important.

Another strand of research on YLL assessments has explored the use of English language proficiency assessments to measure young L2 learners' English language abilities and language development within the context of K–12 school settings in the United States (e.g., Bailey & Heritage, 2014; Hauck, Pooler, Wolf, Lopez, & Anderson, 2017). One major focus of this line of research has addressed theoretical and practical issues concerning the assessment of YLLs who need to develop adequate academic English language proficiency in order to access the content of school curriculum and to support their performances on content assessments in English (Llosa, 2011; Snow & Katz, 2014).

Recommendations for Practice

Age Appropriate Task and Text Types

The developmental characteristics of YLLs have a considerable influence on the design and development of age-appropriate tasks and text types for YLL assessments (Nikolov, 2016). Children's cognitive abilities develop considerably from preschool to early adolescence. When testing language proficiency, early adolescents would have a higher-level of cognitive maturity than the preschoolers in conceptual skills and a better ability to apply learned knowledge to new situations. These cognitive skills can help older learners better deal with more abstract concepts or topics and complete more complicated tasks. The changes in cognitive abilities and the development of high-order cognitive skills as children age imply that the cognitive demands of tasks imposed on older and younger learners may differ and those differences should be considered when designing tasks for YLLs of different age groups. Expectations for developmentally appropriate language growth in YLLs can be found in a variety of resource documents. Two that are recommended for further examination are:

- Common European Framework of Reference for Languages (CEFR) Bank of supplementary descriptors: This document provides language competence descriptors for students in the age ranges 7–10 and 11–15.
  (see: https://www.coe.int/en/web/common-european-framework-reference-languages/bank-of-supplementary-descriptors)
- WIDA English Language Development Standards: This document has been formally adopted by 40 US states and territories. It describes English language development expectations for students in grades K–12.
  (see: https://wida.wisc.edu/sites/default/files/resource/2012-ELD-Standards.pdf)

Key test-development processes that can support the creation of age-appropriate topics, texts, and tasks include involving classroom educators throughout the authoring and review stages of test development (So, 2014). Classroom educators are the best judges of developmentally and age-appropriate tasks for YLLs, and educator involvement in the topic-generation and review phases of development is essential. Educators are able to identify inappropriate directions, concepts, and language that may be too challenging or abstract for YLLs.

In addition to the important role educators play in the development of age-appropriate topics, texts, and tasks, another valuable development step is conducting cognitive labs (Beatty & Willis, 2007). Observations in cognitive labs allow test developers and researchers to gather information about issues that impact task performance and test administration, and to identify problems with task design. Cognitive labs involve the mock administration of test tasks to representative groups of YLLs. During cognitive labs, YLLs respond to test tasks, and after the administration, learners are interviewed (in English or the learner's L1) to determine whether the learners could understand task instructions, process the input, interpret associated pictures, and respond to the task. In general, the labs allow the researchers or test developers to get a sense of how accessible the learners find the task and whether there are confusing or overly difficult aspects of the task (Szpotowicz & Campfield, 2016). Findings from cognitive labs can provide evidence to support claims that test tasks provide cognitively-appropriate levels of demand for YLLs.

Children in the elementary years, roughly between ages 5 and 12, generally have attention spans as short as ten to fifteen minutes, particularly in the youngest grades (McKay, 2006). This means that language assessment tasks that are longer than fifteen minutes may adversely impact YLLs' task engagement and performance. As with attention span, younger learners up to age 8 or 9 have limited working memory capacities and will face challenges if presented with tasks that require the learners to perform several activities within a limited timeframe. Assessment tasks that require very young learners to listen to stimulus materials, process the information, and recall and reproduce source materials might not be age-appropriate.

Many YLLs, especially those in elementary schools, or those whose L1 literacy skills are in a language that uses an alphabet significantly different from that of English, may demonstrate emerging levels of literacy in English. While research has found that learners may use knowledge of print in one language to inform and support their learning of print literacy in another language (Roberts & Neal, 2004), YLLs can be presented with a range of challenges when faced with a reading or writing test in a language they are beginning to learn.

Due to the likelihood that many YLLs will have emerging levels of literacy, thought should be given to the textual input that is provided. Test developers should specify font sizes, text layout, sentence length, and overall passage length, likely employing an appropriate set of text readability indices, which can be challenging to apply meaningfully for the youngest learners. Also, tasks that are designed to assess comprehension at the word and character level are appropriate for these YLLs. Tasks appropriate for the assessment of the subskills that contribute to emerging literacy can be challenging to design and develop without the guidance of experienced grade-level educators and/or child psychologists who are familiar with how children learn to read. Tasks that focus on reading and/or writing at the sentence and discourse levels may not be developmentally appropriate for some YLLs.

Importance of Scaffolding

Scaffolding is a key pedagogical concept that refers to the tools that teachers provide to learners to help them carry out some tasks that are challenging. Hauck et al. (2017) listed several scaffolding techniques that can help young learners to do their best:

- model how to respond to a question;
- break down a task into steps or parts;
- provide key words needed to answer;
- provide a sentence frame, a sentence starter, or graphic organizer; and
- allow for re-prompting if a student does not give a complete or extended answer on speaking tasks.

These scaffolding techniques provide important support to students and are especially useful for students at beginning levels of language proficiency. They may be gradually removed from assessments that target more proficient or older learners. Thus, SLA researchers giving tests to YLLs should be careful to provide sufficient and appropriate scaffolding and support to ensure low performance on a test task is a result of a child's lack of knowledge or skill in the language, and not from a lack of understanding how to do the task; this is important because some YLLs may be challenged by attempting certain tasks without help, which is an age (cognitive-development-level) appropriate (i.e., expected) behavior.

Visual and multimodal support are other types of scaffolding techniques that can be incorporated within an assessment task for YLLs (Gottlieb, 2013). Visual support may be used to provide context to test input, to introduce and explain key vocabulary, to demonstrate who is speaking during test audio input, to explain to YLLs where to focus their attention, and to provide answer options, instead of traditional text-based response options. The use of illustrations and pictures can also serve to soften the assessment experience and to make the content more approachable, familiar, and engaging for YLLs.

While visual support can enhance the testing experience for YLLs and help them do their best, test designers, developers, and researchers must take care that the graphics do not introduce construct irrelevant variance. Graphics that provide too much support to students may lead students to the correct answer with little need for students to process language. On the other hand, for very young learners, pictures that do not align with the texts in the assessment tasks can confuse the very young who are starting to understand the association between pictures and texts (Bialystok, 2001; Winke et al., 2018). Thus, all graphics that appear on the assessment should be subject to review by classroom educators, test developers, and children who are the same age as those who will be tested.

Appropriateness of Delivery and Response Modes

The growth of computer-delivered tests, encompassing the delivery of test content on devices as varied as laptops, tablets, and mobile phones has caused test developers to consider which delivery modes they consider valid for YLLs (Kim, Lee, Chapman, & Wilmes, 2019). Another consideration is which response modes may be considered appropriate. Is it acceptable to ask young learners to type a response to a writing task? Will they perform better if they write out a response by hand? When responding to a speaking task, will learners perform better when interacting with a human interlocutor? Do they need to know the interlocutor? Or is it acceptable for young learners to respond to computer-delivered speaking tasks and have their spoken responses recorded for automated scoring? There are multiple issues around which test designers, developers, and SLA researchers must construct policies appropriate for young learners, and these policies should be supported by research. In addition, there are issues of score consistency and comparability if assessments are to be offered in multiple delivery and response modes.

While answers to these questions are beyond the scope of this chapter, we recommend that stakeholders in any assessment context examine the evidence that supports claims of comparability of an assessment that is offered in more than one delivery or response mode. Studies of mode effects within the context of YLL assessments are rare (Berninger, Abbott, Augsburger, & Garcia, 2009; Bishop, Lee, & Sahin, 2018; Connelly, Gee, & Walsh, 2007), but the few studies that are available do not tell a straightforward story. Perhaps an unsurprising finding is that some young learners lack familiarity with computers and that proficiency with typing interacts with language development to introduce potential construct irrelevant variance in the measurement of writing skills. Recent research by Bishop et al. (2018) showed that raters may exercise different scoring behaviors when rating young learners' spoken responses elicited from face-to-face testing and computer-delivered testing. The study implied that when administering speaking tests to YLLs in different delivery modes, raters need to ensure the comparability and quality of the rating process and procedures between the different test modes.

Responses and Implications for Scoring

YLL responses to constructed response tasks need special consideration when determining the appropriate scoring criteria and protocols (Wolf et al., 2016). Many YLLs are in the very early stages of their second- or foreign-language development and may produce very short, simple responses to productive language tasks. Rubrics must be appropriately designed to allow raters to distinguish between responses at the single-word, word and phrase, and sentence levels. For the very young, non-verbal responses may need to be considered as age- and situation-appropriate displays of communicative competence (i.e., head nods, showing yes to a stranger via a hand up with three fingers). Rubrics designed to evaluate the spoken or written language of older learners will likely not be appropriately nuanced to discriminate between levels of performance of beginner YLLs (Gu & Hsieh, 2019).

YLLs' written responses may be characterized by emerging orthographic control, resulting in common (age-appropriate) "mistakes" in letter formation, creative and phonetic spelling, lack of punctuation and recognizable sentence boundaries, and some very short responses. In addition to creating a rubric that can successfully discriminate between written responses from the target population, test developers must be trained to recognize these expected characteristics of emerging literacy, and to give credit where YLLs have produced age-appropriate original word-level or phrase-level responses. Raters will need to be trained to process YLL written responses for meaning, especially when responses are written by hand and challenging to decode due to the child's difficulties with spelling and letter formation.

As with the evaluation of writing proficiency, evaluating YLLs' spoken language also requires an appropriate rubric and tailored training for raters. YLLs' spoken responses are often characterized by short and fragmented speech at the word or phrase level and may lack organizational coherence (Hsieh & Wang, 2019). Raters must be trained to decode and evaluate YLL spoken performances based on reasonable, age-delimited expectations, focusing on the overall communicative effectiveness of the child's output. Raters should avoid penalizing YLL performance when grammatical or morphological errors (e.g., subject-verb agreement, verb tenses) do not severely hinder comprehension. These types of errors are often developmentally appropriate, even for L1 YLLs, and should be considered as typical characteristics of YLL speech. And finally, how scores are reported to young children is of importance. Instead of scores, positive awards (such as stars or badges) may be given with more awards indicating higher levels of performance, which may help sustain motivation.

Future Directions

Assessing YLLs is complex and challenging, and necessitates the knowledge of child SLA, and an understanding of the interrelated socio-cognitive developments that enable YLLs to expand their linguistic repertoires and conceptual understanding. Here we offer some suggestions for SLA researchers who need to assess the language learning of YLLs, and for future research on this topic in general. From the theoretical perspective, one area that is of particular interest pertains to the need for a better understanding of YLL language development. As previous research indicated, we consider the use of learner corpora and data-driven approaches to rating scale development as promising directions for future research. Another area that needs more detailed analysis is how YLLs process various assessment tasks. Because of children's developing cognition, insights into how YLLs of different ages process information embedded in assessment tasks can help test developers and researchers identify issues surrounding task design that may not be relevant or explicit in adult L2 assessments.

From a practical perspective, there is no doubt that test developers and applied linguists need more empirical research on how to appropriately administer tests to young learners, especially the very youngest (i.e., five to eight years old), given their limited cognitive development. This is important because SLA researchers and applied linguists need to map out the trajectories of YLLs so that the children's classroom instruction and educational language policies can be informed by the observed developmental paths. That mapping can only be done with reliable and accurate measurements. More research is needed to examine how to improve the quality of scoring processes and to provide clearer guidance and procedures for ensuring the comparability of test results derived from different delivery modes. Finally, the field needs to explore ways of generating score reports that offer useful feedback to teachers, parents, and policy makers on children's language learning and growth. We are hopeful that by gaining a deeper understanding in these areas, as well as by furthering applied linguist's knowledge in the theoretical issues that we have discussed in this paper, the field can better serve the needs of YLLs and stimulate new ideas and innovations in testing the L2 of YLLs.

Testing Tips

- Researchers should not assume that methods utilized in studies on adults or young adults will be appropriate for YLL populations. For example, complexity, accuracy, and fluency (CAF) measures used to analyze adult spoken and written language may not always be appropriate for analyzing the language produced by YLLs. Caution should be taken when using CAF measures to validate tests for young learners.
- Due to the developmental profiles of students throughout the school year, research should be conducted, whenever possible, at the same time period as when an operational assessment will be administered. For example, a test administered to students at the beginning of a school year cannot assume any content knowledge of material to be taught within that year's curriculum. Timing of research, specifically data collection, should align with instruction and testing within the school year.
- For very young learners (K–2), researchers should be aware of developmental differences across populations of interest. These very young learners are characterized by language developmental

profiles that are unpredictable and uneven (Barac & Bialystok, 2012), with some students demonstrating rapid growth in oral language skills, while others will make only very slow progress with literacy growth.

- Observational protocols, cognitive interview protocols, and surveys (for students and parents) should take into account both students' target language and home language(s). Surveys and interview questions that are delivered in the target language may not be accessible to YLLs. Researchers should consider translation of survey and interview questions of the students', and where relevant, the parents' home language(s).

Recommended Readings

Hasselgreen, A., & Caudwell, G. (2016). *Assessing the language of young learners*. Equinox.

This book presents concrete examples of assessment tasks in the domains of reading, writing, speaking, listening, vocabulary, and grammar, and practical suggestions on how to test these skills for different young learner age groups.

Nikolov, M. (Ed.) (2016). *Assessing young learners of English: Global and local perspectives*. Springer. https://doi.org/10.1007/978-3-319-22422-0

This edited volume outlines the current status of the assessment of young EFL learners and includes empirical studies in the development and validation of young learner language assessments.

Wolf, M. K., & Butler, Y. G. (Eds.) (2017). *English language proficiency assessments for young learners*. Routledge.

This edited volume presents the theoretical basis and assessment frameworks for young language learners and covers a wide range of topics in the assessment of young learners in both international and the US contexts.

References

Bailey, A. L. (2017). Progressions of a new language: Characterizing explanation development for assessment with young language learners. *Annual Review of Applied Linguistics*, *37*, 241–263. https://doi.org/10.1017/S0267190517000113

Bailey, A. L., Blackstock-Bernstein, A., Ryan, E., & Pitsoulakis, D. (2016). Data mining with natural language processing and corpus linguistics: Unlocking access to school children's language in diverse contexts to improve instructional and assessment practices. In S. ElAtia, D. Ipperciel, & O. R. Zaïane (Eds.), *Data mining and learning analytics: Applications in educational research* (pp. 255–275). John Wiley & Sons. https://doi.org/10.1002/9781118998205.ch15

Bailey, A. L., & Heritage, M. (2014). The role of language learning progressions in improved instruction and assessment of English language learners. *TESOL Quarterly*, *48*(3), 480–506. https://doi.org/10.1002/tesq.176

Barac, R., & Bialystok, E. (2012). Bilingual effects on cognitive and linguistic development: Role of language, cultural background, and education. *Child Development*, *83*(2), 413–422. https://doi.org/10.1111/j.1467-8624.2011.01707

Beatty, P. C., & Willis, G. B. (2007). Research synthesis: The practice of cognitive interview. *Public Opinion Quarterly*, *71*(2), 287–311. https://doi.org/10.1093/poq/nfm006

Berninger, V. W., Abbott, R. D., Augsburger, A., & Garcia, N. (2009). Comparison of pen and keyboard transcription modes in children with and without learning disabilities. *Learning Disability Quarterly*, *32*(3), 123–141. https://doi.org/10.2307/27740364

Bialystok, E. (2001). *Bilingualism in development: Language, literacy, and cognition*. Cambridge University Press.

Bishop, K., Lee, S., & Sahin, S. (2018, October 12–13). *A mixed-methods investigation into the rating contexts of ACCESS for ELLs 2.0 speaking domain*. [Paper presentation]. East Coast Organization of Language Testers (ECOLT) Conference, Princeton, NJ, United States.

Blom, E. (2019). Domain-general cognitive ability predicts bilingual children's receptive vocabulary in the majority language. *Language Learning*, *69*(2), 292–322. https://doi.org/10.1111/lang.12333
Butler, Y. G. (2009). Issues in the assessment and evaluation of English language education at the elementary school level: Implications for policies in South Korea, Taiwan, and Japan. *Journal of Asia TEFL*, *6*(2), 1–31.
Butler, Y. G., & Lee, J. (2010). The effects of self-assessment among young learners of English. *Language Testing*, *27*(1), 5–31. https://doi.org/10.1177/0265532209346370
Cheng, L., & Curtis, A. (2004). Washback or backwash: A review of the impact of testing on teaching and learning. In L. Cheng, Y. Watanabe, & A. Curtis (Eds.), *Washback in language testing*. Lawrence Erlbaum Associates.
Chik, A., & Besser, S. (2011). International language test taking among young learners: A Hong Kong case study. *Language Assessment Quarterly*, *8*(1), 73–91. https://doi.org/10.1080/15434303.2010.537417
Cho, Y., & So, Y. (2014). *Construct-irrelevant factors influencing young English as a foreign language (EFL) learners' perceptions of test task difficulty (ETS RM-14-04)*. Educational Testing Service.
Connelly, V., Gee, D., & Walsh, E. (2007). A comparison of keyboarded and handwritten compositions and the relationship with transcription speed. *British Journal of Educational Psychology*, *77*, 479–492. https://doi.org/10.1348/000709906X116768
Dunn, L. M., & Dunn, D. M. (2007). The Peabody picture vocabulary test (4th ed.). NCS Pearson.
Gottlieb, M. (2013). *Essential actions: A handbook for implementing WIDA's framework for English language development standards*. Board of Regents of the U of Wisconsin System.
Gu, L., & Hsieh, C.-N. (2019). Distinguishing features of young English language learners' oral performance. *Language Assessment Quarterly*, *16*(2), 180–195. https://doi.org/10.1080/15434303.2019.1605518
Gu, L., & So, Y. (2017). Strategies used by young English learners in an assessment context. In M. K. Wolf & Y. G. Butler (Eds.), *English language proficiency assessments for young learners* (pp. 118–135). Routledge.
Hauck, M. C., Pooler, E., Wolf, M. K., Lopez, A., & Anderson, D. (2017). Designing task types for English language proficiency assessments for K-12 English learners in the U.S. In M. K. Wolf & Y. G. Butler (Eds.), *English language proficiency assessments for young learners* (pp. 79–95). Routledge.
Hsieh, C.-N. (2016). Examining content representativeness of a young learner language assessment: EFL teachers' perspectives. In M. Nikolov (Ed.), *Assessing young learners of English: Global and local perspectives* (pp. 262–284). Springer. https://doi.org/10.1007/978-3-319-22422-0_5
Hsieh, C.-N., & Wang, Y. (2019). Speaking proficiency of young language students: A discourse-analytic study. *Language Testing*, *36*(1), 27–50. https://doi.org/10.1177/0265532217734240
Hung, Y.-J. (2018). Group peer assessment of oral English performance in a Taiwanese elementary school. *Studies in Educational Evaluation*, *59*, 19–28. https://doi.org/10.1016/j.stueduc.2018.02.001
Kim, A. A., Lee, S., Chapman, M., & Wilmes, C. (2019). The effects of administration and response modes on Grade 1–2 students' writing performance. *TESOL Quarterly*, *53*(2), 482–513. https://doi.org/10.1002/tesq.495
Lakshmanan, U. (2009). Child second language acquisition. In W. C. Ritchie & T. K. Bhatia (Eds.), *The new handbook of second language acquisition* (pp. 377–399). Emerald.
Lee, S., & Winke, P. (2018). Young learners' response processes when taking computerized tasks for speaking assessment. *Language Testing*, *35*(2), 239–269. https://doi.org/10.1177/0265532217704009
Llosa, L. (2011). Standards-based classroom assessments of English proficiency: A review of issues, current developments, and future directions for research. *Language Testing*, *28*(3), 367–382. https://doi.org/10.1177/0265532211404188
McKay, P. (2006). *Assessing young language learners*. Cambridge University Press.
Nikilov, M. (2016). A framework for young EFL learners' diagnostic assessment: 'Can do statements' and task types. In M. Nikolov (Ed.), *Assessing young learners of English: Global and local perspectives* (pp. 63–92). Springer. https://doi.org/10.1007/978-3-319-22422-0_5
Oliver, R., & Azkarai, A. (2017). Review of child SLA: Examining theories and research. *Annual Review of Applied Linguistics*, *37*, 62–76. https://doi.org/10.1017/S0267190517000058
Papp, S., Rixon, S., Saville, N., & Weir, C. J. (2018). *Examining young learners: Research and practice in assessing the English of school-age learners*. Cambridge University Press.
Papp, S., & Walczak, A. (2016). The development and validation of a computer-based test of English for young learners: Cambridge-English young learners. In M. Nikolov (Ed.), *Assessing young learners of English: Global and local perspectives* (pp. 139–190). Springer. https://doi.org/10.1007/978-3-319-22422-0_5
Philp, J., Borowczyk, M., & Mackey, A. (2017). Exploring the uniqueness of child second language acquisition (SLA): Learning, teaching, assessment, and practice. *Annual Review of Applied Linguistics*, *37*, 1–13. https://doi.org/10.1017/S0267190517000174

Roberts, T., & Neal, H. (2004). Relationships among preschool English language learner's oral proficiency in English, instructional experience and literacy development. *Contemporary Educational Psychology*, *29*(3), 283–311. https://doi.org/10.1016/j.cedpsych.2003.08.001
Snow, M. A., & Katz, A. M. (2014). Assessing language and content. In A. J. Kunnan (Ed.), *The companion to language assessment*. John Wiley & Sons. https://doi.org/10.1002/9781118411360
So, Y. (2014). Are teacher perspectives useful? Incorporating EFL teacher feedback in the development of a large-scale international English test. *Language Assessment Quarterly*, *11*(3), 283–303. https://doi.org/10.1080/15434303.2014.936936
Szpotowicz, M., & Campfield, D. E. (2016). Developing and piloting proficiency tests for Polish young learners. In M. Nikolov (Ed.), *Assessing young learners of English: Global and local perspectives* (pp. 109–137). Springer.
Verhagen, J., & Leseman, P. (2016). How do verbal short-term memory and working memory relate to the acquisition of vocabulary and grammar? A comparison between first and second language learners. *Journal of Experimental Child Psychology*, *141*, 65–82. https://doi.org/10.1016/j.jecp.2015.06.015.
Winke, P., Lee, S., Ahn, J. I., Choi, I., Cui, Y., & Yoon, H.-J. (2018). The cognitive validity of child English language tests: What young language learners and their native-speaking learners and their native-speaking peers can reveal. *TESOL Quarterly*, *52*(2), 274–303. https://doi.org/10.1002/tesq.396
Wolf, M. K., Guzman-Orth, D., Lopez, A., Castellano, K., Himelfarb, I., & Tsutagawa, F. (2016). Integrating scaffolding strategies into technology-enhanced assessments of English learners: Task types and measurement models. *Educational Assessment*, *21*(3), 157–175. https://doi.org/10.1080/10627197.2016.1202107

39

Testing the L2 of Learners with Specific Learning Difficulties

Judit Kormos & Lynda B. Taylor

Background

Evidence of second language (L2) competence is frequently required in academic and professional contexts and, hence, the test-taking population is both growing and changing. A large number of language proficiency tests have become high-stakes with important consequences for test-takers' life chances, career prospects and immigration status. It is paramount, therefore, that every care is taken to ensure valid and fair tests for everyone including test-takers with specific learning difficulties (SpLDs), who constitute around 10% of the global population (OECD, 2008). As educational opportunities around the world are made more accessible for learners with various specific needs, the number of individuals with SpLDs taking language proficiency tests is increasing (Tsagari & Spanoudis, 2013). It is therefore essential that neither the test design nor test implementation procedures create an unfair barrier for these students.

According to the 5th edition of the Diagnostic and Statistical Manual of Mental Disorders of the American Psychiatric Association (DSM-5, APA, 2013), SpLDs are of neurological origin and result in persistent difficulties to learn or use specific academic skills. Although DSM-5 views various sub-types of SpLDs as overlapping constructs and classifies them under a joint umbrella term, it also recognizes the need for specific sub-categories of SpLDs in the areas of reading, writing, and numeracy. Within the category of reading difficulties, DSM-5 distinguishes word-level decoding problems (dyslexia) and higher-level text comprehension problems. Individuals with SpLDs also demonstrate weaknesses in the areas of working memory, executive functioning (planning, organizing, strategizing, and paying attention), processing speed, and phonological processing (for a comprehensive discussion see APA, 2013). The cognitive skills which are affected by SpLDs also play an important role in the success of L2 learning and can influence how students perform on various assessment tasks (for a review see Kormos, 2017). Therefore, a key question is how test designers can ensure fairness for candidates with SpLDs without compromising the validity of the test, particularly the meaningfulness of test score outcomes. This issue is of high relevance for dyslexic test-takers whose SpLD is reading-related and for this reason the main focus in this chapter will be on dyslexic language learners.

Transparency and accessibility in the design and development of language tests is a direct result of a quest for ethics in assessment (Shohamy, 1997; Taylor, 2012). The concept of fairness in language testing is "inherently an ethical one" (Kunnan, 2010, p. 187). The aim of ensuring fairness in assessment is to prevent tests inflicting harm on test-takers, including candidates with SpLDs, and to maximize the opportunities for all test-takers to perform to their best. An important theoretical issue in the field of language testing that is particularly relevant for the assessment of L2 skills of candidates with SpLDs is the complex relationship between validity and fairness (see Kunnan, 2004). Kunnan (2004) argued that a test is only valid if it is fair, and consequently, the concept of validity can be considered to embrace fairness. Kane (2010) also claimed that fairness and validity are strongly inter-related yet he considered them distinct constructs. Importantly, Kane pointed out that no valid interpretations and decisions can be made based on the scores of an assessment tool that creates a systematic negative or positive bias towards specific groups of test-takers.

One of the first systematic, comprehensive and still currently used definitions of test fairness was provided by the American Educational Research Association (1999). In their conceptualization, fairness entails four important components: lack of bias, equitable treatment in the testing process, equality in the outcomes of testing, and fairness as an opportunity to learn. First, a test can be characterized as being unbiased if it has no "construct irrelevant components that result in systematically lower or higher scores for identifiable groups of examinees" (American Educational Research Association (AERA), 1999, p. 76). Bias can be generated by the content and the response format of a test. Therefore, during test design, special attention needs to be paid to the presentation of test content and the selection of response formats in order to allow test-takers with SpLDs to display their L2 skills. Second, to ensure equitable treatment in the assessment, the context and purpose of the assessment need to be considered carefully. With regard to SpLDs, it is essential that tests are administered under testing conditions (e.g., time limits, physical environment) that do not prevent candidates with disabilities from performing to the best of their ability. Third, equality in outcomes of testing can be achieved if it can be demonstrated that specific sub-groups of test-takers with similar levels of ability (e.g., those from different language or ethnic background) perform similarly on the tests. Finally, fairness as an opportunity to learn can be achieved by providing test-takers with equal opportunities for test preparation. For students with SpLDs this means having access to appropriately designed learning and test preparation materials.

Although the Principles of Good Practice of the Association of Language Testers in Europe (2020) explicitly state that "fairness is an overriding concern in all aspects of assessment," in some cases this principle can be difficult to implement in test design and administration, particularly for candidates with disabilities. The Guidelines for Practice of the International Language Testing Association (https://www.iltaonline.com/page/ILTAGuidelinesforPractice) highlight that developers and administrators of tests are responsible for designing and administering the assessment in a manner that does not disadvantage test-takers. In some cases, therefore, special arrangements are required to enable candidates with disabilities to display their L2 knowledge and skills in an assessment context. These special arrangements, often referred to as "accommodations" or "adjustments," can be categorized based on how they make appropriate provision for a test that is valid and accessible to groups of learners with varying physical or cognitive disabilities (e.g., visual/hearing impairment, dyslexia). Accommodations (e.g., Braille version, extra time allocation) seek to ensure that the test is carefully adapted to be accessible to groups of test-takers with particular disabilities while still maintaining validity in terms of construct relevance and thus the meaning and usefulness of score outcomes, i.e., to "minimise the impact of those test-taker attributes that are irrelevant to the construct being measured" (Taylor & Nordby Chen, 2016, p. 378). A further term—"modifications"—is generally used when test content or presentation are modified in a way that affects the construct validity of the test.

Key Concepts

Specific learning difficulties: Persistent difficulties in learning or using specific academic skills, which are neurological in origin (DSM-5, APA, 2013).

Fairness: Fairness in testing entails four important components: lack of bias, equitable treatment in the testing process, equality in the outcomes of testing, and fairness as an opportunity to learn.

Accommodations: These are adjustments (e.g., time extension) that assist test-takers with disabilities to complete the test "without other confounding influences of test format, administration, or responding" (Hollenbeck, Tindal, & Almond, 1998, p. 175) and without affecting the validity of the test.

Modifications: These are special arrangements (e.g., allowing a student to listen to reading text) offered for candidates with disabilities that increase the accessibility of the test, but have an effect on the validity of the assessment.

Universal test design: This aims to ensure that a test is accessible to everyone.

Key Issues

Some Theoretical Considerations

One of the key theoretical issues in assessing candidates with SpLDs is determining how special arrangements may impact on the construct being assessed and to what extent that is acceptable or desirable as far as the meaning and usefulness of any test score outcomes are concerned. This decision-making process requires a careful analysis of the test content, test delivery, and test scoring procedures in relation to the construct and the specific language skills and processes that underlie it, as well as the interpretation of scores resulting from test-takers' performance on the test. For example, the issue of fairness when assessing the reading comprehension of test-takers with dyslexia is particularly difficult because dyslexic individuals' disability manifests itself in slow and inaccurate word-level decoding (DSM-5, APA, 2013), which then might have a negative impact on their sentence and text-level comprehension. Therefore, in some teaching and assessment contexts, dyslexic students are allowed to listen to a text while they read on the assumption that this read-aloud assistance will improve their text comprehension. However, written word-level decoding, which is not tested when a read-aloud assistance is given, is an integral component of the reading construct (e.g., Khalifa & Weir, 2009), and hence the read-aloud assistance is a modification rather than an accommodation (Hansen, Mislevy, Steinberg, Lee, & Forer, 2005). In contrast, offering candidates with SpLDs extra time for answering reading comprehension questions does not change the construct being tested, and thus can be considered an accommodation.

Another key question in relation to special arrangements is whether they risk advantaging test-takers with disabilities over those without disabilities, resulting in differential gains for disabled candidates. Accommodations are intended to facilitate attainment in the skill being assessed while at the same time ensuring that test-takers receiving such provision are not given unfair advantage over other candidates and that the user of the test certificate is not misled about the nature of the candidate's attainment. According to the *interaction hypothesis*, in a valid test special arrangements should only have an impact on the scores of students with SpLDs and should not influence the results obtained by students with no SpLDs (Zuriff, 2000). If everyone benefits from a special arrangement, it means that test-takers in general may not be able to display the best of their abilities under standard test administration conditions, and hence the validity of the test can be called into question. For this reason, some experts in educational measurement have called for a *universal test design*, "which mandates that tests be constructed and administered more flexibly so that accommodations become unnecessary" (Sireci, Scarpati, & Li, 2005). Although in theory the principle of universal test design should contribute to creating more inclusive and ethical tests, unfortunately the practicalities in test production and delivery are likely to constrain the design of fully flexible tests.

Given the continuing need for special arrangements for certain test-taker groups, it is important to consider how accommodations might be differentially beneficial for test-takers with disabilities. According to the *differential boost hypothesis* (Fuchs & Fuchs, 1999), accommodations might not impact the construct being assessed if they result in more gains for students with disabilities than their non-disabled peers. It is important, however, to ascertain that there are no ceiling effects when examining differential boost in test scores. In other words, one needs to exclude the possibility that non-disabled test-takers already score so high in the standard administration condition that they cannot further increase their scores when they perform in the special arrangement condition (Koenig & Bachman, 2004).

Evidence and Insights from Empirical Research

In general, decisions about the nature and extent of modifications to standard language test content and delivery tend to be based upon the judgment of qualified and experienced test development staff, informed by insights from educational and other professional bodies working in a given area of disability. Taylor (2012) highlights the significant ethical, logistical, and measurement challenges involved in undertaking empirical research into accommodated tests or conducting test validation studies among groups of test-takers with disabilities. Given the inherent difficulty of conducting large-scale experimental studies involving quantitative methodologies, there have been calls for a greater focus on carrying out more qualitative or mixed-methods research in this area (Geranpayeh & Taylor, 2013; Taylor, 2012).

In the field of general educational assessment, two types of special arrangements have been widely researched: time-extensions and read-aloud. The policy of granting extra examination time allows candidates with SpLDs either a longer period for the completion of the test and/or more frequent breaks during the test (Cortiella, 2005). Read-aloud assistance offers students with SpLDs the opportunity to listen to a text read out to them while simultaneously reading it. As read-aloud is a modification that has an impact on the validity of the test, its use is less frequent in high-stakes assessments of text comprehension, but it is often applied in classroom contexts (Bottsford-Miller et al., 2006).

Košak-Babuder, Kormos, Ratajczak, and Pižorn (2018) examined how read-aloud assistance benefits dyslexic and non-dyslexic test-takers. Young Slovenian learners of English were administered four tasks adapted from a standardized battery of Slovenian national English language tests. Non-dyslexic and dyslexic participants completed two language comprehension tasks in reading-only mode, one task with read-aloud assistance, and one task in a listening-only condition. Košak-Babuder et al.'s results showed that young dyslexic L2 learners benefited from the read-aloud assistance when the input text was more difficult but gained no advantage in comparison with their non-dyslexic peers when the input text had a higher readability index, that is, when the text was easier.

Time extension, which is a frequently granted accommodation, is assumed to benefit students with SpLDs as they tend to decode written texts and the accompanying comprehension tasks more slowly and, due to working memory limitations, might need to reread information to remember it. A meta-analysis of previous studies by Gregg and Nelson (2012) seems to support the beneficial effects of time-extension as it showed that test-takers with SpLDs achieved significantly higher scores in L1 literacy skills tests under an extended time condition than did students with no SpLDs. A later re-analysis of the effect of time-extension in L1 literacy and numeracy tests by Cahan, Nirel, and Alkoby (2016), however, indicated that time-extension policies can unfairly disadvantage non-disabled candidates who would also benefit from extra time. Their results revealed that approximately half of the non-disabled test-takers would have gained higher scores if they had been given extended time to complete the assessment.

Another type of accommodation is when the response format of certain test tasks or components is changed in a way that does not affect the construct being assessed. This type of accommodation might offer test-takers the opportunity to respond in another modality, such as answering reading comprehension questions in speech rather than in writing. It can also include the use of scribes to whom students dictate their responses, or the use of word-processors instead of handwriting. To date, little research is available on these types of accommodations, and all of the existing studies have focused on L1 writing assessment. For example, Berger and Lewandowski (2013) found that the essay length and scores of both students with and without SpLDs increased when they were allowed to use a word processor in comparison with when they wrote by hand. Word processing tools can increase the fluency of writing and assist in the editing, revision, and monitoring processes of composing. Therefore, it is hoped that word processing tools will soon become part of universal test design in language tests for computer literate populations.

Adjustments in the presentation format of a test are also commonly offered to students with SpLDs. Test-takers can request that the test should be typed using specific font types, spacing and background. The British Dyslexia Association (2014) has a detailed list of accessibility guidelines for the presentation of reading materials. Unfortunately, most evidence on the beneficial effects of these accessibility features is based on subjective preference reports and solid empirical support for their benefits is currently lacking. For example, Kuster et al. (2018) found that font type had no effect on the L1 word-reading accuracy of dyslexic children; the children had higher preference for a sans-serif font type (Ariel) than for a serif font type (Times New Roman), but there was no link between reading performance and font preference. Another controversial issue is the use of colored overlays, which is often recommended for dyslexic individuals. In Henderson, Tsogka, and Bishop's (2013) study dyslexic students reported significantly higher rate of visual stress when reading texts in traditional formats than non-dyslexic ones. Nonetheless, the provision of colored overlays did not result in improvements in reading comprehension or reading speed. A systematic research review by Griffiths, Taylor, Henderson, and Barrett (2016) also revealed that the beneficial effects of colored overlays are small and likely to be due to placebo effects.

Stakeholder Perspectives

One way of improving our understanding of the effectiveness of special arrangements for test-takers with disabilities is through the study of *test impact*, specifically the investigation of impact as it concerns particular stakeholder groups (Hawkey, 2006). Key stakeholders include not only test-takers themselves, but also language teachers, test writers, and test administrators. Studies reporting on the use of special arrangements for candidates with SpLDs remain relatively limited, suggesting that this dimension of impact is worthy of further consideration.

Shaw and Weir (2007) and Taylor and Khalifa (2013) report some of the work in this area from the perspective of a large UK-based examinations board which administers a wide range of internationally recognized English language proficiency tests. Shaw and Weir (2007) describe an investigation into the provision of a separate marking special arrangement for candidates with dyslexia in some of its writing tests, motivated by concerns over theoretical validity, equity, and practicality. The board concluded that the separate marking of dyslexic test-takers' writing performance (i.e., ignoring all spelling errors) was not appropriate in a language-focused test even though it was common practice in content-focused assessment. Additional time was considered to be the most appropriate provision for test-takers with dyslexia.

Taylor and Khalifa (2013) explored test impact on a range of stakeholders involved in accommodations offered in tests by Cambridge Assessment English by triangulating a documentary review of examination board policy and practice with survey and interview data from test administrators, test writers, test examiners, and test-takers. Areas highlighted for attention and possible improvement included: the extent and nature of special arrangements information provided to all stakeholders; the importance of sustained and comprehensive training (e.g., for test centre staff and examiners); the complex logistics of implementation; the challenge of achieving a consistent, professional, and fair approach; and possible future avenues for research. Views varied over whether all candidates who receive extra time do actually need it or use it and this suggests an area for potential research, perhaps through observational studies. Both test developers and examiners appeared to suggest that task comparability across differing accommodated formats is also worthy of investigation.

Despite the fact that special arrangements can entail considerable extra work, inconvenience, and extra expense, as well as present significant challenges for those involved, all stakeholder groups in Taylor and Khalifa's study confirmed the positive impact of test accommodations in terms of benefits to learners, their teachers, and families. This was echoed in test-takers' testimonials on the special arrangements provision. Since the challenge of meeting the often unique configuration of assessment needs of each test-taker with a disability, in a manner that is reliable, valid, and equitable, should not be underestimated, it is encouraging to hear the comments made by the test-takers on the suitability and the appropriate match they experienced between the special arrangement provision offered and their individual requirements.

The particular value of this type of research lies in the way it explores the impact of assessing students with disabilities through the voices of differing stakeholder groups involved in the process. Such research will hopefully deepen our understanding of the roles and needs of such groups and thus contribute to the body of literature in the relatively under-researched area of language assessment for students with disabilities, including those with SpLDs. There are, of course, other key stakeholders who could (and should) be canvassed for their views, including disability organizations who offer advice to examination boards, and test users who have to interpret scores from adapted tests.

Recommendations for Practice

Learners with SpLDs might not be able to achieve the same learning objectives as their peers, especially in the area of second language writing and reading. Therefore, if possible, the learning targets should be adjusted to their individual strengths and weaknesses, and assessment goals and tasks might need to be modified. This can ensure that test-takers with SpLDs experience success, and that their motivation and self-esteem does not deteriorate. To illustrate, in non-standardized low-stakes writing tests, L2 learners with dyslexia might be exempted from the evaluation of their spelling skills or might be allowed to use spell checkers. This approach is more challenging to implement in high-stakes tests where knowledge of spelling may be part of the writing construct being assessed; it could perhaps be resolved, however, if all test-takers, not just those with SpLDs, were allowed access to a spell checker, reflecting the universal design principle.

Both in testing and research contexts, it is also important to consider the timing of assessment and research tasks. Even though many real-life L2 use situations are not constrained by time, most assessments and research contexts have time limits. Students with SpLDs might be slower readers, might process information less quickly than their peers, and might also need more time for writing. However, as research evidence suggests, the benefits of extra time for test-takers with SpLDs might be limited and often other candidates' performance would also be enhanced by extended time (Cahan et al., 2016). Therefore, task designers in classroom, research, and assessment contexts alike, should consider carefully what the optimal time is for completing tasks that allow even slower learners to display the best of their knowledge. Until such universal design features can be implemented, the practice of time extensions should be continued and decisions on extra time should take into account factors such as the students' reading, writing, and information processing speed. As learners with SpLDs sometimes get exhausted and lose focus more quickly than their peers, they should also be offered the option of taking short breaks during the test or research.

Additional adjustments might need to be offered to students with SpLDs to ensure the accessibility of test and task content. Earlier in the chapter we discussed the benefits of read-aloud assistance, which aids comprehension of written texts (Košak-Babuder et al., 2018). Although this results in the modification of the reading construct, its use might be considered in low-stakes classroom assessment, and in teaching and certain research contexts. The multi-modal presentation of test and task instructions (e.g., aural as well as written rubrics, use of visual symbols or pictures) might also universally help students understand what they need to do in a test or a research task and can potentially reduce construct-irrelevant variance resulting from confusion about tasks (cf. Winke et al., 2018). It is also often recommended that tests and teaching material should be printed on colored paper in larger font size and with more generous spacing, and colored overlays are also provided to assist students who experience visual stress. Despite the fact that no solid empirical evidence exists that these visual modifications improve text comprehension, many individuals with SpLDs express a preference for using them and this preference should not be ignored. They have no negative impact on reading speed or comprehension and are relatively easy and cheap to provide, hence their use as a special arrangement should be continued. As students with SpLDs tend to have smaller working memory and shorter attention spans, test and task designers might also need to consider the length of written and aural input texts in a test or a research task. A potentially useful adjustment in this regard can be breaking up reading or listening texts into shorter sections followed by items requiring a response. Computer-based rather than paper-based tests and tasks can facilitate this approach by presenting textual input and test items into more manageable chunks screen by screen.

The response format of a test or a research instrument also needs to allow students with SpLDs to perform to the best of their abilities. Language learners with SpLDs might also benefit from more selected response formats such as matching or underlining instead of gap-fill or short-answer tasks. The computer-based delivery of tests and tasks may make this approach easier, while computer-adaptive tests can perhaps be more readily tailored to the individual needs of some students with SpLDs. Many students with SpLDs find it particularly challenging to listen and read or listen and write at the same time. In listening tests, therefore, previewing the questions, listening to the text more than once and/or having additional time to read the test items might be beneficial. The use of scribes who write down students' answers and the practice of allowing students to record their response orally instead of writing can also be considered.

Decisions about best practice can be informed through professional advice from disability organizations and other examining bodies, though this may sometimes be complex given inconsistencies in national and international disability legislation. Finally, the growing and significant role of assistive technology in L2 learning and assessment contexts should not be underestimated in the future.

Testing Tips

- It is important to leave sufficient time for all candidates to complete tests where time pressure is not part of the construct to be assessed.
- Multi-modal presentation of test instructions might help test-takers understand how to perform the test tasks.
- The visual layout of tests should follow accessibility guidelines.
- Test-takers with SpLDs display their knowledge better in tasks that have selected response formats.
- Previewing questions before listening input helps candidate with SpLDs to focus their attention on relevant parts of the text to be comprehended.

Recommended Readings

Kormos, J. (2017). Chapter 5: Assessing the language skills of students with specific learning difficulties. In J. Kormos, *The second language learning processes of students with specific learning difficulties* (pp. 94–111). Routledge.

This chapter gives an overview of issues surrounding the fair and valid assessment of test-takers with SpLDs. It also elaborates how different types of special arrangements can eliminate barriers that test-takers with SpLDs might face in different assessment contexts.

Tsagari, D. & Spanoudis, G. (Eds.). (2013). *Assessing L2 students with learning and other disabilities*. Cambridge Scholars.

This book is an excellent collection of research articles on assessing the language skills and attainment of L2 learners and multilingual language users with disabilities in a wide variety of contexts.

Tsagari, D. & Sperling, I. (2017). Assessing SLLs with SpLDs: Challenges and opportunities for equity in education. In E. Piechurska-Kuciel et al. (Eds.), *At the crossroads: Challenges of foreign language learning, second language learning and teaching* (pp. 175–188). Springer. https://doi.org/10.1007/978-3-319-55155-5_1

This chapter summarizes discussions and research findings in the field of language assessment for second language learners (SLLs) with SpLDs, identifying key stakeholders who are closely connected to successful assessment. The chapter also explores issues in external and classroom-based assessment in need of attention and highlights research areas for the improvement of assessment of SLLs with SpLDs.

References

American Educational Research Association, American Psychological Association, National Council on Measurement in Education, Joint Committee on Standards for Educational and Psychological Testing (U.S.). [AERA/APA/NCME] (1999). *Standards for educational and psychological testing*. AERA.

American Psychiatric Association. (2013). *Diagnostic and statistical manual of mental disorders* (5th ed.). https://doi.org/10.1176/appi.books.9780890425596

Association of Language Testers in Europe. (2020). *ALTE Principles of Good Practice*. https://www.alte.org/resources/Documents/ALTE Principles of Good Practice Online (Final).pdf

Berger, C. L., & Lewandowski, L. (2013). The effect of a word processor as an accommodation for students with learning disabilities. *Journal of Writing Research, 4*(3), 261–280. https://doi.org/10.17239/jowr-2013.04.03.2

Bottsford-Miller, N., Thurlow, M. L., Stout, K. E., & Quenemoen, R. F. (2006). *A comparison of IEP/504 accommodations under classroom and standardized testing conditions: A preliminary report on SEELS Data* (Synthesis Report 63). University of Minnesota, National Center on Educational Outcomes. https://files.eric.ed.gov/fulltext/ED495884.pdf

British Dyslexia Association. (2014). *Dyslexia style guide*. https://www.bdadyslexia.org.uk/common/ckeditor/filemanager/userfiles/About_Us/policies/Dyslexia_Style_Guide.pdf

Cahan, S., Nirel, R., & Alkoby, M. (2016). The extra-examination time granting policy: A reconceptualization. *Journal of Psychoeducational Assessment, 34*(5), 461–472. https://doi.org/10.1177/0734282915616537

Cortiella, C. (2005). *No child left behind: Determining appropriate assessment accommodations for students with disabilities*. National Center for Learning Disabilities, Inc.

Fuchs, L. S., & Fuchs, D. (1999). Fair and unfair testing accommodations. *School Administrator, 56*(10), 24–29.

Geranpayeh, A., & Taylor, L. (Eds.). (2013) *Examining listening: Research and practice in assessing second language listening*. UCLES/Cambridge University Press.

Gregg, N., & Nelson, J. M. (2012). Meta-analysis on the effectiveness of extra time as a test accommodation for transitioning adolescents with learning disabilities: More questions than answers. *Journal of Learning Disabilities, 45*(2), 128–138. https://doi.org/10.1177/0022219409355484

Griffiths, P. G., Taylor, R. H., Henderson, L. M., & Barrett, B. T. (2016). The effect of coloured overlays and lenses on reading: A systematic review of the literature. *Ophthalmic and Physiological Optics, 36*(5), 519–544. https://doi.org/10.1111/opo.12316

Hansen, E. G., Mislevy, R. J., Steinberg, L. S., Lee, M. J., & Forer, D. C. (2005). Accessibility of tests for individuals with disabilities within a validity framework. *System*, *33*(1), 107–133. https://doi.org/10.1016/j.system.2004.11.002

Hawkey, R. (2006). *Impact theory and practice: Studies of the IELTS test and progetto lingue 2000*. UCLES/Cambridge University Press.

Henderson, L. M., Tsogka, N., & Snowling, M. J. (2013). Questioning the benefits that coloured overlays can have for reading in students with and without dyslexia. *Journal of Research in Special Educational Needs*, *13*(1), 57–65. https://doi.org/10.1111/j.1471-3802.2012.01237.x

Hollenbeck, K., Tindal, G., & Almond, P. (1998). Teachers' knowledge of accommodations as a validity issue in high-stakes testing. *Journal of Special Education*, *32*(3), 175–183. https://doi.org/10.1177/002246699803200304

Kane, M. T. (2010). Validity and fairness. *Language Testing*, *27*(2), 177–182. https://doi.org/10.1177/0265532209349467

Khalifa, H., & Weir, C. (2009). *Examining reading: Research and practice in assessing second language reading*. Cambridge University Press.

Koenig, J. A., & Bachman, L. F. (2004). *Keeping score for all: The effects of inclusion and accommodation policies on large-scale educational assess*. National Academies Press.

Kormos, J. (2017). *The second language learning processes of students with specific learning difficulties*. Routledge.

Košak-Babuder, M., Kormos, J., Ratajczak, M., & Pižorn, K. (2018). The effect of read-aloud assistance on the text comprehension of dyslexic and non-dyslexic English language learners. *Language Testing*, *36*(1), 51–75. https://doi.org/10.1177/0265532218756946

Kunnan, A. J. (2004). Test fairness. In M. Milanovic & C. Weir (Eds.), *European language testing in a global context*: *Proceedings of the ALTE Barcelona conference* (pp. 27–48). Cambridge University Press.

Kunnan, A. J. (2010). Test fairness and Toulmin's argument structure. *Language Testing*, *27*(2), 183–189. https://doi.org/10.1177/0265532209349468

Kuster, S. M., van Weerdenburg, M., Gompel, M., & Bosman, A. M. (2018). Dyslexie font does not benefit reading in children with or without dyslexia. *Annals of Dyslexia*, *68*(1), 25–42. https://doi.org//10.1007/s11881-017-0154-6

Organization for Economic Co-operation and Development. (2008). Annual report. https://www.oecd.org/newsroom/40556222.pdf

Shaw, S. D., & Weir, C. J. (2007). *Examining writing: Research and practice in assessing second language writing*. UCLES/Cambridge University Press.

Shohamy, E. (1997). Testing methods, testing consequences: Are they ethical? Are they fair? *Language Testing*, *14*(3), 340–349. https://doi.org/10.1177/026553229701400310

Sireci, S. G., Scarpati, S. E., & Li, S. (2005). Test accommodations for students with disabilities: An analysis of the interaction hypothesis. *Review of Educational Research*, *75*, 457–490. https://doi.org/10.3102/00346543075004457

Taylor, L. (2012). Accommodation in language testing. In C. Coombe, P. Davidson, B. O'Sullivan, & S. Stoynoff (Eds.), *The Cambridge guide to second language assessment* (pp. 307–315). Cambridge University Press.

Taylor, L., & Khalifa, H. (2013). Assessing students with disabilities: Voices from the stakeholder community. In G. Spanoudis & D. Tsagari (Eds.), *Assessing L2 students with learning and other disabilities* (pp. 229–252). Cambridge Scholars.

Taylor, L., & Nordby Chen, N. (2016). Assessing students with learning and other disabilities/special needs. In D. Tsagari & J. Banerjee (Eds.), *Handbook of second language assessment* (pp. 377–395). Mouton De Gruyter.

Tsagari, D., & Spanoudis, G. (2013). *Assessing L2 students with learning and other disabilities*. Cambridge Scholars.

Winke, P., Lee, S., Ahn, J. I., Choi, I., Cui, Y., & Yoon, H. J. (2018). The cognitive validity of child English language tests: What young language learners and their native-speaking peers can reveal. *TESOL Quarterly*, *52*(2), 274–303. https://doi.org/10.1002/tesq.396

Zuriff, G. E. (2000). Extra examination time for students with learning disabilities: An examination of the maximum potential thesis. *Applied Measurement in Education*, *13*(1), 99–117. https://doi.org/10.1207/s15324818ame1301_5

40

Testing Heritage Language Learners

Young-A Son

Background

According to the 2009-2013 American Community Survey, about 21% of the United States population speaks a language other than English at home (United States Census Bureau, 2015). For over two decades, this number has steadily increased from about 47 million in 2000 to 63.2 million in 2014 (Caramota & Ziegler, 2015). Many researchers have described a similar trend in the number of heritage speakers in many regions of the world (e.g., Ndhlovu & Willoughby, 2017). At the same time, this growing number of heritage speakers has had a major impact on language education, as many of these speakers seek formal instruction of their heritage language. In fact, language educators have reported an increase in enrollment rates of heritage language learners (HLLs) in their language classrooms (e.g., Beaudrie, Ducar, & Potowski, 2014). This change of learner demographics from traditional Foreign Language Learners (FLLs) to HLLs in language courses has sparked increasing scholarly attention in describing HLLs' linguistic abilities and pedagogical needs.

Broadly speaking, much of the research on HLLs can be divided into two major strands of research. On the one hand, researchers have been interested in identifying areas in language development that differentiate HLLs from FLLs. These studies have mostly investigated how timing, amount, and quality of input that HLLs receive influence their linguistic outcomes in phonology, vocabulary, and morphosyntax (e.g., Laleko & Polinsky, 2013; Montrul, 2016; Montrul & Perpiñán, 2011; O'Grady, Lee, & Cho, 2001). Thus, this type of research has typically described the HL proficiency in terms of discrete linguistic features. On the other hand, a second area of research popular in the HLL domain has concentrated on identifying HLLs' pedagogical needs and ways to address them (e.g., Beaudrie, Ducar, & Potowski, 2014; Carreira, 2017; Carreira & Kagan, 2018; Polinsky, 2016). These studies have generally taken a more holistic view in describing HLL's language abilities in terms of broader concepts of language competence, such as listening, reading, speaking, and writing. Overall, both strands of research have significantly contributed to our understanding of how HLL acquire language and the main factors that could influence their language development and maintenance.

Despite these major advancements in heritage language acquisition (HLA) research, one major point of concern which numerous researchers (e.g., Kagan & Dillon, 2012; Malone, Peyton, & Kim, 2014; Polinsky, 2016; Son, 2017) have noted, is the limited number of studies that focus on testing HLLs, particularly the development of HL tests and validation of their uses. Like much of the research in SLA, a large body of literature in HLA considers language proficiency a key moderating factor that has strong implications for how learners' linguistic outcomes in phonological or morphological tests, grammaticality judgment tests, or results on performance tests can be interpreted. It is critical, then, that language proficiency is accurately measured in order to also have an accurate interpretation of research findings. Nevertheless, there has been an overall lack of understanding on how HL proficiency can be measured accurately and reliably. In part, these difficulties in assessing HL proficiency may be rooted from the complexity and overall variability of defining who these learners are and how they differ from FLLs. In addition, due to the limited availability of instruments designed specifically to test HLLs, most of these studies have resorted to using instruments originally designed for FLLs without prior validation for such uses. Thus, the score interpretations of these tests have rarely been validated in terms of how appropriate they are in describing HLLs' proficiency.

Key Concepts

Heritage Language Learners (HLLs): From a language pedagogy standpoint, HLLs can be defined as learners who seek formal education on a minority language which they have been in contact with at home or in a community where the language is spoken. These learners are bilinguals who may speak or at least understand their minority and majority language.

Heritage Language Acquisition (HLA): The process in which HLLs learn (or sometimes re-learn) their HL. Montrul (2016) explains HLA in terms of its similarities to first acquisition (e.g., early exposure to the language, naturalistic setting) and second acquisition (e.g., developmental and transfer errors, typically incomplete acquisition, fossilization).

Heritage language proficiency: Valdés (2001) situates HLLs in a bilingual continuum where on one extreme, the heritage language (HL) is the dominant language, and on the other extreme, the majority language is the dominant language. Bilinguals who were dominant in one language might change to being dominant in the other language.

Key Issues

Defining and Identifying HLLs

One of the major difficulties when testing and assessing HLLs has been defining who they are (Kondo-Brown, 2010; Malone et al., 2014). Due to differences in the amount and quality of experience that HLLs have with their HL, researchers have found the task of classifying these learners into a single group, while setting them apart from the FLL group, very challenging. Furthermore, as Kagan and Dillon (2012) noted, different strands of research have used varying definitions and terminologies to describe the HLL population. The lack of consensus on the definition of HLLs has created an additional set of challenges when trying to test these learners' linguistic abilities, as the claims made about HLLs' proficiency are inevitably associated with how we define them and adequately differentiate them from FLLs and/or native speakers (NS).

Perhaps the most used and cited HLL definitions are those proposed by Valdés' (2001), which are based on two different perspectives. From the perspective of endangered languages and HL maintenance, HLLs are defined more broadly as "individuals [who] have a historical and personal connection to the language" (Valdés, 2001, p. 38). From the pedagogical perspective, HLLs are characterized as "student[s] who [are] raised in a home where a non-English language is spoken, who speak or at least understand the language, and who [are] to some degree bilingual in that language and in English" (Valdés, 2001, p. 38). In other words, the first perspective focuses on the personal connection to the HL, where familial or ancestral roles are particularly important (Van Deusen-Scholl, 2003), while the second one is more oriented towards proficiency in the HL. Although these definitions refer specifically to the US context where English is the dominant language, they have also been used in studies that include HLLs in other contexts.

In addition to the lack of consensus on the definition of HLLs, there has also been considerable variability in the design and selection of tools and methods that can accurately and reliably elicit the information needed to classify learners as HLLs or FLLs. Some studies have categorized learners according to how language programs placed them into separate tracks (i.e., HLL- or FLL-track), without providing much detail on what that initial classification in tracks was based on. Other studies used interviews to elicit information about learners' linguistic backgrounds. However, due to time constraints in collecting and analyzing such extensive interview data, only a few studies (e.g., Beaudrie & Ducar, 2005; Oh & Au, 2005) have employed this methodology for the sole purpose of identifying HLLs.

The most common instrument used in HLA research to identify HLLs has been background questionnaires (Son, 2017). These questionnaires usually consist of items that elicit learners' linguistic background information, with the most common questions focusing on: (a) place of birth and age of arrival to the host country, which are often open-ended questions directed to both learners and their parents; and (b) language contact and/or use, which includes questions about learners' use of the target language with different family members as well as within multiple contexts (e.g., watching TV, listening to music). The number and type of items included in the questionnaires ultimately depends on the purpose of the study for which they are being used. Questionnaires that are used as an initial stage to separate HLLs and FLLs for purposes of placement testing tend to be shorter and composed of discrete items such as yes/no statements or Likert-scale items (e.g., Fairclough, Belpoliti, & Bermejo, 2010). Beaudrie and Ducar (2012), for example, used 14 yes/no statements which explored learners' childhood and current target language use/contact. If learners answered affirmatively to three or more statements, they were classified as HLLs. For research oriented towards investigating the factors that predict HL maintenance, the questionnaires are typically lengthier and also include items examining HLL's ethnic identity as well as their motivation and attitudes towards the heritage culture and language (e.g., Alarcón, 2010; Jensen & Llosa, 2007; Kim, 2006).

Although questionnaires can be a practical tool for describing learners' linguistic background and for quickly classifying learners into different groups, oftentimes studies have not been completely clear about how they have interpreted the results. Except for surveys that include yes/no statements, where the number of affirmative statements is counted, it is not clear how answers to other types of questionnaires translate into HLL-status. In particular, researchers have not sufficiently discussed how to classify learners in a non-dichotomous way (i.e., HLLs vs. non-HLLs), when learners share many aspects of both HLLs and FLLs.

On the whole, there has been great theoretical and methodological variability in the way HLA research has described, identified, and classified HLLs. When these methodological inconsistencies are present across studies within the same area of research, they may hinder the systematic accumulation of research knowledge (Norris & Ortega, 2012). For this reason, it is important for research in HLA to be more specific and transparent in terms of their rationale for defining HLLs in a certain way, and for choosing a given methodology or instrument to categorize these learners into different groups.

Testing Heritage Language Learners

Research on the development of HL tests and the validation of their uses has been very limited and has tended to focus mostly on the design and implementation of placement tests for language programs (Llosa, 2014). In contrast, the measurement of HL proficiency for research purposes has received much less scholarly attention and the documentation of the ways in which these tests can be designed and their uses can be validated has been scarce. This section explores some of the most popular approaches for testing HLLs.

Placement Tests. As increasing numbers of HLLs enroll in language courses, program directors and language educators alike have underscored the need to design and implement placement tests that can appropriately place their students into different curricular levels and ensure their success in the program. For this reason, most of the published research related to HL testing has focused on the development of placement tests. Language programs have implemented different methods for placing their students, for example, self-placements, informal interviews, standardized tests, and in-house placement tests (Llosa, 2014).

Due to the variability in the way different language programs design their curriculum and define their course levels, in-house language tests are the preferred approach for placing HLLs. These tests are usually composed of discrete items such as multiple-choice, lexical-recognition, or fill-in-the-blank items, which assess reading, listening, grammar, or vocabulary skills, as well as performance-based items such as writing compositions or interviews. Several researchers (e.g., Fairclough, 2012; Kagan, 2005) have recommended including both types of items in the placement tests so that learners have the opportunity to show their abilities in different skills. Additionally, Sohn and Shin (2007) advised to implement a more effective scoring method, such as setting cut-off scores for each different section within a test, to avoid overcompensating learners for one specific language skill they are particularly good at. Another important characteristic of these tests is the extent to which they reflect program-specific expectations and curricular designs. As noted in Son (2017), there are two main types of placement tests for HLLs: curriculum-based or curriculum-neutral. The former type of placement test articulates program-specific goals, needs, and requirements (e.g., Beaudrie & Ducar, 2012; Potowski, Parada, & Morgan-Short, 2012), while the focus of the latter type of placement test is more generic, and thus is not program-specific (e.g., Fairclough, 2006; Fairclough, Belpoliti, & Bermejo, 2010).

Furthermore, most of the published research on the development of HLL placement tests has emerged from programs with two separate tracks for HLLs and FLLs. While some programs have chosen to divide learners into HLLs versus FLLs at the initial stage, like in Beaudrie & Ducar (2012), others—like in Potowski et al. (2012)—have proposed an adaptive test that tests both learner groups together at an initial stage and then later separates them according to their heritage status and proficiency level. That is, the latter placement test groups together lower proficiency HLLs and FLLs into a mixed classroom, and separate higher proficiency level learners into different classrooms according to their heritage-status and language ability.

Despite the rapid proliferation of studies on HLL placement tests, there are still some areas in need of more research. First, there has been lack of published work concerning the design of placement tests that would serve mixed classrooms. Carreira (2017) indicated that many language programs have insufficient resources to provide HL courses, and thus resort to teaching both HLLs and FLLs in one single classroom. Future research will need to focus on placement testing for mixed classrooms. Perhaps, one of the main foci of these studies should be the interpretation of test results for different language learners. Second, most of the research on this topic has emerged from Spanish HL programs, and thus more scholarly attention should be directed to the development of tests for other HL programs, especially for Less Commonly Taught Languages. Finally, there has been a general misunderstanding of what validation means and what it entails. For the most part, validity has been considered a quality inherent to the test rather than to the test uses and test score interpretations. More updated validity models, including the Argument-Based Approach to Validation or Evidence-Centered Design, that follow the most recent Standards for Educational and Psychological Testing should be implemented in future validation efforts for these placement tests (see also Chapelle, Chapter 2; Révész & Brunfaut, Chapter 3, this volume).

Self-Assessment Questionnaires. Self-assessment questionnaires have been another useful tool to estimate how proficient HLLs are when performing different tasks in multiple contexts. They have predominantly been used in HL research that focuses on HLLs' ethnic identity, motivations, and attitudes towards the HL. These questionnaires have often been used in combination with other indicators of proficiency like curricular level and/or scores on other tests. A number of differences can be observed between the questionnaires across different studies, in terms of their length, type of item used, and their content. Some studies have included only four to five broad can-do statements regarding HLLs' ability to understand, speak, read, and write in the HL, using a Likert-scale from 1 to 5 (e.g., Laleko & Polinsky, 2013), from none to fluent (e.g., Beaudrie & Ducar, 2005), or from native-like to non-native-like (e.g., Alarcón, 2010). Other studies contain a number of detailed questions, including HLLs' use of the HL as well as their ability to perform specific tasks in the HL (Kim, 2006). In addition, while most studies have designed instruments consisting of Likert-scale type items (e.g., Kang & Kim, 2012), a few studies also included open-ended questions requesting HLLs to provide lengthier explanations of their abilities in certain contexts (e.g., Jensen & Llosa, 2007). The Likert-scale type items have been particularly useful for studies aiming to find patterns across different types of HLLs (i.e., low- or high-proficiency HLLs).

On the whole, self-assessments can provide meaningful insights into HLLs' HL proficiency, and more importantly, they are uniquely advantageous as they can elicit information on HLLs' own perception of their linguistic abilities. However, the differences in the design of self-assessment questionnaires across studies has impeded the generalizability of results and a more comprehensive interpretation of them. Furthermore, there is only limited understanding of the ability of HLLs to appropriately and accurately self-assess their proficiency. Some studies (e.g., Martin, Swender, & Rivera-Martinez, 2013; Swender, Martin, Rivera-Martinez, & Kagan, 2014) found that Russian and Spanish HLLs tend to overestimate their speaking ability. Interestingly, Kang and Kim (2012) suggested that the under- and over-estimation of HL proficiency might be connected to HLLs' ethnic identification to the heritage culture. Their results indicated that Korean HLLs who strongly identified with the heritage culture tended to overestimate their speaking ability, while those who had a weak ethnic identity underestimated their speaking proficiency. Gatti and O'Neil (2017), in addition, found strong positive correlations between Korean HLLs' self-perceived proficiency in writing and their actual performance on the ACTFL WPT. They indicated that in comparison with Chinese and Spanish HLLs, Korean HLLs had the strongest correlation between perceived and actual writing proficiency. In sum, HLLs' ability to self-report their language competence appears to be at times unpredictable, and numerous variables may influence the outcomes of these self-assessments. Therefore, these self-ratings need to be interpreted with caution when being used as indicators of HL proficiency.

Standardized Tests of Language Proficiency. Scores on standardized language proficiency tests are another commonly used way to indicate HL proficiency. In the US context, one of the most frequently used proficiency tests is the ACTFL Oral Proficiency Interview (OPI) (Long, Gor, & Jackson, 2012) or any variation of this test, including the computer-based OPI, the OPIc (Martin et al., 2013; Swender et al., 2014) and the Simulated Oral Proficiency Interview (SOPI; Kagan & Friedman, 2003). These are standardized tests of oral proficiency, where learners are asked to interact with a certified ACTFL interviewer, a computer avatar, or a digital recording. Certified raters carry out the rating of the speech samples according to the ACTFL guidelines. Several studies (e.g., Beaudrie & Ducar, 2005; Kagan & Friedman, 2003) have described HLLs' linguistic abilities in terms of these proficiency guidelines, as they are highly prevalent and influential in the foreign language education community in the US.

Another standardized test that has been commonly used to measure Spanish HLLs' language proficiency is the Diploma de Español como Lengua Extranjera (DELE) or some adaptation of this test (e.g., Montrul & Ionin, 2012; Torres & Sanz, 2015). DELE is a standardized test that certifies individuals as having mastery in the Spanish language (DELE, 2006) according to the Common European Framework of Reference (CEFR). Another example of a standardized test reported in the HL literature is the Test of Proficiency in Korean (TOPIK; Kim, 2006).

Multiple advantages have been associated with the use of these standardized tests in the HL literature. First, these tests are readily available and well known among SLA researchers and the language education community. Therefore, researchers can either administer the test or ask their participants to self-report their scores on these tests if they have already taken them. Second, all of the above-mentioned standardized tests and guidelines include in their test use description the assessment of HLLs or of learners from different backgrounds. The TOPIK, for example, is described as a test for both Korean FLLs and *overseas Koreans* (i.e., HLLs). As a result, these tests have been considered a useful tool for measuring both HLLs and FLLs, especially for research focused on the comparison of these learner groups.

Nevertheless, there has also been a lot of debate around the use of these tests for assessing HLLs. In the case of the ACTFL OPI or the ACTFL proficiency guidelines, several scholars (e.g., Fairclough, 2006; Draper & Hicks, 2000; Valdés, 1989) have argued against their use as these tests have been initially designed for FLLs, and thus have been based on a different type of language development continuum. Furthermore, as Valdés (1989) pointed out, these guidelines do not take into consideration the different language varieties that HLLs might use. By contrast, others (e.g., Kagan, 2005; Martin et al., 2013; Swender et al., 2014) have provided arguments in support of the use of the ACTFL tests and guidelines for measuring HL proficiency. They have asserted that the guidelines describe several criteria of assessment, which include not only accuracy but also function and content, and therefore can be used for assessing both learner types. Moreover, if the main goal is to assess how functional HLLs are in communicating in a language, rather than to compare between the performances of learners and NSs, then there is no need for separate assessment criteria for HLLs and FLLs. In terms of language varieties, Kagan and Friedman (2003) indicated that HLLs of languages other than Spanish, such as Russian, mostly use and are exposed to the standard variety of the language, at least in the US context.

Regarding the DELE, Carreira and Potowski (2011) have criticized its use for assessing HLLs, as it is restricted to the assessment of vocabulary and morphology. They have questioned its appropriateness in studies that use it as a tool to match proficiency levels of HLLs and FLLs, particularly when the research focus is on language skills other than vocabulary and morphology. Without additional measurements (e.g., speaking proficiency), they discouraged the use of DELE for assessing HLLs. In addition, another practical disadvantage of the majority of these standardized tests is that they are not publicly available and can be very costly to use in research.

Recommendations for Practice

As one of the main recommendations to advance research on the assessment of learner knowledge, Norris and Ortega (2012) proposed that the SLA research community "move away from individual researchers pursuing their own versions of assessing learner knowledge and [move] toward the realization of research as a cumulative and cooperative endeavor" (p. 586). This proposition still resonates with research on language learner assessment today and certainly applies to the testing of specific learner populations, such as the HLLs. In order to further advance research on HLA, studies will need to consolidate their definitions and methodologies of defining and classifying HLLs, as well as on how to measure HLLs' language proficiency. In this way, research findings will be more generalizable and a more comprehensive interpretation of these findings will be possible. Furthermore, there needs to be more transparency and adequate justification for choosing certain definitions and approaches to classifying learners, as well as indicators of language proficiency. Oftentimes, the lack of information on the rationale for these decisions hinders the replicability of the studies.

Another important recommendation is that prior to utilizing instruments to assess HLLs, there should be proper validation of such uses. In particular, more research should be conducted to examine the appropriateness of using standardized proficiency tests for testing HLLs. Future studies will need to rigorously examine the implications of using tests originally designed for FLLs to assess HLLs. At the same time, these studies should also determine whether the interpretation of tests results can be the same for both learner populations. In addition, there is a critical need for instruments designed to measure global language proficiency for HL research purposes, as language proficiency is a major moderating factor in HLA studies. Shortcut measures of proficiency, like cloze tests, C-tests, or elicited imitation tests (EITs) have gained increasing popularity in SLA research and have been considered a viable solution to this need (Norris, 2018). Nevertheless, these instruments will also need to be evaluated in terms of their appropriateness for assessing HLLs.

Moreover, the field of HLA would benefit considerably from collaborating with the field of second language testing, specifically for more appropriate validation practices of instruments used to test HLLs. Rather than asking questions such as "Is this test valid?" it would be more fruitful and accurate to ask "To what extent are these test uses valid?" or "To what extent are these test interpretations valid for X and Y purposes?" As stated by the 2014 *Standards*, validity is not a property of the test itself but rather an evaluation of the interpretations for specified uses of the test (see also Chapelle, Chapter 2; Révész & Brunfaut, Chapter 3, this volume). Accordingly, future research on the development of tests for HLLs, whether for programmatic purposes or research purposes, should clearly articulate the purpose of the test and the different claims that are made based on the test results (Bachman, 2005), as well as provide the evidence needed to support such claims.

Testing Tips

In addition to following the *Standards for Educational and Psychological Testing* (AERA, APA & NCME, 2014), when testing heritage language learners' (HLLs') proficiency it is *crucial* to determine:

(1) Who are the HLLs that will get tested?
(2) What criteria make them HLLs?
(3) Are these criteria grounded on previous research?
(4) What instruments can be used to examine whether learners meet these criteria?

When using existing instruments to measure HLLs' proficiency, consider:

(1) Were these instruments designed for the purposes of testing HLLs?
(2) Have these instruments been appropriately validated for the purpose of testing this specific learner population?

If not, the results should be interpreted with caution, and most likely not be used for high-stakes decisions. An ancillary research path could be used to pilot the instruments on HLLs and to report on the reliability and validity of such instruments for HLLs.

Recommended Readings

Kagan, O., & Dillon, K. (2012). Heritage languages and L2 learning. In S. M. Gass & A. Mackey (Eds.), *The Routledge handbook of second language acquisition*, (pp. 491–505). Routledge.

The authors provide a comprehensive review of the HL literature by situating HL research and instructional practices within the SLA and bilingualism domain.

Llosa, L. (2014). Assessing heritage language learners. In A. J. Kunnan (Ed.), *The companion to language assessment* (pp. 440–453). Wiley-Blackwell.

This book chapter mainly reviews studies focused on placement tests for HLLs and describes the most commonly used approaches to place HLLs in different curriculum levels.

Carreira, M., & Kagan, O. (2018). Heritage language education: A proposal for the next 50 years. *Foreign Language Annals*, *51*(1), 152–168.

This article offers a comprehensive review of heritage language studies in the last 20 years and provides proposals for advancing HLL research, instruction, and institutionalization.

References

Alarcón, I. (2010). Advanced heritage learners of Spanish: A sociolinguistic profile for pedagogical purposes. *Foreign Language Annals*, *43*(2), 269–288. https://doi.org/10.1111/j.1944-9720.2010.01078.x

Bachman, L. F. (2005). Building and supporting a case for test use. *Language Assessment Quarterly*, *2*(1), 1–34. https://doi.org/10.1207/s15434311laq0201_1

Beaudrie, S., & Ducar, C. (2005). Beginning level university heritage programs: Creating a space for all heritage language learners. *Heritage Language Journal*, *3*(1), 1–26.

Beaudrie, S., & Ducar, C. (2012). Language placement and beyond: Guidelines for the design and implementation of a computerized Spanish heritage language exam. *Heritage Language Journal*, *9*(1), 77–99. https://doi.org/10.1111/j.1944-9720.2006.tb02278.x

Beaudrie, S., Ducar, C., & Potowski, K. (2014). *Heritage language teaching: Research and practice*. McGraw-Hill Education.

Caramota, S., & Ziegler, K. (2015, October). *One in five U.S. residents speaks foreign language at home*. https://cis.org/sites/default/files/camarota-language-15.pdf

Carreira, M. (2017). The state of institutionalization of heritage languages in postsecondary language departments in the United States. In O. Kagan, M. Carreira, & C. Hitchins Chik (Eds.), *The Routledge handbook of heritage language education: From innovation to program building* (pp. 347–362). Routledge. https://doi.org/10.4324/9781315727974

Carreira, M., & Kagan, O. (2018). Heritage language education: A proposal for the next 50 years. *Foreign Language Annals*, *51*(1), 152–168. https://doi.org/10.1111/flan.12331

Carreira, M., & Potowski, K. (2011). Commentary: Pedagogical implications of experimental SNS research. *Heritage Language Journal*, *8*(1), 134–151. http://www.international.ucla.edu/media/files/carreira-potowski-eight-one-dm-vrp.pdf

DELE. (2006). *Diplomas of Spanish as a foreign language*. http://www.dele.org/

Draper, J., & Hicks, J. (2000). Where we've been; what we've learned. In J. Webb & B. Miller (Eds.), *Teaching heritage language learners: Voices from the classroom* (pp. 15–35). ACTFL.

Fairclough, M. (2006). Language placement exams for heritage speakers of Spanish: Learning from students' mistakes. *Foreign Language Annals*, *39*(4), 595–604. https://doi.org/10.1111/j.1944-9720.2006.tb02278.x

Fairclough, M. (2012). A working model for assessing Spanish heritage language learners' language proficiency through a placement exam. *Heritage Language Journal*, *9*(1), 121–138.

Fairclough, M., Belpoliti, F., & Bermejo, E. (2010). Developing an electronic placement examination for heritage learners of Spanish: Challenges and payoffs. *Hispania*, *93*(2), 273–291.

Gatti, A., & O'Neill, T. (2017). Who are heritage writers? Language experiences and writing proficiency. *Foreign Language Annals*, *50*(4), 734–753. https://doi.org/10.1111/flan.12291

Jensen, L., & Llosa, L. (2007). Heritage language reading in the university: A survey of students' experiences, strategies, and preferences. *Heritage Language Journal*, *5*(1), 98–116.

Kagan, O. (2005). In support of a proficiency-based definition of heritage language learners: The case of Russian. *International Journal of Bilingual Education and Bilingualism*, *8*(2–3), 213–221. https://doi.org/10.1080/13670050508668608

Kagan, O., & Dillon, K. (2012). Heritage languages and L2 learning. In S. M. Gass & A. Mackey (Eds.), *The Routledge handbook of second language acquisition* (pp. 491–505). Routledge.
Kagan, O., & Friedman, D. (2003). Using the OPI to place heritage speakers of Russian. *Foreign Language Annals*, *36*(4), 536–545. https://doi.org/10.1111/j.1944-9720.2003.tb02143.x
Kang, H., & Kim, I. (2012). Perceived and actual competence and ethnic identity in heritage language learning: A case of Korean-American college students. *International Journal of Bilingual Education and Bilingualism*, *15*(3), 279–294. https://doi.org/10.1080/13670050.2011.626846
Kim, E. (2006). Heritage language maintenance by Korean-American college students. In K. Kondon-Brown (Ed.), *Heritage language development: Focus on East Asian immigrants* (pp. 175–208). John Benjamins Publishing Co.
Kondo-Brown, K. (2010). Curriculum development for advancing heritage language competence: Recent research, current practices, and a future agenda. *Annual Review of Applied Linguistics*, *30*, 24–41. https://doi.org/10.1017/s0267190510000012
Laleko, O., & Polinsky, M. (2013). Marking topic or marking case: A comparative investigation of heritage Japanese and heritage Korean. *Heritage Language Journal*, *10*(2), 178–202.
Llosa, L. (2014). Assessing heritage language learners. In A. J. Kunnan (Ed.), *The companion to language assessment* (pp. 440–453). Wiley-Blackwell. https://doi.org/10.1002/9781118411360.wbcla121
Long, M. H., Gor, K., & Jackson, S. (2012). Linguistic correlates of second language proficiency. *Studies in Second Language Acquisition*, *34*(1), 99–126. https://doi.org/10.1017/s0272263111000519
Malone, M., Peyton, J., & Kim, K. (2014). Assessment of heritage language learners: Issues and directions. In T. Wiley, J. Peyton, D. Christian, S. Moore, & N. Liu (Eds.), *Handbook of heritage, community, and Native American languages in the United States* (pp. 349–358). Routledge. https://doi.org/10.5860/CHOICE.52-0672
Martin, C., Swender, E., & Rivera-Martínez, M. (2013). Assessing the oral proficiency of heritage speakers according to the ACTFL proficiency guidelines 2012–speaking. *Heritage Language Journal*, *10*(2), 211–225.
Montrul, S. (2016). *The acquisition of heritage languages*. Cambridge University Press. https://doi.org/10.1017/cbo9781139030502.002
Montrul, S., & Ionin, T. (2012). Dominant language transfer in Spanish heritage speakers and L2 learners in the interpretation of definite articles. *The Modern Language Journal*, *9*(1), 70–94. https://doi.org/10.1111/j.1540-4781.2012.01278.x
Montrul, S., & Perpiñán, S. (2011). Assessing differences and similarities between instructed heritage language learners and L2 learners in their knowledge of Spanish tense-aspect and mood (TAM) morphology. *Heritage Language Journal*, *8*(1), 90–133.
Ndhlovu, F., & Willoughby, L. (2017). Migration, heritage languages, and changing demographics in Australia. In O. Kagan, M. Carreira, & C. Hitchins Chik (Eds.), *The Routledge handbook of heritage language education: From innovation to program building* (pp. 22–32). Routledge. https://doi.org/10.4324/9781315727974
Norris, J. M. (2018). Developing and investigating C-tests in eight languages: Measuring proficiency for research purposes. In J. M. Norris (Ed.), *Developing C-tests for estimating proficiency in foreign language research* (pp. 7–33). Peter Lang.
Norris, J. M., & Ortega, L. (2012). Assessing learner knowledge. In S. M. Gass & A. Mackey (Eds.), *The Routledge handbook of second language acquisition* (pp. 573–589). Routledge.
O'Grady, W., Lee, M., & Cho, M. (2001). The acquisition of relative clauses by heritage and non-heritage learners of Korean as a second language: A comparative study. *Journal of Korean Language Education*, *12*(2), 283–294.
Oh, J., & Au, T. (2005). Learning Spanish as a heritage language: The role of sociocultural background variables. *Language, Culture and Curriculum*, *18*(3), 229–241. https://doi.org/10.1080/07908310508668744
Polinsky, M. (2016). Looking ahead. In D. Pascual y Cabo (Ed.), *Advances in Spanish as a heritage language* (pp. 325–345). John Benjamins Publishing Co.
Potowski, K., Parada, M., & Morgan-Short, K. (2012). Developing an online placement exam for Spanish heritage speakers and L2 students. *Heritage Language Journal*, *9*(1), 51–76.
Sohn, S., & Shin, S. (2007). True beginners, false beginners, and fake beginners: Placement strategies for Korean heritage speakers. *Foreign Language Annals*, *40*(3), 407–418. https://doi.org/10.1111/j.1944-9720.2007.tb02866.x
Son, Y.-A. (2017). Towards useful assessment and evaluation of heritage language learning. *Foreign Language Annals*, *50*(2), 367–386. https://doi.org/10.1111/flan.12273

Swender, E., Martin, C., Rivera-Martínez, M., & Kagan, O. (2014). Exploring oral proficiency profiles of heritage speakers of Russian and Spanish. *Foreign Language Annals*, *47*(3), 423–446. https://doi.org/10.1111/flan.12098

Torres, J., & Sanz, C. (2015). Is there a cognitive advantage for Spanish heritage bilinguals? A first look. *Heritage Language Journal*, *12*(3), 292–309.

United States Census Bureau. (2015, October 28). *Detailed languages spoken at home and ability to speak English for the population 5 years and over: 2009–2013*. https://www.census.gov/data/tables/2013/demo/2009-2013-lang-tables.html

Valdés, G. (1989). Teaching Spanish to Hispanic bilinguals: A look at oral proficiency testing and the proficiency movement. *Hispania*, *72*(2), 392–401. https://doi.org/10.2307/343163

Valdés, G. (2001). Heritage language students: Profiles and possibilities. In J. K. Peyton, D. A. Ranard, & S. McGinnis (Eds.), *Heritage languages in America: Preserving a national resource language in education* (pp. 37–77). Delta Systems and the Center for Applied Linguistics.

Van Deusen-Scholl, N. (2003). Toward a definition of heritage language: Sociopolitical and pedagogical considerations. *Journal of Language, Identity, and Education*, *2*(3), 211–230. https://doi.org/10.1207/s15327701jlie0203_4

41

Testing Sign Language Learners

Tobias Haug, Eveline Boers-Visker & Beppie van den Bogaerde

Background

Sign language research is a relatively young field within linguistics compared to the study of spoken languages like English or German. It started in the late 1950s with the study of American Sign Language (ASL) phonology (Stokoe, 1960). Contemporary sign language linguistics concerns all sub fields (phonology, morphology, etc.) of individual sign languages, and crosslinguistic comparisons amongst sign languages and between sign languages and spoken languages (e.g., Pfau, Steinbach, & Woll, 2012). Sign language studies also cover many topics in an increasing number of disciplines, yielding novel interdisciplinary research. Lately, there is an added focus on the acquisition of sign languages by hearing adult learners and on assessing sign language proficiency in all users.

Deaf Community and L1 Sign Language Users (Heterogeneity)

Deaf communities around the world are not homogeneous (Woll & Ladd, 2011), but members do share characteristics like using a sign language and recognizing shared customs and values, the total of which is often called Deaf Culture. The core of each community is usually their local sign language, but fluency differs greatly amongst deaf people due to various factors like age of (diagnosis of) deafness and subsequent intervention (e.g., Gregory, 2017), duration of deafness, degree of deafness, choice of input language(s) offered during the language acquisition years (Fitzpatrick et al., 2016; Mellon et al., 2015), besides other factors that are generally important for all children in L1 acquisition, e.g., quality and quantity of language input, education of parents and child, parents' socio-economic status, etc. (Clark, 2009).

Most of the factors specific to the high variance in sign fluency have to do with the early years of language acquisition (e.g., Campbell, MacSweeney, & Woll, 2017). From 0–5 years children need rich input of and full access to a natural language in order to be able to acquire a first language (L1). A child born deaf in a hearing family is at danger of being in a language deprived environment when only spoken language is offered and no sign language. Even though, since the early 2000s, many deaf children manage to achieve better spoken language skills (Spencer & Marschark, 2005), natural sign languages present a host of benefits for deaf children, especially to prevent and reduce language deprivation (cf. Hall, Hall, & Caselli, 2019). When they have also learned a sign language, they become bimodal-bilinguals (Müller de Quadros, Lillo-Martin, & Chen Pichler, 2015). Deaf children growing up with a full sign language as L1 acquire that language effortlessly, and learn a spoken/written language as a second language, with varying success. Hearing children of deaf parents (codas) are part of the deaf communities too and are often also bimodal-bilinguals (Lillo-Martin, Müller de Quadros, Chen Pichler, & Fieldsteel, 2014). Because of growing interest in societal changes, for instance changing attitudes to human diversity, disabilities, and human rights, more hearing people are learning a signed language, which also asserts its influence on the linguistic environment of deaf people.

Considering all these factors, it is no wonder that the sign language fluency of deaf people is highly variable.

Second Modality and Second Language Acquisition

People who learn a sign language after acquiring a spoken language are considered M2L2-learners: learners of a second language in a second modality. Like unimodal learners (M1), M2L2-learners can use the knowledge of their L1 in the L2 acquisition process. However, in addition they have to learn features that are unique to the sign language modality, e.g., the use of space to express grammatical relations, the use of the body and facial expressions (i.e., non-manuals), and the simultaneous coordination of manual and non-manual devices. The use of the hands, body, and face is not totally new to learners though, since people using spoken languages use gestures accompanying their speech (Kendon, 2004) and use body actions, for instance when telling a story. Thus, M2L2-learners are faced with the challenge to acquire new modality-specific features, but can utilize their existing multimodal knowledge as well.

A major difference in sign languages is that they have far more iconicity than spoken languages, i.e., the relation between the form of a sign and its meaning can be apparent. Examples are the signs DRINK, READ and LOOK-AT[1] from Sign Language of the Netherlands (NGT), see Figure 41.1.

Since the iconic aspect in sign vocabulary seems to support L2 learning, a large proportion of the research on M2L2-learning has focused on the facilitating of hindering effects of sign iconicity (e.g., Ortega, 2017).

There is little research on the acquisition of grammatical features, although recently some researchers have begun to investigate the learning of grammatical features that are unique to the manual-visual modality (e.g., Ferrara & Nilsson, 2017).

Sign Language Test Research

Research in sign language tests, targeted at both children and adults, is a rather young field which originated in the late 1990s in the US (e.g., Strong & Prinz, 1997). So far, most published studies

Figure 41.1 Example of iconic signs DRINK (left), READ (middle), LOOK-AT (right) (pictures reproduced with permission).

on sign language tests target children acquiring a sign language as L1 (e.g., Herman, Holmes, & Woll, 1999). Testing adult learners of a signed language as foreign or second language has only recently become an issue through the increasing implementation and awareness of the Common European Framework of Reference (Council of Europe, 2020) in sign language teaching in higher education, such as in sign language interpreter programs.

Most published studies on sign language tests focus on their development and on methodological issues (e.g., Haug & Mann, 2008). Very little has been done on other issues, such as rater behavior or test-takers' feedback. This state of research in sign language testing is influenced by the fact that many sign languages are under-documented and under-resourced (e.g., no corpus or reference grammar is available).

Key Concepts

***Sign languages*:** Languages produced by the hands, face and body and perceived visually. Sign languages are transmitted in the manual-visual modality.

***Spoken languages*:** Languages produced by the vocal channel and perceived aurally. Spoken languages are produced in the oral-aural modality.

***M2L2-learners*:** Learners with a spoken language background learning a signed language as a second language. These learners acquire a new language (L2) in a new modality (M2).

***Sign iconicity*:** A direct relation between the form and the meaning of a sign.

***Gestures*:** Actions of the hands, body and face, used to communicate. Gestures can accompany, replace of complement speech (co-speech gestures) as well as signs.

Key Issues

State of Sign Language Acquisition/M2L2 Research

In the absence of any research on sign language pedagogy, the pioneers who started to teach sign languages four decades ago based their curricula (and consequently, their tests) on their intuitions and on existing research on teaching spoken languages as a second language (Quinto-Pozos, 2011). The limited body of research that has since appeared has focused on three main areas: phonology, lexical acquisition, and morpho-syntax. We will briefly recapitulate the most important results in these three areas.

Research on Phonological Acquisition. The acquisition of formational parameters of signs is the area that has attracted the most attention. Because of the modality divergence between the spoken L1 and the signed L2 target language, learners are not, or less, able to use their L1 phonological knowledge in learning signed language. They have to become sensitized to the phonological system (e.g., the inventory of handshapes, locations, movements, orientations, and non-manual phonological features). This sensitivity, as well as the sensorimotor skills to produce and understand signs, need to be developed. Mirus and colleagues (2001) observed that hearing non-signers tended to proximalize the signs they were asked to imitate. Rosen's (2004) analysis of learners' production data revealed substitutions, displacements, additions, deletions and mirroring of movements. The movement parameter appears to be the most difficult to perceive and produce, followed by the handshape parameter. The location parameter is less prone to mistakes (Bochner, Christie, Hauser, & Searls, 2011).

Research on Lexical Acquisition. Several studies have addressed the question of whether the fact that a relative high number of signs are iconically motivated facilitates word learning. For M2L2-learners, the resemblance between form and meaning (e.g., when signing EAT, DRINK (see Figure 41.1), DRIVE, HOUSE) can serve as a mnemonic aid in early stages (Baus,

Carreiras, & Emmorey, 2013). Ortega (2017) points out that although iconicity aids memorization of meaning, it can hinder the acquisition of the phonological elements. Ortega and Morgan (2015) analyzed data of hearing learners' imitations of arbitrary and iconic signs prior to the start of their first British Sign Language (BSL) course, and after eleven weeks of instruction. The results revealed that the participants made more phonological errors when imitating an iconic sign. It seems that if learners have access to the *meaning* of a sign, they pay less attention to the *form*.

In a recent one-year longitudinal study Williams and colleagues (2018) investigated how novice M2L2-learners acquired vocabulary during the first year of ASL instruction. The results of the fMRI study indicated that the ability to acquire and process phonology (e.g., to decompose signs and make phonological contrasts) correlates with successful lexical learning.

Research on the Acquisition of Morpho-Syntactic Features. The manual-visual modality allows signers to exploit the space around the body to express topographical and grammatical relations. Modality-specific linguistic structures include the use of classifier predicates in which the handshape unit denotes salient characteristics of the referent (see Figure 41.2); directional verbs that move between the grammatical subject and object; and conveying feelings, thoughts, speech, and actions of a referent (constructed action and constructed dialogue). M2L2-acquisition of these and other grammatical constructions is under-researched, although the number of published papers and conference papers is increasing. Ferrara and Nilsson (2017) investigated the acquisition of classifier predicates and concluded that these constructions are difficult to master. This might be attributed to the fact that classifier constructions as manifested in sign languages are complex constructions that do not occur in spoken languages, and consequently are novel structures for M2L2-learners (Sandler & Lillo-Martin, 2006).

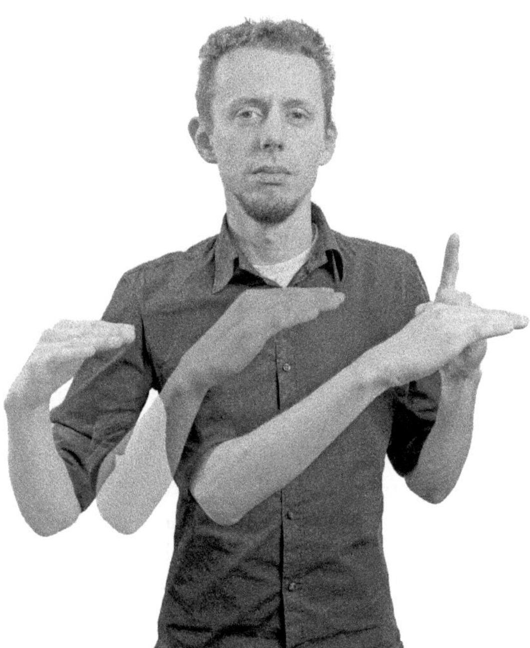

Figure 41.2 Example of a classifier construction (the right hand depicts a member of the class of vehicles (e.g., a car), the left hand depicts a member of the class "long-cylinder-shaped referents" (e.g., a pole or a person)) (picture by Annette Jansen; ©Research Center for Social Innovation).

State of Sign Language Testing and Application

In this section we present a brief overview of the current state of sign language testing and application in M2L2 practice.

A current inventory[2] shows that 24 tests have been developed to assess children's L1, for the following languages: ASL, Australian Sign Language (Auslan), BSL, German Sign Language (DGS), French Sign Language (LSF), Italian Sign Language (LIS) and NGT (see Enns et al., 2016). As far as we know, only four L2 sign language tests have been developed and some of them are available to be used in tertiary education:[3]

1. The Aachen Test for German Sign Language Competence
   The ATG can be applied for the following areas, e.g., (1) diagnosis of children's language development, (2) monitoring sign language development in school, (3) linguistic self-assessment of deaf adults, (4) DGS assessment for hearing parents with deaf children, (5) assessment for hearing professionals working in the deaf field, e.g., interpreters, teachers for the deaf, speech therapists, etc.[4]
2. The Sign Language Proficiency Interview
   The SLPI (see also 3.) uses a conversational approach with the purpose to assess sign language communication skills (considering both function and form) and to support people in the development of their sign language communication skills.[5]
3. The American Sign Language Discrimination Test
   The American Sign Language Discrimination Test (ASL-DT) is intended to measure the language proficiency of adults learning ASL as a second language (L2). The test uses a paired-comparison discrimination task to evaluate learners' ability to discern phonological and morpho-phonological contrasts in ASL (i.e., linguistic similarity and dissimilarity within the context of minimal pairs).[6]
4. Vocabulary size tests for Swiss German Sign Language (*Deutschschweizerische Gebärdensprache*, DSGS)
   The two vocabulary size tests, one using the methodology of a Yes/No test (a self-report), the other one a translation test from written German into DSGS (L1 into L2), assess the vocabulary size of beginning learners of DSGS (level A1 according to the CEFR) (Haug, 2017).

Development and application of valid and reliable morpho-syntactic L2 assessment tools are also rare. Designing sign language tests remains a problem due to aforementioned issues, like lack of grammatical descriptions and small numbers and high variability in L1 users, creating uncertainty about target forms. Possibly as a consequence, evaluating the functional use of sign language in M2L2-learners is becoming more and more the norm, also in accordance with today's insights into L2 learning (Council of Europe, 2018). However, the focus on grammar-oriented teaching and assessment is re-emerging and slowly the M2L2 field is growing towards a blend of pragmatic and grammatical assessment, as for instance shown in the SLPI's adaption into NGT for assessment in university students (Van den Broek-Laven, Boers-Visker, & van den Bogaerde, 2014). With an increase in learners interested in sign languages, the issue of sign language testing and application is prioritized nowadays in academia and practice, which promises rapid development and advances for the near future. International collaboration between linguists, test developers, and teachers in language teaching programs is currently underway (e.g., SIGNGRAM;[7] Haug et al., 2016; Pyfers, 2017), and will surely contribute to the expansion of valid tests.

Assessing Phonology and Lexicon. Traditionally, L2 sign language learners were provided with long lists of sign vocabulary. Comprehension of the vocabulary could be tested for instance by the teacher producing a sign (e.g., LOOK-AT, Figure 41.1) and the learner writing down the meaning in glosses. For production, learners were sometimes provided with a list of glosses (e.g., LOOK-AT, DRINK) and subsequently were to produce the target signs on camera, which could then be assessed for phonological and lexical correctness. Nowadays, advanced filming, archiving and interactive techniques to study sign language production and comprehension exist (Orfanidou, Woll, & Morgan, 2015). However, assessments of M2L2-signers' comprehension and production at the phonological and lexical levels are often ad hoc and local, meaning that they are available in teaching programs in different countries, but they are barely researched and are not published.

Assessing Morpho-Syntax. There are few tests available focusing on morpho-syntax. Since sign languages share some devices (e.g., the use of classifiers, agreement verbs, constructed action, and dialogue) sign language tests such as the SLPI (see above) could be adapted for other sign languages, provided that the language specific grammatical features (e.g., word order, non-manual grammatical features, classifier inventory) are taken into account.

Recommendations for Practice

Due to the paucity of available tests, curriculum developers often face the challenge of developing their own sign language tests. This section describes resources and practical advice regarding sign language test development.

Resources for Sign Language Test Development and Use

The availability of existing materials for developing sign language tests is sparse. One example is the output from the project *ProSign: Sign languages for professional purposes* (Leeson, Haug, Rathmann, Sheneman, & van den Bogaerde, 2018), a project of the European Center for Modern Languages (ECML) in Graz. The available material is an adapted version of the testing cycle (McNamara, 2000), which describes different steps and procedures in developing language tests. The testing cycle is available in International Sign and English on the website of the ECML,[8] enriched with concrete examples of different sign language tasks.

Other resources for developing sign language tests are available online as guidelines (Haug et al., 2016) or publications in journals or book chapters (e.g., Mann & Haug, 2014).

Test Development and Assessment Literacy

When adapting an existing test for another language (e.g., adapting an English proficiency test for German) both linguistic and cultural differences should be considered and accounted for in the test-design. For sign languages, there is an extra layer of complexity: the modality affords the use of iconic structures. This, and the fact that sign languages lack a written form, as well as the limited availability of (signed) literature, pose challenges in both test construction and the rating process. As a consequence, in addition to basic assessment literacy (i.e., knowledge about validity, reliability, etc.), sign language assessment literacy should include awareness of the caveats induced by the modality. Boers-Visker and Hammer (in press) have provided a matrix (SLASS-DM) with an overview of issues that affect sign language assessment. In Table 41.1 we display part of this matrix, concerning validity and reliability.

Developers and raters should be aware of the risk that the elicitation materials could provoke gestural behavior that resembles sign language structures. An example is provided in Figure 41.3a, where the student's productions depicted could be linguistic as well as gestural. Figure 41.3b is an example of a target-picture that could elicit different (correct) alternative productions: The signer could depict the situation from an observer-perspective (providing a general overview, using a classifier construction) or from the perspective of either the boy riding the

Table 41.1 Part of the sign language assessment-design matrix (SLASS-DM) (adapted from Boers-Visker & Hammer, in press)

	Sign Language Production	*Sign Language Understanding*
Reliability	• Impossible to be anonymous: risk of examiner bias. • Lack of rubrics: difficult to achieve good agreement between examiners. • Multiple ways of expressing similar meanings in sign language.	• Language variation affects understanding considerably. • Student's response in glosses requires clear guidelines on gloss conventions. • Lack of freely available texts: difficult to obtain comparable texts for assessment.
Validity	• Lack of clear norms based on evidence from L1-signers and M2L2-learners of sign language. • Interference of gestural behavior: risk of overestimating skills. • Risk of giving away grammatical information when using symbols (e.g., arrows to denote movement of action).	• Risk of overestimating skills if the proportion of iconic signs and grammatical features is relatively high. • Risk of overestimating skills if proportion of mouthings is high. • Risk of over-dependency on memory skills (impossibility to watch and write simultaneously).

bike or one of the persons sitting on the bench. This requires either a very explicit instruction to the test-taker (what is expected) or a flexible rating procedure (considering different options being correct). If the target in Figure 41.3c were used in a test, there is risk that the arrow gives away the grammatical structure, since the targeted linguistic expression includes a movement between the locations of the referents in space. Similarly, the iconicity of the language might bias comprehension tests, since some iconic signs (see Figure 41.1) could be easily guessed by naive non-signers. Moreover, the mouthings (i.e., the simultaneous voiceless articulation of a word during sign articulation) accompanying signs can bias comprehension, as test-takers could use their lip-reading skills to infer meaning. Test developers should thus carefully select the target materials to prevent "iconicity-bias."

The absence of a written language forces developers to either use depictive materials (e.g., photos, pictures, cartoons), to use the written L1, or to present questions or instructions in sign language. The latter can be problematic in low-level tests, and might cause bias in terms of measurement (e.g., the signer must be able to comprehend well in order to perform a production task). Depictive materials on the other hand can be either over-simplistic, or might target only a subset of skills (e.g., a cartoon elicits narration skills, but not communication skills).

Examples of Sign Language Tests in the Light of Technological Developments

Technological developments in recent decades have had an impact on sign language teaching and assessment. On the hardware side, faster Internet connections have improved the possibilities to upload and share signed videos remotely through a university's learning system. Both server space and local storage space (like hard drives) have become more affordable to handle larger amounts of (video) data. Mobile devices in conjunction with apps like WhatsApp, Skype, or even social media like Facebook, can be used for sign language learning, for example, by sharing new signs someone saw at a presentation in a Facebook or WhatsApp chat with fellow-students.

Technology allows the development of web-based sign language tests (e.g., Hauser, Paludneviciene, Riddle, Kurz, Emmorey, & Contreras, 2016) not only in a summative framework, but also for formative assessment purposes. One example is the web-based vocabulary size test which uses a methodology of a Yes/No test. The learner has to indicate whether s/he does or

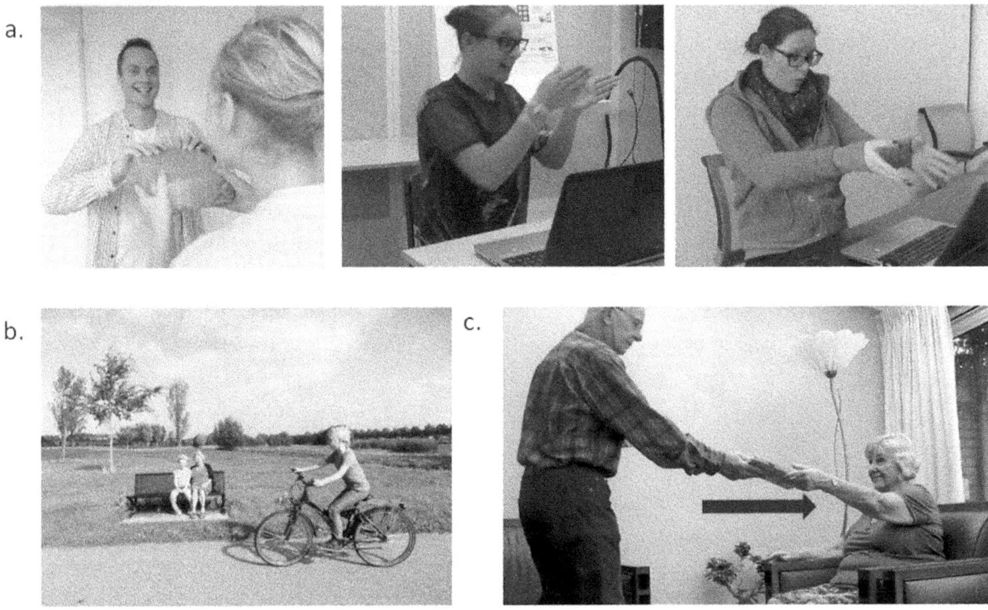

Figure 41.3 Examples of target materials that can cause bias (pictures ©Eveline Boers-Visker, used with permission).

does not know a sign that is shown on video. Such a test has been developed for DSGS, but is not yet being used operationally (Haug, 2017). However, the results are promising and this test could be used by M2L2-learners of DSGS as one possible instrument for (self-)assessment.

To conclude, the increasing interest in sign languages and the deaf community they are used in requires deeper insights into the structures of these sign languages, at all linguistic levels. Besides fuller descriptions of the sign language varieties used by L1 users, there is a need for pedagogy research and test development studies in order to cater to the growing number of hearing people who want to learn a sign language as a foreign language. In recent years, a start has been made on developing L2 sign language tests, but so far only for very few sign languages. The manual-visual modality (M2) in which sign languages are produced and perceived afford benefits of gestural experience in hearing M2L2-learners, as well as iconic aspects in the lexicon and in the grammar. However, these same aspects pose extra challenges for test developers: There is no simple translation or adaptation from spoken language L2 tests to sign language tests. New ways need to be found in order to test M2L2 hearing learners of a signed language with representative assessment methods. Innovative technologies increasingly enable test developers to create such opportunities to assess learners' L2 production and comprehension. The field of M2L2 sign language assessment urgently needs exchange of information about the development of tests, even when they are under construction, to combine our knowledge and enable collaboration in further innovating assessment tools.

Testing Tips

- Develop or adapt your sign language tests with deaf people from your local deaf community who are experienced in sign language teaching.

- Select elicitation materials with care given the iconicity of sign language; ensure that you measure sign language and not gestural behavior.
- The cycle of development and evaluation should be short, and well documented, especially with a view to the fact that sign languages have no written form. Develop a format to archive signed materials, including test items and rubrics (either written or signed), with explicit metadata.
- In the absence of validated tests, focus on formative assessment, employing students' own signed/written reflections and teachers' experiences in targeted areas that need development, for example, via the European Language Portfolio (ELP) which has specifically been developed for sign languages within the ProSign 2[9] project at the European Center for Modern Languages, Graz. Evaluate the use of the ELP with students and teachers, and use the results to further develop tests.

Notes

1 DRINK ('to drink') is an example of a sign language gloss, a translated label reflecting a principal aspect of the meaning of a sign. Glosses are typically written in small caps.
2 http://www.signlang-assessment.info/index.php/home-en.html
3 http://www.signlang-assessment.info/index.php/tests-of-l2-learning.html
4 http://www.signlang-assessment.info/index.php/aachen-test-for-basic-german-sign-language-competence---adult-version.html
5 http://www.signlang-assessment.info/index.php/sign-language-proficiency-interview.html
6 http://www.signlang-assessment.info/index.php/american-sign-language-discrimination-test.html
7 https://parles.upf.edu/llocs/cost-signgram/about-action
8 https://www.ecml.at/ECML-Programme/Programme2012-2015/ProSign/Assessment/tabid/1766/Default.aspx
9 https://www.ecml.at/ECML-Programme/Programme2016-2019/SignLanguageInstruction/tabid/1856/language/en-GB/Default.aspx

Recommended Readings

Woll, B. (2013). Second language acquisition of sign language. In C.A. Chapelle (Ed.), *The encyclopedia of applied linguistics*. Blackwell Publishing Ltd. https://doi.org/10.1002/9781405198431.wbeal1050

This paper provides an overview of the acquisition of a sign language as a second or foreign language.

Bochner, J. H., Samar, V. J., Hauser, P. C., Garrison, W. M., Searls, J. M., & Sanders, C. A. (2016). Validity of the American Sign Language Discrimination Test. *Language Testing*, *33*(4), 473–495. https://doi.org/10.1177/0265532215590849

This paper discusses validity evidence of a test for ASL.

www.signlang-assessment.info

Resource website of tests for adult learners of a sign language.

References

Baus, C., Carreiras, M., & Emmorey, K. (2013). When does iconicity in sign language matter? *Language and Cognitive Processes*, *28*(3), 261–271. https://doi.org/10.1080/01690965.2011.620374

Bochner, J. H., Christie, K., Hauser, P. C., & Searls, J. M. (2011). When is a difference really different? Learners' discrimination of linguistic contrasts in American Sign Language. *Language Learning*, *61*(4), 1302–1327. https://doi.org/10.1111/j.1467-9922.2011.00671.x

Boers-Visker, E., & Hammer, A. (in press). Language assessment literacy in second sign language assessment contexts. In T. Haug, W. Mann, & U. Knoch (Eds.), *Handbook of language assessment across modalities*. Oxford University Press.
Campbell, R., MacSweeney, M., & Woll, B. (2017). Cochlear implantation (CI) for prelingual deafness: The relevance of studies of brain organization and the role of first language acquisition in considering outcome success. *Frontiers in Human Neuroscience, 2014*(8), 834. https://doi.org/10.3389/fnhum.2014.00834
Clark, E. (2009). *First language acquisition*. Cambridge University Press.
Council of Europe (2020). *Common European Framework of Reference for Languages: Learning, teaching, assessment. Companion Volume*. Council of Europe. https://rm.coe.int/common-european-framework-of-reference-for-languages-learning-teaching/16809ea0d4
Enns, C., Haug, T., Herman, R., Hoffmeister, R. J., Mann, W., & Mcquarrie, L. (2016). Exploring signed language assessment tools in Europe and North America. In M. Marschark, V. Lampropoulou, & E. K. Skordilis (Eds.), *Diversity in deaf education* (pp. 171–218). Oxford University Press.
Ferrara, L., & Nilsson, A. L. (2017). Describing spatial layouts as an L2M2 signed language learner. *Sign Language & Linguistics, 20*(1), 1–26. https://doi.org/10.1075/sll.20.1.01fer
Fitzpatrick, E. M., Hamel, C., Stevens, A., Pratt, M., Moher, D., Doucet, S. P., Neuss, D., Bernstein, A., & Na, E. (2016). Sign language and spoken language for children with hearing loss: A systematic review. *Pediatrics, 137*(1), 1–17. https://doi.org/10.1542/peds.2015-1974
Gregory, S. (2017). *Deaf children under two years: Diagnosis and intervention*. BATOD (British Association of Teachers of the Deaf). https://www.batod.org.uk/information/deaf-children-under-two-years-diagnosis-and-intervention/
Hall, M. L., Hall, W. C., & Caselli, N. K. (2019). Deaf children need language, not (just) speech. *First Language, 39*(4), 367–395. https://doi.org/10.1177/0142723719834102
Haug, T. (2017). *Development and evaluation of two vocabulary tests for Swiss German Sign Language* (Unpublished master's thesis). Lancaster University, Lancaster, UK.
Haug, T., & Mann, W. (2008). Adapting tests of sign language assessment for other sign languages—A review of linguistic, cultural, and psychometric problems. *Journal of Deaf Studies and Deaf Education, 13*(1), 138–147. https://doi.org/10.1093/deafed/enm027
Haug, T., Mann, W., Boers-Visker, E., Contreras, J., Enns, C., & Rowley, K. (2016). *Guidelines for sign language test development, evaluation, and use* (V. 1.1). http://www.signlang-assessment.info/
Hauser, P. C., Paludneviciene, R., Riddle, W., Kurz, K. B., Emmorey, K., & Contreras, J. (2016). American Sign Language comprehension test: A tool for sign language researchers. *Journal of Deaf Studies and Deaf Education, 21*(1), 64–69. https://doi.org/10.1093/deafed/env051
Herman, R., Holmes, S., & Woll, B. (1999). *Assessing BSL development: Receptive skills test*. Forest Books.
Kendon, A. (2004). *Gesture: Visible action as utterance*. Cambridge University Press.
Leeson, L., Haug, T., Rathmann, C., Sheneman, N., & Bogaerde, B. van den. (2018). *The implementation of the Common European framework of reference (CEFR) for signed languages in higher education—Results of an international survey* (Survey report). https://www.researchgate.net/publication/326059817_Survey_Report_from_the_ECML_Project_ProSign_Sign_Languages_for_Professional_Purposes_The_Implementation_of_the_Common_European_Framework_of_Reference_CEFR_for_Sign_Languages_in_Higher_Education_Result
Lillo-Martin, D., Müller de Quadros, R, Chen Pichler, D., & Fieldsteel, Z. (2014). Language choice in bimodal bilingual development. *Frontiers in Psychology, 5*. https://doi.org/10.3389/fpsyg.2014.01163
Mann, W., & Haug, T. (2014). Mapping out guidelines for the development and use of sign language assessment: Some critical issues, comments and suggestions. In D. Quinto-Pozos (Ed.), *Multilingual aspects of signed language communication and disorders* (pp. 123–139). Multilingual Matters.
McNamara, T. (2000). *Oxford introductions to language study: Language testing*. Oxford University Press.
Mellon, N. K., Niparko, J. K., Rathmann, C., Mathur, G., Humphries, T., Napoli, D. J., Handley, T., Scambler, S., & Lantos, J. D. (2015). Should all deaf children learn sign language? *Pediatrics, 136*(1), 170–176. https://doi.org/10.1542/peds.2014-1632
Mirus, G., Rathmann, C., & Meier, R. P. (2001). Proximalization and distalization of sign movement in adult learners. In V. Dively, M. Metzger, S. Taub, & A. M. Baer (Eds.), *Signed languages: Discoveries from international research* (pp. 103–119). Gallaudet University Press.
Müller de Quadros, R., Lillo-Martin, D., & Chen Pichler, D. (2015). Bimodal bilingualism: Sign language and spoken language. In M. Marschark & P. E. Spencer (Eds.), *The Oxford handbook of deaf studies in language* (pp. 181–196). Oxford University Press.
Orfanidou, E., Woll, B., & Morgan, G. (2015). *Research methods in sign language studies*. John Wiley.

Ortega, G. (2017). Iconicity and sign lexical acquisition: A review. *Frontiers in Psychology*, *8*, 1280. https://doi.org/10.3389/fpsyg.2017.01280
Ortega, G., & Morgan, G. (2015). Phonological development in hearing learners of a sign language: The influence of phonological parameters, sign complexity, and iconicity. *Language Learning*, *65*(3), 660–688. https://doi.org/10.1111/lang.12123
Pfau, R., Steinbach, M., & Woll, B. (2012). *Sign language: An international handbook*. DeGruyter.
Pyfers, L. (Ed.). (2017). *Sign language teaching in Europe: Report & recommendations*. EUD. http://www.signteach.eu/BOOK/SignLanguageTeachinginEurope2017.pdf.
Quinto-Pozos, D. (2011). Teaching American Sign Language to hearing adult learners. *Annual Review of Applied Linguistics*, *31*, 137–158. https://doi.org/10.1017/S0267190511000195
Rosen, R. S. (2004). Beginning L2 production errors in ASL lexical phonology. *Sign Language & Linguistics*, *7*(1), 31–61. https://doi.org/10.1075/sll.7.1.04beg
Sandler, W., & Lillo-Martin, D. (2006). *Sign language and linguistic universals*. Cambridge University Press.
Spencer, P. A., & Marschark, M. (2005). *Advances in spoken language development of deaf and hard-of-hearing children*. Oxford University Press.
Stokoe, W. C. (1960). Sign language structure: An outline of the visual communication system of the American deaf. *Studies in Linguistic Occasional Papers*, *8* [revised edition (1978)]. Linstok Press.
Strong, M., & Prinz, P. M. (1997). A study on the relationship between American Sign Language and English literacy. *Journal of Deaf Studies and Deaf Education*, *2*(1), 37–46.
Van den Broek-Laven, A., Boers-Visker, E., & Bogaerde, B. van den. (2014). Determining aspects of text difficulty for the Sign Language of the Netherlands (NGT) functional assessment instrument. *Papers in Language Testing and Assessment*, *3*(2), 53–75.
Williams, J. T., Darcy, I., & Newman, S. D. (2018). Neural substrates of sign language vocabulary processing in less-skilled hearing M2L2 signers: Evidence for difficult phonological movement perception. *Bilingualism: Language and Cognition*, *21*(3), 550–562. https://doi.org/10.1017/S1366728917000347
Woll, B., & Ladd, P. (2011). Deaf communities. In M. Marschark & P. E. Spencer (Eds.), *The Oxford handbook of deaf studies, language, and education*. Oxford Handbooks Online. https://doi.org/9780199750986.013.0012

Part VI

Measurement Principles for SLA Researchers

42

Statistical Modeling of SLA Theories

Connecting Test Performance to Construct

Yo In'nami & Akira Murakami

Background

Statistical analysis in second language acquisition (SLA) has largely taken place within the *null hypothesis significance testing* (NHST) paradigm (Plonsky, 2013) and, among NHST techniques, has especially been based to a large extent on comparing means between groups (e.g., t-test, ANOVA). This trend extends to language testing, where variables are systematically manipulated, and the effects of these variables on test scores are examined using NHST. The goal of NHST in this respect is to understand what contributes to variability in test scores. In addition to NHST, however, a given field generally observes an increased use of the statistical modeling techniques other than simple group-mean comparison methods as it matures (Rodgers, 2010a). A model may or may not explain a phenomenon of interest, and one model may explain the phenomenon better than another model. Sometimes, the grand mean is the best model. The point is that statistical modeling allows researchers to more directly specify processes of interest (Cavagnaro, Myung, & Pitt, 2013).

However, quantitative analytical techniques in SLA and language testing have rarely been discussed from the perspective of statistical modeling, presumably because these fields have used only a limited number of models to date. Perhaps as a result, the recent surge of interest among SLA researchers in better data analysis (e.g., Plonsky, 2014) has been largely confined to the enhancement of group-mean comparison methods through such measures and techniques such as effect sizes, confidence intervals, and meta-analysis (e.g., Norouzian & Plonsky, 2018; Plonsky & Oswald, 2012; but see also Plonsky & Oswald, 2017). Statistical modeling nevertheless holds promise for its ability to potentially allow applied linguists to answer questions to which traditional NHST techniques cannot readily provide answers. We believe that second language (L2) researchers are likely to benefit from the use of various statistical modeling techniques to better connect performance to construct. Note that the frequentist group-mean comparison techniques in the way currently used in SLA and language testing research typically fall within the NHST paradigm, and each NHST technique can generally be considered as a type of statistical modeling. Our claim is not that statistical modeling should be used instead of group-mean comparison or NHST but that it is more fruitful to conceptualize quantitative analytical techniques in terms of statistical models, which require analysts to give careful thoughts to the mechanism of the phenomenon of their interests and the structure of the data as a result, than to understand them solely within NHST.

Key Concepts

Null-hypothesis significance testing (NHST): A framework for testing a hypothesis using a null hypothesis, in which the effect of the variable of interest is assumed to be zero. Analysts then compute the probability of obtaining the observed or more extreme data given the null hypothesis (i.e., *p*-value). The null hypothesis is deemed unlikely when the calculated *p*-value is low.

Statistical modeling: Statistical models are generally understood to be idealized ways to describe reality (Pearl, 2009) that are closely related to underlying theoretical models (Collins, 2006). In statistical models, there is no need to explicitly state the null hypothesis, which is usually unjustifiable on theoretical grounds (cf. Long, 2012). Researchers instead compare competing models, and in this sense, all the compared models are alternative hypotheses (Long, 2012).

Key Issues

Statistical models represent a data-generation process of scientific inquiry and can test whether a given variable is relevant to the process more directly than NHST can (Lang, Sweet, & Grandfield, 2017). The models may not include all potentially relevant variables or account for those variables in exactly the same manner as they behave in the population, but statistical models are still useful insofar as they help researchers better understand the target phenomenon and address questions of interest.

The difference between statistical modeling and NHST is not computational but philosophical in nature (Rodgers, 2010b; cf. the box above). For example, suppose researchers want to examine whether there is a difference in learners' mean scores across Times 1 through 5. In NHST, the researchers test the null hypothesis, which states that there is no difference in learners' mean scores across these times. If the null hypothesis is rejected, analysts often support the alternative hypothesis that there is a difference in learners' mean scores across Times 1 through 5. If the analysis fails to reject the null hypothesis, it is often interpreted as indicating that the data are not informative enough to adopt the alternative hypothesis. In statistical modeling, in contrast, analysts might compare two linear models: one that assumes a consistent increase (or decrease) in the mean score (i.e., slope > 0 or < 0) and another that assumes no change in the value (i.e., an intercept-only model). The two models are then fitted to the data and their goodness-of-fit and/or predictive accuracy are compared to determine which model better explains the data. The null hypothesis is not explicitly stated during this process. Also, in statistical modeling, analysts can compare more than two models. Another model that might be tested in the above example is a model that assumes non-linear growth, such as a U-shaped change in scores.

Using statistical modeling does not mean that NHST has no role in L2 research. Rather, statistical modeling subsumes NHST because the null hypothesis is a statistical model with the null effect of a given parameter (Rodgers, 2010b). In a similar vein, NHST is useful for model comparison from the statistical modeling perspective and should be retained as part of statistical modeling (Lang et al., 2017; Rodgers, 2010b). From the NHST perspective, model comparison in the above example of linear development examines whether the difference in the goodness-of-fit between the two models can be assumed to be zero. In other words, the null hypothesis states that the model assuming a linear change in the scores and that assuming no change are equally capable of explaining the observed data, while its rejection suggests that the more flexible former model better explains the data.

Nevertheless, statistical modeling has a clear benefit in comparison to NHST—ecological validity (Lang et al., 2017). Statistical models are more holistic than NHST. They account for the entire system, while NHST is inevitably simpler, matches less well to reality, and only tests individual parameters without taking account of their contexts (Lang et al., 2017; Rodgers, 2010b). For instance, suppose one wishes to test the difference in mean reaction time between two groups of words (e.g., cognates versus non-cognates) in a lexical decision task in L2 learners sampled from a range of proficiency levels. Potential sources of variation, apart from the word group, include learners' proficiency, within-participant trial number (e.g., practice effects), variation across the participants, and variation across individual words, all of which should be incorporated into the analysis in some way. Besides their influence on the mean reaction time, however, the variability of reaction time has been claimed to decrease as learning progresses (e.g., Heathcote, Brown, & Mewhort, 2000). Analysts, therefore, can build a statistical model that allows the variance to vary across learners' proficiency levels and trial numbers. Alternatively, they can build two models, one that allows the variability of reaction time to vary across the said variables and the other that does not, and compare the two to investigate whether the prediction of decreasing variability holds in their data. Statistical models can be specified flexibly in this manner to reflect the assumed mechanism of the phenomenon. The holistic approach of this kind is more difficult to achieve with NHST, in which one might need to, for example, compare the reaction time at each proficiency level separately.

The flexibility of statistical modeling has recently been further enhanced due to the spread of Bayesian statistical modeling (e.g., Kruschke, 2012) and the associated development of probabilistic programming languages, such as Stan (Carpenter et al., 2017). These developments allow researchers to not only use existing modeling methods (e.g., mixed-effects regression models) but also develop their own models. Readers are referred to Lee and Wagenmakers (2013) for examples of flexible Bayesian modeling in psychology, many of which have straightforward applications to L2 research. Considering these developments, we echo Carlin and Chib (1995), who wrote that "the class of candidate models for a given data set now appears limited only by the user's imagination" (p. 473).

Recommendations for Practice

The benefits of statistical modeling over group-mean comparison techniques are especially prominent in the analysis of longitudinal data. For example, in statistical modeling, it is straightforward to model a development where observations are not evenly spaced or do not occur at the same time for all learners (Collins, 2006), whereas data of this kind are not readily analyzable with t-tests or analyses of variance (ANOVAs). Since L2 acquisition is an essentially longitudinal phenomenon, longitudinal data should be the standard data type in SLA research; however, although longitudinal data analysis has received attention in areas like education and some fields of psychology (e.g., Singer & Willett, 2003), L2 researchers may have little experience analyzing longitudinal data quantitatively (but see Barkaoui, 2014).

Below, we introduce two statistical modeling frameworks commonly used in longitudinal data analysis. The first is a mixed-effects regression model that can analyze group- and individual-level development simultaneously. Potential drawbacks of observed variable modeling, such as that done in typical mixed-effects regression models, as opposed to latent-variable modeling, include (a) that the modeling assumes that there is no measurement error in the independent variables, and (b) that the modeling lacks the flexibility brought by the inclusion of latent variables with multiple indicators (e.g., Lang et al., 2017). Thus, the second type of model we will introduce, multilevel structural equation modeling, is a latent variable model that overcomes this issue by separately modeling constructs and measurement errors.

Mixed-Effects Regression Modeling

A common issue in longitudinal data analysis is that observations are correlated/situated/nested within each learner. In other words, the value of the dependent variable (e.g., article accuracy in learner essays) can be more or less predicted based on which learner produced the essay because a learner with higher ability to use articles accurately tends to use articles more accurately than a learner with lower ability. Table 42.1 provides another example, from Sasaki, Mizumoto, and Murakami (2018), who examined how 37 Japanese learners of English developed their L2-writing-strategy use over four time points; the researchers found one of the strategies examined, global planning (the "overall planning of the content of the text to be written" [Sasaki et al., 2018, p. 294]), was more widely used among high-proficiency learners than among low-proficiency learners. Global planning use was partly predicted by who wrote a given essay; that is, the global planning use varied significantly among individuals, and, in this sense, the data were learner-dependent. Similarly, Table 42.1 shows the data structure of Barkaoui and In'nami (2019), who investigated longitudinal change in the test scores of 1000 learners of various backgrounds taking the Pearson Test of English (PTE) Academic. Because users often make high-stakes decisions on the basis of the interpretations of the scores of these tests, the researchers assumed it was possible that learners who initially obtained lower scores worked harder and improved more than high-proficient learners. Here, too, the scores were partly predicted by which learner took the test. Note that, in Table 42.1's Examples A and B, responses at the time points are nested within learners. The responses are defined as a lower-level or "Level 1" variable, while learners are at a higher level and are defined as a "Level 2" variable. Responses at Level 1 within learners are similar to each other (as they are from the same learner), and this entails dependency of the data.

Table 42.1 Examples of dependent data structures

Example A.				
Level 2 (Learner)	*Learner 1*	*Learner 2*	...	*Learner 37*
Level 1 (Response per time point)	--Time 1, global planning score --Time 2, global planning score --Time 3, global planning score --Time 4, global planning score	--Time 1, global planning score --Time 2, global planning score --Time 3, global planning score --Time 4, global planning score	...	--Time 1, global planning score --Time 2, global planning score --Time 3, global planning score --Time 4, global planning score
Example B.				
Level 2 (Learner)	*Learner 1*	*Learner 2*	...	*Learner 1000*
Level 1 (Response per time point)	--Time 1, proficiency score --Time 2, proficiency score --Time 3, proficiency score	--Time 1, proficiency score --Time 2, proficiency score --Time 3, proficiency score --Time 4, proficiency score --Time 5, proficiency score --Time 6, proficiency score --Time 7, proficiency score		--Time 1, proficiency score --Time 2, proficiency score --Time 3, proficiency score

Note. Example A shows the data structure of Sasaki, Mizumoto, and Murakami (2018). Example B shows the data structure of Barkaoui and In'nami (2019).

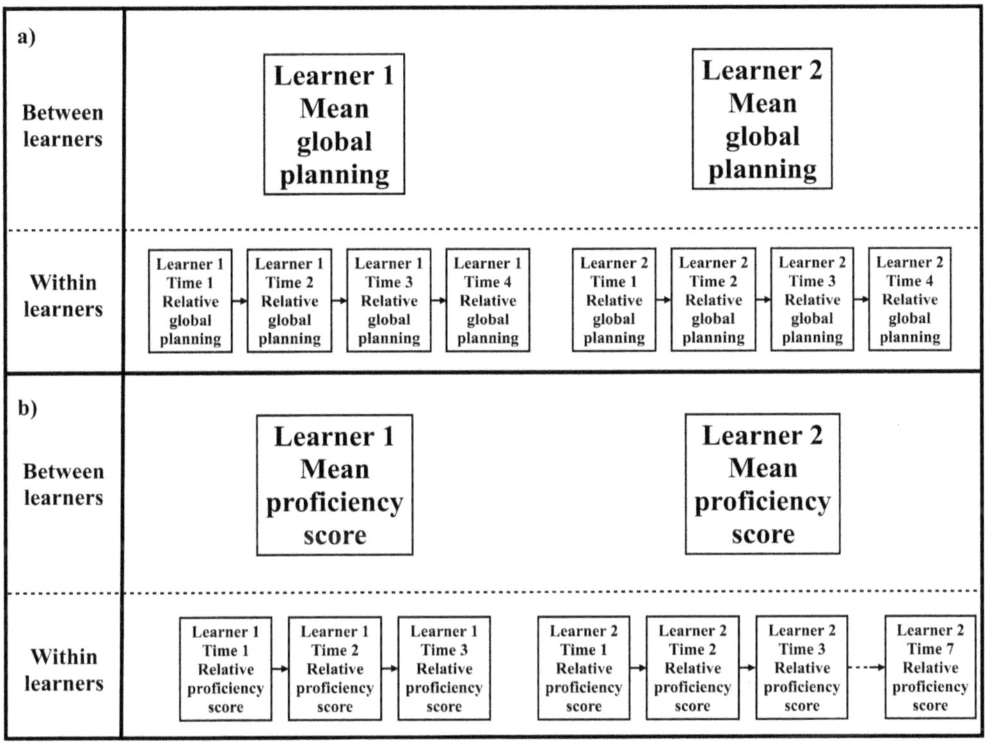

Figure 42.1 Mixed-effects models in Sasaki, Mizumoto, and Murakami (2018) and Barkaoui and In'nami (2019). Note: The models in Figure 42.1 are for illustration purposes and are not exactly the same as specified in statistical software.

Such dependency of data can be accounted for by mixed-effects models. A mixed-effects model partitions variance into multiple levels (e.g., Hox et al., 2018); for instance, it partitions total variability of data into (i) variability across native language (L1) groups, (ii) variability across learners within the same L1 group, and (iii) variability within learners, the last of which includes variability attributable to longitudinal development (cf. Murakami, 2016). In Examples A and B in Table 42.1, the total variability of the data is partitioned into variability across learners and variability within learners, as shown in Figure 42.1, where the between-learner level represents the mean scores of learners, whereas the within-learner level represents the deviation of each time point from the mean of the learner. In this manner, mixed-effects models allow researchers to model development at both the group level and the individual level. Modeling development at both levels is particularly important, given that the aggregated developmental pattern can differ from the learning curves of the individual learners that constitute the group (Heathcote et al., 2000; Murakami & Alexopoulou, 2016).

A strength of mixed-effects models is that each level of variability can be quantified and explained. However, it is important that researchers be aware of the level of the variability that they are trying to explain. If, for example, researchers are interested in the effects of L1 typology on an outcome measure, then between-L1 variability is the level they will be interested in, and they will need many typologically diverse L1 groups to better quantify and explain the role of L1 typologies, as the inferences they can draw depend on the variability in L1 typology present in the data. If a researcher is interested in the effects of learners' proficiency, on the other hand, between-learner variability (i.e., individual variation) is the level of interest, and many learners of different proficiency levels will be necessary to better understand how proficiency relates to an outcome measure, as otherwise the variability in the outcome variable cannot be linked with the variability in proficiency. In this manner, if researchers incorporate learners as random effects (i.e., if researchers allow their values for the dependent variable to vary), the researchers can look into individual variation by disentangling inter- and intra-learner variability. Interaction between the learner and other variables (modeled as random slopes) represents individual variation in the effects of those variables.

A relevant distinction is the one between time-varying variables, whose values can change over time (e.g., number of hours learning the L2 per week), and time-invariant variables, whose values remain the same (e.g., place of birth) (e.g., Long, 2012; Singer & Willett, 2003) across the timespan of the given dataset. Time-varying variables can explain both intra- and inter-learner variability, while time-invariant variables usually only explain variability between learners. As the type of variables—time-varying or time-invariant—dictates the level of interpretation—intra- and/or inter-learner variability, researchers should be fully aware which variables in their datasets are time-varying and time-invariant.

A useful technique related to the distinction between time-varying and time-invariant variables is within-learner centering (Hoffman & Stawski, 2009). In many cases, a time-varying predictor can explain both between-learner variability and within-learner variability, but researchers may need to separate the two. For instance, if the amount of time learners needed to write an essay is positively correlated with the lexical diversity of the essays (operationalized as, say, measure of textual lexical diversity, MTLD) in longitudinal data, including multiple learners, this positive correlation could mean any of the following:

- the essays of learners who wrote slowly tended to be more lexically diverse than those of learners who wrote quickly (the between-learner interpretation);
- individual learners were able to write more lexically diverse essays when they spent more time on them (the within-learner interpretation), or;
- both of the above.

One way to disentangle these effects is to use within-learner centering. Let us say that there are two learners, A and B, who wrote four essays each. The time they spent on writing each essay is shown under the "minutes" column of Table 42.2.

Table 42.2 Example of within-learner centering

Learner A	
Minute	Centered
14	–3
16	–1
18	1
20	3
Mean: 17	
Learner B	
Minute	Centered
24	–3
26	–1
28	1
30	3
Mean: 27	

To perform within-learner centering, researchers calculate the mean of the target variable within each learner (i.e., 17 and 27) and then subtract the mean from the individual value of the learner (e.g., 14 – 17 = –3). Instead of the target variable (Minutes), we can now enter two variables separately into statistical models:

- the by-learner mean (17 for Learner A and 27 for Learner B), representing between-learner differences, and;
- the mean-subtracted variable (–3, –1, 1, and 3 for Learners A and B), representing within-learner change.

In this manner, two variables, one representing between-learner differences and the other representing within-learner change, can be entered separately into the model. Although between-learner differences are observed (i.e., Learner A wrote more quickly than Learner B), the within-learner relative change in the time they spent writing an essay is the same (i.e., Learners A and B were similar in the way the time they spent writing essays changes chronologically). The key here is to create variables that represent the information of interest; see Sasaki et al. (2018) for an application of this technique in L2 writing research.

Another issue rather unique to modeling longitudinal data that has received little attention in L2 research (but see Meulman, Wieling, Sprenger, Stowe, & Schmid, 2015, and Wieling, 2018) is the *autocorrelation* of errors (Baayen, van Rij, de Cat, & Wood, 2018; Sóskuthy, 2017). Errors correlate when something other than the construct that is being measured causes responses/scores/data to be related to each other. An error is the difference between the true value and the predicted value by a statistical model and is approximated by the residual, or the difference between the observed value and the predicted value. The residual of a data point is negative when the predicted value is larger than the observed value. It would be positive in the opposite case. Autocorrelation refers to the correlation of errors between chronologically neighboring observations. To illustrate a case of autocorrelation, let us say that a learner has written 20 essays, and a researcher is interested in the relationship between MTLD and noun phrase length (i.e., whether writings with higher MTLD tend to include longer or shorter noun phrases) in those essays. The researcher fits a linear regression model to the 20 MTLD values against the 20 values of noun phrase length and computes the residual for each observation (Figure 42.2A). Figure 42.2B shows the scatter plot between noun phrase length and MTLD, and the numbers in the figure correspond to the time column in Figure 42.2A. The line is the simple regression line and the dashed lines represent residuals. Since time was (deliberately) not included in the model, however, time and residuals are not independent. Figure 42.2C shows that residuals tend to be negative in the first half of the essays, while they tend to be positive in the latter half. Indeed, if the residuals at Time t are correlated with those at Time t + 1 (Lag 1) or t + 2 (Lag 2), the correlations are moderately strong (Figure 42.2D). Figure 42.2E shows such autocorrelations at different lags. If the errors are autocorrelated (at any or all lags), then there is systematicity in the residuals, which indicates that the observations are *not* independent (Wieling, 2018). Remember that observations are independent if the occurrence of one provides no information about the occurrence of the other. Thus, autocorrelation indicates the assumption of observation-independence is likely to be violated and suggests that there is an echo in the data—that the occurrence of one data point provides some information about another. Autocorrelated errors are problematic because they could lead to spurious "significant" *p*-values. The bam function in the mgcv package (Wood, 2017) in R offers two tools to tackle autocorrelated errors (Baayen et al., 2018; Sóskuthy, 2017): (i) using more complex models (e.g., adding random smooths) to account for the systematic patterns in the residuals so that the resulting residuals are less systematic, and (ii) specifying the first-order autoregressive models, AR(1), that take lag-1 autocorrelation into account in the calculation of *p*-values and other relevant statistics. Readers are referred to Sóskuthy (2017) for practical tutorials on handling autocorrelated errors.

A. Raw Data, Fitted Values, and Residuals

Time	Noun Phrase Length	MTLD	Fitted	Residual
1	3.58	56.6	59.3	-2.74
2	4.15	50.4	60.5	-10.09
3	4.88	56.3	62.1	-5.78
4	3.55	59.4	59.3	0.07
⋮	⋮	⋮	⋮	⋮
20	4.82	69.7	61.9	7.76

B. Scatter Plot Between Noun Phrase Length and MTLD

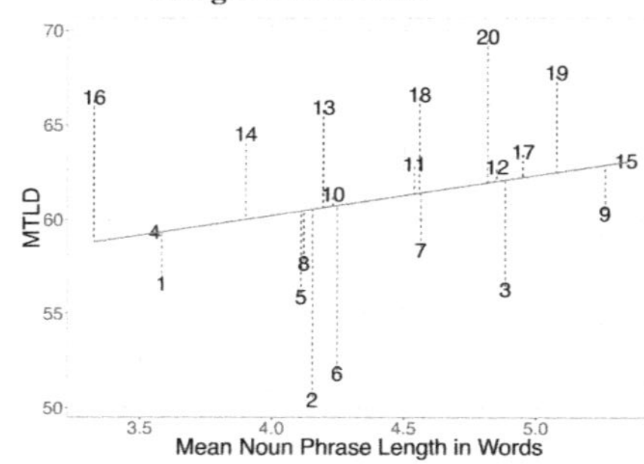

C. Residuals Across Time

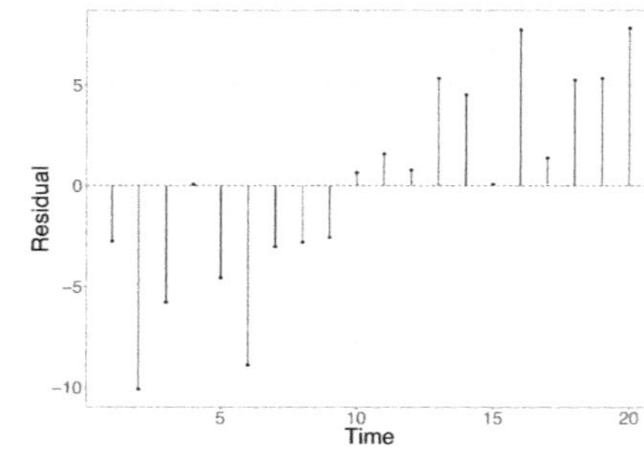

D. Residuals and Lagged Residuals

(a) Residual at Time t	(b) Residual at Time t + 1	(c) Residual at Time t + 2
-2.74	-10.09	-5.78
-10.09	-5.78	0.07
-5.78	0.07	-4.55
⋮	⋮	⋮
5.25	5.33	7.76

Correlation between (a) and (b): 0.58 → Lag 1 autocorrelation
Correlation between (a) and (c): 0.44 → Lag 2 autocorrelation

E. Correlogram Showing Autocorrelations

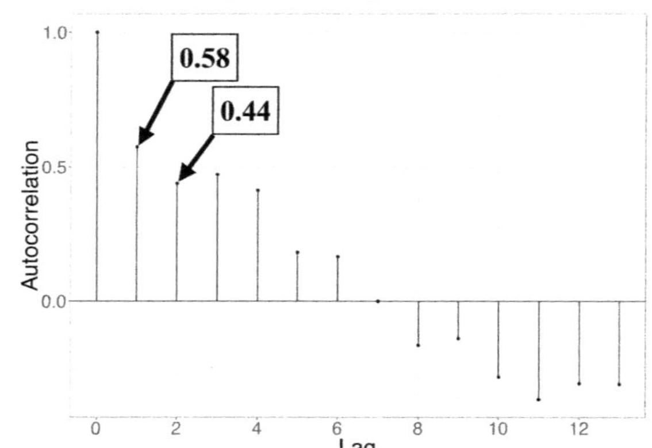

Figure 42.2 Autocorrelations.

Multilevel Structural Equation Modeling

Another approach to examining change is to use multilevel structural equation modeling (SEM), which researchers use to model group- and individual-level changes (as they can with mixed-effects regression modeling) while additionally and flexibly modeling various features, such as unobserved/latent variables (also called factors) and measurement errors (e.g., Finch & Bolin, 2017; Little, 2013; Stapleton, 2013). As its name suggests, multilevel SEM is a multilevel version of SEM. Some readers may be familiar with (basic) SEM, which is a combination of factor analysis and regression, that has been used in SLA and language testing (see e.g., the studies cited in Barkaoui, 2014; see also Hancock & Schoonen, 2015). When data are taken from clustered groups of individuals, they are dependent, as shown in Table 42.1, and violate the assumption of independence of responses. If such data are analyzed using SEM, *t*-test, or ANOVA, the standard errors of parameters (e.g., paths, factor loadings) will be underestimated, revealing spurious statistically significant results by chance (i.e., a Type I error; e.g., Hox et al., 2018). This problem is addressed in multilevel SEM, as in mixed-effects regression modeling, but with more flexibility.

Similar to the graphical representation of the mixed-effects regression models in Figure 42.1, the total variability of the data is partitioned into variability across and variability within learners. However, three unique features of multilevel SEM compared with mixed-effects regression modeling merit discussion. First, more accurate modeling is made possible with multilevel SEM by incorporating measurement error into the independent variables of the model. Researchers normally assume that there is no measurement error in independent variables (i.e., that they can measure constructs perfectly) when using mixed-effects regression models (Lang et al., 2017). For example, in Sasaki et al. (2018), one of the predictors of learners' use of global planning strategies was L2-writing ability, measured by L2-writing-composition scores. As it is not possible to measure constructs, such as writing ability, directly and perfectly, one approach is to consider error in the measurement. The error may, for example, include topic familiarity and raters' marking consistency. In this way, error can be included in the model in multilevel SEM; this allows researchers to examine whether and to what extent L2 writing ability predicts global planning, while separately estimating the measurement error from the construct. If these two are not separately modeled, it is not clear to what extent change in global planning may be due to L2 writing ability—the focal construct—or due to error.

Second, in addition to modeling measurement error, researchers can more accurately model constructs by introducing latent variables. For instance, Sasaki et al. (2018) measured global planning by whether participants reported having used the strategy in stimulated retrospective protocols. The authors videotaped the protocol session and coded the protocol. On top of the video-based measurement, global planning could also have been represented by participants' performance measured by self- and teacher assessments. Thus, global planning could be represented by three measures: participants' protocols coded by the authors and self- and teacher assessments of performance. Using multiple measures helps measure constructs more accurately. Note that latent-variable scores are a very specific type of score (e.g., factor scores). Just because scores measure something reportedly unobservable does not make them inherently latent-variable scores.

Third, introducing latent variables and measurement errors in models allows researchers to examine change at the level of latent variables, not observed variables, while considering measurement error. In addition to global planning, Sasaki et al. (2018) examined the development of two other writing strategies: local planning (which they defined as "planning what to write next without any sense of the overall picture of the composition to be formed" [p. 294]) and L1-to-L2 translation ("translating or attempting to translate the idea generated into the L2" [p. 294]). As writing is a complex process in which various strategies interact, it would be interesting to examine how these three strategies are correlated with each other and how they are related causally (mediation analysis; e.g., whether global planning leads to local planning, which in turn leads to L1-to-L2 translation). Such correlational and causal relationships can be examined using multilevel SEM while controlling for measurement error. These three unique features of multilevel SEM meet the demands of SLA researchers and language testers who want to rigorously examine longitudinal change to better connect performance to construct.

Testing Tips

- In analyzing quantitative data for L2 research, consider employing statistical modeling as the analytical framework, rather than opting for group-mean comparison.
- Pay attention to the level of variability that you are interested in explaining, and make sure that you have sufficient sample size at that particular level of concern.
- Be careful of autocorrelated errors in longitudinal data analysis.
- Model latent variables and measurement errors to examine changes in performance. Measure the construct your study is focused on by using multiple instruments or indices. Considering these two issues would allow for a more accurate measurement of the construct.

Recommended Readings

Hox, J., Moerbeek, M., & van de Schoot, R. (2018). *Multilevel analysis: Techniques and applications* (3rd ed.). Routledge.

The authors describe how to analyze longitudinal data using mixed-effects modeling with user-friendly HLM software. The authors explain how each variable is entered into the regressions; data and tutorials are available on Hox et al.'s website (https://multilevel-analysis.sites.uu.nl/).

Long, J. D. (2012). *Longitudinal data analysis for the behavioral sciences using R*. SAGE Publications.

This book provides handy tutorials on the use of mixed-effects models for longitudinal data analysis with R. It also covers several useful topics that are not usually discussed in the L2 literature (e.g., multimodel inference).

Finch, W. H., & Bolin, J. E. (2017). *Multilevel modeling using Mplus*. CRC Press.

Finch and Bolin provide a detailed explanation of multilevel Structural Equation Modeling (SEM) and how to conduct it using Mplus software.

References

Baayen, R. H., van Rij, J., de Cat, C., & Wood, S. (2018). Autocorrelated errors in experimental data in the language sciences: Some solutions offered by generalized additive mixed models. In D. Speelman, K. Heylen, & D. Geeraerts (Eds.), *Mixed-effects regression models in linguistics* (pp. 49–69). Springer.

Barkaoui, K. (2014). Quantitative approaches for analyzing longitudinal data in second language research. *Annual Review of Applied Linguistics*, *34*, 65–101. https://doi.org/10.1017/S0267190514000105

Barkaoui, K., & In'nami, Y. (2019). Using multilevel modeling to examine changes in second language test scores over time. In V. Aryadoust & M. Raquel (Eds.), *Quantitative data analysis for language assessment volume II: Advanced methods* (pp. 171–189). Routledge.

Carlin, B. P., & Chib, S. (1995). Bayesian model choice via Markov Chain Monte Carlo methods. *Journal of the Royal Statistical Society: Series B (Methodological)*, *57*(3), 473–484.

Carpenter, B., Gelman, A., Hoffman, M., Lee, D., Goodrich, B., Betancourt, M., Brubaker, M., Guo, J., & Riddell, A. (2017). Stan: A probabilistic programming language. *Journal of Statistical Software*, *76*(1). https://doi.org/10.18637/jss.v076.i01

Cavagnaro, D. R., Myung, J. I., & Pitt, M. A. (2013). Mathematical modeling. In T D. Little (Ed.), *Oxford handbook of quantitative methods* (Vol. 1, pp. 437–452). Oxford University Press.
Collins, L. M. (2006). Analysis of longitudinal data: The integration of theoretical model, temporal design, and statistical model. *Annual Review of Psychology*, *57*, 505–528. https://doi.org/10.1146/annurev.psych.57.102904.190146
Finch, W. H., & Bolin, J. E. (2017). *Multilevel modeling using Mplus*. CRC Press.
Hancock, G. R., & Schoonen, R. (2015). Structural equation modeling: Possibilities for language learning researchers. *Language Learning*, *65*(S1), 160–184. https://doi.org/110.1111/lang.12116
Heathcote, A., Brown, S., & Mewhort, D. J. K. (2000). The power law repealed: The case for an exponential law of practice. *Psychonomic Bulletin & Review*, *7*(2), 185–207. https://doi.org/10.3758/BF03212979
Hoffman, L., & Stawski, R. S. (2009). Persons as contexts: Evaluating between-person and within-person effects in longitudinal analysis. *Research in Human Development*, *6*(2–3), 97–120. https://doi.org/10.1080/15427600902911189
Hox, J., Moerbeek, M., & van de Schoot, R. (2018). *Multilevel analysis: Techniques and applications* (3rd ed.). Routledge.
Kruschke, J. K. (2012). *Doing Bayesian data analysis: A tutorial with R, JAGS, and Stan* (2nd ed.). Academic Press.
Lang, K. M., Sweet, S. J., & Grandfield, E. M. (2017). Getting beyond the null: Statistical modeling as an alternative framework for inference in developmental science. *Research in Human Development*, *14*(4), 287–304. https://doi.org/10.1080/15427609.2017.1371567
Lee, M. D., & Wagenmakers, E.-J. (2013). *Bayesian cognitive modeling*. Cambridge University Press.
Little, T. D. (2013). *Longitudinal structural equation modeling*. Guilford.
Long, J. D. (2012). *Longitudinal data analysis for the behavioral sciences using R*. SAGE Publications.
Meulman, N., Wieling, M., Sprenger, S. A., Stowe, L. A., & Schmid, M. S. (2015). Age effects in L2 grammar processing as revealed by ERPs and how (not) to study them. *PLos One*, *10*(12), e0143328. https://doi.org/10.1371/journal.pone.0143328
Murakami, A. (2016). Modeling systematicity and individuality in nonlinear second language development: The case of English grammatical morphemes. *Language Learning*, *66*(4), 834–871. https://doi.org/10.1111/lang.12166
Murakami, A., & Alexopoulou, T. (2016). Longitudinal L2 development of the English article in individual learners. In A. Papafragou, D. Grodner, D. Mirman, & J. Trueswell (Eds.), *Proceedings of the 38th annual meeting of the Cognitive Science Society* (pp. 1050–1055). Cognitive Science Society.
Norouzian, R., & Plonsky, L. (2018). Eta- and partial eta-squared in L2 research: A cautionary review and guide to more appropriate usage. *Second Language Research*, *34*(2), 257–271. https://doi.org/10.1177/0267658316684904
Pearl, J. (2009). *Causality: Models, reasoning, and inference* (2nd ed.). Cambridge University Press.
Plonsky, L. (2013). Study quality in SLA: An assessment of designs, analyses, and reporting practices in quantitative L2 research. *Studies in Second Language Acquisition*, *35*(4), 655–687. https://doi.org/10.1017/S0272263113000399
Plonsky, L. (2014). Study quality in quantitative L2 research (1990–2010): A methodological synthesis and call for reform. *The Modern Language Journal*, *98*(1), 450–470. https://doi.org/10.1111/j.1540-4781.2014.12058.x
Plonsky, L., & Oswald, F. L. (2012). How to do a meta-analysis. In A. Mackey & S. M. Gass (Eds.), *Research methods in second language acquisition: A practical guide* (pp. 275–295). Blackwell Publishing.
Plonsky, L., & Oswald, F. L. (2017). Multiple regression as a flexible alternative to ANOVA in L2 research. *Studies in Second Language Acquisition*, *39*(3), 579–592. https://doi.org/10.1017/S0272263116000231
Rodgers, J. L. (2010a). Statistical and mathematical modeling versus NHST? There's no competition! *Journal of Modern Applied Statistical Methods*, *9*(2). https://doi.org/10.22237/jmasm/1288584120
Rodgers, J. L. (2010b). The epistemology of mathematical and statistical modeling: A quiet methodological revolution. *American Psychologist*, *65*(1), 1–12. https://doi.org/10.1037/a0018326
Sasaki, M., Mizumoto, A., & Murakami, A. (2018). Developmental trajectories in L2 writing strategy use: A self-regulation perspective. *The Modern Language Journal*, *102*(2), 292–309. https://doi.org/10.1111/modl.12469
Singer, J. D., & Willett, J. B. (2003). *Applied longitudinal data analysis: Modeling change and event occurrence*. Oxford University Press.
Sóskuthy, M. (2017). *Generalised additive mixed models for dynamic analysis in linguistics: A practical introduction*. https://arxiv.org/abs/1703.05339
Stapleton, L. M. (2013). Multilevel structural equation modeling with complex survey data. In G. R. Hancock & R. O. Mueller (Eds.), *Structural equation modeling: A second course* (pp. 521–562). Information Age Publishing.

Wieling, M. (2018). Analyzing dynamic phonetic data using generalized additive mixed modeling: A tutorial focusing on articulatory differences between L1 and L2 speakers of English. *Journal of Phonetics*, *70*, 86–116. https://doi.org/10.1016/j.wocn.2018.03.002

Wood, S. N. (2017). *Generalized additive models: An introduction with R* (2nd ed.). Chapman and Hall/CRC.

43

Using Equivalent Test Forms in SLA Pretest-Posttest Design Research

Yuichi Suzuki & Rie Koizumi

Background

Pretest-posttest experimental design is essential when the aim is to identify the effects of different treatments on second language (L2) acquisition. This experimental research design typically requires two or more test forms (e.g., pretest, immediate posttest, and delayed posttest). These test forms should be interchangeable in terms of content, difficulty, and other characteristics. Forms that have such equivalency are called equivalent forms, alternate forms, or parallel forms (Henning, 1987).[1] They facilitate consistent score interpretations and thus help in objectively assessing L2 development over time.

Equivalent test forms also minimize a threat to the internal validity of pretest-posttest design used in experimental research (Brown, 1988). When participants are administered the same test before and after the treatment, the experience gained during the first test may influence the performance on the second test. This effect is called a *practice effect*. It refers to "the fact that taking two tests with the same or similar content may result in a higher score on the second test, despite there being no increase in ability in the skill being measured" (Davies et al., 1999, p. 148).[2] The discussions provided in this chapter focus on practice effects observed when the same test is used in pretest-posttest design. There are at least three major sources of practice effects: (a) test-takers remember (some elements of) test item content; (b) test-takers notice some patterns or intentions of researchers in the tests and learn a strategy to perform on the test better; and (c) they get used to the test situation and perform better for the second time. It may not be possible to completely eliminate the second and third possibility by using equivalent test forms. These risks, however, can be reduced by including many filler test items and inserting a longer interval between multiple test administrations. These unintended and undesirable practice effects jeopardize the interpretations of score changes from one test to the next. In other words, practice effects make it impossible to fairly assess learning gains that can be attributed to the experimental treatment. This concern is equally important for observational studies where the development of L2 learners is being tracked. In order to minimize practice effects, researchers should be equipped with several methodological options, such as using equivalent test forms. The appropriate use of equivalent test forms and related techniques contributes to scientifically rigorous research in both fields of second language acquisition (SLA) and language testing (LT).

In the sections that follow, researchers will be given advice on how to design equivalent test forms for a pretest-posttest design study and to account for the equivalence of test forms and their use from experimental and statistical points of view (e.g., counterbalancing and test equating). This will be followed by a brief overview of the current practice in using equivalent test forms in a subdomain of instructed SLA research to demonstrate that they are insufficiently exploited. Finally, some recommendations for using equivalent test forms in SLA and LT research are given.

Key Concepts

***Practice effect*:** The influence of one test on the next one when the same test is given multiple times to the same participants. Practice effect is also called recall effect, memory effect, test order(ing) effect, carryover effect, and test familiarity effect.

***Equivalent forms*:** Test forms that have very similar content, difficulty, and other pertinent characteristics. Test development based on test specifications and statistical analysis is required to ensure equivalency of test forms. Equivalent forms are also called alternate or parallel forms.

***Test equating*:** A statistical method of adjusting scores on multiple test forms to ensure that they can be used interchangeably.

Key Issues

Here, the nuts and bolts of equivalent test design and its use are discussed in relation to three stages of research. In the test design phase, researchers need to create test forms to assess the same construct for the same purpose, with the same content and statistical specifications, to the best of their abilities. In the pilot testing phase, they should examine the actual psychometric characteristics of the test forms to demonstrate evidence of equivalency. In the main study, they should implement a design that ensures test equivalency by using counterbalancing techniques.

Test Design

Development of language tests requires test specifications (see Green & Fulcher, Chapter 7, this volume) to account for how tests can measure target constructs (e.g., target linguistic ability). Based on these specifications, multiple test forms that contain different items but fulfill very similar item characteristics are created. The test specifications typically include detailed descriptions of content areas, format, difficulty, the number of test items, ratios of different item types, item order, and how to administer the test and score the responses, as well as specifications on any other pertinent elements, such as test directions (Davies et al., 1999).

By covering some of these key features of test design, we explain how to create equivalent test forms in this section. For illustration purposes, we focus on grammar tests because the acquisition of grammatical knowledge remains one of the most researched linguistic domains in SLA research. Outcome measures for the acquisition of linguistic rules can be broadly categorized into: (a) controlled tests, where target linguistic rules are obligatorily tested for receptive or productive use; and (b) free production tests, where test-takers are given control over the linguistic features they use for production (Norris & Ortega, 2000). Examples of controlled tests are a grammaticality judgment test (GJT), an oral elicited imitation (EI) test, a text reconstruction test, a translation test, a picture matching test, and multiple-choice test. Free production tests typically include an oral/written narrative test and an interview test.

In controlled tests, researchers can take a stricter control of learners' responses than in production tests. For instance, one of the widely used tests, a GJT, typically requires participants to read or listen to a single sentence and to judge whether the sentence is grammatically correct (Spinner & Gass, 2019). Equivalent forms of GJT should therefore have the same number of test items (e.g., 40),[3] as well as equal proportion of item types (e.g., 20 grammatical and 20 ungrammatical items, with a balanced number of items related to targeted constructs, such as 10 past-tense, 10 past-perfect, and 20 filler items), and the order of test items should be (pseudo-)randomized across forms. In addition, other factors should be also controlled across test forms, such as sentence length (e.g., number of words, syllables, and audio stimulus lengths, when necessary) and lexical difficulty of stimulus sentences (e.g., frequency, familiarity).

While these rules seem straightforward, creating equivalent forms is challenging. For instance, when a GJT is designed to assess learners' knowledge of subjunctive past perfect in English, similar test items for equivalent test forms can be constructed in several ways. Suppose that the item (A) below is the baseline that contains verb form error (i.e., the correct form is "had taken"). A rule of thumb is to create a sentence that is not too different nor too similar to the baseline. Higher similarity between test items increases interchangeability of test scores across forms, but it tends to increase practice effects. Lower similarity can reduce practice effects; however, if test items differ significantly in many aspects, their equivalency becomes questionable. This point is illustrated below.

A) If my father took the car, he would have come here earlier. (Baseline)
B) If my father had taken the car, he came here earlier. (Inappropriate)
C) If my mother took the car, she would have come here earlier.
D) If my mother took the car, she would have left home later.
E) If my mother took the picture, she would have kept it here.
F) If my mother helped my father, he would have been very happy.

Apparently, item (B) has some resemblance to the baseline item (A), but it may not constitute a good equivalent item because the target is different (the error is in the main clause rather than the subordinate clause). Thus, the remaining items, (C) to (F), are better candidates as an equivalent item for item (A). While the number of words and lexical difficulty are controlled, the degree of similarity decreases from (C) to (F). The items (C) and (D) include the same verb phrase ("took the car") in the subordinate clause. However, while the same verb phrase is used in the main clause in item (C), it is changed in (D). In comparison, the item (E) is more different from the baseline. While the same verb "took" is retained, the object is changed ("took the picture") and the main clause is also modified. In the item (F), the target verb phrase is completely changed ("helped my father"). Unless researchers are also interested in the acquisition of verb form (irregular inflection as in "took" vs. regular inflection as in "helped"), item (F) is most likely to alleviate practice effects, while measuring the knowledge of subjunctive past perfect.

Many decisions have to be made when constructing similar GJT items for equivalent forms. Thus, it is essential to explicitly report in research articles how items in equivalent forms were constructed and justify the chosen strategy. For instance, researchers can select item (C) or (D), if their aim is to assess the direct effect of treatment on the verb phrases (e.g., "took the car") practiced in the treatment, and/or if participants' English proficiency is limited. While GJT is a receptive test, a production test such as EI test (i.e., wherein participants listen to a sentence and repeat it under certain time pressure) may require more careful construction. For one reason, learners may find it difficult to repeat the sentence under time pressure for the first time, but would likely perform better on the second test simply due to the practice effect (rather than as a result of gaining grammatical knowledge of a specific construction). If some tests are more susceptible to practice effects, researchers can create a different test form using more dissimilar sentences. Of course, researchers cannot be certain how practice effects pertaining to different tests for a given study develop. That is why it is critical to evaluate test form equivalency by conducting a pilot study, which is discussed in the next section.

When it comes to free production tests of grammatical knowledge, the elicitation of target grammatical structures can be the key aspect of a certain pretest-posttest research design. Test developers should make sure that participants are equally likely to use targeted grammatical structure in different test forms, as this will allow the development of grammatical knowledge to be assessed in the natural context of language production. Prompts (e.g., picture, short passage, and questions) are typically used to elicit spoken and written production. They should be given, prior to the main experiment, to a group of participants (e.g., native speakers, or a sample of L2 learners similar to the population targeted by the main study). Preliminary analysis should determine the usability of each prompt by evaluating some criteria, which can be guided by the previous research (e.g., eight out of ten participants used the target structure for a prompt). Some problematic items will be discarded along the way.

Finally, it is worth noting that there is an emerging interest in developing controlled, real-time sentence processing tests utilizing different measures (e.g., reaction time and eye-movement) as measures of implicit grammatical knowledge (Suzuki, 2017). For instance, Godfroid (2016) conducted one of the first studies in which a reaction-time test called the *word-monitoring test* was used as a part of a pretest-posttest design in instructed L2 research. Readers can easily imagine that developing multiple equivalent forms for this type of test requires much more effort and careful construction than traditional tests like GJTs. Moreover, as reaction-time and eye-movement measures are highly sensitive and more susceptible to extraneous variables (e.g., lexical access speed, predictability of cues, visual prompts) than traditional measurements, pilot studies should also be designed and conducted more rigorously to verify test equivalence prior to the main experiment (see Isbell & Rogers, Chapter 29, this volume).

Pilot Testing

Once similar multiple test forms are created, researchers need to check if these forms are actually equivalent by administering them to a trial sample drawn from the target population (see Green, Chapter 11, this volume, for more information on pilot testing). Three main methods of inspecting test equivalency are presently in use.

The method of *equivalency* is the strictest of the three and requires the test forms to have (a) the same means, (b) the same standard deviations (*SD*s), and (c) strong correlations with each other (i.e., equivalent-forms reliability) or the same correlations with other tests (Bae & Lee, 2011; Henning, 1987). These assumptions should be always verified by administering multiple test forms to the same group. Whether means, *SD*s, and correlations are the same should be established by significance tests, such as *t* test, with preferably very small effect sizes indicating small differences between test forms. We argue that the three conditions are equally important, although the third type of evidence for correlations is sometimes considered to be optional (see AERA, APA, & NCME, 2014, p. 35, for an example). Furthermore, the third condition (c) can be investigated more rigorously by examining an internal structure of each test form through structural equation modeling, e.g., by checking for the same factor loadings, factor variances, and factor covariances (Bae & Lee, 2011). See Weir and Wu (2006) for an example of this method.

Second, in the method based on *random parallel test forms*, multiple forms are developed using an "item bank" with a large pool of test items that conform to the same test specifications (see Oswald, Friede, Schmitt, Kim, & Ramsay, 2005, for an illustration). These test items are piloted and often analyzed through item response theory (IRT; Henning, 1987), and their item characteristics (e.g., item difficulty, item discrimination) are known. When creating test forms, researchers would randomly select the same number of items for each test form from within each band of item difficulty, with the items balanced on item discrimination as well. This procedure works best when there are more items in the item bank. Since this procedure may produce slight variations across test forms, especially if there are not enough items in the item bank, it is advisable to check their characteristics using the approach explained in the first method.

The third method is based on *test equating*, which enables researchers to equate test forms by transforming test form scores "onto a common scale which allows for comparison" across test forms (Davies et al., 1999, p. 199). In this case, test forms may have different means and *SD*s, but their scores can be used comparably by employing a conversion table (see Stewart & Gibson, 2010, for an example). According to Kolen and Brennan (2014), equating "adjusts for differences in difficulty among forms that are built to be similar in difficulty and content" (p. 2). Test form equating is performed in three steps (Kolen & Brennan, 2014).

- First, scores from one form are related to a common score scale, which is constructed based on the results (e.g., means) from a norm group (e.g., using linear or nonlinear transformation). Then, as part of this first step, a conversion table is created, delineating the relationship between each raw score of the form and its corresponding scale score.
- Second, raw scores on a new form (e.g., Form Y) are usually equated to those on the old form (Form X). This second step (in which new form scores are equated to the old form scores) involves multiple phases, such as selecting and implementing an appropriate equating design, choosing statistical techniques for equating estimation, and examining the equating quality. Interested readers can consult Kolen and Brennan's (2014) comprehensive guide on the statistical equating methods based on raw scores as well as IRT.
- Third and last, a revised conversion table is generated by adding the information derived from the second step. Table 43.1 illustrates the scale score derived from the raw scores pertaining to three test forms. In this case, Form X is one point easier than Form Y and is one point more difficult than Form Z, to which the scale scores are adjusted. Thus, by using the scale scores, the three test form scores can be represented on a common scale and used interchangeably.

When administering two test forms for equating, there are three options for participant group selection (Kolen & Brennan, 2014). In one approach, two whole test forms are administered to the same participants, with the order of test forms counterbalanced. In the second approach, only a representative sample of items from two forms (called anchor or common items) is administered to two different groups, and the remaining items of two test forms are presented to one of the two groups. In the third approach, participants are randomly assigned to one of the forms: This can be done by distributing test forms sequentially, e.g., in the order of seating. These groups of participants are considered equivalent, allowing test scores to be compared across the test forms.

While the first option requires a smaller number of participants, having to take two tests can be overwhelming. In contrast, the second approach requires only one testing event; nonetheless, this strategy requires advanced planning, including careful selection of anchor items that represent overall test content and its statistical characteristics (e.g., item difficulty, which is estimated

Table 43.1 Conversion table of three test forms in a hypothetical situation

Scale score	*Form X raw score*	*Form Y raw score*	*Form Z raw score*
⋮	⋮	⋮	⋮
25.0	20	19	21
25.5	21	20	22
26.0	22	21	23
26.5	23	22	24
27.0	24	23	25
⋮	⋮	⋮	⋮

before the test equating) and inserting common items in the same locations across forms. The third option can be applied to more than two forms without increasing the test-taking time; however, it necessitates a larger number of participants to obtain stable results. In all the three approaches, equating can be conducted not only in the pilot testing phase, but also after the main test administration and before the main analysis (Wendler & Walker, 2016). Although checking the equivalency of test forms may appear tedious, it is indispensable for ensuring test equivalency statistically.

Counterbalancing Test Forms

Counterbalancing (i.e., systematically allocating equivalent forms to different groups) is another key aspect of pretest-posttest research design, as it helps control for unknown confounding factors over multiple testing occasions (e.g., practice effects). It involves a systematic assignment of multiple test forms to different testing events (e.g., pretest and posttests). Suppose that L2 experimental research involves pretest, posttest I, and posttest II with two treatment conditions. Without counterbalancing, for instance, all participants are given Form A in the pretest, with Form B and Form C adopted in posttest I and posttest II, respectively. This fixed matching between forms and test occasions involves an inherent risk that a test form may be easier or more difficult than the others due to practice effects.

As shown in Table 43.2, when counterbalancing three test forms, researchers can randomly assign participants into six groups within each condition. A technique called a diagram-balanced Latin square design can reduce the required number of groups for counterbalancing (see Keppel & Wickens, 2004, for details). With this technique, when the number of test forms (k) is even, then only k groups are necessary. When the number of test forms is odd, then $2 \times k$ groups are necessary. For example, in using four test forms, researchers should use four groups (not 24), while 10 groups are sufficient for five test forms (not 120).

Assuming that multiple test forms are randomly distributed to groups, counterbalancing can help neutralize the practice effect, from administering multiple test forms. In other words, counterbalancing increases the confidence of interpreting the average score changes from pretest to posttests as an indicator of L2 development for different groups.

Use of Equivalent Test Forms in L2 Form-Focused Instruction Research

In this section, we report a small literature survey that examined how equivalent test forms have (not) been used in L2 research. Since a comprehensive review of pertinent literature was unfeasible, we focused on the subdomain of instructed L2 research. Thus, we selected the study conducted by Goo, Granena, Yilmaz, and Novella (2015) as it is the most recent comprehensive meta-analysis on L2 form-focused instruction. In this work, the authors reviewed 34 empirical studies published in 1980 through 2011 that met the following criteria: (1) research involved a (quasi-)experimental pretest-posttests research design; (2) the effects of different treatments

Table 43.2 An example of counterbalancing of three test forms for pretest, and posttest I and II

	Group 1	*Group 2*	*Group 3*	*Group 4*	*Group 5*	*Group 6*
Pretest	Form A	Form A	Form B	Form B	Form C	Form C
Posttest I	Form B	Form C	Form A	Form C	Form A	Form B
Posttest II	Form C	Form B	Form C	Form A	Form B	Form A

Note: Complete counterbalance requires 12 groups (two conditions × six groups).

(e.g., explicit and implicit grammar instruction) were compared; and (3) research targeted the development of specific L2 features (e.g., grammatical, pragmatic, lexical areas).

For this assessment, we selected 15 experiments (see the references indicated with asterisks; note that these 15 are specifically Andringa et al. 2011; Benati, 2004; Ellis, 2007; Ellis et al. 2006; Kang, 2010; Koike & Pearson, 2005; Kubota, 1994; Kubota, 1996; Leow, 1998; Loewen & Erlam, 2006; Muranoi, 2000; Rosa & Leow, 2004; Sauro, 2009; Sheen, 2007; Tode, 2007) from these 34 empirical studies, which involved the assessment tasks employed on at least three occasions (e.g., pretest, posttest I and posttest II). The authors coded all 15 experiments for (a) the existence of multiple test forms (no different test form vs. more than one test forms vs. all different test forms). If multiple test forms are used, we further coded for (b) content equivalence, (c) item difficulty equivalency, (d) pilot testing (e.g., whether equivalent-forms reliability was computed), and (e) counterbalancing (counterbalancing vs. no counterbalancing).

The analyses of these 15 studies revealed that (a) in more than half of these cases, the researchers employed identical forms for pretest and multiple posttests. Specifically, no use of different forms is identified in nine studies,[4] at least two different forms (e.g., pretest and immediate posttest were different, but the pretest and the delayed posttest were identical) in three studies, and all test forms were different in three studies. In terms of (b), among the six studies in which different forms were used, how different forms were controlled for content similarity was explicitly stated in only four cases.

However, it was more difficult to identify evidence of (c) difficulty equivalency.[5] In only two of the six studies, a clear description of the process employed was provided for controlling item difficulty. These studies coincided with the ones that reported conducting (d) pilot testing (Benati, 2004; Tode, 2007). In one study (Benati, 2004), "the three versions were balanced in terms of difficulty and vocabulary during a pilot experiment" (p. 216). In the other case (Tode, 2007), the author provided the explanation of a pilot study, stating that its aim was checking equivalent-forms reliability and indicating that the random parallel test method was employed. In the pilot phase, Tode (2007) created six equivalent test forms (which served as a pretest and five posttests) and administered six tests to a group of students in the same school (i.e., another sample from the target population). These six forms were created by selecting test items from a large pool of items with estimated difficulty. Tode (2007) reported that "all Pearson correlations among the six forms … [were] over .90" (p. 19). The creation of six forms in the pilot study is commendable, as it allowed the author to interpret the test score differences straightforwardly. Overall, however, none of the authors of the 15 studies included in the current methodological review examined means, *SD*s, and correlations or conducted test equating, which are two of the three available methods for ensuring test equivalency (see the Pilot Testing section).

In terms of (e), counterbalancing was not employed in any of the six studies in which researchers used different test forms. This is another unfortunate finding of this methodological review.

Overall, the current analysis clearly suggests that methodological and reporting practices in the L2 research domain are deficient (cf., Plonsky, Marsden, Crowther, Gass, & Spinner, 2020). Given the importance and impact of meta-analyses in form-focused L2 instruction research (e.g., Goo et al., 2015; Norris & Ortega, 2000), it is surprising to find that, in a significant number of empirical studies in this field, the authors failed to assure the assumption of test equivalence. As the current analysis is far from comprehensive, the practices in other domains are unknown. However, we emphasize that creating, using, and providing detailed descriptions of equivalent test forms is an important aspect of SLA pretest-posttest research design. Moreover, given that this approach is not consistently adopted, there is immediate need for establishing guidelines for constructing and using equivalent forms. To adhere to procedures to adequately use equivalent test forms, expertise in the LT field (test development, interpretation, and use, see Carr, 2011, for instance) benefits researchers when they critically analyze and interpret previous studies as well as their studies from methodological and measurement perspectives. Interdisciplinary collaboration across SLA and LT fields is thus an effective means to improve the quality of research.

Recommendations for Practice

Test Design

Researchers should first develop detailed test specifications for multiple test forms and should always report them in publications to demonstrate test equivalence. Asking for external content reviews in advance would help identify problems with test items and test forms, such as inadequate items and extreme content overlaps (AERA, APA, & NCME, 2014). It is also noteworthy that many linguistic journals allow the contributing authors to upload all test items used in their studies as a supplementary online material. Similarly, such materials can be uploaded to a digital depository, such as IRIS (Marsden, Mackey, & Plonsky, 2016). Such materials should also be shared with reviewers as an additional equivalence check.

Pilot Testing

Whenever using new test forms, researchers should conduct a pilot study, as this would allow them to examine the features of each form prior to the main test administration. For the pilot study, it is recommended to include 20–30% more items into the forms than would be employed in the main research, as some problematic items may have to be excluded for numerous reasons (e.g., low item discrimination, attractiveness of options in a multiple-choice format, items of free production test failing to elicit target structures). During this pilot testing, the order of the item presentation should be carefully determined and the order of form presentation should be counterbalanced when multiple forms are administered to the same group, to minimize ordering effects that may skew the analyses of test form equivalency. Note that as long as situations allow, counterbalancing should be conducted prior to the test administration for test form equivalency, because post-hoc counterbalancing may not completely eradicate test difficulty-level differences across test forms.

Test Administration

In the main study, counterbalancing of test forms is recommended. This can be easily achieved, especially when tests are administered by a computer. Although it is practically more difficult in conducting paper-and-pencil tests in classroom settings, different forms can still be given to different participants. In addition to random assignments of multiple test forms, when a covariate is available (e.g., proficiency test score), researchers are advised to assign participants into groups to ensure that the scores on the covariate will be equivalent. This is an additional measure that helps reduce unexpected sources of threat to internal validity. Furthermore, researchers may conduct more rigorous statistical analysis to take into account a factor of counterbalancing (see Keppel & Wickens, 2004). The main advantage of this strategy stems from stricter statistical control over unexpected confounding factors and greater statistical power; however, computation can be complex and a larger sample size is often required.

When multiple equivalent tests are not available (this is unfortunate but often the case in many SLA studies as shown above), counterbalancing of test forms is mandatory at minimum to compare the scores *at the group level*. It is important to note that interpreting *individuals' score changes* may not be meaningful without the tests that are equated properly prior to the main experiment. If test forms are equated, no counterbalancing may not be needed because practice effects can be measured by employing a control group. In any case, explicit reasonable justifications for counterbalancing and non-counterbalancing are necessary for supporting adequate score interpretations and uses of multiple test forms in pretest-posttest research design. In addition to counterbalancing, considering measurement errors and statistical artifacts (regression to the mean and standard error of difference) is also essential, but is often overlooked in interpreting results in pretest–posttest designs (see Koizumi, In'nami, Azuma, Asano, Agawa, & Eberl, 2015; McKay & Plonsky, Chapter 44, this volume).

Testing Tips

- Create and report test specifications for multiple test forms in publications to account for test equivalence.
- Conduct a pilot study to check the features of each test form prior to the main test administration.
- Report some indices (e.g., equivalent-forms reliability) of multiple test forms to support test equivalence.
- Counterbalancing of test forms is recommended.

Notes

1 Although these three form types may sometimes be distinguished by definitions (e.g., AERA, APA, & NCME, 2014), they are considered the same in this chapter.
2 Repeated testing can also lead to lower scores due to fatigue and decreased motivation.
3 Researchers sometimes use a smaller number of items for a pretest, e.g., when participants are likely to know little about target linguistic rules and a large number of items are likely to lead to undesirable outcomes, such as demotivation and fatigue. In this case, proportions of correct items are compared.
4 In three studies, researchers simply used the same items but changed the item order for different forms; we coded these studies as "no different test form."
5 For example, Muranoi (2000) stated that "Item sequences were shuffled and several content words were replaced with others equally familiar to the students" (p. 642). We found it difficult to conclude that this author controlled "difficulty" (slightly different from familiarity) of items in the study, and thus coded it as "no explanation of difficulty equivalence."

Recommended Readings

Dorans, N. J., Moses, T. P., & Eignor, D. R. (2010). Principles and practices of test score equating. *ETS Research Report Series*, *RR-10-29*. Educational Testing Service. https://doi.org/10.1002/j.2333-8504.2010.tb02236.x

This resource gives a concise overview of best practices and potential pitfalls in the equating process.

Kolen, M. J., & Brennan, R. L. (2014). *Test equating, scaling, and linking: Methods and practices* (3rd ed.). Springer.

This book is a complete summary of what researchers should know to apply theory of test equating into practice.

LaFlair, G. T., Isbell, D., Gutierrez-Arvizu, M. N., May, L. D. N., & Jamieson, J. (2017). Test equating in small language programs. *Language Testing*, *34*(1), 127-144. https://doi.org/10.1177/0265532215620825

This study compares different equating methods, considering their accuracy and usability in small-scale settings where multiple test forms are needed.

References

(Asterisks indicate 15 studies included in the methodological synthesis.)

American Educational Research Association (AERA), American Psychological Association (APA), & National Council on Measurement in Education (NCME). (2014). *Standards for educational and psychological testing*. AERA.

*Andringa, S., de Glopper, K., & Hacquebord, H. (2011). Effect of explicit and implicit instruction on free written response task performance. *Language Learning*, *61*(3), 868–903. https://doi.org/10.1111/j.1467-9922.2010.00623.x

Bae, J., & Lee, Y.-S. (2011). The validation of parallel test forms: 'Mountain' and 'beach' picture series for assessment of language skills. *Language Testing*, *28*(2), 155–177. https://doi.org/10.1177/0265532210382446

*Benati, A. (2004). The effects of structured input activities and explicit information on the acquisition of the Italian future tense. In B. VanPatten (Ed.), *Processing instruction: Theory, research and commentary* (pp. 187–206). Lawrence Erlbaum.

Brown, J. D. (1988). *Understanding research in second language learning: A teacher's guide to statistics and research design*. Cambridge University Press.

Carr, N. T. (2011). *Designing and analyzing language tests*. Oxford University Press.

Davies, A., Brown, A., Elder, C., Hill, K., Lumley, T., & McNamara, T. (1999). *Dictionary of language testing*. Cambridge University Press.

*Ellis, R. (2007). The differential effects of corrective feedback on two grammatical structures. In A. Mackey (Ed.), *Conversational interaction in second language acquisition: A collection of empirical studies* (pp. 339–360). Oxford University Press.

*Ellis, R., Loewen, S., & Erlam, R. (2006). Implicit and explicit corrective feedback and the acquisition of L2 grammar. *Studies in Second Language Acquisition*, *28*(2), 339–368. https://doi.org/10.1017/S0272263106060141

Godfroid, A. (2016). The effects of implicit instruction on implicit and explicit knowledge development. *Studies in Second Language Acquisition*, *38*(2) 177–215. https://doi.org/10.1017/S0272263115000388

Goo, J., Granena, G., Yilmaz, Y., & Novella, M. (2015). Implicit and explicit instruction in L2 learning. In P. Rebuschat (Ed.), *Implicit and explicit learning of languages* (pp. 443–482). John Benjamins.

Henning, G. (1987). *A guide to language testing: Development, evaluation, research*. Heinle & Heinle.

*Kang, H. S. (2010). Negative evidence and its explicitness and positioning in the learning of Korean as a heritage language. *The Modern Language Journal*, *94*(4), 582–599. https://doi.org/10.1111/j.1540-4781.2010.01093.x

Keppel, G., & Wickens, T. D. (2004). The single-factor within-subject design: Further topics. In G. Keppel (Ed.), *Design and Analysis: A Researcher's Handbook* (4th Ed.) (pp. 369–400). Prentice Hall.

*Koike, D. A., & Pearson, L. (2005). The effect of instruction and feedback in the development of pragmatic competence. *System*, *33*, 481–501. https://doi.org/10.1016/j.system.2005.06.008

Koizumi, R., In'nami, Y., Azuma, J., Asano, K., Agawa, T., & Eberl, D. (2015). Assessing L2 proficiency growth: Considering regression to the mean and the standard error of difference. *Shiken*, *19*(1), 3–15. http://teval.jalt.org/node/16

Kolen, M. J., & Brennan, R. L. (2014). *Test equating, scaling, and linking: Methods and practices*. Springer Science & Business Media.

*Kubota, M. (1994). The role of negative feedback on the acquisition of the English dative alternation by Japanese college students of EFL. *Institute for Research in Language Teaching Bulletin*, *8*, 1–36. https://files.eric.ed.gov/fulltext/ED386023.pdf

*Kubota, M. (1996). The effects of instruction plus feedback on Japanese university students of EFL: A pilot study. *Bulletin of Chofu Gakuen Women's Junior College*, *18*, 59–95. https://files.eric.ed.gov/fulltext/ED397641.pdf

*Leow, R. P. (1998). The effects of amount and type of exposure on adult learners' L2 development in SLA. *The Modern Language Journal*, *82*(1), 49–68. https://doi.org/10.1111/j.1540-4781.1998.tb02593.x

*Loewen, S., & Erlam, R. (2006). Corrective feedback in the chatroom: An experimental study. *Computer Assisted Language Learning*, *19*(1), 1–14. https://doi.org/10.1080/09588220600803311

Marsden, E., Mackey, A., & Plonsky, L. (2016). The IRIS repository: Advancing research practice and methodology. In A. Mackey & E. Marsden (Eds.), *Advancing methodology and practice: The IRIS repository of instruments for research into second languages* (pp. 1–21). Routledge.

*Muranoi, H. (2000). Focus on form through Interaction enhancement: Integrating formal instruction into a communicative task in EFL classrooms. *Language Learning*, *50*, 617–673. https://doi.org/10.1111/0023-8333.00142

Norris, J. M., & Ortega, L. (2000). Effectiveness of L2 instruction: A research synthesis and quantitative meta-analysis. *Language Learning*, *50*(4), 417–528. https://doi.org/10.1111/0023-8333.00136

Oswald, F. L., Friede, A. J., Schmitt, N., Kim, B. H., & Ramsay, L. J. (2005). Extending a practical method for developing alternate test forms using independent sets of items. *Organizational Research Methods*, *8*(2), 149–164. https://doi.org/10.1177/1094428105275365

Plonsky, L., Marsden, E., Crowther, D., Gass, S., & Spinner, P. (2020). A methodological synthesis and meta-analysis of judgment tasks in second language research. *Second Language Research*, 36(4), 583–621. https://doi.org/10.1177/0267658319828413
*Rosa, E. M., & Leow, R. P. (2004). Awareness, different learning conditions, and second language development. *Applied Psycholinguistics*, *25*(2), 269–292. https://doi.org/10.1017/S0142716404001134
*Sauro, S. (2009). Computer-mediated corrective feedback and the development of L2 grammar. *Language Learning & Technology*, *13*(1), 96–120. https://www.lltjournal.org/item/2656
*Sheen, Y. (2007). The effect of focused written corrective feedback and language aptitude on ESL learners' acquisition of articles. *TESOL Quarterly*, *41*(2), 255–283. https://doi.org/10.1002/j.1545-7249.2007.tb00059.x
Spinner, P., & Gass, S. (2019). *Using judgments in second language acquisition research*. Routledge.
Stewart, J., & Gibson, A. (2010). Equating classroom pre and post tests under item response theory. *SHIKEN: JALT Testing & Evaluation SIG Newsletter*, *14*(2), 11–18. http://hosted.jalt.org/test/ste_gib1.htm
Suzuki, Y. (2017). Validity of new measures of implicit knowledge: Distinguishing implicit knowledge from automatized explicit knowledge. *Applied Psycholinguistics*, *38*(5), 1229–1261. https://doi.org/10.1017/S014271641700011X
*Tode, T. (2007). Durability problems with explicit instruction in an EFL context: The learning of the English copula be before and after the introduction of the auxiliary be. *Language Teaching Research*, *11*(1), 11–30. https://doi.org/10.1177/1362168806072398
Weir, C. J., & Wu, J. R. W. (2006). Establishing test form and individual task comparability: A case study of a semi-direct speaking test. *Language Testing*, *23*(2), 167–197. https://doi.org/10.1191/0265532206lt326oa
Wendler, C. L. W., & Walker, M. E. (2016). Practical issues in designing and maintaining multiple test forms. In S. Lane, M. R. Raymond, & T. M. Haladyna (Eds.), *Handbook of test development* (2nd ed., pp. 433–449). Routledge.

44

Reliability Analyses

Estimating Error

Todd H. McKay & Luke Plonsky

Background

Constructs of interest in second-language (L2) research are almost never directly measurable. Applied linguists create tools, therefore, that allow them to estimate and quantify the constructs' presence. However, there is error in all measurements, and certain types (and amounts) of error are expected. Score reliability, the focus of this chapter, allows one to understand the extent of error in applied linguists' measures. Without evidence that scores are consistent at the level expected, researchers cannot begin to make claims about the object of their measurement, much less its relationship with another variable.

Let's say that one wants to measure the weight of a bag of dates at the supermarket. If the person obtains the same weight for the bag when they measure it three times, then they can claim that the weight of the bag is *consistent across measurements*; they can claim that the measurements are *reliable*. However, if the person obtains different weights for the bag each time they measure it, then the weight of the bag is *inconsistent* across measurements; they can claim that the measurements are *unreliable*, with the extent of the unreliability being dependent on how different the weights from the measurement tool (in this case, the fruit and vegetable scale at the supermarket) actually were. Some slight measurement variation (inconsistency) may be expected or deemed acceptable. For example, if three different spring-loaded supermarket scales measured the dates as .501, .498, and .511 pounds respectively, a person may tolerate that measurement variation: The person could be fairly confident, for the purposes of using a half-pound of dates in a recipe, that the measurement is accurate enough.

Much like the weight measurements for the bag of dates, the scores applied linguists use in L2 research are reliable only to the extent that they are consistent enough for the purposes for which they are used. And if scores are not consistent enough, applied linguists should be wary about making interpretations on the basis of those scores. In other words, as it is often said in the measurement literature as well as in applied linguistics (e.g., Brown, 2014), reliability is a necessary but insufficient condition for validity.

One can see the relationship between score reliability and validity claims by revisiting the example with the bag of dates. Let's say that our shopper now has two bags of dates; one bag has ten dates, and the other has twenty dates. After measuring each bag of dates a hundred times using various scales, the person estimates that the weight of the ten-date bag is half a pound, and the weight of the twenty-date bag is one pound. The sets of measurements for each bag of dates were consistently within .02 pounds. Because the sets of measurements were reliable for each bag of dates, the person can use this evidence to support the claim that the twenty-date bag weighs twice as much as the ten-date bag (the shopper's validity claim). If the scales had indicated substantial variability in weight measurements, however, such a claim would be in question. It is much the same with measuring L2 learner knowledge. A lack of consistency in applied linguists' measures—of grammatical knowledge, motivation, or target-language contact, for example—necessarily poses a threat to the claims applied linguists want to make about the constructs of interest in their research.

Unacceptable inconsistency in measurement not only poses an abstract threat to the validity of one's observations; unreliability is also of major concern because it lowers or *attenuates* the effect sizes applied linguists often seek as the primary object of their research. The reason for this is quite simple: unreliability (or measurement error) necessarily contributes non-construct-relevant variance (i.e., noise) into scores. Such noise then obscures one's ability to observe information (i.e., the signal) in the data.

Certain amounts of measurement error are unavoidable or natural, however. When the error or unreliability in set of scores is (a) minimal and (b) unexplainable or seemingly random in nature, researchers can imagine it not being there. For example, suppose that a group of researchers at an international English-medium university (i.e., they teach their courses in English) wants to examine the correlation between their prospective students' IELTS and TOEFL writing proficiency test scores. The researchers have on hand both sets of test scores from 200 prospective undergraduate students who were native speakers of Bangla. The correlation that the researchers observed was moderate: $r = .70$. However, when researching the internal reliabilities test scores, they found that IELTS writing-test scores have, on average, a reliability estimate of .85 (www.ielts.org/en-us/teaching-and-research/test-performance), and the TOEFL writing-test scores have, on average, a reliability estimate of .80 (www.ets.org/s/toefl/pdf/toefl_ibt_research_s1v3.pdf). Considering the exams, the researchers assume that the unreliability (or measurement error) within each set of scores is minimal and perhaps natural. This is because humans score the tests, and getting reliabilities above .80 or .85 would be difficult indeed. Thus, the researchers took the score reliabilities into account and applied a correction for attenuation (see Osborne, 2003). By doing so, they estimated that the relationship between the 200 students' sets of scores may be closer to $r = .85$. They are able to consider the attenuated correlation because the two tests' score-reliability estimates are rather high; they could view measurement error as stemming from non-controllable (random) human factors that are probably natural to human-rated testing. Reliability coefficients in L2 research are more often in the .70–.90 range (Plonsky & Derrick, 2016), and, when they are, this type of correction may be generally recommended as an additional reliability estimation technique (see Frey, Pedroni, Mata, Rieskamp, & Hertwig, 2017). In other words, the researchers, in a paper based on their findings, could report both correlation coefficients—.70 unattenuated and .85 attenuated—and write that they assume the true association between the two sets of scores is within that range. Thus, understanding score reliability and its relationship to observed effects is important because it can impact claims researchers make on the basis of those effects.

Before going any further, we must note that reliability is an estimate derived from the scores, which are in turn derived from the test (and its context of administration) by the sample; it is not an absolute value of the test. Wording such as "the test is reliable" and "the reliability of the test" is commonly used by applied linguists, but this language is misleading and causes problems in research practice. Better language may be something like, "the reading tests scores' reliability estimate was .58 (coefficient α) in X and Y's research" (see comments on assessment-related claims and warrants in Chapelle, Chapter 2, this volume). Language about test reliability can lead people to use test scores without considering the unique test administration context and the sample's characteristics. Researchers should always report the reliabilities for the scores they obtain regardless of the number of test takers in their sample. However, researchers should also keep in mind that, with few test takers, a reliability estimate may be more inaccurate than if the estimate had been obtained from a larger group of test takers; one thing researchers with small test-taker samples can do is to obtain bootstrapped reliability estimates or collect estimates from similar groups of test takers over time and compare them (provided test items and other aspects of the test administration are similar).

Approaches to Reliability and Error

Thus far we have been discussing reliability without making reference to the various theories in which it is grounded. The dominant theory in SLA by far is classical test theory (CTT), in which reliability is based on properties of random variables and assumptions regarding the nature of error in scores (see Traub, 1994). If researchers administer a willingness-to-communicate (WTC) questionnaire to a group of students, according to CTT, the researchers can never know the students' actual WTC score (their *true* score). However, all other things constant, if the researchers take enough measurements of students' WTC, students' WTC scores (and their error scores) will have certain properties; the scores obtained on the WTC (the *observed* scores) will cluster around the true score, and error introduced into scores due to aspects of the test administration, the students, and the test itself will wash out (sum to zero). Therefore, in CTT, the observed reliability estimate for a set of scores is the best approximation of the true score after accounting for error.

The basic formula for CTT score reliability is $O = T + E$ wherein an observed (O) score is equal to the true score (T) plus error (E). Put simply, this formula states that students have a real WTC, and researchers try to measure that value by gathering responses to questionnaire items; students' WTC manifests in their responses. However, the measurement of students' WTC is not perfect, and aspects of the test administration, students, and the instrument (among other factors) affect how closely the observed score approximates a student's true score; these aspects introduce error into the measurement, which is reflected in the error term and, consequently, the observed score.

CTT also makes assumptions about the nature of error in scores. Error introduced into measurements can be systematic or unsystematic. Systematic error refers to error that systematically affects the measurement of scores. For example, if someone weighs herself multiple times, and she wears a 50 pound (23 kilogram) backpack each time, then the backpack systematically affects the observed weight measurements. Similarly, if researchers administer a vocabulary test to students multiple times, and they sometimes administer the test at 4:00 AM and sometimes at 4:00 PM, most students will be extra tired when taking the test at 4:00 AM, which will affect their observed vocabulary scores; therefore, *time of day* introduces systematic error into observed scores because it introduces error (variance) each time we seek to measure students' vocabulary knowledge. Unsystematic error refers to random error that affects the measurement of scores. In applied linguistics, researchers and teachers all know that, at any given test administration, students will be more or less awake, or more or less hungry, or in a better or worse mood. The test designers might be concerned with wording in one or two test items and may wonder if all students will interpret the directions in the same way. Teachers may be wary of construction noise from outside the classroom that could be heard during the test administration and so on. These aspects of test administration that are present in applied linguistics research and pedagogical practice due to the realities of everyday life are sources of unsystematic or random error.

Key Concepts

Artifact: Error that is person-made or arti-factually introduced into sets of scores.

Attenuation: A reduction in an observed relationship due to measurement error or other statistical artifacts (e.g., range restriction).

Classical test theory: An approach to estimating score reliability based on the properties of random variables and assumptions regarding the nature of error in scores.
Reliability estimation method: The specific formula used to compute a reliability coefficient.
Reliability type: The family of estimation methods used to determine score consistency and score *un*reliability due to different sources of error.

Applied linguists must also make a distinction between different types of reliability, each of which seeks to identify and quantify different sources of error (Schmidt & Hunter, 2015). The most common type of reliability found in SLA is referred to as internal-consistency, which helps a researcher estimate how interrelated item scores are on a test. Two other commonly used methods, inter-rater and inter-coder estimation methods, are concerned with ratings and coded data; these forms can be used when researchers want to examine the consistency of rating or coding responses due to factors associated with the raters or the coders (e.g., biases, severity). Other methods include stability (e.g., test-retest; see Cronbach, 1947) and equivalent forms. When estimating score reliability, it is imperative that researchers use the type that is most suitable for their study's design and that will provide the most trustworthy indication of the impact of relevant sources of error.

Key Issues

Reporting of Reliability Coefficients

One of the most common issues related to reliability in L2 research is, simply, that it often goes unreported. When researchers fail to report score reliability in applied linguistics, "it is unclear whether researchers have improperly conducted their studies or conducted their research properly and simply failed to report what they did" (Whittington, 1998, p. 187). Reliability estimates were observed, for example, in only 16%, 28%, and 40% of the primary studies synthesized by Plonsky, Marsden, Crowther, Gass, and Spinner (2020), Derrick (2016), and Plonsky and Ghanbar (2018), respectively. Failing to report reliability coefficients and their corresponding confidence intervals compromises progress in L2 research in at least two ways (see Fan & Thompson, 2001; Thompson, 2003). First, a reliability coefficient is an indication of not only the consistency of scores, but the degree to which measurements are unreliable due to different sources of error. For example, if scores on a cloze test are wildly different across repeat administrations to similar groups of test-takers, then the test designers have little evidence to support the claim that cloze-test items elicit scores that people can use to measure a specified construct. A reliability coefficient provides an indication to readers of the extent to which scores are consistent and likely unaffected by sources of error introduced by poor instrumentation, problems in the study's design, idiosyncrasies in the group of test-takers, and so on. Second, as we noted in this chapter's introduction, score reliability directly influences a study's effects. For example, if a researcher reports a small effect size and no reliability coefficient for test scores on the measured variables, then it is difficult to know if the effect is actually small or if it has simply been attenuated by score unreliability. A third motivation for reporting reliability estimates concerns meta-analyses (statistical techniques for aggregating the quantitative data from multiple studies), which often use reliability estimates to apply psychometric corrections to the effect sizes being aggregated (see Schmidt & Hunter, 2015). In the absence of information about reliability, it is obviously not possible to do so.

The second major score-reliability issue is the failure to report the reliability type and estimation method used to compute the reliability coefficient. That is, it is not sufficient to simply report a reliability estimate. It is also necessary to indicate which type of reliability is being provided (i.e., internal consistency, inter-rater, intra-rater, or stability reliability [i.e., test-retest]) and which method is being used (e.g., coefficient α, omega, KR-20, Pearson correlation). Failure to do so greatly limits researchers' ability to interpret findings in light of the error that is present because different indices carry different assumptions and interpretations. For example, although omega and coefficient α both estimate internal consistency, only the latter assumes that scores measure the same thing and that errors are uncorrelated (McNeish, 2018). Errors correlate when something other than the construct researchers intend to measure results in scores being related (for example, when test items are worded similarly). When these assumptions are not met, α is attenuated. Similarly, some coefficients are more conservative than others. Built into the formula for Cohen's κ, for instance, is a correction for chance agreement often found when working with nominal variables.

It is not sufficient to simply report reliability estimates and their corresponding type and index. Like any other statistic, it is also necessary to interpret reliability coefficients and the scores they affect. In order to assist researchers in doing so, Plonsky and Derrick (2016) meta-analyzed reliability coefficients across 537 primary studies in 16 applied linguistics journals over a five-year period. The final sample consisted of 2,244 reliability estimates, each of which was also coded for features related to sample demographics, research contexts, instrument design (e.g., number of items, response type), and reliability type. Among other results, the median estimates for instrument, inter-rater, and intra-rater reliability were found to be .82, .92, and .95, respectively. Researchers can use these benchmark reliability estimates as a starting point to guide their interpretations as to the reliability of the scores they elicit in their studies and the extent to which error was introduced into scores; for example, if a research team obtains an intra-rater reliability estimate of .93, they might interpret this estimate to mean that some error in the scores they obtained was due to raters in their study, and the degree of score (un)reliability was similar to that obtained from samples in other applied linguistics studies. Several other reliability generalization meta-analyses have been conducted since then as a means to inform individual domains of L2 research.

The fourth and final major reporting-related reliability issue is the failure to make tests and other instruments available. Aside from the importance of adhering to principles of open science (e.g., Marsden & Plonsky, 2018; McKay, 2016) and supporting potential replications (Marsden, Mackey, & Plonsky, 2016), making instruments available allows readers to make more informed interpretations about researchers' claims. For example, a researcher may administer a C-test to a group of students in order to create different proficiency groups on the basis of C-test scores. In the study, the researcher reports that KR-20 internal consistency reliability was .84 and interprets the estimate as being acceptable for the study's purposes. If the researcher makes their C-test available, readers can learn that the estimate was high because the C-test consisted of 150 items or blanks. (All other things being equal, scales with a greater number of items have higher reliability than those with fewer.) Just as importantly, making the instrument available allows research consumers to judge the validity of the test score use. They can look at the reading passage in the C-test and ponder whether the test directions were clear, whether the reading passage was at the right level of difficulty for the test takers, whether the test was fair, and whether researchers were ethical in their research.

Modern Approaches to Measurement

Our discussion thus far has centered on CTT, which is in many ways the default approach to assessing reliability in L2 research. There are other measurement approaches aside from CTT, however. And although these approaches are used less commonly outside of language-testing circles in applied linguistics, they have advantages over CTT that make learning to use them worthwhile.

One modern approach to measurement is generalizability theory, or "G" theory (Cronbach, Rajaratnam, & Gleser, 1963; Cronbach et al., 1972; Schoonen, Chapter 45, this volume.) G-theory provides several improvements over CTT. For example, whereas CTT can only account for a single source of error, G theory allows the researcher to take multiple sources into account simultaneously and to consider any possible interactions between different sources of error (Thompson, 2003).

A second modern measurement approach is item response theory, or IRT (Lord & Novick, 1968). IRT is a set of statistical models that are used to analyze response patterns to test items in order to scale both test-takers and test items. There are a number of advantages to using IRT as a measurement approach in L2 research. First, IRT models place both test-takers and items on the same scale, allowing researchers to determine not only how much of a construct of interest is exhibited by individual test-takers, but also the extent to which individual test items elicit the construct of interest. In Figure 44.1 below, created with Wright Map (Torres Irribarra & Freund, 2014), a histogram of test-takers' scores is shown on the left, and item scores are shown on the right. Figure 44.1 shows that, the higher up a test-taker is on the scale (moving upwards in the histogram), the more likely that person is to respond correctly to test items at and below their level (more on this in a moment). Similarly, items 1–10 move up the scale as we move from left to right, indicating that more of a construct of interest (or ability) is needed to respond correctly to items 6–10 (most test-takers in this example are likely to correctly respond to items 1–5). Second, although CTT reliability estimates can be computed from IRT model results, a useful counterpart to score reliability in IRT is test or item information. The test information function is a measure of how much information researchers obtain from scores on individual test items (Frey, 2018). When test items are "lined up" with test-takers' ability levels, the researchers have more information with which to estimate test-takers' ability levels, and the re is a higher likelihood that the test takers will respond correctly or incorrectly to test items; in short, estimates of test-taker level

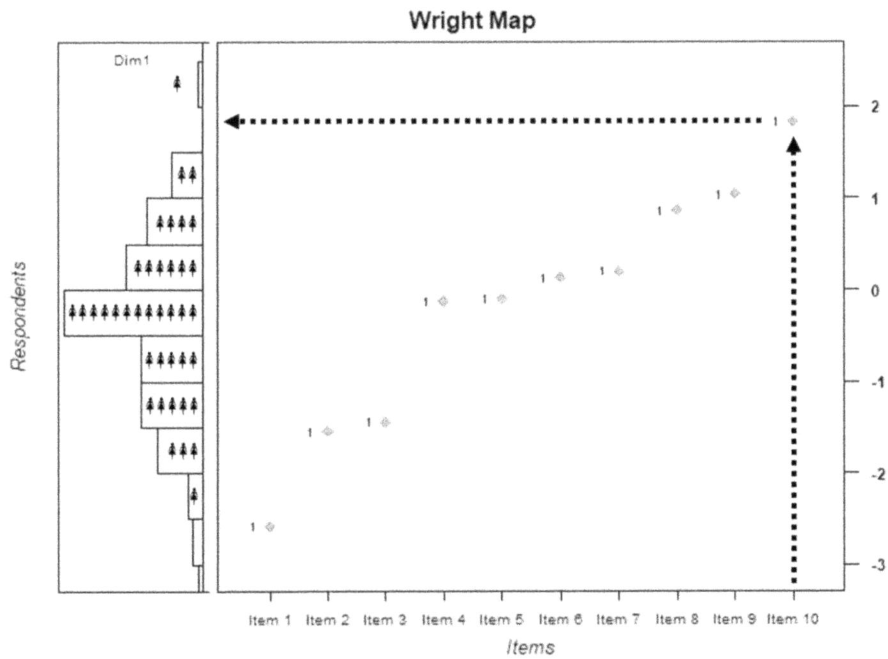

Figure 44.1 Wright map of a ten-item test with 100 test-takers

and item scores at that level are more precise. Thus, for the person at the top of the Wright map in Figure 44.1, estimates of their scores are less precise (have more error) because item 10 is about the only item at their level. However, there is greater test information for estimating scores around 0 because there are more test-takers and items at that level.

Other Methods Within CTT

Another key issue worth noting here is the widespread use of only a select few CTT estimation methods. As noted by Derrick (2016) and Plonsky and Derrick (2016), L2 researchers rely quite heavily on coefficient α for internal consistency and on percent agreement, and Cohen's κ for estimating the reliability of ratings. Are these statistics the most appropriate ones for L2 research? If scores vary in the extent to which they measure a construct, then researchers should consider using omega (ω) (McDonald, 1999). If items on a test are grouped according to content or difficulty, they should consider using stratified α. If scores are not continuous data, then researchers should consider using ordinal α. If scores are obtained from items of different formats, researchers should consider using standardized α. After factor analyzing scores, researchers can use maximal reliability (Hancock & Mueller, 2001) in which items are weighted by their loading or *contribution* to the overall scale score. Score reliability estimates using these methods can be computed with packages in R, such as with User Friendly Science (Peters, 2018). For an overview of a few alternative estimation methods, see Hattie (1985), McNeish (2018), and Osburn (2000).

Reliability Methods and Study Artifacts

As we have been discussing throughout this chapter, measurement artifacts, such as measurement error, obscure applied linguists' understanding of the constructs they study. There are formulas that, when applied conscientiously, allow researchers to estimate true scores (and other statistics) in the absence of error and other artifacts (i.e., an idealized scenario), such as range restriction. Recalling the CTT formula for observed scores (O) as $O = T + E$, this procedure attempts to cancel out the error term (E) such that the observed score is equal (or very close to equal) to the true score (T).

Imagine, for example, that a study of the relationship between L2 anxiety (variable x) and proficiency (variable y) found an (uncorrected) correlation between these two variables of $r = .4$. If researchers know that the reliability of x and y are .80 and .90, respectively, and if the researchers are confident that those reliabilities are good given the constructs and measurements (meaning that the unexplained error is theoretically acceptable, is random, and not attributable to construct irrelevant variables), then the researchers can then apply the following formula: $rxy_{\text{corrected}} = rxy_{\text{observed}}$ / square root of the reliability of x * reliability of y. The corrected (unattenuated) correlation is then estimated to be $r = .53$ instead of $r = .4$. (For a recent example of this correction being applied in SLA research, see Teimouri, 2017).

Recommendations for Practice

A first recommendation for SLA and language testing researchers, as well as practitioners, is to carefully consider the nature of your data and research questions in order to select an appropriate reliability statistic. Table 44.1 provides an overview of reliability measures, explains when (not) to use them, and directs to further readings.

Secondly, a particularly fruitful direction for the field involves a greater role for meta-analysts who are in a unique position with respect to reliability. We would thereby recommend that meta-analysts and methodological synthesists continue to examine reliability estimates in the domains they investigate by coding for the presence of such data and any interpretations thereof. We also

Table 44.1 Types of reliability statistics

Statistic	*When to use?*	*References (R package)*
Internal consistency: Error due to test items		
Coefficient (Cronbach's) alpha (α)	When all item scores measure a single construct. *Note*: • When computed on binary data, will equal the KR-20 coefficient. • Influenced by the number of items on the test. • Not good on scores from speeded tests or test with items ordered in terms of difficulty.	• Thompson (2003) for an accessible introduction. • Cronbach (1951) for detailed description. • **`psych`** • **`userfriendlyscience`**
Stratified alpha (α)	When items on a test are grouped such that their scores measure different facets of a same construct (e.g., subgroups of items or testlets to measure knowledge of reading).	• Cronbach, Schoenemann, & McKie (1965) for detailed description. • **`Sirt`**
Standardized alpha (α)	When items on a test consist of different formats.	• Falk & Savalei (2011) for detailed description. • **`psych`**
Kuder Richardson 20 (KR-20)	When item scores are binary (0 or 1). *Note*: • KR-20 and Cronbach's α coefficients will be the same when computed on binary data. Researchers can use Cronbach's α instead of KR-20 on binary data. • Influenced by the number of items on the test. • Not good on scores from speeded tests or test with items ordered in terms of difficulty.	• Kuder & Richardson (1937) for detailed description. • **`psych`**
Kuder Richardson 21 (KR-21)	When researchers want to know score unreliability due to test items. *Note*: • KR-21 assumes that all test items are of about the same difficulty (i.e., item facility or proportion correct), which is difficult to meet in practice. • Influenced by the number of items on the test. • Not good on scores from speeded tests or test with items ordered in terms of difficulty	• Kuder & Richardson (1937) for detailed description.
Omega hierarchical (ω_h)	When all item scores measure a single construct. *Note*: • May be more accurate when some item scores measure a construct "less than" others.	• McDonald (1999) for detailed description. • **`psych`**

(*Continued*)

Table 44.1 (*Continued*)

Statistic	*When to use?*	*References* (R `package`)
Split–half reliability	When item scores measure a single construct. *Note*: • Split–half reliability involves splitting test items into two halves, usually by odd vs. even or first vs. second halves, and then correlating the two sets of scores. • Because test items are halved, the test length is adjusted (back to its original length) with the Spearman–Brown formula. • Not good on scores from speeded tests or tests in which items have been ordered by difficulty.	• Frey (2018) for a short description. • **psych**
Parallel forms reliability: Error due to test forms		
Pearson's product–moment correlation coefficient (*r*)	When researchers want to determine the relationship between two sets of continuous scores. *Note*: • Scores should be linear, normally distributed, and contain no extreme outliers.	• Laerd Statistics (2019c) for a good SPSS overview. • **psych** • **userfriendlyscience** • (and *many* other packages)
Polychoric correlation (PCC)	In situations similar to Pearson correlation, but with discretized scales. *Note*: • PCC may be more accurate than other methods when there are fewer rating categories (e.g., 4-point scale) and performances (Morgan et al., 2014).	• Salkind (2010) for a general overview. • **polycor**
Polyserial correlation (PSC)	When researchers are interested in the relationship between two sets of scores when one set is continuous and the other is discretized. *Note*: • Scores should be normally distributed.	• Olsson, Drasgow, & Dorans (1982) for a detailed description. • **CTT** • **psych**
Spearman's rho (ρ)	When researchers want to determine the relationship between two sets of ordinal ratings. Or, when the assumptions for the Pearson's *r* are not met.	• Spearman (1904) for a detailed description. • Laerd Statistics (2019b) for a good SPSS overview. • **irr**
Kendall's tau (τ)	When researchers want to determine the relationship between two sets of ordinal ratings, like Spearman's ρ; however, Kendall's τ is useful when assumptions for Spearman's ρ are not met, scores come from a small sample of test-takers, or there are too many same ratings for pairs to run Spearman's ρ.	• Laerd Statistics (2019d) for a good SPSS overview. • **irr** • **psych**

(*Continued*)

Table 44.1 (Continued)

Statistic	*When to use?*	*References (R package)*
Test–retest reliability: Many of the correlation coefficients described in this table can be used to compute test–retest reliability.		
Inter-rater reliability		
Intraclass correlation coefficient (ICC)	When researchers are interested in the relationship between ratings of multiple (three or more) raters. There are multiple ICCs, and which to use depends on the research design.	• Shrout & Fleiss (1979) for detailed description. • **psych**
Maxwell's RE coefficient	When researchers are interested in the relationship between the binary ratings (0, 1) of two raters.	• Maxwell (1977) for detailed description. • **irr**
Percent agreement	When researchers want to determine what proportion of ratings are the same across raters. *Note*: • More clunky to compute the more raters are included in calculations. • Does not account for the fact that raters might assign the same rating by chance.	• Numerous examples that show how to compute percent agreement can be found online. • **irr**
Extended or adjacent agreement	When researchers want to determine what proportion of ratings fall within 1+ rating category across raters. Researchers might be less interested in exact ratings and instead want to understand what proportion of ratings cluster about a point on a scale; this information might be useful when a scale has many categories.	• See Powers (2000) for a comparison of agreement methods, including adjacent agreement. • **irr**
Polychoric correlation (PCC)	In situations similar to Pearson correlation. *Note*: PCC may be more accurate than other methods when there are fewer rating categories (e.g., 4-point scale) and performances (Morgan et al., 2014).	• Salkind (2010) for a general overview. • **polycor**
Cohen's kappa (κ)	When researchers want to determine the relationship between categorical ratings of two raters. *Note*: • Sometimes, two raters might give a performance the same rating by chance; Cohen's κ takes chance ratings into account. • High agreement between ratings can lead to a lower Cohen's κ.	• Cohen (1960) for detailed description. • **irr** • **psy** • **psych**

(*Continued*)

Table 44.1 (*Continued*)

Statistic	*When to use?*	*References (R* `package`*)*
Brennan-Prediger's G-Index (GI)	When researchers want to determine the relationship between categorical ratings of two or more raters. *Note*: • GI is more accurate than Cohen's κ when there is a high rate of agreement between ratings.	• Brennan & Prediger (1981) for a detailed description. • `irrCAC`
Gwet's first-order agreement coefficient (AC_1)	When researchers want to determine the relationship between categorical ratings of two raters. *Note*: • Gwet's AC_1 is more accurate than Cohen's κ when there is a high rate of agreement between ratings.	• Gwet (2008a) for a detailed description. • `irrCAC`
Fleiss' kappa (κ)	When researchers want to determine the relationship between ratings of two or more raters. Ratings should be categorical and independent. Additionally, rated items (e.g., a random selection of essays) and raters (e.g., panel judges) should be randomly selected.	• Fleiss (1971) for detailed description. • Laerd Statistics (2019a) for a good SPSS overview. • `irr`
Krippendorff's alpha (α)	When researchers want to determine the relationship between ratings of two or more raters. This statistic is particularly useful when ratings consist of continuous data.	• Krippendorff (1980) for detailed description. • `irr`
Spearman's rho (ρ)	When researchers want to determine the relationship between two sets of ordinal ratings. Or, when the assumptions for the Pearson's *r* are not met.	• Spearman (1904) for a detailed description. • Laerd Statistics (2019b) for a good SPSS overview. • `irr`
Intra-rater reliability: Researchers should choose the relevant inter-rater reliability method to compute *intra*-rater reliability coefficients (see Gwet, 2008b). Error due to intrapersonal factors.		

Note: This list is not exhaustive; additional methods can be found in the *R* packages' documentation. Methods and references in this table were synthesized from the references, including those in the *R* packages' documentation. Researchers should check score assumptions for each method. Readers should refer to Chalmers (2018) for information on ordinal alpha, described in the chapter.

see value in maintaining efforts to synthesize reliability coefficients via *reliability generalization meta-analysis* as a means to estimate measurement error at the domain level. Such evidence (e.g., Marsden et al., 2018; Plonsky & Kim, 2016; Plonsky & Derrick, 2016; Saito & Plonsky, 2019) can be used to aid interpretation of meta-analytic effects, push for greater transparency, make recommendations for improvements to instrumentation, and provide a point of reference for future interpretations of score reliability.

As the availability of appropriately derived reliability estimates increases over time, we also encourage primary and secondary researchers to consider applying psychometric corrections to estimates to account for measurement error (e.g., Schmidt & Hunter, 2015). In doing so, however, we would caution against the temptation to engage in overly technical analyses that may reach greater levels of precision but that may limit interpretability (Oswald & Plonsky, 2010). As mentioned above, we also caution against the potential for "over-correction" which might be introduced when corrections are applied that incorporate very low reliability coefficients (e.g., below .7).

As the primary source of methodological training, graduate programs in applied linguistics also bear a responsibility for improving score-reliability issues in the field. Studies have shown that many researchers have a poor understanding of measurement, and measurement does not figure prominently in doctoral programs (see Fan & Thompson, 2001; Gonulal, Loewen, & Plonsky, 2017; Loewen et al., 2014). Offering little methodological training with respect to measurement practice is detrimental to the field because high quality empirical research is precisely what enables applied linguists to make valid claims and, hence, to develop the discipline. Therefore, perhaps our most important recommendation is that program directors and researcher trainers devise ways to incorporate measurement training into their curricula. If such content cannot be covered "in house," programs should consider advising graduate students to enroll in courses on measurement in affiliated departments such as Education or Psychology.

Testing Tips

For researchers

- Aim for transparency throughout the process of designing, conducting, and reporting, and in decisions that pertain to participants, measures, and analyses.
- In terms of the actual reliability estimates: Researchers should clearly state the type of reliability analysis and the specific method being used for all measured variables, not just composite scores. Furthermore, if multiple dimensions or sub-scales are identified (through factor analytic techniques, for example), for most estimation methods, estimates should be calculated and reported for each sub-scale.
- Check the assumptions of reliability estimates (e.g., unidimensionality for coefficient α) and report confidence intervals around those estimates.
- Interpret reliability coefficients. In doing so, researchers can consider (a) reliability as observed field-wide (Plonsky & Derrick, 2016), (b) reliability estimates from previous administrations of the same instrument, (c) estimates by similar tools, (d) the stakes of the testing situation (the higher the stakes, the higher the reliability must be), (e) whether the measure was piloted and any improvements that resulted, and (f) the effect that error may have had on the validity of the measure and, more broadly, of the entire study.
- Make known: (a) the definitions of the constructs that the measured variables operationalize; (b) item-response formats (multiple choice vs. fill-in-the-blank); (c) the structure of the data being analyzed (categorical, ordinal, continuous, and the scale and possible range); and (d) information about how the items are organized on a test.
- Make instruments, data, and code available to the broader L2-research community.
- Keep learning! There are always more conceptual and methodological tools the L2 researcher can add to his/her toolkit, and every new tool improves the field as a whole.

For journal editors and reviewers

- Require authors of empirical studies to report, at a minimum, three different types of score-reliability information: (a) basic score-reliability information for each construct measured; (b) a description of the participants whose scores were used to derive score-reliability interpretations;

(c) an interpretation of study effects with respect to score reliability. The unreliability in scores due to measurement error lowers observed effects; therefore, without an estimate of score reliability, the exact nature of observed effects cannot be determined.

- Journal editors could consider applying reliability-related standards to articles submitted for publication (e.g., Appelbaum et al., 2018) or at least giving greater consideration to measurement error when making decisions on manuscripts. Adding such standards would increase awareness about score-reliability issues for both readers and those who submit their work for publication.

For synthesists and meta-analysts

- Assess, acknowledge, and interpret the reliability of coding schemes at both the item and instrument level (see Coding section in Plonsky et al., 2020).
- Cooper and Dent (2011) noted that meta-analysts "face the same ethical issues faced by quantitative methodologists [...] in a different context." To ensure trustworthy interpretations, meta-analysts need to embrace the notion of transparency. We recommend that all meta-analysts make available not only their coding schemes, but also their data and any code that was used to analyze that data.

Recommended Readings

Linacre, J. M. (2012). *Winsteps tutorial 1*. http://www.winsteps.com/a/winsteps-tutorial-1.pdf

For those interested in item response theory, the author guides the user in installing IRT software as well as analyzing and interpreting scores analyzed with the Rasch IRT model.

Osburn, H. G. (2000). Coefficient alpha and related internal consistency reliability coefficients. *Psychological Methods*, *5*(3), 343–355. https://doi.org/10.1037/1082-989X.5.3.343

The author discusses coefficient α and 10 additional internal consistency reliability-estimation methods. The author examines conditions in which methods over and underestimate score reliability.

Thompson, B. (2003). A brief introduction to generalizability theory. In B. Thompson (Ed.), *Score reliability: Contemporary thinking on reliability issues* (pp. 43–58). SAGE Publications.

The author provides a very accessible introduction to generalizability theory and its advantages.

References

Appelbaum, M., Cooper, H., Kline, R. B., Mayo-Wilson, E., Nezu, A. M., & Rao, S. M. (2018). Journal article reporting standards for quantitative research in psychology: The APA Publications and Communications Board task force report. *American Psychologist*, *73*(1), 3–25. https://doi.org/10.1037/amp0000191

Brennan, R. L., & Prediger, D. J. (1981). Coefficient kappa: Some uses, misuses, and alternatives. *Educational and Psychological Measurement*, *41*(3), 687–699. https://psycnet.apa.org/doi/10.1177/001316448104100307

Brown, J. D. (2014). Classical theory reliability. In A. J. Kunnan (Ed.), *The companion to language assessment* (pp. 1–17). John Wiley. https://doi.org/10.1002/9781118411360.wbcla054

Chalmers, R. P. (2018). On misconceptions and the limited usefulness of ordinal alpha. *Educational and Psychological Measurement*, *78*(6), 1056–1071. https://doi.org/10.1177%2F0013164417727036

Cohen, J. (1960). A coefficient of agreement for nominal scales. *Educational and Psychological Measurement*, *20*(1), 37–46. https://doi.org/10.1177%2F001316446002000104

Cooper, H., & Dent, A. (2011). Ethical issues in the conduct and reporting of meta-analysis. In A. T. Panter & S. K. Sterba (Eds.), *Handbook of ethics in quantitative methodology* (pp. 417–443). Routledge.

Cronbach, L. J. (1947). Test 'reliability': Its meaning and determination. *Psychometrika*, *12*, 1–16. https://doi.org/10.1007/BF02289289

Cronbach, L. J. (1951). Coefficient alpha and the internal structure of tests. *Psychometrika, 16*, 297–334. https://doi.org/10.1007/BF02310555

Cronbach, L. J., Gleser, G. C., Nanda, H., & Rajaratnam, N. (1972). *The dependability of behavioral measurements: Theory of generalizability for scores and profiles*. John Wiley.

Cronbach, L. J., Rajaratnam, N., & Gleser, G. C. (1963). Theory of generalizability: A liberalization of reliability theory. *British Journal of Statistical Psychology, 16*(2), 137–163. https://doi.org/10.1111/j.2044-8317.1963.tb00206.x

Cronbach, L. J., Schoenemann, P., & McKie, D. (1965). Alpha coefficient for stratified-parallel tests. *Educational and Psychological Measurement, 25*(2), 291–312. https://psycnet.apa.org/doi/10.1177/001316446502500201

Derrick, D. (2016). Instrument reporting practices in second language research. *TESOL Quarterly, 50*(1), 132–153. https://doi.org/10.1002/tesq.217

Falk, C. F., & Savalei, V. (2011). The relationship between unstandardized and standardized alpha, true reliability, and the underlying measurement model. *Journal of Personality Assessment, 93*(5), 445–453. https://doi.org/10.1080/00223891.2011.594129

Fan, X., & Thompson, B. (2001). Confidence intervals about score reliability coefficients, please: An EPM guidelines editorial. *Educational and Psychological Measurement, 61*(4), 517–531. https://psycnet.apa.org/doi/10.1177/00131640121971365

Fleiss, J. L. (1971). Measuring nominal scale agreement among many raters. *Psychological Bulletin, 76*(5), 378–382. https://psycnet.apa.org/doi/10.1037/h0031619

Frey, B. B. (2018). Test information function. In B. B. Frey (Ed.), *The SAGE encyclopedia of educational research, measurement, and evaluation*. SAGE Publications. https://doi.org/10.4135/9781506326139

Frey, R., Pedroni, A., Mata, R., Rieskamp, J., & Hertwig, R. (2017). Risk preference shares the psychometric structure of major psychological traits. *Science Advances, 3*. https://doi.org/10.1126/sciadv.1701381

Gonulal, T., Loewen, S., & Plonsky, L. (2017). The development of statistical literacy in applied linguistics graduate students. *International Journal of Applied Linguistics, 168*, 4–32. https://doi.org/10.1075/itl.168.1.01gon

Gwet, K. L. (2008a). Computing inter-rater reliability and its variance in the presence of high agreement. *British Journal of Mathematical and Statistical Psychology, 61*(1), 29–48. https://doi.org/10.1348/000711006X126600

Gwet, K. L. (2008b). Intrarater reliability. In R. D'Agostino, L. Sullivan, & J. Massaro (Eds.), *Wiley encyclopedia of clinical trials* (pp. 473–485). John Wiley. https://doi.org/10.1002/9780471462422.eoct631

Gwet, K. L. (2019). *irrCAC: Computing chance-corrected agreement coefficients (CAC)*. R package version 1.0. https://CRAN.R-project.org/package=irrCAC

Hancock, G. R., & Mueller, R. O. (2001). Rethinking construct reliability within latent variable systems. In R. Cudeck, S. du Toit, & D. Sorbom (Eds.), *Structural equation modeling: Present und future—A Festschrift in Honor of Karl Joreskog* (pp. 195–216). Scientific Software International.

Hattie, J. (1985). Methodology review: Assessing unidimensionality of tests and items. *Applied Psychological Measurement, 9*, 139–164. https://doi.org/10.1177/014662168500900204

Krippendorff, K. (1980). *Content analysis: An introduction to its methodology*. SAGE Publications.

Kuder, G. F., & Richardson, M. W. (1937). The theory of the estimation of test reliability. *Psychometrika, 2*, 151–160. https://doi.org/10.1007/BF02288391

Laerd Statistics. (2019a). Fleiss' kappa using SPSS statistics. *Statistical Tutorials and Software Guides*. https://statistics.laerd.com/spss-tutorials/fleiss-kappa-in-spss-statistics.php

Laerd Statistics. (2019b). Spearman's rank-order correlation. *Statistical Tutorials and Software Guides*. https://statistics.laerd.com/spss-tutorials/spearmans-rank-order-correlation-using-spss-statistics.php

Laerd Statistics. (2019c). Pearson's product–moment correlation using SPSS statistics. *Statistical Tutorials and Software Guides*. https://statistics.laerd.com/spss-tutorials/pearsons-product-moment-correlation-using-spss-statistics.php

Laerd Statistics. (2019d). Kendall's tau-b using SPSS Statistics. *Statistical Tutorials and Software Guides*. https://statistics.laerd.com/spss-tutorials/kendalls-tau-b-using-spss-statistics.php

Loewen, S., Lavolette, E., Spino, L. A., Papi, M., Schmidtke, J., Sterling, S., & Wolff, D. (2014). Statistical literacy among applied linguists and second language acquisition researchers. *TESOL Quarterly, 48*(2), 360–388. https://doi.org/10.1002/tesq.128

Lord, F. M., & Novick, M. R. (1968). *Statistical theory of mental test scores*. Addison–Wesley.

Marsden, E., Mackey, A., & Plonsky, L. (2016). Breadth and depth: The IRIS repository. In A. Mackey & E. Marsden (Eds.), *Advancing methodology and practice: The IRIS repository of instruments for research into second languages* (pp. 1–21). Routledge.

Marsden, E., & Plonsky, L. (2018). Data, open science, and methodological reform in second language acquisition research. In A. Gudmestad & A. Edmonds (Eds.), *Critical reflections on data in second language acquisition* (pp. 219–228). John Benjamins.
Maxwell, A. E. (1977). Coefficients of agreement between observers and their interpretation. *British Journal of Psychiatry*, *130*(1), 79–83. https://doi.org/10.1192/bjp.130.1.79
McDonald, R. P. (1999). *Test theory: A unified approach*. Lawrence Erlbaum Associates.
McKay, T. H. (2016). *Let's be clear: Towards a culture of open data-sharing in applied linguistics*. https://sites.google.com/site/toddhavilandmckay/
McNeish, D. (2018). Thanks coefficient alpha, we'll take it from here. *Psychological Methods*, *23*(3), 412–433. https://doi.org/10.1037/met0000144
Olsson, U., Drasgow, F., & Dorans, N. J. (1982). The polyserial correlation coefficient. *Psychometrika*, *47*, 337–347. https://doi.org/10.1007/BF02294164
Osborne, J. (2003). Effect sizes and the disattenuation of correlation and regression coefficients: Lessons from educational psychology. *Practical Assessment, Research & Evaluation*, *8*(11). https://pareonline.net/getvn.asp?v=8&n=11
Osburn, H. G. (2000). Coefficient alpha and related internal consistency reliability coefficients. *Psychological Methods*, *5*(3), 343–355. https://psycnet.apa.org/doi/10.1037/1082-989X.5.3.343
Oswald, F. L., & Plonsky, L. (2010). Meta-analysis in second language research: Choices and challenges. *Annual Review of Applied Linguistics*, *30*, 85–110. https://doi.org/10.1017/S0267190510000115
Peters, G. (2018). *userfriendlyscience: Quantitative analysis made accessible*. R package version 0.7.2. https://doi.org/10.17605/osf.io/txequ
Plonsky, L., & Derrick, D. J. (2016). A meta-analysis of reliability coefficients in second language research. *The Modern Language Journal*, *100*(2), 538–553. https://doi.org/10.1111/modl.12335
Plonsky, L., & Ghanbar, H. (2018). Multiple regression in L2 research: A methodological synthesis and guide to interpreting R2 values. *The Modern Language Journal*, *102(*4), 713–731. https://doi.org/10.1111/modl.12509
Plonsky, L., & Kim, Y. (2016). Task-based learner production: A substantive and methodological review. *Annual Review of Applied Linguistics*, *36*, 73–97. https://doi.org/10.1017/S0267190516000015
Plonsky, L., Marsden, E., Crowther, D., Gass, S., & Spinner, P. (2020). A methodological synthesis of judgment tasks in second language research. Advanced online publication. *Second Language Research*, *36*(4), 583–621. https://doi.org/10.1177/0267658319828413
Powers, D. E. (2000). *Computing reader agreement for the GRE® writing assessment*. Research Memorandum, ETS. https://www.ets.org/Media/Research/pdf/RM-00-08-Powers.pdf
Saito, K., & Plonsky, L. (2019). Measuring the effects of second language pronunciation teaching revisited: A proposed measurement framework and meta-analysis. *Language Learning*, *69*(3), 652–708. https://doi.org/10.1111/lang.12345
Salkind, N. J. (2010). Polychoric correlation coefficient. In N. J. Salkind (Ed.), *Encyclopedia of research design*. SAGE Publications. https://dx.doi.org/10.4135/9781412961288
Schmidt, F. L., & Hunter, J. E. (2015). *Methods of meta-analysis: Correcting error and bias in research findings*. SAGE Publications.
Shrout, P. E., & Fleiss, J. L. (1979). Intraclass correlations: Uses in assessing rater reliability. *Psychological Bulletin*, *86*(2), 420–428. https://psycnet.apa.org/doi/10.1037/0033-2909.86.2.420
Spearman, C. (1904). The proof and measurement of association between two things. *American Journal of Psychology*, *15*(1), 72–101. https://psycnet.apa.org/doi/10.2307/1412159
Teimouri, Y. (2017). L2 selves, emotions, and motivated behaviors. *Studies in Second Language Acquisition*, *39*, 681–709. https://doi.org/10.1017/S0272263116000243
Thompson, B. (2003). A brief introduction to generalizability theory. In B. Thompson (Ed.), *Score reliability: Contemporary thinking on reliability issues* (pp. 43–58). SAGE Publications.
Torres Irribarra, D., & Freund, R. (2014). *WrightMap: IRT item-person map with ConQuest integration*. http://github.com/david-ti/wrightmap
Traub, R. E. (1994). *Reliability for the social sciences: Theory and applications*. SAGE Publications.
Whittington, D. (1998). How well do researchers report their measures? An evaluation of measurement in published educational research. *Educational and Psychological Measurement*, *58*, 21–37. https://doi.org/10.1177/0013164498058001003

45

Measurement Generalizability

Considerations on Reliability and Validity

Rob Schoonen

Background

Suppose investigations found out that Johnny from Marshbrook wrote a poor composition on March 12, 2019. Most of us would shrug and probably would not find the information worth remembering, although we might worry about Johnny. Questions that may be triggered by the above observation will almost all be questions about generalizability. Is the poor writing performance typical for Johnny, that is: in new assignments will his performance be poor again? Is Johnny typical of a certain group or population of writers? Did he have bad luck with the unattractive topic of the writing assignment that was administered, or maybe with the rater who judged his performance unfavorably? This simple example concerns an individual writer, but it is good to realize that most of the time the data in applied linguists' and language testers' L2 research is compiled from language performances of individual writers, speakers, readers, and listeners. These performances are susceptible to all the effects mentioned and to more than those effects, thus affecting the analyses and conclusions of our studies.

In scientific research, scientists, including applied linguists and language testers, search for valid and generalizable knowledge. This is largely dependent on the generalizability of the measurements, which is the main focus of this chapter. Some level of measurement generalizability is required in order to be able to make predictions about a new performance. In other words, can we expect Johnny to write a poor essay next time around, because he is a poor writer, or could it be that his next writing product is above expectations, or rated more favorably, and then what would that mean for computation of, for example, correlations between the measured variables?

Key Concepts

Universe of admissible observations: This is the (large) set of possible observations that we as researchers are willing to accept as measurement of the construct concerned. The admissible observations are described in terms of one or more facets, e.g., items, raters, interviewers, occasions.

Objects of measurement: The objects that are measured and of which the individual differences are the target of measurement. Usually it concerns persons, but it could be any kind of object, such as texts or utterances.

Fixed and random facets: Facets constitute the relevant dimensions of the measurement and as such sources of measurement error. If there is a large number of conditions in a facet which can be considered as interchangeable, then the facet is random (e.g., raters); if the number of conditions in the study exhausts the number in the universe of admissible observations and/or if they cannot be considered interchangeable, then the facet is fixed (e.g., L1 vs. FL).

Absolute and relative decisions: Scores can be used to make two kinds of decisions. When the decision pertains to only the rank ordering of, and the individual differences between candidates, this is a relative decision. However, if the scores are used to indicate a person's absolute level of performance, this is an absolute decision.

Universe of generalization: Usually researchers aim to generalize from their measurements to the full universe of admissible observations, but it may be the case that there is a fixed facet involved, or that a researcher deliberately focuses on a fixed number of conditions of a facet. In those cases, the universe of generalization is also restricted to just those conditions.

Key Issues

It is obvious that the choices applied linguists and language testers make concerning the measurement of language proficiency are crucial to the claims they can make about participants' levels of proficiency, especially if they want to make individual or group comparisons or compare performance with a preset standard, as is the case in admission testing (Kane, 2003). If a candidate fails an admission test with just two points, the test-score users will want to be sure that a new testing task would lead to the same conclusion about the candidate's level. Likewise, when researchers test hypotheses about the efficacy of foreign language training programs, they do not want the conclusions to be dependent on the particular test administration. It is important that the testing results are generalizable and allow the score users to make valid predictions. Various features of the testing task could affect the test outcomes, and therefore the generalizability of the results. To be able to counter unwanted effects of task or other features of the measurement, researchers need to know where these effects come from. Potentially all features of a task may affect candidates' responses, but some will have a larger effect than others. Considering wanted and unwanted effects, such as treatment effects and measurement errors respectively, we have to bear in mind that "it is the variances of the errors that are additive, rather than the errors themselves, [and] it is especially important to control the larger sources of errors" (Kane, 2003, p. 95–96). Therefore, the challenge for researchers is to investigate which features of a testing procedure cause the major error variance in the elicited language performance.

Generalizability studies (G-studies) can estimate how much task features affect candidates' test performances. The estimates can only be made if researchers include multiple tasks in their studies and the tasks differ on the features that may cause variation in performance. If a feature is constant across tasks, this is considered a so-called hidden facet of the testing tasks; no effect of this feature will be noticed. This may be a deliberate choice, but may also occur unconsciously, being unaware of the features that make a difference in the measurement of the proficiency concerned. For example, when researchers have all of the speaking performances rated by one and the same rater, the researchers will not be able to investigate or estimate the effect of rater in this measurement. The generalizability of the research outcomes across raters will remain unknown, and "rater" should be considered a hidden facet. It is these and related issues that are well addressed within generalizability theory (Cronbach, Gleser, Nanda, & Rajaratnam, 1972; Brennan, 2001; Shavelson & Webb, 1991). These questions seem to be just *technical issues* in applied linguistics research, but, as is often the case, presumed technical issues end up to be related to serious substantive questions, such as: What exactly is the construct that needs to be measured? Who should be considered acceptable raters of speaking performances?

In the remainder of this chapter, I will briefly introduce G-theory, and describe how this theory can contribute to the improvement of measurements in applied linguistics and SLA research, and how G-theory can help address validity questions.

Generalizability Theory

The usefulness of Generalizability theory or G-theory is best illustrated with reference to the measurement of productive language proficiency, because these assessments are usually clearly multi-faceted. The features of a measurement, as discussed above, are called *facets* in G-theory. These facets may introduce additional variance in scores, which may obscure the score variance of interest, i.e., variance due to the objects of measurement. In SLA research, the object of measurement will be the language learner in most cases.

In the assessment of writing proficiency one can obviously distinguish between tasks and raters as facets of the assessment. Another facet could be the writing mode: handwritten with paper and pen versus word-processed on a computer. Some writers might benefit more from the word processing mode than others, which makes the writing mode another potentially important facet of the assessment of writing proficiency. When measuring writing proficiency in language learning research, researchers probably want to claim that the candidates are proficient writers (or not), irrespective of the rater, of whether the candidates write with a pen on paper or with a keyboard and computer, and of the specifics of the writing task. However, this last facet may not be self-evidently included in the claim about writing proficiency. In this example, the facet of task is not very well specified, and could refer to the topic of the assignment, but also to the genre of the writing. Usually we regard the effect of topic as unwanted, whereas we may want to distinguish between, for example, narrative and persuasive writing. Successful persuasive writing might require certain writing subskills that not all successful narrative writers possess. Researchers may not want to generalize from narrative to persuasive writing. At the same time, researchers may expect that a proficiently written, high-quality text that is recognized as such by rater A, will also be recognized by rater B. Although this generalization across raters is not guaranteed, this certainly is a generalization all researchers expect to hold. With regard to the writing genres, persuasion versus narration, test-score users may be more inclined to accept that individual differences are affected by tasks. Basically, researchers are then postulating (partially) different constructs: persuasive writing ability versus narrative writing ability. Here, generalizability and validity concerns meet, and it becomes evident that researchers are dealing with two sides of the same coin.

To estimate the magnitude of the effects of raters, writing mode, topic, or any other facet of the measurement, researchers can resort to G-theory as a psychometric approach very well-suited to deal with multi-faceted measurements. Contrary to classical testing theory (CTT), a G-study can estimate the *error* components for each facet separately, and subsequently, in a Decision-study (or D-study), a researcher can design new measurements and calculate the expected generalizability of the new measurement given the number of raters and tasks included.

Terminology and Concepts. As an introduction to G-theory, I want to briefly introduce a few concepts and terms that are part of this approach (see also Key Concepts). In G-theory, researchers have to define a *universe of admissible observations*. In other words, what is acceptable as a measure of, for example, speaking proficiency, and can the measurement used in the research be considered a random sample of this universe of admissible observations? It is the delineation of this universe that leads the researchers back to theoretical considerations. Do they accept the repeating of sentences as an admissible observation of speaking proficiency (as in elicited imitation; see Yan, Maeda, Lv, & Ginther, 2016)? Most people will be inclined to respond with *No* to the previous question, although others may be able to think of contexts where this measure is acceptable, especially if one defines speaking proficiency as the ability to pronounce the target language appropriately.

In G-theory, a candidate's proficiency level is theoretically defined as the average score on all presumed admissible observations, the so-called *universe score* (cf. CTT's so-called *true score*[1]). However, in reality researchers cannot make all admissible observations; they have to work with a (very) limited sample of observations, which at best consists of a few speaking tasks of which the performances are rated by two or three raters. Still, researchers want to make claims about candidates' general speaking proficiency, i.e., the individual differences in the *universe score* for speaking. The observed individual differences in scores are (unwantedly) affected by the specifics of the tasks and raters. The limitations of the task(s) and raters involved in the measurement add to the error in the measurement. Most of the measurements in applied linguistics research are multi-faceted, whether it is the facet of the sentences in a sentence repetition task or the facet of raters who score candidates' performances. These facets can be *random* or *fixed* (see Key Concepts). In a writing assessment, applied linguists usually consider the topics candidates have to write about as a random selection of all admissible topics. Thus, topic can be considered a *random facet*, and the goal is to generalize from the topics the candidate wrote about to all possible topics, constituting the universe of admissible observations. This is different from a *fixed facet*, which has a limited number of levels, like the levels "word-processing" or "paper-and-pencil" of the facet "writing mode." Researchers normally do not see these two writing modes as a random sample from a whole range of writing modes, but they may see the two as exhaustive for the currently existing writing modes. Researchers may decide to generalize to just these two writing modes. Therefore the *universe of generalization* is confined to just these two writing modes in such a context.

When researchers want to generalize on the basis of their observations, they need to take into account whether the decisions they make and which need to be generalizable are *absolute* or *relative*. Obviously, *absolute* decisions are important when candidates are required to pass a certain entrance level, or when claims are made about the level of development. In these cases, researchers want new measurements to represent the same level of difficulty as the first measurement. Here, high correlations between tests and retests are not enough; the actual scores should be at the same level (see Suzuki & Koizumi, Chapter 43, this volume). This not only implies that tasks are expected to be equally difficult, but also that the raters involved are equally strict or lenient across measurements (see Pill & Smart, Chapter 13, this volume). In applied linguistics, researchers usually study individual differences, and thus the stability of relative positions of candidates in the samples suffices. For instance, the most strongly motivated learners are expected to be the fastest learners. This observation should be replicable with new measurements, and this can be achieved, ignoring the absolute level of the scores. Generalizability theory distinguishes between *absolute* and *relative* decisions, contrary to CTT, and describes two types of reliability or generalizability coefficients, that is the *generalizability coefficient* $E\rho^2$ for relative decisions (cf. CTT), and the *index of dependability*, coefficient Φ, which indeed takes the absolute level of scores into account. In both cases, the coefficients are ratios of the variance due to person as the objects of measurement (universe score variance, σ_p^2) and the variance due to person plus the error variance. The difference between the coefficients is that in the first case of relative decisions, error is defined as every effect that affects the ranking of the candidates, while in the second case of absolute decisions, error is defined as every effect that affects the ranking of the candidates or the level of scores per se. In (1) σ_δ^2 refers to differences in ranking that occur with measurements, whereas in (2) σ_Δ^2 refers to the differences in the ranking and level of the scores.

$$E\rho^2 = \frac{\sigma_p^2}{\sigma_p^2 + \sigma_\delta^2} \tag{1}$$

$$\Phi = \frac{\sigma_p^2}{\sigma_p^2 + \sigma_\Delta^2} \quad (2)$$

The magnitudes of the various variance components are estimated using variance analytic techniques, and different components add to the two types of error variance. σ_δ^2, including variance components that affect the ordering of candidates, consists of the interactions of a facet and person (see also Table 45.1). For absolute decisions, all effects that affect score levels are included in the error term (σ_Δ^2) to calculate the dependability coefficient Φ.

The first step in establishing the generalizability of a measurement is to estimate the magnitude of variance components due to the facets of the measurement compared to that due the object of measurement (person). Once the amount of variance that can be attributed to the facets is known, one can make not only estimates of the generalizability of the measurement at hand, but also estimates for newly designed measurements (D-study). A researcher may wonder, for example, what the effect is of reducing the number of raters, but increasing the number of speaking tasks, or vice versa? This kind of answer is highly valuable in planning future studies. The variance due to person (or any other object of measurement) (σ_p^2) will not change, but the error terms will change in new designs of the assessment. If tasks have a great impact on candidates' performance, i.e., constitute a large variance component, it seems fair to include multiple tasks in the measurement, because the end result, the average performance over these multiple tasks, will be a far better estimate of a candidate's universe score than the score on a single task. On the other hand, if tasks do not constitute a large variance component, that is, if different tasks lead to (more or less) the same score, little can be gained by adding more tasks to the measurement, as they will provide similar information. To be able to make such decisions, researchers need to include at least two levels of a facet in their (initial) measurements (G-study). They cannot just observe language performance elicited with a single task, rated by a single rater, and still make generalizing claims about the persons' language proficiency. Such claims would lack external validity and be unwarranted. Contrary, the more observations are made, the smaller the error variance will be, and the better the generalizability is. The precise computation of the error components is dependent on the research design and the kind of decisions the test-score users want to make; the formulas are beyond the scope of this chapter, but below is a simple example for an assessment with two facets (tasks and raters). In this example, Dutch students responded to three EFL writing assignments, and these writing performances were rated holistically by two raters each, but by different panels of two raters for each assignment: Assignment 1 was rated by Rater 1 and 2; Assignment 2 was rated by Rater 3 and 4, and Assignment 3 by Rater 5 and 6. In other words, raters were *nested* within tasks (see Brennan, 2001; Shavelson & Webb, 1991). The criterion or

Table 45.1 Variance components (σ^2) for EFL writing performances by Dutch secondary school students and their percentage of the total amount of variance (%)

Source of variance	*EFL writing scores (N = 249)*	
	σ^2	%
Person (p)	53.13	47.91
Task (t)	1.29	1.16
Rater within task (r:t)	1.31	1.18
Person by task (pt)	31.46	28.37
Person by rater within task and error (pr:t,e)	23.71	21.38

Adapted from Schoonen (2012).

focus of rating was whether the students had fulfilled the functional writing task appropriately, and the raters were provided with a scale of benchmark essays with given scores (Schoonen, 2012). The variance components reported in Table 45.1 were estimated with GENOVA (Crick & Brennan, 1983), a software package from the suite of programs developed by Brennan and colleagues to compute generalizability indices, and which can deal with various research designs, including nested facets.

The results in Table 45.1 show that almost 48% of the variance in the writing scores can be attributed to individual differences in the presumed universe scores of the students (person). The main effect of task is negligible, so the averages of the scores per task are more or less equal, which could mean that the tasks are equally difficult, but in this case the lack of a task main effect is probably due to the scoring procedure. The three scales with benchmark essays were all centered around 100, and thus make for equal score levels. This is very much different for the interaction of person by task; this interaction accounts for over 28% of the variance, which means that individual differences between the students are strongly dependent on the task that one is looking at. Rater differences are small, which suggests that the raters were well trained and all kept to the average level that was suggested by the benchmark scales. The final component (pr:t,e) is substantial again, which could mean that the rater pairs differed in their appreciation of individual performances, or in other words, that individual differences are very much dependent on the rater involved. However, this latter component is confounded with all remaining error components that cannot be teased apart from the facets in this design. Therefore, the results need to be interpreted with caution. The results in Table 45.1 constitute a G-study, and based on these variance components, a D-study can be conducted. In a D-study, the size of the error components of new measurements with different numbers of tasks or raters is estimated and thus the expected generalizability can be established (see below). In this case with the nested design, the possibilities are slightly limited, because the G-study does not provide separate estimates of the main effect of rater and the interaction of person by rater. For this design with two facets (and the nesting), the error component for absolute decisions is defined by all the facets of the measurement, both as interaction effects of the facets with person and as main effects (see (3)). For the computational derivations, see Cronbach et al. (1972), Shavelson and Webb (1991) or Brennan (2001), among others. It will be obvious from the formula in (3) that the more tasks (n_t) are included in the measurement, the smaller the individual error components become, and thus the smaller the overall error component becomes. The same goes for an increase of the number of raters (n_r). If researchers use just a single random task rated by a single random rater, all denominators in (3) will be 1 and thus the absolute error component (σ_Δ^2) will add up to 57.76 (1.29+1.31+31.46+23.71). The dependability coefficient Φ will be the person variance (σ_p^2) as a proportion of the total variance (person+error): 53.13/(53.13+57.76) =.4791 (see Table 45.1)[2].

$$\sigma_\Delta^2 = \frac{\sigma_t^2}{n_t} + \frac{\sigma_{r:t}^2}{n_r n_t} + \frac{\sigma_{pt}^2}{n_t} + \frac{\sigma_{pr:t,e}^2}{n_r n_t} \quad (3)$$

When the scores of assessment are for relative decisions (see above), that is, when researchers are interested in just individual differences, and not in absolute score levels as is often the case in SLA research, task difficulty and rater severity do not really matter, and these components literally drop out of the equation. All components that do not interact with individual differences (*p*) are ignored in the formula for the error component in relative decisions (see (4)). Again, if researchers stick to a single random task and a single random rater, the overall relative error (σ_δ^2) then is 55.17 (31.46+ 23.71) and the generalizability ($E\rho^2$) the proportion of the person variance of the total of person and relative error: 53.13/(53.15+55.17) = .4906. In this example, Φ and $E\rho^2$

are quite similar, but in cases where task difficulty and/or rater severity are more variable, these two indices can diverge substantially.

$$\sigma_{\delta}^{2} = \frac{\sigma_{pt}^{2}}{n_t} + \frac{\sigma_{pr:t,e}^{2}}{n_r n_t} \tag{4}$$

In planning new research, the estimates of a G-study can be very helpful in designing the measurements, as most will be gained when the effect of a large error component can be reduced. For example, if researchers choose to administer three tasks in a writing assessment ($n_t = 3$), each one rated by a single, random rater ($n_r = 1$), applying formula (3) shows that the amount of absolute error will drop to 19.25, thus making Φ= 53.15/(53.15+19.25) = .7340, and the amount of relative error, applying formula (4), will drop to 18.39, creating a generalizability ($E\rho^2$) of .7429. These indices are usually considered acceptable for research purposes. However, when the researcher opts for a single task administration and hires three raters, the index of dependability Φ is expected to be .56 and the generalizability $E\rho^2$ .57. Little is gained by the increased number of raters, certainly if researchers compare this to what was gained by adding tasks to the measurement. It is therefore important to design measurements based on good information. However, psychometrics may not be the only concern of the researcher, as hiring more raters burdens a project budget in a different way than administering more tasks. In the latter case, the researcher requires more effort of the participants involved in the study.

Generalizability in Applied Linguistics Research

A brief review of the applied linguistics literature confirms that in most cases adding tasks to a language assessment enhances generalizability more than adding raters does.

In a study on L2 pronunciation, Van Weeren and Theunissen (1987) investigated the generalizability of the assessment of German and French pronunciation. Their *tasks* were the items that participants had to read aloud and which were scored by raters. Results showed that there was a substantial person-by-item interaction for French with a small effect for rater differences. For German, results were more complicated because of a person-by-item-by-rater interaction and residual effect which is difficult to interpret. But for both languages, more observations (items) increased the generalizability notably. Lee (2006) and Van Moere (2006) studied the assessment of speaking proficiency, and both reported large person-by-task interactions. In Lee's study, 11 speaking tasks and a pool of 22 raters were involved, and the person-by-task interaction was one of the major variance components, again suggesting that the individual differences in presumed speaking proficiency are to a large extent dependent on the task that is used to measure the (L2) speaking proficiency. Van Moere (2006) did not investigate task *per se* as a facet of speaking proficiency, but rather he investigated *occasion*. The Japanese EFL students in the latter study took an oral group test twice. Occasion represented different topics that were discussed and different interlocutors and group dynamics. However, these can all be considered valid facets of the universe of admissible observations. It turned out that the person-by-occasion interaction was substantial and larger than the person-by-rater interaction. Therefore, assessment outcomes were very much dependent on the occasion concerned, and multiple occasions (or group conversations) should be recommended. For an example of a study in which rater effects were larger than the task effects, see Bachman, Lynch, and Mason (1995).

The measurement of writing proficiency is as multifaceted as is the measurement of speaking proficiency. Several studies investigated the effect of task on the generalizability of the writing scores. For example, Gebril (2009) found relatively large task effects in comparison to the observed rater effects, in the measurement of the writing proficiency of Egyptian EFL students.

Similar findings are reported by Schoonen (2005) and (2012) for primary and secondary school writing, respectively. The results differ slightly according to the kind of tasks investigated (independent or integrated), the aspects rated (*Content and organization* or *Language use*), the scoring procedures (*holistic* or *analytic*), and languages involved (L1 or EFL) (Gebril, 2009; Schoonen, 2005; 2012). For instance, Schoonen (2012) found that EFL writing scores (i.e., related to individual differences between EFL writers) were more generalizable than participants' L1 writing scores.

In SLA studies, researchers are often concerned about rater reliability. This is a valid concern that needs to be addressed, and the rater reliability (or generalizability) needs to reported, but there is a larger threat in the form of limited generalizability that comes from the use of a single (or too few) task(s). Given the often relatively large person-by-task interactions and small person-by-rater interactions, one could argue that raters usually recognize proficient performance, but test-takers, however, are dependent on the characteristics of the elicitation task to be able to display their speaking or writing proficiency. This is confirmed by a synthesis of generalizability studies, conducted by In'nami and Koizumi (2016); based on 20+ datasets for both speaking and writing measurements, they concluded that person-by-task interactions are larger than person-by-rater interactions. Task effects seemed to be slightly larger in writing than in speaking measurements. The interactions seem to be increased if analytic scoring procedures are applied.

Recommendations for Practice

It is important that researchers sample enough performance data of (second) language learners from the universe of admissible observations, including relevant tasks, raters, occasions, and other facets that are relevant. This is paramount to get a fair indication of a learner's language level. Also, within the context of correlational research, one has to question to what extent the correlations found between variables are dependent on the tasks with which the variables are measured, e.g., "Is the correlation between lexical diversity and syntactic complexity the same when both scores come from task A, as when they are derived from task B?" In multivariate G-analyses, the variance components of multiple measures are attributed to the object and facets of measurement, but also the correlations between the variables involved are estimated; these estimates represent the correlation between the candidates' universe scores for the variables concerned, which implies that the estimates are not attenuated by measurement error. Moreover, the analyses also provide information about the variability of the correlation estimates, which is dependent on the (number of) tasks involved in the measurement. The analysis of the generalizability of multiple scores or score profiles, and the correlation between the scores, was already introduced in the early days of G-theory (Cronbach et al., 1972), and further elaborated upon by Brennan (2001). Examples of the application of the multivariate extension can be found in Brennan et al. (1995), Lee (2006), Sawaki (2007), and Xi (2007). Xi (2007) used multivariate G-analyses to investigate the score profiles of candidates who took the Test of English as a Foreign Language (TOEFL). Score profiles consisted of scores for *topic development*, *language use*, and *delivery*. Xi found that correlations between the three analytic scores varied across the six tasks that were involved. These varying correlations also affected the weighting of the three aspects in the composite score that is commonly computed on the basis of analytic scores. From a more theoretical SLA perspective, it is also meaningful to know to what extent the balance or unbalance in score profiles of candidates is true (un)balance in the universe scores, and to what extent it is related to measurement error in the observed scores; see Han (2016) for a similar approach in the study of interpreter performances tested for certification. In Han's study, analytic scores differed in their dependability, and composite scores varied according to the design of the measurement in terms of number of tasks and raters. The results also showed that the intended weighting scheme for the composite score was not effectively reproduced. Sawaki (2007) found similar discrepancies in a study of analytic speaking scores of a test battery of Spanish as an L2. Within the set of five analytic scores, *grammar* weighted for 33% instead of the intended 20%, at the expense of *pronunciation*, *organization*, *vocabulary*, and *cohesion*. Multivariate G-studies may help prevent such unwanted situations from occurring in the next data collection.

Generalizability and Validity

It may be obvious that for the external validity of research and the meaningful testing of SLA or applied linguistics hypotheses, generalizable measurements are essential. However, as is often the case with methodological issues, there is a theoretical, substantive question underlying the generalizability of the measurements. Researchers have to decide on the *universe of admissible observations* or, as Deville and Chalhoub-Deville (2006) put it, on the distinction between " good" and "bad" variability, trying to avoid construct-irrelevant variance, but also construct-underrepresentation (Messick, 1989). If, for example, task specific topical knowledge plays a large role in generating individual differences in a speaking measurement, this might be considered "bad" variance, assuming that the topical knowledge is construct-irrelevant. At the same time, in striving for a homogeneous set of speaking tasks that are interchangeable, a researcher might opt for one specific genre of tasks and thus not sample the universe of admissible observations properly, which may lead to construct-underrepresentation (see also In'nami & Koizumi, 2016). This balancing act between too broad and too narrow construct definitions requires theorizing about the constructs involved, and conducting fundamental research into the relevant parameters of the language ability that steers the (target) language use and response behavior (Bachman & Palmer, 1996; Borsboom, Mellenbergh, & Van Heerden, 2004). It is not for psychometrics to decide which variability is good or bad, but in order to understand person-by-facet interactions, applied linguists and language testers should either aim at defining relatively narrow universes of generalization that will have small person-by-facet interactions, or design studies with multiple facets and multiple observations per facet to disentangle the effects of the different facets, such as task and genre (Bouwer, Béguin, Sanders, & Van den Bergh, 2015) or task and occasion (Huang, 2009). Generalization to broad constructs can only be valid if they are based on a large number of observations, compared to the number of observations that is needed for generalization to a relatively narrowly defined construct (Chapelle, 2006). At the end of the day, applied linguists and language testers need to know whether Johnny from Marshbrook (see Background) is a poor writer in need of remedial teaching, or just had bad luck with the topic or rater assigned.

Testing Tips

- Collect a good amount of performance samples from the language learners, resulting from relevant tasks, raters, occasions, and other relevant facets.
- Try to use multiple testing formats in your assessment of the abilities concerned. Multiple testing formats will increase the generalizability of the findings and thus the external validity of your study. It prevents from mono-method bias.
- In language performance assessment, such as speaking and writing measurement, it is usually more important to increase the number of tasks to be administered than to hire more raters.

Notes

1 In classical testing theory, a theoretical concept of *true score* is postulated which is the expected score of a person on a test if the person were tested on a large number of occasions, such that random measurement error is averaged out. For a comparison of reliability coefficients from CTT and G-theory, see Brennan (2001).

2 On a more substantive note, generalizability of lower than .50 is very undesirable and researchers should strive for higher generalizability indices. What is acceptable as a dependability or generalizability coefficient very much depends on the measurement context and the stakes involved, but will typically be in the range of .70–.90.

Recommended Readings

Shavelson, R. J. & Webb, N. M. (1991). *Generalizability theory. A primer*. SAGE Publications.

This book is a well-written and pleasant introduction to G-theory, starting from the very basics, but also including conceptual considerations.

Brennan, R. L. (2001). *Generalizability theory*. Springer.

This book on G-theory is very comprehensive and very technical. It provides all the statistical considerations in G-theory, for simple and complex measurement designs. It also briefly introduces the programs of the GENOVA suite.

Chalhoub-Deville, M., Chapelle, C. A., & Duff, P. (2006). *Inference and generalizability in applied linguistics. Multiple perspectives*. John Benjamins.

This edited volume provides many interesting chapters on the conceptual, theoretical, and methodological considerations concerning generalizing in language research.

References

Bachman, L. F., Lynch, B. K., & Mason, M. (1995). Investigating variability in tasks and rater judgements in a performance test of foreign language speaking. *Language Testing*, *12*(2), 238–257. https://doi.org/10.1177/026553229501200206

Bachman, L. F., & Palmer, A. S. (1996). *Language testing in practice: Designing and developing useful language tests*. Oxford University Press.

Borsboom, D., Mellenbergh, G. J., & Van Heerden, J. (2004). The concept of validity. *Psychological Review*, *111*(4), 1061–1071. https://doi.org/10.1037/0033-295X.111.4.1061

Bouwer, R., Béguin, A., Sanders, T., & Van den Bergh, H. (2015). Effect of genre on the generalizability of writing scores. *Language Testing*, *32*(1), 83–100. https://doi.org/10.1177/0265532214542994

Brennan, R. L. (2001). *Generalizability theory*. Springer.

Brennan, R. L., Gao, X., & Colton, D. A. (1995). Generalizability analyses of work keys listening and writing tests. *Educational and Psychological Measurement*, *55*(2), 157–176. https://doi.org/10.1177/0013164495055002001

Chapelle, C. A. (2006). L2 vocabulary acquisition theory: The role of inference, dependability and generalizability in assessment. In M. Chalhoub-Deville, C. A. Chapelle, & P. Duff (Eds.), *Inference and generalizability in applied linguistics: Multiple perspectives* (pp. 47–64). John Benjamins.

Crick, J. E., & Brennan, R. L. (1983). *Manual for GENOVA: A generalized analysis of variance system* (No. ACT Technical Bulletin No. 43). ACT.

Cronbach, L. J., Gleser, G. C., Nanda, H., & Rajaratnam, N. (1972). *The dependability of behavioral measurements: Theory of generalizability for scores and profiles*. John Wiley & Sons.

Deville, C., & Chalhoub-Deville, M. (2006). Old and new thoughts on test score variability: Implications for reliability and validity. In M. Chalhoub-Deville, C. A. Chapelle, & P. Duff (Eds.), *Inference and generalizability in applied linguistics. Multiple perspectives* (pp. 9–25). John Benjamins.

Gebril, A. (2009). Score generalizability of academic writing tasks: Does one test method fit it all? *Language Testing*, *26*(4), 507–531. https://doi.org/10.1177/0265532209340188

Han, C. (2016). Investigating score dependability in English/Chinese interpreter certification performance testing: A generalizability theory approach. *Language Assessment Quarterly*, *13*(3), 186–201. https://doi.org/10.1080/15434303.2016.1211132

Huang, C. (2009). Magnitude of task-sampling variability in performance assessment: A meta-analysis. *Educational and Psychological Measurement*, *69*(6), 887–912. https://doi.org/10.1177/0013164409344550
In'nami, Y., & Koizumi, R. (2016). Task and rater effects in L2 speaking and writing: A synthesis of generalizability studies. *Language Testing*, *33*(3), 341–366. https://doi.org/10.1177/0265532215587390
Kane, M. (2003). Generalizability theory. *International Journal of Testing*, *3*(1), 95–100. https://doi.org/10.1207/S15327574IJT0301_6
Lee, Y.-W. (2006). Dependability of scores for a new ESL speaking assessment consisting of integrated and independent tasks. *Language Testing*, *23*(2), 131–166. https://www.doi.org/10.1191/0265532206lt325oa
Messick, S. (1989). Validity. In R. L. Linn (Ed.), *Educational measurement* (3rd ed., pp. 13–103). American Council on Education/Macmillan.
Sawaki, Y. (2007). Construct validation of analytic rating scales in a speaking assessment: Reporting a score profile and a composite. *Language Testing*, *24*(3), 355–390. https://doi.org/10.1177/0265532207077205
Schoonen, R. (2005). Generalizability of writing scores: An application of structural equation modeling. *Language Testing*, *22*(1), 1–30. https://doi.org/10.1191/0265532205lt295oa
Schoonen, R. (2012). The validity and generalizability of writing scores: The effect of rater, task and language. In E. van Steendam, M. Tillema, G. Rijlaarsdam, & H. van den Bergh (Eds.), *Measuring writing: Recent insights into theory, methodology and practices* (pp. 1–22). Series in Writing (Vol. 27). Brill. https://doi.org/10.1163/9789004248489_002
Shavelson, R. J., & Webb, N. M. (1991). *Generalizability theory: A primer*. SAGE Publications.
Van Moere, A. (2006). Validity evidence in a university group oral test. *Language Testing*, *23*(4), 411–440. https://doi.org/10.1191/0265532206lt336oa
Van Weeren, J., & Theunissen, T. J. J. M. (1987). Testing pronunciation: An application of generalizability theory. *Language Learning*, *37*(1), 109–122. https://doi.org/10.1111/j.1467-1770.1968.tb01314.x
Xi, X. (2007). Evaluating analytic scoring for the TOEFL® Academic Speaking Test (TAST) for operational use. *Language Testing*, *24*(2), 251–286. https://doi.org/10.1177/0265532207076365
Yan, X., Maeda, Y., Lv, J., & Ginther, A. (2016). Elicited imitation as a measure of second language proficiency: A narrative review and meta-analysis. *Language Testing*, *33*(4), 497–528. https://doi.org/10.1177/0265532215594643

Index

Page numbers in *italics* indicate figures and page numbers in **bold** indicate tables.

For Product Safety Concerns and Information please contact our EU
representative GPSR@taylorandfrancis.com
Taylor & Francis Verlag GmbH, Kaufingerstraße 24, 80331 München, Germany

www.ingramcontent.com/pod-product-compliance
Ingram Content Group UK Ltd.
Pitfield, Milton Keynes, MK11 3LW, UK
UKHW050234200926
475702UK00020B/3019
* 9 7 8 0 3 6 7 6 4 0 4 9 1 *